A-Bombe
Ian Anderson
Dr. Rachel Armstrong
Jason Bailey
Phil Baines
Tom Balchin
Barnbrook
Keith Bates
Mario Beernaert
David Berlow
Phil Bicker
Erik van Blokland
Lo Breier
Neville Brody
Matthew Butterick
Barbara Butterweck
Margaret Calvert
David Carson
Matthew Carter
Jose Chamorro
Scott Clum
Coil Graphics
John Critchley
David Crow
Vera Daucher
Barry Deck
eBoy
Paul Elliman
Naomi Enami
Florian Fossel
Tobias Frere-Jones
Fuel
Function
Olöf Birna Gardarsdottir
Malcolm Garrett
Adam Graveley
Lucas de Groot
Peter Grundy
Lee Hasler
Zaid Hassan
Frank Heine
Florian Heiß
Katsuhiko Hibino
Tom Hingston
RAD HOC
Lucy Hutchinson
Sylke Janetzky
Sam Jones
Asgeir Jónsson
Tibor Kalman
Jeffrey Keedy
Max Kisman
M&Co
Bruce Mau
Rory McCartney
Russell Mills
François Moissette
Moniteurs
Vaughan Oliver
Natalija Nikpalj Polondak
John Randle
Lucienne Roberts
Just van Rossum
Pablo Rovalo
Stefan Sagmeister
Peter Saville
Anna-Lisa Schönecker
Pierre di Sciullo
Darren Scott
Erik Spiekermann
Simon Staines
Francis Stebbing
Ian Swift
Paul Sych
Jake Tilson
Tomato
Alexei Tylevich
Gerard Unger
Chu Uroz
Rick Valicenti
Rick Vermeulen
Volcano Type
Petra Waldeyer
WD+RU
Martin Wenzel
Brett Wickens
Bob Wilkinson
Marina Willer
Cornel Windlin
Jon Wozencroft
Ian Wright
Xplicit ffm

TASCHEN

Hohenzollernring 53, D-50672 Köln
www.taschen.com

ISBN 978-3-8365-2501-5

What is FUSE

Launched in 1990, FUSE is ostensibly a quarterly magazine, assembled in London and originally published by FontShop International. Each issue is comprised of a plain carton box containing a disc with four or more fonts on it, plus five printed posters. Each issue is given a theme related to various underlying tendencies in communications and the consequences of them. Four designers, from both the type industry plus other fields, are commissioned to explore the given theme through the design of a typeface. Each designer then takes that typeface into creative application through the design of a poster or animation. The four designs are accompanied by a written editorial, and the addition of any number of unpredicted extra fonts.

That is the pragmatic description of FUSE as a material product. But that doesn't say anything about FUSE.

At its root, FUSE has always been intended to be an exploration. It is a laboratory, a space where practitioners and non-practitioners are invited to enter and experiment with the visual language forms we use. In a way, it is little more than a catalyst, and each publication is like a white paper, a research document revealing new explorations.

FUSE takes as its base the concept that all language is fluid, not fixed, that digital distribution systems allow us to disseminate ideas that are alterable, especially in the visual form.

Taken from the opening address by Neville Brody at FUSE98, San Francisco (CONTINUES ON PAGE 358)

Contents

About this book

FUSE 1-20 is an anthology of the FUSE project since its initial edition in 1991.

This is the first time that all editions of FUSE have been collected and published in one place, a point of visual and historical reference. Limited print runs, obsolete technologies and 20 years of software developments have meant that before now FUSE has never been seen in its complete form.

We have decided to stay true to the various editions as they first appeared, and for this reason the book has been split into two main sections. Part 1 features FUSE editions 1-18. The editorial essays and font descriptions are faithful to the text as it appeared on the original editorial posters. Any editorial changes made illustrate the shifting versions of desktop publishing standards.

FUSE editions 19 and 20 accompany this book in poster form, with the fonts and editorial content downloadable online with the key card included in the box.

FUSE 1-20: Foreword Neville Brody

20 years, 20 issues, 100 printed posters, 114 fonts!

From its inception 21 years ago, FUSE has always been a battleground of experimentation, a laboratory of thought and language where discussion of far wider issues would find form in form, in the very structures in which we place our systems for the distribution of expression and fact. Edging continually between familiarity and abstraction, this liquid space allowed new configurations to erupt through the intense questioning and dismantling of conventional tools and structures of communication. If society is to be fluid, it demands constant evolutionary language systems which are able to undermine all attempts to fix the status quo in an exploitary stasis through hypnosis. 'Anti' matters.

In a world of generic mediocrity and corporate obeyance, new flowers of exuberance bloom in dark crevices. FUSE is a breach in the wall, a genetic mutation from which new lifeforms can spring. Our language is our being, and our thoughts are conditioned by our languages; only by extension can we expand our boundaries of possibility. What started out as a raw, explosive exploration of typographic language enabled by digital technology, later developed sophistication and layering.

The twenty years of FUSE feels like an unexpected burst of creative shards. Some fonts were vandalistic, some decorative, some playful. Some were investigative, some architectural, some joyful... All were intrinsically both questions and possibilities. Alternating between the emotive and formalistic, they offered visions into new spaces enabled by new languages. Their forms were aligned in structures and motives that allow new thoughts. Many succeeded, some failed, and the experiment continues. Never before has FUSE been so relevant and so necessary.

Introduction 1

This aspect of "the sacred" can seem to feel sacred because no equivalent in the modern world seems to be – this is a setback. Is it true that we experience disembodiment, alienation, a psychic loss of power... the slow disappearance of poetry? Few would admit it, for to do so would be a heresy in the space shuttle of contemporary communication.

FUSE 1-20: The Circle and the Square **Jon Wozencroft**

The difference between analogue and digital is most often framed around a change of formats – from vinyl to CD, celluloid and VHS to DVD, and most recently paperback to Kindle. This glosses over a more fundamental switch in terms of reproduction and pattern generation, and points to the reason why typography became a crucial context in which to investigate this.

One might start with a demonstration of what has happened to the letter 'O'. In *Garamond*, the curve and harmonic structure feeds off centuries of development, in digital, a set of squares/pixels gives the eye the illusion that it is not seeing pixels... It looks like an 'O' but it isn't an 'O'. It's a different order of construction, resolving itself to look like the letter 'O'. Blame the sans serif precedent that took less than 40 years to become *Helvetica* and *Univers*, whose 'O' uses a perfect circle just asking to be smashed!

Digital systems are based on a high order of optical illusion. It is some kind of magic, but put to the wrong purpose... In the realm of the fantastic, the scheme of contemporary life makes you see one thing when you've actually seen another, and it extends everywhere and forms the root point of our perceptual malaise. Instinctively we don't believe in anything any more. Who would – who except the religious? For the rest of us, the world was meant to have ended on 21 May 2011, but it didn't. We are living in a world of Endless Change.

"The technique of reproduction detaches the reproduced object from the domain of tradition". [1]

Following the publication of the first *Graphic Language* book, I spent a good year in 1989/90 researching and writing outlines for what we proposed as its follow-up – *The Death of Typography*. This had as its genesis a page Brody had done for the Touch *Ritual* project in 1986; it was also, for us, a riposte to the flame of fame that fell over our studio practice following the busy year of publication and the V&A exhibition in 1988... In that short interval, we'd been experimenting with what the PC and the dot-matrix printer had to offer. Not a great deal as far as we were concerned, and it still seems to me the strangest accident that computers first fell upon graphic designers, before film-makers, musicians and artists.

We were interested in print processing – moving between type specimen book and photocopier, to graph paper and Rotring, pushing typographic forms into various distressed states. The project being a passion, Brody would mention *The Death of Typography* in interviews while I sat under a tree on Hampstead Heath looking for clues in history, philosophy and in particular the communication strategies of WW2: between Goebbels and Churchill's 'Black Propaganda' unit, this was a time of great resonance with what we see happening in today's culture.

I just googled "Death of Typography". It's out there on repeat, and there is of course no mention of the 1986 version, which is poetic justice. The real challenge was to form some update of Walter Benjamin's seminal text, 'The Work of Art in the Age of Mechanical Reproduction'. Substitute 'Digital Experience' for 'Mechanical Reproduction' and the conclusion is/was that it is a nigh impossible task when communications systems mutate at such a speed.

Digital typography seemed a backwards step from what we were doing by hand and it took many months before we saw how it could be turned into another dimension. The work, all of a sudden, was reinvigorated by the direct challenge to how we should understand visual language.

Some would take *The Death of Typography* literally and like T.S. Eliot's 'idiot questioner' demand "What do you mean?". We were never able to come up with an effective one liner. At the same time, dialogues were opening up concerning the paperless office, the end of the book and virtual reality; the first synopsis of nanotechnology had just been published by Drexler; [2] to say nothing of the *End of History* and *A Thousand Plateaus*. [3]

Theory went into overdrive at this point, but it had as much in common with the aftermath of WW2 as it did a way forward with digital. Adorno and Warhol would both understand 'rhizomes', they just failed to use that word.

In printed media, words that once had to be sent into the future could all of a sudden be sent in real-time. The fax machine, born to us in 1987, was a marriage between printing and digital/telephony, more than a telegram, as instant as TV.

There was no email, no Internet, aside from the localised JANET system used in academia. The fax machine seemed to be the future, and look what happened to that.

It was nevertheless a catalyst... The fax, not the facts – heat-sensitive paper, square formations like the earlier gravure printing process, which upon contact with the paper stock blurred, and on enlargement became a new aesthetic of seductive fragmentation, as soft-edged as today's imagery is hard and virtually lifeless.

FUSE is a buried narrative of this wild time, when "you know something is happening but you don't know what it is" (B. Dylan).

An intention we tried to insist upon was for the project to be "a forum" for discussion; we hoped for a vigorous debate – this was always abbreviated and any perspective has not been possible until now. Criticisms came from traditionalists who never acknowledged that we were fully aware of tradition. Instead, it turned viral, and for the time we managed to do it, FUSE was fairly out of control and always a last-minute panic to finish.

The hare became a tortoise. No longer do "all roads lead to Rome". The lines to cyberspace go round in circles.

"Limit gives form to the limitless". [4]

In older civilisations, its people prized a circular formation over the square. There was such a thing as a square circle, made up of the harmonic alignment of measurement and number – this much can be divined from an analysis of the mathematics and sacred geometry that gave rise to the Golden Section and the Pythagorean notion of cosmic harmony, which graphic designers can still call upon despite the modern world of metric values and DIN sizes. "It also led to their endeavours to realise the harmonies of such proportions in the patterns of daily life, thereby elevating life to an art". [5] Actually, not many contemporary graphic designers have the first idea about the Golden Section, and why should they, if it is no longer a key module of every Foundation course?

Stone circles can be visited across the British Isles that pay testament to an earlier perception of what is radiant and progressive concerning the human relationship with forms. Astronomy, astral projection, ritual... such practices point to intuition and divination as essential survival skills. "Every stone circle had an affinity with a certain part of the human body... and forms a common feature of poetic expression". [6]

This aspect of "the sacred" can seem to feel sacred because no equivalent in the modern world seems to be – this is a setback. Is it true that we experience disembodiment, alienation, a psychic loss of power... the slow disappearance of poetry? Few would admit it, for to do so would be a heresy in the space shuttle of contemporary communication. A pixel can never claim to be anything but a drop in the ocean, but it causes ripples, forms circles in its wake, and we have yet to find the best way of living in a liquid state.

This recent transition from the circle to the square is as crucial a turning point in terms of "the future" as the Romans were to Ancient Britain. It questions everything in its wake, and has this amazing new

We are still no closer to being "digitally literate" than we were 20 years ago. So it's not so much about intuition, it's about processing power and the coverage you can get across networks, Facebook and Twitter, where in spite of the supposed ease of connectivity, everything has got more "random" and ephemeral in depth.

quality of being able to be drowned by itself, without ever actually disappearing. It's not so much the End of History as the Beginning of the Endless Change. Facts and figures get mutated in the ongoing dialogue of reality and its fictions.

The ancients must have been short-sighted, given the ease with which the Roman invaders of Britain in 43AD used square formations to conquer tribal chieftains and clans, with their 'tortoise' formations in battle, and town squares and straight roads in peacetime... Or far-sighted, in relation to what would develop thousands of years later. The Romans built their roads on the existing "straight tracks" of the prehistoric way of connecting each sacred site to the other. In doing so, they set the template for horse and cart, for railways, for tarmac, where the old could smother the new in its latest form – power becomes diluted – but the power is still there nonetheless, struggling to break through the cracks in the paving stones.

Before PC, nobody got their hands on the modelling tools easily except the select few. The personal computer changed everything in a way the typewriter and electric guitar once promised to, but never did on the same scale. We are still no closer to being "digitally literate" than we were 20 years ago. So it's not so much about intuition, it's about processing power and the coverage you can get across networks, Facebook and Twitter, where in spite of the supposed ease of connectivity, everything has got more "random" and ephemeral in depth.

A culture of pixels and cut-off corners is a very different proposition to the Roman idea of city squares, the forum, and even the later garden cities of post-war modernism. These were also designed on the grand scale, visible and practical to every citizen and a testament to a hopeful future. Nowadays our pixellated universe is more like a vanishing point that everybody has their way of searching for, however they might feel their way through the antimatter.

We had a conversation in Tokyo in 1990 when we were starting FUSE: Tokyo is for the London eye a city of complete craziness just as speed-dominated then as

Moonbase Alpha was a frequent choice for techno flyers in the 1990s and *Reactor* a favourite of fine art contexts; ... the fonts ended up in the most surreal of contexts, from corporate logos to doctors' surgeries.

it is now :) – the level of information surrealism... an extraordinary wonderland of what was going on and what might come out on screen. You could see speed and time folding in on itself. Later I found out it was a lot to do with the benzene petrol fumes in the air. We concluded that the solution to working together was to work in parallel, and FUSE was an exemplar of this.

FUSE 1 is basically a blast against the universe. It's naïve as all manifestos generally are; but from FUSE 2 *RUNES* onwards we dedicated ourselves to pursuing the work into something more enduring than a magazine. In any respect we shot ourselves in the foot; we started to release editions on a regular basis, but this soon became unsustainable and in the end FUSE has the legacy of still being a work in progress.

We always had a problem... Thinking of who to ask... trying to invite women designers... You can see where this situation was by looking at FUSE 3/9/12... It can look like a club but this was just the reality of getting FUSE out. We had the difficulty of trying to convince many people to make work for us beyond a few allies, and (you're not going to believe this), quite a few of the designers included in this collection didn't want to do it at first. If you're thinking of "why didn't so-and-so do a font for FUSE?", well there's a good chance we asked them and they declined!

Looking back on these works there is also a strong undercurrent to what has subsequently become an obsession in graphic design, from "The Designer as Author" argument of the late '90s to all these recent concentrations on Design History of who's who and what's forgotten.

When we started, we got acres of press, and sold out the 3000 editions with ease. As the project deepened, we'd struggle to sell 500 because everyone wanted it for free.

The time-based nature of FUSE is our biggest achievement. It is still in flower, and not properly recorded; though *Moonbase Alpha* was a frequent choice for techno flyers in the 1990s and *Reactor* a favourite of fine art contexts; *White No Sugar* was one of many that won an award for type design and the fonts ended up in the most surreal of contexts, from corporate logos to doctors' surgeries.

Revisiting the texts one would be forgiven for assuming that FUSE represents a pessimistic vision of the future. The surrealism of the situation – concerning representation and reproduction we felt ours to be a moment on a par with the photography/ painting schism of the beginning of the last century – should not obscure the sense of adventure we felt. As for the future, when we look at our children we can see signs of a digital awareness we never had, nor could ever have had. So we hold our breath.

One day in 1991, I was abstracting the *Akzidenz Grotesk* font under the PMT machine for a logo I was doing for Kudos Productions, a London-based TV company. Brody said to me, "What are you doing, I can do that on the computer"...

Blur, a font that Brody configured overnight, became a guiding form of the FUSE project. I saw it recently in a foreign country, being used as the typeface for an optician's shop frontage.

Reference:
1. *Illuminations*, Walter Benjamin, Harcourt, Brace and World Inc. 1968 **2.** *Engines of Creation: The Coming Era of Nanotechnology*, Erik Drexler, Fourth Estate 1987 **3.** *The End of History and the Last Man*, Francis Fukuyama, Penguin 1993; *A Thousand Plateaus: Capitalism and Schizophrenia*, Gilles Deleuze and Felix Guattari, Continuum (New Ed.) 2004 **4. & 5.** *The Power of Limits*, György Doczi, Shambhala Publications 1981 **6.** *The New View Over Atlantis*, John Michell, Thames and Hudson 1983; *The Dimensions of Paradise*, John Michell, Thames and Hudson 1988

The FUSE box, the set of four posters, the editorial insert, postcard and the 700K floppy disk for FUSE 1 *INVENTION*

FUSE 1-20: Wreckers of Typographic Civilisation
Adrian Shaughnessy

For graphic designers encountering the first issues of FUSE, there was a sense of new terrain being opened up: a sense of two explorers – Brody and Wozencroft – striding out into the icy steppes of the new digital kingdom. The reports they sent back – housed in modest cardboard boxes – were prophetic and often shocking.

Wozencroft's texts fizzed with provocations that sometimes read like science fiction, but which now, more than 20 years later, demonstrate an uncanny ability to define the big questions that preoccupy us currently – the cultural impact of information technology, surveillance, propaganda, genetics and the Internet, amongst other topics. At the same time, under Brody's art direction, early FUSE stuck pins in the eyes of typo traditionalists and gleefully invited the displeasure of graphic design's self-appointed ruling elite by simultaneously showing how typography, thanks to the computer, had become open to all-comers *and* showing how it had been freed from its traditional purpose of conveying linguistic meaning.

The visuals in early editions of FUSE derived their power to shock from the attempts by Brody, Wozencroft and their collaborators to coerce the new tools – software, keyboards, output systems – into making the statements they so urgently wanted to broadcast. The work was often raw and unpolished, and some of it shows immaturity, but something happened around the publication of FUSE 10: graphic expression jumped the digital firebreak and crossed from haphazard experimentation into controlled expression. It's there for all to see in the pages of this book: a moment of digital transubstantiation when the users achieved mastery of the tools and conjured up visual statements of substance and integrity that can be compared with other peak moments in graphic design history.

Writing in FUSE 10, Wozencroft identified the reasons for this breakthrough: "For some time we have been talking about our intention to create an outlet that uses the keyboard more as a musical instrument or palette of colours, and not to restrict its potential to the endless refinement, sophistication or abstraction of Roman letterforms." From then onwards, Brody and Wozencroft – and the many designers and typographers they invited to collaborate with them – demonstrated a new mastery of the digital tools and networks; they showed, more compellingly than ever before, how computerised design could be used to make a new future for visual and semantic communication that went beyond Roman letterforms and which species-jumped from the printed page to the electronic screen.

Brody has also spoken about this moment: interviewed by Rick Poynor in *Eye* (No. 6, 1992), he was asked if he had reached a "point of fluency with the computer where you are the master..." Brody replied: "Absolutely. I even remember the night it happened. It was 11:30 and I had been sitting attacking the machine. I suddenly realised that I was in control and there had been a definite switchover."

Amongst today's designers, the role of digital technology has gained almost universal acceptance. To be against the computer in design now is to be heretical, but there was a time when the digital way – the DTP revolution – was seen as evidence that the barbarians had entered the citadel. Paul Rand, in an essay called 'Computer, Pencils and Brushes' (1992) noted that "... the language of the computer is the language of technology, not the language of design. It is also the language of production. It enters the world of creativity only as an adjunct, as a tool – a time-saving device, a means of investigating, retrieving, and executing tedious jobs – but not the principal player." Brody, in the pages of FUSE and

They showed, more compellingly than ever before, how computerised design could be used to make a new future for visual and semantic communication that went beyond Roman letterforms and which species-jumped from the printed page to the electronic screen.

elsewhere, set about proving that the computer could play a far more central role in design than Rand envisaged.

Even an astute commentator such as the American designer Michael Rock – hardly a warp and weft traditionalist – could allow himself a bat-squeak of regret at the prospect of typography falling into the hands of the new digital infidels. Writing about FUSE in *Eye* (No. 15, 1994), he said: "Type will never again be produced by a guild-like fraternity; the craft republicanism and labour unionism that characterised letter-making are gone forever. But as exciting as the results of the type revolution have been, it is hard not to feel a speck of remorse for the decimation of another craft, and another organised group of craftsmen, by a handful of young punks with personal computers."

Hallowed notions of type as secret craft and as an 'invisible' vessel tasked only with imparting linguistic meaning (the 'crystal goblet' of typographic lore) were elbowed aside by the flailing geometric elbows of Brody and other 'young punks with personal computers'. More than anyone working in graphic design in the 1980s and '90s, Brody contributed to the foregrounding of typography. He turned type into visual expression. This is not to say that expressive type did not exist in the pre-Brody era. The Constructivists of the 1920s and the psychedelic poster artists of the 1960s both made use of outrageous letterforms in ways that challenged notions of typographic orthodoxy. But these anti-formalist conceits were used primarily as a transportation system for messages, instructions and announcements. What Brody and others did was to create – in the words of Michael Rock – "a new typographic rhetoric ... that sees the letterform as a site for visual experimentation and the alphabet as a screen on to which designers project their creativity."

But they did something else. They showed how it was possible to be a designer of typefaces and, at the same time, a graphic designer. Up until this pivotal moment, practitioners were mostly one or the other. But new software such as Fontographer gave designers the tools to avoid the laborious process of creating entire fonts by hand, with their numerous qualities such as optical scaling and unified family structures. Here was a generation that could – at will – create their own fonts, typefaces and letterforms, thus freeing themselves from extant typographic systems. It also meant that this work – most notably in Brody's own case – acquired a signature that was uniquely that of the designer. The designer who used his or her own fonts was more of a designer/author than those designers who relied on pre-existing fonts.

Other graphic designers prior to the digital eruption of the 1980s and '90s had made their own letterforms – most famously Wim Crouwel. *New Alphabet* (1967), created in response to the arrival of the first screen-based communication systems, is perhaps the most celebrated example of Crouwel's typefaces. But *New Alphabet* was an exception, and it was rare for Crouwel to make an entire alphabet – he usually only drew the letters he needed to make specific words; it was only in the 1990s, with the arrival of digitisation, that font house The Foundry could approach Crouwel and offer to turn his letterforms into working fonts.

Digitisation meant something else, too: it meant interaction. Thanks to the personal computer, it was now possible for users to control the means – and modes – of communication. FUSE is full of 'typefaces' that are user-generated. David Crow's typeface *Mega Family 2* functioned like a set of drawing tools, allowing users to make portraits: "The font functions as a game", he wrote in FUSE 16, "for one or two players and suggests a move towards leisure-based activity as a cellular growth within what we understand as typography. Its rules are self-generated and not imposed." John Critchley's *Mutoid* (FUSE 10) used the keyboard to contain "a series of interchangeable body parts – heads, legs and torsos – which can be combined to form a collection of 'mutant' figures. Create your own creature!"

Brody and Wozencroft, and their collaborators – designers such as Cornel Windlin, David Crow, Pierre Di Sciullo and others – used FUSE as a platform to confront typographic dogma. They showed how type could be used in the same way that an illustrator uses lines, squiggles, shading and shapes to make abstract or semi-abstract, visual declarations: sometimes

FUSE's greatest achievement, however, might be the stinging rebuke it offers to the widely held view that graphic design lacks the ability to critique itself, and is a zone of stylistic posturing and self-promotion. Critics and historians have routinely decried the lack of depth and substance that designers contribute to the design discourse. FUSE, it seems to me, is one of the few effective rebuttals of that assertion.

clear in their intention, at other times ambiguous, illustrators were free from the need to make semantic sense in a way that graphic designers were not. Brody and his collaborators, and thousands of graphic designers who came after them, land-grabbed some of that freedom. They used amorphous blobs, meandering lines, jagged and contorted bitmaps with the same freedom enjoyed by illustrators. They made a new disenfranchised typography for the age of the image – and even more importantly, for the age of screen-based communication.

FUSE's mix of texts and visual experimentation was a potent brew. Wozencroft's essays were Ballardian investigations into the stuff that surrounds us. Rarely celebratory, often prescient, they acted as fiery manifestos for a group – thinking graphic designers – who were questioning their symbiotic relationship with business and consumerism. To the vast majority of designers, in thrall to the Thatcher/Reagan consumer boom, Wozencroft's tone must have seemed almost traitorous; but to others, his words provided a blueprint for contrarian thinking.

His texts displayed an easy unforced erudition: in one essay ('Runes', FUSE 2) he references Etruscan script, Norse legend, the tree languages of Welsh and Irish Druids, SS insignia and uniforms, Heavy Metal LPs, 'New Age' culture, green issues, Gaia philosophy and LED train indicators. Elsewhere he writes with an informed sense of social justice: "Once, the direction of social policy was towards the disadvantaged – today, it seeks to consolidate the comfort of the restless middle class (stuck as always between two extremes, wealth and poverty – a perfect breeding ground for such ideas as the National Lottery and private health insurance)." Here, as he does in other FUSE essays, Wozencroft is engaging with social issues within a graphic design publication in a way that was rare at the time, but which now, post-banking crises, is more commonplace.

FUSE's greatest achievement, however, might be the stinging rebuke it offers to the widely held view that graphic design lacks the ability to critique itself, and is a zone of stylistic posturing and self-promotion. Critics and historians have routinely decried the lack of depth and substance that designers contribute to the design discourse. FUSE, it seems to me, is one of the few effective rebuttals of that assertion, and yet it is rarely mentioned when graphic design culture is mentioned, and only a handful of designer-authored publications can match the textual and visual ambition of Brody and Wozencroft's self-publishing venture – perhaps only *Emigre* can be named in the same breath.

It is not only in the ideological and polemical realm that FUSE has suffered neglect. Modern typography has produced few successors to Brody's spurt of naked invention. Today's typographers seem only to have eyes for the formalism of the past: typographic conservatism is the norm. This is a development that the early FUSE contributor Jeffrey Keedy predicted. Writing in FUSE 4 (1992), he noted: "To avoid the mortality of style many designers today have revived the dead. The typographic cadavers are brought back from the distant past (classical mummies), the recent past (zombie moderns) or patched together, à la Frankenstein, with recently dug-up parts (post-mortem-modern). No matter what the approach, it all comes down to the same thing, a kind of typographic necrophilia. Instead of wasting time perfecting an exquisite corpse, type designers should be excited by new digital possibilities, just as the Industrial Age designers were about their technological advances."

In interviews and in his new role as educator, Brody has made repeated calls for his successors to be 'excited by new digital possibilities' and to 'think dangerously'. It is his express wish that someone will undertake to emulate the work he started 20 years ago. He wants to hear again the wrecking ball smashing into the walls of typographic civilisation, but he is not confident it will happen. Instead, most typography seems only to aspire to match the sterile tones of shopping music as we go about our daily task of, to quote Wozencroft, drifting through "a seamless quilt of shopping malls, banking services, telecom centres, restaurants and bars that keep the modern nomads occupied and animated in no man's land."

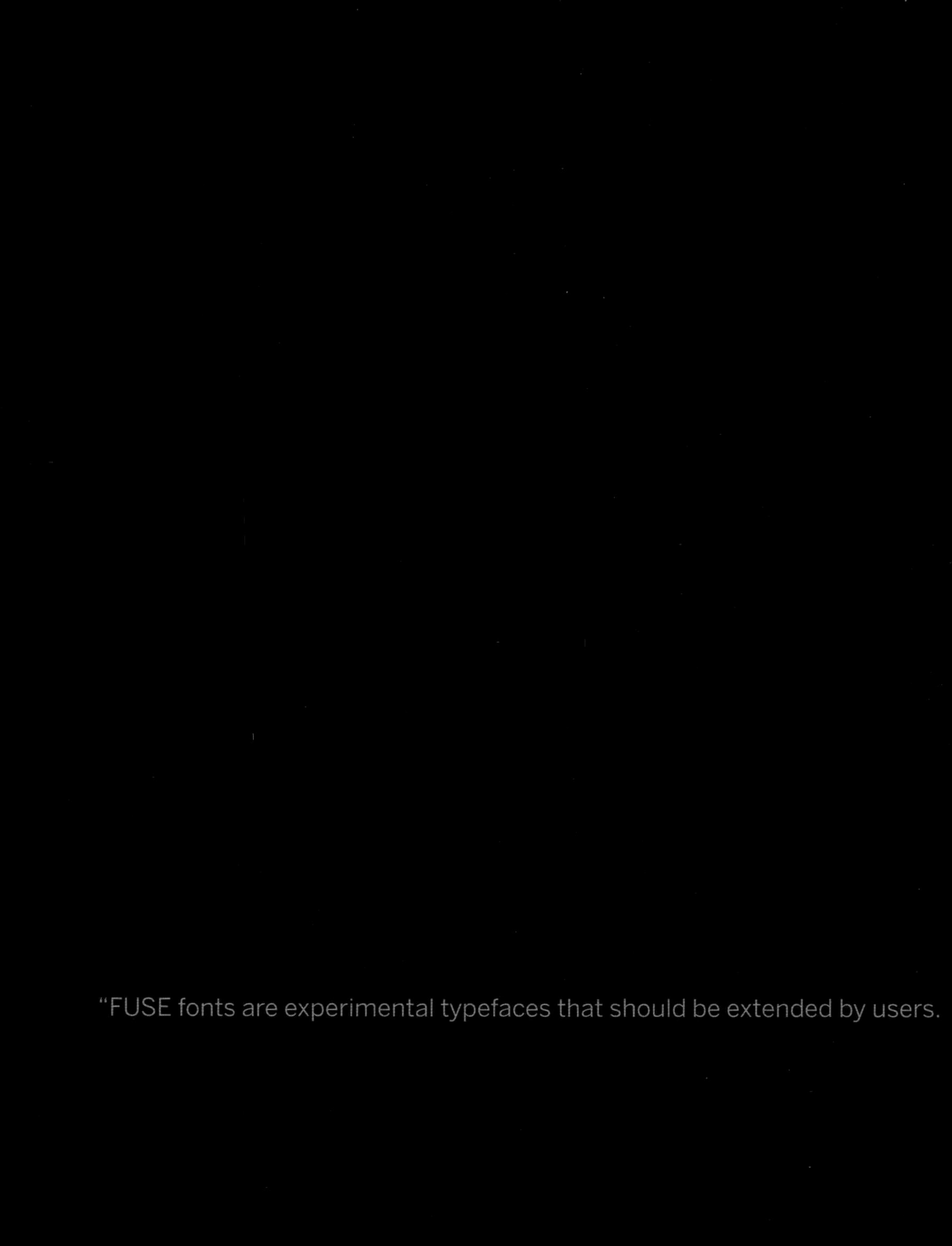

“FUSE fonts are experimental typefaces that should be extended by users.

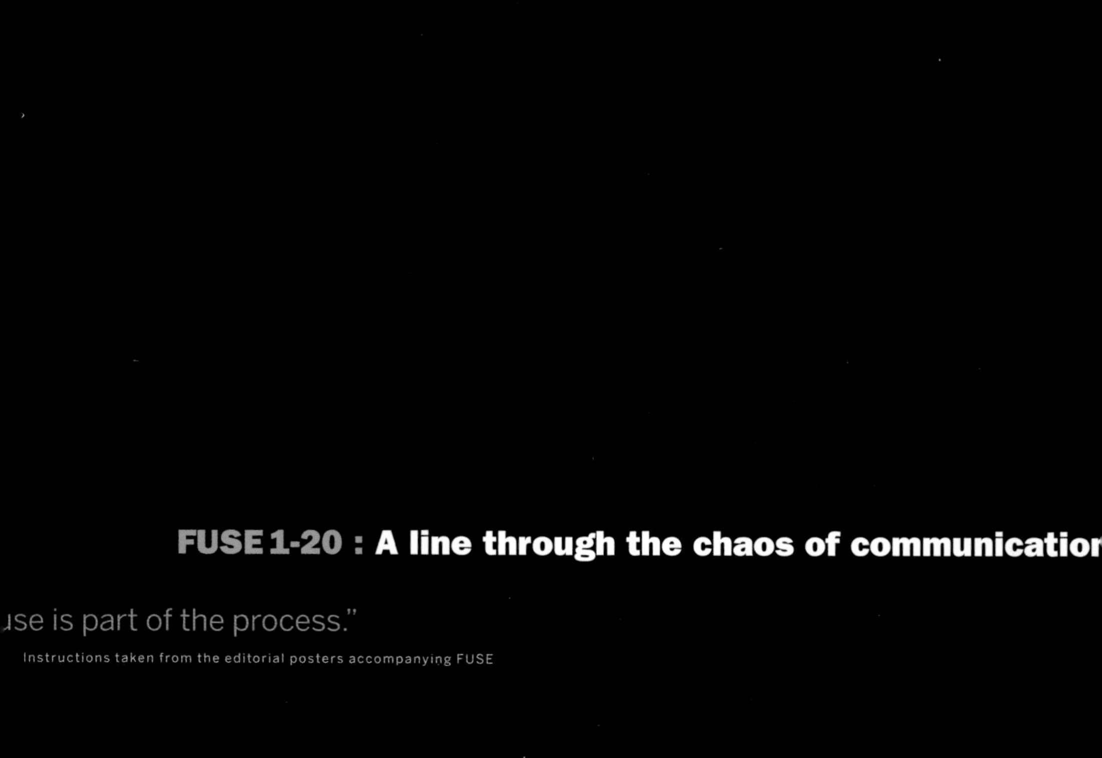

FUSE 1-20 : A line through the chaos of communicatio

use is part of the process.”

Instructions taken from the editorial posters accompanying FUSE

FUSE

FUSE
2
RUNES

FUSE
3

FUSE
7
CRASH

FUSE
RELIGION

AUTO 9
FUSE

SUPERSTITION
FUSE

14 CYBER
FOUR A2 POSTERS WITH THEIR ACCOMPANYING EXPERIMENTAL
MACINTOSH® COMPATIBLE POSTSCRIPT® FONTS DESIGNED EXCLUSIVELY BY:
'MONITEURS' RICK VERMEULEN BRETT WICKENS 'XPLICIT FFM'
+ R.C.A. STUDENTFUSE WINNERS FRANCIS STEBBING & VERA DAUCHER
FUSE

15 CITIES
FUSE

FUSE
4
EXUBERANCE

VIRTUAL
FUSE
5

FUSE
6

FUSE
10
FREEFORM

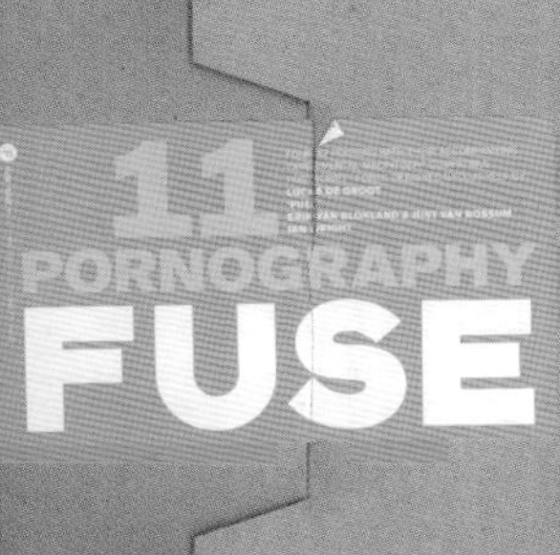

11
PORNOGRAPHY
FUSE

PROPAGANDA
FUSE
12

FUSE
16

FUSE
17
ECHO

FUSE
18

FUSE

FUSE 1: Why FUSE? Jon Wozencroft

IN

SUMMER 1991

VENTION

Over the last decade, the technical changes that have taken place in typography and typesetting have made a deep impression upon the state of language, yet outside the design profession, the power of typography is barely recognised. We are surrounded by typographic information whose influence upon our everyday environment is largely taken for granted. Perhaps this is also a form of refusal by those who, already bombarded by an obsessive and possessive media, see little benefit in getting further involved in its machinations. It is time for a fresh approach. FUSE is an interactive medium that provides the opportunity to publish an experimental font which does not need to be an 'ultimate statement', one to be appreciated or dismissed – the idea is to provide a framework for a new way of looking at language that can be adapted differently by every person who chooses to participate in this creative process. A dynamic new forum for typography will stimulate a new sensibility in visual expression, one grounded in ideas, not just image.

The Trouble with Type

Most education systems fail to provide even a basic training in media techniques and processes: it seems that the Information Age cannot persist without promoting its opposite, Disinformation, which feeds on ignorance and exclusion. Therefore in spite of the growth of information technology, it seems unlikely that typography will become a burning educational issue when standards of world literacy are themselves in such decline.

Why does typography appear so marginal? The choice of typeface is the first message of any communication and colours perception of the information it gives form to. From an early age, we are taught that typeset words should demand our attention (but never how, or why), and from then on, we perceive typography as something no more remarkable than water is to fish. In fact, we no longer see it. Consequently, mediocrity is accepted as the norm, good typography will be as rare as ever and the myths that have built up around type design will go unchallenged.

Typography has been practised as if it were an occult art. A century after the birth of printing in Europe, very few type-founders were actually allowed by law to produce moveable type even though it was in great demand. As recently as 1855, the English founder Figgins remarked, 'the art had been perpetuated by a kind of Druidical or Masonic induction from the first'.[1] When metal type did become freely available at the end of the 19th century, it was not long before the modernist movement started to promote the new sans serif letter forms as a way of returning to the principles of 'pure' typography. Tschichold was later to reflect that it "had shocking parallels with the teachings of National Socialism and Fascism", but the influence of *The New Typography* is still very much with us.

Traditionally, typographers have made the trade a closed shop. 'Pure' typography in all cases means 'only' typography – typographers alone know what typography can achieve, so no one else can be allowed to achieve it! The protective jargon of point sizes, leading and kerning compounds this insularity and supports the typographer's monastic aura.

The Digital Nightmare

But in effect, typographers maintain a schizophrenic existence, motivated by the ongoing quest for the Perfect Typeface whilst driven to meet the demands of printers, publishers and advertisers for whom the perfect typeface is simply the one that helps to sell their message best.

The perfect typeface does not in fact exist. Types that we now look upon as "classic faces" were, in their own time, innovations that were as often vilified as they were praised. In the mid-18th century, John Baskerville's perfectionism in his printing and typefounding business was so frequently derided by his peers that, lacking any financial return and fearing starvation, he was forced to abandon his work. A century later, William Morris was to call Bodoni's typefaces "shatteringly hideous". Not surprisingly, on their introduction in the late 1920s, sans serif typefaces such as *Futura* and *Kabel* deeply offended the conservative typographers of the day; as expressions of a new European sensibility, they found greater success in the United States.

Typography continues to be an innately conservative medium, resisting anything that challenges the familiarity of its 'classical' past; whilst there is no doubt that this past has provided a wealth of practical alphabets that highlight a fine balance between form and function, typography is not immune to change. In Britain, the power and restrictive practices of the Graphic Arts' Trade Union, the N.G.A., have been cast aside by new technology and anti-Union legislation, yet other areas such as the archaic copyright laws that apply to type design remain inadequate – as a number of post-war typographers, especially Hermann Zapf, have found to their cost. Digital technology throws this problem into sharp focus. It is as problematic to prevent the piracy of digitised typefaces as it is to prevent home taping of LPs and CDs – but this has done nothing to stem the tide of type.

The best way to encourage a new generation of type designers is to break open typography's closed circle, to question its traditions and to support risk-taking. The function of typography has changed – the power of television has long since broken its monopoly as a means of distributing information. Legibility is as important as ever, but it must also be linked to broader considerations of perception and recognition. With over 4000 typefaces readily available for the computer we seem to be spoilt for choice, but most of these typefaces were created for a different society with different thoughts, which it needed to communicate in different ways to ourselves. It is time that we looked for something different – without taking the easy option of creating typefaces that only illustrate the computer screen's lack of resolution.

The computer will encourage designers to create new ways of using the alphabet – but first we must clear the cobwebs that cover the type that has so quickly been digitalised and dumped in the system folder. Otherwise we will be left deeper in a digital nightmare, plundering as many hot metal typefaces as possible to compensate for our lack of imagination. We will pretend to be in command of our language, but will actually be locked in a museum.

Reference:

1. Alexander Lawson, *Anatomy of a Typeface*, Hamish Hamilton 1990

FUSE 1

FUSE IS A NEW VENTURE IN TYPE DESIGN, CONTAINING FOUR EXPERIMENTAL FONTS DIGITISED FOR MACINTOSH. THE FUSE DISC IS ACCOMPANIED BY FOUR A2 POSTERS SHOWING EACH TYPEFACE IN CREATIVE APPLICATION.

ISSUE ONE FEATURES FOUR BRITISH DESIGNERS :
PHIL BAINES
NEVILLE BRODY
MALCOLM GARRETT
IAN SWIFT

PRODUCED BY FONTSHOP INTERNATIONAL
AND DISTRIBUTED EXCLUSIVELY
THROUGH THE FONTSHOP NETWORK

FONTSHOP BELGIUM
MAALTECENTER BLOK C
DERBYSTRAAT 247
9051 ST. DENIJS-WESTREM
(GENT), BELGIUM
TEL: (32) 91 202620
FAX: (32) 91 203445

FONTSHOP CANADA
401 WELLINGTON ST. WEST
TORONTO,
ONTARIO M5V 1E8
CANADA
TEL: (1) 416 348 9837
FAX: (1) 416 593 4318

FONTSHOP HOLLAND
LAAN VAN BEEK
& ROYEN 1D
3701 AH ZEIST, HOLLAND
TEL: (31) 3404 32366
FAX: (31) 3404 24952

FONTSHOP ITALY / ROGER BLACK INC.
VIA MASOTTO 21
20159 MILANO, ITALY
TEL: (39) 2 7000 1176
FAX: (39) 2 7010 4199

FONTSHOP SWEDEN
TEGNÉRGATAN 37
111 61 STOCKHOLM,
SWEDEN
TEL: (46) 8 21 52 00
FAX: (46) 8 21 28 80

FONTWORKS UK
65-69 EAST ROAD
LONDON N1 6AH,
UNITED KINGDOM
TEL: (44) 71 490 5390
FAX: (44) 71 490 5391

FONTSHOP U.S.A.
TEL: (1) 617 227 9181
FAX: (1) 617 723 6432

FUSE

Over the last decade, the technical changes that have taken place in typography and typesetting have made a deep impression upon the state of language, yet outside the design profession, the power of typography is barely recognised. We are surrounded by typographic information whose influence upon our everyday environment is largely taken for granted. Perhaps this is also a form of refusal by those who, already bombarded by an obsessive and possessive media, see little benefit in getting further involved in its machinations.

WHY FUSE?

It is time for a fresh approach. FUSE is an interactive medium that provides the opportunity to publish an experimental font which does not need to be an 'ultimate statement', one to be appreciated or dismissed - the idea is to provide a framework for a new way of looking at language that can be adapted differently by every person who chooses to participate in this creative process. A dynamic new forum for typography will stimulate a new sensibility in visual expression, one grounded in ideas, not just image.

THE TROUBLE WITH TYPE

Most education systems fail to provide even a basic training in media techniques and processes: it seems that the Information Age cannot persist without promoting its opposite, Disinformation, which feeds on ignorance and exclusion. Therefore in spite of the growth of information technology, it seems unlikely that typography will become a burning educational issue when standards of world literacy are themselves in such decline.

Why does typography appear so marginal? The choice of typeface is the first message of any communication and colours perception of the information it gives form to. From an early age, we are taught that typeset words should demand our attention (but never how, or why), and from then on, we perceive typography as something no more remarkable than water is to fish. In fact, we no longer see it. Consequently, mediocrity is accepted as the norm, good typography will be as rare as ever and the myths that have built up around type design will go unchallenged.

Typography has been practiced as if it were an occult art. founders were actually allowed by law to produce moveable type even though it was in great demand. As recently as 1855, the English founder Figgins remarked, 'the art had been perpetuated by a kind of Druidical or Masonic induction from the first'[1]. When metal type did become freely available at the end of the 19th Century, it was not long before the modernist movement started to promote the new sans serif letterforms as a way of returning to the principles of 'pure' typography. Tschichold was later to reflect that it "had shocking parallels with the teachings of National Socialism and Fascism", but the influence of *The New Typography* is still very much with us.

Traditionally, typographers have made the trade a closed shop. 'Pure' typography in all cases means 'only' typography - typographers alone know what typography can achieve, so no-one else can be allowed to achieve it! The protective jargon of point sizes, leading and kerning compounds this insularity and supports the typographer's monastic aura.

But in effect, typographers main-tain a schizophrenic

FUSE 1

Issue 1 - Summer 1991

Contains four A2 posters each accompanied by an experimental Macintosh compatible Postscript font designed exclusively by

Phil Baines, Neville Brody, Malcolm Garrett and **Ian Swift**

THE DIGITAL NIGHTMARE

existence, motivated by the ongoing quest for the Perfect Typeface whilst driven to meet the demands of printers, publishers and advertisers for whom the perfect typeface is simply the one that helps to sell their message best.

The perfect typeface does not in fact exist. Types that we now look upon as "classic faces" were, in their own time, innovations that were as often vilified as they were praised. In the mid-18th Century, John Baskerville's perfectionism in his printing and typefounding business was so frequently derided by his peers that, lacking any financial return and fearing starvation, he was forced to abandon his work. A century later, William Morris was to call Bodoni's typefaces "shatteringly hideous". Not surprisingly, on their introduction in the late 1920s, sans serif typefaces such as Futura and Kabel deeply offended the conservative typographers of the day; as expressions of a new European sensibility, they found greater success in the United States.

Typography continues to be an innately conservative medium, resisting anything that challenges the familiarity of its 'classical' past; whilst there is no doubt that this past has provided a wealth of practical alphabets that highlight a fine balance between form and function, typography is not immune to change. In Britain, the power and restrictive practices of the Graphic Arts' Trade Union, the N.G.A, have been cast aside by new technology and anti-Union legislation, yet other areas such as the archaic copyright laws that apply to type design remain inadequate - as a number of post-war typographers, especially Hermann Zapf, have found to their cost. Digital technology throws this problem into sharp focus. It is as problematic to prevent the piracy of digitised typefaces as it is to prevent home taping of LPs and CDs - but this has done nothing to stem the tide of type.

The best way to encourage a new generation of type designers is to break open typography's closed circle, to question its traditions and to support risk-taking. The function of typography has changed - the power of television has long since broken its monopoly as a means of distributing information. Legibility is as important as ever, but it must also be linked to broader considerations of perception and recognition. With over 4000 typefaces readily available for the computer we seem to be spoilt for choice, but most of these typefaces were created for a different society with different thoughts, which it needed to communicate in different ways to ourselves. It is time that we looked for something different - without taking the easy option of creating typefaces that only illustrate the computer screen's lack of resolution.

The computer will encourage designers to create new ways of using the alphabet - but first we must clear the cobwebs that cover the type that has so quickly been digitalised and dumped in the system folder. Otherwise we will be left deeper in a digital nightmare, plundering as many hot metal typefaces as possible to compensate for our lack of imagination. We will pretend to be in command of our language, but will actually be locked in a museum.

Reference[1]
Alexander Lawson, *Anatomy of a Typeface*, Hamish Hamilton 1990

F Can You...?
PHIL BAINES

F STATE
NEVILLE BRODY

F STEALTH
MALCOLM GARRETT

F MAZE 91
IAN SWIFT

Phil Baines was born in Kendal in the English Lake District in 1958. Since studying Graphic Design at St. Martin's School of Art and at the Royal College of Art between 1982 and '87, he has worked as a freelance designer for various clients, including Monotype Typography and The Craft's Council. He teaches letterpress techniques one day a week at Central St. Martin's College of Art & Design in London and is currently editing and designing *Rookledge's International Handbook of Type Designers*, due to be published in late 1991.

Can You (and Do You Want to) Read Me? *My original drawings for this typeface were done some eight years ago, based on research by Brian Coe into how much of a letter need be visible to be recognised. His original alphabet - see Herbert Spencer's* Visible Word *(Lund Humphries, 1969, p.62) - was a monoline sans serif. I changed it to a 'modern' and found that, thanks to the serifs, further pruning could take place and continuous strokes could form the characters, rather than the separate strokes of his original.*

Looking at the drawings again recently, I decided it was worth taking further; firstly, the modern serifs and thins were too stark and contrasting - a Clarendon proved better, its larger serifs giving clues and greater weight to strong characters. The next stage involved ignoring the objectivity of the original and looking at the letters from a purely subjective, visual point of view. Further pruning then took place to emphasise the new shapes, and some letters (to break up the hitherto consistent x-height) were reduced to only their bottom halves.

The punctuation is, in part, a response to ideas in design which suggest its abolition except within continuous text. I like punctuation and wanted to make it very prominent. The word space is almost a reference to the 'body' of metal type - here it helps to isolate the words and thus reinforce recognition.

I have no plans for an upper case but suggest that, if one is needed, complete lower-case characters are used from Adobe Clarendon Light. The F Can You...? characters in non-standard positions on the Macintosh keyboard are - ff (Option 4), fi (option 5), ffl (Shift 3), fl (option shift l), and æ (Op. ').

Neville Brody did his best to avoid typography until he was forced to look for new ways of treating type whilst Art Director of *The Face* between 1982-86. During this time he designed a series of typefaces, of which the recently published *Industria* and *Typeface Six* are the best known. Having since been Art Director of *Arena*, *Per Lui* and *Lei* magazines, he is presently Art Director of *Actuel*. Recent commissions have included the station identity for Premiere, a national German TV channel, and the 1991 calendar for Parco, one of the largest department stores in Tokyo. A Thames and Hudson book was published to co-incide with a touring exhibition of his work, which has so far been seen in England, Scotland, Germany and Japan. Brody runs his own studio in London.

State *The idea is to get inside the structure of the alphabet and to accentuate the shapes that are inherent in written language. The negative shapes are given equal prominence to the positive, an attempt to diffuse the power of language and the hierarchy imposed by typographic rules. Perhaps for this reason, the typeface is not practical for day-to-day use. Readability is a conditioned state. I wanted to take the role of typography away from a purely subservient, practical role towards one that is potentially more expressive and visually dynamic. There are no special characters and presently no lower-case is planned. The font is designed to have no letter spacing, and ideally it should be set with no line space. I decided not to include a complete set of punctuation marks and accents, prefering people to create their own if needed.*

Malcolm Garrett is design director of the UK consultancy Assorted Images. He studied typography at Reading University 1974-75 and Graphic Design at Manchester Polytechnic between 1975 and '78. In 1977 he began a long period of working with the music industry, with clients such as Buzzcocks, Simple Minds, Culture Club and Duran Duran. In 1983, Garrett formed a partnership with Kasper de Graaf, former editor of *New Sounds New Styles*, to develop the wider potential of the creative team at Assorted Images along with an increasing commitment to the use of electronic design tools. Garrett has judged for the D&AD annual awards each year from 1988 to 1990; a book of his work is planned for later this year, to coincide with an exhibition in Tokyo and at the Design Museum in London.

Stealth *This typeface is designed primarily for use as initials alongside a sans serif text, and, like Japanese characters, these letters work equally well in either a horizontal or vertical format. The initial aim of the design was to reduce each character to a single continuous line, but for reasons of aethetics and legibility I chose to make a few exceptions. It is a single case font, although there are some random alternative characters for no other reason than personal whim (to be found under lower-case e, t and x).*

The characters rigidly adhere to a grid made up of two concentric circles of different diameters; I wanted the character height to seem inconsistent, with the letters not quite balanced within their containing squares. This marriage of structure and incongruity appealed to me. The classical references inherent in the notion of initial caps, and the use of non-aligning characters to complement non-aligning numerals are other interesting aspects of this strictly modernist font.

Ian Swift studied Graphic Design at Manchester Polytechnic between 1983-86 before joining *The Face* and then *Arena*, for whom he became Art Director in 1990. Swifty currently runs his own studio in London, specializing in work for dance labels Talking Loud and SBK Records. He has been design director of the quarterly Jazz magazine *Straight No Chaser* since 1989.

Maze 91 *Maze - labyrinth, network of paths and hedges designed as a puzzle for those who try to penetrate it; (fig) confusion, confused mass, etc. Bewilder, confuse (AMAZE).*

Maze was created primarily on the Fontastic Plus programme - its bitmap feel was developed from a font I designed over two years ago, Block Extra. *Once I had outlined the font, I started chopping chunks off the sides, toiling with the idea of how much type you actually needed to make a letter legible.*

Readability was no great concern. The abstract quality is something I like, and the font can still be read even if it is a bit of a struggle. I butted the characters together so that without any spacing the words are more like abstract shapes.

NEVILLE BRODY & JON WOZENCROFT EDITORIAL POSTER

POSTSCRIPT TECHOSPEC

Bitmap fonts are responsible for screen display, and are installed in your system folder using Apple's Font/DA Mover. Check your Macintosh Utilities for details. You can also open the font suitcase file with a font management utility, eg. Suitcase II. Screen display is most accurate for the sizes installed in the system folder, but your Macintosh can compute any other size from those installed. Screenfonts (as they're also called) take up a lot of space on your system disk, so it's best only to install the sizes you actually need.

Outline fonts - Printer fonts are defined by outlines which are resolution independent and can be scaled to any size supported by your application. The quality of the output depends on the printer - from medium resolution LaserWriter to high resolution film recorders. The outline fonts have to be kept *loose* in the system folder, not in a folder of their own. Again, your Macintosh manual provides more information. Never alter the names of font files as the Macintosh looks for abbreviations with five letters followed by another three letters.

Installing Bitmap fonts After inserting the FUSE disk, open the Font/DA Mover supplied with your system. Click on the right hand Open button, then on Drive. Select the faces and sizes you want to install, and click Copy. Finally, click Close.

Installing Outline fonts - Install the outline fonts by copying the files into your system folder. Leave them loose in the system folder.

Automatic downloading - Most applications will automatically download the fonts needed to print a document, as long as the appropriate outline font files are present in the system folder.

Manual downloading If several documents use the same fonts, it can save printing time to initially download the fonts manually, using the Apple LaserWriter font utility.

SUBMIT

The role of FUSE is to promote typographic innovation. We welcome your input - if you would like to present your own experimental type design and poster for inclusion in a future edition, please write to FUSE at the address below submitting, if not a digitised typeface on disc, then a clear proposal and outline of your idea, enclosing in both cases an SAE/IRC. We also plan to expand this section to include examples of your own manipulations of published FUSE fonts, any experimental type that you have created but have no plans to digitise, and to publish any critique or comment you have on typography. Is it type that's getting more distressed by photocopiers and fax machines or is it us? What's the idea behind backward-kerning? Tell us what you have seen that has impressed and inspired you!

FOR THE FUTURE

FUSE is published quarterly and distributed through the FontShop network. Future editions of FUSE will include new typefaces from as many origins as possible, linked to themes that range from the secret alphabets of Runes to electromagnetism, 'virtual typography' and the effects of digital information. Each FUSE is published in a limited edition; be sure to reserve a copy by contacting the FontShop in your area.

ACHTUNG!

FUSE fonts do not include a full set of upper and lower case characters, though each type design has been duplicated so that it works in both cases; nor does every font cover a full range of accents and special characters. Fuse fonts are experimental typefaces that should be extended by users. Abuse is part of the process.

Issue 1 - Summer 1991
Editor & text by Jon Wozencroft; design by Neville Brody.
Published & © 1991 by FSI GmbH.
Typefaces and Posters © 1991 the designers.
FSI, Bergmannstraße 102, 1000 Berlin 61, Germany.
Fuse, Top Floor Studio, 65 - 69 East Road, London N1 6AH, England

FUSE 1: Phil Baines Can You...?

Can You (and Do You Want to) Read Me?
My original drawings for this typeface were done some eight years ago, based on research by Brian Coe into how much of a letter need be visible to be recognised. His original alphabet – see Herbert Spencer's *Visible Word* (Lund Humphries, 1969, p.62) – was a monoline sans serif. I changed it to a 'modern' and found that, thanks to the serifs, further pruning could take place and continuous strokes could form the characters, rather than the separate strokes of his original. Looking at the drawings again recently, I decided it was worth taking further; firstly, the modern serifs and thins were too stark and contrasting – a *Clarendon* proved better, its larger serifs giving clues and greater weight to strong characters. The next stage involved ignoring the objectivity of the original and looking at the letters from a purely subjective, visual point of view. Further pruning then took place to emphasise the new shapes, and some letters (to break up the hitherto consistent x-height) were reduced to only their bottom halves. The punctuation is, in part, a response to ideas in design which suggest its abolition except within continuous text. I like punctuation and wanted to make it very prominent. The word space is almost a reference to the 'body' of metal type – here it helps to isolate the words and thus reinforce recognition. I have no plans for an upper case but suggest that, if one is needed, complete lower-case characters are used from *Adobe Clarendon Light*. The *Can You...?* characters in non-standard positions on the keyboard are – ff (Option 4), ffi (Op. shift 5), ffl (Op. 6), ℗ (Op. P), [ ] (( )), æ (Op. ').

FUSE 1: Neville Brody State

The idea is to get inside the structure of the alphabet and to accentuate the shapes that are inherent in written language. The negative shapes are given equal prominence to the positive, an attempt to diffuse the power of language and the hierarchy imposed by typographic rules. Perhaps for this reason, the typeface is not practical for day-to-day use. Readability is a conditioned state. I wanted to take the role of typography away from a purely subservient, practical role towards one that is potentially more expressive and visually dynamic. There are no special characters and presently no lower-case is planned. The font is designed to have no letter spacing, and ideally it should be set with no line space. I decided not to include a complete set of punctuation marks and accents, preferring people to create their own if needed.

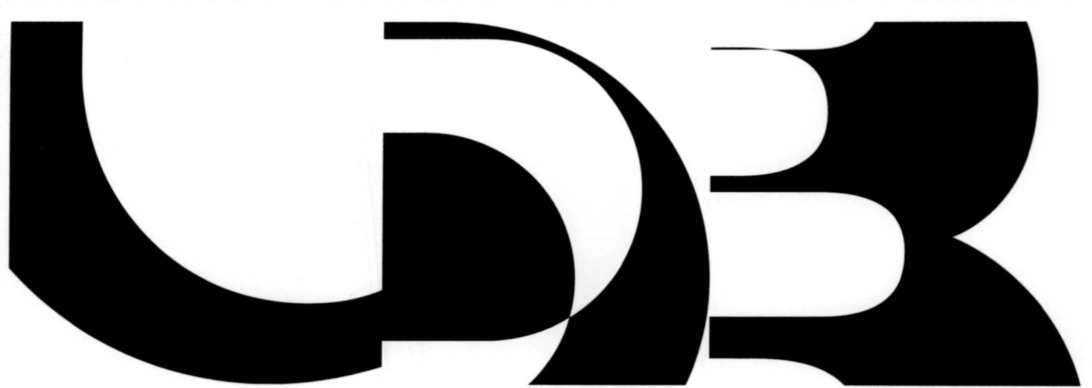

POSTER DESIGN **NEVILLE BRODY** TYPEFACE **FF STATE** POSTER ©1991 FONTSHOP INTERNATIONAL ©1991 NEVILLE BRODY

USE
M
X
7 G 2 1 8
5
0 3
4 + 9
HIST-
ORY BE
IT - LONGS
TO
TODAY
ÉZÇß V
Q
K T
J
THE ?
! ?WEI
FUTU-
RE
FUSE
DIFF
USE

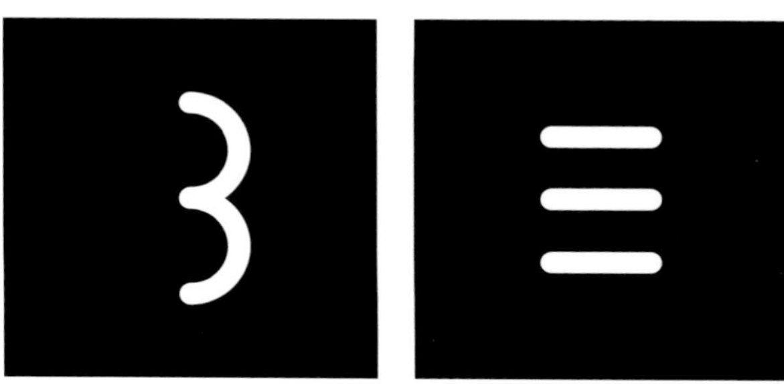

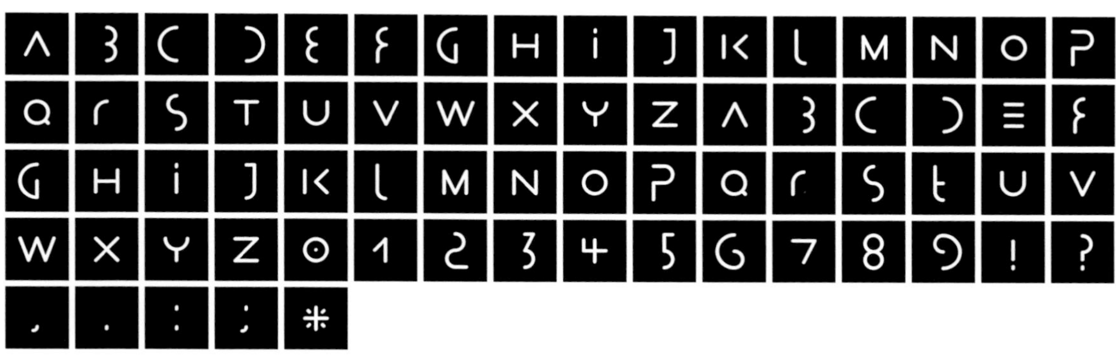

FUSE 1: Malcolm Garrett Stealth

This typeface is designed primarily for use as initials alongside a sans serif text, and, like Japanese characters, these letters work equally well in either a horizontal or vertical format. The initial aim of the design was to reduce each character to a single continuous line, but for reasons of aesthetics and legibility I chose to make a few exceptions. It is a single case font, although there are some random alternative characters for no other reason than personal whim. The characters rigidly adhere to a grid made up of two concentric circles of different diameters; I wanted the character height to seem inconsistent, with the letters not quite balanced within their containing squares. This marriage of structure and incongruity appealed to me. The classical references inherent in the notion of initial caps, and the use of non-aligning characters to complement non-aligning numerals are other interesting aspects of this strictly modernist font.

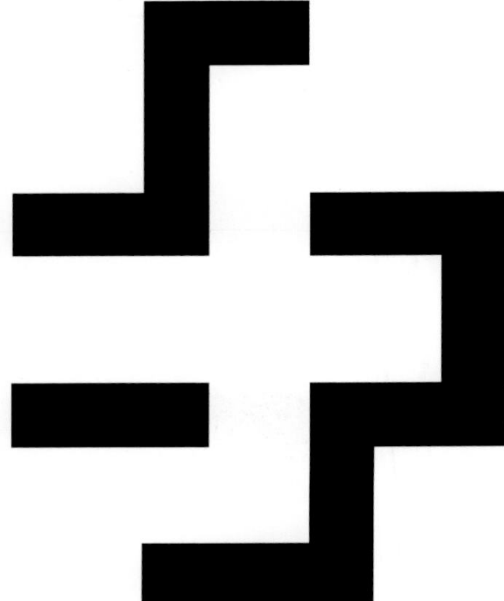

FUSE 1: Ian Swift Maze 91

Maze – labyrinth, network of paths and hedges designed as a puzzle for those who try to penetrate it; (fig.) confusion, confused mass, etc. Bewilder, confuse (AMAZE). *Maze* was created primarily on the Fontastic Plus program – its bitmap feel was developed from a font I designed over two years ago, *Block Extra*. Once I had outlined the font, I started chopping chunks off the sides, toiling with the idea of how much type you actually needed to make a letter legible. Readability was no great concern. The abstract quality is something I like, and the font can still be read even if it is a bit of a struggle. I butted the characters together so that without any spacing the words are more like abstract shapes.

0123456789

POSTER DESIGN IAN SWIFT TYPEFACE FF MAZE91 POSTER ©1991 FONTSHOP INTERNATIONAL ©IAN SWIFT

FUSE

FUSE 2: Wind Blasted Trees: A Short History of Runes

Jon Wozencroft

RUNES

Before the Latin alphabet had taken over Europe, a magical alphabet was in common use – but its potential for lateral thought so disturbed the Church that its practitioners would later be branded as witches and burnt at the stake.

A satellite in space can single out and photograph a car number plate anywhere on the earth's surface. Electronic impulses reach computer ports that give instantaneous information on the latest grain prices. DNA technology has told us more about the origins of the human species in the last few years than researchers and explorers have been able to tell us in the last 2000. So that mystery might remain mystery, it is therefore just as well that some areas of human knowledge and endeavour fall beyond the grip of scientific rationalisation and explanation.

Before the Latin alphabet had taken over Europe, a magical alphabet was in common use which claimed powers that are these days rarely acknowledged to be possible (or even credible) in our present state of language. 'Runes' is the name given to a range of European scripts that probably date back to the 2nd or 3rd century AD. They are said to illuminate the unspoken and the spaces between words – as channels to the intuitive realm that exists before and beyond words, they are able to reveal 'information' whose use demands lateral thinking.

Runes were derived neither from Latin nor Greek letterforms (although this has, in the past, been suggested and rejected by scholars), and whilst a few show similarities to the Etruscan alphabet developed in Central and Northern Italy (c.500 BC), the origins of most runes are still unclear. They may have been developed when sigils (magically encoded signs) used in rock carvings and divination magic were matched to certain transalpine characters from the Etruscan script, but according to Norse legend in the *Hàvamàl*, the act of synthesis which enabled them to be used by humans came when the god Odin spent nine days and nights in self-crucifixion "hanging on the wind-blasted tree" where, at the peak of his self-torturing ritual (common to all shamanist practice), the runes were revealed to him and "screaming, I took them, then I fell back from that place".

Legends abound concerning the genesis of all languages. For example, Hermes is said to have invented the Greek alphabet after watching the shapes and patterns created by the beating wings of cranes who "make letters as they fly", but it is more likely that, thanks to established trading routes, both the Greek and the Hebrew alphabets were developed from the Phoenician model around the 8th centuries BC.

Runes have always been associated with magic. The Nordic/Anglo-Saxon word *run*, the Icelandic *runar* and the high-German *runa* are connected to the Gothic *runa*, meaning "mystery" and "secret". This is the source behind the modern German word *raunen*, "to whisper". In modern Irish, *rún* means both "a secret" and "a resolution", which connects to the Anglo-Saxon practice of using runes for decision-making: before Christianity, counsels held in England were called *the Runes*. However, runic scripts are primarily so-called because the Teutons (for whom runes can be considered the 'national' text) sought to attribute magical powers to the inscriptions and symbols carved on armour, jewellery, tombstones and so on. Runes were used to gain advantage in contests and battles, for legal purposes, for healing, for safe passage, to increase intelligence, to protect, for love and seduction. Runic calendars were developed in the form of tablets of wood or bone, as swords or as staves that varied in height – from walking sticks to stacks as tall as those who used them. In Norway they were called *Primstaves*, *prim* being "golden number", and in Denmark *Rimstocks*, from *rim*, "calendar", *stock*, "stick".

Again, it is unclear to what extent the use of runes was 'religiously' restricted, nor how widespread was their use as a 'normal' means of communication. We also like to believe that the runes have been passed down intact, in spite of their variations. Three principal runic systems have survived – the Elder Futhark (meaning "alphabet", referring to the initial letters F-U-T-H-A-R-K of the runic script), the Anglo-Saxon and the Northumbrian – plus an extended system of 38 runes. The Anglo-Saxon and Elder Futhark runes can also be inverted to give different meanings. The possibilities for interpretation are complex enough. Whatever we think we know must always be balanced with our ignorance of their exact origins.

We know that runes do have a phonetic basis and are not simply ornamental. Germanic forms of speech were carried to the British Isles in the 5th and 6th century AD by heathen invaders, the Angles, Saxons and Jutes, causing the great modification to Old English of vowel mutation which increased the 24 Teutonic runes to 33 in the Anglo-Saxon runic alphabet. This was important to the development of the present Roman alphabet. The Anglo-Saxon runes then influenced the adaptation of the Roman alphabet to Old English, thus establishing the tripartite Latin/Old English/German (Runic) core in Modern English. (The impact of French language was not felt until after the Norman invasion of England.) A runic poem from King Alfred's time shows this merging starting to take shape:

> Thorn byth thearle scearp thegna gehwylcum,
> Anfengys yfyl, ungemetun rethe
> Manna gehwylcum the him mid resteth.
>
> (Thorn is most sharp to every man,
> Its assault evil, enormously harsh
> To any man who rests upon it.)

Closely related to runes are the tree languages of the Druids based in Wales and Ireland where the names of trees and their 'qualities' are matched to individual letters and the times of year. Runes share strong affinities with another tree language, the Oghams, a script that was more or less restricted to the Celtic-speaking peoples of Britain. The Gaelic word *ogham* refers to a form of cryptic speech in which the names of letters could replace the letters. One theory suggests that they were originally a finger-alphabet invented by the Druids as a private signalling code which was later translated into a written form, based on a letter-unit of 5 dashes – an early form of numerology. Again, this was predominantly used for

FUSE2

FUSE : THE NEW VENTURE IN TYPE DESIGN. IT CONTAINS FOUR EXPERIMENTAL FONTS DIGITISED FOR MACINTOSH. THE FUSE DISC IS ACCOMPANIED BY FOUR A2 POSTERS SHOWING EACH TYPEFACE IN CREATIVE APPLICATION.

FUSE TWO, *RUNES*, FEATURES FOUR DUTCH DESIGNERS :
MAX KISMAN
GERARD UNGER
ERIK VAN BLOKLAND
JUST VAN ROSSUM

inscriptions, but later, wherever ogham texts were found, they sufficiently disturbed the Christian Church that the sign of the cross was imposed upon them. Some occultists still believe the oghams to have been the written language of Atlantis.

Whilst Irish and Roman missionaries went to considerable lengths to suppress the runic script in the 7th and 8th centuries, runes were in use in England for about 500 years. They were in even more widespread use and lasted much longer in Scandinavia and Iceland, whose "Futhark" eventually had to remedy its phonetic shortcomings by the use of dotted runes (hence the range of accents in modern Scandinavian languages). Elsewhere, after the 13/14th century, the use of runes diminished, except in remote areas such as Gotland that had evaded the grip of the Latin Church. By the time of the witch trials that took place across Northern Europe during the Middle Ages, anyone who even dared to write in runes could expect to be burnt at the stake. Is it conceivable that a typeform might once again induce such dread and superstition?

In spite of their prohibition, in most parts of Europe the use of runes survived for some time in the rural tradition. However, as signifiers not only of paganism but of 'black magic', they were increasingly marginalised and forced underground – where, having been outlawed, their magical powers became even more focused. Runes thus remained active in occult circles – and in such a setting they were "rediscovered" hundreds of years later by Hitler who wished to appropriate their links with Teutonic mythology and use their magical properties to promote his own tyrannical purpose. The Nazi use of runes is an extreme example that it is worthwhile to consider alongside present arguments concerning the correct usage of language and the notion of freedom of expression. Runes were applied to Nazi medals, to SS insignia and uniforms, to the crests painted onto Panzer tanks, etcetera. The Nazi abuse of the occult has compounded the fear of magic in Western civilisation, a fear that dates back to the rise of Christianity, the beginnings of urban settlement and mankind's quest to control nature. And it is this recent abuse that has consolidated the association of runes with satanism, when historically, the opposite is true: runes have predominantly been used as a medium for insight and for liberation.

Today, in support of their dark associations, you might find runes used on the cover of a Heavy Metal LP. However, with the ascendency of 'New Age' culture, green issues, and Gaia philosophy, in our quest for purism we are brought back into contact with ways of seeing and their languages that previously our forefathers have attempted to eradicate. The magical properties of runes will transcend previous abuse if present and future practitioners follow simple guidelines – to research, to reflect and to respect their potential. As part of the ongoing process of urban breakdown and renewal, ecology will soon have to be applied to language, and the question of mental pollution confronted.

In fact, runic forms are already widespread. They were initially developed as markings that could easily be inscribed on wood, on stone or on metal with straight lines and angles. We have come full circle. The digitalisation of the alphabet, in effect, means that it becomes increasingly runic (cf. dot-matrix and bitmap typefaces, the resolution of type when processed through a fax machine, LED train indicators and signboards). The traffic signs that mean 'One Way' and 'No Stopping' use runic symbols. Following on from the multinational logo of the SS, corporate logos have become increasingly runic. Proof-reading symbols on manuscripts are runic. A prescription from the doctor's surgery is in such an illegible scrawl it can be said to be runic. And just as technical jargon, subcultural dialect and fashionable 'in-words' form exclusion zones within a language, so does the diaspora of modern life insist upon esoteric written counterparts. Hip-hop graffiti is runic. Marks left as coded signs on buildings by gypsies are runic. Recently, there was an article in the English press describing how burglars have developed a runic style of markings to denote which properties were worth breaking into, whether they had guard dogs, whether or not the owners were on holiday, etc., etc. New language is generated when and where it is needed. But it is also generated when and where new

As part of the ongoing process of urban breakdown and renewal, ecology will soon have to be applied to language, and the question of mental pollution confronted.

technologies and products seek to improve the *distribution* of language: a loop with which we are in danger of hanging ourselves.

All and any language has magical and ritual foundations. The need for a new medium of communication to illuminate the transformational processes that foreshadow its creation is a precondition. Were the potential for transformation not to be apparent, the new language would never survive its incubation. Nevertheless, a language once it has gained dominion over all others to become a 'world language' becomes less an agent for change, and instead, consolidates its hold (as it must do, for 'world language' is rarely the first language of its speakers). Its basis in magic is appeased by the familiarity that arises from centuries of usage. Furthermore, the transformational processes are increasingly taking place on technological, rather than human terms.

The ability of modern languages to assimilate anything that serves their hegemony is yet to be seriously questioned. The (American) English language, through information technology, is being as fervently applied as the Roman language was with the rise of Christianity. With a greater understanding and appreciation of runes, we come to a closer awareness of the possibilities inherent in our own language. We need to rediscover the pretexts of 'ancient' languages, even if we do not swallow them whole, if we are to develop letterforms that re-empower our communicative possibilities in the present climate.

Reference:

1. David Diringer, *The Alphabet*, Hutchinson 1948 **2.** Robert Graves, *The White Goddess*, Faber & Faber 1961 **3.** Nigel Pennick, *The Secret Lore of Runes*, Rider Books 1991

TECHNOSPEC

Bitmap fonts are responsible for screen display, and are installed in your system folder using Apple's Font/DA Mover. Check your Macintosh Utilities for details. You can also open the font suitcase file with a font management utility, eg. Suitcase II. Screen display is most accurate for the sizes installed in the system folder, but your Macintosh can compute any other size from those installed. Screenfonts (as they're also called) take up a lot of space on your system disk, so it's best only to install the sizes you actually need.

Outline fonts - Printer fonts are defined by outlines which are resolution independent and can be scaled to any size supported by your application. The quality of the output depends on the printer - from medium resolution LaserWriter to high resolution film recorders. The outline fonts have to be kept *loose* in the system folder, not in a folder of their own. Again, your Macintosh manual provides more information. Never alter the names of font files as the Macintosh looks for abbreviations with five letters followed by another three letters.

Installing Bitmap fonts - After inserting the FUSE disk, open the Font/DA Mover supplied with your system. Click on the right hand Open button, then on Drive. Select the faces and sizes you want to install, and click Copy. Finally, click Close.

Installing Outline fonts - Install the outline fonts by copying the files into your system folder. Leave them loose in the system folder.

Automatic downloading - Most applications will automatically download the fonts needed to print a document, as long as the appropriate outline font files are present in the system folder.

Manual downloading - If several documents use the same fonts, it can save printing time to initially download the fonts manually, using the Apple LaserWriter font utility.

SUBMIT

The role of FUSE is to promote typographic innovation. We welcome your input - if you would like to present your own experimental type design and poster for inclusion in a future edition, please write to FUSE at the address below submitting, if not a digitised typeface on disc, then a clear proposal and outline of your idea, enclosing in both cases an SAE/IRC. We will continue to expand this section to include examples of your own manipulations of published FUSE fonts, any experimental type that you have created but have no plans to digitise, and to publish any critique or comment you have on typography.

CONTACT

FUSE is published quarterly and distributed through the FontShop network. Future editions of FUSE will include new typefaces from as many origins as possible, linked to themes that range from information surrealism to electromagnetism, 'virtual typography' and the effects of digital information. Each FUSE is published in a limited edition - reserve a copy by contacting the FontShop in your area.

BITTE...

FUSE fonts do not include a full set of upper and lower case characters, though each type design has been duplicated so that it works in both cases; nor does every font cover a full range of accents and special characters. Fuse fonts are experimental typefaces that should be extended by users. Abuse is part of the process.

Issue 1 - Summer 1991
Editor & text by Jon Wozencroft;
design by Neville Brody.
Published & © 1991 by FSI GmbH.
Typefaces and Posters © 1991 the designers.

FSI, Bergmannstraße 102,
1000 Berlin 61, Germany.

Correspondence to FUSE,
65 - 69 East Road,
London N1 6AH, England

FUSE

Fuse in the Runic alphabet

FUSE 2 RUNES

Issue 2 - Autumn 1991

Contains four A2 posters each accompanied by an experimental Macintosh compatible Postscript font designed exclusively by **Max Kisman, Gerard Unger, Erik van Blokland** and **Just van Rossum**

Plus essays on **Runes** by Jon Wozencroft and **Chocolate letters** by Gerard Unger

Wind Blasted Trees : A Short History of Runes

Before the Latin alphabet had taken over Europe, a magical alphabet was in common use - but its potential for lateral thought so disturbed the Church that its practitioners would later be branded as witches and burnt at the stake.

Runic or Futhark Alphabet

2

DECODER
DIKODER

GERARD UNGER D'CODER

MAX KISMAN LINEAR KONSTRUKT

Consulting runestacks in 16th Century Scandinavia

3

NEVILLE BRODY & JON WOZENCROFT EDITORIAL PAMPHLET FEATURING GERARD UNGER

Manna gehwylcum the him mid resteth.
(Thorn is most sharp to every man.
Its assault evil, enormously harsh
To any man who rests upon it.)

Closely related to runes are the tree languages of the Druids based in Wales and Ireland where the names of trees and their 'qualities' are matched to individual letters and the times of year. Runes share strong affinities with another tree language, the Oghams, a script that was more or less restricted to the Celtic-speaking peoples of Britain. The Gaelic word *ogham* refers to a form of cryptic speech in which the names of letters could replace the letters. One theory suggests that they were originally a finger-alphabet invented by the Druids as a private signalling code which was later translated into a written form, based on a letter-unit of 5 dashes - an early form of numerology. Again, this was predominantly used for inscriptions, but later, wherever ogham texts were found, they sufficiently disturbed the Christian church that the sign of the cross was imposed upon them. Some occultists still believe the oghams to have been the written language of Atlantis.

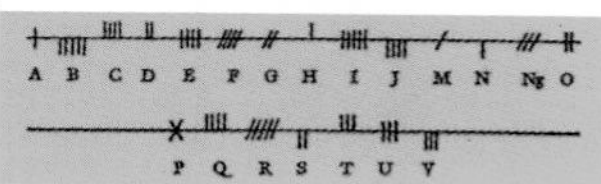

The Ogham alphabet

Whilst Irish and Roman missionaries went to considerable lengths to suppress the runic script in the 7th and 8th Centuries, runes were in use in England for about 500 years. They were in even more widespread use and lasted much longer in Scandinavia and Iceland, whose "Futhark" eventually had to remedy its phonetic shortcomings by the use of dotted runes (hence the range of accents in modern Scandinavian languages). Elsewhere, after the 13/14th Century, the use of runes diminished, except in remote areas such as Gotland that had evaded the grip of the Latin church. By the time of the witch trials that took place across Northern Europe during the Middle Ages, anyone who even dared to write in runes could expect to be burnt at the stake. Is it conceivable that a typeform might once again induce such dread and superstition?

In spite of their prohibition, in most parts of Europe the use of runes survived for some time in the rural tradition. However, as signifiers not only of paganism but of 'black magic', they were increasingly marginalised and forced underground - where, having been outlawed, their magical powers became even more focused. Runes thus remained active in occult circles - and in such a setting they were "rediscovered" hundreds of years later by Hitler who wished to appropriate their links with Teutonic mythology and use their magical properties to promote his own tyrannical purpose. The Nazi use of runes is an extreme example that it is worthwhile to consider alongside present arguments concerning the correct usage of language and the notion of freedom of expression. Runes were applied to Nazi medals, to SS insignia and uniforms, to the crests painted onto Panzer tanks, etcetera. The Nazi abuse of the occult has compounded the fear of magic in Western civilisation, a fear that dates back to the rise of Christianity, the beginnings of urban settlement and mankind's quest to control nature. And it is this recent abuse that has consolidated the association of runes to satanism, when historically, the opposite is true: runes have predominantly been used as a medium for insight and for liberation.

Today, in support of their dark associations, you might find runes used on the cover of a Heavy Metal LP. However, with the ascendency of 'New Age' culture, green issues, and Gaia philosophy, in our quest for purism we are brought back into contact with ways of seeing and their languages that previously our forefathers have attempted to eradicate. The magical properties of runes will transcend previous abuse if present and future practitioners follow simple guidelines - to research, to reflect and to respect their potential. As part of the ongoing process of urban breakdown and renewal, ecology will soon have to be applied to language, and the question of mental pollution confronted.

In fact, runic forms are already widespread. They were initially developed as markings that could easily be inscribed on wood, on stone or on metal with straight lines and angles. We have come full circle. The digitalisation of the alphabet, in effect, means that it becomes increasingly runic (cf. dot-matrix and bitmap typefaces, the resolution of type when processed through a fax machine, LED train indicators and signboards). The traffic signs that mean 'One Way' and 'No Stopping' use runic symbols. Following on from the multinational logo of the SS, corporate logos have become increasingly runic. Proof reading symbols on manuscripts are runic. A prescription from the doctor's surgery is in such an illegible scrawl it can be said to be runic. And just as technical jargon, subcultural dialect and fashionable 'in-words' form exclusion zones within a language, so does the diaspora of modern life insist upon esoteric written counterparts. Hip-hop graffiti is runic. Marks left as coded signs on buildings by gypsies are runic. Recently, there was an article in the English press describing how burglars have developed a runic style of markings to denote which properties were worth breaking into, whether they had guard dogs, whether or not the owners were on holiday, etc. etc. New language is gen-erated when and where it is needed. But it is also generated when and where new technologies and products seek to improve the *distribution* of language: a loop with which we are in danger of hanging ourselves.

All and any language has magical and ritual foundations. The need for a new medium of communication to illuminate the transformational processes that foreshadow its creation is a precondition. Were the potential for transformation not to be apparent, the new language would never survive its incubation. Nevertheless, a language once it has gained dominion over all others to become a 'world language' becomes less an agent for change, and instead, consolidates its hold (as it must do, for 'world language' is rarely the first language of its speakers). Its basis in magic is appeased by the familiarity that arises from centuries of usage. Furthermore, the transformational processes are increasingly taking place on technological, rather than human terms.

The ability of modern languages to assimilate anything that serves their hegemony is yet to be seriously questioned. The (American) English language, through information technology, is being as fervently applied as the Roman language was with the rise of Christianity. With a greater understanding and appreciation of runes, we come to a closer awareness of the possibilities inherent in our own language. We need to rediscover the pretexts of 'ancient' languages, even if we do not swallow them whole, if we are to develop letterforms that re-empower our communicative possibilities in the present climate.

Reference: 1. David Diringer, *The Alphabet*, Hutchinson 1948. 2. Robert Graves, *The White Goddess*, Faber & Faber 1961. 3. Nigel Pennick, *The Secret Lore of Runes*, Rider Books 1991.

Chocolate Runes

As soon as the grain had been harvested and turned into flour, cakes in the shapes of runes were made and eaten as offerings to Odin, god of literacy.

ERIK VAN BLOKLAND NIWIDA
JUST VAN ROSSUM FLIXEL

FUSE 2: Chocolate Runes Gerard Unger

About 2000 years ago, the Dutch (or the original inhabitants of Holland) made rune-shaped cakes, a custom that is now connected with Saint Nicolas but was originally a ritual that celebrated the Norse god Odin, one of whose gifts to man was the runic script. In North and Northwestern Europe, Odin (Wotan) was one of the gods of the Teutons. He rode a miraculous horse and wore a hat on his head whilst wielding a magic spear. He was the god of literacy and of poetry. He was god of the wind and therefore of sailors and of harvests, and because of that, also of fertility, of lovers and of children, and so on.

As soon as the grain had been harvested and turned into flour, cakes in the shapes of runes were made and eaten as offerings to Odin. It was believed that the eating of these cakes made one literate. Around the year 600 AD, however, Pope Gregory the Great decreed that following the conversion of the heathens to Christianity, their religious figures and customs must be subtly transformed into Roman Catholic equivalents.

The qualities of Saint Nicolas as well as his anniversary in late autumn matched those of Odin remarkably well. The saintly bishop who hitherto had never ridden a horse was thus mounted, the spear replaced with a crozier and the hat with a mitre.

Nicolas lived and worked in the Southwestern part of Asia Minor (now Turkey). It is not known when or where he was born, but he died as the Bishop of Myra about the year 340 on the 6th of December. For two hundred years he remained obscure; then he began to take on saintly aspects and to have popular legends associated with him. For example, he is supposed to have saved three young army officers from an unjust sentence, to have rescued sailors during a storm, and to have miraculously provided the inhabitants of Myra with grain during a famine. On saving a group of pilgrims at sea, fragrant and medicinal oils were said to have sprung from his grave. The remarkable feats attributed to Saint Nicolas led him to become the patron saint of such diverse professions as sailors, fishermen and shipbuilders, grain and wine merchants, perfumers, bankers, lovers, students and, of course, children.

After the Great Schism of 1054, the religious world was divided into the Roman Catholic and Greek Orthodox Churches and St. Nicolas became far more popular in the East than in the West. Think of Nicolas as the name of Russian Tsars and also of the famous punchcutter from Hungary, Nicolas Kis. But in 1087, his remains were taken from Myra and St. Nicolas was reburied in Bari, Italy, and from then on he was established as a fully-fledged saint in the Roman Catholic Church.

When the Netherlands became Protestant in the 16th century, the authorities tried to ban the feast of St. Nicolas, but the custom proved to have deeper roots than the Roman Catholic and Protestant religions and thus it endured.

So in Holland, confectioners still make large letters of puff pastry, filled with almond paste. The Dutch tradition of typophagy – the eating of chocolate letters – came later, after 1825, when the Dutchman Coenraad van Houten invented a means to make chocolate solid.

Chocolate letters play an important part in the party held on the eve of St. Nicolas, the 5th of December, when poems and rhymes are read prior to the unwrapping of a present. Such rhymes are meant to mock their recipient, allowing the speaker, for one evening, to make public someone's unfavourable characteristics.

As soon as the grain had been harvested and turned into flour, cakes in the shapes of runes were made and eaten as offerings to Odin. It was believed that the eating of these cakes made one literate.

The presents are often packed in an elaborate way, to make them look like something else.

Of the chocolate letters that are eaten (usually one's own initials), those in the form of "bamboo" type or Egyptian clipped serifs are the most favoured. The public does not seem to want modern typefaces. For a long time it was impossible to make chocolate letters with the smooth curves of a classic serif face thanks to the construction and soldering of the metal mould used to manufacture them. With today's plastic moulds, problems persist with the cooling of the chocolate, the maintenance of a uniform thickness, weight and stem width. Another consideration is that squared-off typefaces fit neater in their presentation box. In any case, the Egyptians are associated with homeliness, warmth, the feeling of a good bite on a solid serif. Other faces definitely taste less good.

Because here it is not a question of readability, but of edibility.

Reference:

1. Gerard Unger, adapted from a lecture given at Type 90, Oxford, 1990

information communication modification
recognition identification

FUSE 2: Max Kisman Linear Konstrukt

Linear Konstrukt is based on the Roman alphabet, though the characters are reduced to basic, simple shapes – runic shapes. The capitals are underlined lower-case, and the numbers are overlined. I made the initial designs for *Linear Konstrukt* as a screen font in 1986 for a project on future societies. It's an example of what could be a 'dialect'or 'code' alphabet, which in the future might appear in small-scale societies, reserved for one particular group only, signifying a closed community. It would be used for internal communication, externally revealing only the group identity. Thanks to the easy availability of computer systems and communications media, dialect alphabets will become increasingly common in magazines, on posters, local TV and computer games.

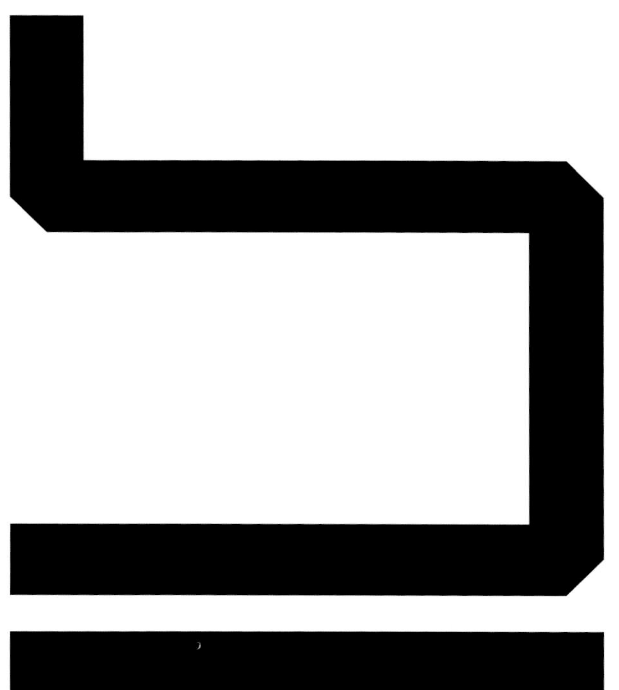

FUSE 2: Gerard Unger D'coder

D'coder is the raw material, the most basic ingredients of letters: arcs and straight lines. The other shapes will work in characters like *a*, *g* and *s*, and suggest less conventional letterforms. And think of what you always wanted to do with a giant full stop and comma. To use these elements you have to ask yourself the following – "how little do you need to make yourself understood?" and "how little do readers require to get wise?". Runes were never possible with curves; the technology would not allow it. Here, the curves are very much my curves and appear in all my typefaces; they are not lazy *Béziers* which throw themselves onto the screen without finesse. Use them as you will, though I would greet any attempt to take these arcs and bars as the inspiration and basic material with which to make your own letterforms.

TO READ A TEXT
IS TO MAKE
YOUR OWN TEXT OF IT

DECODER

1 2 3 4 5 6 7 8 9 10

Typeface: Decoder, Poster © 1991 FSI GmbH © Gerard Unger

FUSE 2: Erik van Blokland Niwida

Niwida (which in German is phonetic for "never again") was produced from a faxed original. The orientation of the reader is important – *Niwida* looks like information, you can recognise the symbols, but they are so deteriorated and taken out of context that you are not sure where to start. I thought it was a dubious task to develop an alternate set of symbols to the letters that make up the Latin alphabet. What good is a type that no one can read? Do we create such a type to visualise an already existent set of ideas, or do we want to distance ourselves by using a code we keep secret to exclude others from our communication? In that case, is the secrecy implied by what we have to impart, or do we just want to be different? What I think distinguishes runes from other scripts is that you feel the presence of information, even if you cannot read them. Runes look to be full of meaning on the outside, but hide it on closer examination. The symbols are old, misread and often misused.

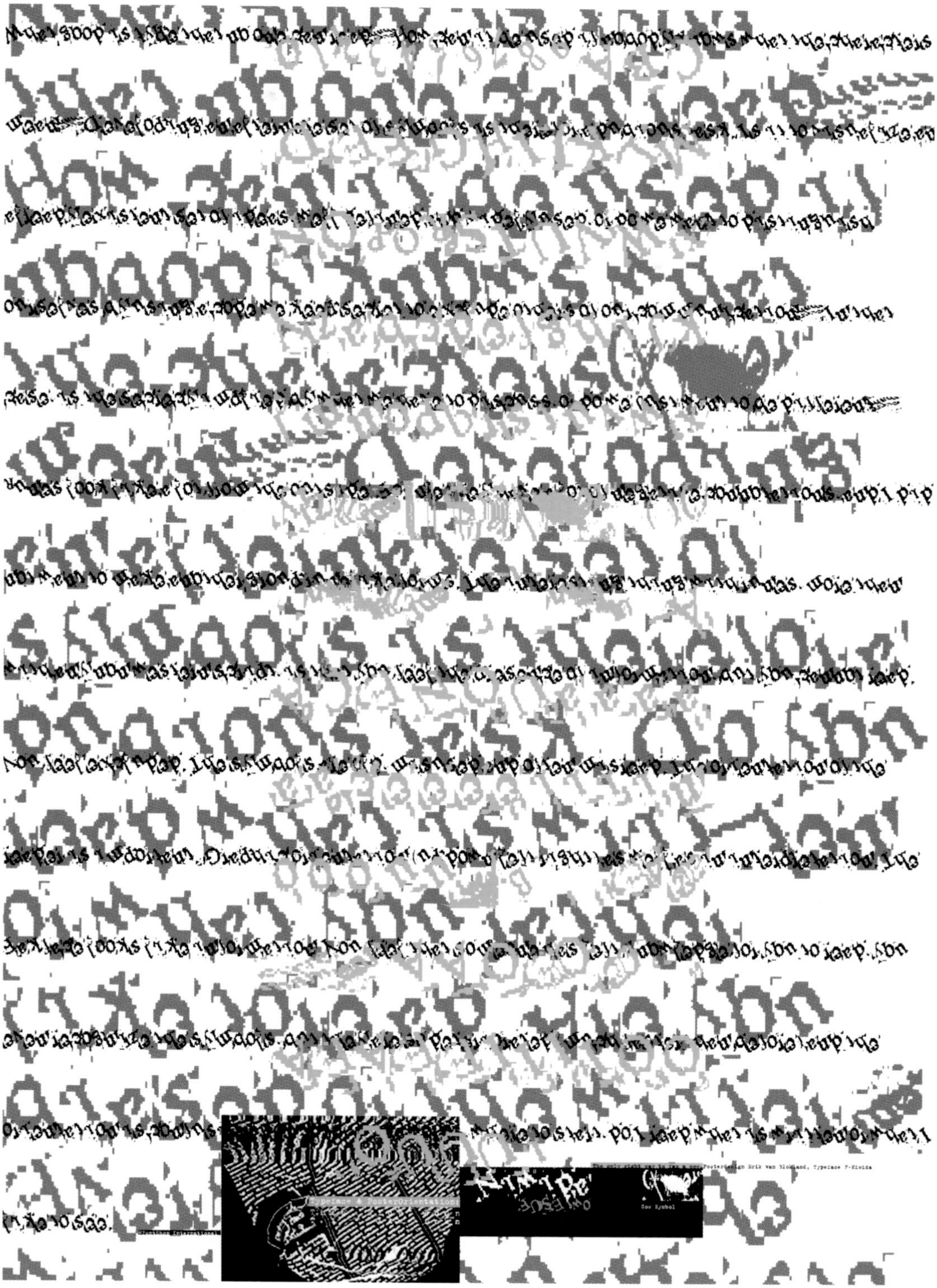
Typeface & PosterOrientation:
Cow Symbol
The only right way to fax a cow. Posterdesign Erik van Blokland, Typeface F-Hiwida

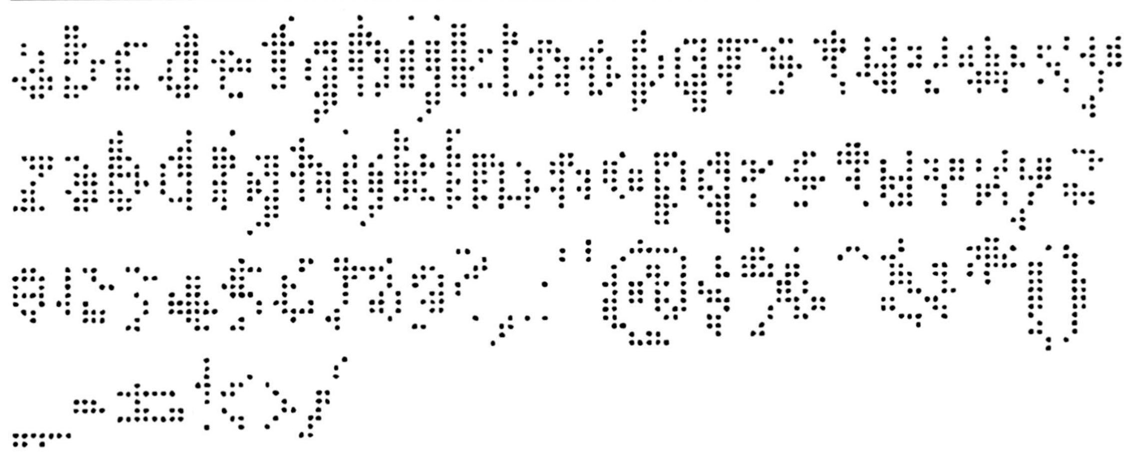

FUSE 2: Just van Rossum Flixel

Flixel has as its basis a bitmap font similar to *Geneva* 9pt., but narrower. It was transferred to a slightly higher resolution, which caused some distortion. Next, all the pixels were "shaken", so that some got random positions. All the pixels were then isolated and enlarged, but this was not done very precisely so each pixel became a dot that differed slightly from the rest. *Flixel* – flickering pixels – was inspired by those LED display bars you often see in shop windows. At a glance, these LED displays look very sophisticated and hi-tech, which is why people are so attracted to them. Nowadays, this method of displaying text is more or less obsolete, not only from a technological point of view – there are now so many in use that people no longer find them exciting. Strangely enough, hi-tech is still associated with coarse resolution bitmap images and letters even though today's technology is capable of much better. Bitmap letterforms are the runic letters of our times. In the future we will look at these characters and wonder why there was ever a need for making such primitive and illegible type.

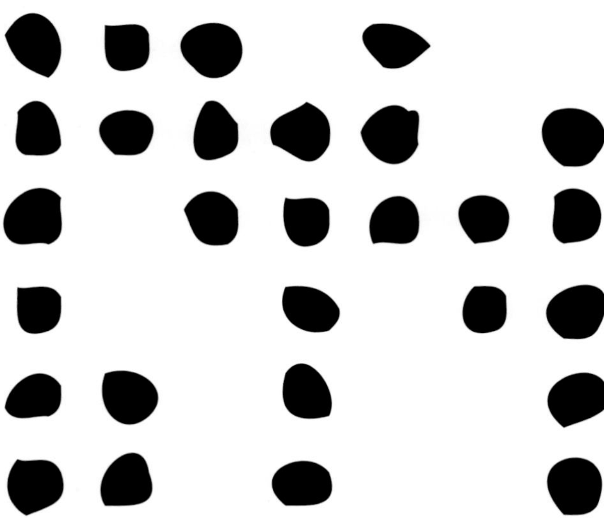

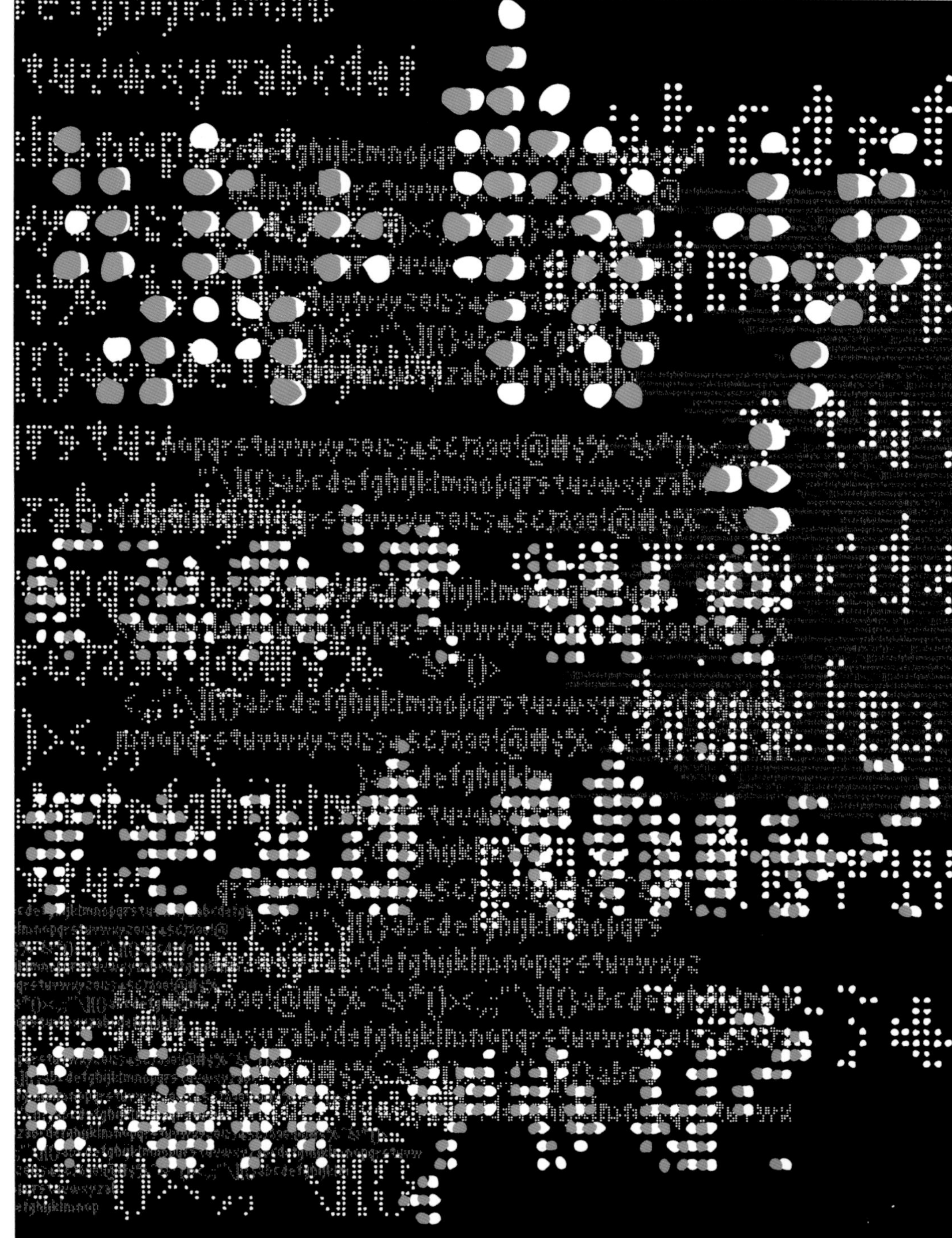
copyright1991, just van rossum for fuse/fsi

FUSE

FUSE 3: Point to Line and Plane... Jon Wozencroft

SPRING 1992

(DIS)INFORMATION

You've been held up at work. You rush home, check the ansaphone for any messages, and shove your belongings into a suitcase. A moment's peace – *think again, double check* – and having remembered to pick up your passport, you dash out of the door and head for Heathrow.

Travelling to an airport need not be that much of a strain, provided that time is on your side, and it is not some God-awful flight at six in the morning. To get away is pure excitement, and even better if you can turn any waiting into dreamtime. But especially in negative situations, when your thoughts, intentions and fantasies compete in your mind with the things you may have forgotten to pack, your senses are in a fragile state, just when you need a full deck and an open hand. You have passed GO, and for the next few hours everything will be complicitly connected to everything else, and if the linearity gets broken, well this could spell delay. And delay is the enemy of Progress.

Oh to be in Amsterdam, sucking tulips, where the airport is a mere twenty-odd minutes from the centre. For taxis you need an off-peak departure time, plenty of patience, and of course the dosh, especially if you are in New York. To make that flight, nothing is better than a lift from a friend, but even this would do you little good in Tokyo, where there is often no way through the gridlock – there, you are forced to allow half a day for a 25-mile journey in the 'airport limousine'.

But you are in London. Down the Tube. The trek along the Piccadilly Line has more stops than a milk-round. The walls are thick with advertising, yet one in particular hits your unbelieving eye, tiresomely telling you that "when you've caught the train, you've caught the plane" – your first true taste of the aspiration behind information – to be instantaneous. But you have been standing on this platform for nearly ten minutes now, and there is no sign of any light coming through this tunnel.

The platform indicator says **Heathrow 3 min**, the platform itself is packed. You wonder that maybe London Transport forbids any number above 7 to appear on the signboard, but more likely it is because the operator has been on double-shift, begins to suffer from RSI, and really meant to key in 18. A click on the wire tells you that a platform announcement is approaching, and here it comes, screeching like a Stuka through the speakers, a completely unintelligible act of noise terrorism in the name of Customer Service. The passengers wince. An infant wails. You can feel the stress swimming through the station.

Recent research by a group of ophthalmologists who have studied the effects of stress on eyesight concluded that, based on the example of Tottenham Court Road station, a rush-hour commuter's sense of vision might suffer by as much as 50% under such conditions. The symptoms are by no means confined to the Tubes – **stress** is totally related to the awareness of cut-out points along any route or network, and your ability to glide across them. Here, stuck at Green Park, under heavy luggage and late for the plane, by the time you get to Heathrow the station name-plates will have become no more than a blur.

Another command punctures the air, if you can call it that, this strange blend of dust, sweat and electrical faults. "Please let the passengers off the train first"; this is in secret code, so the passengers – sorry, customers – take their cue and stampede for the doors. As you gasp your way to a seat, you yearn again for the world upstairs – not at street level, but up there, cruising at 29,000 ft., far above the clouds. You remind yourself that at any time, there are well over 100,000 passengers already in flight, high in the skies, possibly enjoying a shrink-wrapped croissant, and if the Atomic Energy Authority is to be believed, in planes whose NO_2 emissions hit the ozone layer hardest, the effect of their fumes 30 times that of a car on the road.

Nonetheless, by now you might wish you were driving, but you're on the train and easily distracted: too distracted to read, so you complement the disengagement of your senses by staring into space, listening (or rather having to hear) the clatter of the train tracks, the tinny rattle of cheap headphones, and the guard proclaiming in a voice that successfully blends routine with astonishment... "This is a Heathrow train".

Perhaps the glimmer of glee in the guard's voice betrays an unspoken ambition: he hopes, some day, to move upwards and onwards to become a Tone of Voice in the shiniest shop-window of controlled climates, the airport departure hall. Imagine – the distance from the General Public, the thrill of pushing those switches that can instantly put your gospel into a foreign language and, above all, a blissful amount of announcements to make, each with its own subtle cadence; this needs careful training to allow your personal voice to co-exist with the clipped neutrality that information demands of it. Nevertheless, the **DING!** sounds help break the boredom and keep the people *moving*. This is *the* model environment, where only the chosen get the chance to be a small but satisfying side-show in a major film, say *Terminator 2*, because here, too, it is clunk/click every trip. And with all that design to support you.

The French writer and weapons analyst, Paul Virilio, insists... "*People are no longer citizens, they are passengers in transit*". Visit an airport, free of the pressures of baggage checks, boarding times, connecting flights, and you can observe the catalogue of parallel realities kept in line within the miniature city – a seamless quilt of shopping malls, banking services, telecom centres, restaurants and bars that keep the modern nomads occupied and animated in no man's land. These days, the pleasure of travel is not only to arrive, but also to be wilfully detached from the process, somehow in a daze, though not vacant (in spite of the tempting bargains that blare at you), but neither in any particular place. Simply – to be about to board. The airport authorities blend the buzz you might get from an expensive afternoon's shopping with a sharp dose of Nationalism, but when the seat-belt sign goes up, you can simultaneously be everywhere. So the next thing the cabin crew will do is to serve you a drink, as advertised.

But first of all the formalities. British Airways promise with a marketing blast that they will be "Clearing the path from A to B", but they never tell you about the rest of the alphabet, the typefaces, let alone the dingbats. If by chance you ever fly from new-improved Stansted,* your technoblur will be well catered for – there is no way you can miss the giant arrows, the numbers and toilet signs, for this is **People Traffic Control** for the

British Airways promise with a marketing blast that they will be "Clearing the path from A to B", but they never tell you about the rest of the alphabet, the typefaces, let alone the dingbats.

future. But wherever you fly from, before you settle down in your seat number to enjoy the drink and the familiar forms of an in-flight magazine, you must wade through a torrent of typography. All you really need is a ticket, your passport and the boarding card, but that would be too boring. Thus you travel through this maze of external information, carrying your necessary belongings, yet only at three stages do you actually intersect with the real reason you are here.

Your broken trolley somehow navigates its way to the security checks, and here is where dingbats and signboards get serious for a while. The PTC could well get personal, for you must realise that rubber gloves are never far away. This particular zone is free of service industry retouching, the techno does it automatically, but after the hilarity of Skyshops and the triumph of the check-in, you try hard to keep a straight face. To smile like an idiot and suppress it at the same time is a common condition, but awkward – it might be giving the game away if there's a coke mule just behind you. So you stay hollow. You concentrate on being the luggage, and the luggage being you – the perfect, virtual state of the telecommuter. Scanners need scannees. And after all, this is what we're here to learn. We *will* become magnetic.

And your prize? A clean bill of health from the metal detector? But of course, the Duty Free shops, where it is their duty to overcharge you, and if a bottle of Scotch or a dab of Dior does not grab you, well, then go stand next to a Rothmans ad. Smoke. Read a book. Get the GameBoy out. Play Tetris.

Watch the on-screen timetable.

Do anything. This is no place to be unoccupied. And in any case, from here on it is easy – a moving conveyor belt to help you to the Gate Number, elsewhere perhaps a shuttle-car, and then the wizzy whirr of the engines as you come aboard.

*Stansted, modernised in 1991, is London's "third airport". It was designed by Richard Rogers, well known as the architect of the fabulous Lloyd's Building in the City of London. At Stansted, the idea is that you arrive at the front gate, walk through the automatic doors, and then proceed in a straight line towards your departure point. In the meantime, there is plenty to preoccupy you.

You see, you cannot, must not, be allowed any quiet.

Silence verboten!

Is it not so that every air traveller, even for that nanosecond, will at some point in the journey think of the plane crash? – and this has little to do with the encouragement you get from the safety demonstration. Logic has nothing to do with it. After King's Cross and more small fires than a gas showroom, London Underground is the more likely accident waiting to happen. As for the roads, death matches the traffic. But to conjure the power of that one word, Lockerbie, all signals and all sense go into a tailspin. No signboard has yet to summon up a symbol to deal with such thoughts. They're working on it. If the blip drops off the radar-screen, then where will we be?

All these shifts in perception are linked to stages of movement across the grid. The grid is illuminated. It's all "high Art". The information is a cocktail of hard/soft, concrete/plastic, real/imagined. On JAL, there is a computer screen in your cabin that changes every ten minutes, showing your position, altitude, temperature, and your distance to the nearest city, marked out on a map. The pilot does not speak: the passengers like it better that way.

Airports perform technology's circus tricks for us, and at the same time they are development sites where new techniques can freely operate, unfastened from their ideologies. As a result, can it be any surprise that they are prime targets for terrorism? From Kandinsky to NASA, the mapping out of land and space has been achieved, so the energies of information technology are now devoted to the mapping out of time – "geography is replaced by chronography". It is as if you had hailed that taxi: a privatised version of your journey here, but vivid and true to the cause. The meter goes tick tick tick.

SPACE = TIME = MONEY.

It is clear that the connection between (information) technology and the creation of stress is residual. The connection between (information) technology and the *manufacture and calibration* of stress is embryonic, but as a result, we still have some possibility to interact, to understand and hopefully intercept the applications. If we are feeling brave, to interrupt.

Reality, after all, is itself no more than an agreement made through communication. When the destination is reached, you always hear the same instruction – "Please remain seated until the aircraft has come to a complete standstill" – and just as on the Underground, every time the message is relayed, the message is ignored. Is this small defiance a hope for the future, a final refusal to be pinned to our seats? Have the passengers, by now, become so stupefied by information that they cannot tell the difference between a semi-polite request and a direct order? Or shall we soon be boxed in good and proper, fumbling for a virtual key to open a virtual lock?

NEVILLE BRODY ISSUE POSTER

FUSE
the newest forum
for experimental
typography
The third
edition
includes 4 new
Macintosh compatible
typefaces on disc, with
four A2 posters
showing each font in
creative application
FUSE 3
DISINFORMATION
features
ERIK SPIEKERMANN
BARBARA
BUTTERWICK
MARTIN WENZEL
CORNEL WINDLIN
Aa
DISINFORMATION

FUSE 3: Information Design: Who needs it, what is it, and the Catch 22? **Erik Spiekermann**

If you tell somebody that you're a graphic designer, the normal reaction will be "ah, so you design all those posters and book jackets?". If you are no such lucky designer, then you've got record covers and letterheads or, as a last resort, advertising. Nobody has ever heard of an information designer and, in fact, nobody ever ought to – apart from potential clients, of course.

For the same can be said about information design as the things people used to say about children: they should be seen, and not heard. In other words, if a building is designed badly, it will need an elaborate signage system to send people to their required destination. If it is a building with character, well-designed and transparent in a philosophical sense, it will not need much more than its numbers on the doors.

This is the domain of the information designer: when things become too complex, when an artificial environment defies common sense, when technical requirements supercede human effort, someone has to intervene. Designing information could be described as translating a message, from one language or medium into another, from official or technical jargon into plain English, from complicated diagrams into a straightforward listing.

By virtue of having to make things plain to everybody, information design has to be about designing a *process* rather than just a message. What good would it be to rearrange stupid questions and silly explanations into a nice-looking layout and print it in pretty colours when all the wrong questions are asked in the wrong order? Those clients who expect a designer to come up with no more than another fancy picture without him or her interfering with the actual contents should not go to an information designer, because they might end up being talked out of the job altogether and it'll get left to the presentation people.

The only problem is, however, that such designers are few and far between. Who would volunteer to design forms for the Inland Revenue if he could make a living designing glossy brochures instead? And who wants to spend his time hanging around train stations trying to establish what sort of information passengers need and where it should be placed? It is indeed the sad truth that a lot of people doing these sort of jobs would rather do the other ones, which, incidentally, also pay a lot more. But if you lack a talent for illustration, if you can't come up with an exciting slogan or fascinating visual concept, then you're still good enough to design EXIT signs for the Tube. At least, that seems to be the popular misconception and, unfortunately, it often rings true. Most "good" designers hate those "necessary" jobs and leave them to printers, typesetters, engineers, bureaucrats, architects. Consequently information design gets a bad name.

But what do we need? Is it not enough to put a few words on some bits of wood, hang them from the ceiling and expect people to find their own way around? And are paper forms not doomed in any event? There is, after all, already something called "information anxiety". We suffer from an overload of messages, all trying to make us look, listen and react.

But some messages are more equal than others. It would not be the end of the world if we missed one of those amazing bargains we see plastered all over the shop, but it could well be curtains if we failed to find the "Way Out" sign in the Tube before the smoke engulfed us – as happened at King's Cross. Have you ever tried to fit snowchains to the tyres of your car whilst kneeling on a wet road, in the dark, in the freezing cold? And hadn't you wished some clever

If you tell somebody that you're a graphic designer, the normal reaction will be "ah, so you design all those posters and book jackets?". If you are no such lucky designer, then you've got record covers and letterheads or, as a last resort, advertising. Nobody has ever heard of an information designer and, in fact, nobody ever ought to – apart from potential clients, of course.

person had printed the instructions on something more permanent than paper which quickly became soaking wet and illegible the minute you got it out of the plastic bag? How many video recorders have you tried to set up, only to discover that every time you needed to know something, it wasn't in the instruction booklet – or at least, you couldn't find it under the obvious heading? I won't even mention road-maps, motorway signs, electricity bills or tax forms. And these contain information which may not excite you or even interest you, but it'll cost you money, health or sanity not to find out what they say and what they want from you.

Seeing how often the process of informing us is left in the hands of people with no interest in the results of that process and with no qualification or talent to write a coherent sentence, let alone a comprehensible one, it seems incredible that information design is not the biggest growth industry in the country. But it's a Catch 22 situation: we never know what we miss until someone shows us, and we never know how we depend on good information until we go or do wrong.

Good information design will inform by convincing, not by persuading. One thing it could learn from advertising is that nothing convinces people more than by being entertained. I look forward to forms that are fun to fill out, signs that make me smile and instructions that I will read in bed, for my amusement.

Issue 3 - Spring 1992

Contains four A2 posters each accompanied by an experimental Macintosh compatible Postscript font designed exclusively by

Erik Spiekermann,

Martin Wenzel,

Cornel Windlin,

Barbara Butterweck

Essays on **Air Travel** by Jon Wozencroft;
Information Systems by Erik Spiekermann

DISINFORMATION
Photographs taken in London and Berlin by Wozencroft, Siebert and Haswell.
Design by Neville Brody studio.
Editor: Jon Wozencroft.
Published & © 1992 by FSI GmbH.
Typefaces and Posters © 1992 the designers.

FSI, Bergmannstraße 102,
1000 Berlin 61, Germany.

Correspondence to FUSE,
65 - 69 East Road,
London N1 6AH, England

READ ON

Paul Virilio's writing is published by Editions Gallimard and Les Cahiers du Cinema in Paris. In translation, the best starting points are *Pure War* (Semiotexte, USA) and *War and Cinema* (Verso, UK). For Erik Spiekermann's ideas on information presentation, *Rhyme and Reason, A Typographic Novel*, is published by Berthold, Berlin. Put together like a Mac user's handbook, *Information Anxiety* is by Richard Saul Wurman, published in the UK by Pan.

SUBMIT/CONTACT

The role of FUSE is to promote typographic innovation. We welcome your input - if you would like to present your own experimental type design and poster for inclusion in a future edition (and/or any feedback you have on the supplied fonts), please write to FUSE at the address below submitting, if not a digitised typeface on disc, then a clear proposal and outline of your idea, enclosing in both cases an SAE/IRC. We would like to see structural changes to the ways we might use the alphabet, and less abstractions of existing typefaces! FUSE is published quarterly and distributed through the FontShop network. Future editions of FUSE will include new typefaces from as many origins as possible, linked to themes that range from information surrealism to electro magnetism and 'virtual typography'. Each FUSE is published in a limited edition - reserve a copy by contacting the FontShop in your area.

MEIN HERR...

FUSE fonts do not necessarily include a full set of upper and lower case characters, nor does every font cover a full range of accents and special characters - check the option keys in any case, you never know what you might find! Fuse fonts are experimental typefaces that should be extended by users. Abuse is part of the process.

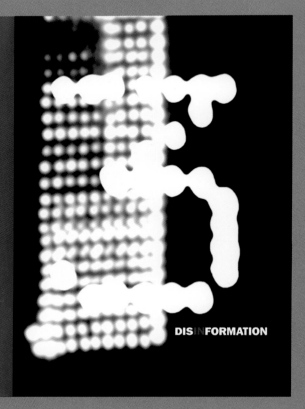

FUSE 3

DISINFORMATION

Point to Line and Plane...

You've been held up at work. You rush home, check the ansaphone for any messages, and shove your belongings into a suitcase. A moment's peace - think again, double check - and having remembered to pick up your passport, you dash out of the door and head for Heathrow.

NEVILLE BRODY STUDIO & JON WOZENCROFT EDITORIAL PAMPHLET FEATURING ERIK SPIEKERMANN

arrive, but also to be wilfully detached from the process, somehow in a daze, though not vacant (in spite of the tempting bargains that blare at you), but neither in any particular place. Simply - to be about to board. The airport authorities blend the buzz you might get from an expensive afternoon's shopping with a sharp dose of Nationalism, but when the seat-belt sign goes up, you can simultaneously be everywhere. So the next thing the cabin crew will do is to serve you a drink, as advertised.

But first of all the formalities. British Airways promise with a marketing blast that they will be "Clearing the path from A to B", but they never tell you about the rest of the alphabet, the typefaces, let alone the dingbats. If by chance you ever fly from new-improved Stansted*, your technoblur will be well catered for - there is no way you can miss the giant arrows, the numbers and toilet signs, for this is PEOPLE **TRAFFIC CONTROL** for the future. But wherever you fly from, before you settle down in your seat number to enjoy the drink and the familiar forms of an in-flight magazine, you must wade through a torrent of typography. All you really need is a ticket, your passport and the boarding card, but that would be too boring. Thus you travel through this maze of external information, carrying your necessary belongings, yet only at three stages do you actually intersect with the real reason you are here.

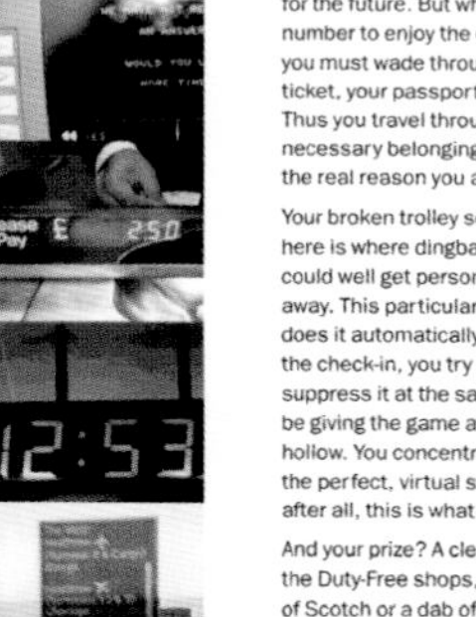

Your broken trolley somehow navigates its way to the security checks, and here is where dingbats and signboards get serious for a while. The PTC could well get personal, for you must realise that rubber gloves are never far away. This particular zone is free of service industry retouching, the techno does it automatically, but after the hilarity of Skyshops and the triumph of the check-in, you try hard to keep a straight face. To smile like an idiot and suppress it at the same time is a common condition, but awkward - it might be giving the game away if there's a coke mule just behind you. So you stay hollow. You concentrate on being the luggage, and the luggage being you - the perfect, virtual state of the telecommuter. Scanners need scanees. And after all, this is what we're here to learn. We *will* become magnetic.

And your prize? A clean bill of health from the metal detector? But of course, the Duty-Free shops, where it is their duty to overcharge you, and if a bottle of Scotch or a dab of Dior does not grab you, well, then go stand next to a Rothmans ad. Smoke. Read a book. Get the GameBoy out. Play Tetris.

Watch the on-screen timetable.

Do anything. This is no place to be unoccupied. And in any case, from here on it is easy - a moving conveyor belt to help you to the Gate Number, elsewhere perhaps a shuttle-car, and then the wizzy whirr of the engines as you come aboard.

*Stansted, modernised in 1991, is London's "third airport". It was designed by Richard Rogers, well-known as the architect of the fabulous Lloyd's Building in the City of London. At Stansted, the idea is that you arrive at the front gate, walk through the automatic doors, and then proceed in a straight line towards your departure point. In the meantime, there is plenty to preoccupy you.

You see, you cannot, must not, be allowed any quiet.

SILENCE VERBOTEN!

Is it not so that every air traveller, even for that nanosecond, will at some point in the journey think of the plane crash? - and this has little to do with the encouragement you get from the safety demonstration. Logic has nothing to do with it. After King's Cross and more small fires than a gas showroom, London Underground is the more likely accident waiting to happen. As for the roads, death matches the traffic. But to conjure the power of that one word, Lockerbie, all signals and all sense go into a tailspin. No signboard has yet to summon up a symbol to deal with such thoughts. They're working on it. If the blip drops off the radar-screen, then where will we be?

All these shifts in perception are linked to stages of movement across the grid. The grid is illuminated. It's all "high Art". The information is a cocktail of hard/soft, concrete/plastic, real/ imagined. On JAL, there is a computer screen in your cabin that changes every ten minutes, showing your position, altitude, temperature, and your distance to the nearest city, marked out on a map. The pilot does not speak: the passengers like it better that way.

Airports perform technology's circus tricks for us, and at the same time they are development sites where new techniques can freely operate, unfastened from their ideologies. As a result, can it be any surprise that they are prime targets for terrorism? From Kandinsky to NASA, the mapping out of land and space has been achieved, so the energies of information technology are now devoted to the mapping out of time - "geography is replaced by chronography". It is as if you had hailed that taxi: a privatised version of your journey here, but vivid and true to the cause. The meter goes tick tick tick.
SPACE = TIME = MONEY.

It is clear that the connection between (information) technology and the creation of stress is residual. The connection between (information) technology and the *manufacture and calibration* of stress is embryonic, but as a result, we still have some possibility to interact, to understand and hopefully intercept the applications. If we are feeling brave, to interrupt.

Reality, after all, is itself no more than an agreement made through communication. When the destination is reached, your always hear the same instruction - "Please remain seated until the aircraft has come to a complete standstill" - and just as on the Underground, every time the message is relayed, the message is ignored. Is this small defiance a hope for the future, a final refusal to be pinned to our seats? Have the passengers, by now, become so stupified by information that they cannot tell the difference between a semi-polite request and a direct order? Or shall we soon be boxed in good and proper, fumbling for a virtual key to open a virtual lock?

Jon Wozencroft 11:42:33 7-1-92

Information Design:
Who needs it, what is it, and the Catch 22?

If you tell somebody that you're a graphic designer, the normal reaction will be "ah, so you design all those posters and book jackets?". If you are no such lucky designer, then you've got record covers and letterheads or, as a last resort, advertising. Nobody has ever heard of an information designer and, in fact, nobody ever ought to - apart from potential clients, of course.

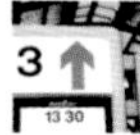

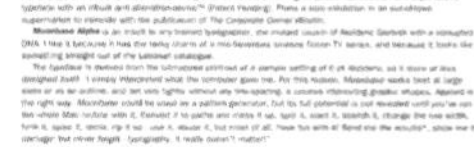

Moonbase Alpha CORNEL WINDLIN

Dearjohn BARBARA BUTTERWECK

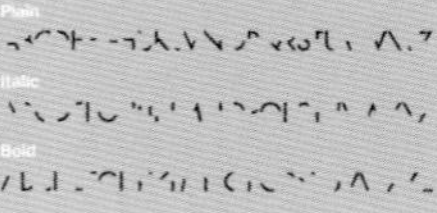

DEARJOHN REGULAR

DEARJOHN BOLD

DEARJOHN ITALIC

FUSE 3: Barbara Butterweck DearJohn

DearJohn splits a Futura-like typeface into three modular segments, which gives users infinite choice in combining these various parts, their size, weight and colour. The three *DearJohn* groups are connected to the typestyle menu, plain, bold and italic. The plain font contains the most characteristic part of each letter – start by writing your text, then select the *DearJohn regular*, make a copy or clone the text box and place it over the original, then change the style of the copied/cloned text into italic or bold. Continue this process until the desired combinations are achieved. Then serve. Thanks to Claudia Kipp, Günter Pawlak and Prof. Gerd Fleischmann for their help.

DEAR

JOHN

ABCDEFGHIJKLMNOPQRSTUVWXYZ

ABCDEFGHIJKLMNOPQRSTUVWXYZ

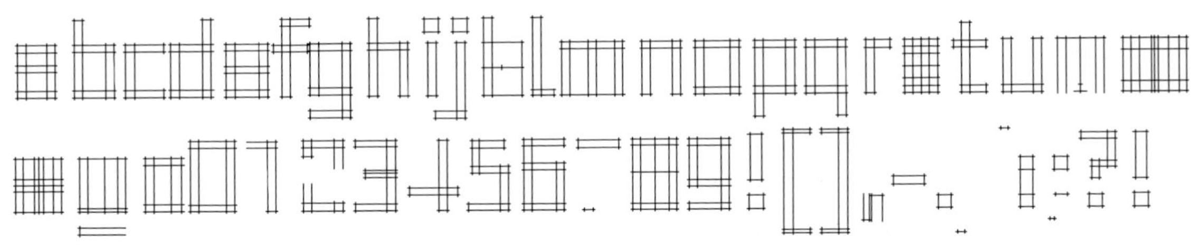

FUSE 3: Erik Spiekermann Grid

Grid is not a typeface, *Grid* is the construction behind the typeface. When I draw type (which I always start doing as a pencil sketch), after I've worked out the basic measurements and proportions (how high the lower-case characters are compared to the caps, how wide the downstroke is on the lower-case *h*, and how much thinner the horizontal stroke on the lower-case *o* is), I draw up a rough grid with those proportions to help me sketch. I might cross the lines of that grid to allow for round shapes or points to overhang, and I may ignore the grid altogether after the first trials, but it is always a good starting point. *Grid* is therefore nothing more than a starting point for someone else wanting to draw a typeface. They can use the guidelines as reference to the extreme points of the characters, i.e. the ones on both sides as well as on top and bottom. Apart from that there are also some indications of intersections for diagonal strokes (as in *v* or *z* and the start or finish of some horizontal lines (as in *t* or *f*). Where curves join and how they are shaped is up to everybody's imagination. Lastly, as befits real grids, I have not drawn any diagonal guides at all, nor any round ones.

!abcdefghijklmnopqrstuvwxyz 1234567890[.,;:-]?!

DESIGN **ERIK SPIEKERMANN** TYPEFACE F GRID © **FONTSHOP** INTERNATIONAL 1992

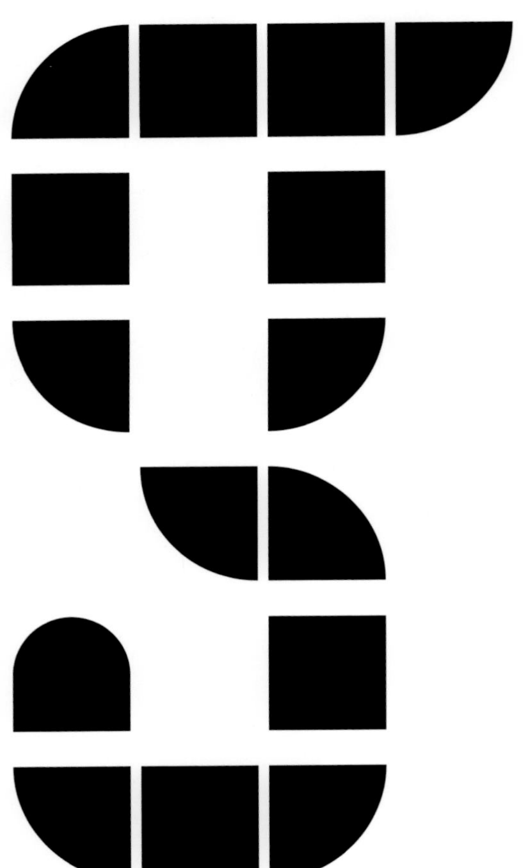

FUSE 3: Martin Wenzel InTegel

I started work on *InTegel* in December 1991. The idea was to give the user 18 different pixels that can be assembled into a typeface whose characters can be combined in any number of ways.

Tegel is a district of Berlin, and Flughafen Tegel its principal airport. With the font *InTegel* you have to work line by line to construct the letterforms: thus, to create the letter g, type 2!!4/!-!-/5-4/-53/7-!/5!4 (- is a space, / is a carriage return). All characters have a uniform width. I created the pictograms, designed by Alexandra Poleschal, to combine them with the pixels to create some kind of display for an office, a café, a shop, or even an airport.

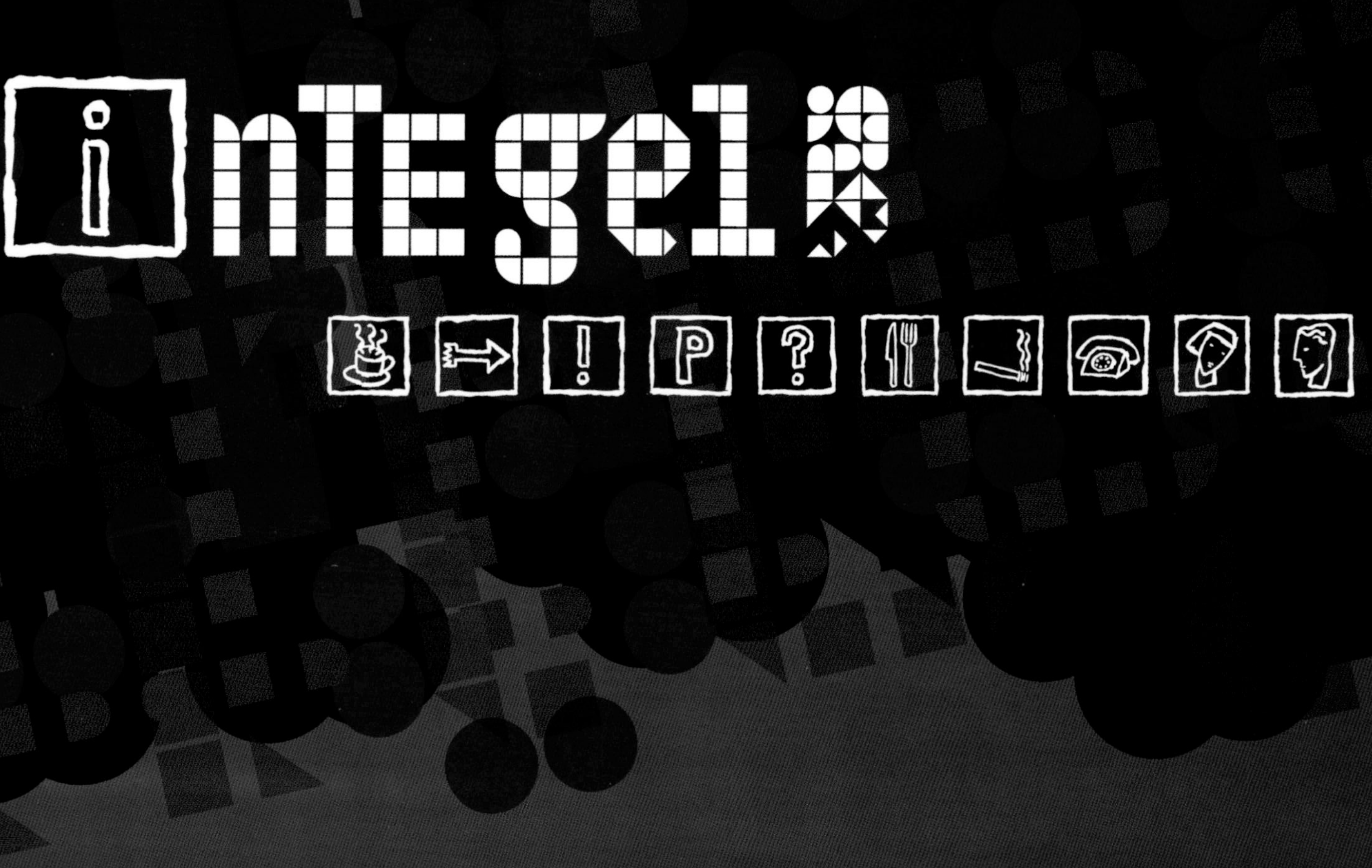
inTegel
font © Martin Wenzel
pictograms © Alexandra Polešal
Berlin 1992

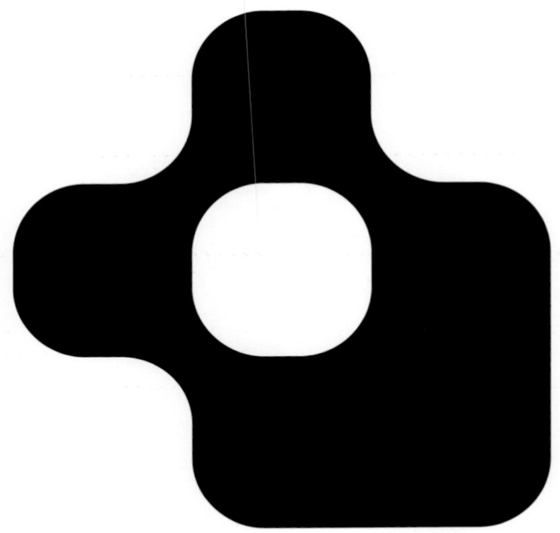

ABCDEFGHIJKLMNOPQRSTUVWXYZ

abcdefghijklmnopqrstuvwxyz®©å

0123456789,.:;"{}!?@£$%^+*()_+-=

FUSE 3: Cornel Windlin Moonbase Alpha

Moonbase Alpha is an insult to any trained typographer, the mutant cousin of *Akzidenz Grotesk* with a corrupted DNA. I like it because it has the tacky charm of a mid-Seventies science fiction TV series, and because it looks like something straight out of the Letraset catalogue. The typeface is derived rom the bitmapped print-out of a sample setting of 6pt. Akzidenz, so it more or less designed itself – I simply interpreted what the computer gave me. For this reason, *Moonbase* works best at large sizes or as an outline, and set very tightly without any line-spacing, it creates interesting graphic shapes. Applied in the right way, *Moonbase* could be used as a pattern generator, but its full potential is not revealed until you've run the whole Mac routine with it. Convert it to paths and mess it up, split it, slant it, stretch it, change the line width, funk it, spike it, remix, rip it up – use it, abuse it, but most of all, have fun with it! Send me the results, show me the damage; but never forget – typography, it really doesn't matter!

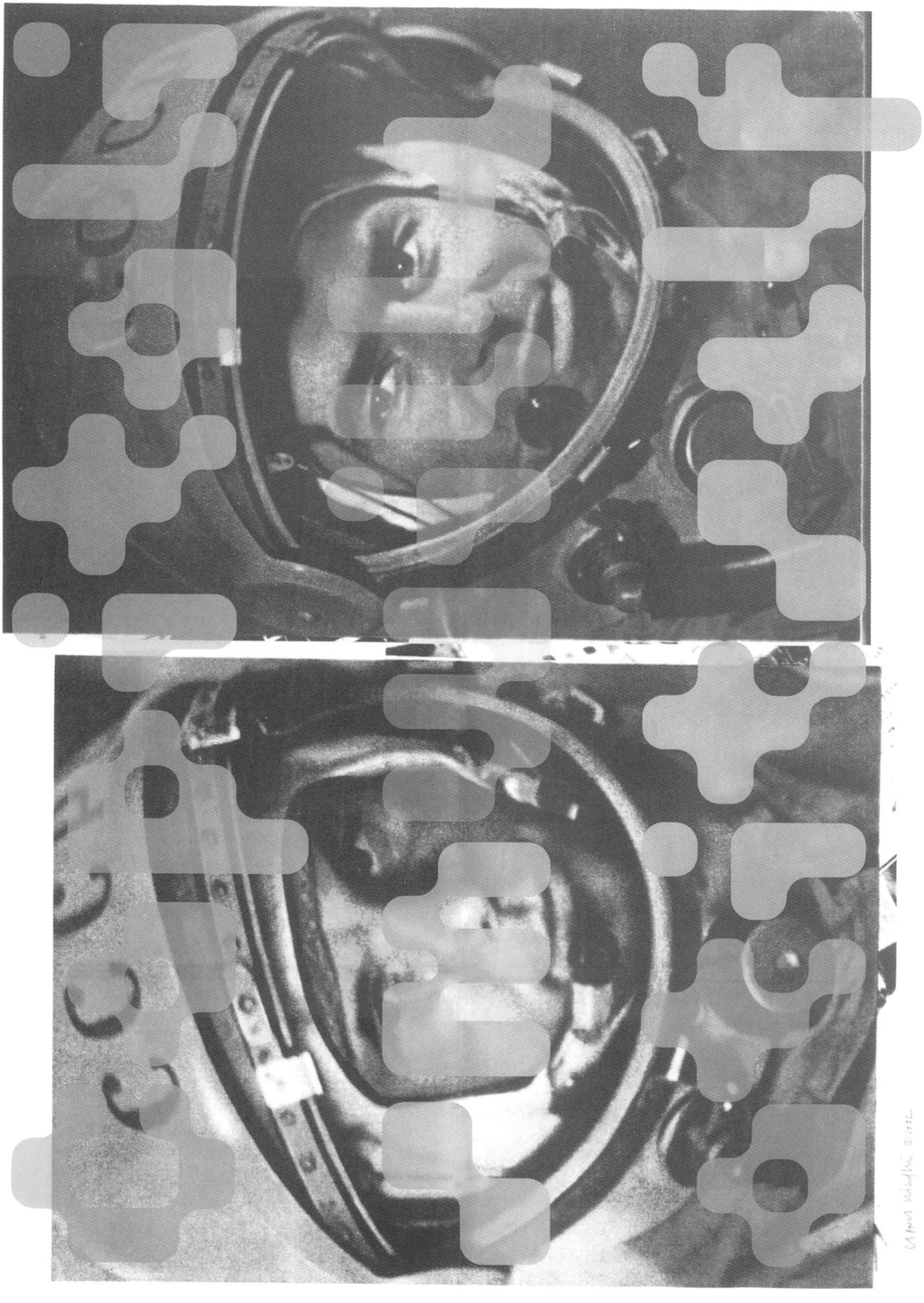

© 1992

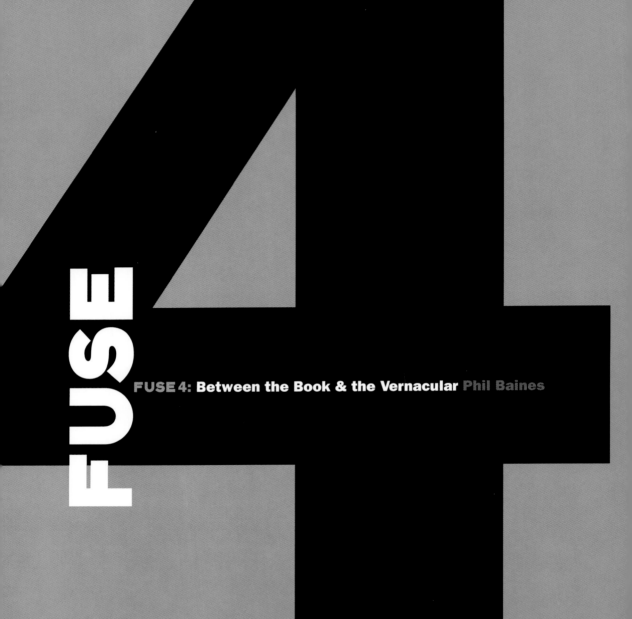

FUSE

FUSE 4: Between the Book & the Vernacular Phil Baines

SUMMER 1992

EXUBERANCE

There is a long heritage of decorated letters. The initial letters that form the carpet pages of the Gospels of Kells, Durrow and Lindisfarne for instance, are all developed to the extent where the text is subservient to the richness and detail of the overall design. Despite this, after the first printed book appeared in 1455, typography began to concentrate on the functional aspects of readability above all else. It was Stanley Morison who wrote: *Typography is the efficient means to an essentially utilitarian and only incidentally æsthetic end [...] if readers do not notice the consummate reticence and rare discipline of a new type it is probably a good letter.* Until the end of the eighteenth century, the norm to which typography aspired was that of the book, and when (and if) we are taught typography, it is generally in this spirit.

In England, the growth of commerce and the development of advertising in the late eighteenth and early nineteenth century gave this idea of function a new twist. The contemporary book types – the so-called 'moderns' – could not shout loud enough in their bid to sell lottery tickets or entertainments: something more was needed. The development of the **fat faces** (c.1796), and the invention of **sans serifs** (1815), **egyptians** (1816), and **clarendons** (1845), fulfilled this need and enabled typography to shake off the fetters of the book. The impact of the single word became more important than the silent, linear comprehension of an entire page. Somewhere between the book printers' typography and the vernacular, a whole new world developed, one where novelty and adornment were explored for their own sake.

Once this basic menu of shapes had appeared, anything was possible. All the founders produced versions of these faces, and soon after, reissued them in new and startling guises: shaded, angled, outlined, inlined, three-dimensional, and every possible combination thereof. New forms appeared too – highly decorated and more exuberant still – with names and classifications we no longer recognise: *Tuscan*, *Italian*, *Grecian*, *Rounded*, *Antique*, *Latin*, *Runic*, *Rustic* and *Monastic*. These letters were not for education, but for effect and adornment. All questioned the accepted notions of legibility and, in the process, they pushed type manufacturing technology to its limits.

Until the 1830s, when mechanical routing allowed the mass production of large (but much simpler) wooden type, all type was produced in metal. Large sizes of the more decorative and flamboyant metal type originated as wood-engravings and thus show the characteristics of that medium. They were used to reproduce matrices in typemetal, from which casts were made for such applications as posters and handbills. Original engravings of twenty-three full alphabets (some of which appeared in the 1836 specimen books of Wood & Sharwoods) have survived and are now in the collection of the St. Bride Printing Library in London. They are fairly standard letterforms with shadow treatment, but their whole surface is covered by illustrations: fruit, masonic symbols, farmyard scenes or abstract decoration.

The new letterforms, catalysed by commerce and an interest in antiquity – the first sans serifs, for instance, were an attempt to capture the spirit of early Roman letterforms – were by no means confined to work on paper. The fat faces and sturdy *clarendons* proved ideal for casting in metal and became synonymous with the railways and heavy industry. The retail environment seized on letterforms with glee and made them perform unprecedented feats of embellishment and distortion; flamboyant letters, such as the *Tuscans,* found a home etched, printed, mirrored and gilded on glass. As the century progressed, further exploration of letter shapes occurred as new media were exploited, the possibilities of silhouette explored and whenever the opportunity arose to work on a large scale.

Exuberance was not just to do with the particular type design but with how many different types you could use together, either on a broadside or, better still, the outside of a building. The sign-writer and fly-poster combined to cover every possible surface with letters, cajoling, exhorting or pleading for attention.

Exuberance of spirit in mainstream typography died away at the turn of the century with a revival of interest in the letter during forms of the incunabula. Type manufacturers this century have concentrated on producing countless new versions of old faces, and serious designers have turned their noses up at anything tainted with personality.

Today, it seems as though exuberance is permissible in our work, but not in the type itself. Type design is thirty-something, it's left home, got a wife, children, a car, an overdraft and a mortgage. **Sad**. Exuberance was something that happened in its youth, down the pub with its mates on a Friday night... or was it?

Some further reading:

1. James Mosley, "English Vernacular", in *Motif* 11, 1963 **2.**James Mosley, "Display Types", in *Motif* 13, 1967 **3.** Michael Twyman, *Printing 1770–1970*, Eyre & Spottiswoode, 1970 **4.** Nicolette Gray, *Nineteenth Century Ornamented Typefaces*, Faber & Faber, 1976 **5.** *Ornamented Types: prospectus*, I.M. Imprimit/St. Bride's, 1990

FUSE
EXUBERANCE
The newest forum for experimental typography. This fourth edition includes 4 new Macintosh compatible typefaces on disc, with four A2 posters showing each font creatively
FUSE 4 EXUBERANCE
features
DAVID BERLOW
BARRY DECK
JEFFREY KEEDY
RICK VALICENTI

FUSE 4: A Type of Death Jeffrey Keedy

Ornament is crime. Typeface designers today are Modernist law-abiding citizens who police their forms within the strict confines of function. By abstaining from the excesses of the material world, they have learned to live with less, but they think it is more. By devoting themselves to 'good design' and professional practices they have reached that state of grace known as legibility. Our time is the timeless time. We have taken the best from the past and perfected it.

But this was not always the case. Long ago, in the Industrial Age, when type was made of metal, wood and sweat, there were no regulations and all the typographic rules were swelled and decorated. No expression was left unstated, no gimmick or trick untried. It was every type designer for himself and no holds barred. In those rough and tumble days, letters were three-dimensional and cast long dark shadows across the page. Others were so elegantly affected or grossly contorted that one could get altogether lost in them.

Today, you can readily spot these ridiculous old types in the occasional antique-shop, sign or when the circus comes to town. They're only put to use in order to remind us of a splendidly decadent past, long dead and almost forgotten.

Like the grand old Victorian mansions in horror films, these typefaces are haunted by ghosts and they have different voices; some elegant and frail; some brazen and oppressive; and others pompous and ridiculous. Even so, all of them can be heard and they tell the story of their time. Will our types speak clearly of our age when we are long gone? Will they reflect a lust for life, a passion for new possibilities? Or just a pessimistic retrenchment into the timeless zone of legibility?

In the Industrial Age, type designers started all the fashions for 'artistic printing'. Today no self-respecting type designer would condescend to an interest in something as fleeting and ephemeral as fashion or future. Why bother when one can lay claim to timelessness? For practitioners in a relatively obscure artform, the lure of eternity is strong. Why be Number One for a year when you can be in the Top 10 till the end of time?

Of course we don't truly believe it's possible to do something that is timeless, it's just a bit of rhetoric we use when history makes us feel small. It's something we say to build ourselves up; it gives us courage. After all, who would want to admit to making tomorrow's ghosts?

To avoid the mortality of style many designers today have revived the dead. The typographic cadavers are brought back from the distant past (classical mummies), the recent past (zombie moderns) or patched together, à la Frankenstein, with recently dug-up parts (post-mortem-modern).

No matter what the approach, it all comes down to the same thing, a kind of typographic necrophilia. Instead of wasting time perfecting an exquisite corpse, type designers should be excited by new digital possibilities, just as the Industrial Age designers were about their technological advances. We should be expressing the vicissitudes of our time instead of continuing a methodical meltdown into one perfect *Helvetica*. The only way to breathe new life into old faces is to introduce new ones that in turn will grow old. This is the natural course of change that ensures the inevitability of style.

The concept of timelessness is the desire to escape this reality. To be timeless one merely has to be like Peter Pan and refuse to grow up, or at least refuse to acknowledge the passage of time. This immature strategy is at the core of most of what is uninteresting in typographic practice today. It is the legacy of an exhausted Modernism that refuses to die.

Like the grand old Victorian mansions in horror films, these typefaces are haunted by ghosts and they have different voices; some elegant and frail; some brazen and oppressive; and others pompous and ridiculous. Even so, all of them can be heard and they tell the story of their time.

In its early years, Modernism courted capitalist consumerism (Modernism knew a meal ticket when it saw one). Today however, Modernism and consumerism have been married so long it is hard to tell them apart. But this sanctuary of domestic bliss has a couple of skeletons in its closet. They are exuberance and decoration, the two (illegitimate?) babies Modernism threw out with the bathwater so it could have consumerism to itself. That's when Modernism began its slow decline. Consumerism might run itself into the ground, unless exuberance and decoration come back from the vernacular (where they have done quite well on their own) and help redefine a newly styled consumerism. If exuberance and decoration were admitted to the high culture club of 'serious' type design, then maybe designers would see Modernism for the zombie it really is.

All type families have skeletons in their closets and ghosts as well. So make your typography for today; let it speak to us in the voice of this moment. And accept the fact that it will haunt us in the future. After all, you're not afraid of ghosts... are you?

Submit/Contact

The role of **Fuse** is to promote typographic innovation. We welcome your input. If you would like to present your own experimental type design and poster for inclusion in a future edition (and/or any feedback you have on the supplied fonts) please write to **Fuse** at the address below, submitting, if not a digitised typeface on disk, then a clear proposal and outline of your idea, enclosing in both cases an SAE/IRC. We would like to see structural challenges to the way we might use the alphabet, and not abstractions of existing typefaces! Fuse is published quarterly and distributed through the FontShop network.

Future editions will include new typeface designs from as many origins as possible, linked to themes that range from information surrealism to electro-magnetism and 'virtual typography'. Each **Fuse** is published in a limited edition, reserve your copy by contacting your local FontShop.

Mein Gott!

Fuse fonts do not necessarily contain a full set of upper and lower case characters, nor does every font contain a full range of accents and special characters: check the option keys, you never know what you might find! **Fuse** typefaces are experimental typefaces that should be extended by users. Abuse is part of the process.

Exuberance

FUSE Issue 4, Summer 1992.

Contains four A2 posters each accompanied by an experimental Macintosh® compatible PostScript® typeface designed exclusively by

David Berlow, Barry Deck, Jeffrey Keedy & Rick Valicenti,

plus essays by Phil Baines & Jeffrey Keedy.

Exuberance

FUSE

Between the book & the vernacular

There is a long heritage of decorated letters. The initial letters that form the carpet pages of the Gospels of Kells, Durrow and Lindisfarne for instance, are all developed to the extent where the text is subserviant to the richness and detail of the overall design. Despite this, after the first printed book appeared in 1455, typography began to concentrate on the functional aspects of readability above all else. It was Stanley Morison who wrote: **Typography is the efficient means to an essentially utilitarian and only incidentally asthetic end [...] if readers do not notice the consummate reticence and rare discipline of a new type it is probably a good letter.** Until the end of the eighteenth century, the norm to which typography aspired was that of the book, and when (and if) we are taught typography, it is generally in this spirit.

In England, the growth of commerce and the development of advertising in the late eighteenth and early nineteenth century gave this idea of function a new twist. The contemporary book types—the so-called 'moderns'—could not shout loud enough in their bid to sell lottery tickets or entertainments: something more was needed. The development of the **fat faces** (c.1796), and the invention of **sans serifs** (1815), **egyptians** (1816), and **clarendons** (1845), fulfilled this need and enabled typography to shake off the fetters of the book. The impact of the

Top: Fat Face, early 19c. **Middle:** Five-Line Pica, Sans-Serif, Figgins, 1835. **Bottom:** Fifteen Lines Egyptian, early 19c.

Yurnacular In February of this year, as Berlow waited impatiently for some friends to come out of a jewellry shop in Colorado, he spotted a hand-lettered sign in the window of a rafting adventure company. Upon closer inspection Berlow determined the sign to be highly expressive of the American typographic vernacular. Crude in contrast, impoverished in shape and hopelessly misaligned, it was truly an American classic. It became the basis for [illegible] After passing through several versions, the face became hopelessly illegible and was thus complete.

Berlow recommends that [illegible] be used in small point sizes for important legal documents, British Rail buffet car menus and IBM PC-compatible application program user documentation. Above nine point, Berlow suggests that the face be negatively tracked for yet greater compactness and, of course, to save paper.

David Berlow began his career in the type industry in 1977 with Mergenthaler Linotype where he developed such legible typeface revivals as New Century Schoolbook and New Caledonia. He moved to the newly formed Bitstream Inc. in 1982 before forming The FontBureau Inc. with Roger Black in 1989. The Font Bureau have developed over 200 typefaces, new designs and revivals for custom clients, the retail market and for equipment manufacturers like Apple Computer Inc.

Berlow has won no major awards and is not a member of any prestigious organisation. His hobbies include taking time off, collecting rubber bands and counting grains of sand.

Yurnacular DAVID BERLOW

Caustic Biomorph BARRY DECK

Caustic Biomorph Decoration evolves in response to a continual visual sampling of daily life in conjunction with a culture's dominant notions of beauty, often rooted in the technical means by which it is produced. Today the media environment mixes with American neighbourhoods, as homeless encampments and discarded packages multiply in open view. Whilst our culture's definition of beauty is continually rewritten by marketing consultants in the service of greedy corporate executives, our ability to produce style is expanding, exceeded only by our perpetual desire to consume it.

I think of **CAUSTIC BIOMORPH** as a battle-scarred veteran of this stormy techno-cultural evolution: my own acid-eaten response to the decay so visible in American cities today. It is a typeface appropriate for the words **AMALGAMATED CHEMICAL CORPORATION, RE-ELECT BUSH**, or even **IF YOU LIVED HERE YOU'D BE HOME BY NOW.**

Barry Deck grew up in an American suburb, where he contemplated world domination while mowing the lawn. After studying briefly at six different colleges and pursuing almost as many majors, he settled on graphic design as 'a creative way to make money'. In 1986 he took his first job at a a firm where work was routinely typeset in Goudy, then centred. He worked there for only six months before realising the fatal flaw in his career choice. The next autumn, he found himself enrolled at California Institute of the Arts where he caught on to a particularly loud-mouthed rationale for his hyper-individualism in design.

Today he can't hold a job and does everything he can to make ends meet. In addition to designing type, Barry does photo-illustration, graphic design and even design production.

single word became more important than the silent, linear comprehension of an entire page. Somewhere between the book printers' typography and the vernacular, a whole new world developed, one where novelty and adornment were explored for their own sake.

Once this basic menu of shapes had appeared, anything was possible. All the founders produced versions of these faces, and soon after, reissued them in new and startling guises: shaded, angled, outlined, inlined, three-dimensional, and every possible combinations thereof. New forms appeared too—highly decorated and more exuberant still—with names and classifications we no longer recognise: Tuscan, Italian, Grecian, Rounded, Antique, Latin, Runic, Rustic and Monastic. These letters were not for education, but for effect and adornment. All questioned the accepted notions of legibility and, in the process, they pushed type manufacturing technology to its limits.

Until the 1830's, when mechanical routing allowed the mass production of large (but much simpler) wooden type, all type was produced in metal. Large sizes of the more decorative and flamboyant metal type originated as wood-engravings and thus show the characteristics of that medium. They were used to reproduce matrices in typemetal, from which casts were made for such applications as posters and handbills. They are fairly standard letterforms with shadow treatment, but their whole surface is covered by illustrations: fruit, masonic symbols, farmyard scenes or abstract decoration.

The new letterforms, catalysed by commerce and an interest in antiquity—the first sans serifs for instance, were an attempt to capture the spirit of early Roman letterforms—were by no means confined to work on paper. The fat faces and sturdy clarendons proved ideal for casting in metal and became synonymous with the railways and

Top: Five-Line Pica, White, Figgins. **Middle:** Perspective, Figgins, 1836. **Bottom:** Five-Line Pica Antique Open.

NEVILLE BRODY/PHIL BAINES & JON WOZENCROFT EDITORIAL PAMPHLET FEATURING PHIL BAINES & JEFFREY KEEDY

SIDE

heavy industry. The retail environment seized on letterforms with glee and made them perform unprecedented feats of embellishment and distortion; flamboyant letters such as the Tuscans, found a home etched, printed, mirrored and gilded on glass. As the century progressed, further exploration of letter shapes occurred as new media were exploited, the possibilities of silhouette explored and whenever the opportunity arose to work on a large scale.

Exuberance was not just to do with the particular type design but with how many different types you could use together, either on a broadside or, better still, the outside of a building. The sign-writer and fly-poster combined to cover every possible surface with letters, cajoling, exhorting or pleading for attention.

Exuberance of spirit in mainstream typography died away at the turn of the century with a revival of interest in the letter during forms of the incunabula. In the UK, type manufacturers this century have concentrated on producing countless new versions of old faces, and serious designers have turned their noses up at anything tainted with personality. In America however, there was a resurgence of decorative lettering by Rick Griffin & Co, used to promote the psychedelic playpen of mid 60's science fiction. Its effect was international.

Today, it seems as though exuberance is permissible in our work, but not in the type itself. Type design is thirtysomething, it's left home, got a wife, children, a car, an overdraft and a mortgage. **Sad.** Exuberance, was something that happened in it's youth, down the pub with it's mates on a friday night...or was it?

Phil Baines

Some further reading

Nicolette Gray, Nineteenth Century Ornamented Typefaces, Faber & Faber, 1976. **James Mosley,** English Vernacular, in Motif 11 (1963); Display Types in Motif 13, 1967, and Ornamented Types: Prospectus, I.M. Imprimit/St Bride's, 1993. **Michael Twyman,** Printing 1770–1970, Eyre & Spottiswoode, 1970.

Top: Five-Line Pica, Italian, Caslon, 1810. **Middle:** (Tuscan) Marr, 1853. **Bottom:** Sixteen Line Ornamented No.1, Wood & Sharwoods, 1838.

A type of death

Ornament is crime. Typeface designers today are Modernist law-abiding citizens who police their forms within the strict confines of function. By abstaining from the excesses of the material world, they have learned to live with less, but they think it is more. By devoting themselves to 'good design' and professional practices they have reached that state of grace known as legibility. Our time is the timeless time. We have taken the best from the past and perfected it.

But this was not always the case. Long ago, in the Industrial Age, when type was made of metal, wood and sweat, there were no regulations and all the typographic rules were swelled and decorated. No expression was left unstated, no gimmick or trick untried. It was every type designer for himself and no-holds barred. In those rough and tumble days, letters were three-dimensional and cast long dark shadows across the page. Others were so elegantly affected or grossly contorted that one could get altogether lost in them.

Today, you can readily spot these ridiculous old types in the occasional antique-shop, sign or when the circus comes to town. They're only put to use in order to remind us of a splendidly decadent past, long dead and almost forgotten.

Like the grand old Victorian mansions in horror films, these typefaces are haunted by ghosts and they have different voices; some elegant and frail; some brazen and oppressive; and others pompous and ridiculous. Even so, all of them can be heard and they tell the story of

Top: Eight Line Ornamented No.4, Wood & Sharwoods, c.1842. **Middle:** Five Line Pica Ornamented, Marr, c.1853. **Bottom:** Fifteen Line Ornamented, No.2, Wood & Sharwoods, 1838.

their time. Will our types speak clearly of our age when we are long gone? Will they reflect a lust for life, a passion for new possibilities? Or just a pessimistic retrenchment into the timeless zone of legibility?

In the Industrial Age, type designers started all the fashions for 'artistic printing'. Today no self-respecting type designer would condescend to an interest in something as fleeting and ephemeral as fashion or future. Why bother when one can lay claim to timelessness? For practitioners in a relatively obscure artform, the lure of eternity is strong. Why be Number-One for a year when you can be in the Top-10 'till the end of time?

Of course we don't truly believe it's possible to do something that is timeless, it's just a bit of rhetoric we use when history makes us feel small. It's something we say to build ourselves up; it gives us courage. After all, who would want to admit to making tomorrows' ghosts?

To avoid the mortality of style many designers today have revived the dead. The typographic cadavers are brought back from the distant past (classical mummies), the recent past (zombie moderns) or patched together, à la Frankenstein, with recently dug-up parts (post-mortum-modern).

No matter what the approach, it all comes down to the same thing, a kind of typographic necrophilia. Instead of wasting time perfecting an exquisite corpse, type designers should be excited by new digital possibilities, just as the industrial age designers were about their technological advances. We should be expressing the vicissitudes of our time instead of continuing a methodical melt-down into one perfect Helvetica. The only way to breathe new life into old faces is to introduce new ones that in turn, will grow old. This is the natural course of change that insures the inevitability of style.

Top: Enamelled Metal Sign, 19c. **Middle:** Cast Iron Street Name Plates, Godmanchester, 19c. **Bottom:** Glass Pub Mirror, London, 19c.

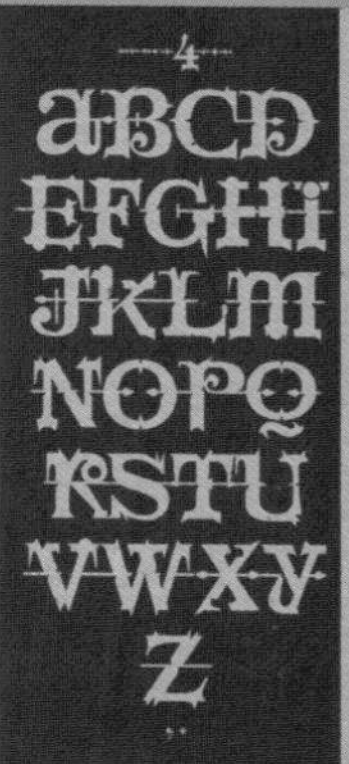

LushUS **JEFFREY KEEDY**

LushUS is the typeface that inebriated itself on exuberant excess, then told history to go fuck itself. Born an illegitimate typeface, the result of a repressed Victorian orgy whose participants were Egyptian, Tuscan, Ornamental and...who knows what else,

LUSHUS was banned from the Typophiles Club for explaining in depth how to insert a crystal goblet up one's backside, to reveal rather than contain the beautiful contents. Obviously, LUSHUS is tormented by a desire to be what it knows it can never be—modern!

There are decorative ornaments in the number keys **(1-7)** except for the 4. Please feel free to add ornamentation to this typeface: **more is not a bore.**

Mr. Keedy is a graphic designer living in Los Angeles. His clients include the Museum of Contemporary Art, Los Angeles Contemporary Exhibitions, Santa Monica Museum of Art and other such artsy-fartsy organisations. He also designs typefaces soon to be released through his company 'Cipher'. Currently he is Acting Program Director in Graphic Design at California Institute of the Arts.

Uck N Pretty **RICK VALICENTI**

Uck N Pretty was created by Rick Valicenti as the perfect collection of organic letterforms to express just about any emotion in this 'modern-post-modern, pre-millennium, early-paradigm shift world'.

Exuberance Abounds! Uck N Pretty makes headlines fun again. Each character has the right number of points for you, the designer, to pull and push in any direction that your turbo-techno-psychedelic imagination desires. Try it once and you'll feel the magic of the **new age.** (Remember: **Don't Kill Pretty**)

There are seven extra characters under the following **Option** keys: **a, r, e double space, 1, v, T, & S.**

Rick Valicenti lives and works in Chicago. He is principal and principle of Thirst, a group devoted to the creation of Art with Function. Thirst clientele vary in their respective businesses, but all share a deep commitment to design's ability to make a difference.

The concept of timelessness is the desire to escape this reality. To be timeless one merely has to be like Peter Pan and refuse to grow up, or at least refuse to acknowledge the passage of time. This immature strategy is at the core of most of what is uninteresting in typographic practice today. It is the legacy of an exhausted Modernism that refuses to die.

In its early years, Modernism courted capitalist consumerism (Modernism knew a meal ticket when it saw one). Today however, Modernism and consumerism have been married so long it is hard to tell them apart. But this sanctuary of domestic bliss has a couple of skeletons in its closet. They are exuberance and decoration, the two (illegitimate?) babies Modernism threw out with the bathwater, so it could have consumerism to itself. That's when Modernism began its slow decline. Consumerism might run itself into the ground, unless exuberance and decoration come back from the vernacular (where they have done quite well on their own) and help redefine a newly styled consumerism. If exuberance and decoration were admitted to the high culture club of 'serious' type design, then maybe designers would see Modernism for the zombie it really is.

All type families have skeletons in their closets and ghosts as well. So make your typography for today; let it speak to us in the voice of this moment. And accept the fact that it will haunt us in the future. After all, you're not afraid of ghosts...are you?

Mr. Keedy

Top: Glass, Wheel Cut & Gilded, Bride Lane Public House, London, 1917 **Middle:** Wrought Iron Sign, Queen's Hotel, Hornsey, 19c. **Bottom:** Northampton, (photographed 1962).

FUSE 4: David Berlow Yurnacular

In February 1992, as Berlow waited impatiently for some friends to come out of a jewellery shop in Colorado, he spotted a hand-lettered sign in the window of a rafting adventure company. Upon closer inspection Berlow determined the sign to be highly expressive of the American typographic vernacular. Crude in contrast, impoverished in shape and hopelessly misaligned, it was truly an American classic. It became the basis for *Yurnacular.*

After passing through several versions, the face became hopelessly illegible and was thus complete. Berlow recommends that Yurnacular be used in small point sizes for important legal documents, British Rail buffet car menus and IBM PC-compatible application program user documentation. Above nine point, Berlow suggests that the face be negatively tracked for yet greater compactness and, of course, to save paper.

A VERY EXHUBERANT

FAT FACE WITH CELLULITE AND LIPOSUCTION.

TYPE FOR TODAY.

LATE IN THE TWENTIETH CENTURY, A NEW AGE OF TYPOGRAPHIC EXUBERANCE SAW THE REBIRTH OF DECORATION. USING FORMS INSPIRED BY THE DECAY AND GARBAGE THAT DOMINATED THE LANDSCAPE AT THAT POINT IN HISTORY, TYPOGRAPHERS MADE LETTERS THAT SPEAK TO US IN THE LANGUAGE OF DECAY. TYPOGRAPHY FOR A LANGUAGE IN DISREPAIR AND A SOCIETY IN DECLINE.

DESIGN: BARRY DECK

TYPEFACE F CAUSTIC BIOMORPH EXTRA BOLD

R 1992 FONTSHOP INTERNATIONAL

C 1992 BARRY DECK

ABCDEFGHIJKLMN
OPQRSTUVWXYZ
0123456789!?,.;:'

FUSE 4: **Barry Deck** Caustic Biomorph

Decoration evolves in response to a continual visual sampling of daily life in conjunction with a culture's dominant notions of beauty, often rooted in the technical means by which it is produced. Today the media environment mixes with American neighbourhoods, as homeless encampments and discarded packages multiply in open view. Whilst our culture's definition of beauty is continually rewritten by marketing consultants in the service of greedy corporate executives, our ability to produce style is expanding, exceeded only by our perpetual desire to consume it. I think of *Caustic Biomorph* as a battle-scarred veteran of this stormy techno-cultural evolution: my own acid-eaten response to the decay so visible in American cities today. It is a typeface appropriate for the words AMALGAMATED CHEMICAL CORPORATION, RE-ELECT BUSH, or even IF YOU LIVED HERE YOU'D BE HOME BY NOW.

aBCDEFGHIJKLM
NOPQRSTUVWXYZ
4 ! , . &

FUSE 4: Jeffrey Keedy LushUS

LushUS is the typeface that inebriated itself on exuberant excess, then told history to go fuck itself. Born an illegitimate typeface, the result of a repressed Victorian orgy whose participants were *Egyptian, Tuscan, Ornamental* and... who knows what else, *LushUS* was banned from the Typophiles Club for explaining in depth how to insert a crystal goblet up one's backside, to reveal rather than contain the beautiful contents. Obviously, *LushUS* is tormented by a desire to be what it knows it can never be – modern! There are decorative ornaments in the number keys (**1 to 7**) except for the 4. Please feel free to add ornamentation to this typeface: **more is not a bore**.

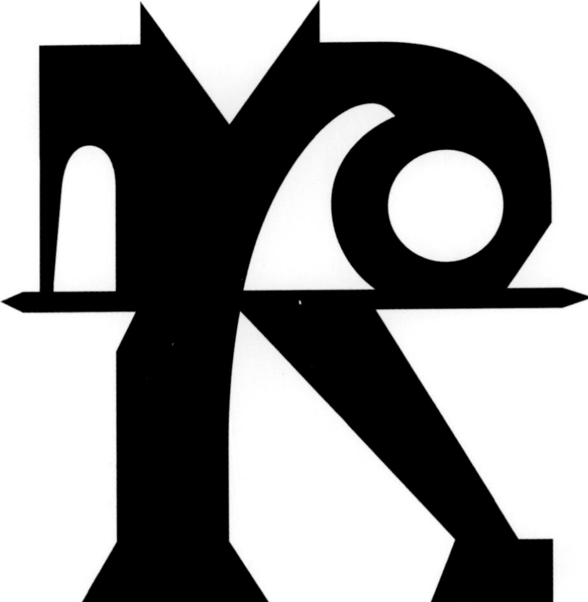

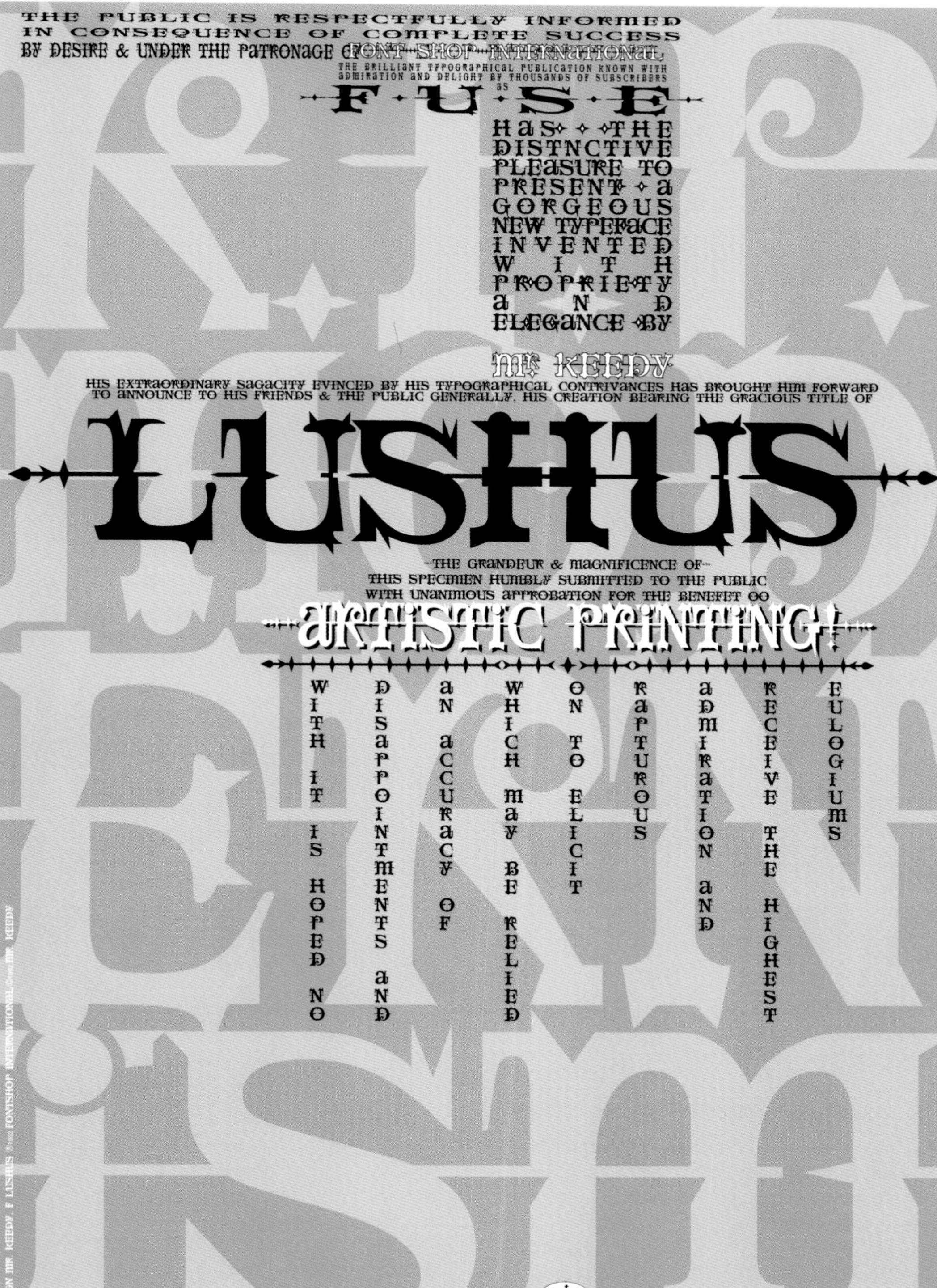
THE PUBLIC IS RESPECTFULLY INFORMED
IN CONSEQUENCE OF COMPLETE SUCCESS
BY DESIRE & UNDER THE PATRONAGE OF FONT SHOP INTERNATIONAL
THE BRILLIANT TYPOGRAPHICAL PUBLICATION KNOWN WITH ADMIRATION AND DELIGHT BY THOUSANDS OF SUBSCRIBERS
AS
F·U·S·E
HAS THE DISTNCTIVE PLEASURE TO PRESENT A GORGEOUS NEW TYPEFACE INVENTED WITH PROPRIETY AND ELEGANCE BY
MR KEEDY
HIS EXTRAORDINARY SAGACITY EVINCED BY HIS TYPOGRAPHICAL CONTRIVANCES HAS BROUGHT HIM FORWARD
TO ANNOUNCE TO HIS FRIENDS & THE PUBLIC GENERALLY, HIS CREATION BEARING THE GRACIOUS TITLE OF
LUSHUS
THE GRANDEUR & MAGNIFICENCE OF
THIS SPECIMEN HUMBLY SUBMITTED TO THE PUBLIC
WITH UNANIMOUS APPROBATION FOR THE BENEFIT OO
ARTISTIC PRINTING!
WITH IT IS HOPED NO
DISAPPOINTMENTS AND
AN ACCURACY OF
WHICH MAY BE RELIED
ON TO ELICIT
RAPTUROUS
ADMIRATION AND
RECEIVE THE HIGHEST
EULOGIUMS
DESIGN MR KEEDY F LUSHUS FONTSHOP INTERNATIONAL MR KEEDY
4

FUSE 4: Rick Valicenti Uck N Pretty

Uck N Pretty was created by Rick Valicenti as the perfect collection of organic letterforms to express just about any emotion in this "modern-post-modern, pre-millennium, early-paradigm shift world". Exuberance Abounds! *Uck N Pretty* makes headlines fun again. Each character has the right number of points for you, the designer, to pull and push in any direction that your turbo-techno-psychedelic imagination desires. Try it once and you'll feel the magic of the **new age**. (Remember: **Don't Kill Pretty**) There are seven extra characters under the following **Option** keys: **a, r, e double space, 1, v, T, & S.**

FONT SHOP INTERNATIONAL
RICK VALICENTI

5

FUSE

FUSE 5: The Great Escape Jon Wozencroft

LATE SUMMER 1992

VIRTUAL

Virtual Reality, don't you just love it. Everyone's hoping that you will, because even before zero point one percent of us have tried it, the phrase is being used as a media buzzword to keep us believing that yes, in spite of it all, we can look forward to a fun-filled future.

Ever since man began to believe he could control and transcend his environment, we have passed through various versions of virtual reality. We are, and always have been, living in the imaginary world of our own perceptions. Paradox is everywhere: a car window sticker that says Friends of the Earth; "Deaf Pride" graffiti'ed onto a poster promoting a mass rally for the latest evangelist, who promises to cure people of their disabilities live on stage. It's a suspect idea, virtual reality, because deep down we know we've got it already, everywhere around us, but for some, spurred on by the last decade's success of selling us things we already own, such as water, gas and electricity, it's an opportunity not to be missed. Scientists, who increasingly need public relations to explain away the technoscape's darker legacy, can now join forces with a PR industry frantically searching for its own version of $E=mc^2$ to give substance to their bag of tricks. Of course with any new technology we are promised liberation, and from this there is truly no escape. But before it becomes widely available, the media will perform its brand of everyday hijack and *describe the experience before anyone has the chance to find out for themselves.* What you want is information, but what you are given is data, opinions and psychobabble. It's amazing what they think they can get away with.

Virtual reality works by presenting each eye with a different image, making it seem three-dimensional; when you move your head, the image around you changes, with real-time computer graphics recreating the scene in front of you 25 times a second, creating the illusion that you are moving around *inside* what is actually a stationary external world. According to the inventor of the term VR, Jaron Lanier, "we should think of the human being as a kind of spy submarine moving around in space, gathering information. This creates a picture of perception as an active activity [*sic*], not a passive one". When researchers and manufacturers of virtual machines talk about their quest "to personalise and humanise technology", they stress the interactive nature of VR (though reading a book or driving a car never warranted this term) and the "immersive" quality of the experience. By this they mean that VR should be convincing and engrossing, but it's strange that this should be so highlighted – who buys a car without an engine?

And where does that leave dreaming? Virtual reality reminds me of an episode from TV's *The Twilight Zone* where the clock stops and life is put on hold. *"I'm trying to connect you"*... Immersed in the VR world, the rest of civilisation might as well be in suspended animation whilst you navigate your way across nowhere land. William Bricken, principal scientist at the Human Interface Technology Laboratory in Seattle, observed the behaviour of 20 people who had spent 10 hours on a VR machine; he noted that "VR affects dreaming strongly – it seems to provide tools for the control of the dream-life within the dream. The trouble is that we don't have the faintest clue what is going on". But such details do not seem to bother Bob Jacobson of World Design, another VR developer based in Seattle: "we only have a finite amount of time to prove the worth of what we're doing. I would say let's go for performance, not worry about the minutiae of what we're doing". His argument is based on economics: "the Japanese don't think about that sort of thing".

Some scientists are beginning to 'talk down' our supercharged expectations, warning that current technology is still at a primitive stage and that even the best VR displays can emulate just one fiftieth of the detail of the human eye – that's a car with a top speed of 3 mph. In fact, the VR helmet or 'headset' renders its user legally blind: whilst wearing it, you would only be able to read the top row of letters on an optician's wallchart. Thus in order to receive your virtual reward, you must first concede that the real world is now "the other side", no more than a blur.

Virtual reality works by presenting each eye with a different image, making it seem three-dimensional; when you move your head, the image around you changes, with real-time computer graphics recreating the scene in front of you 25 times a second, creating the illusion that you are moving around *inside* what is actually a stationary external world.

At the University of Manchester's National Advanced Robotics Research Centre, technical director Bob Stone agrees that current VR machines are far too slow; he says the minimum frame speed needed for a convincing scene is about 60 fps – ideally, he recommends frame rates of 200 fps, which is some way off. In the meantime, other developers (there are only about 20 laboratories worldwide working exclusively on VR) talk of the user's need for "cognitive plasticity", in other words our ability to form patterns from crude outlines.[1]

This is what we should be doing with the very idea of virtual reality. "Given the rate of development of VR technologies, we don't have a great deal of time to tackle questions of morality, privacy, personal identity and the prospect of fundamental change in human nature" says Howard Rheingold.[2] J.G. Ballard reckons "virtual reality represents the greatest step in human evolution", but in another breath he warns, "when VR comes on stream, we'll immerse ourselves in an ocean of rubbish". As for pollution, environmentalists tell us that we have thirty years in which to save the planet, yet we've barely started to address the damage caused by *mental* pollution, the long-term effects of TV, or what the great investment into an electro-magnetic digital future is going to do to our brains and to our bodies.

There *are* positive aspects. VR might prove to be crucial to medicine, architecture and manufacturing, especially for training operators to carry out complex or dangerous tasks. In the business world, you would be able to create virtual presentations in an electronic work-place, cutting down on staff, expense accounts and travel costs. Salesmen could be replaced by 2D robots (the screen display is mightier than the suit). And designers would never have to meet their clients.

But as if it were a new Hollywood blockbuster, VR is principally being proclaimed for its potential to enhance entertainment, a fantasy factory that can fire the imagination and promote self-awareness all at the same time. VR is reality made safe. It's like Dionysian rituals, the alphabet, cinema, cities and money markets never existed, as if funny strokes and squiggles on a piece of rag, pulp or cloth never allowed us "to interact with other people almost as if it were part of the real world". And as if language itself wasn't *always* virtual.

As for our identities, increasingly we choose to express ourselves through objects, brand-names, pop groups... you name it. Well part of the trouble is, *we don't*. It all comes pre-packaged. We move around "gathering information" subject to a man-made structure whose orders and signposts predetermine our path. Concepts, icons and constructs are presented to us from on high, honed, and at such speed that our spy submarines rarely go below periscope depth. Preoccupied by surface activity, we glimpse the outlines and are shown brief excerpts, forever fitting fragments together in order to make sense of this external world. In this respect, we can begin to understand the full effect of the digital conversion. *There is no longer any such thing as the full picture.* It has been abolished. In its place comes a pixellated image of reality, in which we are always trying to join the dots.

"If, against all the evidence, men dream of original and brilliantly thought-out machines, it is because they despair for their own originality, or prefer to part with it in favour of the sheer pleasure of machines that grant them this by proxy. Firstly, what these machines do is offer the spectacle of thought, and men, as they manipulate them, devote themselves more to this spectacle of thought than to thought itself".[3]

"Welcome if you've just joined us"! This morning I went to get the paper, and on the contents list, up there with the masthead, lo and behold if it's not the words themselves – virtual reality for the breakfast table. This, however, turned out to be no more than a short review of a new film, *The Lawnmower Man*, in which a village idiot gets injected with strange fluids by a mad professor. Well knock me down with a paperweight if it doesn't transpire that old Joe Dimwit turns into a super-genius who goes off on God knows what "amazing" and "spectacular" virtual reality trips, and

J.G. Ballard reckons "virtual reality represents the greatest step in human evolution", but in another breath he warns, "when VR comes on stream, we'll immerse ourselves in an ocean of rubbish".

then it all goes wrong (until the happy ending), causing the cinema-going public in America (and now England) to queue up by the coachload for a sneak preview of their near future. The only character in the film to actively question VR, the professor's wife, Caroline, quickly melts into the background. Edited out. Despite this, the film has a message struggling to break free, one that warns of the military tendency where the baddies get their hands on the technology and stop us, the common or garden Joe, from having a good trip and reaching enlightenment into the bargain. Between the source and the signal, however, what you are left with is a bad film that reeks of a bandwagon.

You could say that VR is just about money and marketing (the film, which cost "just" $8.5m to make, has already grossed over $35m and there's the video to come), you could say that it's only a tool, don't get excited (but so is the car, so is a gun, and look where they got us) – what worries me is the way that VR and its apostles connect with a host of social malaises whilst promising a deliverance from them. Caroline says "it may be the future to you, but it's the same old shit to me".[4]

There will simply be more of it. We won't have to worry if there's nothing on the telly, nor bother with the lengthy rituals of seduction, because from virtual sex to virtual armageddon it'll all be on tap. The Victorian age prided itself on its public works – hospitals, sewers, the distribution of water (and pollution); the present age concentrates its energies on the distribution of entertainment. If you're born in the U.S.A., by the time you are 16 years old you will have spent half a year of your life watching TV commercials – 4380 hours of hard sell.

It is easy to forget that any good film, book or record is a leap forward into a virtual reality, surprising and empowering us with new possibilities. Perhaps it's because we are lazy, maybe it's because we are now addicted to finding ever more sensational sensations. One reason why *The Lawnmower Man* has been so popular is thanks to its (albeit fleeting) virtual sex sequence. You cannot help but notice how the steamy scenes have been stacking up in Hollywood's recent

NEVILLE BRODY STUDIO & JON WOZENCROFT EDITORIAL POSTER

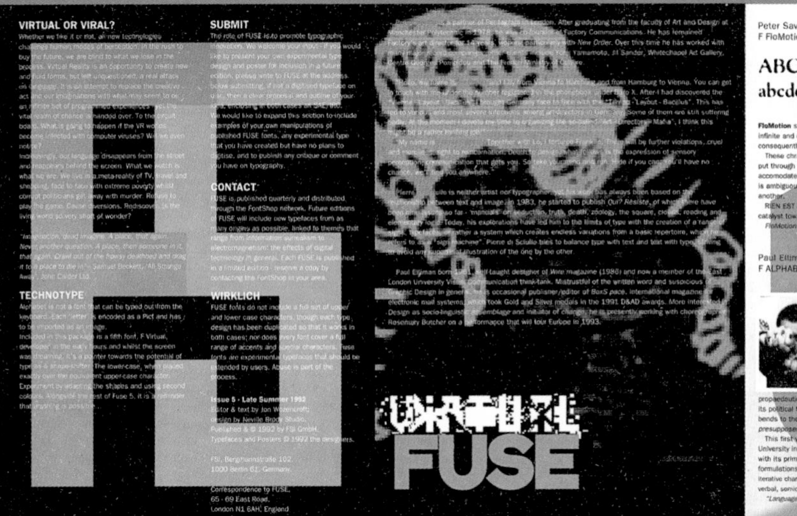
VIRTUAL OR VIRAL?
SUBMIT
CONTACT
TECHNOTYPE
WIRKLICH
VIRTUAL
FUSE
Peter Saville
F FloMotion
ABCDEFGHIJKLMNOPQRSTUVWXYZ
abcdefghijklmnopqrstuvwxyz
Paul Elliman
F ALPHABET
Lo Breier/Florian Fossel
F Spherize
Pierre Di Sciullo
F Scratched Out

output, yet there is still a strong sense of puritan attitudes in films like *Basic Instinct*, and of course the backdrop of AIDS, making the idea of guilt and risk-free sex irresistible. Hope for the future? It's the digital update of an age-old male fantasy. It's a complement to those urban encounters where you meet people and then never see them again. It also brings to mind the scenario in Yevgeny Zamyatin's *We*, written in 1920, the forerunner of both *Brave New World* and *1984*.

In *We*, D-503 keeps a diary of his life in a glass-enclosed city, The One State, where The Benefactor appoints Sexual Days upon which the inhabitants get a Personal Hour of privacy, the Right of Blinds, for which they must obtain a certificate by exchanging their "pink tickets", which are themselves rationed. D-503 writes that "having subordinated Hunger, The One State launched an offensive against the other sovereign of the universe – against Love, that is. 'Every number has the right of availability, as a sexual product, to any other number'. And that's all there is to it".[5]

Obviously most people will jump at the chance that blocked drains, boredom and sexual repression be banished from their lives, so it's little wonder that virtual reality has so rapidly become a concept that we swallow whole. Science Fiction, from H.G. Wells to Ballard, from *Dr. Who* to *Aliens 3*, is usually about mutants and nasty monsters whose sole mission is to mosch us, so it comes as most welcome when *the edge* is a cliff-face that we would all queue up for to jump off.

The reality is, as always, even more bizarre, but I thought I'd better try it. The only publicly accessible VR machine in England is at London's Trocadero, itself a controlled climate (a glass-enclosed city) that wires you up with video banks, flashing neon and the sound of electronic toys. I was very much hoping to be proved wrong... but this brief encounter was a let-down. You put on a helmet still sweaty from the brow of the last space cadet, you only have a joystick and a firing button, and it's like a screen displaying a bog-standard video game being shoved against your nose. Deeply unconvincing, yet you can at least glimpse where the technology's heading. We've all been softened up for this, by TV, by sitting at the front when you see a film on 70mm, by the way fast e/di/tin/g is now used in advertising. Kids who have been brought up with computer games, I wonder what they would make of it? Perhaps it's all second nature (*against nature?*). If there were to be any considered planning as to how this new technology might be applied, you would hope that the virtual worlds themselves were more psychotropic than psychotic. But the market is neutral. War, death and destruction is "what sells", so in the Trocadero's VR world, you find yourself in a walled city with an electrified perimeter fence, populated by marauding prisoners out to get you.

The thing is, you only know whether you've 'died' or not when your money has run out and the screen displays your score. Fake death, it would seem, is still better than real life. If you are unhappy with who you are, soon you will be able to discover what it is like to be a (virtual) member of the opposite sex, a (virtual) nymph or a (virtual) neanderthal. So much for the Hindu philosophy of reincarnation: soon you will be able to be anything or anyone you like all for one credit! It's a way of denying mortality, a way of avoiding physical existence and all the pain that can go with it – a way of flipping the coin on some of the greatest breakthroughs in 20th-century thought and perception – Gurdjieff, Jung, Duchamp (make your own list)... The 'real' is just too risky: the way forward is back to control.

The problem of our age is the problem of limits, where, by whom, or indeed if they should be drawn. In no time, VR technology will also link up with the innovations being made with "brain machines" that enable the human brain's RAS centre to be bypassed – the area that acts as a distribution centre for all the sensory information we receive, allowing us to make choices about any information's relative importance (such as... *bleep*... the phone rings while you are reading this). This is truly to open the flood gates, with VR as an electronic Ark into which we can offload problems ranging from drug abuse and AIDS to over-population, keeping people docile, domesticated and off limits. In other words, this creates a picture

You put on a helmet still sweaty from the brow of the last space cadet, you only have a joystick and a firing button, and it's like a screen displaying a bog-standard video game being shoved against your nose.

of active passivity. Choose your prison with the necessary comforts! Death is your parole! This is not what I call progress.

It took over a millennium for the alphabet to translate itself into one of Shakespeare's plays, so there is every possibility that somewhere in the future a truly magical development will come out of VR. But what will happen in the short term is that our present "playback culture" (exemplified from compact disc re-issues to karaoke nights) will be replaced by the fast-forward version. Software developers will come up with all kinds of futuristic scenarios that give us the illusion that we can intercept the future, that we are moving forward as a species. Hope becomes mathematic. Faith is made redundant.

And to hold a critical eye against such developments as virtual reality is to risk to be a killjoy, pessimist, and to fall victim to another scourge of our times – media-induced cynicism. However, before VR comes on stream, we have the advent of multimedia to contend with – the ability to create new forms of instant animation. On the one hand, this might function merely to prepare us for VR's perceptual world, but it also gives us the chance to use its possibilities to build a bridge, across which we can steer the way VR develops. VR might even prove to be a gift, a form of protest, one that forces us to reconfront what's really out there... as people do in wartime.

Reference:
1. For a good overview of the current state of VR technology, see Charles Arthur's article "Did Reality Move for You?" in *New Scientist* No. 1822, 23 May 1992 **2.** Howard Rheingold's book, *Virtual Reality*, is published by Secker & Warburg **3.** Jean Baudrillard, *Xerox and Infinity*, Touchepas UK, published in French in the collection *La Transparence du Mal*, Editions Galilée, Paris **4.** *The Lawnmower Man* is advertised as "The world's first virtual reality film". Where does that leave *2001*, *Dr. Strangelove*, *Apocalypse Now*, *Eraserhead*, *Star Wars* and so on... not to mention *The Player*? **5.** *We* is published in paperback in the U.K. by Penguin Books

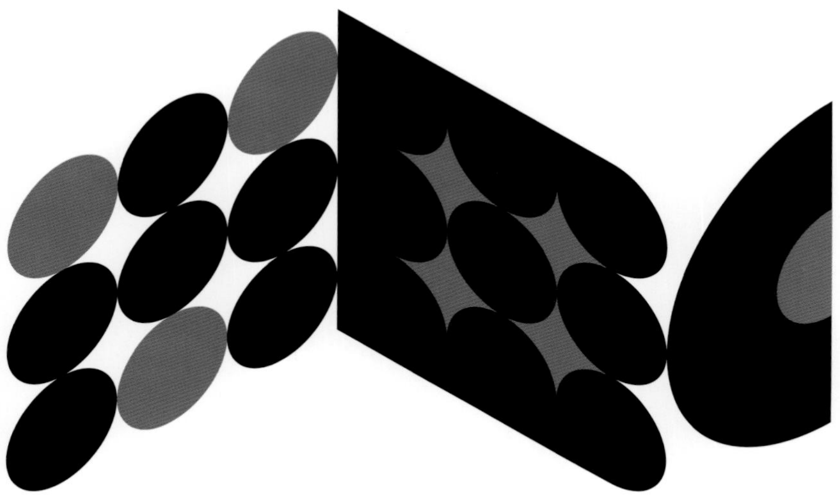

FUSE 5: Neville Brody Bonus Font Virtual

Fuse 5 available from :

FontShop Austria
Seidengasse 26
1070 Wien
(02 22) 523 29 46, -47
Fax (02 22) 523 29 47 22

FontShop Belgium
Maaltecenter Blok C
Derbystraat 247
9051 St. Denijs-Westrem
(091) 20 26 20
Fax (091) 20 34 45

FontShop Canada
401 Wellington St. West
Toronto, Ontario M5V 1E8
1-800-36-Fonts
416 408 3828
Fax 416 593 4318

FontShop Germany
BergmannstraBe 102
1000 Berlin 61
(030) 69 00 62 62
Fax (030) 69 00 62 77

FontShop Holland
Laan van Beek
en Royen 1b
3701 AH Zeist
(0 34 04) 323 66
Fax (0 34 04) 249 52

FontShop Italy
Via Masotto 21
20159 Milano,
(2) 7010-0555
Fax (2) 7010 0585

FontShop Sweden
Tegnérgatan 37
111 61 Stockholm
(08) 21 52 00
Fax (08) 21 28 80

FontWorks UK
65-69 East Road
London N1 6AH,
(071) 490 5390
Fax (71) 490 5391

Virtual c Neville Brody / Published 1992 by FontShop International
VIRTUALFUSE
5
FEATURING
PETER SAVILLE
LO BRIER
PAUL ELLIMAN
PIERRE DI SCIULLO
A NEW VISUAL LANGUAGE EMERGES FROM BEHIND THE SCREEN...
Fuse is a new venture in type design, containing
four experimental fonts digitised for Macintosh.
The fuse disc is Accompanied by four A2 posters
showing each typeface in creative application.
Produced by Fontshop International
and distributed exclusively
through the Fontshop network

ABCDEFGHIJKLMNOPQRSTUVWXYZ
abcdefghijklmnopqrstuvwxyz0123456789
,.:;’!?()-

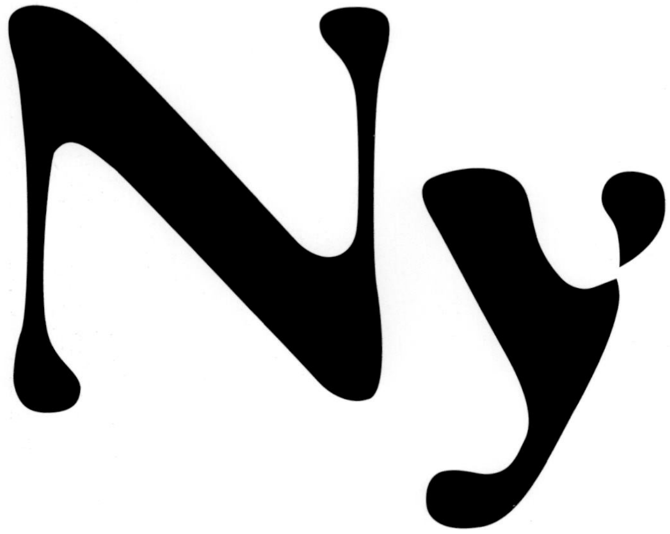

FUSE 5: Peter Saville FloMotion

FloMotion started with the premise that the future may not be exclusively sans serif... The scope of VR is infinite and obviously timeless, so I began to wonder about technology's simulation of history and consequently of classicism – how it might look in the unresolved blur that is as yet the VR screen field. These characters were drawn from the shapes that remained after a 'traditional' serif typeface had been put through blur and then further reduced by contrast adjustments.

The objective was to accommodate VR's low-res and create a 'simulated neo-classic'. The forms that evolved have a liquidity that is ambiguous: are the words emerging or deconstructing – slowly transforming from one message into another? RIEN EST DURABLE DANS CE MONDE is from *Caractères de L'Imprimerie* (1742); the font has been a catalyst towards creating a neo-neo classic series of type and ornament, virtual Fournier. *FloMotion* was developed with the help of Mette Heinz.

RIEN DE
DURABLE DANS
CE MONDE

F FloMotion ©Design by Peter Saville + Mette Heinz, Pentagram Published by Fontshop International

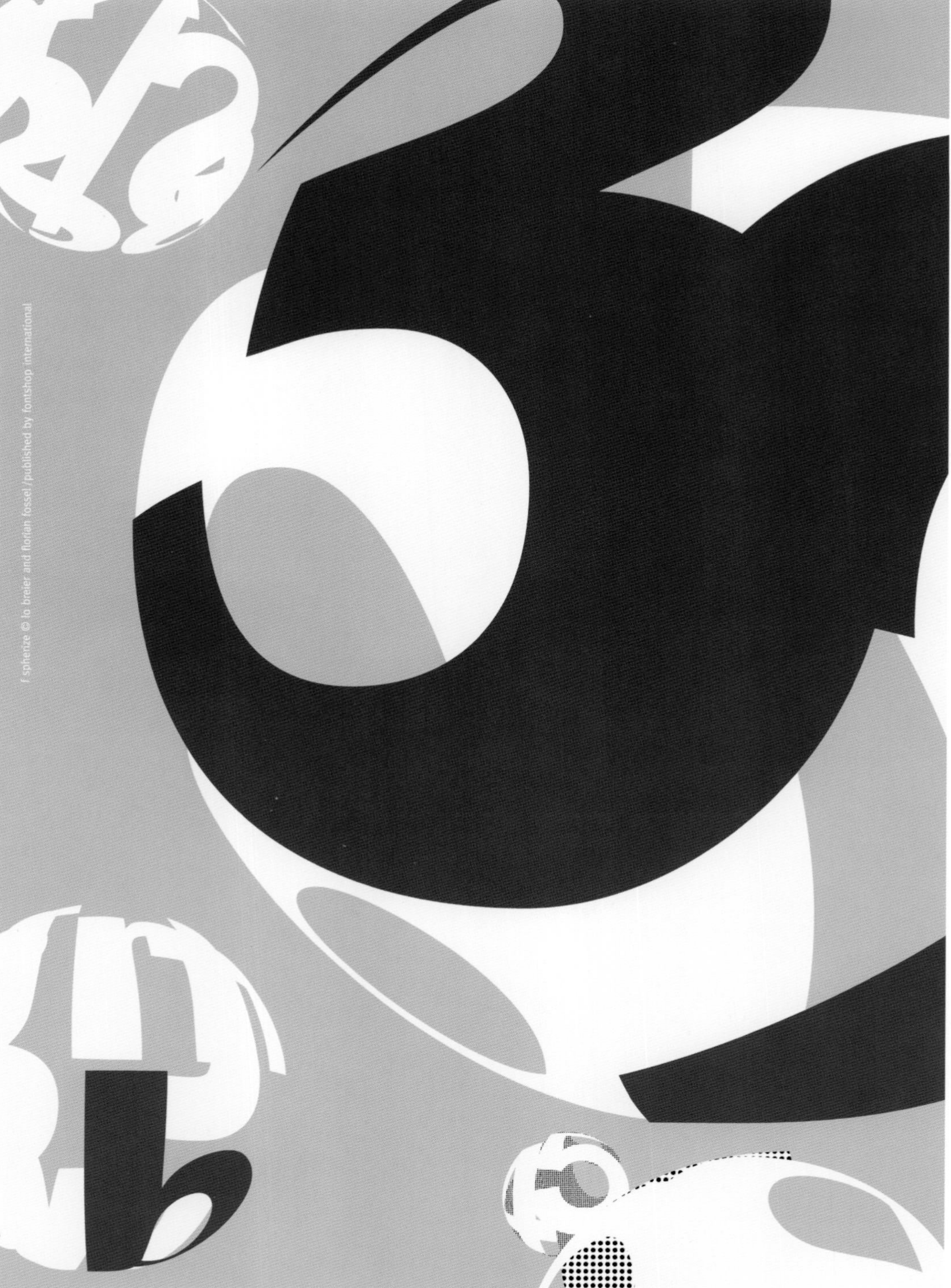
f sphenze © lo breier and florian fossel/published by fontshop international

FUSE 5: Lo Breier & Florian Fossel Spherize

Is there anyone out there who is not yet sick of *Franklin*? (*Yes, me – Ed.*). You come across it everywhere – *Franklin, Franklin, Franklin*. Wherever one reads. From here to Tokyo. Catching sight of *Franklin* almost makes one explode. Or rather, *Franklin* explodes. So would you please take a closer look at this: it is our revenge on *Franklin*. We simply blew it up. Plop. The end. No more. And here's the result: *Spherize*. The type comes post-*Franklin*, this is *Virtual Franklin, Franklin of The Third Kind*, spreading out into space, flashing in timeless space, immense like the matrix, where letters whizz through time and space. *Vibrant Franklin*. (*That's enough Franklin – Ed.*). For the man of the world, because it's round, just like the world. Planetary round. Dome-shaped like the continents. Typo balls. Powerful as cannonballs. Sweet, soft and tender like *Mozartkugeln*. Revenge must be taken!

FUSE 5: Paul Elliman Alphabet

Alphabet rethreads the links and separations between written, spoken and associative language. Language is a system and as such lays itself open to be *smashed*. We treat language as one of the last lines of security, like the ground we stand on, a dependable defence and an unimpeachable link with reality. This is a mistake – to undermine the things we depend upon is our only option in the unchallenged autocratic state. MEDIA SURVEILLANCE SWEEPS LANGUAGE... *Larger than life*; scrolling back to re-edit Historical past and pre-scanning/pre-inventing the future. Virtual Reality Technology is the processed experience gone big-time, *opening doors that are not there*. This is its charm: designers merely take up the slack. Outside *The Studio*, we might accept that Television offers certain propaedeutical benefits; since its tendency to displace/disengage us will surely be superseded by VRTech, its political forms should be somewhat anticipated. Back inside (*The Studio*), the race into virtual space bends to the illusion of *Neutral Technology* (as does the flight from it). *"Any exploration of the alphabet presupposes an exploration of the connections between writing and language"* – Gerstner. This first version of *Alphabet* was realised as a performance for 26 people in a photo-booth at London University in June 1992. By recodifying the codification of language in a way that merges written language with its primal form (spoken? expressed?), language is reset to expand towards a multiplicity of equivalent formulations – like the n-space under matrix transformation. An open proposal, *Alphabet* moves out along an iterative channel towards analphabetic/ultra-alphabetic thought; open to expression and interpretation, verbal/non-verbal, semio-linguistic and limitless: *larger than language*.

"Language is not dependent on writing" – de Saussure.

Alphabet

Tu peux également la lire.

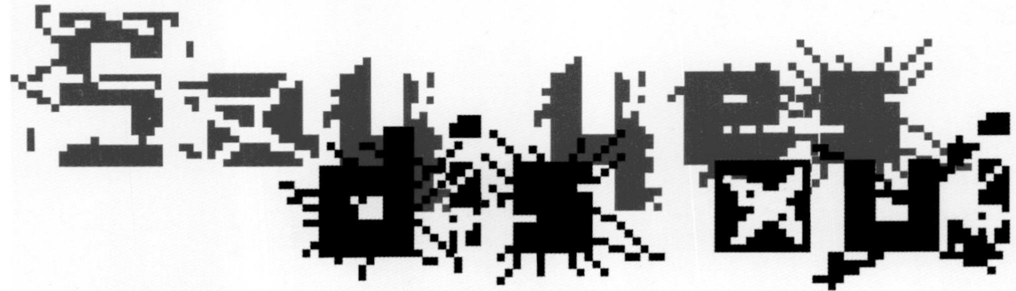

Tu ne seras jamais déçu
You'll never be disappointed

Whenever you want wherever you want
Quand tu veux où tu veux

Avec tes yeux
With your eyes

Your skin will never wear out
Ta peau ne s'usera pas

Tes dents sont blanches
My teeth are white

It's ready
C'est facile

Sur le velours des écrans
On the velvet of the screens

Did you see it ?
Tu as vu ?

Reste avec moi
Stay with me

You can try with your tongue as well
Tu peux essayer avec ta langue aussi

Tu as tout le temps
You have plenty of time

I'm free
Je suis disponible

J'ai juste besoin d'un peu d'énergie
I just need a little energy

What will you give me in exchange ?
Que me donneras-tu en échange ?

FUSE 5: Pierre di Sciullo Scratched Out

Scratched Out (*Minimum Rayé*) was initially designed as a bitmap font which served as the basis for numerous deformations and metamorphoses. Each letter is angrily erased, crossed out, punched, spoilt and scratched... However, it is possible to read it if you play leapfrog with your eyes. Words are deciphered in spite of their letters – words emerge from letters that refuse to be read. Composed in 1988 during my research into illegibility, I only started to use the font in 1991 for a text on what had to be said and what must not be said about the Gulf War. The media propaganda was so coherent and univocal that, by basically opposing the war, this loathsome consensus might have become respectable. Hence this attempt to react against the very words used in propaganda. Commentators could then use foul and inept expressions such as "surgical strike" without creasing their jackets. I would have liked to hear surgeons remind everyone that their work is about curing and saving life, rather than death and mutilation. Letters rebel against the message they convey. In my poster, *Scratched Out* in effect says: the text is never totally there, it refuses itself, whereas sentences bring comfort. Is it the virtual technology that is imperfect, or does the user need to be warmed up?

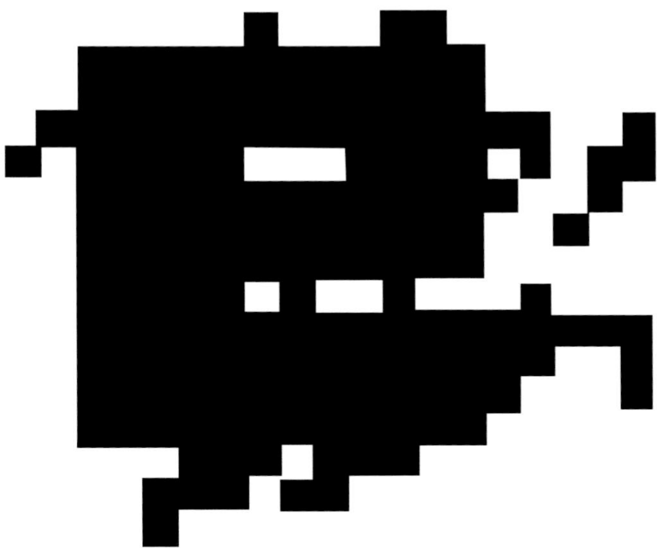

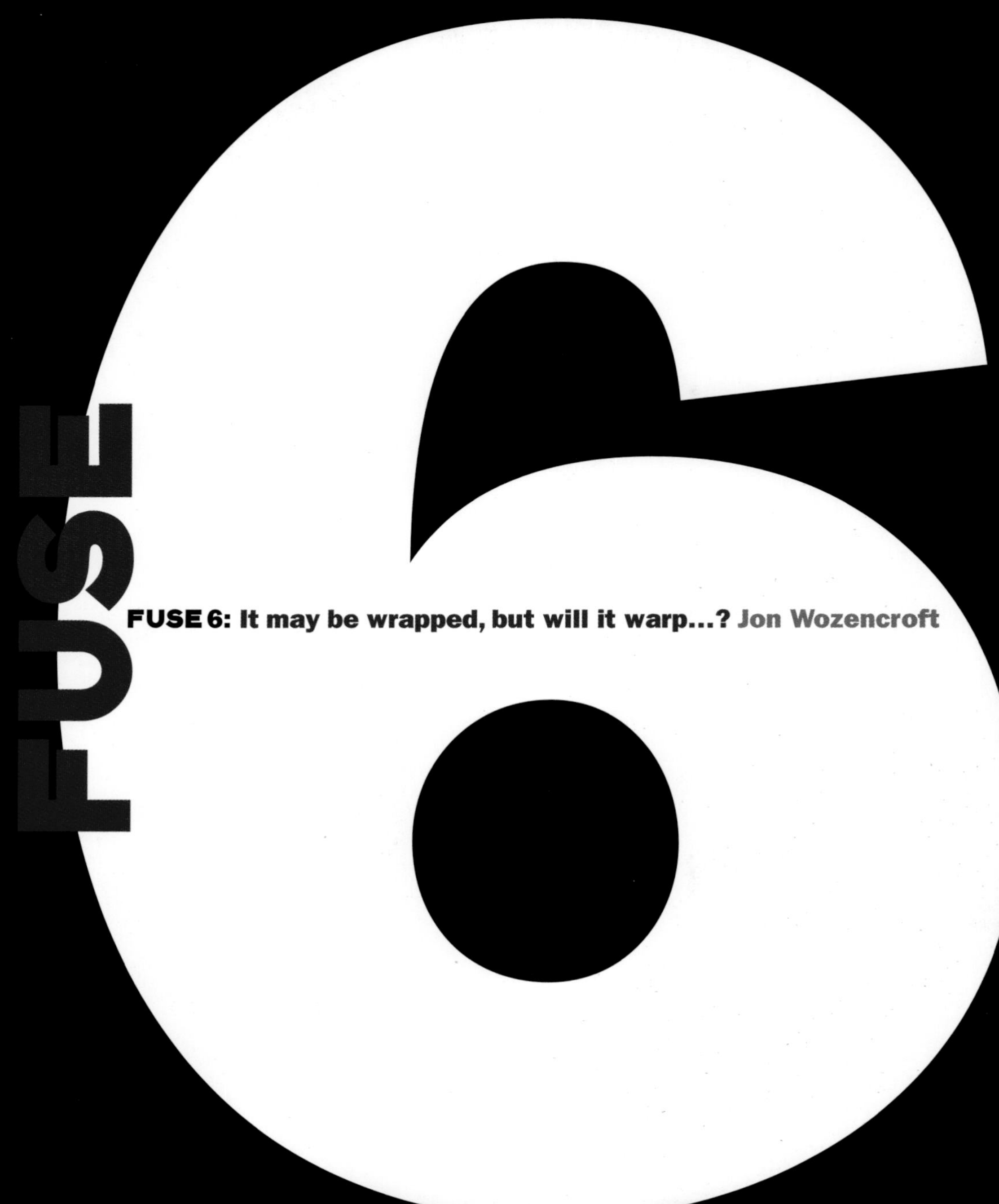
FUSE
6
FUSE 6: It may be wrapped, but will it warp...? Jon Wozencroft

WINTER 1992

CODES

It is too early to predict how, exactly, the conversion from analogue to digital forms is going to effect human communication and interaction on an everyday level. Already, it is possible to send fonts down a telephone line; we will soon be able to publish our own faces on videophones hooked up to all corners of the globe; we can retouch photographs to make smiles flash on full beam, yet the full potential of new technology is still beyond our means, the cutting edge is never accessible, and by its very nature it always will be.

Fundamental changes to the process of transmitting language create fundamental changes in its expression. To have any chance of understanding the impact of digital forms of communication upon the way we use language, we are, paradoxically for such a modern invention, forced to pretend that we are in a *pre*-condition rather than a "post" state. The reduction of words and images to a system based on the binary code is not simply a sophisticated "techno/logical development": it necessitates a revolution in the way we perceive any information. In effect, we have two choices: to blindly go along with it, or to reconsider everything. And if we return to the origins of our language, to phonetics, hieroglyphs, embryo-writing and early alphabets, looking for clues or for archetypes of linguistic change, this is also a form of futurology, but retro-divination. There are drawbacks: we colour the past, lose sight of the present and fall subject to "the disease of tomorrow". And all the time we are compelled to weigh up whether or not anything is *obvious* any more. Education systems are not working, every individual holds 'views' but few are in a position to express them, acronyms, euphemisms, jargon and catchphrases are used to such excess that a direct statement either leaves us speechless or is dismissed as another piece of advertising.

Having mastered the technique of building super-structures and shopping malls, we have forgotten how to build homes. So it is with language. In order to communicate, we designate our thoughts and feeling into prearranged compartments. To articulate means we fill a space and hope to connect. We agree that an owl is not an elephant, but that is as far as it goes – in the main, we navigate a way through broad generalisations. Words, when spoken first person, are primarily sonic devices with endless possibilities for personal pitch change – nuances that cannot be recorded on tape even if they have been registered in real time. The spoken word is standardised to keep pace with new modes of transmission. It becomes another format; as Goebbels noted, "the spoken word is more 'magnetic' in its effect than the written one". The chaos of communication has to be kept tidy, thus as soon as human encounters ceased to be either original or impromptu (which is to say, relatively early on in the day), codes are developed to hold fast the compartments. As the population and diversity of voices increases, so must the codes be made more rigid. Until communication, powered by mass media forms which expressly rely upon the concept of hidden (if not invisible) information, consists only of codes... then codes of codes of codes. Pastiche and self-referential terms become our staple diet – "garbage in, garbage out", as the saying goes. And we shout to make ourselves heard.

In the best of all possible worlds, nothing needs to be recorded because the experience of it is always available. As soon as a civilisation devotes its energies to upholding (and thus redefining) its "heritage", a storage problem arises – just like the housing crisis. As soon as the exposure and availability of any item or idea is restricted by the need to control the amount of people who wish to be exposed to it, the need to capture this information and to replicate it results. Words and ideas, like cities, become overpopulated. In this way, communication is no longer guided by the desire to emancipate, but the need to edit. The notion that, in today's marketplace, any product or message has to be "commercial" in order to achieve "a high profile" is often the kiss of death as far as meaning is concerned (and as for irony?!). This is the age of Convenience, no matter what the cost.

Since different peoples evolve different solutions to their societies' needs for information storage, codes are as old as written language. In the beginning, everybody knew them – we presume. And if they did not, does this mean that language has always involved exclusion? Who knows? In spite of the fact that DNA research can now tell us more about the origins of man than ever before, we really have not got a clue. So rather than speculate, we can at least say that all forms of writing are a means of information storage. Anything stored needs to be codified. Is there an essential difference between early man, who made knots in a length of fabric as a mnemonic device, and modern man, who types letters on a keyboard and saves them on a hard disk?

As a noun, the first meaning of "code" is a legal one. The word then develops to refer to a system or collection of rules of any sort. The lines you are now reading are of course in code, yet those of us who fall within the demographic range of the Roman alphabet and the English language have, from an early age, been instructed in the use of this code; its tradition as a common denominator determines that we would never consider it to be cryptic (from the Greek *kryptos*, 'secret'). Following this line, nor can Chinese/Arabic/Russian etc. be assigned such a status, yet their alphabets are so unfamiliar to us that any written messages presented in these languages might as well be cryptographic.

At what point does a language become a code? Perhaps the dividing line *is* simply based on familiarity, and we have been misled by too many post-war spy films into thinking codes to be the privy of James Bond, Smiley's people, the government, the military, *The Prisoner*, and to gain access to these codes involves our crawling through a ventilation shaft, hoping that the guards will not be roused. To press further for a distinction, the idea that all information in the public domain must be made familiar in style in order to appeal to a specific ("target") audience, and judicial, state and military information be encoded and "made classified" creates a class system based on the relative ability of the reader or audience

At what point does a language become a code? Perhaps the dividing line *is* simply based on familiarity, and we have been misled by too many post-war spy films into thinking codes to be the privy of James Bond, Smiley's people, the government, the military, *The Prisoner*, and to gain access to these codes involves our crawling through a ventilation shaft, hoping that the guards will not be roused.

to receive and interpret the coded information. Codes are like camouflage: they are founded on the twin precepts of display and concealment. The distribution, or SEND, is all important. The method or process of disseminating information, the "reaching out", the lying that is part and parcel of this process, demands that there be codes; and if this form of **containment** is insufficient, more direct forms of censorship can be called upon.

There is so much information vying for our attention that, inevitably, techniques are used to compress it into smaller loads, using codes to replace what may seem to be excess, complex or redundant wordage. This "compression" is also regulated by time: deadlines, clearance, desk space, the available slot. In the same breath, the world's information is increasingly articulated in one language – electronumerical U.S. English (its very self a hybrid) – so that every message becomes one that begs to be deciphered and then relocated and renewed using another code. Ours is a translation game.

The game has more losers than winners. The pressure of codification makes ('amateur') users of language turn (or retreat) to metaphors to 'fill out' and rebuild their flattened mental environment. The reduction of complex ideas to 'basic' dimensions demands that we juggle signs around, twist them and redecorate. Then we wonder why, and how, we become confused.

The need to conceal and guard information is an ancient one. An early example AD is the so-called Caesar Alphabet, a basic method of transposing letters so that A becomes D and B translates to E. This, to be exact, is not a code but a cipher. A code works on complete words or phrases, and a cipher upon individual letters; there are two principal techniques – transposition and substitution. ('Cipher' comes from the Arabic *sifr*, meaning the arithmetical zero, and in this sense it has passed down into English to mean "a mere nothing, a worthless person".) As for the word "code", it now strikes us most often in its cybernetic sense (and is thereby better termed as a *formula*). This meaning did not enter the language until 1946. Accordingly, the noun merges with its verb. This linguistic shift is closely related to the progressive emphasis during the 20th century on the use of codes in wartime – a hijack performed by the military. Just as Alan Turing's improvised techniques cracked the German Enigma code, so was his later prototype for "intelligent machines" adapted to compromise peacetime. The very ability to mechanise message sending and receiving creates the capacity for 'Total War'. In turn, the possibility for artificial intelligence makes real life artificial. The apparent need to now define words in almost any context, from ad campaigns to essays, is proof enough that as far as our language is concerned, we are still in the dug-out.

5. *Cinemat. and Television.* The end of a session of filming or recording

1974. M. AYRTON *Midas Consequence* 1. 63 Other cars are heard starting up out of shot and the lights on the pergola go off so I assume it's a wrap and the crew is listening to the director saying something consequential and busy about tomorrow's call. **1980** J. KRANTZ *Princess Daisy* xii. 191 'Right... it's a wrap.'... The large lights, cameras, sound equipment and other tools of the trade were quickly stowed away. **1983** *Listener* 23 June 18/2 The Director says: 'Cut! Thank you, Ben, that's a wrap – there is no more filming.'

FUSE 6: The Fast Lane Jon Wozencroft

In "the information age", codes are thought to be essential to make the flow of data more efficient. But this has gone no way to solving the traffic problem. In fact, a surfeit of codified information only makes matters worse.

OMERTA
BRAILLE
MORSE
ERM
MATA HARI
JOSEF K
THE IRON CURTAIN
THE CONVERSATION
CIA/KGB
ROMEO OSCAR FOXTROT TANGO
THE HIGHWAY CODE
COMPUTERS
OCCUPIED EUROPE
LED
TIMECODES
TELEPHONE NUMBERS
DNA
BLOOD GROUP
THE BODY SHOP
DRESS SENSE
SAMPLING RATES
MARKET RESEARCH
OPINION POLLS
CIRCULATION FIGURES
OZONE EMISSIONS
TIC TAC TOE
BATTLESHIPS
MI5/MI6
METEOROLOGY
AGENT ORANGE
ALGEBRA, LOG BOOKS & MATRICES
POSTMODERNISM
BARCODES
E-NUMBERS
BRIAN ENO
THE THESAURUS
FRACTALS
DESIGN
DRUG DEALING
DIALECTS AND SLANG
SUBCULTURE
THE ZIMMERMAN TELEGRAM
THE OFFICIAL SECRETS ACT
THE ROYAL FAMILY
UNEMPLOYMENT FIGURES
NEWSPRINT
THE ENNEAGRAM
CATHOLICISM
VHS/PAL/NTSC
REMOTE CONTROLS
PHONE BILLS
TAX RETURNS AND N.I.
THE BIBLE
STILL LIFE PAINTINGS
MODERN ART
INSURANCE CLAIMS
ADVERTISING
ARCHITECTURE
FLOCK WALLPAPER
AIRLINE TICKETS
MAPS
THE FULL CLASSIFIED RESULTS SERVICE
AN AIRPORT CHECK-IN DESK
CASHPOINT MACHINES
TRAFFIC WARDENS
HOW-TO-DO-IT MANUALS
ASTROLOGY
GRAPHOLOGY
OMNIOLOGY
"ARE YOU ON THE PILL?"
SCIENCE
THE SWASTIKA
ALPHABETS
POLICE RECORDS
BODY LANGUAGE
CREDITS AT THE END OF THE FILM
A POLITICAL SPEECH
NADSAT
ANSAPHONE MESSAGES
VODAPHONES
WALT DISNEY
THE SATANIC VERSES
PROPAGANDA
POCKET CALCULATOR
PSION ORGANISER
TV RECONSTRUCTIONS
THE INDEX TO A BOOK
CROWDS
CRITICS
MILES DAVIS' TRUMPET
NEWSREADERS' VOICES
FOOTSIE SHARE INDEX
CARBON
THE USE OF THE LETTER 'X'
A NEW HAIRCUT
WORLD RECORDS
GMT
MARLIN FITZWATER (OR CNN)
PC
E
FOOTBALL TEAM KITS
FRUIT MACHINES
CONTRAFLOW SYSTEMS
ACID
FAKE FUR
ACTION REPLAYS
ZIP CODES & DIRECT MAIL
LEAN CUISINE
DOC MARTENS
LISTS SUCH AS THIS
501'S
95.8 FM
A YELLOW CARD FOR DISSENT
HANDWRITING
MADONNA NUDE
REVOLUTIONS
DAN QUAYLE
THE AUTUMN STATEMENT
THE RECESSION
"A LEVEL PLAYING FIELD"
REMEMBRANCE DAY POPPIES
DCC/MINI DISK
IN-JOKES
NUMBER SIX
007
THE BOUNCING BALL
NEO-(VEGETARIAN)ISMS
SELL-BY-DATE
THE ENGLAND MANAGER
FURRY DICE
IKEA
ARNIE'S MUSCLES
THE 4-4-2 FORMATION
RAGGA/RAP/TECHNO/GRUNGE ETC.
VATICAN SMOKE SIGNALS
JOHN 13:16
1905
TIMESHIFT RECORDING
ROADWORKS ON THE M25
A FLAG FOR OFFSIDE
ANARCHY *(IN THE UK)*
THE SWISS JUDGES
WAYNES WORLD
AIR TRAFFIC CONTROL
"LA NORVÈGE, NUL POINTS"
A POKER DECK
BRITISH RAIL PLATFORM ANNOUNCEMENTS
DEMOLISH SERIOUS CULTURE
"AT THE END OF THE DAY"
MTV
H_3O
TELEPATHY
FISH AND CHIPS
TRAFFIC LIGHTS
"SPARE 10P?"
CODEX
MALCOLM X
ROADSIGNS
BONO/STING/PHIL COLLINS ETC.
50% OFF - BARGAIN!
SUBTITLES
DEPECHE MODE
MOTORWAYS AND ROADS
CODES

JOHN CRITCHLEY FOR NEVILLE BRODY STUDIO & JON WOZENCROFT EDITORIAL POSTER

THE FAST LANE

In "the information age", codes are thought to be essential to make the flow of data more efficient. But this has gone no way to solving the traffic problem. In fact, a surfeit of codified information only makes matters worse.

SUBMIT
The role of FUSE is to promote typographic innovation and confusion. We welcome your input - if you would like to present your own experimental type design and poster for inclusion in a future edition, please write to FUSE at the address below submitting, if not a digitised typeface on disc, then a clear proposal and outline of your idea, enclosing in both cases an SAE/IRC. We would also like to see any examples of your own manipulations of published FUSE fonts, any experimental type that you have created but have no plans to digitise, and any critique or comment you have on typography.

FUSE fonts do not include a full set of upper and lower case characters, though each type design has been duplicated so that it works in both cases; nor does every font cover a full range of accents and special characters. Fuse fonts are experimental typefaces that should be extended by users. Abuse is part of the process.

CONTACT
FUSE is published quarterly and distributed through the FontShop network. Future editions of FUSE will include new typefaces from as many origins as possible, linked to themes that question the effects of digital technology in general and attempt to 'open up' its possibilities. Each FUSE is published in a limited edition - reserve a copy by contacting the FontShop in your area.

WIDERSTAND
To use *F morsig*, load and then open the program, click message, and type in the text you wish to send. You could turn your screen to face the window - each letter you have typed will be converted to short and long flashes, each in its own colour, which is random through the alphabet. This colour code appears in different shades of grey on a black and white screen. Word spaces appear as black in both cases.

V1

Issue 6 - Winter 1992
Editor & text by Jon Wozencroft.
Design by John Critchley for Neville Brody Studio.
Published & © 1992 by FSI GmbH.
Typefaces and Posters © 1992 the designers.

FSI, Bergmannstraße 102,
1000 Berlin 61, Germany.

Note new address!
Correspondence: FUSE editorial,
Unit 2 White Horse Yard,
78 Liverpool Road,
London N1 0QD, England.
Fax +44 (71) 704 2447.

FUSE

CODES

It may be wrapped, but will it warp...?

It is too early to predict how, exactly, the conversion from analogue to digital forms is going to effect human communication and interaction on an everyday level. Already, it is possible to send fonts down a telephone line; we will soon be able to publish our own faces on videophones hooked up to all corners of the globe; we can retouch photographs to make smiles flash on full beam, yet the full potential of new technology is still beyond our means, the cutting edge is never accessible, and by its very nature it always will be.

Fundamental changes to the process of transmitting language create fundamental changes in its expression. To have any chance of understanding the impact of digital forms of communication upon the way we use language, we are, paradoxically for such a modern invention, forced to pretend that we are in a *pre-condition* rather than a "post" state. The reduction of words and images to a system based on the binary code is not simply a sophisticated "techno/logical development"; it necessitates a revolution in the way we perceive any information. In effect, we have two choices: to blindly go along with it, or to reconsider everything. And if we return to the origins of our language, to phonetics, hieroglyphs, embryo-writing and early alphabets, looking for clues or for archetypes of linguistic change, this is also a form of futurology, but retro-divination. There are drawbacks: we colour the past, lose sight of the present and fall subject to "the disease of tomorrow". And all the time we are compelled to weigh up whether or not anything is *obvious* anymore. Education systems are not working, every individual holds 'views' but few are in a position to express them, acronyms, euphemisms, jargon and catchphrases are used to such excess that a direct statement either leaves us speechless or is dismissed as another piece of advertising.

Having mastered the technique of building superstructures and shopping malls, we have forgotten how to build homes. So it is with language. In order to communicate, we designate our thoughts and feelings into prearranged compartments. To articulate means we fill a space and hope to connect. We agree that an owl is not an elephant, but that is as far as it goes - in the main, we navigate a way through broad generalisations. Words, when spoken first person, are primarily sonic devices with endless possibilities for personal pitch change - nuances that cannot be recorded on tape even if they have been registered in real time. The spoken word is standardised to keep pace with new modes of transmission. It becomes another format; as Goebbels noted, "the spoken word is more 'magnetic' in its effect than the written one". The chaos of communication has to be kept tidy, thus as soon as human encounters ceased to be either original or impromptu (which is to say, relatively early on in the day), codes are developed to hold fast the compartments. As the population and diversity of voices increases, so must the codes be made more rigid. Until communication, powered by mass media forms which expressly rely upon the concept of hidden (if not invisible) information, consists only of codes... then codes of codes of codes. Pastiche and self-referential terms become our staple diet - "garbage in, garbage out", as the saying goes. And we shout to make ourselves heard.

In the best of all possible worlds, nothing needs to be recorded because the experience of it is always available. As soon as a civilization devotes its energies to upholding (and thus redefining) its "heritage", a storage problem arises - just like the housing crisis. As soon as the exposure and availability of any item or idea is restricted by the need to control the amount of people who wish to be exposed to it, the need to capture this information and to replicate it results. Words and ideas, like cities, become overpopulated. In this way, communication is no longer guided by the desire to emancipate, but the need to edit. The notion that, in today's marketplace, any product or message has to be "commercial" in order to achieve "a high profile" is often the kiss of death as far as meaning is concerned (and as for irony?!). This is the age of Convenience, no matter what the cost.

Since different peoples evolve different solutions to their societies' needs for information storage, codes are as old as ancient language. In the beginning, everybody knew them we presume. And if they did not, does this mean that language has always involved exclusion? Who knows? In spite of the fact that DNA research can now tell us more about the origins of man than ever before, we really have not got a clue. So rather than speculate, we can at least say that all forms of writing are a means of information storage. Anything stored needs to be codified. Is there an essential difference between early man, who made knots in a length of fabric as a mnemonic device, and modern man, who types letters on a keyboard and saves them on a hard disk?

As a noun, the first meaning of 'code' is a legal one. The word then develops to refer to a system or collection of rules of any sort. The lines you are now reading are of course in code, yet those of us who fall within the demographic range of the Roman alphabet and the English language have, from an early age, been instructed in the use of this code; its tradition as a common denominator determines that we would never consider it to be cryptic (from the Greek *kryptos*, 'secret'). Following this line, nor can Chinese/Arabic/Russian etc. be assigned such a status, yet their alphabets are so unfamiliar to us that any written messages presented in these languages might as well be cryptographic.

At what point does a language become a code? Perhaps the dividing line *is* simply based on familiarity, and we have been misled by too many post-war spy films into thinking codes to be the privy of James Bond, Smiley's people, the government, the military, *The Prisoner*, and to gain access to these codes involves our crawling through a ventilation shaft, hoping that the guards will not be roused. To press further for a distinction, the idea that all information in the public domain must be made familiar in style in order to appeal to a specific ("target") audience, and judicial, state and military information be encoded and "made classified" creates a class system based on the relative ability of the reader or audience to receive and interpret the coded information. Codes are like camouflage: they are founded on the twin precepts of display and concealment. The distribution, or SEND, is all important. The method or process of disseminating information, the "reaching out", the lying that is part and parcel of this process, demands that there be codes; and if this form of **containment** is insufficient, more direct forms of censorship can be called upon.

There is so much information vying for our attention that, inevitably, techniques are used to compress it into smaller loads, using codes to replace what may seem to be excess, complex or redundant wordage. This "compression" is also regulated by time: deadlines, clearance, desk space, the available slot. In the same breath, the world's information is increasingly articulated in one language - electronumerical U.S. English (its very self a hybrid) - so that every message becomes one that begs to be deciphered and then relocated and renewed using another code. Ours is a translation game.

The game has more losers than winners. The pressure of codification makes ('amateur') users of language turn (or retreat) to metaphors to "fill out" and rebuild their flattened mental environment. The reduction of complex ideas to 'basic' dimensions demands that we juggle signs around, twist them and redecorate. Then we wonder why, and how, we become confused.

The need to conceal and guard information is an ancient one. An early example AD is the so-called Caesar Alphabet, a basic method of transposing letters so that A becomes D and B translates to E. This, to be exact, is not a code but a cipher. A code works on complete words or phrases, and a cipher upon individual letters; there are two principal techniques - transposition and substitution. ('Cipher' comes from the Arabic *cifr*, meaning the arithmetical zero, and in this sense it has passed down into English to mean "a mere nothing, a worthless person"). As for the word 'code', it now strikes us most often in its cybernetic sense (and is thereby better termed as a *formula*). This meaning did not enter the language until 1946. Accordingly, the noun merges with its verb. This linguistic shift is closely related to the progressive emphasis during the 20th Century on the use of codes in wartime - a hijack performed by the military. Just as Alan Turing's improvised techniques cracked the German Enigma code, so was his later prototype for "intelligent machines" adapted to compromise peacetime. The very ability to mechanise message sending and receiving creates the capacity for 'Total War'. In turn, the possibility for artificial intelligence makes real life artificial. The apparent need to now define words in almost any context, from ad campaigns to essays, is proof enough that as far as our language is concerned, we are still in the dug-out.

5. *Cinema and Television.* The end of a session of filming or recording.

OMERTA
BRAILLE
MORSE
ERM
MATA HARI
JOSEF K.
THE IRON CURTAIN
THE CONVERSATION
CIA/KGB
ROMEO OSCAR FOXTROT TANGO
THE HIGHWAY CODE
COMPUTERS
OCCUPIED EUROPE
LED
TIMECODES
TELEPHONE NUMBERS
DNA
BLOOD GROUP
THE BODY SHOP
DRESS SENSE
SAMPLING RATES
MARKET RESEARCH
OPINION POLLS
CIRCULATION FIGURES
OZONE EMISSIONS
TIC TAC TOE
BATTLESHIPS
MI5/MI6
METEOROLOGY
AGENT ORANGE
ALGEBRA, LOG BOOKS & MATRICES
POSTMODERNISM
BARCODES
E-NUMBERS
BRIAN ENO
THE THESAURUS
FRACTALS
DESIGN
DRUG DEALING
DIALECTS AND SLANG
SUBCULTURE
THE ZIMMERMAN TELEGRAM
THE OFFICIAL SECRETS ACT
THE ROYAL FAMILY
UNEMPLOYMENT FIGURES
NEWSPRINT
THE ENNEAGRAM
CATHOLICISM
VHS/PAL/NTSC
REMOTE CONTROLS
PHONE BILLS
TAX RETURNS AND N.I.
THE BIBLE
STILL LIFE PAINTINGS
MODERN ART
INSURANCE CLAIMS
ADVERTISING
ARCHITECTURE
FLOCK WALLPAPER
AIRLINE TICKETS
MAPS
THE FULL CLASSIFIED RESULTS SERVICE
AN AIRPORT CHECK-IN DESK
CASHPOINT MACHINES
TRAFFIC WARDENS
HOW-TO-DO-IT MANUALS
ASTROLOGY
GRAPHOLOGY
OMNIOLOGY
"ARE YOU ON THE PILL?"
SCIENCE
THE SWASTIKA
ALPHABETS
POLICE RECORDS
BODY LANGUAGE
CREDITS AT THE END OF THE FILM
A POLITICAL SPEECH
NASSAT
ANSAPHONE MESSAGES
VODAPHONES
WALT DISNEY
THE SATANIC VERSES
PROPAGANDA
POCKET CALCULATOR
PSION ORGANISER
TV RECONSTRUCTIONS
THE INDEX TO A BOOK
CROWDS
CRITICS
MILES DAVIS' TRUMPET
NEWSREADERS' VOICES
FOOTSIE SHARE INDEX
CARBON
THE USE OF THE LETTER 'X'
A NEW HAIRCUT
WORLD RECORDS
GMT
MARLIN FITZWATER (OR CNN)
PC
E
FOOTBALL TEAM KITS
FRUIT MACHINES
CONTRAFLOW SYSTEMS
ACID
FAKE FUR
ACTION REPLAYS
ZIP CODES & DIRECT MAIL
LEAN CUISINE
DOC MARTENS
LISTS SUCH AS THIS
801'S
95.8 FM
A YELLOW CARD FOR DISSENT
HANDWRITING
MADONNA NUDE
REVOLUTIONS
DAN QUAYLE
THE AUTUMN STATEMENT
THE RECESSION
"A LEVEL PLAYING FIELD"
REMEMBRANCE DAY POPPIES
DCC/MINI DISK
IN-JOKES
NUMBER SIX
007
THE BOUNCING BALL
NEO
(VEGETARIANISMS
SELL BY DATE
THE ENGLAND MANAGER
FURRY DICE
IKEA
ARNIE'S MUSCLES
THE 4-4-2 FORMATION
RAGGA/RAP/TECHNO/GRUNGE ETC.
VATICAN SMOKE SIGNALS
JOHN 13/16
1965
TIMESHIFT RECORDING
ROADWORKS ON THE M25
A FLAG FOR OFFSIDE
ANARCHY *(IN THE UK)*
THE SWISS JUDGES
WAYNE'S WORLD
AIR TRAFFIC CONTROL
"LA NORVÈGE, NUL POINTS"
A POKER DECK
BRITISH RAIL PLATFORM ANNOUNCEMENTS
DEMOLISH SERIOUS CULTURE
"AT THE END OF THE DAY"
MTV
H2O
TELEPATHY
FISH AND CHIPS
TRAFFIC LIGHTS
"SPARE 10p?"
CODEX
MALCOLM X
ROADSIGNS
BONO/STING/PHIL COLLINS ETC.
50% OFF - BARGAIN!
SUBTITLES
DEPECHE MODE
MOTORWAYS AND ROADS
CODES

F DR No-B

In code, legibility is not an issue. **DR. No-B** is a series of logos based on the Roman alphabet, a corporate code of dots and dashes or a system of icons to convey more than language. It is 'toy-digital'. The salespitch is that **DR. No-B** is "beyond semantics", in reality it is... *join the AA here... today's temperature 30°... your train has been delayed - sorry for the inconvenience this will cause you... no smoking... wednesday 4 united 0 - 90 mins... sale! all items half price... change given... delayed further... engaged... london to berlin - save £50... happy birthday from all your friends... queue here... touchdown!... your train has been cancelled.*

Information can tell you nothing - **DR.No-B** has the power to tell you less.

F Box

The Fuse 6 assignment has redeveloped the way I perceive typography at the moment. Because of my background in jazz studies, I am constantly trying to merge the two media, jazz and type. **F Box** is an expression of sound, as if it were a tuning fork vibrating at a given pitch. The irregular letterforms within the grid suggest a more spontaneous interpolation, as one would find in improvised music.

Basically, a wide variety of typestyles are currently available, none of which seem to centre upon getting the appropriate message across - rather, the well-worn is served up as something new. I cannot fall in with this. I believe that to get heard, you have to make a little noise, noise whose frequencies move beyond the normal wavelengths. The noise may be cacophony to some - just as John Coltrane's saxophone might once have sounded - *so be it.*

F morsig

The inspiration for **F morsig** starts with the truism "The alphabet is nothing more than a code". The purity of this code has suffered from far too many intellectual/stylistic/designed toolboxes in the name of "communication design". One only need look at the increasing block of shitty typefaces in the guise of new and supposedly experimental typefaces to ask the question... "why?". The simple and beautiful purity of symbols is the basis for **F morsig**, with its implications as a digital "typeface".

The Morse Code was developed and used as an international telegraphic system which assigned dots and dashes to letters and numerals, which were then sent and received as short and long sounds, or flashes of light. This system finds its match in the computer's binary composition of plus and minus, on and off. Here, the relationship between the archaic and the contemporary is significant - it illustrates the direct romance that **F morsig** embraces.

The code reduces the act of communication to the essential message, like sharpening a pencil and writing a letter to a friend. **F morsig**'s pencil is now Hypercard - it can be used and seen only on screen, there is no sound, and it is impossible to print. Communication with this code is determined by the user's thoughts and **F morsig**'s pencil.

F morsig was constructed with Hypercard help from Aad van Dommelen.

Hypercard animation not available on disk for legal reasons.

F Schrift

The word 'Schrift' is a modification of the German word for 'typeface' - *schrift*. Similar modifications can be found in every letter of this alphabet, which, for the moment, has spared the capital letters. Starting with the regular letterforms, I rearranged the elements of each lowercase character and numeral.

The idea is to create a new, foreign face that is based on the latin alphabet. **F Schrift** is condensed, with negative numbers designed especially for things like telephone books, listings magazines, bills, forms and any kind of invoice that is best kept in code.

F DR No-B

abcdefghijklmnopqrstuvwxyz
1234567890.,!?&$:

F Schrift

F morsig

F Box

Ian Anderson

"My name is Ian Anderson. I was born in Croydon before England won the World Cup and now I'm lucky enough to be here with you. Somewhere in between came Thunderbirds, Captain Scarlet, Scooby Doo, The Trigan Empire, Bubblegum and Andy Warhol; Dave & Ansel Collins, Slade, Roxy Music, Parlifunkadelicament, The Clash, The Pop Group, Eno, On-U and Miles Davies; the Young Socialists, the Anti-Nazi League, the Marx Brothers and Russian Constructivism; Infra Red Helicopters, Voodoo Voodoo magazine, a Philosophy degree, playing records for money and managing bands; Nobby, friends & family, Fulham, Sheffield Wednesday and DR Sokka; Helvetica, Burroughs, technology, "Crush", Tokyo and sci-fi consumerism.

I never studied design formally, I am not a typographer, I hate religion, I love my wife and **I love my Designers Republic.**"

Paul Sych

"I spent three years at the Ontario College of Art in Toronto, and because of my interest in jazz, I studied concurrently at York University, doing a Jazz Studies Program. Having left college, I worked for a number of design companies, most recently with Reactor. As senior Art Director, I began to explore and concentrate on type design - however, my work there was restricted by the need to maintain the 'look' that Reactor had already established for itself.

I felt there to be an ample opportunity in Toronto to develop my own look, or 'voice', hence the creation of Faith - a leap, as it were, into the unknown. The main emphasis is still on typography - a discipline that seems to be in decline in Canada. At the moment, Faith can count almost every major advertising agency in Canada amongst its clients: the campaigns we have worked on include Coca Cola, General Motors, MacDonalds, Letraset and IBM. My work has been featured in issues of Print Magazine, International Design, Step by Step... It is possible to challenge even the most conservative of clients, and doing this has opened up many opportunities for me to provide a voice in Canada and elsewhere."

Rick Vermeulen

"Briefly... Born 1950. Studied design at the College of Fine Arts in Rotterdam from 1967-72. In-house designer at publishers Bert Bakker in Amsterdam from 1975 until 1977. In 1979, co-founded Hard Werken Magazine, and since 1981, one of the partners along with Gerard Hadders, Willem Kars, Tom van den Haspel and Bart Jan Jansen.

The design company evolved out of the magazine to become a multi-disciplinary organisation working within the areas of corporate, literature, packaging and interior design, with a full time staff of fifteen. My main work is for print - catalogues for museums, book jackets, magazine and book design, architectural monographs, posters, postage stamps, etc. Hard Werken works on an international level and has become known for its outspoken attitude to the design industry. Hard Werken designers have lectured at educational institutions in Europe and the United States - the Rietveld Academy in Amsterdam, Les Ateliers Paris, Cranbrook Academy of Art, Cal Arts in LA, amongst others."

Martin Wenzel

"Born of the 6th of June (1969) in Berlin. Still living there. 2 years experience in digital typographic design. Has designed several faces, including Marten for FontShop International."

Detail set in F DR No-8 by Ian Anderson, F Box by Paul Sych, F Schirft by Martin Wenzel, F morsig by Rick Vermeulen.

FUSE is published by FontShop International and is available exclusively from the following outlets :

FontShop Austria
Seidengasse 26
A-1070 Wien
(02 22) 523 29 46, -47
Fax (02 22) 523 29 47 22

FontShop Benelux
Maaltecenter Blok D
Derbystraat 119
B-9051 St.-Denijs-Westrem
(091) 20 65 98
Fax (091) 20 34 45

FontShop Canada
401 Wellington Street West
Toronto, Ontario M5V 1E8
1-800-36-FONTS
Local (416) 348 9837
Fax (416) 593 4318

FontShop Germany
Bergmannstraße 102
1000 Berlin 61
(030) 69 00 62 62
Fax (030) 69 00 62 77

FontShop Italy
Via Masotto 21
20133 Milano
(2) 7010 0555
Fax (2) 7010 0585

FontWorks UK
65-69 East Road
London N1 6AH
(071) 490 2002
Fax (071) 490 5391

Still available :

FUSE 1 featuring
PHIL BAINES, NEVILLE BRODY, MALCOLM GARRETT and IAN SWIFT

FUSE 2 featuring
GERARD UNGER, ERIK VAN BLOKLAND, MAX KISMAN, and JUST VAN ROSSUM

FUSE 3 featuring
BARBARA BUTTERWECK, ERIK SPIEKERMANN, MARTIN WENZEL and CORNEL WINDLIN

FUSE 4 featuring
DAVID BERLOW, BARRY DECK, JEFFREY KEEDY and RICK VALICENTI

FUSE 5 featuring
LO BREIER, PAUL ELLIMAN, PETER SAVILLE and PIERRE DI SCIULLO

FUSE

The newest forum for experimental typography. This sixth edition includes 4 new Macintosh compatible typefaces on disc, with four A2 posters showing each font in creative application.

FUSE 6: CODES
features
IAN ANDERSON
PAUL SYCH
MARTIN WENZEL
RICK VERMEULEN
plus one extra font

FUSE 6: Neville Brody Bonus Font **Code Bold**

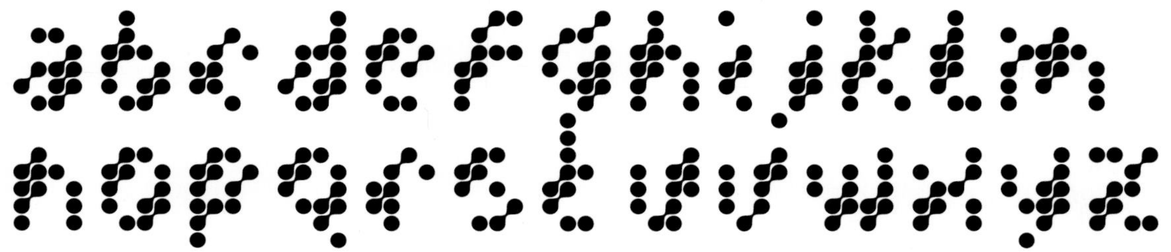

FUSE 6: Ian Anderson Dr No-B

In code, legibility is not an issue. *Dr No-B* is a series of logos based on the Roman alphabet, a corporate code of dots and dashes or a system of icons to convey more than language. It is 'toy-digital'. The sales pitch is that *Dr No-B is* "beyond semantics", in reality it is... join the AA here... today's temperature 30°... your train has been delayed – sorry for the inconvenience this will cause you... no smoking... Wednesday 4 united 0 – 90 mins... sale! All items half price... change given... delayed further... engaged... London to Berlin – save £50... happy birthday from all your friends... queue here... touchdown!... Your train has been cancelled. Information can tell you nothing – *Dr No-B* has the power to tell you less.

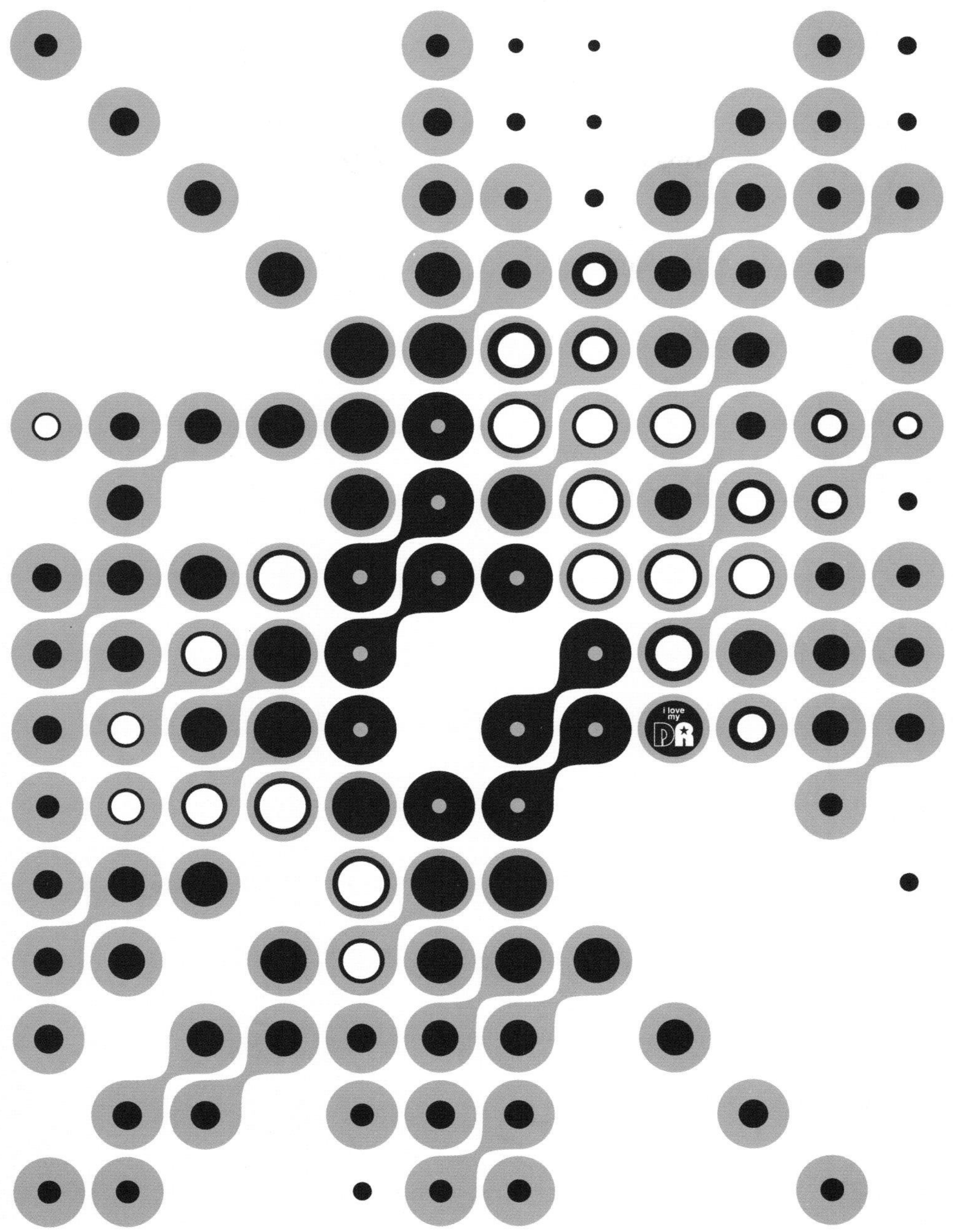

data D-CODE information typeface:(F) dr.no-b

Ludi-cypher: IAN ANDERSON 4 THE DESIGNERS REPUBLIC. ©1992 THE DESIGNERS REPUBLIC. ℗1992 FONTSHOP

HEY! EYE! TECHNI-THANKS: MG

FUSE 6: Paul Sych Box

The FUSE 6 assignment has redeveloped the way I perceive typography at the moment. Because of my background in jazz studies, I am constantly trying to merge the two media, jazz and type. *Box* is an expression of sound, as if it were a tuning fork vibrating at a given pitch. The irregular letterforms within the grid suggest a more spontaneous interpellation, as one would find in improvised music. Basically, a wide variety of typestyles are currently available, none of which seem to centre upon getting the appropriate message across – rather, the well-worn is served up as something new. I cannot fall in with this. I believe that to get heard, you have to make a little noise, noise whose frequencies move beyond the normal wavelengths. The noise may be cacophony to some – just as John Coltrane's saxophone might once have sounded – *so be it*.

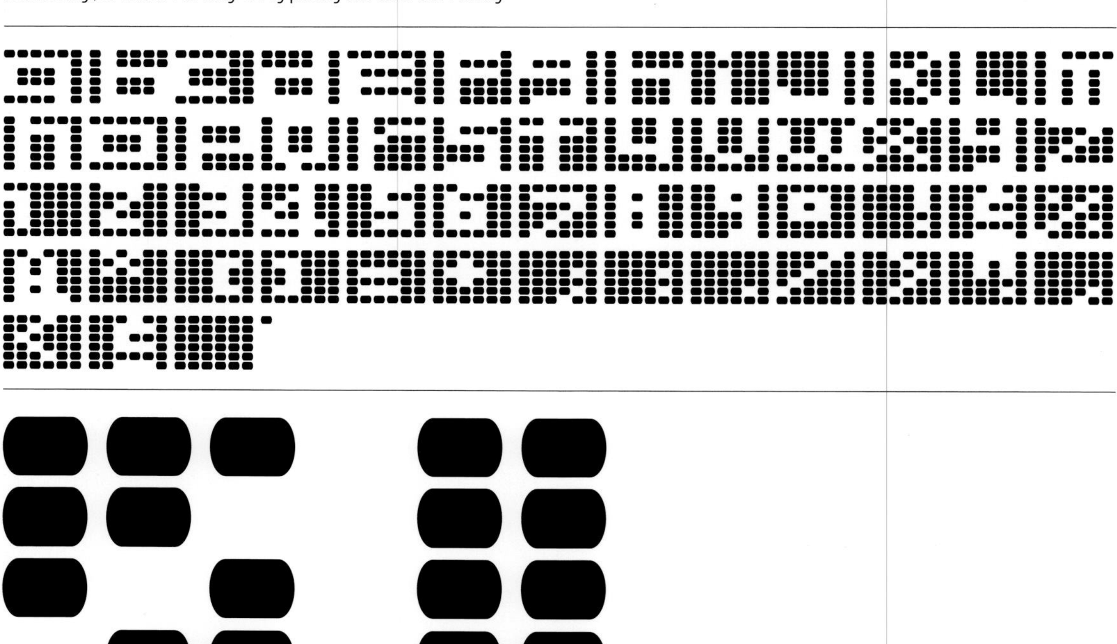

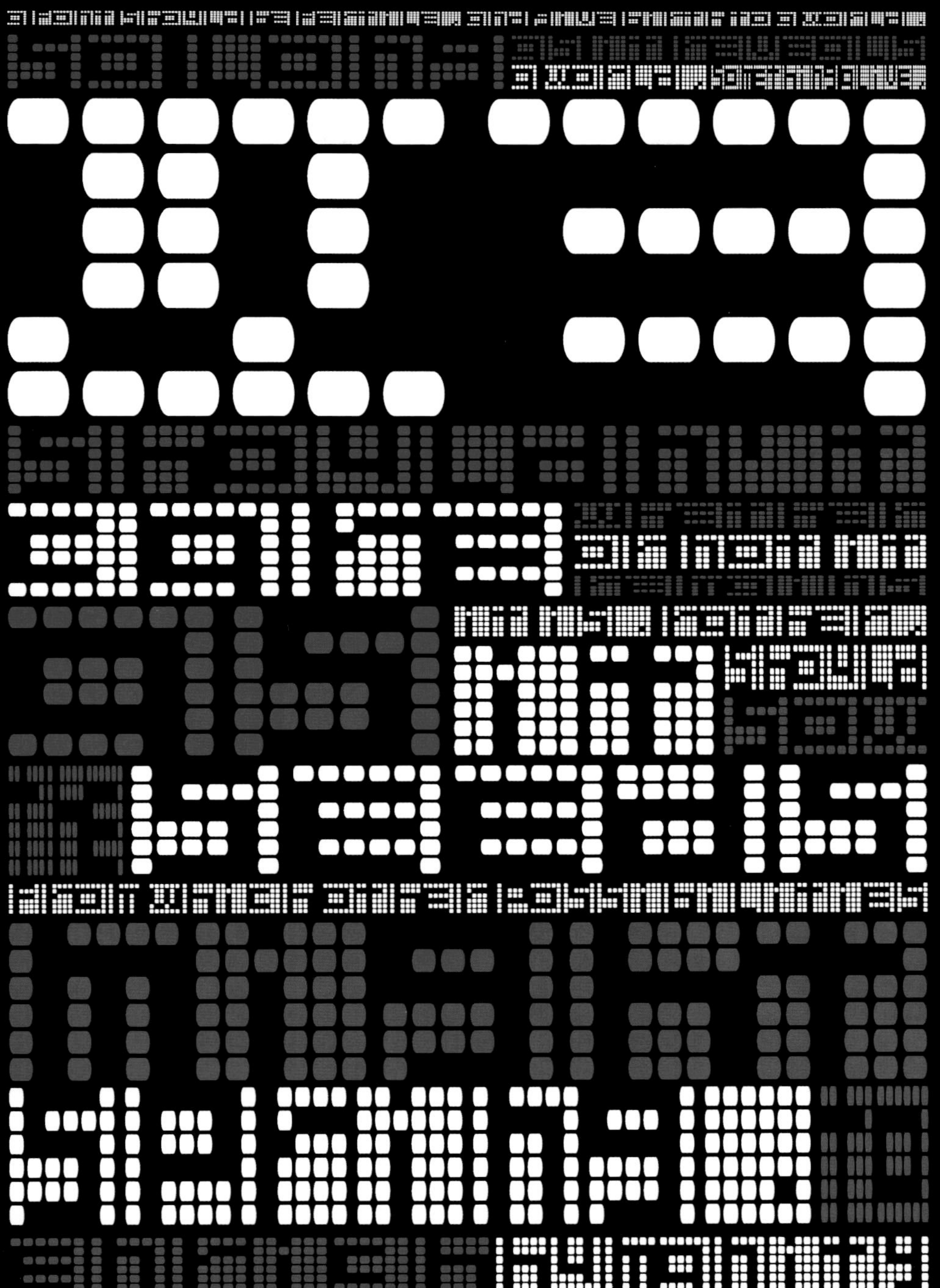

abc

FUSE 6: Martin Wenzel Schirft

The word 'Schirft' is a modification of the German word for 'typeface' – *Schrift*. Similar modifications can be found in every letter of this alphabet, which, for the moment, has spared the capital letters. Starting with the regular letterforms, I rearranged the elements of each lower-case character and numeral. The idea is to create a new, foreign face that is based on the latin alphabet. *Schirft* is condensed, with negative numbers designed especially for things like telephone books, listings magazines, bills, forms and any kind of invoice that is best kept in code.

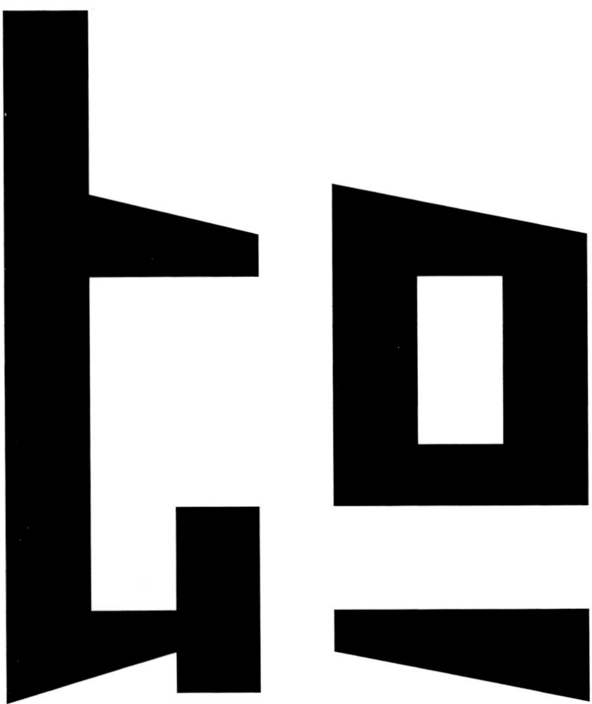

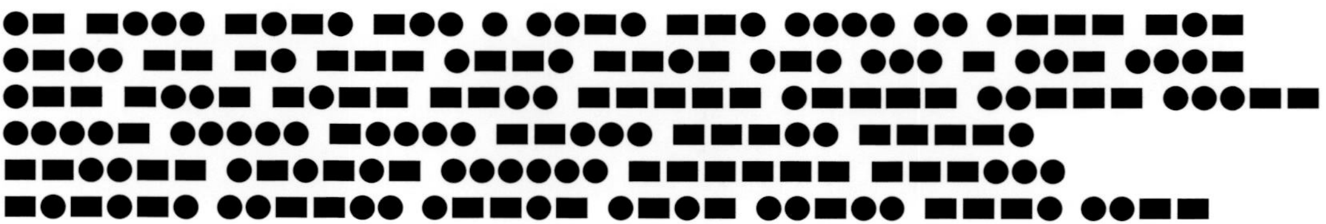

MORSIG USED HYPERCARD SOFTWARE TO TRANSLATE TEXT INPUT INTO A SEQUENCE OF FLASHING COLOURS THAT PULSED LIKE A PSYCHEDELIC MORSE CODE. IT CAN BE IMAGINED – OR LIKENED TO THE OPENING SEQUENCE OF KUBRICK'S FILM OF *A CLOCKWORK ORANGE*.

FUSE 6: Rick Vermeulen Morsig

At the last minute, it was not possible to publish Rick Vermeulen's Morsig *program in FUSE 6 due to an ambivalent copyright situation regarding the software that had been used to generate the "typeface". Here it is, in its basic form.*

The inspiration for *Morsig* starts with the truism "The alphabet is nothing more than a code". The purity of this code has suffered from far too many intellectual/stylistic/designed toolboxes in the name of "communication design". One only need look at the increasing block of shitty typefaces in the guise of new and supposedly experimental typefaces to ask the question... "why?". The simple and beautiful purity of symbols is the basis for *Morsig*, with its implications as a digital "typeface".

The Morse Code was developed and used as an international telegraphic system which assigned dots and dashes to letters and numerals, which were then sent and received as short and long sounds, or flashes of light. This system finds its match in the computer's binary composition of plus and minus, on and off. Here, the relationship between the archaic and the contemporary is significant – it illustrates the direct romance that *Morsig* embraces.

The code reduces the act of communication to the essential message, like sharpening a pencil and writing a letter to a friend. *Morsig*'s pencil is now Hypercard – it can be used and seen only on screen, there is no sound, and it is impossible to print. Communication with this code is determined by the user's thoughts and *Morsig*'s pencil. Ideally, every workstation should have *Morsig*. Type in your text message, turn your computer screen towards the window, and flash forth to your neighbours. Light up the city with the colourful mantras of *Morsig*, and put down that mobile phone! *Morsig* was constructed with help from Aad van Dommelen.

.- a
-... b
-.-. c
-.. d
. e
..-. f
--. g
.... h
.. i
.--- j
-.- k
.-.. l
-- m

n -.
o ---
p .--.
q --.-
r .-.
s ...
t -
u ..-
v ...-
w .--
x -..-
y -.--
z --..

I get a lot of thoughts in the morning,
I write them all down,
if it wasn't for that,
I'd forget them in a while.

And lately I've been thinking about a good friend,
I'd like to see more of. (oh yeah)

I think I make a call.

I wrote the number down,
but I've lost it,
so, I searched in my pocketbook,
I couldn't find it,
so, I sat down and concentrated
on the number,
and slowly it came to me,
so, I dialed it,
and I let it ring a few times,
there was no answer,
so, I let it ring a little more,
still no answer,
so, I hung up the telephone,
got some paper,
and sharpened up a pencil
And wrote a letter to my friend.

.---- 1
..--- 2
...-- 3
....- 4
..... 5
-.... 6
--... 7
---.. 8
----. 9
----- 0

. ...
; -.-.-.
, .-.-.-
: ---...
? ..--..
! --..--
" --..--
' .----.
/ ------

Busy Doin' Nothing
(B. Wilson)

Poster Design,
Typeface: morsig © 1992
Rick Vermeulen

FUSE 7: Pandemonium Jon Wozencroft

FUSE

SPRING 1993

CRASH

"A language is an implement quite as much as an implement of stone or steel; its use involves social consequences; it does things to you just as a metal or a machine does things to you. It makes new precision and also new errors possible".
H.G. Wells, *In Search of Hot Water*

"War is a terrible thing, and so few people realise it..."
Private Peter McGregor, 14th Bn Argyll and Sutherland Highlanders, killed on the Western Front on 13 September 1916, in his last letter home to his wife

On the outbreak of World War One in 1914, there was no need for conscription. Earl Kitchener's 'Call to Arms' was fully answered by men who anticipated a brisk, spectacular, triumphant campaign.

By the time conscription was introduced in 1916, some two million men in the U.K. had 'taken the King's shilling', and in a unique feature of warfare, local communities (especially from the North) formed 'Pals' batallions, customised fighting units ready to give their all for the cause.

The optimism did not last. Marching off to the front, a fresh recruit heard "a raucous and anonymous voice" from a troop of soldiers returning on leave: "you came of your own accord. You didn't have to be fetched. You *bloody* fools". The effect of battles such as the Somme wiped out whole communities. 'The Bradford Pals', 'The Altrincham Pals', 'The Grimsby Chums' – overnight, local pride turned to local grief as newspapers printed double-page spreads, day in, day out, listing the fallen. At the front, Lance Sergeant Elmer Cotton recorded "the trench after the dead... a ghastly sight... red with blood like a room papered in crimson while equipment lay everywhere".[1] Like cinema, the new century had barely started. The world would never be the same again.

"Abandon all hope, ye who enter the hell of images"
Abel Gance, quoted by Paul Virilio, *War & Cinema*, Verso 1989

An icy afternoon in early February 1993. A man is hurrying along one of London West End's busiest streets, carrying a dufflebag, looking surreptitiously from left to right. He stops, all of a sudden, crouches down to unzip the bag and quickly picks out the contents – videotapes – before thrusting them into the hands of bewildered, suspicious passers-by, imploring "Go On – Take it! Take it!". His eyes lend fever to the words. Several pedestrians accelerate away from the scene, just as they might upon spotting a collection-box or person-with-a-clipboard; handouts, likewise, are not to be trusted. In spite of this, having swiftly offloaded about 20 tapes, the man picks up the empty bag, looks up, and then rushes off into the crowd, down into the nearby Tube station. Vanished.

The videotape is about 20 minutes long. It catalogues the unbroadcast horrors of "ethnic cleansing" against Muslims in Bosnia. A catalogue of corpses. Men with torched-out faces, death by torture with a flamethrower. Images of once-pregnant women, their stomachs cut open to settle a bet between soldiers on the sex of the unborn child. Hollow-eyed men, their genitals cut off and mounted in rows, on an improvised chipboard trophy case. These are some of the nastiest images of violence you've ever seen; horrors that have yet to be contained by History. Little is left to the imagination: the assumption being that these images of violence should be as direct as possible, *yet another attempt to override any need for the imagination.* In the bottom corner of the screen, a series of timecodes bend and shimmer with the scratch-like picture quality: the menacing reminder that what you are looking at was recorded on 16:7:91 – 16:30. Just to compound the confusion, the way that the bootleg-quality footage hits you straight in the solar plexus before it gets to the brain, the video carries a lamentational voiceover backed up by a funereal classical soundtrack, a blackened muzak. The front frame of the video carries an address in Leicester, middle England, asking for donations. As you scamper back into your skin, questions

In the bottom corner of the screen, a series of timecodes bend and shimmer with the scratch-like picture quality: the menacing reminder that what you are looking at was recorded on 16:7:91 – 16:30.

compete with the viciously vivid scenes you have been watching. How? Why? By whom? For what? Is there not another, equally distortive set of invisibles behind the camera? Let us assume (however wildly) that this footage is typical of what is available, and could conceivably be Serb, Croat, or Muslim in origin, and has been withheld by the major broadcasting stations worldwide. You begin to wonder – is this video a positive example of guerilla information, and its distribution a revolutionary act? Or does it brutalise and weaken more than it empowers, getting us nowhere, faster? As the saying goes, *a little knowledge is a dangerous thing.* As the voiceover went, "he who turns his back on the sufferings of men does not deserve to be called a man". This is happening and what are you going to do about it?

"Get the facts first, you can distort them later"
Billboard poster campaign for the *Financial Times*, March 1993

That same week, the ex-manager of the Scala cinema in London's King's Cross was in court, facing charges in connection with the showing of *A Clockwork Orange* at the cinema last April, billed anonymously as a "Surprise Film" in its advance listings – a necessary precaution, although many could guess what this meant (*the Rave Scene meets Copyright Culture*). Stanley Kubrick, the film's director, had withdrawn it from circulation in the U.K. soon after its release in the early 1970s because of copycat violence. The film has recently been enjoying something of a revival on the big screens of Paris and elsewhere; in Britain it is still banned.

Kubrick's reaction raises the spectre of Responsibility. And since the film's suppression was, unusually, activated by him, it highlights issues that might normally be trapped within the traditional argument (or babble) over state censorship. The author of the book, Anthony Burgess, wrote "neither cinema nor literature can be blamed for original sin. A man who kills his uncle cannot justifiably blame a performance of *Hamlet*. On the other hand, if literature is to be held responsible for mayhem and murder, then the most damnable book of them all is the Bible, the most vindictive piece of literature in existence".[2]

The Scala case has yet to be finally adjudicated. However, should the cinema lose, it faces a fine that might help close it down. All the while, at a screen near you, *Reservoir Dogs*, *Bad Lieutenant*, *Romper Stomper*, *Candyman*, *Man Bites Dog*... It is not as if we need be squeamish. The director of *Reservoir Dogs*, Quentin Tarantino, appeared frequently on TV during the film's pre-release hype, and taking the chance to defend its levels of violence, he said that he wanted "to make a film that showed people what violence was really like", insisting that violence was crucial to "the palette" of any film-maker (i.e. him). Forget *Night and Fog*. TV news. Forget anything Sam Peckinpah directed or Lee Marvin ever starred in, *The Wild Bunch*, *The Killers*... Paint the town red, this would be everything and more! For the media, it was a case of 'follow the locust', and in such cases, historical precedents and contemporary challenges evaporate into thin air.

By and large, everyone was happy. TV stations and their presenters could sleep safely in the knowledge that they were not "promoting violence". Cinema audiences could satisfy their thirst for blood and gore and still think that they were watching something new, approaching a moral tale for our times. The film's producers and distributors could make a killing at the box office. To its credit, *Reservoir Dogs* does indeed carry a moral sting in its tail; a "good movie", but any constructive message against violence was by and large drowned out by the metronome of sensational publicity. Burgess complained that much the same thing had happened to the film and media treatment of his book, which centres upon the choice that has to be made between good and evil. "A vindication of free will had become an exaltation of the urge to sin", he said. In the meantime, *A Clockwork Orange*, arguably the mother of all films about law and order breakdown, remains by and large unseen by the current generation of cinema-goers.

"The marriage of reason and nightmare which has dominated the 20th century has given birth to an even more ambiguous world... We live inside an enormous novel".
J.G. Ballard, Introduction to the French edition of *Crash*, 1974

Kubrick's censorship of his own film remains in deep contrast to Tarantino's "realism". If art should be prophecy, a provocation that can set a context for, if not a healing process, then at least a greater awareness of how this might be activated, all too often the current and simple ambition is to "reflect society". This enables the perpetrators of violent imagery to adopt a "don't blame me" attitude, at the same time as they appear to be in tune with the times.

It is quite easy to ignore and thereby operate beyond criticism when everyone is boxed in by a barrage of publicity. Ultrapropaganda becomes the real horror-show, because now more than ever, any questioning of 'the system' (and those that run it) is seldom accepted and answered directly, and is far more likely to be seen purely as a "public relations problem". *THE FOLLOWING PROGRAMME CONTAINS SCENES THAT SOME VIEWERS MAY FIND DISTRESSING...*

The Heads of Programming for BBC1 and Channel 4 were recently invited onto British TV's one significant viewer response slot, *Right to Reply*, to defend the increasing levels of sex and violence in mainstream broadcasting. (Currently, all these considerations are also shadowed in the U.K. by the recent abduction and murder of a 2-year-old boy, James Bulger, who was frogmarched from a shopping centre in Bootle on Merseyside by a pair of as yet unidentified youths, even though they were 'caught' on video by security cameras.) Both media mandarins took refuge in their upholding of the 9 o'clock 'watershed', as if it were the zero hour, after which any violent imagery might be deemed acceptable because after all, it was the responsibility of parents to make sure that their children were safely tucked up in bed. This is living in cloud-cuckoo-land. Both spoke of the difficulties broadcasters faced when they came to the problem of "catching up with reality" – once again, this sleight of hand whereby producers, in a rare show of unity with their audiences, present themselves as the victims of current events, never the catalysts. At no point did either representative come up with any adequate response to one of the programme's earlier critiques, voiced to them by a viewer, Malcolm Victory.

He said: "*It is strange to me that although studies have for a long time shown a correlation between violent programming and personality disorders the issue is only now at the stage of being debated. The majority of people I have spoken to agree that there is no doubt about it – the only exceptions are the friends I have working in the TV business. The media feel they have 'carte blanche', total freedom, and the pace of programmes, fast editing, explicit violence, manic voiceovers, even subliminal messages, all contribute to stress in society. What they are trying to do is to hold the waning interest of the viewers as their human sensitivities are eroded piece by piece. My children, at 5 years old, have already been exposed to hundreds of murders, and adults raised on 'Andy Pandy' still debate whether the new generation will grow up affected by the new television*".

Where does all this leave that most basic prerogative of 20th-century artists – to use disturbing material for "shock value"? Art *should be* disorientating – with its shock value based on experience (content), rather than fantasy (special effects). There is a subtle line that divides prophecy from threat, and a gulf that separates vision from speculation. Secondly, is it acceptable and/or inevitable that violent images should intensify "in line with the increasing levels of violent crime in society"? Can various standards and safeguards be developed that do not get shouted down by the need to maintain "free speech" (a curious notion in itself, given the current hegemony of market forces as the ultimate form of arbitration). In Britain, the present attempts to place 'restrictions' upon the press are seen purely in terms of censorship: this term is used as a negative replacement for a more straightforward insistence, namely, that those who exert such influence should accept the need for an ECOLOGY. It is clear that our mental environment is, in general, as polluted as the North Sea and as burnt out as a rainforest; can there be any real environmentalism without the recognition of this fact?

Perhaps we like to believe that it is all too far down the line? Is violence a 'normal' feature of everyday life? There can be little dispute that the human fascination with violent death and destruction is a deeply

Ultrapropaganda becomes the real horrorshow, because now more than ever, any questioning of 'the system' (and those that run it) is seldom accepted and answered directly, and is far more likely to be seen purely as a "public relations problem". *THE FOLLOWING PROGRAMME CONTAINS SCENES THAT SOME VIEWERS MAY FIND DISTRESSING...*

ingrained tradition, from gladiatorial spectacles in Roman times, Victorian 'Penny Dreadfuls', to today's *Soaraway Sun*. Colin Wilson remarked, "the history of mankind since about 2500 BC is little more than a non-stop record of murder, bloodshed and violence".[3] And in a recession, violence becomes a key feature – not only can sales figures can be upheld, but responsibility can be diverted from the Government and roundly placed on the shoulders of "the deviant", etc. Jeremy Seabrook wrote of the James Bulger murder, "there is little point Mr. Baker urging parents to teach their children right from wrong, when a more persuasive version comes over the heads of teachers and parents alike: having money is right and not having it is wrong".[4]

If, indeed, there has ever been an era of benevolent urbanity, was it in the early 1950s, when the after-effect of World War and the early promise of the Welfare State created a balance of austerity and optimism that kept the peace? If so, from which quarters are we likely to find the impetus for our present and urgent need for reconstruction, *not deconstruction*? For a while, popular culture did provide the frame for a wealth of poetic licence, from Beckett to Ballard, from Lindsay Anderson to The Beatles and The Stones, but now it has all become product, not potential. Despair has become fashionable. Whilst Western Europe has enjoyed one of its longest periods of peacetime in recent history, the use of "the war metaphor" increases. Information War. The battle for minds. Cynicism is consolidated on a daily basis by the market-led mass media. This means that, despite the politicians who queue-jump to claim "the law and order ticket", today you shock people by having values, by withstanding the brutal saturation of media, *the crash narcotic*, and by refusing to be in awe of the great chain that links celebrity to a shopping basket.

"The forms of a person's thoughts are controlled by inexorable laws of pattern of which he is unconscious".
Benjamin Lee Whorf, quoted by George Steiner, *The Language Animal*, Faber 1970

In the 1660s, John Milton warned in his epic poem, *Paradise Lost*, of the price that would have to be paid for the industrial revolution and the machine age, which he called the building of "Pandemonium, the high capital of satan and his peers", the Palace of all the Devils. Nearly 300 years later, the painter and film-maker Humphrey Jennings undertook to make some sense of this, bringing together a disparate collection of contemporary observations that, in his opinion, documented "the real history of Britain... a history that has never been written... a building that will never be finished" – since it has to be transformed into "a new Jerusalem".[5]

Crushed humanity, and we call it Progress. Jennings concluded: "unless we are prepared to claim special attributes for the poet – the attribute of vision – and unless we are prepared to admit the work of the artist (that is to say the function of 'imagination') as an essential part of the modern world there is no real reason for our continuing to bother with any of the arts any more, or with any imaginary activity. No reasons except money, snobbery, propaganda or escapism".

The use of violence is a manifestation of a deeper malaise – a language problem – fucked-up expressionism. It has intensified and consolidated its hold over the years because, largely, we choose to see it in terms of criminality, an escape into "otherness" – not consciousness, but its substitute. In doing so, we fool ourselves into believing that we can switch in and out of its spellbind. Maybe this is just our way of getting into training for what the future holds: poverty and lack. Some future. Some hold. *How about NOW?*

Reference:

1. Quotations are taken from Malcolm Brown, *Tommy Goes to War*, J.M. Dent & Sons 1978 **2.** For further coverage of the *Clockwork Orange* controversy, see Tony Parson's article, 'Forbidden Fruit', in *The Times Saturday Review*, 30 Jan 1993 **3.** Colin Wilson, *A Criminal History of Mankind*, Grafton Books 1985 **4.** Jeremy Seabrook, 'The Root of All Evil', in *New Statesman & Society* 26-2-93 **5.** Humphrey Jennings (with Charles Madge), *Pandemonium – The Coming of the Machine...*, André Deutsch 1985

Despair has become fashionable. Whilst Western Europe has enjoyed one of its longest periods of peacetime in recent history, the use of "the war metaphor" increases. Information War. The battle for minds. Cynicism is consolidated on a daily basis by the market-led mass media.

JOHN CRITCHLEY FOR NEVILLE BRODY STUDIO & JON WOZENCROFT EDITORIAL POSTER

"A language is an implement quite as much as an implement of stone or steel; its use involves social consequences; it does things to you just as a metal or a machine does things to you. It makes new precision and also new errors possible".
HG Wells, *In Search of Hot Water*

SUBMIT

The role of FUSE is to promote typographic inno-vation and confusion. We welcome your input - if you would like to present your own experimental type design and poster for inclusion in a future edition, please write to FUSE at the address below submitting, if not a digitised typeface on disc, then a clear proposal and outline of your idea, enclosing in both cases an SAE/IRC. We would also like to see any exemples of your own manipulations of published FUSE fonts, any experimental type that you have created but have no plans to digitise, and any critique or comment you have on digital typography.

CONTACT

FUSE is published quarterly and distributed through the FontShop network. Future editions of FUSE will follow themes that question the effects of digital technology, attempting to 'open up' its possibilities. Each FUSE is published in a limited edition- reserve a copy by contacting the FontShop in your area.

MIMOSENHAFT

FUSE fonts do not always include a full set of upper and lower case characters; nor does every font cover a full range of accents and special characters. Fuse fonts are experi-mental typefaces that should be extended by users. Abuse is part of the process. And for those who do no more than rip off the type-faces to use on a techno 12", please at least send us a copy...!

DON'T BELIEVE THE TYPE!

FUSE 7 includes two free fonts.

ISSUE 7 CRASH

Spring 1993
Editor & text by Jon Wozencroft.
Design by John Critchley
for Neville Brody Studio.
Published & © 1993 by FSI GmbH.
Typefaces and Posters © 1992 the designers.

FSI, Bergmannstraße 102,
1000 Berlin 61, Germany.

Correspondence: FUSE editorial,
Unit 2 White Horse Yard,
78 Liverpool Road,
London N1 0QD, England.
Fax +44 (71) 704 2447.

PANDEMONIUM

"War is a terrible thing, and so few people realise it..."
Private Peter McGregor, 14th Bn Argyll and Sutherland Highlanders, killed on the Western Front on 13 September 1916, in his last letter home to his wife.

On the outbreak of World War One in 1914, there was no need for conscription. Earl Kitchener's 'Call to Arms' was fully answered by men who anticipated a brisk, spectacular, triumphant campaign. By the time conscription was introduced in 1916, some two million men in the UK had 'taken the King's shilling', and in a unique feature of warfare, local communities especially from the North formed 'Pals' batallions, customised fighting units ready to give their all for the cause.

The optimism did not last. Marching off to the front, a fresh recruit heard "a raucous and anonymous voice" from a troop of soldiers returning on leave: "you came of your own accord. You didn't have to be fetched. You *bloody* fools". The effect of battles such as the Somme wiped out whole communities, 'The Bradford Pals', 'The Altrincham Pals', 'The Grimsby Chums' - overnight, local pride turned to local grief as newspapers printed double page spreads, day in, day out, listing the fallen. At the front, Lance Sergeant Elmer Cotton recorded "the trench after the dead... a ghastly sight... red with blood like a room papered in crimson while equipment lay everywhere"[1]. Like cinema, the new century had barely started. The world would never be the same again.

"Abandon all hope, ye who enter the hell of images"
Abel Gance, quoted by Paul Virilio, *War and Cinema*, Verso 1989

An icy afternoon in early February 1993. A man is hurrying along one of London West End's busiest streets, carrying a dufflebag, looking surreptitiously from left to right. He stops, all of a sudden, crouches down to unzip the bag and quickly picks out the contents - videotapes - before thrusting them into the hands of bewildered, suspicious passers-by, imploring "Go On - Take it! Take it!". His eyes lend fever to the words. Several pedestrians accelerate away from the scene, just as they might upon spotting a collection-box or person-with-a-clipboard; handouts, likewise, are not to be trusted. In spite of this, having swiftly offloaded about 20 tapes, the man picks up the empty bag, looks up, and then rushes off into the crowd, down into the nearby tube station. Vanished.

The videotape is about 20 minutes long. It catalogues the unbroad-cast horrors of "ethnic cleansing" against Muslims in Bosnia. A catalogue of corpses. Men with torched out faces, death by torture with a flamethrower. Images of once-pregnant women, their stomachs cut open to settle a bet between soldiers on the sex of the unborn child. Hollow-eyed men, their genitals cut off and mounted in rows, on an improvised chipboard trophy case. These are some of the nastiest images of violence you've ever seen; horrors that have yet to be contained by History. Little is left to the imagination; the assumption being that these images of violence should be as direct as possible, *yet another attempt to override any need for the imagination*. In the bottom corner of the screen, a series of timecodes bend and shimmer with the scratch-like picture quality: the menacing reminder that what you are looking at was recorded on 16:7:91 - 16:30. Just to com-pound the confusion, the way that the bootleg-quality footage hits you straight in the solar plexus before it gets to the brain, the video carries a lamentational voiceover backed up by a funereal classical soundtrack, a blackened musak.

The front frame of the video carries an address in Leicester, middle England, asking for donations. As you scamper back into your skin, questions compete with the viciously vivid scenes you have been watching. How? Why? By whom? For what? Is there not another, equally distortive set of invisibles behind the camera? Let us assume (however wildly) that this footage is typical of what is available, and could conceivably be Serb, Croat, or Muslim in origin, and has been withheld by the major broadcasting stations worldwide. You begin to wonder - is this video a positive example of guerilla-information, and its distrib-ution a revolutionary act? Or does it brutalise and weaken more than it empowers, getting us nowhere, faster? As the saying goes, a *little knowledge is a dangerous thing*. As the voiceover went: "he who turns his back on the sufferings of men does not deserve to be called a man". This is happening and what are you going to do about it?

"Get the facts first, you can distort them later"
Billboard poster campaign for the *Financial Times*, March 1993.

That same week, the ex-manager of the Scala cinema in London's Kings Cross was in court, facing charges in connection with the showing of *A Clockwork Orange* at the cinema last April, billed anonymously as a "Surprise Film" in its advance listings - a necessary precaution, although many could guess what this meant (*the Rave Scene meets Copyright Culture*). Stanley Kubrick, the film's director, had withdrawn it from circulation in the UK soon after its release in the early 1970s because of copycat violence. The film has recently been enjoying something of a revival on the big screens of Paris and elsewhere; in Britain it is still banned.

Kubrick's reaction raises the spectre of Responsibility. And since the film's suppression was, unusually, activated by him, it highlights issues that might normally be trapped within the traditional argument (or babble) over state censorship. The author of the book, Anthony Burgess, wrote "neither cinema nor literature can be blamed for original sin. A man who kills his uncle cannot justifiably blame a performance of *Hamlet*. On the other hand, if literature is to be held responsible for mayhem and murder, then the most damnable book of them all is the Bible, the most vindictive piece of literature in existence"[2].

The Scala case has yet to be finally adjudicated. However, should the cinema lose, it faces a fine that might help close it down. All the while, at a screen near you, *Reservoir Dogs, Bad Lieutenant, Romper Stomper, Candyman, Man Bites Dog*... It is not as if we need be squeamish. The director of *Reservoir Dogs*, Quentin Tarantino, appeared frequently on TV during the film's pre-release hype, and taking the chance to defend its levels of violence, he said that he wanted "to make a film that showed people what violence was really like", insisting that violence was crucial to "the palette" of any film-maker (ie., him). Forget *Night and Fog*. TV news. Forget anything Sam Peckinpah directed or Lee Marvin ever starred in, *The Wild Bunch, The Killers*... Paint the town red, this would be everything and more! For the media, it was a case of 'follow the locust', and in such cases, historical precedents and contemporary challenges evaporate into thin air.

By and large, everyone was happy. TV stations and their presenters could sleep safely in the knowledge that they were not "promoting violence". Cinema audiences could satisfy their thirst for blood and gore and still think that they were watching something new, approaching a moral tale for our times. The films producers and distributors could make a killing at the box office. To its credit, *Reservoir Dogs* does indeed carry a moral sting in its tail; a "good movie", but any constructive message against violence was by and large drowned out by the metronome of sensational publicity. Burgess complained that much the same thing had happened to the film and media treatment of his book, which centres upon the choice that has to be made between good and evil. "A vindication of free will had become an exaltation of the urge to sin", he said. In the meantime, *A Clockwork Orange*, arguably the mother of all films about law and order breakdown, remains by and large unseen by the current generation of cinema-goers.

"The marriage of reason and nightmare which has dominated the 20th Century has given birth to an even more ambiguous world... We live inside an enormous novel". J.G. Ballard, Introduction to the French edition of *Crash*, 1974

Kubrick's censorship of his own film remains in deep contrast to Tarantino's "realism". If art should be prophesy, a provocation that can set a context for, if not a healing process, then at least a greater awareness of how this might be activated, all too often the current and simple ambition is to "reflect society". This enables the per-petrators of violent imagery to adopt a "don't blame me" attitude, at the same time as they appear to be in tune with the times.

It is quite easy to ignore and thereby operate beyond criticism when everyone is boxed in by a barrage of publicity. Ultrapropaganda becomes the real horror-show, because now more than ever, any questioning of "the system" (and those that run it) is seldom accepted and answered directly, and is far more likely to be seen purely as a "public relations problem". *THE FOLLOWING PROGRAMME CONTAINS SCENES THAT SOME VIEWERS MAY FIND DISTRESSING*...

The Heads of Programming for BBC1 and Channel 4 were recently invited onto British TV's one significant viewer response slot, *Right to Reply*, to defend the increasing levels of sex and violence in mainstream broadcasting. (Currently, all these considerations are also shadowed in the UK by the recent abduction and murder of a 2-year old boy, James Bulger, who was frogmarched from a shopping centre in Bootle on Merseyside by a pair of as yet unidentified youths, even though they were 'caught' on video by security cameras). Both media mandarins took refuge in their upholding of the 9 o'clock 'watershed', as if it were the zero hour, after which any violent imagery might be deemed acceptable because after all, it was the responsibility of parents to make sure that their children were safely tucked up in bed. This is living in cloud-cuckoo land. Both spoke of the difficulties broadcasters faced when they come to the problem of "catching up with reality" - once again, this sleight of hand whereby producers, in a rare show of unity with their audiences, present them-selves as the victims of current events, never the catalysts. At no point did either representative come up with any adequate response to one of the programme's earlier critiques, voiced to them by a viewer, Malcolm Victory.

He said: *"It is strange to me that although studies have for a long time shown a correlation between violent programming and person-ality disorders the issue is only now at the stage of being debated. The majority of people I have spoken to agree that there is no doubt about it - the only exceptions are the friends I have working in the TV business. The media feel they have 'carte blanche', total freedom, and the pace of programmes, fast editing, explicit violence, manic voiceovers, even subliminal messages, all contribute to stress in society. What they are trying to do is to hold the waning interest of the viewers as their human sensitivities are eroded piece by piece. My children, at 5 years old, have already been exposed to hundreds of murders, and adults raised on 'Andy Pandy' still debate whether the new generation will grow up affected by the new television"*.

Where does all this leave that most basic prerogative of 20th Century artists - to use disturbing material for "shock value"? Art *should be* disorientating - with its shock value based on experience (content), rather than fantasy (special effects). There is a subtle line that divides prophesy from threat, and a gulf that separates vision from speculation. Secondly, is it acceptable and/or inevitable that violent images should intensify "in line with the increasing levels of violent crime in society"? Can various standards and safeguards be developed that do not get shouted down by the need to maintain "free speech" (a curi-ous notion in itself, given the current hegemony of market forces as the ultimate form of arbitration). In Britain, the present attempts to place 'restrictions' upon the press are seen purely in terms of censorship: this term is used as a negative replace-ment for a more straightforward insistence, namely, that those who exert such influence should accept the need for an ECOLOGY. It is clear that our mental environment is, in general, as polluted as the North Sea and as burnt out as a rainforest: can there be any real environmentalism without the recognition of this fact?

Perhaps we like to believe that it is all too far down the line? Is violence a 'normal' feature of everyday life? There can be little dispute that the human fas-cination with violent death and destruction is a deeply ingrained tradition, from gladiatorial spectacles in Roman times, Victorian 'Penny Dreadfuls', to today's *Scarnway Sun*. Colin Wilson remarked, "the history of mankind since about 2500 B.C. is little more than a non-stop record of murder, bloodshed and violence"[3]. And in a recession, violence becomes a key feature - not only can sales figures can be upheld, but responsibility can be diverted from the Govern-ment and roundly placed on the shoulders of "the deviant", etc. Jeremy Seabrook wrote of the James Bulger murder, "there is little point Mr. Baker urging parents to teach their children right from wrong, when a more persuasive version comes over the heads of teachers and parents alike: having money is right and not having it is wrong"[4].

If, indeed, there has ever been an era of benevolent urbanity, was it in the early 1950s, when the aftereffect of World War and the early promise of the Welfare State created a balance of austerity and optimism that kept the peace? If so, from which quarters are we likely to find the impetus for our present and urgent need for recon-struction, *not deconstruction*? For a while, popular culture did provide the frame for a wealth of poetic license, from Beckett to Ballard, from Lindsay Anderson to The Beatles and The Stones, but now it has all become product, not potential. Despair has become fashionable. Whilst Western Europe has enjoyed one of its longest periods of peacetime in recent history, the use of "the war metaphor" increases. Information War. The battle for minds. Cynicism is consolidated on a daily basis by the market-led mass media. This means that, despite the politicians who queue-jump to claim "the law and order ticket", today you shock people by having values, by withstanding the brutal saturation of media, *the crash narcotic*, and by refusing to be in awe of the great chain that links celebrity to a shopping basket.

"The forms of a person's thoughts are controlled by inexorable laws of pattern of which he is unconscious". Benjamin Lee Whorf, quoted by George Steiner, *The Language Animal*, Faber 1970.

In the 1660s, John Milton warned in his epic poem, *Paradise Lost*, of the price that would have to be paid for the industrial revolution and the machine age, which he called the building of "Pandemonium, the high capital of satan and his peers", the Palace of all the Devils. Nearly 300 years later, the painter and film-maker Humphrey Jennings undertook to make some sense of this, bringing together a disparate collection of contemporary observations that, in his opinion, docu-mented "the real history of Britain... a history that has never been written... a building that will never be finished" - since it has to be trans-formed into "a new Jerusalem"[5].

Crushed humanity, and we call it Progress, Jennings concluded: "unless we are prepared to claim special attributes for the poet - the attribute of vision - and unless we are prepared to admit the work of the artist (that is to say the function of 'imagination') as an essential part of the modern world there is no real reason for our continuing to bother with any of the arts anymore, or with any imaginary activity. No reasons except money, snobbery, propaganda or escapism".

The use of violence is a manifestation of a deeper malaise - a language problem - fucked-up expressionism. It has intensified and consolidated its hold over the years because, largely, we choose to see it in terms of criminality - an escape into "otherness" - not consciousness, but its substitute. In doing so, we fool ourselves into believing that we can switch in and out of its spellbind. Maybe this is just our way of getting into training for what the future holds: poverty and lack. Some future. Some hold. *How about NOW?*

Jon Wozencroft

1 - Quotations are taken from Malcolm Brown, *Tommy Goes to War*, J.M.Dent & Sons 1978. 2 - For further coverage of the Clockwork Orange controversy, see Tony Parsons's article, *Forbidden Fruit*, in *The Times Saturday Review*, 30 Jan 1993. 3 - Colin Wilson, *A Criminal History of Mankind*, Grafton Books, 1985 4 - Jeremy Seabrook, *The Root of All Evil*, in *New Statesman & Society* 20.2.93. 5 - Humphrey Jennings (with Charles Madge), *Pandaemonium - The Coming of the Machine*, André Deutsch 1985.

Phil Bicker

As art director of his London-based company, Village, Bicker has sought to encourage and work towards a creative community. Working to the ideals of a collaborative spirit, he has and continues to actively support and collaborate with a new generation of young maverick photographers.

Originally working as an illustrator, he has a strong editorial background having previously been art director at *New Socialist* and *The Face* magazines. Since setting up Village two years ago, he has worked on more diverse projects. Presently he is conciously trying to accentuate the more human elements in his work, whilst developing further ideas through a series of non-design projects.

David Carson

Based in Del Mar California, Carson's work with *Beach Culture* magazine received numerous awards. Here, he has his own design studio, where he currently produces *Ray Gun* magazine. He has been art director for Billboard's *Musician* magazine, a senior designer for Condé Nast's *Self*, and is currently art director at Surfer Publications in Dana Point California. Carson's clients include MTV, Suzuki, Converse shoes, Scripto pens, Sony and Kentucky Fried Chicken.

Tobias Frere-Jones

Born 1970 in New York, graduated from the Rhode Island School of Design in 1992. He is currently working as a type designer for the Font Bureau Inc. in Boston. Previous designs include *Dolores* (FontFont), *Garage Gothic* and *Nobel* (The Font Bureau). He enjoys walking around on train tracks late at night.

Cornel Windlin

Born in in Switzerland in 1964, where he grew up on an unhealthy diet of "understanding and caring Catholicism" and, like most middle-Europeans, very dodgy pop music and outdated afternoon TV shows: *Daktari, Skippy, Flipper* and *the Brady Bunch*. Does anyone remember *Arpad, the Gipsy*?

He studied graphic design and visual communication at the Schule fur Gestaltung in Luzern, where he met Hans-Rudolf Lutz, whom he describes as "the only good teacher I have ever known in my life".

In 1987 he started to work with Neville Brody, and moved to England a year later to join his studio on a permanent basis. Eager to learn about magazine design, he left the Brody Bunch to work for *The Face* magazine in 1990. A year later he set up his own studio and has since been living and working as a freelance art director/designer in London and Zurich.

F Illiterate

Illiterate, the language of the modern primitive, simultaneously creative and destructive, born of speed and urban identity. A grouped mutation of Roman letterforms create symbols which evoke those of cave painting and eastern alphabets. A language where words, not letters, are the basic building blocks.

Illiterate returns us to the physical world, to texture and touch, to human expression and sensitivity no longer shackled by conformity or the colours of our computer screens. Apply its attitude, enjoy its freedom, experiment with its form, go into the real world and discover for yourself.

F Fingers

What will type look like at its point of collapse? I believe we passed that point some time ago. The only natural, logical step would of course be letterforms arrived at by using one's fingers. In this age of "personalised" fonts, how much more personal can one get than one's own fingers?

In addition to the personal aspect of the typeface, aspiring designers could actually use the "Fingerfont" of their favourite designer to better appropriate that designer's particular style.

F Reactor

Last summer, Frere-Jones watched an abandoned building burn to the ground in Providence, Rhode Island. As always, the flames and noise were interesting, but it was the spindly, cracked frame left over that caught his eye on this occasion. Slowly collapsing in the wind, internal structure was all that remained, the order has revealed itself in death.

Burnt and scarred by industrial accidents, type goes into its last death throes. The caps from an otherwise normal typeface have been introduced to the real world of decay and entropy. The lower-case was inspired by Nikolai Tesla's research into sympathetic vibrations. According to Tesla, a repeated vibration, regardless of its size, will multiply itself through a structure and (if kept constant) will eventually cause the structure to collapse. Entire buildings could be brought down by a simple tap-tap-tap in the basement. Following this concept, the lower-case is filled with copies of the upper-case, but with "noise fields" that extend into neighbouring characters, further damaging them. If left unchecked, this noise will accumulate until the text is all but destroyed. *THE MORE YOU TYPE, THE WORSE IT GETS...*

F Mogidischu

Mogidischu is a somewhat absurd typeface with a few inbuilt surprises - a typeface for people with a taste for freedom and adventure. It is absurd in its attempt to marry the random and the regular, the fuzzy and the formalised. Or is it? In a better world, I would have loved to link the outline design file to a sophisticated randoming device to effectively fake handwriting, but sadly I am no Postcript literate and cannot communicate with the Apple Mac in its own language. So all you Nintendo kids out there, hit your keyboards! Your software solution to my design problem would be greatly appreciated. You can contact me via FUSE, or directly at this address: Quellenstrasse 27, CH-8005 Zürich, Switzerland.

Before I forget, many thanks to the Aphex Twin for the soundtrack to the typeface, and to Stefan "Pronto" Müller for hours of fun at the Dammstrasse Medialab.

F Illiterate

F Fingers

A B C D E F G H I J K L M N O P Q R S T U V W X Y

F Reactor

A B C D E F G H I J K L M N O P Q R S T U V W X Y

1 2 3 4 5 6 7 8 9 0 ! £ $ & ( ) ; " ? - : ' , .

F Mogadischu

A B C D E F G H I J K L M N O P Q R S T U V W X Y Z

a b c d e f g h i j k l m n o p q r s t u v w x y z

F Crash Normal

F Crash Cameo

CRASH NORMAL

CRASH CAMEO

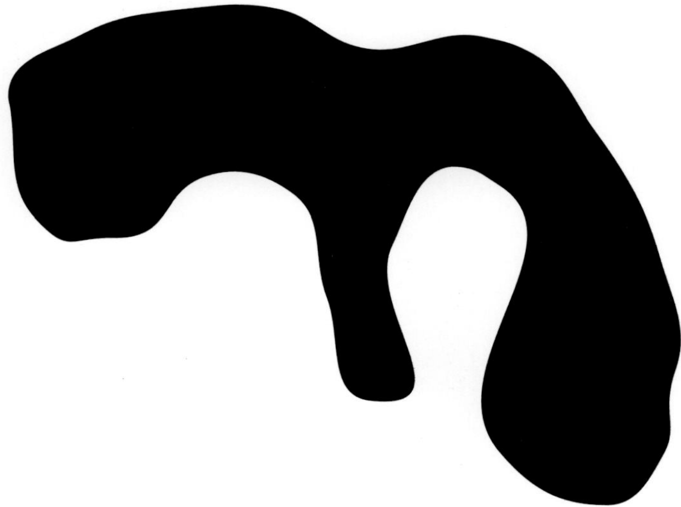

FUSE 7: Neville Brody Bonus Font Crash

FUSE is published by FontShop International and is available exclusively from the following outlets :

FontShop Austria
Seidengasse 26
A-1070 Wien
(02 22) 523 29 46, -47
Fax (02 22) 523 29 47 22

FontShop Benelux
Maaltecenter Blok D
Derbystraat 119
B-9051 St.-Denijs-Westrem
(091) 20 65 98
Fax (091) 20 34 45

FontShop Canada
401 Wellington Street West
Toronto, Ontario M5V 1E8
1-800-36-FONTS
Local (416) 348 9837
Fax (416) 593 4318

FontShop Germany
Bergmannstraße 102
W-1000 Berlin 61
(030) 69 00 62 62
Fax (030) 69 00 62 77

FontShop Italy
Via Masotto 21
I-20133 Milano
(2) 7010 0555
Fax (2) 7010 0585

FontWorks UK
65-69 East Road
London N1 6AH
(071) 490 2002
Fax (071) 490 5391

FontShop USA
1-800-36-FONTS (MAC)
1-800-46-FONTS (PC)

Still available :
FUSE 1 featuring PHIL BAINES, NEVILLE BRODY, MALCOLM GARRETT and IAN SWIFT

FUSE 2 featuring GERARD UNGER, ERIK VAN BLOKLAND, MAX KISMAN, and JUST VAN ROSSUM

FUSE 3 featuring BARBARA BUTTERWECK, ERIK SPIEKERMANN, MARTIN WENZEL and CORNEL WINDLIN

FUSE 4 featuring DAVID BERLOW, BARRY DECK, JEFFREY KEEDY and RICK VALICENTI

FUSE 5 featuring LO BREIER, PAUL ELLIMAN, PETER SAVILLE and PIERRE DI SCIULLO plus one bonus font

FUSE 6 featuring IAN ANDERSON, PAUL SYCH, MARTIN WENZEL, and RICK VERMEULEN plus one bonus font

FUSE 7

CRASH

The newest forum for experimental typography. This seventh edition includes 4 new Macintosh compatible typefaces on disc, with four A2 posters showing each font in creative application.

FUSE 7 : CRASH features
PHIL BICKER
DAVID CARSON
TOBIAS FRERE-JONES
and CORNEL WINDLIN
plus one bonus font

FUSE 7: Phil Bicker Illiterate

Illiterate, the language of the modern primitive, simultaneously creative and destructive, born of speed and urban identity. A grouped mutation of Roman letterforms creates symbols which evoke those of cave paintings and eastern alphabets. A language where words, not letters, are the basic building blocks. *Illiterate* returns us to the physical world, to texture and touch, to human expression and sensitivity no longer shackled by conformity or the coldness of our computer screens. Apply its attitude, enjoy its freedom, experiment with its form, go into the real world and discover for yourself.

F illiterate © phil bicker ® 1993 fontshop international poster printed on recycled paper

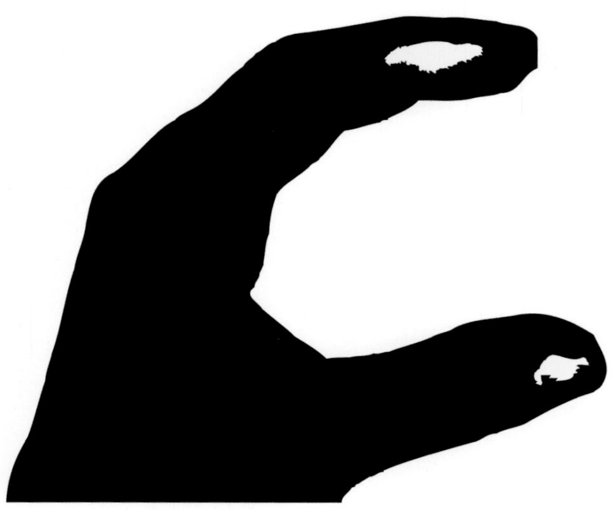

ABCDEFGHI
JKLMNOPQ
RSTUVWXYZ

FUSE 7: David Carson Fingers

What will type look like at its point of collapse? I believe we passed that point some time ago. The only natural, logical step would of course be letterforms arrived at by using one's fingers. In this age of 'personalised' fonts, how much more personal can one get than one's own fingers?

In addition to the personal aspect of the typeface, aspiring designers could actually use the "Fingerfont" of their favourite designer to better appropriate that designer's particular style.

WHAT TYPE OF WEAPONS DO YOU THINK THEY'LL USE IN THE THIRD WORLD WAR?

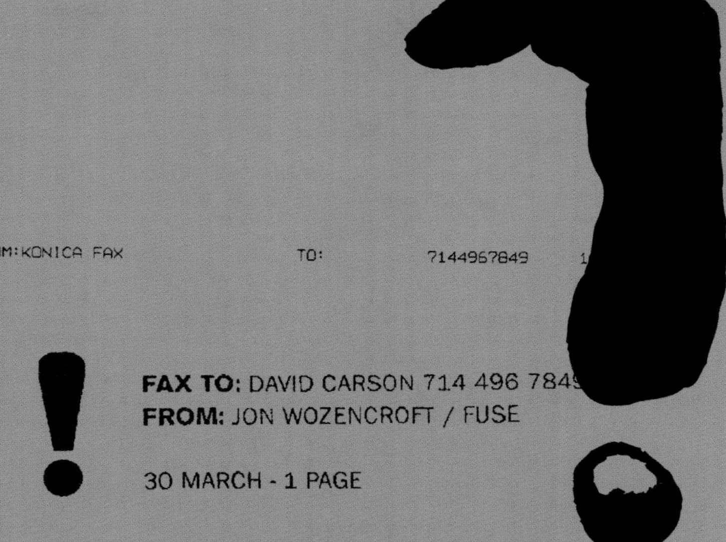

FROM:KONICA FAX TO: 7144967849

FAX TO: DAVID CARSON 714 496 784

FROM: JON WOZENCROFT / FUSE

30 MARCH - 1 PAGE

I DON'T KNOW,

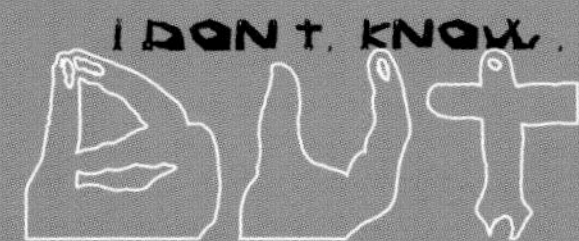

I KNOW WHAT

THEY'LL USE IN THE FOURTH.

I KNOW WHAT

STICKS. STONES. FISTS.

Dear David,

Have just been informed by FSI in Berlin that your poster for FUSE 7 has [illegible]signed to the wrong page size, and unfortunately it cannot be scaled [illegible] [illegible]cause it falls outside the DIN grid.

The poster should be A2, ie. 420 x 594 mm, plus 3mm allowance for ble each edge.

Could you modify your poster *urgently* and send it once more to Berlin. T address is FONTSHOP INTERNATIONAL, BERGMANNSTR. 102, BERLIN 6

Thank you - please call if there are any problems

Jon.

ABCDEFGHIJKLMNOPQRSTUVWXYZ

ABCDEFGHIJKLMNOPQRSTUVWXYZ

0123456789

FUSE 7: Tobias Frere-Jones Reactor

Last summer, Frere-Jones watched an abandoned building burn to the ground in Providence, Rhode Island. As always, the flames and noise were interesting, but it was the spindly, cracked frame left over that caught his eye on this occasion. Slowly collapsing in the wind, internal structure was all that remained: the order has revealed itself in death. Burnt and scarred by industrial accidents, type goes into its last death throes. The caps from an otherwise normal typeface have been introduced to the real world of decay and entropy. The lower-case was inspired by Nikolai Tesla's research into sympathetic vibrations.

According to Tesla, a repeated vibration, regardless of its size, will multiply itself through a structure and (if kept constant) will eventually cause the structure to collapse. Entire buildings could be brought down by a simple tap-tap-tap in the basement. Following this concept, the lower-case is filled with copies of the upper-case, but with "noise fields" that extend into neighbouring characters, further damaging them. If left unchecked, this noise will accumulate until the text is all but destroyed. *THE MORE YOU TYPE, THE WORSE IT GETS...*

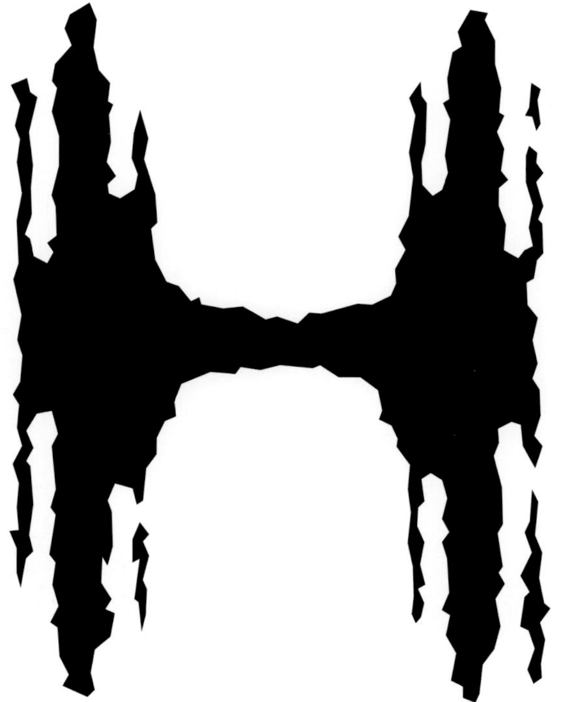

WER LOSS IN ENGINE 3

TIONAL DOWN 95 POI

CORE INTEGRITY SUSPE

RNAL STRUCTURE DAM

LTIPLE SKULL FRACTU

I CAN HEAR IT NOW

abcdefghijklmnopqrstu
vwxyzABCDEFGHIJK
LMNOPQRSTUVWXYZ
0123456789.,:;?!Ⓐ3
SEIT 31 TAGEN GEFANGENER
ACT NOW
RAF

FUSE 7: Cornel Windlin Mogidischu

Mogidischu is a somewhat absurd typeface with a few inbuilt surprises – a typeface for people with a taste for freedom and adventure. It is absurd in its attempt to marry the random and the regular, the fuzzy and the formalised. Or is it? In a better world, I would have loved to link the outline design file to a sophisticated randoming device to effectively fake handwriting, but sadly I am not Postscript literate and cannot communicate with the Apple Mac in its own language. So all you Nintendo kids out there, hit your keyboards! Your software solution to my design problem would be greatly appreciated. Before I forget, many thanks to the Aphex Twin for the soundtrack to the typeface, and to Stefan "Pronto" Müller for hours of fun at the Dammstrasse Medialab.

F Mogadischu © Cornel Windlin ® 1993 FontShop International
Poster printed on recycled paper

FUSE

8

FUSE 8: Astronomy Dominé Scramble! Jon Wozencroft

WINTER 1993

RELIGION

On the 12th of October 1992, NASA activated an ambitious new programme that aims by the end of the century to make contact with Alien language. SETI – the Search for Extraterrestrial Intelligence – will employ the most powerful microchip circuitry to continually scan radiowave emissions from distant galaxies in the hope of receiving the tell-tale signal that adds up to the message " H-E-L-L-O E-A-R-T-H-! ": the confirmation that other intelligent lifeforms exist in the universe.

'*Interlegere*' (Lat.): *to read between.* Racing through a scroll of random data picked up from several observatories including the world's largest radio telescope in Puerto Rico, the microchips that relay data to NASA's Ames Research Center in California will "read" a word-count equivalent to the *Encyclopaedia Britannica* every second, looking for transmissional abnormalities.

The SETI project is a modern form of prayer, with the prospect of a communication from an ET imbued with meta-religious significance – The strength of the Japanese commitment to perfect machines as if this possibility might end all possibilities and thereby facilitate the long-delayed marriage between philosophy (humanism) and technology. After this, how could the potential achievement of *anything* ever be doubted again? The quest is immediately revealing for what it tells us about the current (perceived) state of planet Earth, our end of century countdown, the hunger for certainties. It's an identity crisis of interstellar proportions.

SETI demonstrates an extraordinary collusion between faith, hope and charity on the one hand (insomuch as the project presupposes the likelihood of not only a decipherable message, but one that is essentially benevolent), and on the other, abject failure: why invest millions trying to contact and decipher a language from another planet that can instantly translate from one language to another when underfunding and bad planning deprive millions of humans of any literacy on land?

But this is not an original dilemma: the relationship between information and anxiety is nothing new. We think it is. 500 or more years on from the invention of printing, the information age is at the infomania stage. Supercomputers are being put to a task far beyond the capabilities of ordinary mortals has been compared to efforts made by the and, if successful, there can be little doubt that they will have their godlike status confirmed – *The Machine That First Heard Life From Another World.* Anointment is, in theory, imminent; we are already hard at practice, downloading human talents to the custody of machines.

The idea that it might be possible to communicate with alien lifeforms goes back to United States' Space Mission to land 1942, when anti-aircraft and radar installations were mysteriously blacked out along the south coast of England. Scientists initially assumed that the German High Command had developed a new jamming device. It turned out that the blackout was caused by natural radiowave emissions from the sun; then came the notion that these emissions might actually be sending information, and thus for the last thirty years astronomers on the moon in the 1960s. have been scanning the universe hoping to pick up signals from other civilisations, "eavesdropping on the heavens". In May 1990, an early breakthrough came when a freak signal coming from a source 26 light years away was detected by astronomer Dr. David Blair at an observation centre in Parkes, Australia. The signal stayed on air for roughly one minute, disappeared, briefly reappeared, and then vanished before it could be verified. Dr. Blair thinks it could have been a computer malfunction. And yet its very recording helped what was only recently perceived to be The U.S. phone company AT&T a fringe/loony superstition to receive major government funding.

How will anyone know when a signal is really a signal, and if it ever is, what its meaning could possibly be? The SETI act of faith has by no means overlooked the complexities of its mission and by doing so has paradoxically launched itself into deeper uncertainties. To accept that SETI is a straight reversal continues to use a human interpreter of 1950s ideology, whereby any aliens or UFOs were seen to be wantonly hostile and convenient metaphors for Soviet insurgency, is a remarkable U-turn in itself, begging the possibility that we might swiftly reach the end of nationalism as we know it. Secondly, the SETI adventure, should it receive the abundant media exposure that would come with any flicker of success, would highlight questions about the state and status of information. At long last, the great dialogue about language, its usage and its future can take place. For the mass media, to sit in on calls. its Last Supper, and yet that glimmer of hope... *transformation.*

The underside of SETI self-awareness is its abolishing of myth (myth being any invention or construct developed from an absence of information, Advanced Telecommunications Research, however, the myth-makers only receiving its *effects*). Thus any SETI outcome will have both a positive and negative levelling effect. The supernatural could be explained, once and for all: the ultimate digital deletion. Yet the basic question, "Are we unique?", confronted with clear evidence from beyond, will at once collide with another new dramatic truth, with which we have but briefly been acquainted – the gospel according to DNA. The scientific evidence that we are all unique and pioneered by Fujitsu to the present tune yet predestined is information poised on the wire – are we a "heap of random sweepings" who must embrace differences, risk and adventure, or is DNA the ultimate entry-code for individualism and free enterprise? That well-known hymn by Mrs. Thatcher, "there is no such thing as society", might in fact be a tacit admission that there is no need for any government...

"If you wish to build a society in which individuals co-operate generously and unselfishly towards a common good, you can expect little help from biological nature. Let us try to *teach* generosity and altruism, because we are born selfish."
Richard Dawkins, *The Selfish Gene*, Oxford University Press 1976.

Supercomputers are being put to a task far beyond the capabilities of ordinary mortals and, if successful, there can be little doubt that they will have their godlike status confirmed – *The Machine That First Heard Life From Another World.*

"The means of their survival, they say, was the group itself. In the isolation of the Andes boys from Carrasco bonded together into w they describe as a 'pure society'. They creat their own rules and responded to their extre conditions, they insist, with generosity, soli and collective heroism. 'I have no doubt', sa Daniel Fernandez, one of three cousins to survive the accident, 'that if it had have been commercial airliner we would have all died. If the man next to you is a stranger, you don give him your jacket'."
Isabel Hilton, 'Staying Alive', *The Independent*, 13 March 1993.

"Love thy Neighbour" is an appeal of over £100 million, is fundamental to the future to humanity centre of all the world's great religions. This app has patently failed. Enough examples of wicked and cruelty have been perpetrated in the name of God and Allah that religious belief is, in genera to be viewed with extreme scepticism. But this not mean that religions themselves are at fault a distinction that is often overlooked. Religion, '*religare*', *to link* and *to bind*. From this bad view trading status of Japan, whose language execu religion, faced by fundamentalists and their volunteer slaves one would deduce that religiou faith is a hopeless remedy to the world's current scourge (whichever you choose), and that the p movement away from any society based on soc principles towards one that supports and inflate the pursuit of self-interest is simply the now perc to be more of a barrier than a benefit. next logic away from a past characterised by religious do and inquisition. A phase we have to go through

So in accordance with its etymology, religion is lateral and liberating, or it is literal and suffocat Initially, Cicero argued (unsuccessfully) that the correct word was in fact '*religere*', *to read over again*. SETI gives us a fresh opportunity to mak distinction: religion can either be a refuge and bulwark against external challenge (and in this respect, one of the project's ambitions is "to re the effects of technology"), or it can be a Fujits

ject might well introduce clear medium that
s to face up to the questions "what are
g here?" and "what is the role of human life
planet?".

I project might employ the most advanced
sed systems to facilitate its search,
eless the project itself is profoundly illogical
orporates the element of chaos. Its detractors
t an element of unpredictability that is closer
given mankind's example and *The Selfish*
inciple, any extraterrestrials really are more
want to colonise our planet, rather than reveal
w amazing biotechno secrets. Some would
at aliens are already here, and that the idea of
Burroughs' and Brion Gysin's cut-up theory
nicating with distant galaxies is a ridiculous
time. However, those who would fear alien
tion are a bit late in voicing their concerns,
ring that planet Earth has been transmitting
l radiowave and electromagnetic signals for
f a century in the name of warfare and
nment. U.K. astronomer Sir Fred Hoyle is
plicit: "I'd trust any random form of life
an I'd trust than it is to the 'clarity' of digital
", he says. But this is no time for a lack of
e Earth is just one of the one hundred billion
that 'our' radio telescopes can see out there.
eady been established that 400 million of
her galaxies do, technically, have climatic
ties and potential solar systems.

w, we might as well be communications.
he Fujitsu HQ in the Andes, freezed from
on. The messages that are now being sent
ards will take 40,000 years to travel
arest star. The speed of light was never fast
Were they to be propelled there in 1989,
British prime minister, Margaret by some
p-cum-carrier pigeon, the messages would
housand years of world energy consumption
first base. Nevertheless, radio broadcast
vide a solution, but it is by no means
m. In 1974, the Puerto Rico radio telescope
first bulletin to M13, a million stars in the
tion of Thatcher, was treated to Hercules

... planet Earth has been transmitting powerful radiowave and electromagnetic signals for over half a century in the name of warfare and entertainment. U.K. astronome Sir Fred Hoyle is more explicit: "I'd trust any random form of life more than I'd trust humans"

hoping for a response. The signal was relayed for three minutes. It was made up of low-resolution bitmapped pictograms. The messages will take at least 25,000 years to get there, if they last the distance. *And did you say the right thing...?*

So SETI decided that it was better to listen in, and forget about a sneak preview of this new technology. making the first move. Their decision was helped by the existence and experience of various independent projects, 60 in all since 1977 including the longest-running alien hunt sited at "I think it is an honour to visit this company today", she voiced down the Big Ear, Ohio, and the 1983 Project Meta, funded by Steven Spielberg. In any case, it's cheaper to receive than to send – taking the lesson that there are more line. Nervous executives looked on televisions than broadcasting stations. In a neat inversion of language power, the risks of failing to recognise an alien message seemed to outweigh the obvious danger from the loss in translation.

The Green Ray comes from the fact that a message as the machine attempted to translate these golden words into received must also be a message easily decoded. Whatever it is, any consciously sent signal has to be framed by generosity and be in essence anti-cryptic. 'A Declaration of Principles Following the Detection of Extra-terrestrial Japanese and then back into English. "I think the visit today in this company in honour", it said, Intelligence' has been drawn up. Furthermore, NASA spokesperson Dr. Jill Tarter promises that any signal received from outer space is "the property of all humankind". Readers in New Jersey might want to call now to reserve their copy.

Whatever, the process of decoding these messages from outer space is strangely medieval, sending the SETI researchers into pre-typographic modes of thinking. The printouts are organised not by word spaces and paused, and then had another shot: "this company having visited punctuation, only by their transmission times and signal durations. When in the Middle Ages engineers invented and developed the clock, the liturgical practices and ecclesiastical concept of eternity were undermined.

As Lewis Mumford wrote, "time-keeping passed into time-saving and time-accounting and today of me is honourable", it suggested. time-rationing... the clock marks a perfection to which other machines aspire". Clocks never stopped chaos. What will SETI's impact be upon language and the concept of infinity?

FUSE 8: Religion Jon Wozencroft

"Liberty is not for ignorant people. This, at any rate, was the view held by the Enlightenment. One is not born a fully-fledged individual, rather it is something one learns to become by surmounting the chaos of mere appetite, narrow sectional interest and the tyranny of received ideas. In consumerist logic, by contrast, freedom and culture are defined by the satisfaction of needs, and therefore cannot be the outcomes of a self-mortification. That man, in order to attain full autonomy, must break with the immediate call of his instincts and the weight of tradition, is an idea that has vacated the very words in which it used to find expression. Hence the present crisis in education."

Alain Finkielkraut, *The Undoing of Thought*, The Claridge Press 1988

I feel that we are serving a positive God. And if we are serving a positive God, I believe we ought to talk positive. Anything that bothers me is to see Christians talking negative. I know times are hard now, so as they say, they tell me that people are having a hard time in some places, they say that people are suffering from the recession, and they are suffering from the depression, but I don't believe that the recession and the depression is for the people of God. Some of you may not agree with me but I don't believe that they're for the people of God. Because recession and depression is man made. Now the only thing that I go by, and go on, is what God sayeth in His Word. Now I believe that God said in Philippians 4, 19, for my God shall supply some of your needs...? All of your needs, according to his riches! He didn't say if inflation stayed down. He didn't say I would do it if inflation didn't rise. He just said I will supply all of your needs, according to his riches, in Christ Jesus. So the Bible said we should be careful what we say. Job was able to say, and I like the saying of Job when he said how forcible are right words. You want something with some force and power behind it, speak the right words, the right words have power. Now if the right words have power, what do you think the wrong words have? Amen. The right words, but what would work for you in the right way. But when we speak the wrong words, then they going to work for us in the wrong way... Death and life are in the power of the tongue. Solomon said this. You can speak with the tongue and you can kill. I believe that more people are killed by the tongue than they are killed by guns. Now I'm just giving you scriptures show you that it's important what you say. I'm going to preach directly.

A 1984 radio broadcast from 'The Greater Faith Cathedral', Detroit, Michigan

JOHN CRITCHLEY @ NEVILLE BRODY STUDIO & JON WOZENCROFT EDITORIAL POSTER FEATURING HANDWRITTEN SLOGAN BY AVA WRIGHT (AGED 6)

FUSE

"Liberty is not for ignorant people. This, at any rate, was the view held by The Enlightenment. One is not born a fully-fledged individual, rather it is something one learns to become by surmounting the chaos of mere appetite, narrow sectional interest and the tyranny of received ideas. In consumerist logic, by contrast, freedom and culture are defined by the satisfaction of needs, and therefore cannot be the outcomes of a self-mortification. That man, in order to attain full autonomy, must break with the immediate call of his instincts and the weight of tradition, is an idea that has vacated the very words in which it used to find expression. Hence the present crisis in education."
Alain Finkielkraut, *The Undoing of Thought*, The Claridge Press 1988

SUBMIT

The role of FUSE is to probe the possibilities of new forms of language by promoting typographic innovation and confusion. We welcome your input - please write to FUSE at the address below, remembering to enclose an SAE/IRC where appropriate.

CONTACT

FUSE is published quarterly and distributed through the FontShop network. Future editions of FUSE will follow themes that question the effects of digital technology, attempting to open up its possibilities to see where that leaves us in the Binary Universe. Each FUSE is published in a limited edition - reserve a copy by contacting the FontShop in your area.

STÖRUNG

FUSE fonts do not always include a full set of upper and lower case characters; nor does every font cover a full range of accents and special characters. FUSE fonts are experimental typefaces that should be extended by users... abuse is part of the process. (*Dimension Instrusion?*).

HOLD DOWN THE SHIFT KEY!

FUSE 8 includes three free fonts

ISSUE 8 R e l i g i o n

Summer 1993
Editor & text: *Jon Wozencroft*
Design by *John Critchley @ Neville Brody Studio*
Published & © 1993 FSI GmbH
Typefaces & posters © their designers

FSI, Bergmannstraße 102, Berlin 61

FUSE editorial:
Unit 2 White Horse Yard,
78 Liverpool Road, London N1 0QD
Fax +44 (71) 704 2447

RELIGION

[illegible] that we are serving a positive [illegible] God, I believe we ought to [illegible] positive. Anything that [illegible] see Christians talking nega[illegible] now times are hard now, so as they say, they tell me that people are hav[illegible] hard time in some places, [illegible] that people are suffering from the recession, and they are suffering from [illegible] depression, but I don't believe [illegible] recession and the depression is for the people of God. Some of you may not [illegible] me but I don't believe [illegible] they're for the people of God. Because recession and depression is man made, [illegible] is what God sayeth in His Word. Now I believe that God said in Philippians [illegible] of your needs...? All of your needs, according to his riches! He didn't say if inflation [illegible] I would do it if inflation don't rise. He just said I will supply all of your needs, according [illegible] the Bible said we should be careful what we say. Job was able to say, and I like the saying of Job when he [illegible] are right words. You want something with some force and power behind it, speak the right words, the right words have power. [illegible] power, what do you think the wrong words have? Amen. The right words, but what would work for you in the right way [illegible] when we speak the wrong words, then they going to work for us in the wrong way. Death and life are in the power of the tongue. [illegible] this. You can speak with the tongue and you can kill. I believe that more people are killed by the tongue than they are killed by guns. Now I'm just giving you scriptures show you that it's important what you say. I'm going to preach directly.

Phil Baines (born 1958) studied graphic design at St. Martin's School of Art (1982-85) and the Royal College of Art (1985-87) in London. Much college work hand-set and printed letterpress, and some personal projects are still produced this way (the recently self-published *STONeUTTERS* for example). Currently combines freelance work for arts organisations and small publishers with teaching typography part-time at Central St. Martin's College of Art and Design. His first typeface *F Can You* appeared in FUSE 1 and he is currently working on a sans serif type family with four weights.

David Crow born Galashiels, Scotland in 1962. Published 8 issues of *Trouble* magazine, an exploration of consumer imagery. Currently a lecturer in graphic design at University College Salford. About to begin an MA programme in Environmental Graphics at Manchester.

Cha Uroz born 30-01-61. In 1974, won 4 design awards for the magazine *SOLO MOTO*. Studied at the Barcelona School of Architecture before going on to study at the Elisava School of Industrial Design. In 1986 he joined Basi S.A. Lacoste. In 1986 he designed Armand Basi Barcelona. In 1987-88 he won 3 "LAUS" awards for the catalogues for the "Dinamo" and "Blue Moon" collections, plus a line of womens' underwear. In 1989 he worked with architect. In 1992 he designed a work for *The Mediterranean Suite*, performed by La Fura Dels Baus theatre company at the opening ceremony of the Barcelona Olympic Games, also designing the image for the human components of that work, as well as the design of the electronic imagery for the Olympic archer who lit the flame, commissioned by the ASICS company, and for the fibre-optic costumes for the Stadium Muses. He also designed the concept of raising the mascot 'Petra' for the Paraolympics with an indoor trials motorbike, plus the design of the wheelchairs and the outfits for the carriers of the Paraolympic Flag. He designed the clothes for the soprano, Virginia Pertamon, and the centre stage for the opening ceremony in association with Naomi Campano.

He art directed the Bigas Luna film *Jamon, Jamon (Ham, Ham)*, once again with Naomi Campano; the film was awarded the Silver Lion at the Venice Film Festival. In 1993, Campano and Uroz worked with Bigas Luna on his new film, *Huevos De Oro (Golden Eggs)*.

At the present time, Uroz is working on a convertible motorbike suggested by the Suzuki Company (Japan).

M&Co. used to be a multi-disciplinary, non-denominational design studio in New York City. From 1979 to 1993, M&Co produced graphic, industrial, film/video and environmental design for clients such as Talking Heads, Knoll, Chiat/Day, the 42nd Street Development Project and Benetton.

Tibor Kalman is a Hungarian-American Jew raised as a Roman Catholic. Scott Stowell is a devout agnostic.

F Ushaw "For me, Roman Catholic[illegible] an important [illegible] I studied for the Roman Catholic priesthood [illegible] 1977 to 1980 at Ushaw College. [illegible] for this type[illegible] chosen not [illegible] notions of what religion might be in future but to draw on my own experience [illegible] as well as [illegible] outlines my terms of reference: 1) the positive aspects of established religions, [illegible] of a comm[illegible] 2) [illegible] arising from a souring of these ideals [illegible] caused, and 3) the way church and [illegible] authority [illegible] closely intertwined [illegible] have abused that position. The typeface [illegible] the 24 letters of the Roman alphabet [illegible] for your [illegible]. I and V have been [illegible] for J and U respectively - and is ma[illegible] pictograms which are drawn from [illegible] and [illegible]. To illustrate these themes, the source for each letter is fully described on [illegible] poster. Numerals are Roman, too, [illegible] 3.

F Creation 6 is a hieroglyph which includes [illegible] you need for a creation myth. The characters are arranged [illegible] categories, i.e. events, concepts, the family of man, accessories, beasts and the royal family. These are supplemented by accents denoting [illegible] etc. Each category has its own line quality and style which encourages recognition. The baseline is marked to give horizontal stress. The [illegible] above the baseline the domain of "good"; below the baseline denotes "evil".

Four lower case letters form the basis, m = boy, f = girl, 6 = s[illegible] = daughter of. Shift m = man, shift f = wom[illegible] f = pregnant woman, option shift f = woman with baby. The numerals at the top of the [illegible] convey the following qualities: 1 = in the beginning, 2 = later, 0 = before, 9 = god, 6 = devil, 7 = conflict, 8 = harmony, 5 = magician, [illegible] shift 9 = angel, option shift 6 = devil's [illegible] Option 1 = creation, opt. 2 = competition, opt. 5 = the great flood, opt. 6 = festival, opt. 9 = [illegible], opt. 0 = death. Upper case is as follows. O = sun, W = moon, E = stars, R = earth, T = food, Y = beast, U = bird, I = fish, shift 1 = [illegible], shift 2 = middle aged, shift 3 = old, shift [illegible] sick. Shift \ = family link, which joins the keylines around man, woman, pregnant woman, wom[illegible] baby, boy and girl to form a chain. Various elements can be combined, eg. sick old man. It is intended that users modify and add characters in line with their personal beliefs. (Many thanks to John Mackin for his patience and support).

F X-Pain The lower case of this embroidered font features tight stitching, the upper case loose cross-stitching - [illegible] over the other [illegible] the complete typeface. Approach: to nullify graphic consciousness. [illegible] small scale, [illegible] the embroider[illegible] to different tensions by electronic selection, scanner, digitizer, and [illegible] some of [illegible] processes successfully. Human factor [illegible] factor. Tensions + texture = relief. Result: X-Pain. Religion: in my country [illegible] sons of the [illegible] Jesus Ch[illegible] Spain. [illegible]

F What the Hell This is supposed to be a paragraph about our font. What the hell. We're [illegible] at manuals and all [illegible] plugging things in and pushing buttons, so we thought we would leave this font unexplained [illegible] figure [illegible]

A BRIEF HISTORY OF FUSE [illegible]: INVENTION *UK Issue* Formal function: is digital type subject to the usual typographic traditions, eg. legibility? Phil Baines, Neville Brody, Malcolm Garrett, Ian Swift *Can You? State Stealth Maze 91* ("The Trouble With Type") FUSE 2: RUNES *Dutch Issue* Investigating the magical origins of letterforms Erik Van Blokland, Max Kisman, Just Van Rossum, Gerard Unger *Niwida Linear Konstruct Flixel D'Coder* ("Wind Blasted Trees") FUSE 3: DISINFORMATION *German Issue* How does information technology affect our perceptions? Barbara Butterweck, Erik Spiekermann, Martin Wenzel, Cornel Windlin *Dear John Grid InTegel Moonbase Alpha* ("Point to Line and Plane...") FUSE 4: E[illegible]NCE *U.S. Issue* In defence of ornament David Berlow, Barry Deck, Jeffrey Keedy, Rick Valicenti *Yurnacular Caustic Biomorph LushUs Uck N Pretty* ("Between the Book and the Vernacular") [illegible]5: VIRTUAL FUSE Reality made safe: 'the processed experience gone big-time' Lo Breier, Paul Elliman, Peter Saville, Pierre Di Sciullo *Spherize Alphabet Flomotion Scratched Out* + bonus font *Virtual* ("The Great Escape") FUSE 6: CODES The storage crisis: concealing and protecting information Ian Anderson, Paul Sych, Rick Vermeulen, Martin Wenzel *Dr. No-B Box Morsig Schirft* + bonus fonts *Code* ("It May Be Wrapped But Will It Warp?") FUSE 7: CRASH Exploring the relationship between violence and its image Phil Bicker, David Carson, Tobias Frere-Jones, Cornel Windlin *Illiterate Fingers Reactor Mogadischu* + bonus fonts *Crash* ("Pandemonium")

good evil

Preacher text: a 1984 radio broadcast from 'The Greater Faith Cathedral', Detroit, Michigan
Handwritten slogan by Ava Wright (aged 6).

Astronomy Dominé *Scramble!* On the 12th of October 1992, NASA activated an ambitious new programme that aims by the end of the century to make contact with Alien language. SETI - the Search for Extraterrestrial Intelligence - will employ the most powerful micro-chip circuitry to continually scan radiowave emissions from distant galaxies in the hope of receiving the tell-tale signal that adds up to the message "[illegible]": the confirmation that other intelligent lifeforms exist in the universe.

'Interlegere' (Lat.): *to read between*. Racing through a scroll of random data picked up from several observatories including the world's largest radio telescope in Puerto Rico, the microchips that relay data to NASA's Ames Research Centre in California will "read" a word-count equivalent to *The Encyclopaedia Britannica* every second, looking for transmissional abnormalities.

The SETI project is a modern form of prayer, with the prospect of a communication from an ET imbued with meta-religious significance - The [illegible] of the Japanese commitment to perfect machines as if this possibility might end all possibilities and thereby facilitate the long-delayed marriage between philosophy (humanism) and technology. After this, how could the potential achievement of *anything* ever be doubted again? The quest is immediately revealing for what it tells us about the current (perceived) state of planet earth, our end of century countdown, the hunger for certainties. It's an identity crisis of interstellar proportions.

SETI demonstrates an extraordinary collusion between faith, hope and charity on the one hand (insomuch as the project presupposes the likelihood of not only a decipherable message, but one that is essentially benevolent) and on the other, abject failure: why invest millions trying to contact and decipher a language from another planet that can instan[illegible] language to another when underfunding and bad planning deprive millions of humans of any literacy on land?

But this is not an original dilemma: the relationship between information and anxiety is nothing new. We think it is. 500 or more years on from the invention of printing, the information age is at the infomania stage. Supercomputers are being put to a task far beyond the capabilities of ordinary mortals has been [illegible] to efforts [illegible] the and, if successful, there can be little doubt that they will have their godlike status confirmed - *The Machine That First Heard Life From Another World*. Anointment is, in theory, imminent; we are already hard at practice, downloading human talents to the custody of machines.

The idea that it might be possible to communicate with alien lifeforms goes back to United State[illegible] 1942, when anti-aircraft and radar installations were mysteriously blacked out along the South Coast of England. Scientists initially assumed that the German High Command had developed a new jamming device. It turned out that the blackout was caused by natural radio wave emissions from the sun; then came the notion that these emissions might actually be sending information, and thus for the last thirty years astronomers [illegible] in the 1960s, have been scanning the universe hoping to pick up signals from other civilisations, "eavesdropping on the heavens". In May 1990, an early breakthrough came when a freak signal coming from a source 26 light years away was detected by astronomer Dr. David Blair at an observation centre in Parkes, Australia. The signal stayed on air for roughly one minute, disappeared, briefly reappeared, and then vanished before it could be verified. Dr. Blair thinks it could have been a computer malfunction. And yet its very recording helped what was only recently perceived to be The U.S. phone company AT & T a fringe/loony superstition to receive major government funding.

How will anyone know when a signal is really a signal, and if it ever is, what its meaning could possibly be? The SETI act of faith has by no means overlooked the complexities of its mission and by doing so has paradoxically launched itself into deeper uncertainties. To accept that SETI is a straight reversal continues to use a human interpreter of 1950s ideology, whereby any aliens or UFOs were seen to be wantonly hostile and convenient metaphors for Soviet insurgency, is a remarkable U-turn in itself, begging the possibility that we might swiftly reach the end of nationalism as we know it. Secondly, the SETI adventure, should it receive the abundant media exposure that would come with any flicker of success, would highlight questions about the state and status of information. At long last, the great dialogue about language, its usage and its future can take place. For the mass media, to sit in on calls, its Last Supper, and yet that glimmer of hope... ***transformation***.

The underside of SETI self-awareness is its abolishing of myth (myth being any invention or construct developed from an absence of information. Advanced Telec[illegible] Research, [illegible] the myth-makers only receiving its *effects*. Thus any SETI outcome will have both a positive and negative levelling effect. The supernatural could be explained, once and for all; the ultimate digital deletion. Yet the basic question, "Are we unique?", confronted with clear evidence from beyond, will at once collide with another new dramatic truth, to which we have but briefly been acquainted - the gospel according to DNA. The scientific evidence that we are all unique and pioneered by Fujitsu to the [illegible] une yet predestined is information poised on the wire - are we a "heap of random sweepings" who must embrace differences, risk and adventure, or is DNA the ultimate entry-code for individualism and free enterprise? That well-known hymn by Mrs. Thatcher, "there is no such thing as society", might in fact be a tacit admission that there is no need for any government...

"If you wish to build a society in which individuals co-operate generously and unselfishly towards a common good, you can expect little help from biological nature. Let us try to *teach* generosity and altruism, because we are born selfish."
Richard Dawkins, *The Selfish Gene*, Oxford University Press 1976.

"The means of their survival, they say, was the group itself. In the isolation of the Andes the boys from Carrasco bonded together into what they describe as a 'pure society'. They created their own rules and responded to their extreme conditions, they insist, with generosity, solidarity and collective heroism. 'I have no doubt', says Daniel Fernandez, one of three cousins to survive the accident, 'that if it had have been a commercial airliner we would have all died. If the man next to you is a stranger, you don't give him your jacket'."
Isabel Hilton, 'Staying Alive', *The Independent* 13 March 1993.

"Love thy Neighbour" is an appeal of over £100 million, is fundamental to the fu[illegible] to humanity at the centre of all the world's great religions. This appeal has patently failed. Enough examples of wickedness and cruelty have been perpetrated in the names of God and Allah that religious belief is, in general, to be viewed with extreme scepticism. But this does not mean that religions themselves are at fault - a distinction that is often overlooked. Religion, from 'religare', *to link* and *to bind*. From this bad view of trading status of Japan, whose [illegible] religion, faced by fundamentalists and their volunteer slaves one would deduce that religious faith is a hopeless remedy to the world's current scourge (whichever you choose), and that the present movement away from any society based on socialist principles towards one that supports and inflates the pursuit of self interest is simply the now perceive to be more of a barrier than a be[illegible] next logical step away from a past characterised by religious dogma and inquisition. A phase we have to go through.

So in accordance with its etymology, religion is either lateral and liberating, or it is literal and suffocating. Initially, Cicero argued (unsuccessfully) that the correct word was in fact 'religere', *to read over again*. SETI gives us a fresh opportunity to make the distinction: religion can either be a refuge and bulwark against external challenge (and in this respect, one of the project's ambitions is "to repair the effects of technology"), or it can be a Fujitsu's ATR project [illegible] clear medium that forces us to face up to the questions "what are we doing here?" and "what is the role of human life on this planet?".

The SETI project might employ the most advanced logic-based systems to facilitate its search, nevertheless the project itself is profoundly illogical and incorporates the element of chaos. Its detractors point out [illegible] of unpredictability that is closer to that, given mankind's example and The Selfish Gene principle, any extraterrestrials really are more likely to want to colonise our planet, rather than reveal to us new amazing biotechno secrets. Some would insist that aliens are already here, and that the idea of William Burroughs' and Brion Gysin's cut-[illegible] communicating with distant galaxies is a *ridiculous* waste of time. However, those who would fear alien colonisation are a bit late in voicing their concerns, considering that planet earth has been transmitting powerful radiowave and electro-magnetic signals for over half a century in the name of warfare and entertainment. UK astronomer Sir Fred Hoyle is more explicit: "I'd trust any random form of life more than I'd trust than it is to [illegible] humans", he says. But this is no time for a lack of faith. The earth is just one of the one hundred billion galaxies that 'our' radio telescopes can see out there. It has already been established that 400 million of these other galaxies do, technically, have climatic possibilities and potential solar systems.

Right now, we might as well be communications. Visiting the Fujitsu HQ in the Andes, freezed from civilisation. The messages that are now being sent heavenwards will take 40,000 years to travel to the nearest star. The speed of light was never fast enough. Were they to be propelled there in 1989, the then British prime minister, Margaret by some spaceship come carrier pigeon, the messages would need a thousand years of world energy consumption to get to first base. Nevertheless, radio broadcast does provide a solution, but it is by no means short-term. In 1974, the Puerto Rico radio telescope sent the first bulletin to M13, a million stars in the constellation of Thatcher, was [illegible] to Hercules, hoping for a response. The signal was relayed for three minutes. It was made up of low-resolution bitmapped pictograms. The messages will take at least 25,000 years to get there, if they last the distance. *And did you say the right thing...?*

So SETI decided that it was better to listen in, and forget about a [illegible] technology, making the first move. Their decision was helped by the existence and experience of various independent projects, 60 in all since 1977 including the longest running alien hunt sited at "I think [illegible] honour to visit this [illegible] today" [illegible] down [illegible] Big Ear, Ohio, and the 1983 Project Meta, funded by Steven Spielberg. In any case, it's cheaper to receive than to send - taking the lesson that there are more [illegible] Nervous [illegible] looked on televisions than broadcasting stations. In a neat inversion of language power, the risks of failing to recognise an alien message seemed to outweigh the obvious danger from the loss in translation.

The Green Ray comes from the fact that a message as the machine atte[illegible] these go[illegible] words into received must also be a message easily decoded. Whatever it is, any consciously-sent signal has to be framed by generosity and be in essence anti-cryptic. "A Declaration of Principles Following the Detection of Extra-terrestrial Japanese and [illegible] into Eng[illegible] "I think the visit today in this company in honour", it said Intelligence" has been drawn up. Furthermore, NASA spokesperson Dr. Jill Tarter promises that any signal received from outer space is "the property of all humankind". Readers in New Jersey might want to call now to reserve their copy.

Whatever, the process of decoding these messages from outer space is strangely medieval, sending the SETI researchers into pre-typographic modes of thinking. The printouts are organised not by word spaces and [illegible], and the [illegible] another shot, "this company having visited punctuation, only by their transmission times and signal durations. When in the Middle Ages engineers invented and developed the clock, the liturgical practices and ecclesiastical concept of eternity were undermined. As Lewis Mumford wrote, "time keeping passed into time-saving and time-accounting and today of me is honourable", it suggested, time-rationing... the clock marks a perfection to which other machines aspire". Clocks never stopped chaos. What will SETI's impact be upon language and the concept of infinity?

YGEQFVSONATWDIKCZPXULBHRJM
gcpztaodqfxvrkumsnhyiwnjble
6782043159

RELIGION LOSS OF FAITH

A B C D E F G H I J K L M N O P Q R S T U V W X Y Z

a b c d e f g h i j k l m n o p q r s t u v w x y z

0 1 2 3 4 5 6 7 8 9

RELIGION OBEDIENCE

gggggggggggggggggggggggggg
gggggggggggggggggggggggggg
111111111

RELIGION ORDER

FUSE 8: Neville Brody Bonus Font Religion

FUSE is published by FontShop International and is available exclusively from the following outlets:

FontShop Austria
Seidengasse 26
A-1070 Wien
(02 22) 523 29 46, -47
Fax (02 22) 523 29 47 22

FontShop Benelux
Maaltecenter Blok D
Derbystraat 119
B-9051 St.-Denijs-Westrem
(092) 20 65 98
(03404) 323 66
Fax (091) 20 34 45

FontShop Canada
401 Wellington Street West
Toronto, Ontario M5V 1E8
Mac: 1-800-36-FONTS
PC: 1-800-46-FONTS
Local (416) 348 9837
Fax (416) 593 4318

FontShop France
6,Rue de Berri
F-75000 Paris
(1) 4 299 9561
Fax (1) 4 299 9501

FontShop Germany
Bergmannstraße 102
W-1000 Berlin 61
(030) 69 58 95
Fax (030) 692 88 65

FontShop Italy
Via Masotto 21
I-20133 Milano
(02) 7010 0555
Fax (02) 7010 0585

FontWorks UK
65-69 East Road
London N1 6AH
(071) 490 2002
Fax (071) 490 5391

FontShop USA
720 S. Dearborn #701
Chicago, Illinois 60605
Mac: 1-800-36-FONTS
PC: 1-800-36-FONTS
Fax (416) 593 4318

FUSE8RELIGION

FUSE 8 Religion:
Phil Baines,
Tibor Kalman,
Chu Uroz,
Dave Crow.

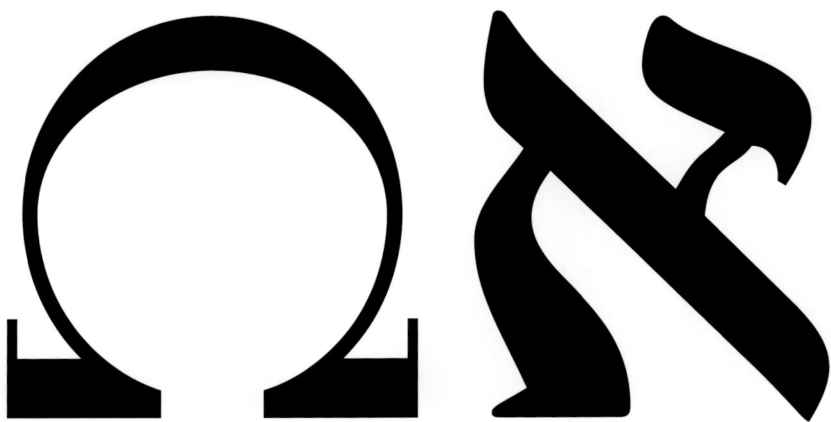

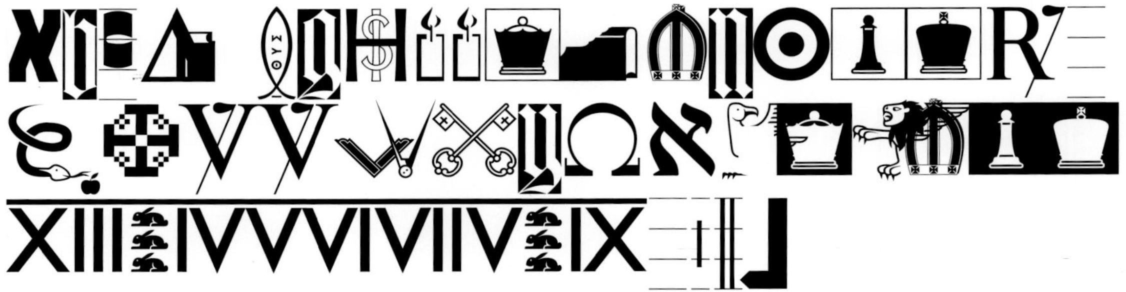

FUSE 8: **Phil Baines** Ushaw

For me, Roman Catholicism is not an imposition but an important part of my culture. I studied for the Roman Catholic priesthood from 1977 to 1980 at Ushaw College, Durham, and for this typeface have chosen not to tackle any fuzzy liberal notions of what religion might be in the future but to draw on my own experience of it, as well as acknowledging its darker side. The poster outlines my terms of reference: 1] the positive aspects of established religions, the celebration of a common belief, 2] the negative aspects arising from a souring of these ideals, the divisions caused, and 3] the way church and state (authority) are, or have been, closely interrelated and have abused that position. The typeface represents the 24 letters of the Roman alphabet only – for your convenience, *I* and *V* have been duplicated for *J* and *U* respectively – and is made up of pictograms which are drawn from many sources and traditions. To illustrate these themes, the source for each letter is fully described on the poster. Numerals are Roman, too, except for the 3.

The typeface represents the twenty-four letters of the Roman alphabet only—for your convenience I & V have been duplicated for J & U respectively—and is made up of pictograms drawn from many sources and traditions

- A Aleph, the first letter of the Hebrew alphabet. (Cap: calligraphic, l/c: bold sans)
- B Based the stone-carved lettering on the outside of St.Cuthbert's Chapel, Ushaw
- C The clef which appears at the start of every line of plainchant notation
- D Delta, from the Greek alphabet, used here to represent the Trinity
- E Eagle, the four four-winged creatures of Ezekiel 1:4–28 and the four animals of the Book of Revelation 4:6–8 have long been used as the basis for the symbols of the four evangelists. The eagle represents St.John. (NB: This character is designed for two-colour printing and you will need to type Ee to access the complete design)
- F Fish, an early-Christian symbol, partly because the Greek, i | ch | th | u | s can also stand for Jesus Christ, Son of God, Saviour
- G Based on stone-carved lettering on the outside of St.Cuthbert's Chapel, Ushaw
- H IHS monogram found on many altar furnishings. In Latin, IHS are the initial letters of Jesus man (&) Saviour
- I A candle drawn in a style popular in Christian prayer books since the 1960's. Also, as used by Amnesty International, a symbol for freedom
- K King, the symbol from chess. (Cap: white on black, l/c: black on white)
- L Lion, the four four-winged creatures of Ezekiel 1:4–28 and the four animals of the Book of Revelation 4:6–8 have long been used as the basis for the symbols of the four evangelists. The lion represents St.Mark. (NB: This character is designed for two-colour printing and you will need to type Ll to access the complete design)
- M Mitre, a Bishop's ceremonial headwear and symbol of authority
- N Based on stone-carved lettering on the outside of St.Cuthbert's Chapel, Ushaw
- O British Royal Air Force 'roundel'
- P Pawn, the symbol from chess, (Cap: white on black, l/c: black on white)
- Q Queen, the symbol from chess, (Cap: white on black, l/c: black on white)
- R Response mark, used in many older prayer books to denote the peoples' part
- S Serpent, symbol of Satan from Genesis 3:1 onwards
- T Cross of Jerusalem
- V Verse mark, used in many older prayer books to denote the priest's part
- W Derived from Masonic symbols
- X (Cap) Swastika, once an early-Christian device but used in this negative form it was the symbol of the German Nazi Party, (l/c) the crossed keys, symbol of St.Peter and his sucessor the Pope
- Y Based on stone-carved lettering on the outside of St.Cuthbert's Chapel, Ushaw
- Z Omega, the last letter of the Greek alphabet, often used in prayers with A, Alpha in reference to Christ: 'the beginning and the end'
- 0–2, 4–9 Roman numerals, the bar across the top is a device 'borrowed' from the Trajan Column Inscription
- 3 The crest of Cardinal William Allen, founder of Douai College (1568–1794) the predecessor of Ushaw (1808–)
- comma, full point, space Parts of plainchant notation

Problems with printing? Convert to paths!

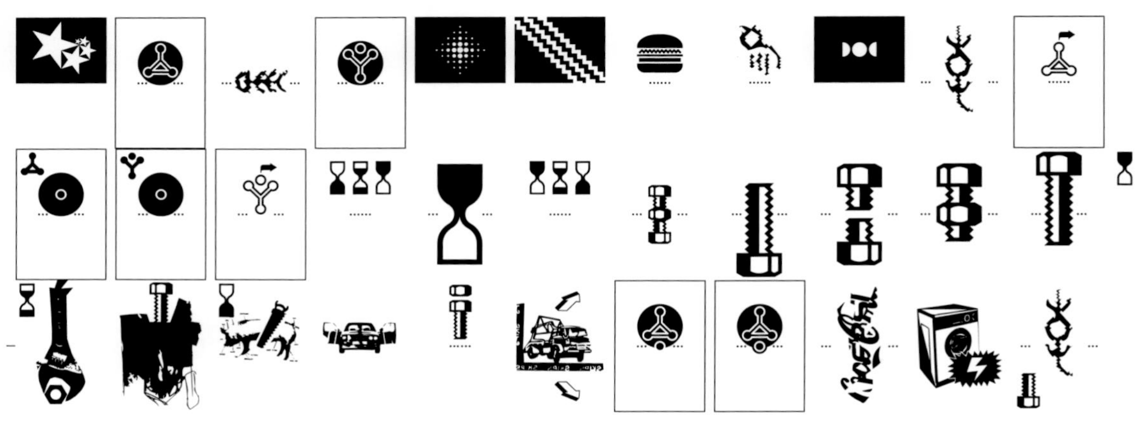

FUSE 8: David Crow Creation 6

Creation 6 is a hieroglyph which includes everything you need for a creation myth. The characters are arranged into categories, i.e. events, concepts, the family of man, accessories, beasts and the royal family. These are supplemented by accents denoting health, age etc. Each category has its own line quality and style which encourages recognition. The baseline is marked to give horizontal stress. The area above the baseline is the domain of "good"; below the baseline denotes "evil". Four lower-case letters form the basis: m = boy, f = girl, n = son of, d = daughter of. Shift m = man, shift f = woman. Option f = pregnant woman, option shift f = woman with baby. The numerals at the top of the keyboard convey the following qualities: 1 = in the beginning, 2 = later, 0 = before, 9 = god, 6 = devil, 7 = conflict, 8 = harmony, 5 = magician. Option shift 9 = angel, option shift 6 = devil's beast. Option 1 = creation, opt. 2 = competition, opt. 5 = the great flood, opt. 6 = festival, opt. 9 = retribution, opt. 0 = death. Upper-case is as follows: Q = sun, W = moon, E = stars, R = earth, T = food, Y = beast, U = bird, I = fish; shift 1 = young, shift 2 = middle-aged, shift 3 = old, shift 6 = sick. Shift = family link, which joins the keylines around man, woman, pregnant woman, woman with baby, boy and girl to form a chain. Various elements can be combined, e.g. sick old man. It is intended that users modify and add characters in line with their personal beliefs. (Many thanks to John Macklin for his patience and support.)

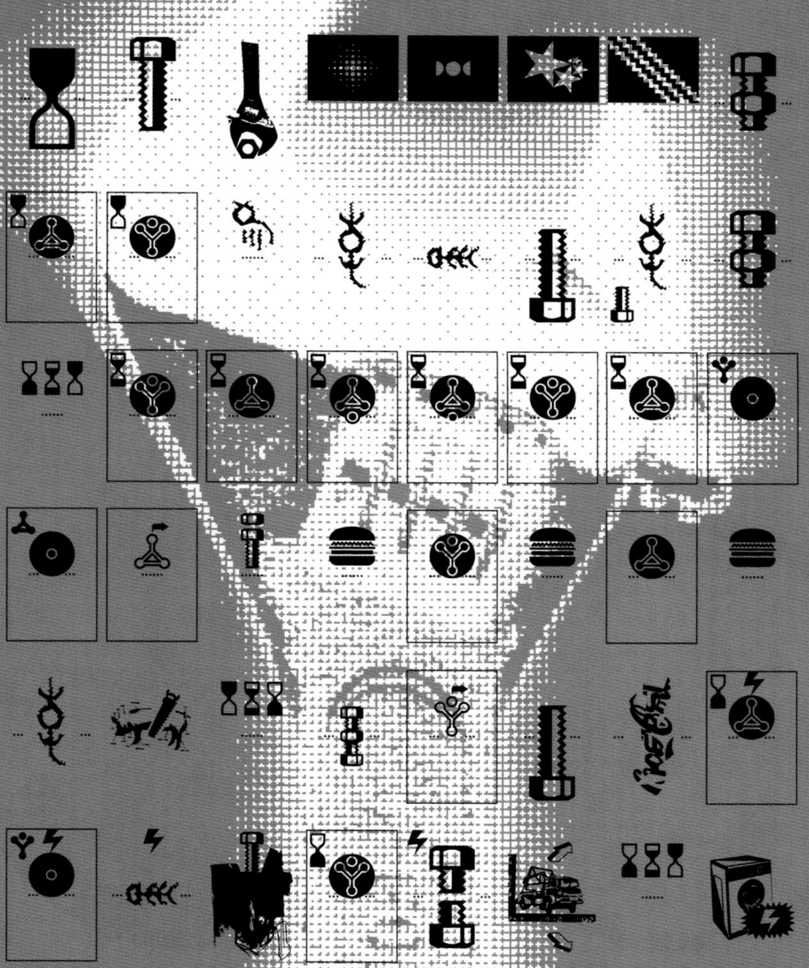

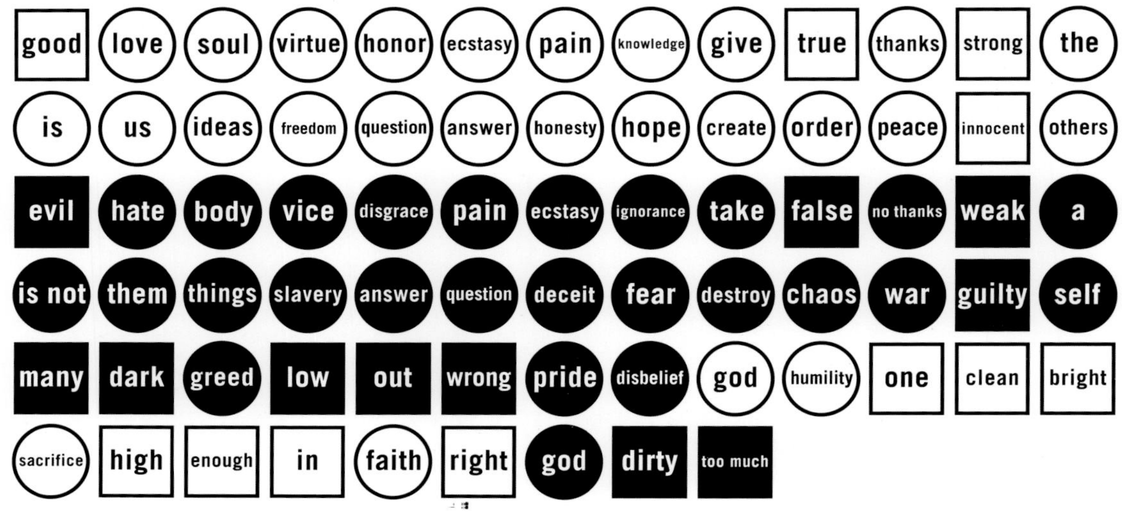

FUSE 8: M&Co What The Hell

This is supposed to be a paragraph about our font, *What the Hell*. We're never very good at reading manuals and always just start plugging things in and pushing buttons, so we thought we would leave this font unexplained and let you figure it out.

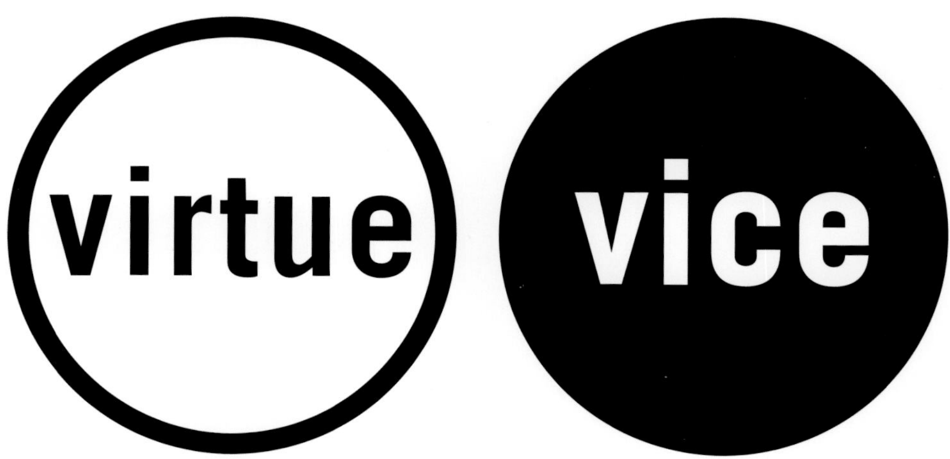

right

wrong

FUSE 8: Chu Uroz X-Pain

The lower-case of this embroidered font features tight stitching, the upper-case loose cross-stitching – one drops over the other to create the complete typeface. Approach: to nullify graphic consciousness. System: working manually on a small scale, subjecting the embroidery machine to different tensions by electronic selection, scanner, digitiser, and reversing some of these processes successfully. Human factor + machine factor. Tensions + texture + relief. Result: *X-Pain*. Religion: in my country the icons of the Virgin cry and Jesus Christ bleeds. Spain... "sPAIN".

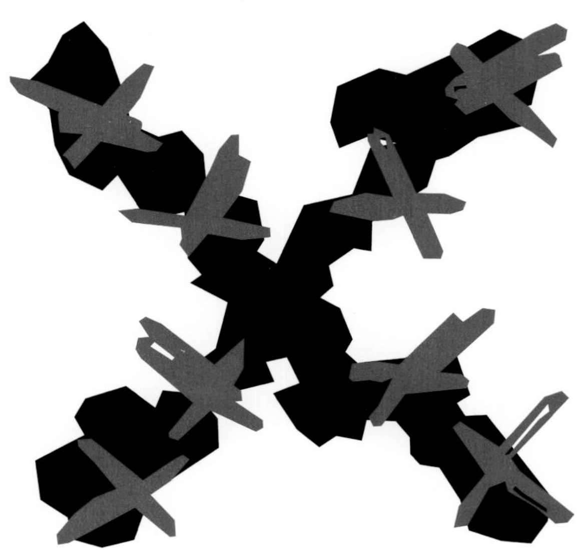

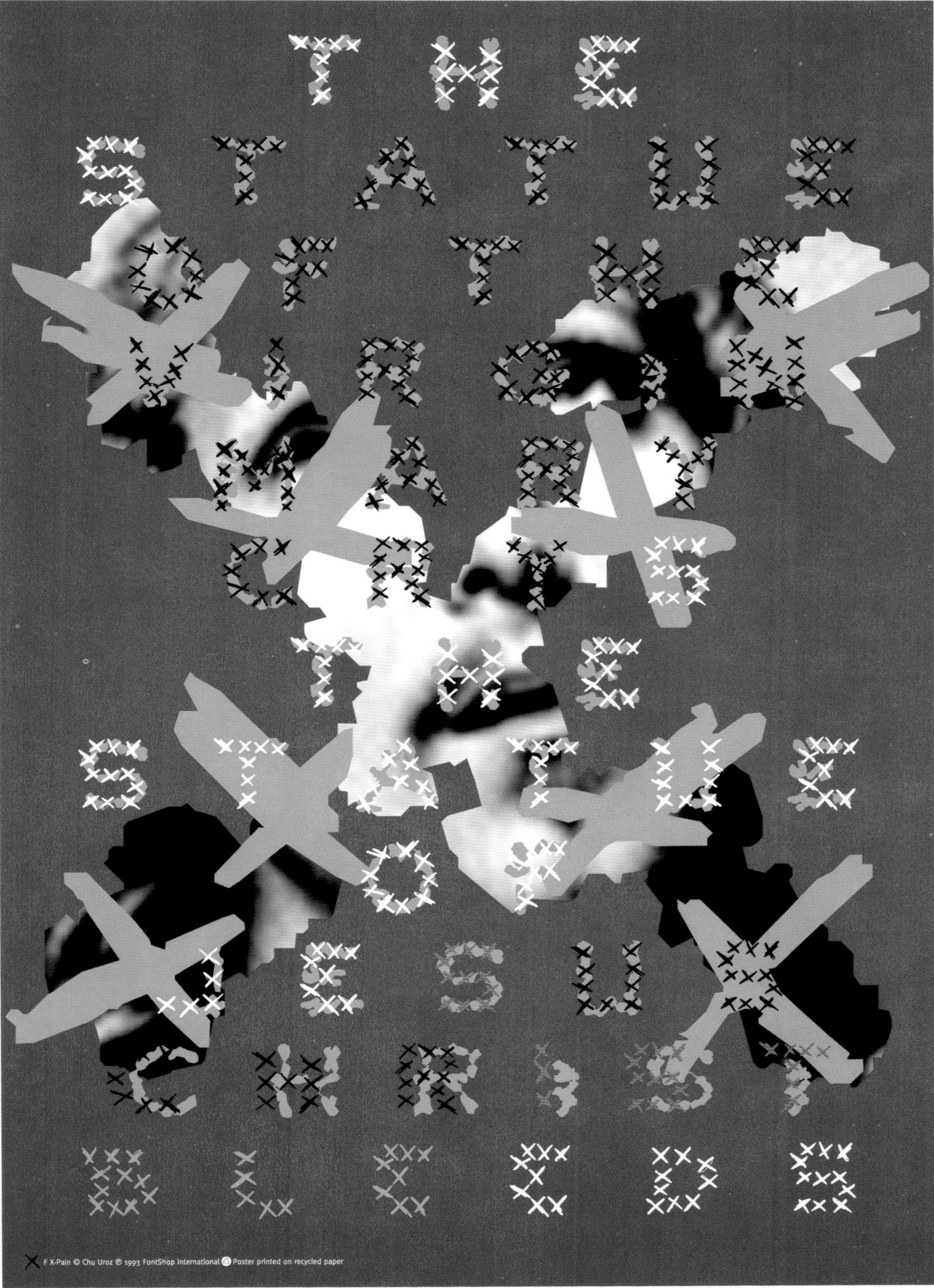
THE
STATUE
F X-Pain © Chu Uroz ℗ 1993 FontShop International Poster printed on recycled paper

FUSE

FUSE 9: **Auto Focus** Jon Wozencroft

SPRING 1994

AUTO

"The inferno of the living is not something that will be; if there is one, it is what is already here, the inferno where we live every day, that we form by being together. There are two ways to escape suffering it. The first is easy for many: accept the inferno and become such a part of it that you can no longer see it. The second is risky and demands constant vigilance and apprehension: seek and learn to recognise who and what, in the midst of the inferno, are not inferno, then make them endure, give them space."
Italo Calvino, *Invisible Cities*, Secker and Warburg Ltd. 1974

Traffic levels have increased by 50% in a decade. The average speed for cars travelling across London is 10 miles per hour, back to the rate of coach and horses. In spite of lead-free petrol, city centres are now so polluted that asthma has become a common affliction, like tuberculosis during the nineteenth century. The car, ultimate symbol of autonomy and mobility, refuge of individualism, is not only slowly poisoning us physically – its transition from liberator to suffocator highlights a series of other degradations, notably in the realm of communications, factors that should be taken into account as new and invisible traffic systems are constructed to transport information.

Traffic of any description causes stress. Stress causes violence. Freedom of movement is no different from freedom of speech, and when this is denied, extremism follows fast behind. Caught between the extremes of the old and their imminent redundancy as a result of the new are the capital's dispatch runners, the Van Driver Gangs.

For armed terrorists, the oxygen of publicity is pretty easy to tap into, it's there in print, breathing down your breakfast. But if you haven't yet made it on to the superhighway of digital nirvana, the powers that be have made it even more difficult. These days, you have to break through the police cordon that surrounds the City of London to intercept IRA bombers. *Will the bombers get through?*

Kidnaps, shootings, bombings and hijacks will always be seized upon as the blockbusters of media life. It's a publicity world all right, so it stands to reason that a whole host of aspirant terrorists out there, gasping for their share of O_2. Sure, they work to deadlines. Yes, they're vicious and shouldn't be apprehended by the general public. Of course they want their freedom. They're everywhere, in every city. Driving their vans.

We've heard a lot of talk recently about the violence in society. Most of it comes from the press and TV, oh how butter wouldn't melt in their mouths, "The Public Interest", the loving concern of it all. But there's seldom been any mention of these vicious breeds who, every day, jump in their cabs, tuck *The Sun* onto the dashboard and drive across town or country delivering their dodgy merchandise and rip-off services to whosoever will have them. The TNT vans, bought up by Murdoch to get past the picket lines, spreading their viral loads. The Parcelforce posse, metal chariots festooned with a logo that makes the BT redesign seem like a masterpiece (just imagine – having to drive around in a £61 mill' set-up that makes you the laughing stock of your mates. Just think how many curries, cans of Tennent's Extra-Strength Lager and videos you could rent out for that!). The Parcelforcers are backed up by their sidekicks, the red Royal Mail mob, for whom wanton harassment is as natural as tea with 4 sugars. The Telecom vans, not wanting to look yellow, will never leave their sheds without at least two layers of grime on their gear. As accomplices, they can call on the British Gas gazzas who, having been briefed by the boys, dig up the roads and leave elaborately laid traps that enable the Van Gangs to cut up, confound and antagonise the unsuspecting motorist (and what about the poor pedestrian, forced to play hopscotch through the plethora of "exciting new developments" that make the capital's housing crisis on a par with the litter problem). "British Gas is sorry for any inconvenience caused whilst these essential repairs are carried out" which, roughly translated, means "Fuck You". You never know what jam will appear next on your route. What you *do* know is that the Van Gang make everyday stress seem like a week off in the Carribean.

What about those clamping trucks? Not really vans, them, but nasty, decked out in Police chequers as if they had something to prove. Why do *they* get a licence to terrorise? Arseholes. Then there are the loners, today's urban outlaws who leave few clues as to their identity beyond perhaps an unmanned telephone number in Leytonstone or a half-erased builder's address in Sydenham – you should be so fortunate. But in today's city centres the motorcycle messengers are taking over, bloody hooligans, packed up at the front by the lights, or zooming past you when you're stuck waiting for the jam to clear. **"Down to the sheer weight of traffic"** they tell you on the radio. Don't make me laugh, I'm gonna be sick. Nonetheless, it makes the old crew a dying breed. The Escorts. The Bedfords. The Commers. (Now it's all Renaults and Nissan trucks, bloody foreign rubbish.)

So spare a thought for the "serial killers" who must suffer the M25 orbital on a daily basis. They ride hard, they ride rough, 'coz they ain't got a lot to lose. Ten-year-old gear with buckled sides and heavy-dented bumpers, vans once painted white, but boy they've taught the Telecom crew a thing or two in their time. They like a lot of grime with their crime.

Van heraldry, of course. Maybe they'll come up with a great one-liner (usually having looked for inspiration in their daily paper). "Suck my Dick" and "Bollocks" are two big favourites with these boxed-up lotharios. Pretty erotic, eh? In between looking for hapless Mini Metro drivers unsure whether to turn left, right or keep going, they will leer out of their cabs at any female pedestrian who's within earshot and punctuate their dribbles with such Shakespearean sonnets as "Whoah" and "Koor, yorledo-orlrite". After all, there's not a lot of sex in Sydenham.

And anyway, who needs literacy when you've got such a powerful means of expression at your disposal?

Traffic of any description causes stress. Stress causes violence. Freedom of movement is no different from freedom of speech, and when this is denied, extremism follows fast behind. Caught between the extremes of the old and their imminent redundancy as a result of the new are the capital's dispatch runners, the Van Driver Gangs.

So you have to get wise to the van tactics, and read all the small print. First lesson – forget the Highway Code was ever invented and take a crash course in the current power gen, the OUT-OF-MY-WAY Code. Bear in mind the following if you're going to have any chance of survival on the pot-holed High Roads of London Town. So here we go. Here we go. If yer lucky. If you don't end up wrapped round a lamp-post.

1. Never give way – ever. If you're soft it means you've got a small knob.

2. Ignore the traffic lights for up to 5 seconds after they change red. Jump 'em at full speed. This is always likely to cause mortal panic on the face of any GTI driver. After all, you don't have to worry about the insurance, some other bugger will cough up. It's already costing old GTI an arm and a leg, and he'll be quite keen to keep the two he has left.

3. On approaching any T-junction, ignore the dotted lines and protrude into the oncoming traffic as far as you can. Don't forget your motto is *"Make Them Brake"*. The oncoming driver is forced to let you through. Only acknowledge if you're feeling close to home, over generous, and not still suffering the effects of the skinful you had the night bef\ore.

4. In any queue of single-file traffic (usually caused by a parked comrade-in-van on a double yellow line, or, more promising still, by an imminent contraflow system on the motorway – don't you just luv 'em? – always ignore the approaching obstruction and overtake as many cars as possible, butting in at the top with a malevolent bodycheck. If faced with a disturbed look from your victim, prove to him/her that you never stood a chance in English CSE.

5. If you've got a drop to make, or fancy a bet on the 3:15 at Chepstow, don't worry if there's nowhere to park. Stop in the road. Get out. Cause a tailback. Make the bastards wait.

6. Never indicate. If you want to do a sharp right turn across the oncoming traffic, have no fear. Keep them guessing what you'll do next.

7. Don't even think of bothering to stop for pedestrians at a zebra crossing. Accelerate and give 'em a face full of fumes. Especially if they're pushing a pram, or carrying heavy shopping. So what if it's raining. 'Coz you're always in a rush. And you don't like your van to get wet.

8. Speed limits are for pooftahs, women and Deux Chevaux drivers.

9. On motorways, or anywhere where you can do over thirty, never keep your distance. Stick to the vehicle in front of you and look as intense as you can. (How long was it since you last saw *Rollerball*? Good film, that.)

10. The patrol car and the emergency services are your friends. When the flashing sirens start up, take your chance to follow that vehicle! Extra glee can be garnished by forcing a prat in a Peugeot 205 onto the pavement.

11. When taking a short-cut through residential areas, don't worry if a set of parked cars allow only one-way traffic – burn on through and make the other car reverse back. This tactic can do wonders for your time sheet!

12. Never worry about keeping in lane. You know where you're going even if no one else does. Back to the pub as soon as you knock off!

"The inferno of the living is not something that will be; if there is one, it is what is already here, the inferno where we live every day, that we form by being together. There are two ways to escape suffering it. The first is easy for many: accept the inferno and become such a part of it that you can no longer see it. The second is risky and demands constant vigilance and apprehension: seek and learn to recognise who and what, in the midst of the inferno, are not inferno, then make them endure, give them space."
Italo Calvino, *Invisible Cities*, Secker and Warburg Ltd. 1974

SUBMIT

The role of FUSE is to probe the possibilities of new forms of language by promoting typographic innovation and confusion. We welcome your input - please write to FUSE at the address below, remembering to enclose an SAE/IRC where appropriate.

CONTACT

FUSE is published quarterly and distributed through the FontShop network. FUSE follows themes that question the effects of digital technology, attempting to open up its possibilities to see where that leaves us in the Binary Universe. Each FUSE is published in a limited edition - reserve a copy by contacting the FontShop in your area.

KURZPARKZONE

FUSE fonts do not always include a full set of upper and lower case characters; nor does every font cover a full range of accents and special characters. FUSE fonts are experimental typefaces that should be extended by users... abuse is part of the process. (Turn a blind eye?).

CABIN DOORS TO MANUAL!

FUSE 9 includes a bonus font

autofuse

ISSUE 9 - Spring 1994
Editor & text: Jon Wozencroft
Design by John Critchley @ Neville Brody Studio
Published & © 1994 FSI GmbH
Typefaces & posters © their designers

FSI, Bergmannstraße 102, Berlin 61

FUSE editorial:
Unit 2 White Horse Yard,
78 Liverpool Road, London N1 0QD
Fax +44 (71) 704 2447

AUTO
autogenous

F TV27HorizontalNormal

I designed *F TV27HN* for the 1992 FUSE Award held in Belgium. I won. It's based on the shapes from a macro-photo taken off a television set: 27, because it is based on a 9*3 grid; horizontal, because the shapes are horizontal. Normal because.

F A26

After designing several typefaces for specific purposes, where maximum legibility was of paramount importance, I felt it would be both fun and a challenge to respond to a brief which required a different approach.

F A26 ends up looking like an alien set of abstract heiroglyphics. The characters are more 'found' than invented and are based on the set of mandatory and warning signs on the UK's road system, designed in 1963 to conform with the protocol proposed by the United Nations World Conference on Road and Motor Transport, held in Geneva in 1949.

Basically, upper-case characters point up and lower-case characters point down. The cropped circles and triangles act as ligatures between characters, which can be adjusted individually, set solid or letter-spaced according to taste.

Drawing *F A26* (by hand) has literally taken a month of Sundays. I am grateful for Richard Doust's technical expertise in translating my specification into a digital format and to John Critchley for his help. I am now convinced that I am missing out on magical time-saving technical know-how.

F Metal

Following the theme of AUTO, I came across the word 'autogenous', meaning self-produced, produced in the same organism and welding (by melting edges together without adding different material). This idea of welding together became the initial key to the font's development. Since I do not possess a computer, the font had to be drawn up by hand prior to the digitising process. I kept it as simple as possible whilst also keeping the idea of sliding metal plates in mind.

F Metal offers the user a multiple choice of parts for each letterform, with the surrounding space as important as the letterform itself. Once the basic parameters were established, I refined the ideas after suggestions from Jon Wozencroft and John Critchley in London. Ideally I wanted to produce each letterform so that it had a graduated dissolve within its shapes, enabling each character to slide out of and over its surrounding 'plates'. This proved to be technically not possible. Instead, I followed the idea of interlocking parts – a kind of abstract mosaic could be generated. The characters have been split into their component parts – positive in upper-case, negative in lower-case.

F Currency

The typeface was borne from a very simple reading of the brief. Random circular selections were extracted from overlapped sans serif and scripts. I like the new tensions created by strictly imposing this formal pattern on some rather emotive calligraphy - a machine finish to manual mark-making.

Mario Beernaert

Born in 1971. Currently studying Graphic Design in St. Lucas, Ghent (in Belgium, the creative desert) after four years of Informatics. I haven't done much of interest yet in graphic design, I'm just starting. I'm working with Cloaca Maxima; our logo is a chicken. I saw Jungle Book yesterday and my next typeface will be called 'Tarzan'. Too bad there's no chicken in it.

Margaret Calvert

Born in South Africa in 1936. Studied Illustration at Chelsea School of Art from 1953 to '57. Joined Jock Kinnear as an assistant designer in 1958 working principally on lettering and signage systems for Gatwick Airport; Britain's new motorways, 1961; the UK's all-purpose roads, 1963; British Rail; British Airports; and the Tyne and Wear Metro in 1981.

Margaret Calvert now works independently and since 1966 she has taught at the Royal College of Art in London, where from 1987 to '89 she was Head of Graphic Design and Acting Course Director from 1989 to '91. She is a member of the Alliance Graphique Internationale.

Russell Mills

Since graduating from the Royal College of Art in 1977 with an MA degree, Russell Mills has worked extensively in many areas, especially those related to the music industry. He has produced numerous record covers for amongst others Brian Eno, David Sylvian, Youssou N'Dour, etc. He has made many book covers, images for editorial, magazine and corporate bodies, stage sets and lighting designs for contemporary dance and rock musicians, video and environmental installations.

He has lectured in art colleges and architectural schools in Europe, America and Japan. His paintings have been exhibited in numerous solo and group shows in the UK, USA, Japan, Germany, France and Denmark. He currently lives and works near Ambleside in Cumbria, the English Lake District.

Vaughan Oliver

Born 1957. Studied Graphic Design, specialising in Illustration at Newcastle-Upon-Tyne under Terry Dowling, who exposed me to his photographs of East European shop-front typography. Touched but not fully comprehending, I was further inspired by the lettering on a Quay Brothers film poster, seen during their college visit. Otherwise missed the History of Typography lectures and was later left to furthering my interest through practical experience, designing drink labels at a packaging design company in London, and through an intuitive and eclectic taste. Today I'm a freelance art director/designer working in the music business, television, publishing and theatre, looking forward to my first interior design commission from France and a personal retrospective exhibition in Los Angeles in September. This project has been my debut with digital technology (partially used) and I might even consider using it again in 1994.

F A26

F Metal

F TV27HN

F Currency

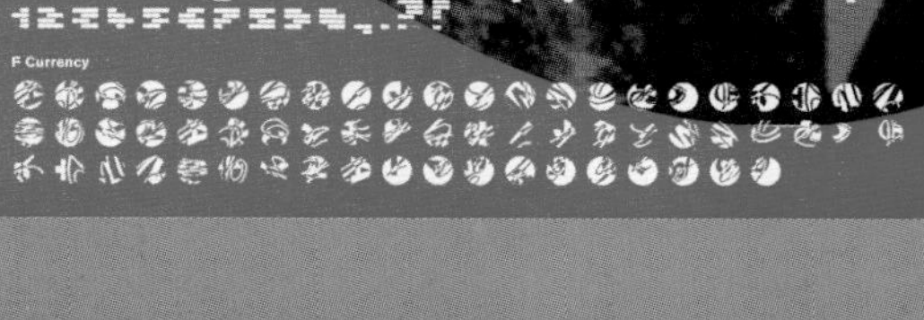

Traffic levels have increased by 50% in a decade. The average speed for cars travelling across London is 10 miles per hour, back to the rate of coach and horses. In spite of lead-free petrol, city centres are now so polluted that asthma has become a common affliction, like tuberculosis during the Nineteenth Century. The car, ultimate symbol of autonomy and mobility, refuge of individualism, is not only slowly poisoning us physically - its transition from liberator to suffocator highlights a series of other degradations, notably in the realm of communications, factors that should be taken into account as new and invisible traffic systems are constructed to transport information.

Traffic of any description causes stress. Stress causes violence. Freedom of movement is no different from freedom of speech, and when this is denied, extremism follows fast behind. Caught between the extremes of the old and their imminent redundancy as a result of the new are the capital's dispatch runners, the Van Driver Gangs.

For armed terrorists, the oxygen of publicity is pretty easy to tap into, it's there in print, breathing down your breakfast. But if you haven't yet made it on to the superhighway of digital nirvana, the powers that be have made it even more difficult. These days, you have to break through the police cordon that surrounds the City of London to intercept IRA bombers. *Will the bombers get through?*

Kidnaps, shootings, bombings and hijacks will always be seized upon as the blockbusters of media life. It's a publicity world alright, so it stands to reason that a whole host of aspirant terrorists out there, gasping for their share of O_2. Sure, they work to deadlines. Yes, they're vicious and shouldn't be apprehended by the general public. Of course they want their freedom. They're everywhere, in every city. Driving their vans.

We've heard a lot of talk recently about the violence in society. Most of it comes from the press and TV, oh how butter wouldn't melt in their mouths. "The Public Interest", the loving concern of it all. But there's seldom been any mention of these vicious breeds who, every day, jump in their cabs, tuck *The Sun* onto the dashboard and drive across town or country delivering their dodgy merchandise and rip-off services to whosoever will have them. The TNT vans, bought up by Murdoch to get past the picket lines, spreading their viral loads. The Parcelforce posse, metal chariots festooned with a logo that makes the BT redesign seem like a masterpiece (just imagine - having to drive around in a £61 mill' set-up that makes you the laughing stock of your mates. Just think how many curries, cans of Tennants Extra Strength Lager and videos you could rent out for that!). The Parcelforcers are backed up by their sidekicks, the red Royal Mail mob, for whom wanton harrassment is as natural as tea with 4 sugars. The Telecom vans, not wanting to look yellow, will never leave their sheds without at least two layers of grime on their gear. As accomplices, they can call on the British Gas gazzas who, having been briefed by the boys, dig up the roads and leave elaborately laid traps that enable the Van Gangs to cut up, confound and antagonise the unsuspecting motorist (and what about the poor pedestrian, forced to play hopscotch through the plethora of "exciting new developments" that make the capital's housing crisis on a par with the litter problem). "British Gas is sorry for any inconvenience caused whilst these essential repairs are carried out" which, roughly translated, means "Fuck You". You never know what jam will appear next on your route. What you *do* know is that the Van Gang make everyday stress seem like a week off in the Carribean.

What about those clamping trucks? Not really vans, them, but nasty, decked out in Police chequers as if they had something to prove. Why do *they* get a licence to terrorise? Arseholes. Then there are the loners, today's urban outlaws who leave few clues as to their identity beyond perhaps an unmanned telephone number in Leytonstone or a half-erased builder's address in Sydenham - you should be so fortunate. But in today's city centres the motorcycle messengers are taking over, bloody hooligans, packed up at the front by the lights, or zooming past you when you're stuck waiting for the jam to clear. [illegible]

[illegible]" they tell you on the radio. Don't make me laugh, I'm gonna be sick. Nonetheless, it makes the old crew a dying breed. The Escorts. The Bedfords. The Commers. (Now it's all Renaults and Nissan trucks, bloody foreign rubbish).

So spare a thought for the "serial killers" who must suffer the M25 orbital on a daily basis. They ride hard, they ride rough, 'coz they ain't got a lot to lose. Ten-year-old gear with buckled sides and heavy-dented bumpers, vans once painted white, but boy they've taught the Telecom crew a thing or two in their time. They like a lot of grime with their crime.

Van heraldry, of course. Maybe they'll come up with a great one-liner (usually having looked for inspiration in their daily paper). "Suck my Dick" and "Bollocks" are two big favourites with these boxed-up lotharios. Pretty erotic, eh? In between looking for hapless Mini-Metro drivers unsure whether to turn left, right or keep going, they will leer out of their cabs at any female pedestrian who's within earshot and punctuate their dribbles with such Shakespearean sonnets as "Whoah" and "Koor, yorledo-orrite". After all, there's not a lot of sex in Sydenham.

And anyway, who needs literacy when you've got such a powerful means of expression at your disposal? So you have to get wise to the van tactics, and read all the small print. First lesson - forget the Highway Code was ever invented and take a crash course in the current power gen, the OUT-OF-MY-WAY Code. Bear in mind the following if you're going to have any chance of survival on the pot-holed High Roads of London Town. So here we go. Here we go. If yer lucky. If you don't end up wrapped round a lamp-post.

1. Never give way - ever. If you're soft it means you've got a small knob.

2. Ignore the traffic lights for up to 5 seconds after they change red. Jump 'em at full speed. This is always likely to cause mortal panic on the face of any GTi driver. After all, you don't have to worry about the insurance, some other bugger will cough up. It's already costing old GTi and arm and a leg, and he'll be quite keen to keep the two he has left.

3. On approaching any T-junction, ignore the dotted lines and protrude into the oncoming traffic as far as you can. Don't forget your motto is *"Make Them Brake"*. The oncoming driver is forced to let you through. Only acknowledge if you're feeling close to some, over generous, and not still suffering the effects of the skinful you had the night before.

4. In any queue of single file traffic (usually caused by a parked comrade-in-van on a double yellow line, or, more promising still, by an imminent contraflow system on the motorway - don't you just luv 'em? - always ignore the approaching obstruction and overtake as many cars as possible, butting in at the top with a malevolent bodycheck. If faced with a disturbed look from your victim, prove to him/her that you never stood a chance in English CSE.

5. If you've got a drop to make, or fancy a bet on the 3.15 at Chepstow, don't worry if there's nowhere to park. Stop in the road. Get out. Cause a tailback. Make the bastards wait.

6. Never indicate. If you want to do a sharp right turn across the oncoming traffic, have no fear. Keep them guessing what you'll do next.

7. Don't even think of bothering to stop for pedestrians at a zebra crossing. Accelerate and give 'em a face full of fumes. Especially if they're pushing a pram, or carrying heavy shopping. So what if it's raining. 'Coz you're *always* in a rush. And you don't like your van to get wet.

8. Speed limits are for pooftahs, women and Deux Chevaux drivers.

9. On motorways, or anywhere where you can do over thirty, never keep your distance. Stick to the vehicle in front of you and look as intense as you can. (How long was it since you last saw *Rollerball*? Good film, that).

10. The Patrol car and the emergency services are your friends. When the flashing sirens start up, take your chance to follow that vehicle! Extra glee can be garnished by forcing a prat in a Peugeot 205 onto the pavement.

11. When taking a short cut through residential areas, don't worry if a set of parked cars allow only one-way traffic - bum on through and make the other car reverse back. This tactic can do wonders for your time sheet!

12. Never worry about keeping in lane. You know where you're going even if no-one else does. Back to the pub as soon as you knock off!

They're not all as hard-hearted as you make out, the Van Driver Gangs, they're not all a bunch of artery-clogged maniacs. What about the taxi drivers? Have you seen the fogs of black shit that come out of their exhausts when they're on the move? What about the bleeding buses?

To say nothing of the juggernauts burning down Holloway Road as if they've *not* seen a gents toilet for a week. Remember, the longer the vehicle, the shorter the temper. Why try to save a minute on your journey by taking a year off your life? Perhaps I'll give it a go. Who can blame us. It's not much of a life.

In fact, all this lot are being increasingly challenged by another more elite breed of OUT-OF-MY-WAY devotees, the company carcasses sat plushly seated in their BMWs and Range Rovers, or, God help them, a Ford Sierra. The pillocks. Car phone on standby, ready at any moment to waste away more time on the expense account lunch hour (the English language being so economical in such matters - lunch-half-the-working-day just doesn't have the same ring to it). Have to stop off to see a man about new garden furniture? No problem. For this lot, no worry about parking tickets - the company can pay. Clamped? Bit of a bugger, we'll travel by taxi. Besides, it's not much hassle if you belong to a Clamp-Club. So you have to remember that behind every Van Driver Gang, there's your Numero Uno, and yes, the big boys know a pay rise when they see one. Post Office, Gas, Telecom, the Leccy lads, all that driving for the end of day privilege of drinking overpriced piss on the premises of some other monopoly. Is it any wonder? Is it any wonder? *Is it any wonder?*

Well I reckon it's quite simple really. If someone's gonna have a go at me, I'm not gonna sit there like some soft prick at an orgy. I'll give as good as I get. But *I* have to do this for a living, the roads are chocka, and it's not my fault the tubes are like cattle trucks. Who do they think I am, the UN Peacekeeping Force?

So what do you think about this new fad, young waistrels coming up to you at the lights and smothering your windscreen with soap? How they get away with it Lord only knows. But have you noticed, they never bother the Van Gang, and we've got the dirtiest windows of the lot. They wouldn't bloody dare. We'd give 'em a 2p bit up the arse. More likely, we'd jump the lights, run 'em down, and they could go and compare notes with the bikers in ward 7. It gets even more depressing when you think that they'd all jump at the chance of holding down a job like ours, up there in the driving seat, world at their feet. Well, the 071 area at the very least.

And the average motorist you have to share the circuit with, getting as bad as you are, are they not, and hardly inspirational if it comes to that? *Do* me a favour. Those back-window stickers like "My other car's a Porsche". Dickheads. "Honk if you bonked last night". Fat chance. Worst of all are those blatant philanthropists who stick a red nose on their front grille and leave it there for the year's duration as a proud advert of the fact that they once gave a few quid to charity. True, a lot of our lot do that too. But what can you say? Not a lot.

And speaking of adverts, now we get to the nub of it, the nitty gritty, if you get my drift. I'm a family man after all, and with that lot going out shopping every hour God sends, telling me about the Special Offers as soon as I get in, well there's no bloody respite. It's one wind-up after another. Just think of the amount of frigging billboards the Van Gang have to go through, the monotony of seeing the same ones over and over again, day-in, day out, day-in, day out, as you go about your duties.

Meant to be in Whitechapel in 15 minutes. More bloody roadworks in Pancras Road. Advert after advert telling me what to think.

Well you can piss off.
Bastard.

NO ONE TELLS ME WHAT TO DO WHEN I'M IN MY VAN!

JOHN CRITCHLEY @ NEVILLE BRODY STUDIO & JON WOZENCROFT EDITORIAL POSTER

They're not all as hard-hearted as you make out, the Van Driver Gangs, they're not all a bunch of artery-clogged maniacs. What about the taxi drivers? Have you seen the fogs of black shit that come out of their exhausts when they're on the move? What about the bleeding buses?

To say nothing of the juggernauts burning down Holloway Road as if they've not seen a gents toilet for a week. Remember, the longer the vehicle, the shorter the temper. Why try to save a minute on your journey by taking a year off your life? Perhaps I'll give it a go. Who can blame us. It's not much of a life.

In fact, all this lot are being increasingly challenged by another more elite breed of OUT-OF-MY-WAY devotees, the company carcasses sat plushly seated in their BMWs and Range Rovers, or, God help them, a Ford Sierra. The pillocks. Car phone on standby, ready at any moment to waste away more time on the expense account lunch hour (the English language being so economical in such matters – lunch-half-the-working-day just doesn't have the same ring to it). Have to stop off to see a man about new garden furniture? No problem. For this lot, no worry about parking tickets – the company can pay. Clamped? Bit of a bugger, we'll travel by taxi. Besides, it's not much hassle if you belong to a Clamp-Club. So you have to remember that behind every Van Driver Gang, there's your Numero Uno, and yes, the big boys know a pay rise when they see one. Post Office, Gas, Telecom, the Leccy lads, all that driving for the end of day privilege of drinking overpriced piss on the premises of some other monopoly. Is it any wonder? Is it any wonder? *Is it any wonder?*

Well I reckon it's quite simple really. If someone's gonna have a go at me, I'm not gonna sit there like some soft prick at an orgy. I'll give as good as I get. But *I* have to do this for a living, the roads are chocka, and it's not my fault the Tubes are like cattle trucks. Who do they think I am, the U.N. Peacekeeping Force?

So what do you think about this new fad, young wastrels coming up to you at the lights and smothering your windscreen with soap? How they get away with it Lord only knows. But have you noticed, they never bother the Van Gang, and we've got the dirtiest windows of the lot. They wouldn't bloody dare. We'd give 'em a 2p bit up the arse. More likely, we'd jump the lights, run 'em down, and they could go and compare notes with the bikers in ward 7. It gets even more depressing when you think that they'd all jump at the chance of holding down a job like ours, up there in the driving seat, world at their feet. Well, the 071 area at the very least.

And the average motorist you have to share the circuit with, getting as bad as you are, are they not, and hardly inspirational if it comes to that? *Do* me a favour. Those back-window stickers like "My other car's a Porsche". Dickheads. "Honk if you bonked last night". Fat chance. Worst of all are those blatant philanthropists who stick a red nose on their front grille and leave it there for the year's duration as a proud advert of the fact that they once gave a few quid to charity. True, a lot of our lot do that too. But what can you say? Not a lot.

And speaking of adverts, now we get to the nub of it, the nitty gritty, if you get my drift. I'm a family man after all, and with that lot going out shopping every hour God sends, telling me about the Special Offers as soon as I get in, well there's no bloody respite. It's one wind-up after another. Just think of the amount of frigging billboards the Van Gang have to go through, the monotony of seeing the same ones over and over again, day in, day out, day in, day out, as you go about your duties.

Meant to be in Whitechapel in 15 minutes. More bloody roadworks in Pancras Road. Advert after advert telling me what to think.

Well you can piss off.

Bastard.

No one tells me what to do when I'm in my van!

FUSE 9: Neville Brody Bonus Font Autosuggestion

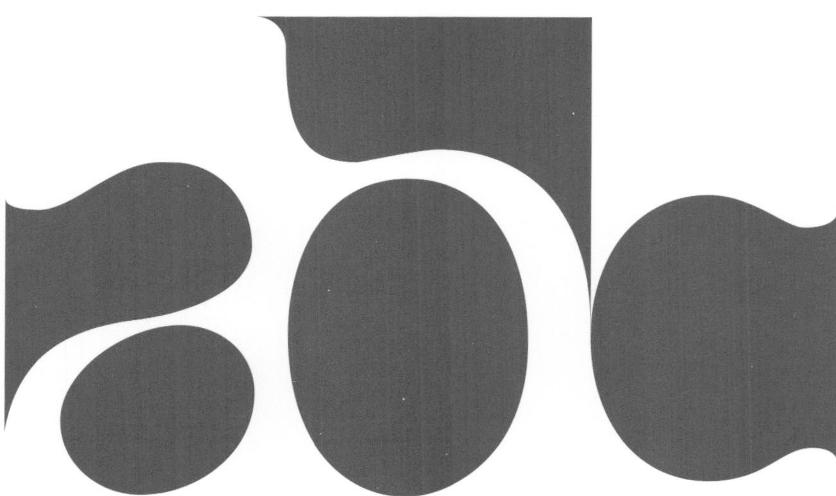

NEVILLE BRODY ISSUE POSTER

FUSE 9: **Vaughan Oliver** Currency

The typeface was born from a very simple reading of the brief. Random circular selections were extracted from overlapped sans serif and scripts. I like the new tensions created by strictly imposing this formal pattern on some rather emotive calligraphy – a machine finish to manual mark-making.

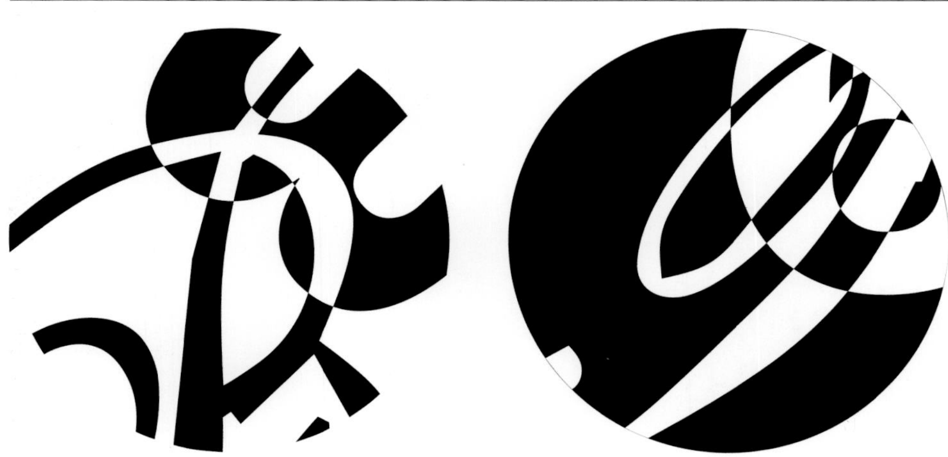

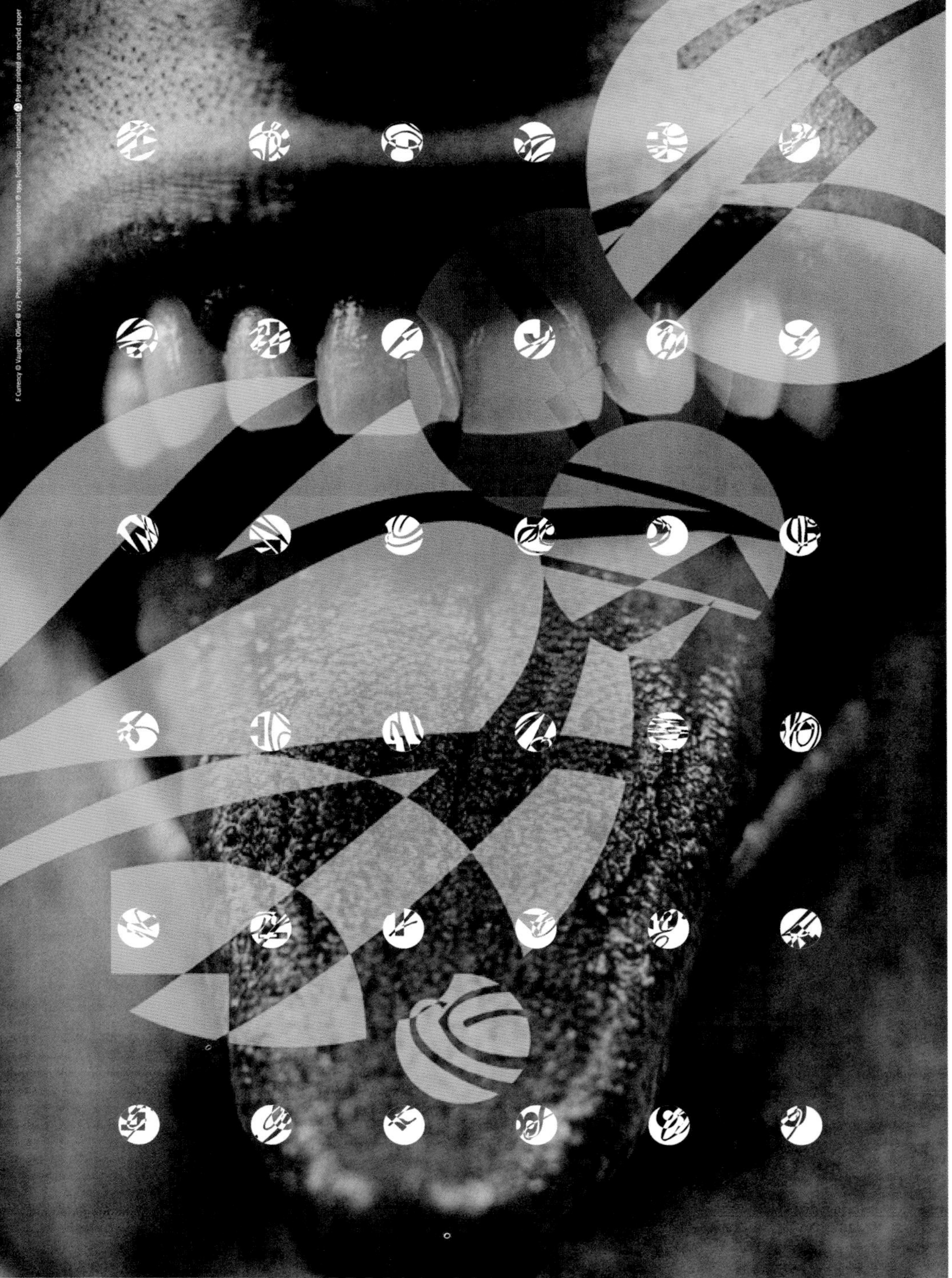
F Currency © Vaughan Oliver © v23 Photograph by Simon Larbalestier © 1994 FontShop International Poster printed on recycled paper

FUSE 9: **Margaret Calvert** A26

After designing several typefaces for specific purposes, where maximum legibility was of paramount importance, I felt it would be both fun and a challenge to respond to a brief which required a different approach. *A26* ends up looking like an alien set of abstract hieroglyphics. The characters are more 'found' than invented and are based on the set of mandatory and warning signs on the U.K.'s road system, designed in 1963 to conform with the protocol proposed by the United Nations World Conference on Road and Motor Transport, held in Geneva in 1949. Basically, upper-case characters point up and lower-case characters point down. The cropped circles and triangles act as ligatures between characters, which can be adjusted individually, set solid or letter-spaced according to taste. Drawing *A26* (by hand) has literally taken a month of Sundays. I am grateful for Richard Doust's technical expertise in translating my specification into a digital format and to John Critchley for his help. I am now convinced that I am missing out on magical time-saving technical know-how.

Margaret Calvert © 1994 FontShop International Poster printed on recycled paper

FUSE 9: **Russell Mills** Metal

Following the theme of AUTO, I came across the word 'autogenous', meaning self-produced, produced in the same organism and welding (by melting edges together without adding different material). This idea of welding together became the initial key to the font's development. Since I do not possess a computer, the font had to be drawn up by hand prior to the digitising process: I kept it as simple as possible whilst also keeping the idea of sliding metal plates in mind. *Metal* offers the user a multiple choice of parts for each letterform, with the surrounding space as important as the letterform itself. Once the basic parameters were established, I refined the ideas after suggestions from Jon Wozencroft and John Critchley in London. Ideally I wanted to produce each letterform so that it had a graduated dissolve within its shapes, enabling each character to slide out of and over its surrounding 'plates'. This proved to be technically not possible. Instead, I followed the idea of interlocking parts – a kind of abstract mosaic could be generated. The characters have been split into their component parts – positive in upper-case, negative in lower-case.

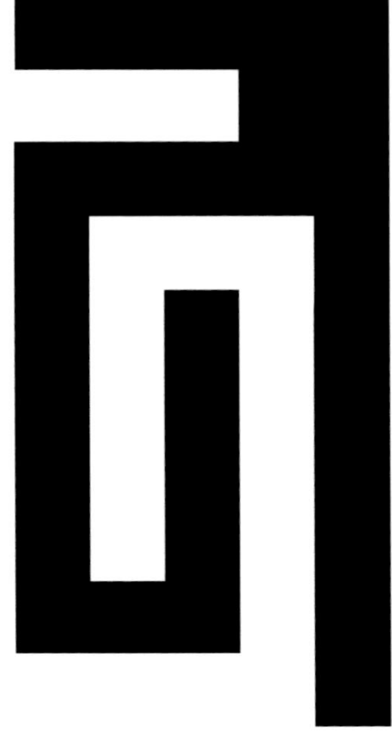

FUSE 9: Mario Beernaert TV27HorizontalNormal

I designed *TV27HorizontalNormal* for the 1992 FUSE Award held in Belgium. I won. It's based on the shapes from a macro-photo taken off a television set; 27, because it is based on a 9x3 grid; horizontal, because the shapes are horizontal. Normal because.

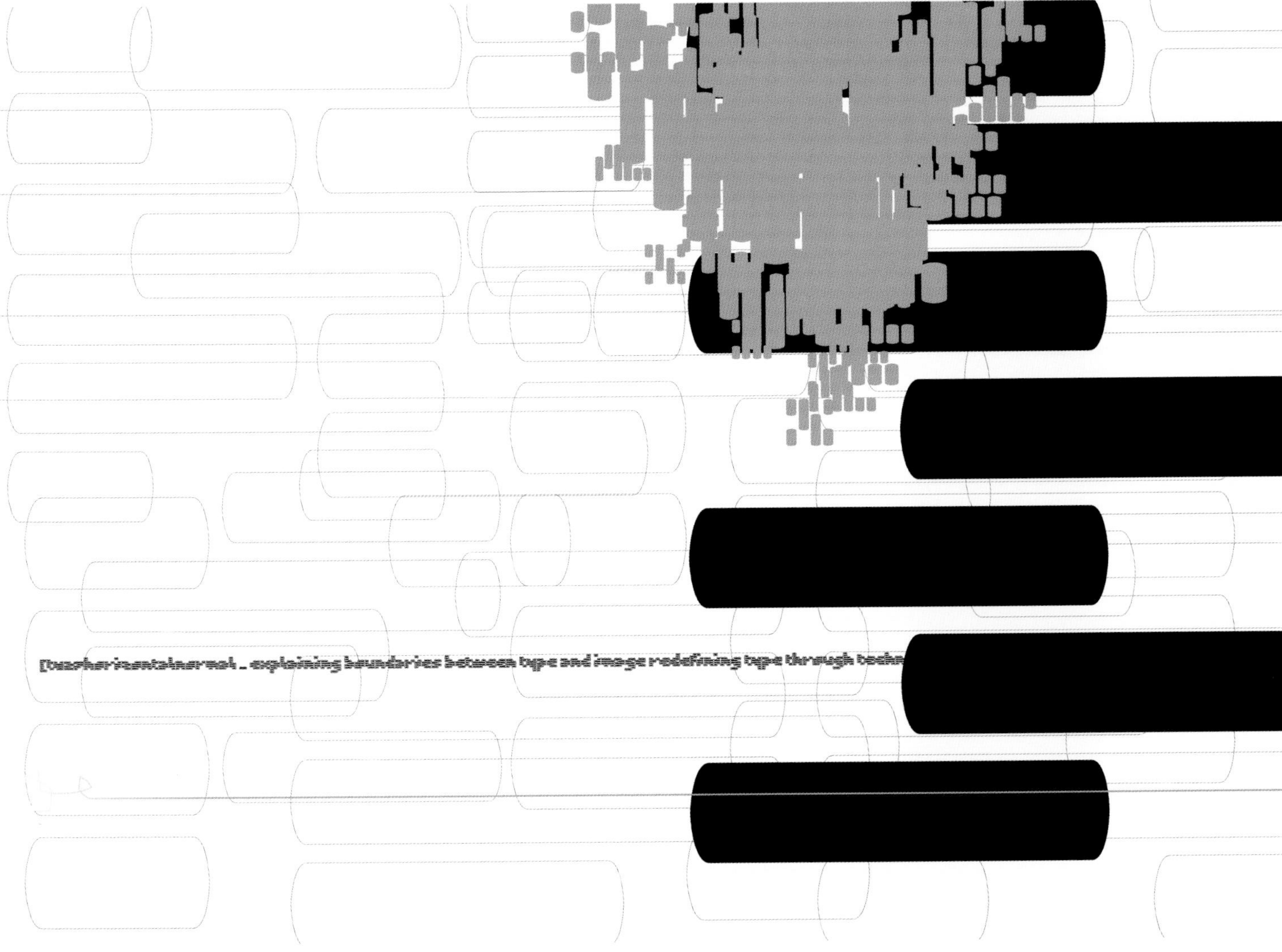
explaining boundaries between type and image redefining type through

FUSE 10: Freeform: A Trojan Horse Jon Wozencroft

FUSE

SUMME

FREEFORM

In the first edition of FUSE, published in May 1991, we called for "a new sensibility in visual expression, one grounded in ideas, not just image". As a response to the wealth of choices afforded by digital typography, many designers have fixed upon the choice of typeface to carry their designs, and FUSE fonts have been a convenient and low-cost means of making an impression. Just as the first sequence of FUSE publications has been based around the transformation of typographic traditions – the question of legibility as applied to the electronic word, the collision of meaning with the need for visual impact, the implications of the digital code upon our use of language... – so has the project quickly collected a fresh cargo of classifications. This is to be expected. Now it is time for the next step, and with a new question comes a new set of tools.

For some time we have been talking about our intention to create an outlet that uses the keyboard more as a musical instrument or palette of colours, and not to restrict its potential to the endless refinement, sophistication or abstraction of Roman letterforms. The metaphor is only a metaphor to the extent that the elements contained within are of course physically soundless. The bandwidth of digital technology nonetheless demands that we leap across these self-imposed borders of expression, and try to find ways of using language that carry the possibilities of new technology along with us, not as is so often the case, with us trailing behind as the language environment is automated, beyond the reach of our touch.

Freeform is a version of a painting by Kandinsky placed alongside an old portrait or landscape, or a score by John Cage played in the Royal Albert Hall in 1948. It takes the language of Mallarmé, James Joyce, William Burroughs, and asks *what would such new writing look like now?* If "language is a virus", then *Freeform* is an antidote to our current complacency as regards the written word.

Type designers developed the sans serif as a response to the dawn of the first machine age. *Freeform* is an impulse that connects to the optical nerve net of cyberspace, whilst rooted in the primary convergence of magic, art and writing.

FUSE 10: Reading Typography Writing Language **Paul Elliman**

"Before people spoke with one another they communicated". Ed Rosenfeld, *Real Time*, Picador 1973.

(26 notes for the introductory essay of a new typewriter manual for computer users.)

1. The Alphabet forms a lifecode of literacy.

2. Thousands of typefaces have emerged since printing was invented – STRANGE TYPE, there is none. Type personifies a routine, all its variations stick close to this theme, i.e. to embody the tyranny of language with a *token* of permanence in an ocean of irregularity. A typeface relies on just two characteristics: *graphetics*, its physical properties, and *graphology*, its expressive qualities. The graphetic aspects of the alphabet have survived the massive historical transition from *reed* to *electronic pulse*, but any dialogue between typography and language seems to have been lost. 'As the Gutenberg typography filled the world the human voice closed down.'[1234567]

3. Even less probable: EXPERIMENTAL TYPE. Although there may be some experimentation with type. (For example legibility is often challenged; a text is obscured perhaps to make a point about literacy: we could say it is difficult to read because *reading is difficult*... touché.) A determined enquiry into, say, the conditions of writing might result in a strategy to empower/enable a typeface with an objective, critical position on language. The problem remains that typography not only supports the artificial structuring of language, it exists for it.

4. A typeface extends the communicative function of the printed word, but only in the same limited way as writing when it functions as an extension, replacement or representation of voice. It comes with no guarantee of *meaning* or the understanding of *presence* (cf. Derrida). It operates in a *silent space* (cf. Ong). A typeface is a new body for a voice long out of its speaker's body, committed to words but indifferent to the language of words, and further estranged from the language of voice. In every language typography provides a service to speech patterns it doesn't even understand.

5. Space is to writing what sound is to speech, the place where it happens. The alphabet is an attempt to phoneticise writing: to imbue it with the *possibility* of gestural presence. Alphabetic typography was, along with cartography, painting, cosmology and physics, swept up by the new wave of 15th-century graphic expression. Inspired by Leonardo and Dürer, and taking the capital letters inscribed on Rome's Trajan column AD 114 as the model of typographic perfection, the printer-publisher-typographers of the Renaissance, among them Aldus Manutius and Luca Paccioli in Venice, Geoffrey Tory and Simon de Colines in Paris, fixed the shape of the alphabet to the foundations of a universal literacy.

6. *Officina Plantinia*, 16th-century printshop and type foundry established in Antwerp by Christopher Plantin, survives intact as the Plantin-Moretus Museum. A breathtaking monument (maybe mausoleum) to typography, but also to the double-edged sword of progress. Workshops such as this brought typography out of the abbey scriptorium. Its punch-makers determined the shape of the modern letter and in doing so systematised language in the service of the state, the church and colonial *fury*. Books might signify learning – foremost they represent power and the luxury of thought (thereby its control).

7. Between the 16th and 19th century, there were few changes in typographic form but a great deal happening in the wake of literacy, from Milton and the freedom of the press, to the Enlightenment and the philosophies of reason. Even the Industrial

If reality, as we recognise it, is confined to the limits of language, typography co-operates by fixing words with a surrogate, redesigned presence, affirmed by the most recognised word in the world: Coke, logo/logos, the typographically enhanced *real thing*.

Revolution did little for typography, but its emphasis on a market economy and the technocratic state delivered mechanised type to the portable computer. In a stage as important to language as both the alphabet's invention and Gutenberg's movable type, typography now moves from the *secular* to the *specular*, as language, the mapping of human experience, sets its own course through virtual worlds. The term typography, a relief printing technique associated with religious codices and the Spanish Inquisition, has become a misnomer in the liquid televisual language of the bitstream.

8. With little or no knowledge of history, contemporary type designers and computer users can easily put a face to the names of Claude Garamond, Christopher Plantin, William Caslon, John Baskerville, Giovanbattista Palatino, Pierre Simon Fournier, François Didot, Giambattista Bodoni etc. Big deal: In the accumulation of time it can be seen that typography puts a face to anything. We should be concerned to distinguish between our design and *the design of our past*.

Language is a Sensation

9. The story of typography is inseparable from the story of language, and its evolution spills through the vascular bundle of humanity's progress. From the first Phoenician alphabet of 22 wedge-shaped, cuneiform characters launched on the banks of the Mediterranean to emerge as Aramaic and Hebrew alphabets, typography was borne between the twin notions of *authorial* and *authority*, in the form of the Scriptures. The Bible, the Koran and Sanskrit, the holy language of India, gave form to the communication of sacramental power, and in the transformation of letters by typographic decoration, writing became a sacred act: intended to preserve the word of God.

10. The 24-character Greek alphabet, containing upper- and lower-case letters, formed the basis of the 19-letter Roman system of the 3rd century BC, inscribed in stone by chisel and gravure. Christianity, surviving the fall of the Holy Roman Empire, maintained both the form of classical writing and the theosophical belief in language as a boundary for human experience.

11. Scribal monks, the first specialist typographers, fixed the anonymous link between writing and reading: they wrote out texts that they had not originated. For 1000 years, from the scriptorium of every abbey, manuscripts were produced, helping Western civilisation to consolidate religious power, restricting reality to the realm of language.

12. The monk designers were trained and employed to 'copy', their creativity centred on the origination of calligraphic letterforms. With goose quill pens, lead pencils and brushes, the Roman letters, based on fonts produced in Italian foundries, were laid down along pre-marked lines using compasses, rulers and set squares. As well as communicating the sacred content of the text, the alphabet with its classical symmetry conveyed ideals of authority and perfection.

13. By the end of the 12th century, scribal art shifted away from the control of the church and books were produced covering a variety of subjects. Scribal workshops appeared, followed by universities where scholars copied the writings of classic Latin authors. The alphabet, a specific writing system requiring very few symbols, enabled the invention of movable type to transform the world. Gutenberg's letterpress, which could simulate handwriting, revolutionised book production and typography, although many scribes resisted printing for much the same reason that publishers today fear the flow of electronic ink. Printed books were banned from many libraries of the late Middle Ages.

14. Unserifed monoline 'Grotesques' appeared in the early 19th century. Homer's 'winged words', having been tamed by writing, now found their letters clipped. Industrial Age type designers reduced the Roman system to its basic skeletal form – a statement of modernist intent that reinforced the significance of the Roman letter. The classical shape was determined largely by the tools of its making: straight-edged, chisel-cut strokes, gliding pen curves, flat brush 'serifs'. This is the basis of our technical understanding and visual recognition of the individual letters, the quads, cross-bars and finials, stems and terminals, tension between counter and mass, the play of loops, lifts and curves, the variable sizes, weights and widths, *the spaces, the separation, the cut off, the void.*

15. The special resonance of letter shapes, and their correlation within the construction of words, gives form to the textile of western script and obscures, by typography, the role of the alphabet, the primary text that intervenes to obstruct or expand the possibilities and nature of text, and therefore of language. Could there ever be a typeface that overtly expressed the implications of the alphabet? What qualities would an experimental font need to even demonstrate a dialogue between the alphabet and our language?

16. ... font X, an invitation to read but not, for once, to write. Analphabet, of broken parts, which, in deference to Plato and the classical dignity of oral language, ought to be named (also because it's a construction of things we rarely bother to call by name, they have no label because they are rarely commercial): escutcheons, grommets, core-winding, curtain weights, coins, stones, buttons, a rubber washer, a pozi-drive, a u-bolt, an o-ring, links, bottle-tops, cup hooks, clamps, trims, sealers, clips, brackets, found sweets, lost keys...

17. A *found font* of almost letters, a dysfunctional community that refuses language, and, before we log(os) on to the digital server stream, mocks the postscript type specialists. Assembled from pieces of metal, stone, polypropylene, zintec; things you don't want to put back in your mouth, it salutes and bids farewell to the Florentine scholars and the first Roman fonts, and is at last readable: Analphabet, an alphabet by auto-suggestion.

Reading, Typography, Writing, Language

18. In the early 1960s, novelist and critic Philippe Sollers established an influential group around the literary magazine *Tel Quel. Tel Quelists* believed in the transformation of society through the 'original revolutionary power' of language, and, citing key 19th

Including fonts by: **Neville Brody, ?, John Critchley, Tobias Frere-Jones, Cornel Windlin, Jon Wozencroft** **Freeform FUSE 10**

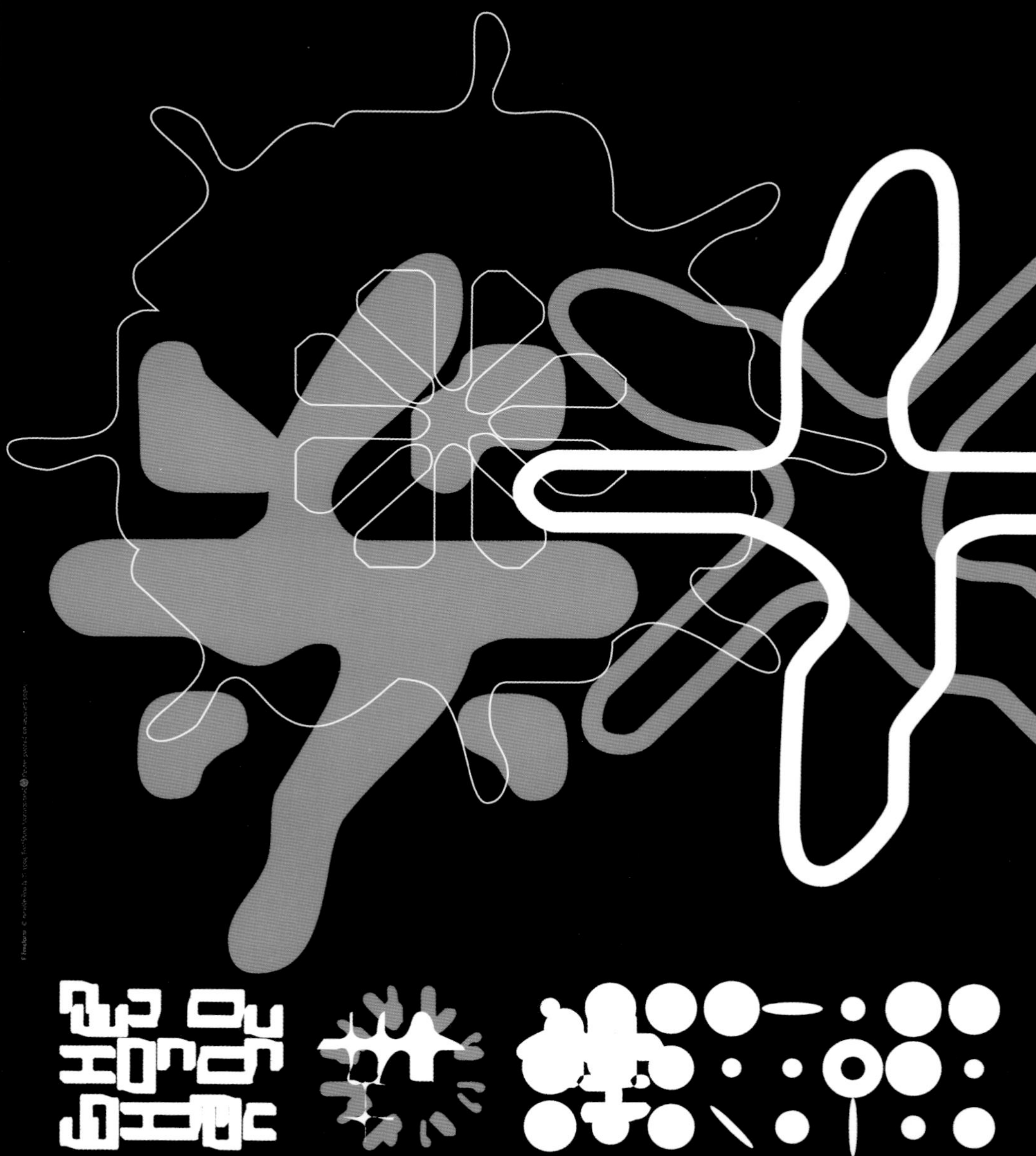

FontShop Austria (0222) 523 29 46 Fax (0222) 523 2947-22 FontShop Benelux (09) 220 65 98 (09) 220 67 25 (09) 221 32 08 Fax (09) 220 34 45 FontShop Canada MAC: 1-800-36-FONTS PC: 1-800-46-FONTS Fax 416-593-4318
FontShop France (1) 43 06 92 30 Fax (1) 43 06 54 85 FontShop Germany (030) 69 58 95 Fax (030) 692 88 65 FontShop Italy (02) 7010 0555 Fax (02) 7010 0585 FontShop Switzerland (044) 3 26 26 Fax (044) 3 26 27
FontWorks UK (071) 490 5390 (071) 490 2002 Fax (071) 490 5391 FontShop US MAC: 1-800-36-FONTS PC: 1-800-46-FONTS Fax 416-593-4318

JON WOZENCROFT EDITORIAL POSTER FEATURING PAUL ELLIMAN

A SENSE OF TYPOGRAPHIC BRUTALISM

F Freeform The font comes as a set of five – the first is comprised of abstract shapes and forms that are positioned on the keyboard according to intended relationships. For example, cap "E" and lower-case "e", cap "F" and lower-case "f" give two springboards into combinations that I have only just started to explore myself. There are 2500 kerning pairs on *Freeform One*, so that each shape has a special interactive relationship with every other shape. The second font is made up of a family of related, I would say organic forms that provide the basis for a more distinct range of contrasts. *Three*, *Four* and *Five* use dot forms of varying sizes and weights… explore as you like, the possibilities are endless. *Freeform is frightening!*

Neville Brody is currently working on a new FontShop International series, *Dirty Faces*, a mid-point between FontFont and *FUSE*. Recent font releases have included *Harlem*, *Tokyo* and *World*. His next project is to create a CD-ROM version of *The Graphic Language of Neville Brody 2*.

F Mutoid The keyboard contains a series of interchangeable body parts – heads, legs and torsos – which can be combined to form a collection of 'mutant' figures. Create your own creature!

John Critchley graduated from Manchester Polytechnic in 1990 and after a brief spell at The Designers Republic in Sheffield, joined Neville Brody Studios where he works on a variety of projects including *FUSE*. Other fonts include *Childs Play*, a series based on childrens' handwriting.

F Fibonacci If you took a typeface and subtracted the alphabet, what would remain? Fibonacci takes written language and boils it down to an interlaced mass: each character has been replaced by fragments of the Golden Section, with weights and orientation dictated by the Fibonacci Series. With the alphabet subtracted, all that remains is the grid, the "grammar" of the system.

The character elements extend in all directions, meshing with each immediate neighbour. Orthogonal treatments are stored in the cap positions, diagonals in the lower-case, and curved sections in figures 0-9. As context changes meaning (both in written and verbal language), each 'character' changes according to its surroundings.

Tobias Frere Jones Born in New York in 1970, graduated from the Rhode Island School of Design in 1992. He is currently working as a senior type designer for The Font Bureau, Inc. in Boston. Previous designs include *Dolores* (FontFont) *Garage Gothic*, *Nobel*, *Cafeteria*, *Reiner Script*, *Stereo*, *Interstate*, *Epitaph*, *Armada* (at the Font Bureau) and *Reactor* (*FUSE 7*).

He relaxes by banging on sheet metal with a sledgehammer, and enjoys chewing on styrofoam.

F Atomic Circle like the braille alphabet is based on a simple encoding of dots within a given area, in this case a circle and its periphery. If you look at the system, it is surprisingly easy to decipher – the dots are always at the place of the eyes in conventional capital letters. The lower-case characters are formally identical to the capitals: the dots, however, are empty. For a better display, the characters are orientated by a dividing line.

Sylke Janetsky 24 years old, born in Neuss and still living there. After leaving school I worked in several theatres in Neuss and Cologne. At present I am studying graphic design – *Atomic Circle* was the result of a student *FUSE* project.

F Robotnik I wanted to find a set of shapes that was not going to be too freeform and not too personal. I have become wary of instant funkiness and inbuilt grunginess. Instead I tried to define cold and technical shapes that only by experimenting and combining and through composition would reveal their potential. They are shapes that always fascinated me and because of *FUSE* I finally managed to make a font of them. I hope *Robotnik* will serve as inspiration; the set can easily be extended. Some of the icons are devoid of meaning, some of them exist in the real world, yet are graphically such strong symbols, I would like to see them out of context in print or on screen. (Also, I have included a new and improved character "e" for my earlier *FUSE 3* font *Moonbase Alpha*, situated on key position 'shift 2', which can be copied into the old font file to create *Moonbase Beta*!).

Cornel Windlin After 5 years in London working for, amongst others, Neville Brody Studios and *The Face*, I am currently running my own studio in Zürich. Recently I have done work for Peter Gabriel, NTT Data Corporation, Museum für Gestaltung Zürich and Kunsthaus Zürich.

Issue 10 – Summer 1994
Editor & text by Jon Wozencroft
26 Notes… by Paul Elliman
℗ & © 1994 FSI GmbH
Typefaces and posters © their designers

FSI, Bergmannstraße 102, Berlin 61

FUSE Editorial:
Unit 2, Whitehorse Yard, 78 Liverpool Road, London N1 0QD. Fax: + 44 (71) 704 2447.

FUSE

FREEFORM A TROJAN HORSE

In the first edition of *FUSE*, published in May 1991, we called for "a new sensibility in visual expression, grounded in ideas, not just image". As a response to the wealth of choices afforded by digital typography, many designers have fixed upon the choice of typeface to carry their designs, and *FUSE* fonts have been a convenient and low-cost means of making an impression. Just as the first sequence of *FUSE* publications has been based around the transformation of typographic traditions – the question of legibility as applied to the electronic word, the collision of meaning with the need for visual impact, the implications of the digital code upon our use of language… – so has the project quickly collected a fresh cargo of classifications. This is to be expected. Now it is time for the next step, and with a new question comes a new set of tools.

For some time we have been talking about our intention to create an outlet that uses the keyboard more as a musical instrument or palette of colours, and not to restrict its potential to the endless refinement, sophistication or abstraction of Roman letterforms. The metaphor is only a metaphor to the extent that the elements contained within are of course physically soundless. The bandwidth of digital technology nonetheless demands that we leap across these self-imposed borders of expression, and try to find ways of using language that carry the possibilities of new technology along with us, not as is so often the case, with us trailing behind as the language environment is automated, beyond the reach of our touch.

Freeform is a version of a painting by Kandinsky placed alongside an old portrait or landscape, or a score by John Cage played in The Royal Albert Hall in 1948. It takes the language of Mallarmé, James Joyce, William Burroughs, and asks *what would such new writing look like now*? If "language is a virus", then *Freeform* is an antidote to our current complacency as regards the written word.

Type designers developed the sans serif as a response to the dawn of the first machine age. *Freeform* is an impulse that connects to the optical nerve net of cyberspace, whilst rooted in the primary convergence of magic, art and writing.

1. 29th May 1994.

2. David Diringer, *The Alphabet – A Key to the History of Mankind*, [illegible] 1948 (see page 22).

3. Alfred Kallir, *Sign and Design*, James Clarke & Co. 1961.

F Restart © Jon Wozencroft © 1994 FontShop International ® Poster printed on recycled paper

F Restart According to the *Independent On Sunday*[1], there were 2300 articles about the Internet published in the UK press during the first nine months of 1993. Of those that I read, all described the Net's digital intercourse as a breakthrough in communications, a dramatic reversal of its originally designed purpose – as an emergency channel that could be used by the US military in the event of a nuclear strike and communication breakdown. Likewise, in the wider context of urban alienation, dislocation, fear of crime etc., cyberspace is proclaimed as a digital nirvana, but once again, the zone is less an open field, more an enclave.

The Internet system has all the immediacy of a phone line, yet it does not demand your immediate response, with the additional benefit that you need never fit a face to its owner's words, nor guage a tone of voice, even if Net users have quickly devised a symbolic replacement in the form of newly-organised punctuation marks (phonetics > pictogram); the written word, both back to basics, yet somehow starved of oxygen. The avowedly more direct and open exchange of information, opinions, and feelings comes about due to the total suppression of the physical self.

Language in cyberspace can be freely contorted, the traditional brake-system of social embarrassment having been removed from the picture, this quality only to be replaced and relocated through the invention of cringe-inducing jargon such as "geek", "flonk" and "moo". Back to the nursery, in effect, the linguistic terms imposed by cyberspace – the Frame, defined as a frontier without limits – grants us a second childhood as far as communicative possibilities are concerned, though such is the requirement that technology sophisticate the circuitry of language that it is tempting to take this extension as being proof of improvement. Never mind the quality, feel the width…

So the motivation behind *Restart* is very simple; why not go all the way? First consideration – what might have happened to our language had the post-war bomb really been dropped, devastating the human race, stripping down the tools of language to a physical, not a digital fundamentalism? Where man had to go in search of water, shelter, food and real human contact, rather than niche-advice and e-mail. How could you be sure that *anyone* was out there? So, assuming that the Roman alphabet in this event would be an instant passport to exclusion, something far more archetypically human is needed.

This was a good opportunity to develop two templates that have intrigued me for the past five years. The first is an ancient sign language from Mas d'Azil, Southern France, belonging to the middle Stone Age, made up of river pebbles painted with peroxide of iron, dots and lines that no expert can fit an explanation to. The shapes and their arrangement is distinctly elemental, and I was intrigued by the idea that a recordable language could be both functionally abstract and directly meaningful: the utopia of a universally appropriate tool-kit! You can see this pebble language in David Diringer's book[2] – some of the elements of *Restart* are facsimiles, though the majority have been redrawn (initially by hand) with the present tense in mind.

Walking down the Charing Cross Road some years ago, I came across a book I had never heard of, nor seen word of since, that dropped its own bombshell into my preconceptions about language. The premise of Alfred Kallir's *Sign and Design*[3] is simple enough – that the alphabet is no more than a procreational device, its every letter based on a symbol of fertility and sexuality. The book investigates the aphabet not simply as an informational code, but as a psychogenetic force. Taking the premise that the past 2000 years have flattened out, if not removed the matriarchal core of language (we still, nevertheless, refer to our 'mother tongue'), *Restart* is an attempt to reconsider these terms. My main preoccupation in drawing *Restart* was not to experiment with the possibility of a 'pure', abstract aesthetic, but to try to focus this sexual and sensual energy, free of the clutter of sexual politics. Distinctly non-techno, expressively soft (even clumsy), the font has a surprising range of combinations that I hope are both powerful and simple. *Restart* might be used as a call-sign, as if it were a post-urban marking, a logo against logocentricity.

READING TYPOGRAPHY WRITING LANGUAGE

PAUL ELLIMAN

"Before people spoke with one another they communicated." Ed Rosenfeld, *Real Time*, Picador 1973.

(26 NOTES FOR THE INTRODUCTORY ESSAY OF A NEW TYPEWRITER MANUAL FOR COMPUTER USERS.)

1. The Alphabet forms a lifecode of literacy.

2. Thousands of type faces have emerged since printing was invented – STRANGE TYPE, there is *none*. Type personifies a routine, all its variations stick close to this theme, ie. to embody the tyranny of language with a *token* of permanence in an ocean of irregularity. A Typeface relies on just two characteristics: *graphetics*, its physical properties, and *graphology*, its expressive qualities. The graphetic aspects of the alphabet have survived the massive historical transition from *reed* to *electronic pulse*, but any dialogue between typography and language seems to have been lost. 'As the Gutenberg typography filled the world the human voice closed down.' [illegible]

3. Even less probable: EXPERIMENTAL TYPE. Although there may be some experimentation with type. (For example legibility is often challenged; a text is obscured perhaps to make a point about literacy: we could say it is difficult to read because *reading is difficult*… touché). A determined enquiry into, say, the conditions of writing might result in a strategy to empower/enable a type face with an objective, critical position on language. The problem remains that typography not only supports the artificial structuring of language, it exists for it.

4. A type face extends the communicative function of the printed word, but only in the same limited way as writing when it functions as an extension, replacement or representation of voice. It comes with no guarantee of *meaning* or the understanding of *presence*. (cf. Derrida). It operates in a *silent space*. (cf. Ong). A type face is a new body for a voice long out of its speaker's body, committed to words but indifferent to the language of words, and further estranged from the language of voice. In every language Typography provides a service to speech patterns it doesn't even understand.

5. Space is to writing what sound is to speech, the place where it happens. The alphabet is an attempt to phoneticize writing: to imbue it with the *possibility* of gestural presence. Alphabetic typography was, along with cartography, painting, cosmology, and physics, swept up by the new wave of 15th century graphic expression. Inspired by Leonardo and Dürer, and taking the capital letters inscribed on Rome's Trajan column AD 114 as the model of typographic perfection, the printer-publisher-typographers of the Renaissance, among them Aldus Manutius and Luca Paccioli in Venice, Geoffrey Tory and Simon de Colines in Paris, fixed the shape of the alphabet to the foundations of a universal literacy.

6. *Officina Plantinia*, 16th century printshop and type foundry established in Antwerp by Christopher Plantin, survives intact as the Plantin-Moretus Museum. A breathtaking monument (maybe mausoleum) to typography, but also to the double edged sword of progress. Workshops such as this brought typography out of the abbey scriptorium. Its punchmakers determined the shape of the modern letter and in doing so systematised language in the service of the state, the church and colonial *fury*. Books might signify learning – foremost they represent power and the luxury of thought (thereby its control).

7. Between the 16th and 19th century, there were few changes in Typographic form but a great deal happening in the wake of literacy, from Milton and the freedom of the press, to the Enlightenment and the philosophies of reason. Even the Industrial Revolution did little for typography, but its emphasis on a market economy and the technocratic state delivered mechanised type to the portable computer. In a stage as important to language as both the alphabet's invention and Gutenberg's movable type, typography now moves from the *secular* to the *specular*, as language, the mapping of human experience, sets its own course through virtual worlds. The term typography, a relief printing technique associated with religious codices and the Spanish Inquisition, has become a misnomer in the liquid televisual language of the bit-stream.

8. With little or no knowledge of history, contemporary type designers and computer users can easily put a face to the names of Claude Garamond, Christopher Plantin, William Caslon, John Baskerville, Giovanbattista Palatino, Pierre Simon Fournier, François Didot, Giambattista Bodoni etc. Big deal: in the accumulation of time it can be seen that typography puts a face to anything. We should be concerned to distinguish between our design and *the design of our past*.

LANGUAGE IS A SENSATION

9. The story of typography is inseparable from the story of language, and its evolution spills through the vascular bundle of humanity's progress. From the first Phoenician alphabet of 22 wedge-shaped, cuneiform characters launched on the banks of the Mediterranean to emerge as Aramaic and Hebrew alphabets, typography was borne between the twin notions of *authorial* and *authority*, in the form of the Scriptures. The Bible, the Koran and Sanskrit, the holy language of India, gave form to the communication of sacramental power, and in the transformation of letters by typographic decoration, writing became a sacred act: intended to preserve the word of God.

10. The 24 character Greek alphabet, containing upper and lower case letters, formed the basis of the 19 letter Roman system of the 3rd century BC, inscribed in stone by chisel and gravure. Christianity, surviving the fall of the Holy Roman Empire, maintained both the form of classical writing and the theosophical belief in language as a boundary for human experience.

11. Scribal monks, the first specialist typographers, fixed the anonymous link between writing and reading: they wrote out texts that they had not originated. For 1000 years, from the scriptorium of every abbey, manuscripts were produced, helping Western civilization to consolidate religious power, restricting reality to the realm of language.

12. The Monk designers were trained and employed to 'copy', their creativity centred on the origination of calligraphic letter forms. With goose quill pens, lead pencils and brushes, the Roman letters, based on fonts produced in Italian foundries, were laid down along pre-marked lines using compasses, rulers, and set squares. As well as communicating the sacred content of the text, the alphabet with its classical symmetry conveyed ideals of authority and perfection.

13. By the end of the 12th century, scribal art shifted away from the control of the church and books were produced covering a variety of subjects. Scribal workshops appeared, followed by universities where scholars copied the writings of classic Latin authors. The alphabet, a specific writing system requiring very few symbols, enabled the invention of movable type to transform the world. Gutenberg's letterpress, which could simulate handwriting, revolutionised book production and typography, although many scribes resisted printing for much the same reason that publishers today fear the flow of electronic ink. Printed books were banned from many libraries of the late Middle Ages.

14. Unserifed monoline 'Grotesques' appeared in the early 19th century. Homer's 'winged words', having been tamed by writing, now found their letters clipped. Industrial-age type designers reduced the Roman system to its basic skeletal form – a statement of modernist intent that reinforced the significance of the Roman letter. The classical shape was determined largely by the tools of its making: straight-edged, chisel cut strokes, gliding pen curves, flat brush 'serifs'. This is the basis of our technical understanding and visual recognition of the individual letters, the quads, cross-bars and finials, stems and terminals, tension between counter and mass, the play of loops, lifts and curves, the variable sizes, weights and widths, *the spaces, the separation, the cut off, the void*.

15. The special resonance of letter shapes, and their correlation within the construction of words, gives form to the textile of western script and obscures, by typography, the role of the alphabet, the primary text that intervenes to obstruct or expand the possibilities and nature of text, and therefore of language. Could there ever be a typeface that overtly expressed the implications of the alphabet? What qualities would an experimental font need to even demonstrate a dialogue between the alphabet and *our* language?

16. …font X, an invitation to read but not, for once, to write. Analphabet, of broken parts, which, in deference to Plato and the classical dignity of oral language, ought to be named (also because its a construction of things we rarely bother to call by name, they have *no* label because they are rarely commercial): escutcheons, grommets, core-winding, curtain weights, coins, stones, buttons, a rubber washer, a pozi-drive, a u-bolt, an o-ring, links, bottle-tops, cup hooks, clamps, trims, sealers, clips, brackets, *found* sweets, lost keys…

17. A *found font* of almost letters, a dysfunctional community that refuses language, and, before we log(os) on to the digital server stream, mocks the postscript type specialists. Assembled from pieces of metal, stone, poly-propaline, zintec: things you don't want to put back in your mouth. It salutes and bids farewell to the Florentine scholars and the first Roman fonts, and is at *last readable*: Analphabet, an alphabet by auto-suggestion.

READING, TYPOGRAPHY, WRITING, LANGUAGE

18. In the early 1960s, novelist and critic Philippe Sollers established an influential group around the literary magazine *Tel Quel*. *Tel Quelists* believed in the transformation of society through the 'original revolutionary power' of language, and, citing key 19th century writers including Mallarmé and Lautréamont, they tried to show how certain radical ideas were subtlety erased from society, and that official language is, ultimately, a means to assert official thought.

19. Contributors to *Tel Quel* pursued the idea that a text has a number of possible readings and therefore no fixed meaning. In severing the link between *authorial* intention and textual *authority*, one can reveal ways in which the reading of a text changes any 'apparent' meaning.

20. By subverting our two most important perceptual codes, the visible and the verbal, the full significance of typography is revealed in the space between what a text says and what it looks like. Nothing demonstrates the myth of neutral technology or focuses the disparity between function and form better than the alphabet.

21. Language emerges from mouths and typography… it is transported by people and by printing. The social life of Typography is such that objects of everyday use become defined through the application of type, and as models they are equally able to convey the dynamics of history, anthropology, linguistics, political science, sociology, economics and so on. If reality, as we recognise it, is confined to the limits of language, typography co-operates by fixing words with a *surrogate*, redesigned presence, affirmed by the most recognised word in the world: Coke, logo/logos, the typographically enhanced *real thing*.

22. The Alphabet is the ultimate cargo cult.

23. Gaps opened up by a technological shift in society encourage new approaches, themes can be developed, not by continually pointing out what is already there, but by targeting the spaces, by addressing the problems, the failings, potential for change, correction, progress and so on. Derrida suggests that our obsession with form derives from a failure or reluctance to keep up with the momentum of 'force', his term for the energy of presence.

24. With the new electronic media, real-time communication at your fingertips, typography finds itself involved in the application of a revised grammatology, the science of writing, of which its theoretical nature, testing the line between thought and language, is explored in the work and ideas of Jacques Derrida, Marshall McLuhan, Walter J. Ong, George Steiner and others, from Harold Innis, McLuhan's teacher and mentor, to Ongian theories about literacy and orality applied to Michael Heim's study of electronic word processing. What is proposed by these ideas, and largely confirmed by digital technology, is a renewal of writing beyond the authority of any official language, or at least a release from its service. For *type-writing* it's the beginning of a messy, cryptic, stutteringly expressive grammatography, based on a firmer alliance between letters and writing.

25. Abcdefghijklmnopqrstuvwxyzzzzzzzzzzz. Typography, sleeping.

26. 1. Marshall McLuhan, *The Gutenberg Galaxy – The Making of Typographic Man*, Routledge & Kegan Paul 1962 2. Jacques Derrida, *Of Grammatology*, Baltimore 1976 3. George Steiner, *Language and Silence*, Faber & Faber 1967 4. Walter J. Ong, *Orality and Literacy – The Technologizing of the Word*, Methuen 1982 5. Michael Heim, *Electric language – A Philosophical Study of Word Processing*, Yale University Press 1987 6. Harold Innis, *The Bias of Communication*, University of Toronto Press 1951 7. Philippe Sollers, *Writing and the Experience of Limits*, [illegible] 1974.

century writers including Mallarmé and Lautréamont, they tried to show how certain radical ideas were subtly erased from society, and that official language is, ultimately, a means to assert official thought.

19. Contributors to *Tel Quel* pursued the idea that a text has a number of possible readings and therefore no fixed meaning. In severing the link between *authorial* intention and textual *authority*, one can reveal ways in which the reading of a text changes any 'apparent' meaning.

20. By subverting our two most important perceptual codes, the visible and the verbal, the full significance of typography is revealed in the space between what a text says and what it looks like. Nothing demonstrates the myth of neutral technology or focuses the disparity between function and form better than the alphabet.

21. Language emerges from mouths and typography... it is transported by people and by printing. The social life of Typography is such that objects of everyday use become defined through the application of type, and as models they are equally able to convey the dynamics of history, anthropology, linguistics, political science, sociology, economics and so on. If reality, as we recognise it, is confined to the limits of language, typography co-operates by fixing words with a surrogate, redesigned presence, affirmed by the most recognised word in the world: Coke, logo/logos, the typographically enhanced *real thing*.

22. The Alphabet is the ultimate cargo cult.

23. Gaps opened up by a technological shift in society encourage new approaches, themes can be developed, not by continually pointing out what is already there, but by targeting the spaces, by addressing the problems, the failings, potential for change, correction, progress and so on. Derrida suggests that our obsession with form derives from a failure or reluctance to keep up with the momentum of 'force', his term for the energy of presence.

24. With the new electronic media, real-time communication at your fingertips, typography finds itself involved in the application of a revised grammatology, the science of writing, of which its theoretical nature, testing the line between thought and language, is explored in the work and ideas of Jacques Derrida, Marshall McLuhan, Walter J. Ong, George Steiner and others, from Harold Innis, McLuhan's teacher and mentor, to Ongian theories about literacy and orality applied to Michael Heim's study of electronic word processing. What is proposed by these ideas, and largely confirmed by digital technology, is a renewal of writing beyond the authority of any official language, or at least a release from its service. For type-writing it's the beginning of a messy, cryptic, stutteringly expressive grammatography, based on a firmer alliance between letters and *writing*.

25. *Abcdefghijklmnopqrstuvwxyzzzzzzzzzzzz. Typography, sleeping.*

26. 1. Marshall McLuhan, *The Gutenberg Galaxy – The Making of Typographic Man*, Routledge & Kegan Paul 1962 **2.** Jacques Derrida, *Of Grammatology*, Baltimore 1976 **3.** George Steiner, *Language and Silence*, Faber & Faber 1967 **4.** Walter J. Ong, *Orality and Literacy – The Technologizing of the Word*, Methuen 1982 **5.** Michael Heim, *Electric language – A Philosophical Study of Word Processing*, Yale University Press 1987 **6.** Harold Innis, *The Bias of Communication*, University of Toronto Press 1951 **7.** Philippe Sollers, *Writing and the Experience of Limits*, Yale University Press 1974

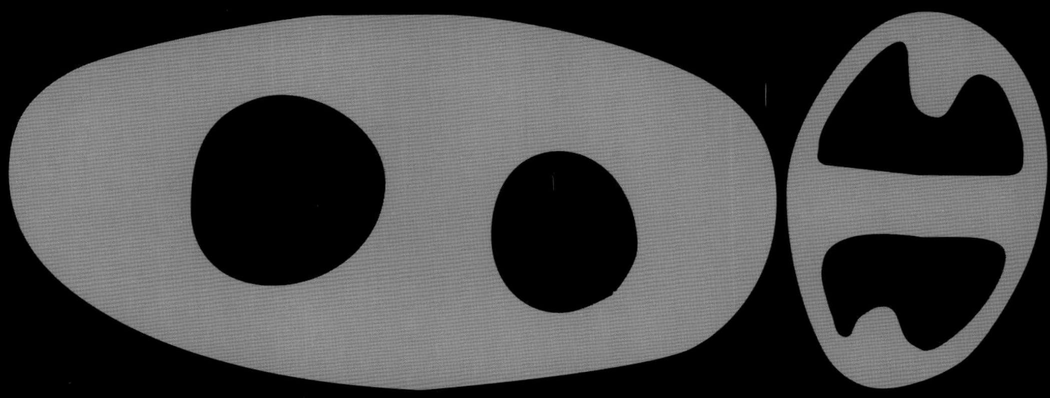

FUSE 10: Jon Wozencroft Restart

According to the *Independent On Sunday*,[1] there were 2300 articles about the Internet published in the U.K. press during the first 9 months of 1993. Of those that I read, all described the Net's digital intercourse as a breakthrough in communications, a dramatic reversal of its originally designed purpose – as an emergency channel that could be used by the U.S. military in the event of a nuclear strike and communication breakdown. Likewise, in the wider context of urban alienation, dislocation, fear of crime etc., cyberspace is proclaimed as a digital nirvana, but once again, the zone is less an open field, more an enclave.

The Internet system has all the immediacy of a phone line, yet it does not demand your immediate response, with the additional benefit that you need never fit a face to its owner's words, nor gauge a tone of voice, even if Net users have quickly devised a symbolic replacement in the form of newly-organised punctuation marks (phonetics > pictogram): the written word, both back to basics, yet somehow starved of oxygen. The avowedly more direct and open exchange of information, opinions and feelings comes about due to the total suppression of the physical self.

Language in cyberspace can be freely contorted, the traditional brake-system of social embarrassment having been removed from the picture, this quality only to be replaced and relocated through the invention of cringe-inducing jargon such as "geek", "flonk" and "moo". Back to the nursery. In effect, the linguistic terms imposed by cyberspace – the Frame, defined as a frontier

What might have happened to our language had the post-war bomb really been dropped, stripping down the tools of language to a physical, not a digital fundamentalism: a search for water, shelter, food and real human contact, rather than niche-advice and e-mail. How could you be sure that *anyone* was out there?

without limits – grants us a second childhood as far as communicative possibilities are concerned, though such is the requirement that technology sophisticate the circuitry of language that it is tempting to take this extension as being proof of improvement. Never mind the quality, feel the width...

So the motivation behind *Restart* is very simple: why not go all the way? First consideration – what might have happened to our language had the post-war bomb really been dropped, devastating the human race, stripping down the tools of language to a physical, not a digital fundamentalism? Where man had to go in search of water, shelter, food and real human contact, rather than niche-advice and e-mail. How could you be sure that *anyone* was out there? So, assuming that the Roman alphabet could be an instant passport to exclusion, something far more archetypically human is needed.

This was a good opportunity to develop two templates that have intrigued me for the past five years. The first is an ancient sign language from Mas d'Azil, Southern France, belonging to the middle Stone Age, made up of river pebbles painted with peroxide of iron, dots and lines that no expert can fit an explanation to. The shapes and their arrangement is distinctly elemental, and I was intrigued by the idea that a recordable language could be both functionally abstract and directly meaningful: the utopia of a universally appropriate tool-kit! You can see this pebble language in David Diringer's book[2] – some of the elements of *Restart* are facsimiles, though the majority have been redrawn (initially by hand) with the present tense in mind.

Walking down the Charing Cross Road some years ago, I came across a book I had never heard of, nor seen word of since, that dropped its own bombshell into my preconceptions about language. The premise of Alfred Kallir's *Sign and Design*[3] is simple enough – that the alphabet is no more than a procreational device, its every letter based on a symbol of fertility and sexuality. The book investigates the alphabet not simply as an informational code, but as a psychogenetic force. Taking the premise that the past 2000 years have flattened out, if not removed the matriarchal core of language

JON WOZENCROFT EDITORIAL FONT POSTER RESTART

(we still, nevertheless, refer to our 'mother tongue'), *Restart* is an attempt to reconsider these terms. My main preoccupation in drawing *Restart* was not to experiment with the possibility of a 'pure', abstract aesthetic, but to try to focus this sexual and sensual energy, free of the clutter of sexual politics. Distinctly non-techno, expressively soft (even clumsy), the font has a surprising range of combinations that I hope are both powerful and simple. *Restart* might be used as a call-sign, as if it were a post-urban marking, a logo against logocentricity.

Reference:

1. 29th May 1994 **2.** David Diringer, *The Alphabet – A Key to the History of Mankind*, Hutchinson's 1948 (see page 22) **3.** Alfred Kallir, *Sign and Design*, James Clarke & Co. 1961

FREEFORM ONE

FREEFORM TWO

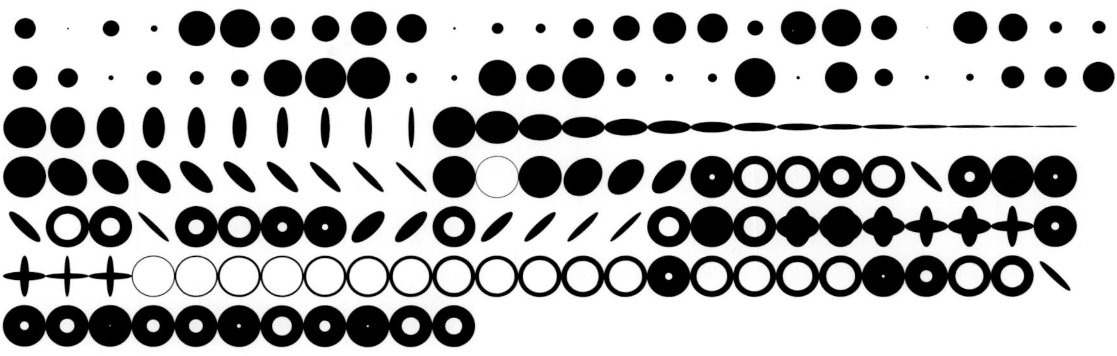

FREEFORM THREE

FUSE 10: Neville Brody Bonus Font Freeform

The font comes as a set of five – the first is comprised of abstract shapes and forms that are positioned on the keyboard according to intended relationships. For example, cap 'E' and lower-case 'e', cap 'F' and lowercase 'f' give two springboards into combinations that I have only just started to explore myself. There are 2500 kerning pairs on *Freeform One*, so that each shape has a special interactive relationship with every other shape. The second font is made up of a family of related, I would say organic forms that provide the basis for a more distinct range of contrasts. *Three, Four* and *Five* use dot forms of varying sizes and weights... explore as you like, the possibilities are endless, *Freeform is frightening!*

FREEFORM FOUR

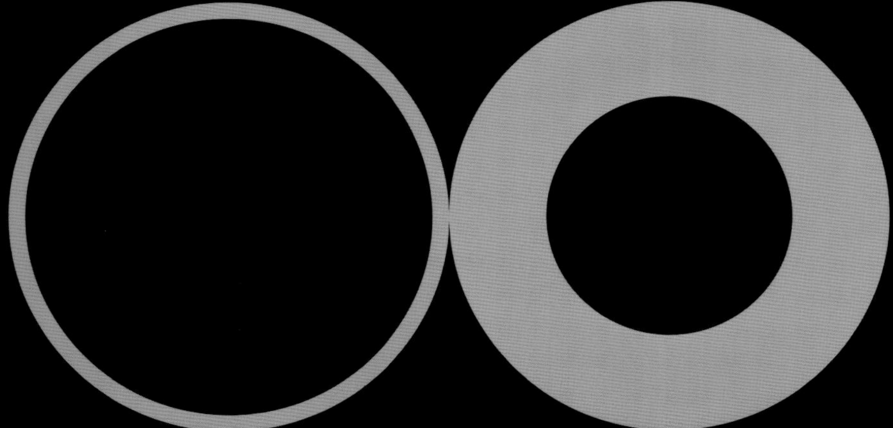

FUSE 10: John Critchley Mutoid

The keyboard contains a series of interchangeable body parts – heads, legs and torsos – which can be combined to form a collection of 'mutant' figures. Create your own creature!

F Mutoid © John Critchley © 1994 FontShop International Poster printed on recycled paper

FUSE 10: Tobias Frere-Jones Fibonacci

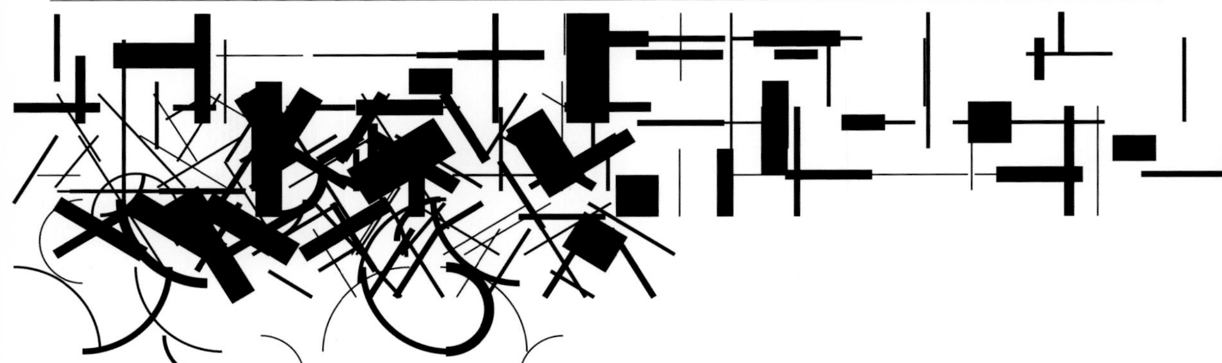

If you took a typeface and subtracted the alphabet, what would remain? *Fibonacci* takes written language and boils it down to an interlaced mass: each character has been replaced by fragments of the Golden Section, with weights and orientation dictated by the Fibonacci Series. With the alphabet subtracted, all that remains is the grid, the essential "grammar" of the system.

The character elements extend in all directions, meshing with each immediate neighbour. Orthogonal treatments are stored in the cap positions, diagonals in the lower-case, and curved sections in figures 0–9. As context changes meaning (both in written and verbal language), each 'character' changes according to its surroundings.

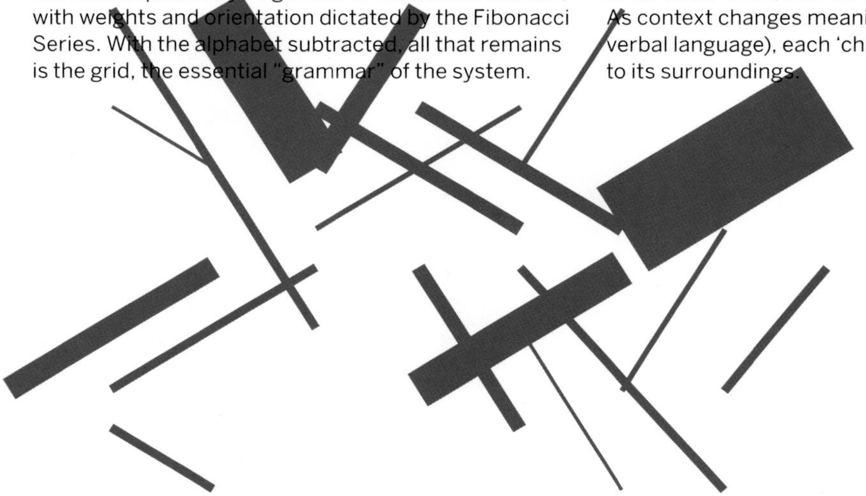

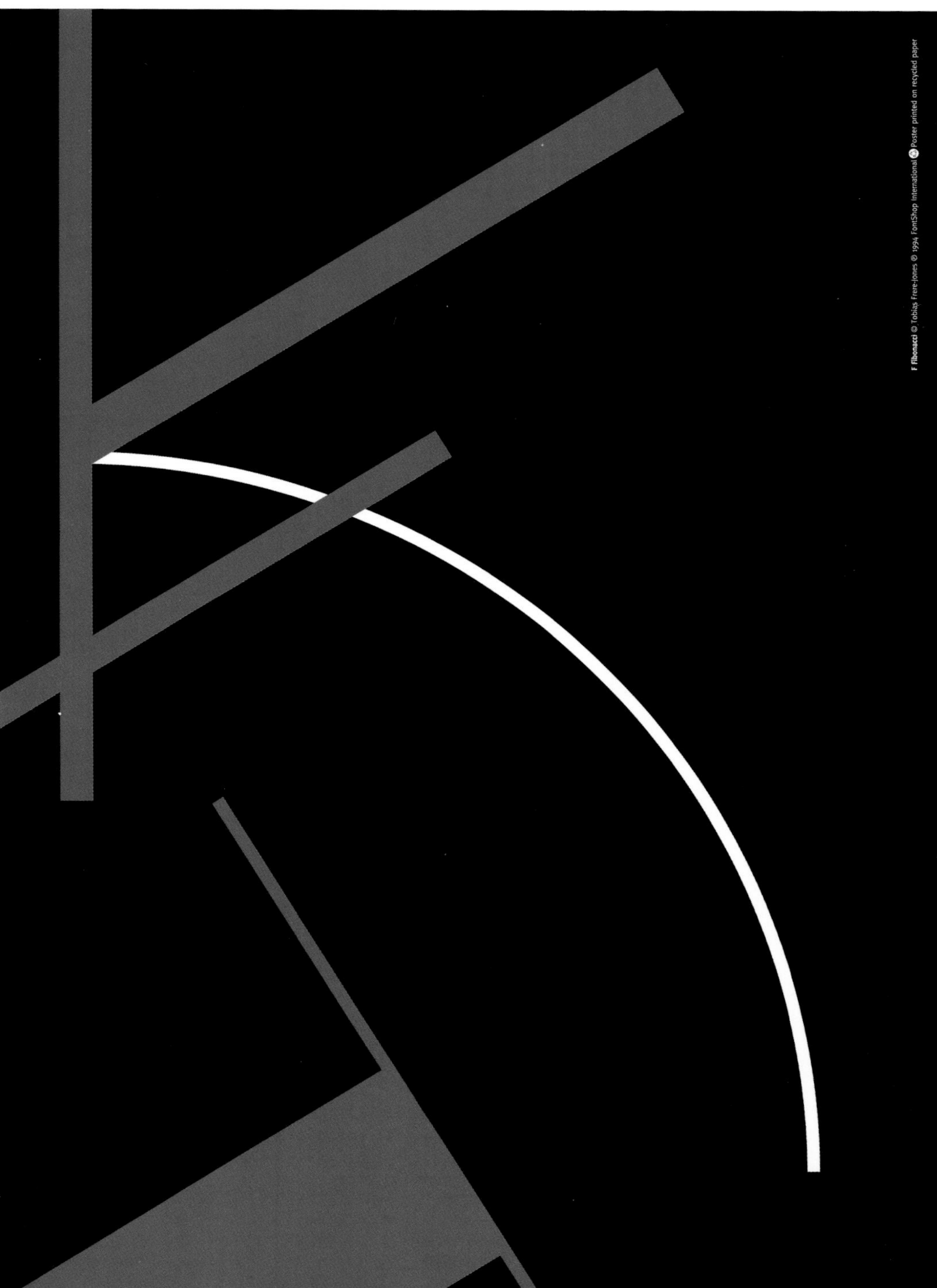
F Fibonacci © Tobias Frere-Jones ℗ 1994 FontShop International Poster printed on recycled paper

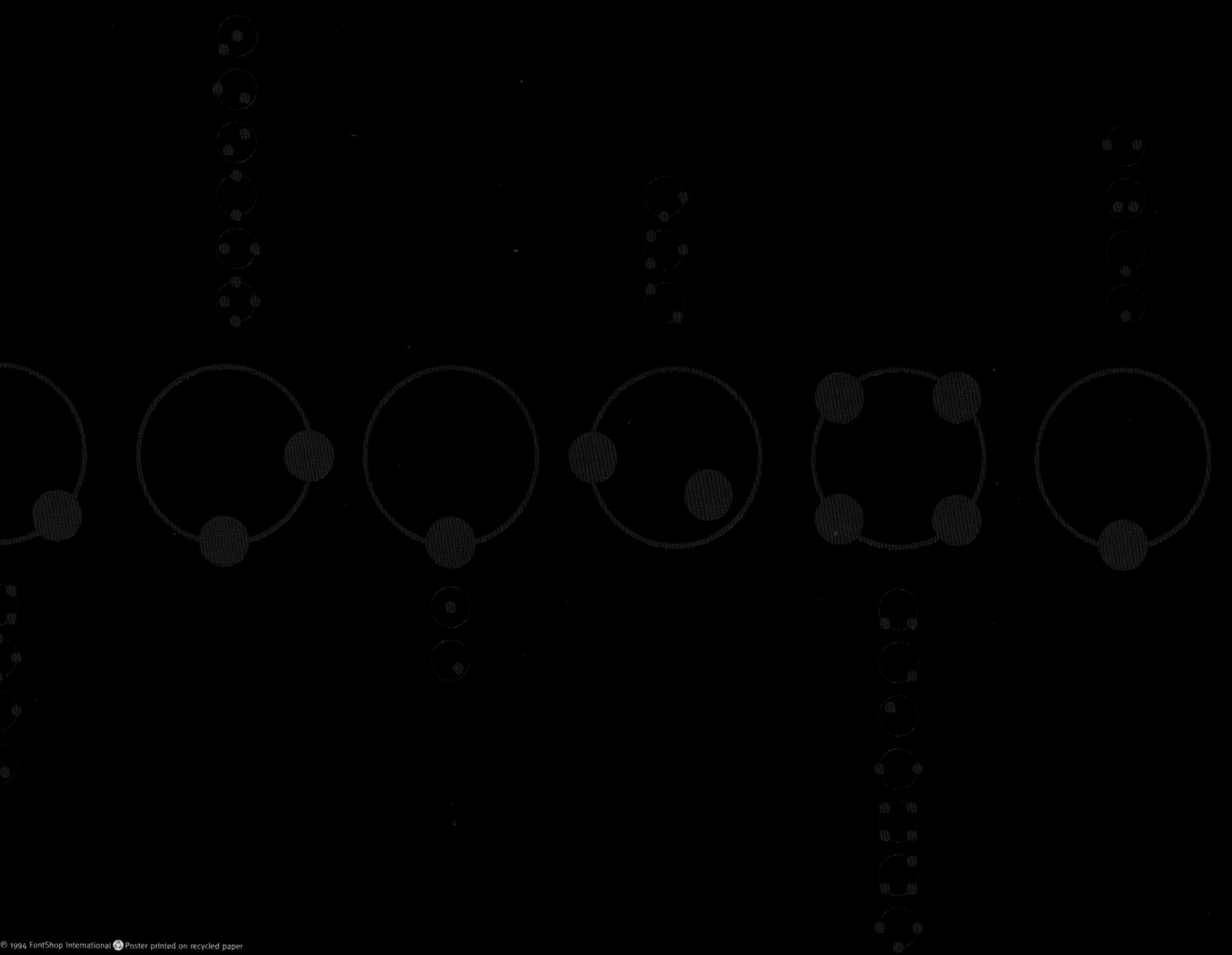
F Atomic Circle © Sylke Janetzky ℗ 1994 FontShop International Poster printed on recycled paper

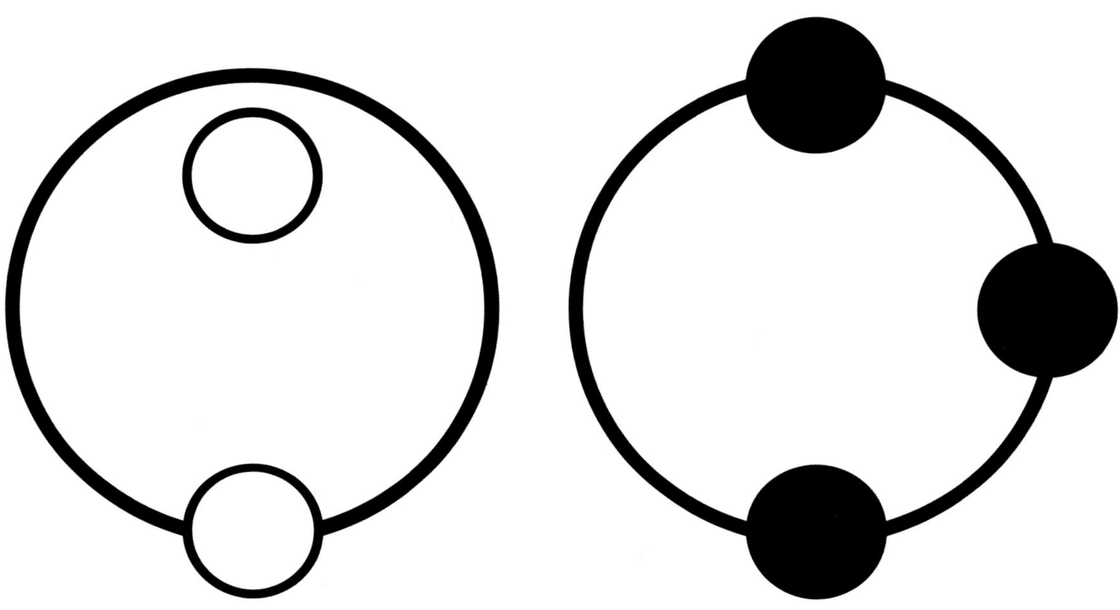

FUSE 10: Sylke Janetzky **Atomic Circle**

Atomic Circle like the braille alphabet is based on a simple encoding of dots within a given area, in this case a circle and its periphery. If you look at the system, it is surprisingly easy to decipher – the dots are always at the place of the eyes in conventional capital letters. The lower-case characters are formally identical to the capitals: the dots, however, are empty. For a better display, the characters are orientated by a dividing line.

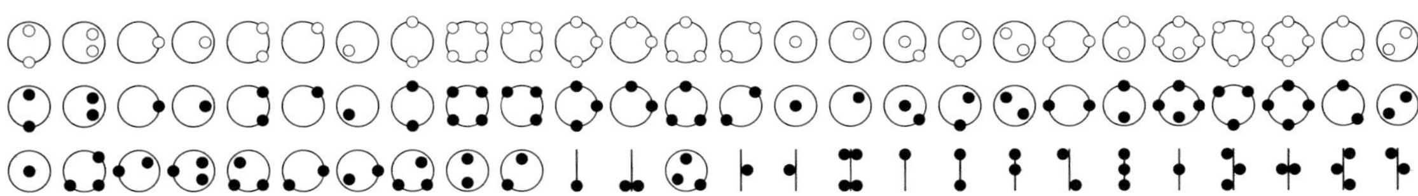

SYLKE JANETZKY WAS THE WINNER OF THE DÜSSELDORF STUDENT PROJECT IN ICELAND

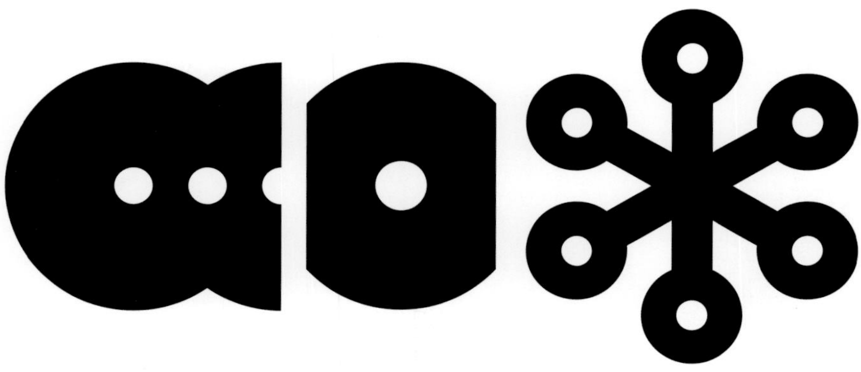

FUSE 10: Cornel Windlin Robotnik

I wanted to find a set of shapes that was not going to be too freeform and not too personal. I have become wary of instant funkiness and inbuilt grunginess. Instead I tried to define cold and technical shapes that only by experimenting and combining and through composition would reveal their potential. They are shapes that always fascinated me and because of FUSE I finally managed to make a font of them. I hope *Robotnik* will serve as inspiration; the set can easily be extended. Some of the icons are devoid of meaning, some of them exist in the real world, yet are graphically such strong symbols, I would like to see them out of context in print or on screen. (Also, I have included a new and improved character 'e' for my earlier FUSE 3 font *Moonbase Alpha*, situated on key position 'shift 2', which can be copied into the old font file to create *Moonbase Beta*!)

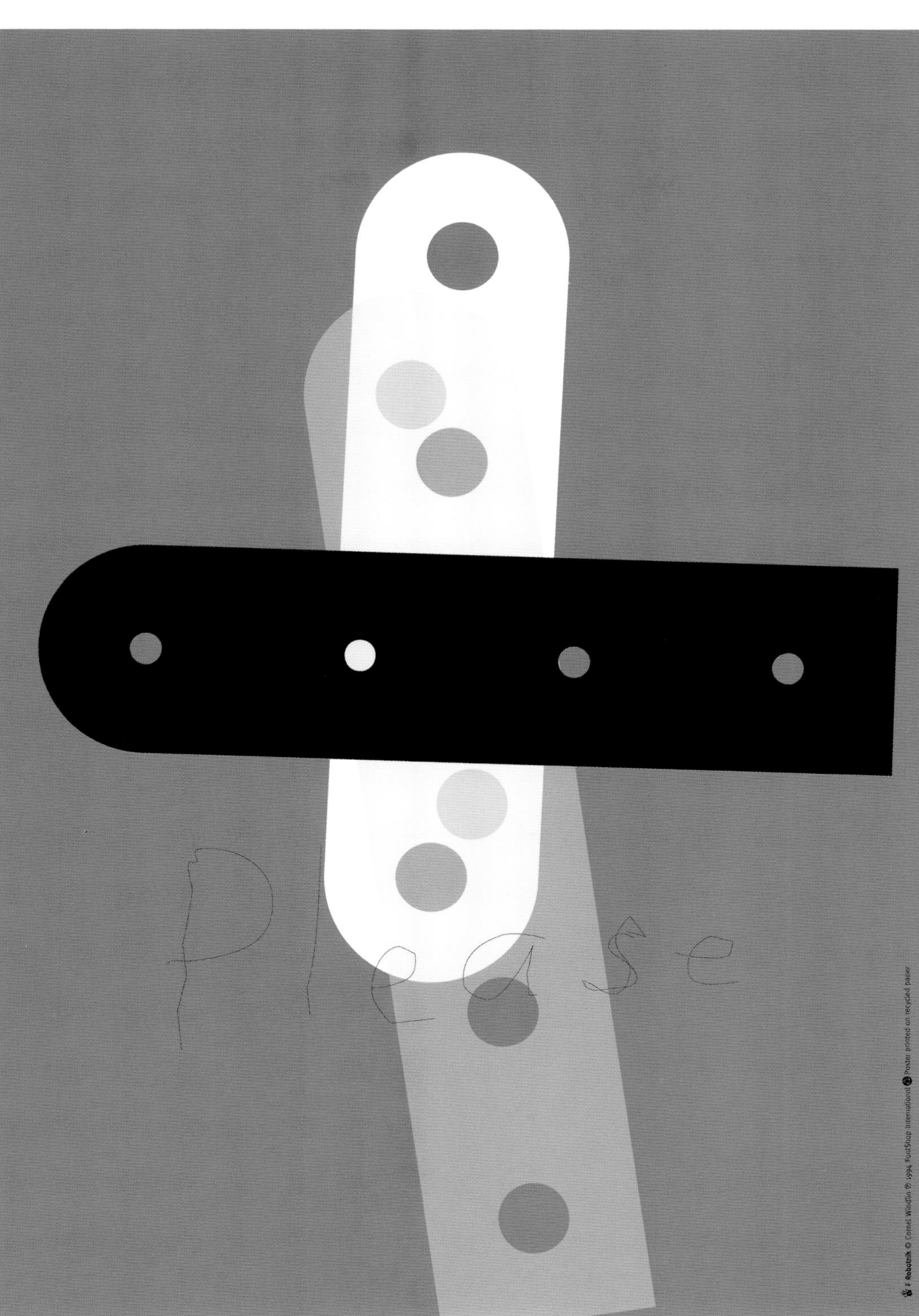
Please
F Robotnik © Cornel Windlin ® 1994 FontShop International Poster printed on recycled paper

FUSE

11

FUSE 11: Extratransubstantiationism Jon Wozencroft

AUTUMN 1994

PORNOGRAPHY

Seizing the space and authority lost by the Church, the mass media took the chalice and became the focal point for a new form of ritual, whose purpose is not to empower an audience, but to keep it docile and subservient. Organised religions provided the framework for systems that could promise liberation in the form of coercion. Candlelight and Holy Communion have been subsumed by the flicker of the screen and the soggy dough of takeaway pizzas. This process and practice of transubstantiation is the 20th century's elemental mutation, affecting every area of communication, open and in need of regular reassessment because the image behind the altar is continually being redrawn.

If the Catholic Church was able to gain dominion through its production and dissemination of a singular image and storyline, in the modern world the message can freely merge with any number of framing devices so that the overriding principle is maintained and reversed at the same time – "believe in us", "stay tuned to this channel", but take nothing at face value. Consequently, it is always necessary to intensify the hue and saturation of the image to create a distinction between today's and yesterday's preoccupation; at the same time, the division between storylines and actual experience becomes more acute, consolidating the twin extremes of wild fantasy and total disbelief. What you are left with is an audience that grows more and more cynical, whilst hungry for the next excitement. Any contrast between the images of Madonna and Whore long since having been lost, obscenity is institutionalised and pornography moves closer to the centre. "We are all prostitutes", indeed, but our collusion with the process also makes pimps of us.

"Ironically, our society makes us believe that sexuality is our dearest secret while at the same time turning it into an instrument of socialisation. As Céline perceived, 'There comes a time when there are no more secrets, or only those made up by the police.' Nature alone, it seems, could have accomplished this miracle of bioengineering: a built-in communication opportunity that could be pleasurable as well. Communication itself is our culture's last ritual, and

verbal exchange our ultimate intercourse... Sexuality is no longer repressed, but no longer desirable... the physicality of sex, like everything else, has been turned into an abstraction.'
Sylvère Lotringer, *Overexposed – Treating Sexual Perversion in America*, Pantheon Books 1988

In its programme previews prior to transmission, the London station Carlton TV proudly announced that they were *not* going to cut the leg-crossing scene in *Basic Instinct* when Sharon Stone flashes her lack of underwear at the wide-eyed police chiefs. There to prove it, next to the programme info, was a nano-clip of the very scene, with Sharon's thigh moving just a notch, as if a door were about to be flung open, revealing the animal of untamed sexuality... "Wednesday, Ten Thirty, on Carlton".

This was pretty rich, coming from a TV channel that, a week previous, had cut a crucial scene from *The Silence of the Lambs* – the one in which Agent Starling discovers the Death's Head moth in the throat of one of Buffalo Bill's victims, in the morgue – making a mockery of how the plot unfolds. Nor was *Basic Instinct* left untampered with, as other scenes fell victim to the censor's knife. But Carlton TV, in a press statement, said that they had decided to leave intact the vital moment *in flagrante*, fearing the backlash of the armchair voyeur should they dare do otherwise.

The nation, according to *The Sun* newspaper, was in any case already "Lotto Blotto", too drunk on the thought of winning the jackpot in the U.K.'s first Lottery Draw. In a demonstration of national solidarity in the face of adversity, like an economic twist of 'The Dunkirk Spirit', 45 million tickets had been sold. To be exact 25 million people had bought them, 57% of the U.K. population over 16, with £49 million being spent in the week prior to the first Draw. *The Sun* printed a large black dot, "charged with psychic energy", which readers could concentrate upon to help them tune in to the winning numbers. More than 20 million people watched the draw, live on BBC1. The state of the nation and the gulf between rich and poor was eclipsed by an expensive advertising campaign and a TV ratings battle.

Any contrast between the images of Madonna and Whore long since having been lost, obscenity is institutionalised and pornography moves closer to the centre. "We are all prostitutes", indeed, but our collusion with the process also makes pimps of us.

The Tory Government was well pleased. After a hail of accusations concerning bribery and corruption amongst its members and ministers, "The Sleaze Factor" that was causing John Major to lurch from one scandal to the next, it seemed as if by magic they were off the hook. Greed had proved itself to be a national, and not strictly a Governmental impulse.

'Pornography' is of Greek origin, meaning "the writing of harlots", yet it did not come to be used until 1857 when the increased visibility of prostitution in Victorian London caused the medical profession to adopt the word as a description of the prostitute lifestyle. The present, most common usage of the word – to condemn images that exceed the boundaries of acceptability – did not gain currency until the late 1960s. In this context the word 'graphic' has less to do with writing, taking on a second sense to mean an 'extreme' or 'vivid' description, almost always related to *images*. "Pornographic" material stretches our ability to classify various feelings in language or through experience and it is thereby convenient as an impulsive branding device in the fantasy world. The word is used far more liberally to refer to any item or phenomenon that incites fear and revulsion: a blank cheque for exaggeration. Its former sexual context has stretched to violence, to politics, to advertising... to anything.

In an essay written in 1975, 'Eros and Image', George Steiner ponders the effect of the dramatic post-war increase in sexual frankness in literature and film – he asks, "What bearing has all this on the life of the imagination?", relating the then-current code of sexual explicitness (this, long before the "sex and shopping" novel of the '80s, Madonna's *Sex* and *Basic Instinct*...) to a more general social, cultural and political malaise – the erosion of privacy, the externalisation of inner experience, the relationship of the individual to the fact of death. "The collapse of taboos has led to a frenetic search for new shocks, for extremes of speech or behaviour as yet unexploited". By contrast, in the closed, corporate environment of the boardroom meeting, we might locate another source of pornography. As a leading film director recently remarked, Hollywood is run by people who care little about cinema, and "knowing more about movies than people in Hollywood isn't a big deal" (Quentin Tarantino). Politics is no longer the domain of politicians, the music business is run by people who don't care about music, the education and health systems are run by Faustian administrations, the art world, like the National Lottery, is run by speculators. And what about the numerous examples where the directors of newly-privatised service companies like British Gas and British Telecom have awarded themselves exorbitant pay increases? The U.K. censors might ban *Natural Born Killers*, but we have plenty of pornography of our own, thank you! Pornography descends directly from power and money, yet the consumers of this effect can be the ones that get blamed for it. The Church – any church – always holds the mirror away from its own face.

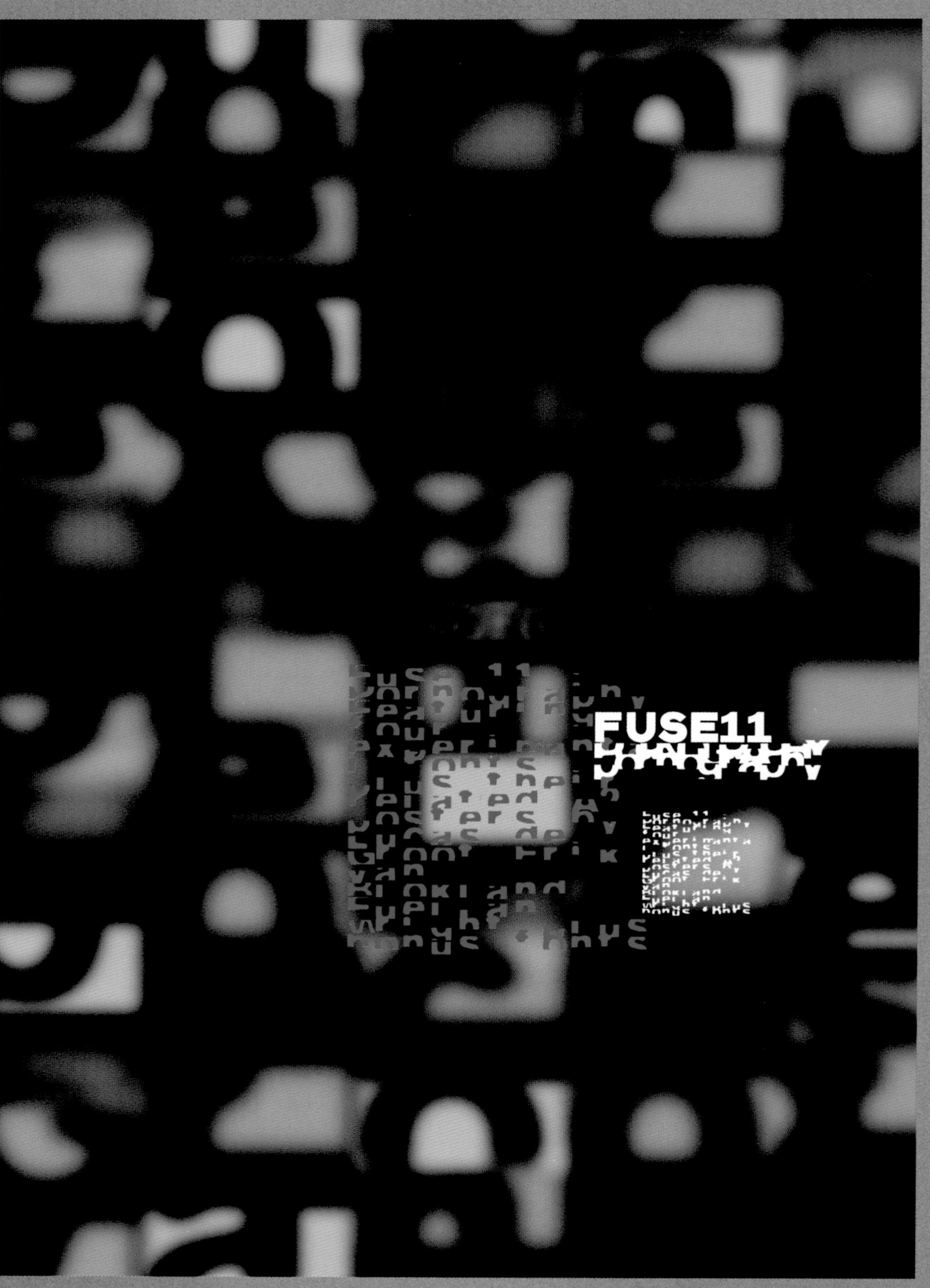
FUSE11

“Any sit-uation you go into deeply enough [illegible]”. Marshall McLuhan

Editor & text: Jon Wozencroft
Designers: John Critchley and Neville Brody @ Research
℗ & © 1994 FSI GmbH
Typefaces and posters © their designers

FSI, Bergmannstraße 102, Berlin 61

Editorial:
Unit 2 Whitehorse Yard, 78 Liverpool Road,
London N1 0QD. Fax: +44 (71) 704 2447.

LUCAS DE GROOT
Move Me MM

“Porno is private and secret, porno happens on the quiet, and it does not come out of the printer. So *Move Me Multiple Master* cannot be fully printed. You can play with it on a corner of your screen whilst nobody is looking and you can hide it when your boss approaches. Many porno letters are based on full colour porno illustrations by a famous type designer. Mac system requirements: Adobe Type Manager 3.8 or 3.0 with the Multiple Master INIT, the Font Creator programme or the XPress MMU (Multiple Master Utilities). Windows system requirements: ATM 3.0.”

Lucas De Groot studied at the Royal Academy of Fine Arts in The Hague under Gerrit Noordzij and then spent four years with the Dutch design group BRS Premsela, mainly on corporate identity work. He taught at the Art Academy in Den Bosch and freelanced before moving to Berlin in 1993 to join *MetaDesign*. A self-confessed font fanatic who spent 5 years on his typeface *Thesis*, he compensates such hard work and sweat with quickly programmed novelty faces.

FUEL
Tape Type

Tape Type is hand drawn using various industrial tapes.

Fuel are Peter Miles, Damon Murray and Stephen Sorrell. A design group based in London's East End.

LETTERROR

“*The Concept*. We were highly embarrassed by this brief and we did not want to talk about it for a long time. The type we made is inspired by cheap signs on the doors of strange bars in bad neighbourhoods, recent URW catalogs and 70s ITC catalogs. Every letter is drawn and designed by us. We made them look like the stuff other nameless tasteless people have made in the last 30 years. The poster follows the same idea – fragments from ill informed, badly thought through designs. All original.

The Idea. First there was type, and then there were people who wanted to make it better. Shadows, screens, outlines, round edges, inlines, glowing, Threee Deee, spaced and stars added. This is not a Fuse font, it is a Turbo FUSE font-GPLi-Grand [plus] – just as a normal off-the-shelf car is not good enough. It has to have spoilers, mags and a stereo the size of a truck. Still the same old car though. This is what most people think type design is all about.

The Idea for real. Porn is not what it seems. The printed material promises many things, but after buying it, there is not much left. Disappointment, emptiness and the feeling that there should be something better. (Being politically correct and all, we heard this from people close to the material, so we do not speak from experience).

Thus there are two sides to the font. There is the part you see on screen, *WhatYouSee*: More, Better, Enhanced, Bigger, Fresher, Hotter, and Cooler. When you try to print this font, what comes out of the printer, *WhatYouGet*, is a boring, empty, ugly contour of what was promised. Nothing you wanted is actually delivered.”

Independent designers from The Netherlands, Erik Van Blokland and Just Van Rossum graduated from the Royal Academy for Fine and Applied Arts in The Hague. After working separately together at various design companies in Europe and the US they are now working separately together under the name of *LettError* (Pronounced Let-Error), still in The Hague. Projects: corporate design, animation and interactive thingies, illustration, animation, TV design, interface design for applications and on-line services, CD covers, music stuff, typography, magazine stuff. They are the creators of the recently-released *Kosmik*, “one of the world's leading Flipper™ fonts”.

“I started off my font (my first ever!) with an idea about body painting – skin contact. Life-sized prints of back, breasts, bollocks and other parts of the body proved impossible to model into a basic alphabet, so like all good pornographers I resorted to using my hand.”

Ian Wright has worked as an illustrator for over 15 years. He has produced record sleeves for artists as diverse as Madness (in the early 80s) and the *Talking Loud* label (in the early 90s). His work is regularly seen in *Esquire* and *Straight No Chaser* magazine. He is best known for his use of hi-tech equipment: “I'm fascinated by fax machines, photocopiers, digital scanners, the Paintbox... They are designed to produce slick, high quality results, but it excites me to use them in the most inappropriate way. I might start with a life drawing, and then process it any number of ways – what I end up with is very low-tech, if not no-tech.” He reads “tons of American crime novels”, is a reggae fanatic and a compulsive record buyer. A collection of his portrait works, *Headcase*, has recently been published in Japan.

NEVILLE BRODY

The typeface is a Hollywood production and it comes in six parts – *Confused, Screwed Up, Regular, Negative Level, Negative Big, Negative*. It explores the gap between what you want to believe is there, and the reality of the situation, the image, and life behind the scenes. Glamour can only exist if what one sees are the edited highlights. Exoticism thrives on an inability to see the whole picture. Show it *whatever it is, as it is*, and you give the game away. Nobody trusts honesty, and everyone hides from freedom. Show a section of the whole, a glimpse, and you have a captive audience, keen to catch the next instalment.

EXTRA[...]STANTIATIONISM!

Seizing the space and authority lost by the Church, the mass media took the chalice and became the focal point for a new form of ritual, whose purpose is not to empower an audience, but to keep it docile and subservient. Organised religions provided the framework for systems that could promise liberation in the form of coercion. Candlelight and Holy Communion have been subsumed by the flicker of the screen and the soggy dough of takeaway pizzas. This process and practice of transubstantiation is the 20th century's elemental mutation, affecting every area of communication, open and in need of regular reassessment because the image behind the altar is continually being redrawn.

If the Catholic Church was able to gain dominion through its production and dissemination of a singular image and storyline, in the modern world the message can freely merge with any number of framing devices so that the overriding principle is maintained and reversed at the same time – “believe in us”, “stay tuned to this channel”, but take nothing at face value. Consequently, it is always necessary to intensify the hue and saturation of the image to create a distinction between today's and yesterday's preoccupation; at the same time, the division between storylines and actual experience becomes more acute, consolidating the twin extremes of wild fantasy and total disbelief. What you are left with is an audience that grows more and more cynical, whilst hungry for the next excitement. Any contrast between the images of Madonna and Whore long since having been lost, obscenity is institutionalised and pornography moves closer to the centre. “We are all prostitutes”, indeed, but our collusion with the process also makes pimps of us.

‘Ironically, our society makes us believe that sexuality is our dearest secret while at the same time turning it into an instrument of socialization. As Céline perceived, “There comes a time when there are no more secrets, or only those made up by the police.” Nature alone, it seems, could have accomplished this miracle of bioengineering: a built-in communication opportunity that could be pleasurable as well. Communication itself is our culture's last ritual, and verbal exchange our ultimate intercourse... Sexuality is no longer repressed, but no longer desirable... the physicality of sex, like everything else, has been turned into an abstraction.’
Sylvère Lotringer, *Overexposed – Treating Sexual Perversion in America*, Pantheon Books 1988.

In its programme previews prior to transmission, the London station Carlton TV proudly announced that they were *not* going to cut the leg-crossing scene in *Basic Instinct* when Sharon Stone flashes her lack of underwear at the wide-eyed police chiefs. There to prove it, next to the programme info, was a nano-clip of the very scene, with Sharon's thigh moving just a notch, as if a door were about to be flung open, revealing the animal of untamed sexuality... “Wednesday, Ten Thirty, on Carlton”.

This was pretty rich, coming from a TV channel that, a week previous, had cut a crucial scene from *The Silence of the Lambs* – the one in which Agent Starling discovers the Death's Head moth in the throat of one of Buffalo Bill's victims, in the morgue – making a mockery of how the plot unfolds. Nor was *Basic Instinct* left untampered with, as other scenes fell victim to the censor's knife. But Carlton TV, in a press statement, said that they had decided to leave intact the vital moment *in flagrante*, fearing the backlash of the armchair voyeur should they dare do otherwise.

The nation, according to *The Sun* newspaper, was in any case already “Lotto Blotto”, too drunk on the thought of winning the jackpot in the UK's first Lottery Draw. In a demonstration of national solidarity in the face of adversity, like an economic twist of ‘The Dunkirk Spirit’, 45 million tickets had been sold. To be exact 25 million people had bought them, 57% of the UK population over 16, with £49 million being spent in the week prior to the first Draw. *The Sun* printed a large black dot, “charged with psychic energy”, which readers could concentrate upon to help them tune in to the winning numbers. More than 20 million people watched the draw, live on BBC1. The state of the nation and the gulf between rich and poor was eclipsed by an expensive advertising campaign and a TV ratings battle.

The Tory Government was well pleased. After a hail of accusations concerning bribery and corruption amongst its members and ministers, “The Sleaze Factor” that was causing John Major to lurch from one scandal to the next, it seemed as if by magic they were off the hook. Greed had proved itself to be a national, and not strictly a Governmental impulse.

‘Pornography’ is of Greek origin, meaning “the writing of harlots”, yet it did not come to be used until 1857 when the increased visibility of prostitution in Victorian London caused the medical profession to adopt the word as a description of the prostitute lifestyle. The present, most common usage of the word – to condemn images that exceed the boundaries of acceptability – did not gain currency until the late 1960s. In this context the word ‘graphic’ has less to do with writing, taking on a second sense to mean an ‘extreme’ or ‘vivid’ description, almost always related to *images*. “Pornographic” material stretches our ability to classify various feelings in language or through experience and it is thereby convenient as an impulsive branding device in the fantasy world. The word is used far more liberally to refer to any item or phenomenon that incites fear and revulsion: a blank cheque for exaggeration. Its former sexual context has stretched to violence, to politics, to advertising... to anything.

In an essay written in 1975, ‘Eros and Image’, George Steiner ponders the effect of the dramatic postwar increase in sexual frankness in literature and film – he asks, “What bearing has all this on the life of the imagination?”, relating the then current code of sexual explicitness (this, long before the “sex and shopping” novel of the 80s, Madonna's *Sex* and *Basic Instinct*...) to a more general social, cultural and political malaise – the erosion of privacy, the externalisation of inner experience, the relationship of the individual to the fact of death. “The collapse of taboos has led to a frenetic search for new shocks, for extremes of speech or behaviour as yet unexploited”.

By contrast, in the closed, corporate environment of the boardroom meeting, we might locate another source of pornography. As a leading film director recently remarked, Hollywood is run by people who care little about cinema, and “knowing more about movies than people in Hollywood isn't a big deal” (Quentin Tarantino). Politics is no longer the domain of politicians, the music business is run by people who don't care about music, the education and health systems are run by Faustian administrations, the art world, like the National Lottery, is run by speculators. And what about the numerous examples where the directors of newly-privatised service companies like British Gas and British Telecom have awarded themselves exorbitant pay increases? The UK censors might ban *Natural Born Killers*, but we have plenty of pornography of our own, thank you! Pornography descends directly from power and money, yet the consumers of this effect can be the ones that get blamed for it. The Church – any church – always holds the mirror away from its own face.

FACING PAGE: NEVILLE BRODY PROMOTIONAL POSTCARD. THIS PAGE: JOHN CRITCHLEY & NEVILLE BRODY @ RESEARCH STUDIOS & JON WOZENCROFT EDITORIAL POSTER

PEEP REGULAR

PEEP CONFUSED

PEEP SCREWED UP

PEEP NEGATIVE

PEEP NEGATIVE BIG

PEEP NEGATIVE LEVEL

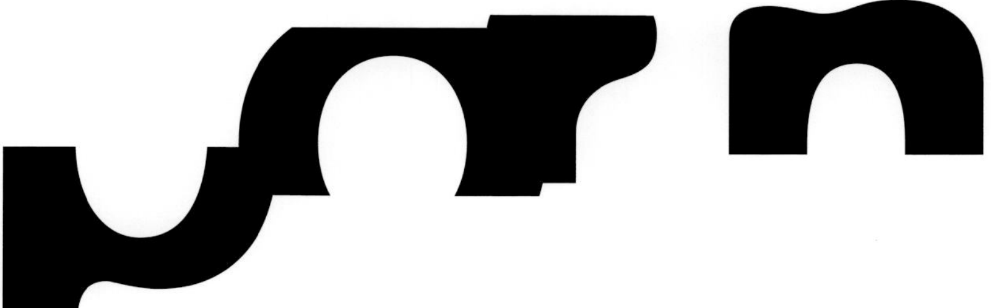

FUSE 11: Neville Brody Bonus Font Peep

The typeface is a Hollywood production and it comes in six parts — *Confused*, *Screwed Up*, *Regular*, *Negative Level*, *Negative Big*, *Negative*. It explores the gap between what you want to believe is there, and the reality of the situation, the image, and life behind the scenes. Glamour can only exist if what one sees are the edited highlights. Exoticism thrives on an inability to see the whole picture. Show it *whatever it is*, as it is, and you give the game away. Nobody trusts honesty, and everyone hides from freedom. Show a section of the whole, a glimpse, and you have a captive audience, keen to catch the next instalment.

F Peep © Neville Brody ® 1994 FontShop International Poster printed on recycled paper

pornography

FUSE11

Fuse 11 : Pornography
Featuring four experimental fonts plus their related A2 posters by Lucas de Groot Erik Van Blokland Fuel Ian Wright plus 6 bonus fonts

ABCDEFGHIJKLMNOPQRSTUVWXYZ

FUSE 11: Lucas de Groot Move Me MM

Porno is private and secret, porno happens on the quiet, and it does not come out of the printer. *So Move Me Multiple Master* cannot be fully printed. You can play with it on a corner of your screen whilst nobody is looking and you can hide it when your boss approaches. Many porno letters are based on full colour porno illustrations by a famous type designer.

ABCDEFGHIJKL

MOVE ME

FUSE 11: Fuel Tape Type

Tape Type is hand drawn using various industrial tapes.

ABCDEFGHIJKLMNOPQRSTUVWXYZ

ABCDEFGHIJKLMNOPQRSTUVWXYZ

1 2 3 4 5 6 7 8 9 0 ! Make Your Own! £ + ; : . , / → ? ←

1234567890

PORNO-GRAPHY NEEDS YOU

F What You See/What You Get © Erik Van Blokland & Just Van Rossum ℗ 1994 FontShop International
OPEN HERE
LETTERROR

ABCdeFgHIJKLmN
OPQRStUVWXYZ
ABCDEFGHIJKLM
NOPQRSTUVWXYZ
0123456789

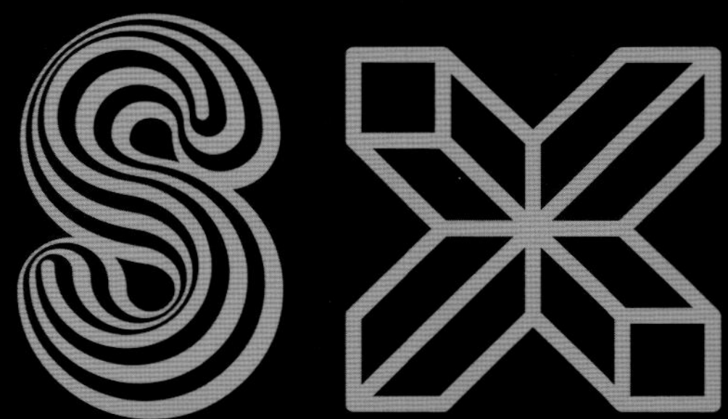

FUSE 11: LettError WhatYouSee/WhatYouGet

The Concept. We were highly embarrassed by this brief and we did not want to talk about it for a long time. The type we made is inspired by cheap signs on the doors of strange bars in bad neighbourhoods, recent URW catalogues and '70s ITC catalogues. Every letter is drawn and designed by us. We made them look like the stuff other nameless, tasteless people have made in the last 30 years. The poster follows the same idea — fragments from ill-informed, badly thought through designs. All original.

The Idea. First there was type, and then there were people who wanted to make it better. Shadows, screens, outlines, round edges, inlines, glowing, Threee-Deee, spaced and stars added. This is not a FUSE font, it is a Turbo FUSE font-GPLi-Grand [plus] – just as a normal off-the-shelf car is not good enough, it has to have spoilers, mags and a stereo the size of a truck. Still the same old car though. This is what most people think type design is all about.

The Idea for real. Porn is not what it seems. The printed material promises many things, but after buying it, there is not much left. Disappointment, emptiness and the feeling that there should be something better. (Being politically correct and all, we heard this from people close to the material, so we do not speak from experience.)

Thus there are two sides to the font. There is the part you see on screen, *WhatYouSee*: More, Better, Enhanced, Bigger, Fresher, Hotter, and Cooler. When you try to print this font, what comes out of the printer, *WhatYouGet*, is a boring, empty, ugly contour of what was promised. Nothing you wanted is actually delivered.

FUSE 11: Ian Wright Hand Job

I started off my font (my first ever!) with an idea about body painting — skin contact. Life-sized prints of back, breasts, bollocks and other parts of the body proved impossible to model into a basic alphabet, so like all good pornographers I resorted to using my hand.

HAND JOB
F Hand Job © Ian Wright © 1994 FontShop International Poster printed on recycled paper

FUSE

An Extra Zero (Careless Type Costs Lives) Jon Wozencroft

PROPAGANDA

The origins of propaganda could be linked to body paintings and tribal rituals, the warrior instinct, predating the Holy Roman Empire and Caesar's "Bread and Circuses" – i.e. synonymous with history itself, "the history of the victors" (Ernst Toller). Before Gutenberg, was there any greater instrument of propaganda than the Holy Bible? In fact the term was not used until much later – it comes from a modern Latin phrase *Congregatio de propaganda fides*, 'The congregation for propagating the faith'. This was first coined in 1622 by a committee of Roman Catholic Cardinals, the Congregation of the Propaganda, who were instructed by the Pope to oversee foreign missionary work.

Propaganda in its political sense was not specified until the 1840s, increasing as the century went on and suggesting the word's close proximity with the development of the press, and later advertising. Nobody spoke of there being such a thing as a 'Propaganda campaign' until 1937, when Koestler applied it to the Madrid Government's attempt to win over the rebels in the Spanish Civil War.

The real action was in Germany. In his capacity to merge the broadcasting media of radio, cinema and the press alongside staged spectacles as massive as anything seen in Ancient Rome, we still think of Goebbels as the exemplar when it comes to manufacturing this "oxygen of publicity". Leni Riefenstahl's 1935 film *Triumph of the Will* is still viewed as the archetype: Triumph of the Drill. Propaganda, an essential part of any religious, political or commercial crusade, hopes to fool us and it seems to succeed in fooling most of the people most of the time. Or does it?

"Perception is the first operation of all our intellectual faculties, and the inlet of all knowledge in our minds... If we will disbelieve everything, because we cannot certainly know all things, we shall do much what as wisely as he who would not use his legs, but sit and perish, because he had no wings to fly."
John Locke, *An Essay on Human Understanding*, 1689

"He insisted on making his own amendments, sometimes changing whole passages... refusing to allow admissions of failure. On one occasion the Army reported having taken 3000 prisoners. Hitler asked, 'Whom do you expect to impress with this figure?' and ordered an extra 0 to be thrown in – then said, 'Don't put 30,000 but 30,723 and everyone will believe an exact count has been made.'"
Michael Balfour, *Propaganda in War*, Routledge & Kegan Paul 1979

PROPAGANDA is like an addiction – it gives an immediate buzz the first time, but repetition dulls the senses, and before you know it, the process is easier to repeat badly – the drive to match and improve upon prior performance persuades users not to give it up. In 1995, propaganda is the art of tailoring the time at hand to think, twinned to the science of persuasion... the first policy used to sell any policy, which makes any success first and foremost a Propaganda Victory. The status quo is upheld by well-honed techniques that nevertheless run the risk of undermining any collective respect for the system. Audiences become attuned to various methods and new ones have to be employed, but as extensions not replacements. However, propaganda is not about masterminds like Adolf Hitler and Joseph Goebbels: it is more reliant upon the machinery that generates it. In this respect, both for propagandist and audience, fatigue reinforces habit.

Any serious crime demands a long drawn-out court case – The Misinformed versus State and Corporations. The evidence accumulates. "Truth will out", with the drawback that vital information enters the public domain years later (at best, in the U.K., under the '30 Year Rule'). By this time it has lost its sharpness and detail, pulled from a dusty cabinet like a faded photograph.

As governments well know, something happens to information during the long decades whilst it is stowed away, waiting, maybe in vain, to see the light of day and the chance of a fair trial for the past and already condemned. The given facts can be extreme and prosecutional – mass murder, or a young squaddie executed for 'desertion' *pour encourager les autres*, or escape routes for known war criminals – but once removed from the volatile context of the present and relocated in an archive, destined for a hardly-to-be-read hardback or even reconfigured for the mass market and Hollywood, strange things happen. It is not that a few key details may have been cut by the censor, or even denials that "it never happened". Time is Chief Editor.

"Truth" has to be unravelled, disentangled from the faltering memories, myths and fictions that have gathered around it. Can a historical truth ever be given the kiss of life, revived and then represented in the present? This is difficult, and nobody likes difficulty. Information becomes an attractive substitute.

The last 20 years have seen the steady declassification of 'sensitive material' relating to WW2, not yet, alas, the full story behind such blockbuster material as Rudolf Hess' 1941 flight to Scotland, but a slow stream that has fuelled numerous books and documentary programmes, currently negotiating the steep curve set up by the 50-year anniversary commemorations. This month, the liberation of Auschwitz. Hardly time to pause for thought: next up, the RAF bombing of Dresden, the prelude to more contrition. Should the Japanese be part of the ritual – can Hiroshima and Nagasaki co-exist with the torture and starvation of Allied POWs? Just as in wartime, the intensity obstructs the grounds for objectivity; however, this short-spaced exposure amidst the long-running controversy might at last connect and make some sense of the maligned caveat that people were "only doing their jobs, obeying orders". There is more to it than that.

Some other central characters, only doing their jobs, have long recorded their deeds in their memoirs – Sefton Delmer, head of 'Black Propaganda' at the Political Warfare Executive in London;[1] Ellic Howe, the PWE's specialist in the manufacture of printed fakes, a man who was able to identify every typeface in use in Western Europe at the time;[2] Michael Balfour, another PWE member, who later became supervisor of the German Information media in the British Zone and Chief Information Officer of the Board of Trade between 1947 and 1964. Their innovations in

As governments well know, something happens to information during the long decades whilst it is stowed away, waiting, maybe in vain, to see the light of day and the chance of a fair trial for the past and already condemned.

the field of subversive operations have hardly been able to compete alongside the Dambuster Raid and the German rocket programme, etc. Their books are all out of print. In any case, the very nature of their work was to conceal the full picture and to promote the acceptance of falsehoods.

Stories circulated: the Germans were dropping rattlesnakes from planes as they bombed England! But it would be a mistake to suppose that black propagandists relied merely on wild rumours to sow fear and doubt. Millions upon millions of leaflets were dropped from the skies: how to perform sabotage, how to feign illness, how to feel envy. Setting the pace for post-war espionage and James Bond gadgetry, Delmer's team came up with ever more sophisticated schemes. Special packs of cigarette papers were printed and distributed in Occupied Europe, their leaves carrying instructions on how to blow up railway junctions, how to forge doctors' prescriptions etc. It made no difference whether these fell into the hands of the Wehrmacht, the Resistance, or foreign workers.

Subversive activities were, initially, in stark contrast to the official line; their success is summed up by their obscurity. In October 1939, as members of the House of Commons were making plain, "the last thing we want to do is embark on any plan, such as the plans in totalitarian states, of propaganda. There is no question of propaganda. It is publicity and by that I mean straight news" (Sir Samuel Hoare). But a day later, Henry Strauss was to say, "There is nothing whatever improper in propaganda" as long as it was "good". Throughout the war, the BBC upheld this benevolent aim with its European Service. But as Ellic Howe makes clear, "until 1941 nobody had the slightest idea of what was possible in the black department. Indeed, as far as the British were concerned, Sefton Delmer created a new concept in psychological warfare". Thus by 1944, on discussing with Stalin dummy operations undertaken by Allied troops before the D-Day landings to fool the Germans into concentrating their firepower in the wrong areas, Churchill came clean when he described truth as "so precious that in wartime she should always be surrounded by a bodyguard of lies".

Ironically, but just as significantly in terms of the peacetime strategies to come, Goebbels was forced by a series of setbacks following the German defeat at Stalingrad to compete with the BBC's "truthful" broadcasts by adopting what he called 'The Policy of Total Frankness' alongside his urge for 'Total War' which he stressed from February 1942 onwards. This was largely the result of the more intense and more successful Allied bombing of German cities. Hitherto, the RAF had pursued the policy of 'precision bombing' selected military targets, which had been a total failure – only 5% of any bombload had come within 5 miles of its chosen destination. Once the Allies turned to the more generalised 'area bombing', they began to cause havoc. Goebbels realised, as Churchill had been forced to realise in Coventry in 1940, and as Japanese officials are having to, this week, after the earthquake that hit Kobe (compared by not a few eye-witnesses to the Tokyo firestorm of 1945), that clear, unadulterated information is the only factor that prevents a devastated population from descending into chaos. The spell is broken. In a climate which has been used to party line, half-truths and forced rumours, this brings double difficulty.

A polluted river does not instantly become a source of spring water.

If wartime is the mother of invention, then the greatest steps forward (or backwards, as is the case) have not been in the realm of weaponry or space travel, but in the manipulation of information – in the space between the codebreaking work at Bletchley Park, [3] and the Black Propaganda unit at Woburn. The idea is to simplify and to sophisticate at one and the same time. The military enjoys the double advantage of being able to fix its initiatives within a temporal frame (1914–18, 1939–45) and, where necessary, to spin them out as Official Secrets.

The residue is relocated in peacetime, tried and tested. Today, every communiqué beyond a secure one-to-one conversation or a small gathering (ie. one that is not tape-recorded) can easily be converted into propaganda. Market research, advertising, product placement and publicity, image processing, soundbite design, the spin doctor and the security services all create camouflage – so much so that even the main protagonists, politicians, frequently appeal for "a level playing field".

The playing field itself has been and long gone: the Western Front, 1914, was the last post of the old order's faith in "fair play" and "gentlemanly conduct", where sport is war and war is sport. In this light, we might conclude that the invention and refinement of the machine gun is the key catalyst that shaped the chemistry of 20th-century communications, not radio, neither television nor the rise of the advertising industry. As populations increase and develop their "standards of living", as the cult of the individual makes the accurate targeting of information more reliant upon expensive and intrusive technologies, it is easy to forget how it all started. "You didn't have to aim, we just fired into them" (a German machine-gunner in 1916). [4] Lord Kitchener's famous recruitment poster, "Your Country Needs You", was no different in this respect. There is so much that we don't know, and knowledge, we are assured, is a dangerous thing. Everyone just hoped they did not turn out to be one of those zeroes, the small print on a densely-typed casualty list.

Reference:

1. Try and locate Delmer's autobiography, *Black Boomerang*, published by Hamish Hamilton in 1962... difficult to find, however, outside major libraries **2.** "I knew its trade name, who originally designed it and when, also who cast and marketed it... I could identify almost any printing type engraved since 1500". Ellic Howe, *The Black Game*, Michael Joseph Ltd. 1982 **3.** See FUSE 6: Codes; also David Khan, *The Codebreakers*, Weidenfeld and Nicholson 1973 **4.** See John Ellis, *The Social History of the Machine Gun*, Pimlico 1993

FUSE 12: Asgeir Jónsson Bonus Font **Dofus**

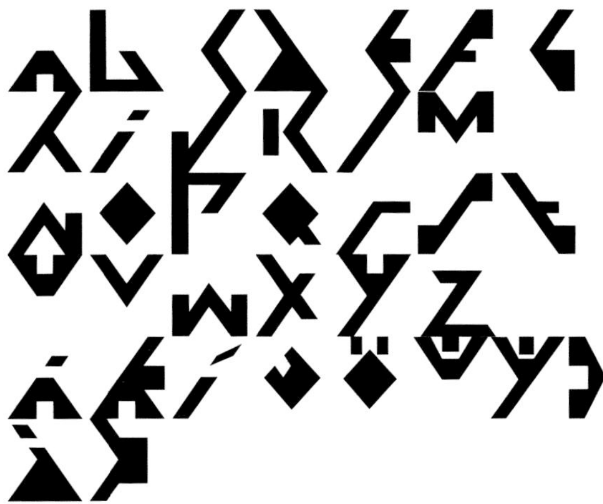

FUSE 12: Olöf Birna Gardarsdottir Bonus Font **XFuse**

FUSE 12 contains more than the usual number of bonus fonts, so here is a brief rundown...

John Critchley – *Ollie* is inspired by the case of Colonel Oliver North, U.S. Marine, who testified to an inquiry into the so-called Iran/*Contra* affair, that all the vital information had been shredded in the interests of national security! Ollie later ran for Senate. This font contains all-American characters only and consists of two pleas, and what's left of the evidence – you be the judge.

Asgeir Jónsson – ***Do*** this, DO that. The thought of having commands hidden behind words has always intrigued me. I looked for a way of constructing the grid that I could build my type upon. First of all, I used capital D and two small o's, but this didn't work, so I used a lower-case d with a lower-case o beneath it. In order to maintain a degree of legibility, I had to break with this system in one or two cases. Some option keys, signs and Icelandic characters I have not had time to finish. Maybe you could do that for me.

Olöf Birna Gardarsdottir – *X* is a basic form. You can either put an *X* next to your choice or cross things out that you don't want. We might imagine the truth is being told, but when propaganda is used, it is easy to be misled.

OLLIE GUILTY

OLLIE NOT GUILTY

OLLIE THE EVIDENCE

FUSE 12: John Critchley Bonus Font Ollie

JOHN CRITCHLEY & JON WOZENCROFT EDITORIAL POSTER

FUSE PROPAGANDA

Matthew Butterick abandoned an early mathematics career at Harvard, for one which has encompassed graphic design, type design, multimedia and programming. He began work as a letterpress printer, then became a type designer, working with Font Bureau and Carter & Cone, producing work for clients such as Apple, Esquire, Microsoft, Rolling Stone and Ziff-Davis. He is the founder of *Atomic Vision*, a new studio which incorporates design and technology for digital media projects, such as Web sites, CD-ROMs and interactive presentations.

Agitprop is not about what some messages may mean by themselves, but what they become in context. Interference can change, accentuate or negate their intended meaning. *Agitprop* is formed from a basic set of 26 shapes under a–z, but each keystroke contains two other shapes which can appear up to four characters away from the centre. Keys A–Z contain the same combinations of symbols, but with three overlay shapes randomly added to change the texture in more severe ways. Shift option a–z contains the symbols alone, and keys 1–3 contain the overlays alone. All have zero width to enable you to control your own propaganda.
email: matthew@atomicvision.com

Malcolm Garrett was director of the design consultancy Assorted Images (London) and consultant designer at Protocol Creative Consultants (Manchester) until 1994. His work involving graphic identity, exhibition design, television graphics, and design for literature of all kinds, as well as for artists such as Duran Duran, Boy George, Simple Minds and more recently Peter Gabriel. His work in TV includes designs for the first three series of *The Last Resort*, and the identity and weekly on-screen graphics for the influential *Network 7*. He is an acknowledged enthusiast of the use of computers in design having worked with Apple, Quantel and Macintosh since the early 80s; he has authored a number of controversial articles in the trade press welcoming new developments in digital publishing. Garrett is now partner with Alasdair Scott in the newly formed interactive media production company AMX digital (London), and he commissioned to develop CD-based multimedia titles for EMI Records, News International and Kodak Image Bank. He designed the recently published Phaidon book, *The Cyberspace Lexicon*.

Instrument explores the 'weighting' of language and the often duplicitous nature of information inherent in written propaganda. Each character is composed of two parts. One, located beneath the lower case keys, is bolder in structure than the other, which is located beneath the upper case keys, though both are made up of seemingly randomised graphic elements. There is therefore a visual imbalance which colours the reading of a text as one switches between the 2 parts. These can also be overlaid to make another complete character set, thus bringing about a 3rd reading. However, because the two are distinctly separate, a purposeful intervention on behalf of the designer is required to make the composition happen. Whilst lower case and upper case forms are discretely legible, their true meaning becomes clearer, but more detailed, once overlaid.

Simon Staines is an art director at the recently formed Research Studios and has worked with clients such as Arena, *The Face* and Acting magazines, ORF and Premiere television channels, *The Guardian*, Chisel and Fiorucci clothing companies, Agfa, Haus der Kulturen der Welt and NCA over the last seven years. He has just finished a project to create several interactive sequences for the forthcoming movies *Hackers* and *Judge Dredd*. He is also a director of the CD-ROM publishing company Digitalogue.

Trojan reflects the difficulty of interpretation in today's media saturated culture, where one man's freedom fighter is another man's terrorist. In a world where the unemployed have become 'job seekers', doublespeak is now reality. It is the role of the viewer to look beyond the hegemony of Western media.

'WD+RU' – Women's Design + Research Unit – is a new design initiative set up by Siân Cook, Liz McQuiston and Teal Triggs, based at Ravensbourne College of Design and Communication. Cook is a consultant designer for NexCompany, amongst others; McQuiston is the author of the recently published *Graphic Agitation*; Triggs is the editor of the upcoming Batsford publication, *Communicating Design*.

Pussy Galore acknowledges the structural conventions of language but uses the technology itself to extend common keyboard functions. The conventional alphabet keys contain a series of ideological statements. By using these in conjunction with the shift and option keys, further visual and verbal references are revealed. In addition, hidden heroines appear as 'surprise' elements throughout. The symbol * denotes several additional layers of information contained on the disk. Here, *Pussy Galore* is presented in simplified form – full representation of the typeface can be found on the accompanying poster. Thanks to Simon Wicker and students at Ravensbourne College of Design and Communication.

FUSE 12 contains more than the usual number of bonus fonts, so here is a brief rundown...

John Critchley – *Ollie* is inspired by the case of Colonel Oliver North, U.S. Marine, who testified to an enquiry into the so-called Iran/Contra affair, but all the vital information had been shredded in the interests of national security. *Ollie* takes on for Senate. This font contains all-American characters only and consists of two pieces, and what's left of the evidence – you be the judge.

Ragnar Jonsson – *Do* this. DO that. The thought of hiding commands hidden behind words has always intrigued me. I looked for a way of constructing the grid that I could build my type upon. First of all, I used capital D and two small o's. But this didn't work, so I used a lowercase d with a lowercase o beneath it. In order to maintain a degree of legibility, I had to break with this system in one of two cases. Some option keys, signs and Icelandic characters I have not had time to finish. Maybe you could do that for me.

Olöf Sirna Gardarsdottir – *X* is a basic form. You can either put an X next to your choice or cross things out that you don't want. We might imagine the truth is being told but when propaganda is used, it is easy to be [illegible].

AN EXTRA ZERO
(CARELESS TYPE COSTS LIVES)

The origins of propaganda could be linked to body paintings and tribal rituals, the warrior instinct, predating the Holy Roman Empire and Caesar's "Bread and Circuses" – ie., synonymous with history itself, "the history of the victors" (Ernst Toller). Before Gutenberg, was there any greater instrument of propaganda than The Holy Bible? In fact the term was not used until much later – it comes from a modern Latin phrase *Congregatio de propaganda fides*, 'The congregation for propagating the faith'. This was first coined in 1622 by a committee of Roman Catholic Cardinals, the Congregation of the Propaganda, who were instructed by the Pope to oversee foreign missionary work.

Propaganda in its political sense was not specified until the 1840s, increasing as the century went on and suggesting the word's close proximity with the development of the press, and later advertising. Nobody spoke of there being such a thing as a 'Propaganda campaign' until 1937, when Koestler applied it to the Madrid Government's attempt to win over the rebels in the Spanish Civil War.

The real action was in Germany. In his capacity to merge the broadcasting media of radio, cinema, and the press alongside staged spectacles as massive as anything seen in Ancient Rome, we still think of Goebbels as the exemplar when it comes to manufacturing this "oxygen of publicity". Leni Riefenstahl's 1935 film *Triumph of the Will* is still viewed as the archetype: Triumph of the Drill. Propaganda, an essential part of any religious, political or commercial crusade, hopes to fool us and it seems to succeed in fooling most of the people most of the time. Or does it?

"Perception is the first operation of all our intellectual faculties, and the inlet of all knowledge in our minds... If we will disbelieve everything, because we cannot certainly know all things, we shall do much what as wisely as he who would not use his legs, but sit and perish, because he had no wings to fly."
John Locke, *An Essay on Human Understanding*, 1689

"He insisted on making his own amendments, sometimes changing whole passages... refusing to allow admissions of failure. On one occasion the Army reported having taken 3,000 prisoners. Hitler asked, 'Whom do you expect to impress with this figure?' and ordered an extra 0 to be thrown in – then said, 'Don't put 30,000 but 30,723 and everyone will believe an exact count has been made.'"
Michael Balfour, *Propaganda in War*, Routledge & Kegan Paul 1979

PROPAGANDA is like an addiction – it gives an immediate buzz the first time, but repetition dulls the senses, and before you know it, the process is easier to repeat badly – the drive to match and improve upon prior performance persuades users not to give it up. In 1995, propaganda is the art of tailoring the time at hand to think, twinned to the science of persuasion... the first policy used to sell any policy, which makes any success first and foremost a Propaganda Victory. The status quo is upheld by well-honed techniques that nevertheless run the risk of undermining any collective respect for the system. Audiences become attuned to various methods and new ones have to be employed, but as extensions not replacements. However, propaganda is not about masterminds like Adolf Hitler and Joseph Goebbels: it is more reliant upon the machinery that generates it. In this respect, both for propagandist and audience, fatigue re-inforces habit.

Any serious crime demands a long drawn-out court case – The Misinformed versus State and Corporations. The evidence accumulates. "Truth will out", with the drawback that vital information enters the public domain years later (at best, in the UK, under the '30 Year Rule'). By this time it has lost its sharpness and detail, pulled from a dusty cabinet like a faded photograph.

As governments well know, something happens to information during the long decades whilst it is stowed away, waiting, maybe in vain, to see the light of day and the chance of a fair trial for the past and already condemned. The given facts can be extreme and prosecutional – mass murder, or a young squaddie executed for 'desertion' *pour encourager les autres*, or escape routes for known war criminals – but once removed from the volatile context of the present and relocated in an archive, destined for a hardly-to-be-read hardback or even reconfigured for the mass market and Hollywood, strange things happen. It is not that a few key details may have been cut by the censor, or even denials that "it never happened". Time is Chief Editor.

"Truth" has to be unravelled, disentangled from the faltering memories, myths and fictions that have gathered around it. Can a historical truth ever be given the kiss of life, revived and then represented in the present? This is difficult, and nobody likes difficulty. Information becomes an attractive substitute.

The last 20 years have seen the steady declassification of 'sensitive material' relating to WW2, not yet, alas, the full story behind such blockbuster material as Rudolf Hess' 1941 flight to Scotland, but a slow stream that has fuelled numerous books and documentary programmes, currently negotiating the steep curve set up by the 50 year anniversary commemorations. This month, the liberation of Auschwitz. Hardly time to pause for thought: next up, the RAF bombing of Dresden, the prelude to more contrition. Should the Japanese be part of the ritual – can Hiroshima and Nagasaki co-exist with the torture and starvation of Allied POW's? Just as in wartime, the intensity obstructs the grounds for objectivity; however, this short-spaced exposure amidst the long-running controversy might at last connect and make some sense of the maligned caveat that people were "only doing their jobs, obeying orders". There is more to it than that.

Some other central characters, only doing their jobs, have long recorded their deeds to their memoirs – Sefton Delmer, head of 'Black Propaganda' at the Political Warfare Executive in London[1]; Ellic Howe, the PWE's specialist in the manufacture of printed fakes, a man who was able to identify every typeface in use in Western Europe at the time[2]; Michael Balfour, another PWE member, who later became supervisor of the German Information media in the British Zone and Chief Information Officer of the Board of Trade between 1947 and 1964. Their innovations in the field of subversive operations have hardly been able to compete alongside the Dambuster Raid and the German rocket programme, etc. Their books are all out of print. In any case, the very nature of their work was to conceal the full picture and to promote the acceptance of falsehoods.

Stories circulated: the Germans were dropping rattlesnakes from planes as they bombed England! But it would be a mistake to suppose that black propagandists relied merely on wild rumours to sow fear and doubt. Millions upon millions of leaflets were dropped from the skies: how to perform sabotage, how to feign illness, how to feel envy. Setting the pace for post war espionage and James Bond gadgetry, Delmer's team came up with ever more sophisticated schemes. Special packs of cigarette papers were printed and distributed in Occupied Europe, their leaves carrying instructions on how to blow up railway junctions, how to forge doctors' prescriptions etc. It made no difference whether these fell into the hands of the Wehrmacht, the Resistance, or foreign workers.

Subversive activities were, initially, in stark contrast to the official line; their success is summed up by their obscurity. In October 1939, as members of the House of Commons were making plain, "the last thing we want to do is embark on any plan, such as the plans in totalitarian states, of propaganda. There is no question of propaganda. It is publicity and by that I mean straight news" (Sir Samuel Hoare). But a day later, Henry Strauss was to say, "There is nothing whatever improper in propaganda" as long as it was "good". Throughout the war, the BBC upheld this benevolent aim with its European Service. But as Ellic Howe makes clear, "until 1941 nobody had the slightest idea of what was possible in the black department. Indeed, as far as the British were concerned, Sefton Delmer created a new concept in psychological warfare". Thus by 1944, on discussing with Stalin dummy operations undertaken by Allied troops before the D-Day landings to fool the Germans into concentrating their firepower in the wrong areas, Churchill came clean when he described truth as "so precious that in wartime she should always be surrounded by a bodyguard of lies".

Ironically, but just as significantly in terms of the peacetime strategies to come, Goebbels was forced by a series of setbacks following the German defeat at Stalingrad to compete with the BBC's "truthful" broadcasts by adopting what he called 'The Policy of Total Frankness' alongside his urge for 'Total War' which he stressed from February 1942 onwards. This was largely the result of the more intense and more successful Allied bombing of German cities. Hitherto, the RAF had pursued the policy of 'precision bombing' selected military targets, which had been a total failure – only 5% of any bombload had come within 5 miles of its chosen destination. Once the Allies turned to the more generalised 'area bombing', they began to cause havoc. Goebbels realised, as Churchill had been forced to realise in Coventry in 1940, and as Japanese officials are having to, this week, after the earthquake that hit Kobe (compared by not a few eye-witnesses to the Tokyo firestorm of 1945), that clear, unadulterated information is the only factor that prevents a devastated population from descending into chaos. The spell is broken. In a climate which has been used to party line, half-truths and forced rumours, this brings double difficulty. A polluted river does not instantly become a source of spring water.

If wartime is the mother of invention, then the greatest steps forward (or backwards, as is the case) have not been in the realm of weaponry or space travel, but in the manipulation of information – in the space between the codebreaking work at Bletchley Park[3], and the Black Propaganda unit at Woburn. The idea is to simplify and to sophisticate at one and the same time. The military enjoys the double advantage of being able to fix its initiatives within a temporal frame (1914–18, 1939–45) and, where necessary, to spin them out as Official Secrets.

The residue is relocated in peacetime, tried and tested. Today, every communiqué beyond a secure one-to-one conversation or a small gathering (ie., one that is not tape-recorded) can easily be converted into propaganda. Market research, advertising, product placement and publicity, image processing, soundbite design, the spin doctor and the security services all create camouflage – so much so that even the main protagonists, politicians, frequently appeal for "a level playing field".

The playing field itself has been and long gone: the Western Front, 1914, was the last post of the old order's faith in "fair play" and "gentlemanly conduct", where sport is war and war is sport. In this light, we might conclude that the invention and refinement of the machine gun is the key catalyst that shaped the chemistry of 20th century communications, not radio, neither television nor the rise of the advertising industry. As populations increase and develop their "standards of living", as the cult of the individual makes the accurate targeting of information more reliant upon expensive and intrusive technologies, it is easy to forget how it all started. "You didn't have to aim, we just fired into them" (A German machine gunner in 1916)[4]. Lord Kitchener's famous recruitment poster, "Your Country Needs You", was no different in this respect. There is so much that we don't know, and knowledge, we are assured, is a dangerous thing. Everyone just hoped they did not turn out to be one of those zeroes, the small print on a densely-typed casualty list.

1. Try and locate Delmer's autobiography, *Black Boomerang*, published by Hamish Hamilton in 1962... difficult to find, however, outside major libraries. 2. "I knew its trade name, who originally designed it and when, also who cast and marketed it... I could identify almost any printing type engraved since 1500" Ellic Howe, *The Black Game*, Michael Joseph Ltd. 1982. 3. See *FUSE 6: Codes*; also David Khan, *The Codebreakers*, Weidenfeld and Nicholson 1973. 4. See John Ellis, *The Social History of the Machine Gun*, Pimlico 1993.

SUBMIT
FUSE explores new possibilities in digital communication but to do this effectively, it is first necessary to diffuse the various 'double binds' and conglomerates of given thought. Once again with *Propaganda*, we come to a point of focus with the definition of the term itself. Given the available space, broad issues are crossed over quickly, but this limitation can also trigger unexpected ideas. So much for form, so for function, the prime intention is to stimulate thought and debate. There is substance and detail for those that will pursue them, but no *fait accomplis*.

CONTACT
FUSE is published quarterly by FontShop International and distributed through the FontShop network.

UNWAHRHAFTIG
FUSE fonts do not always include a full set of upper and lower case characters. They are experimental ideas and should be extended by users... abuse is part of the process!

FUSE EDITORIAL
Unit 2 Whitehorse Yard
78 Liverpool Road London N1 0QD
Fax: +44 (0) 171 704 2447

ISSUE 12
Editor & text: Jon Wozencroft
Design: John Critchley
Main image not in FUSE

FUSE 12: Neville Brody Bonus Font Populist

ABCDEFGHIJKLMNOPQRSTUVWXYZ123456
7890!@£$%^&*()=_+[]{};':"./>?,<§±¡™#¢®§¶

POPULIST SHOUT

a b c d e f g h i j k l m n o p q r s t u v w x y z A B C D E
F G H I J K L M N O P Q R S T U V W X Y Z 0 1 2 3 4 5 6 7 8 9

POPULIST EXCLAIM

0 1 2 3 4 5 6 7 8 9

POPULIST NOISE

POPULIST CONTROL

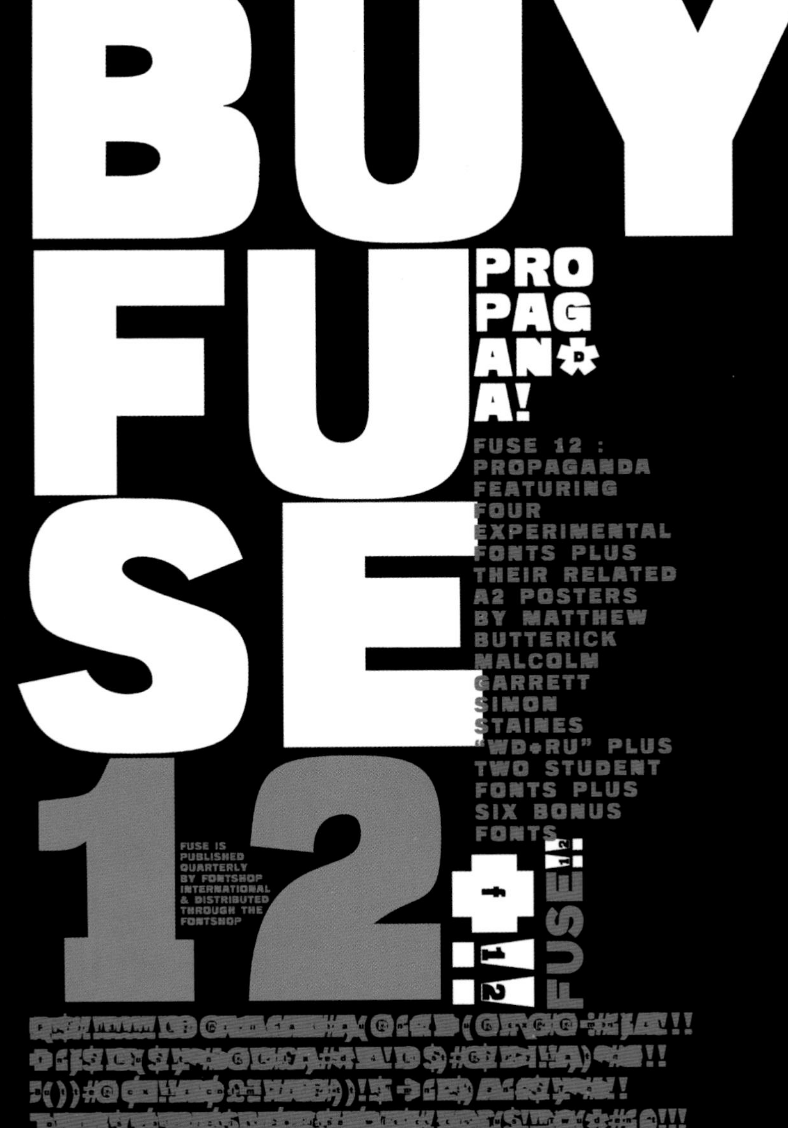
BUY
FUSE
PRO
PAG
AN
A!
FUSE 12 :
PROPAGANDA
FEATURING
FOUR
EXPERIMENTAL
FONTS PLUS
THEIR RELATED
A2 POSTERS
BY MATTHEW
BUTTERICK
MALCOLM
GARRETT
SIMON
STAINES
"WD+RU" PLUS
TWO STUDENT
FONTS PLUS
SIX BONUS
FONTS
12
FUSE IS
PUBLISHED
QUARTERLY
BY FONTSHOP
INTERNATIONAL
& DISTRIBUTED
THROUGH THE
FONTSHOP
FUSE

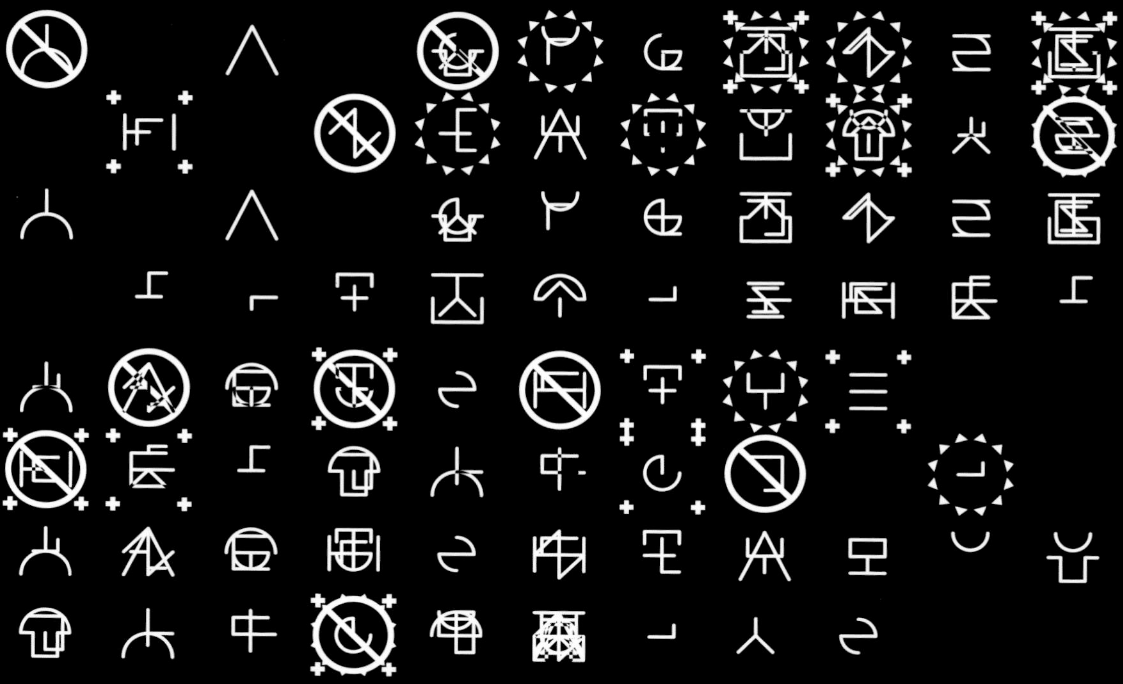

FUSE 12: Matthew Butterick Agitprop

Agitprop is not about what some messages may mean by themselves, but what they become in context. Interference can change, accentuate or negate their intended meaning. *Agitprop* is formed from a basic set of 26 shapes under a-z, but each keystroke contains two other shapes which can appear up to four characters away from the centre. Keys A-Z contain the same combinations of symbols, but with three overlay shapes randomly added to change the texture in more severe ways. Shift option a-z contains the symbols alone, and keys 1-3 contain the overlays alone. All have zero width to enable you to control your own propaganda!

F Agitprop © Matthew Butterick ℗ 1994 FontShop International Poster printed on recycled paper

believe me?
F Instrument © Malcolm Garrett ℗ 1994 FontShop International Poster printed on recycled paper

FUSE 12: Malcolm Garrett Instrument

Instrument explores the 'weighting' of language and the often duplicitous nature of information inherent in written propaganda. Each character is composed of two parts. One, located beneath the lower-case keys, is bolder in structure than the other, which is located beneath the upper-case keys, though both are made up of seemingly randomised graphic elements. There is therefore a visual imbalance which colours the reading of a text as one switches between the 2 parts. These can also be overlaid to make another complete character set, thus bringing about a 3rd reading. However, because the two are distinctly separate, a purposeful intervention on behalf of the designer is required to make the composition happen. Whilst lower-case and upper-case forms are discreetly legible, their true meaning becomes clearer, but more detailed, once overlaid.

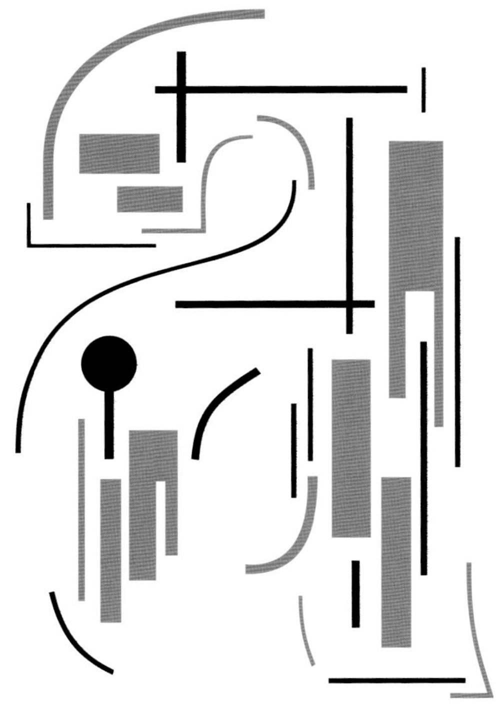

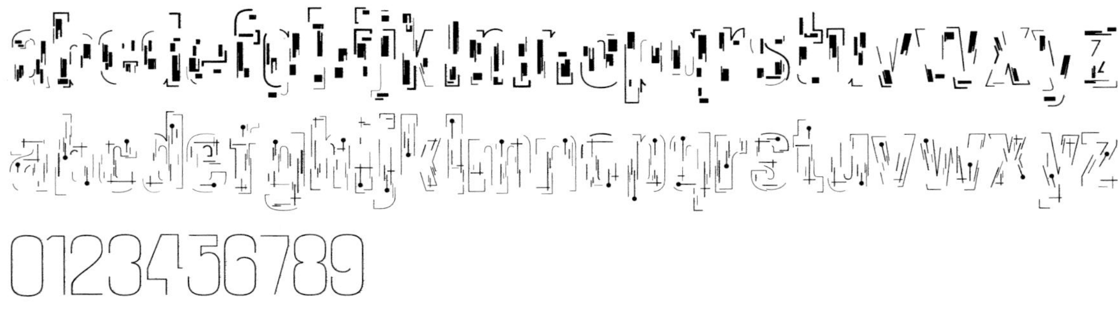

ABCDEFGHIJKLMNOPQRSTUVWXYZ
abcdefghijklmnopqrstuvwxyz 12345
67890!@£$%^&*()=_+[]{};'"\|>?,

FUSE 12: Simon Staines Trojan

Trojan reflects the difficulty of interpretation in today's media-saturated culture, where one man's freedom fighter is another man's terrorist. In a world where the unemployed have become 'job seekers', doublespeak is now reality. It is the role of the viewer to look beyond the hegemony of Western media.

"It is easier to perceive error than to find truth, for the former
lies on the surface and is easily seen, while the latter lies in the
depth, where few are willing to search for it"
Johann Wolfgang von Goethe
F Trojan © Simon Staines ℗ 1994 FontShop International Poster printed on recycled paper

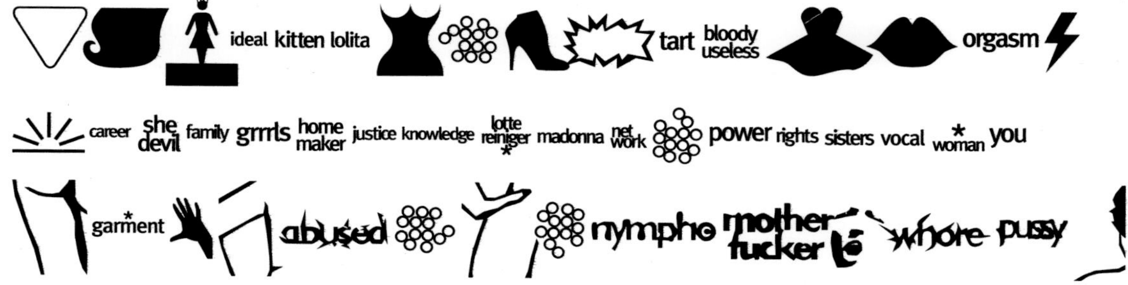

FUSE 12: 'WD + RU' Pussy Galore

Pussy Galore acknowledges the structural conventions of language but uses the technology itself to extend common keyboard functions.

The conventional alphabet keys contain a series of ideological statements. By using these in conjunction with the shift and option keys, further visual and verbal references are revealed. In addition, hidden heroines appear as 'surprise' elements throughout.

The symbol * denotes several additional layers of information contained on the disk. Here, *Pussy Galore* is presented in simplified form – full representation of the typeface can be found on the accompanying poster.

Thanks to Simon Wicker and students at Ravensbourne College of Design and Communication.

Pussy Galore

The Women's Design + Research Unit (WD + RU) has been established to recognize and encourage women workimg internationally in the field of visual graphics including graphic design, typography and multi-media.

con Women's voices have been restricted for too long fine

Empowerment normal
Stereotypes shift
Choices option
Bad Language shift option

* "We wore girdles on our bodies, and girdles on our minds"

* Hidden heroines who have made important contributions to the areas of art, design and film appears as suprise elements- the start of a growning database

* Women and technology are equal parts of the future and, for women, technology is the vehicle for their liberation

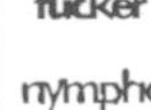

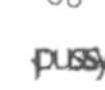

F Pussy Galore © WD + RU ® 1995 FontShop International Poster printed on recycled paper

SUPER FUSE

FUSESUPERSTITION: We Live in Hope Jon Wozencroft

STITION

"Now my charms are all o'erthrown And what strength I have's mine own, Which is most faint."
W. Shakespeare, *The Tempest*, epilogue

Don't sneeze, and if you must, put your hand in front of your mouth. "Bless You". But only mothers and elderly folk say "bless you" these days, and it's not just a question of decorum. Superstition represents old ways of thinking and youth has no such inclination. Superstitious belief has faded away at a similar pace as church attendance in city centres and long before this, face to face with Einstein's equations and the illuminations of electric lighting, superstitious thoughts were held to be an ancient preserve of the pre-modern, parched-skin mentality.

Like rats leaving a sinking ship, *we know better...* This is what we say to ourselves when a black cat dashes out into the road, crossing our path. This is the version we believe when we say something risky, before covering our words with the instinctive insurance policy, "Touch wood" – only to find that the table we're sitting at is solid formica and the chair made out of plastic. So you touch your head, in modest alarm. *Nevermind*. Superstitions are simply the idle brake of a miniature world; and on this planet we want maximum reach, the space beyond NASA, while we track our selves down to invisible detail, the basic DNA.

However, all this assumes that human behaviour has developed alongside the technologies that now define it. With the certainty of scientists, all this assumes that we have no further need for the consensual wisdom of old wives' tales. How can a rabbit's foot compete with nuclear power? What status the four-leaf clover in a world of fractals?

Humanity abhors simple solutions. In fact, the more we advance as a species in terms of material comforts, the more we are returning to the world of superstitions and their familiar slipstream of irrationality. Maybe, for a short time, the Western world really did move away from this sphere – through psychoanalysis, kitchen appliances, James Bond precision (who knows?) – with the revival of uncertainty, superstitions once again come to the rescue. They help us ward off general fears and make sense of the inexplicable. And if they do not seem to work, well "it's a load of old rubbish, isn't it?". "I take it back". Avoid it like the plague.

In fact, this double standard is encoded in the origins of the word itself, coming from the Latin verb *superstare*, 'to stand over'. (Many conflicts in Roman times were settled by hand-to-hand fighting: those who survived the duel were known as *superstites*, 'standing above' the slain.)[1] The current definition of superstition is diffuse – 'standing over a thing in amazement', 'an over-ceremonious attitude to religion', 'the survival of old religious habits in the midst of a new order of things' – all, however, suggest the uneasy relationship between the world of appearances and the world of invisible forces. Like the raver who says, lost for words, "Amazing".

Delving deeper into definition, the verb *stare* is the exact equivalent of the English 'survival'. If at one time all superstitions were measured by the fact that they were not endorsed by any of the great organised religions (with their monopoly on ritual), then the roots are nonetheless identical. Superstition is thus a medium that allows us to channel the primary impulse, the transcendence of death into life lines.

This is made apparent on investigating the origins of a widespread practice: the habit of avoiding walking under ladders. A simple precaution, no doubt, one that removes the possibility of a bucket of paint falling on your head, or in the days before a decent municipal drainage system, something much less fragrant. The superstition actually derives from the days of public hanging, when the executioner would climb a ladder to cut free the victims of the gallows. The combination of ill omen and the practical possibility that a freshly-dead body might come crashing down on top of you leaves an indelible imprint. And on a universal level, walking under a ladder means the breaking of the triangle, symbol of the Holy Trinity, an inauspicious deed whenever and wherever it is committed.

Superstitions do not so much signify fear of the unknown as *fear of the abnormal*. This explains the variety of commonly-held beliefs associated with natural phenomena (the four-leaf clover again) and especially the weather, summed up by "red sky at night, shepherd's delight; red sky in the morning, shepherd's warning". Yellow-grey muck tends to welcome bad luck.

There are countless admonitions about the weather. You could be forgiven for supposing that various superstitions persist simply because their messages rhyme and are easy to remember. The fear of the abnormal, however, is made explicit by another still widely-believed idea: the shock that arises from a shattered mirror (7 years' misfortune) or the broken glass of a framed photograph (imminent death). If a person's image or reflection is their soul, to damage this will block the doors to heaven. In Europe, what you have to do is to pick up all the shards of broken glass and throw them into a fast-moving river to wash away the curse. In America you have to place a $5 bill on the collected fragments whilst making the sign of the cross. Next you have to sing the Star Spangled Banner standing on your head, and then play air guitar to your favourite Nirvana track. Only joking.

But superstition is above all no laughing matter. You cannot laugh. Traditionally, in the perpetual war of mind over matter, it is often difficult to differentiate between careful observance and simple eccentricity. "Beware the Evil Eye", "Don't spill the salt", and "Keep your fingers crossed". Dr. Johnson, the famous man of letters, was prey to a whole host of superstitions... wherever he went he would touch every wooden post, and he would *never* step on the cracks between paving stones. Was he a nutter? Shakespeare, who attributed his success to a 400-year-old lucky bed, coloured his plays with superstitious lore. Was he too off his trolley? In the case of Howard Hughes, superstition mutates into the phobic and obsessive. Such was his fear of germs, he employed various bodyguards, armed with boxes of tissue paper, to guard his airspace against the sudden invasion of a fly.

Delving deeper into definition, the verb *stare* is the exact equivalent of the English 'survival'. If at one time all superstitions were measured by the fact that they were not endorsed by any of the great organised religions (with their monopoly on ritual), then the roots are nonetheless identical.

Any such daredevil insect would have to be clasped and smothered with a Kleenex before being placed in a sterilised container and incinerated. Flying and personal hygiene were Hughes' greatest passions. He was able to make millions of dollars whilst holed up in a hotel bedroom. "I guess it just goes to show, the lie-dream of the casino soul" (The Fall).

Hope is a small town in British Columbia.

"The Feelgood Factor are the three most boring words in the English Language."
John Major, quoted on BBC2 *Newsnight*, 31 March 1995

For commonly-shared beliefs and fears, you can at least depend on the English Language not to be boring, even when it's floundering under the burden of tourism and soundbites. Arcane, yes. Wilfully obscure, most definitely. Never boring. For "fear of the number 13" we have 'triskaidekaphobia'. Not the stuff of night schools. Especially tentacular, this particular foreboding seems to have originated in Scandinavian folklore when the god Loki caused the death of Balder at a gathering of thirteen people (who knows anything of this?), since when, the superstition has spread like a virus into every possible association with the magic number.

In an attempt to restore the balance and have the chance to check whether the lift really *does* get stuck on the 13th floor, there is (according to author Peter Haining) the Thirteen Club whose meetings and activities flout as many superstitions as possible. No horseshoes on their front porches. They have yet it would seem to perish, one by one like actors in an Agatha Christie thriller.

The origins of many superstitions are more difficult to trace, but that only adds to the sense of deliberate mystery (the Greek root of the word 'mystery' means 'to close the lips or the eyes'). Why, for example, must you always offer a symbolic payment should you receive a gift of cutlery? Apparently because a knife will cut the ties of friendship – and money keeps everything on a level footing. Surely there is a perfectly good reason for this custom (still followed religiously by H.M. the Queen, it is said), but what the hell, the main imperative behind all superstitions is straightforward.

We believe them because we want to believe them, and when the Feelgood Factor is pretty low on the Richter scale, then the power of positive thinking brings its own rewards. *All that glistens is not gold.*

Superstition brings us into direct contact with the most metaphysical feature of human existence – *how do thoughts anticipate and influence coming events?* And it is this eternal conundrum that explains why, now, superstitions are making such a comeback in our culture. Everything from *Notes & Queries* newspaper columns, the National Lottery and megavitamins, to daily horoscopes, urban myths and conspiracy theories fits into this pattern.

The most significant difference is the way that superstitions now collude with our modern futurism. Their prime function is not to maintain the connection with the pagan past, but to harden a more urgent and contemporary faith. The mindset travels in the opposite direction. *There must be something just over the horizon that will come to our rescue.* We can safely say that we deploy a vision of the future to immunise ourselves against it. Today's great superstition is "What do I care?". "What can I do about it?". (Loads.) When the laws of probability refuse to weigh in our favour, there is nothing better than an irrational thought, a crazy idea, an abstract abandonment to put things in perspective.

Are both technophilia and technophobia based on superstition? Of course. Is the Internet a hive of rational argument? Hardly. What happens to email in the split second it takes to travel from terminal to terminal? I'd like to think... rubbish. This computer, for one, is full of little green men that feed themselves from the wastebasket. They've already had a full breakfast – two early versions of this poster will keep them going at least until dinner time.

Reference:

1. It is also worth looking at the associations with paganism, folklore, myth and magic. 'Pagan' (*paganus*) not only means 'rustic' or 'villager', but in Roman times meant 'non-militant', the opposite of 'soldier'. 'Folk' was originally used to mean 'a division of the army' ('folklore' was not coined until 1846). 'Myth' once existed as an adjective, meaning 'gentle', and also as a verb, meaning alternately 'to show', 'to notice' and 'to measure'. Only the meaning of 'magic' has remained constant and universal.

In an attempt to restore the balance and have the chance to check whether the lift really *does* get stuck on the 13th floor, there is (according to author Peter Haining) the Thirteen Club whose meetings and activities flout as many superstitions as possible.

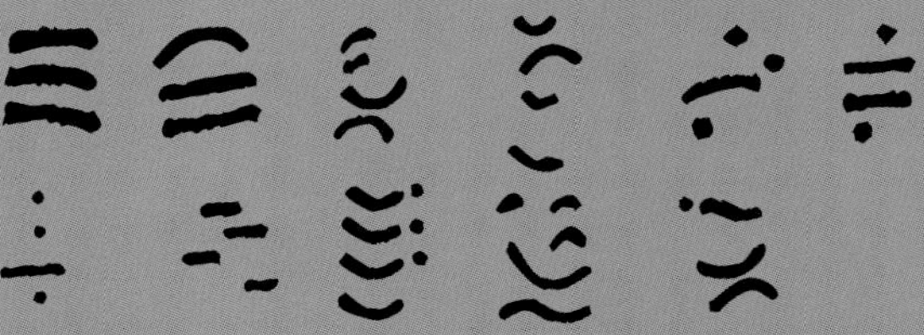

FUSESUPERSTITION: Marina Willer Bonus Font Babel

One of the five winners of the StudentFUSE project at the Royal College of Art, held to coincide with the FUSE 94 conference last November.

FUSESUPERSTITION: Petra Waldeyer Bonus Font Kwarthel

The font comes from the same Düsseldorf project that gave us *Atomic Circle* (published in FUSE 10).

JOHN CRITCHLEY & JON WOZENCROFT EDITORIAL POSTER

WE LIVE IN HOPE

"Now my charms are all o'erthrown
And what strength I have's mine own,
Which is most faint."
W. Shakespeare, *The Tempest*, epilogue.

FUSE SUPERSTITION

SUBMIT

CONTACT

SCHADENFREUDE!

FUSE EDITORIAL

ISSUE THE ONE AFTER 12

ABCDEFGHIJKLMNOPQRSTUVWXYZ
abcdefghijklmnopqrstuvwxyz123456789

RITUAL ONE

RITUAL TWO

ABCDEFGHIJKLMNabcdefghijklmnmo123
ABCDEFGHIJKLMNabcdefghijklmnmo123

RITUAL THREE

RITUAL FOUR

FUSESUPERSTITION: Neville Brody Bonus Font Ritual

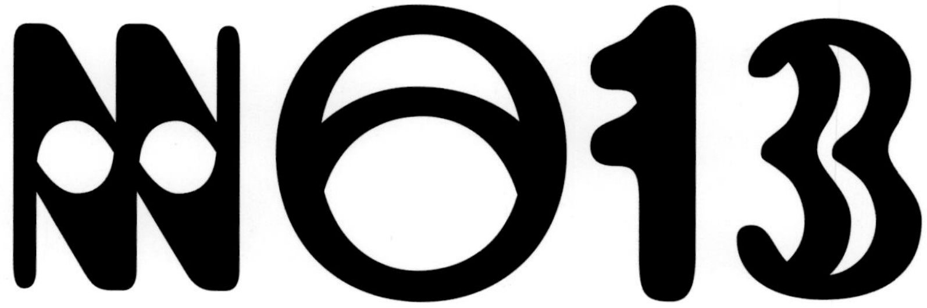

SUPE
RSTIT
ION

Fuse | Superstition
Featuring four experimental fonts
plus their related A2 posters
by Scott Clum, Hibino,
Pablo Rovalo Flores, 'Tomato'.
Plus six bonus fonts.

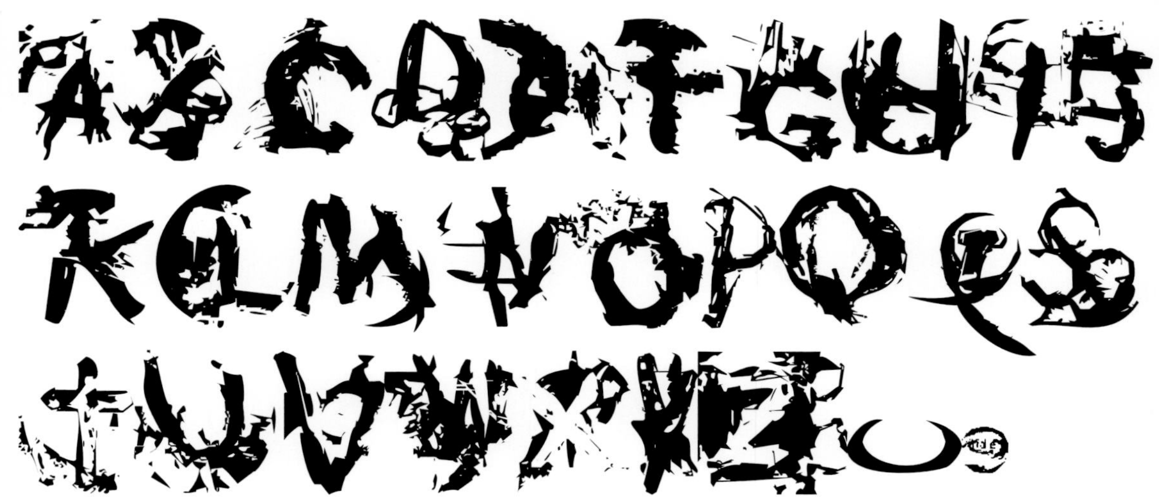

FUSESUPERSTITION: Scott Clum Burnfont

Burnfont is based on the idea that each one of our superstitions is a private religion of delicate balances, each hinging on the other. These characters operate in much the same way, some working better with others, each having its own balance and relationship.

F Burnfont © Scott Clum ® 1995 FontShop International Poster printed on recycled paper

ONMI FONT KATSUHIKO HIBINO ELECTRONIC DESIGN PROPELLER ART WORKS
F Onmi © Hibino ® 1995 FontShop International Poster printed on recycled paper
"	shall be placed where a right angle exists."
"	shall stick it's head into a rectangle."
"	shall calmly stay on the corner of a square."
"	shall never be used alone."
"	shall be on top of a triangle with good balance."
"	looks best in mirror image."
"	brings good luck when surroundeed by double circles."
"	brings a sutable match when when places a black dot in the direction of north west."
"	means the best when shaped by building blocks."
"	shall find a lost object by landing its leg onto ground."
"	brings the best career by scattering into the shape of a circle."
"	shall heal illness when shapped with the elements of dumplings."
"	shall be constructed with five points, then link them with lines and place three curved lines underneath in order to recieve dear children."
"	shall break through cloud to concrete your lost decision."
"	shall heal sty eyes and corn on your foot when blowing a part of o, espcially top left."
"	shall open up financial luck when when building it with a line and D which an eye is placed in it."
"	guarantees safety of a house by placing another Q crushed out of shape."
"	shall bring peace in life by replacing the angled line with dotted line."
"	shall bring good luck in gambling by shooting an arrow into the middle."
"	shall have a man walk on top of it in order to heal pain in legs."
"	shall bring bon voyage by floating a ship on the bottom."
"	with three lines in three level shall be good for you throat."
"	shall bring a winner by placing three circles on top of it."
"	shall solve dispute when constructed with four levels."
"	shall be planted deep into the ground and grow roots in order to bring good luck in moving places."
"	shall be good for everthing when built with three circles."

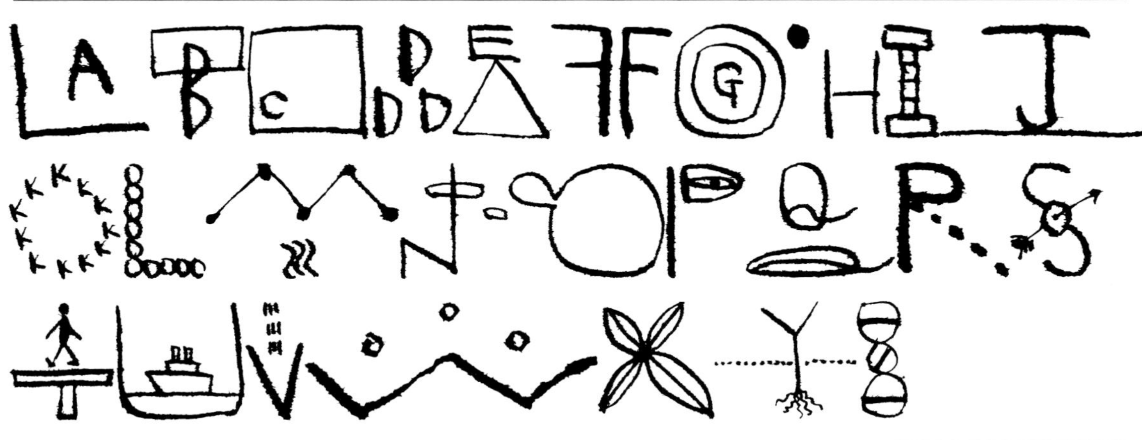

FUSESUPERSTITION: Katsuhiko Hibino Onmi

Onmi is a specially created term which means "Holy Font" – no such word exists in Japanese. While meanings get transformed in time, *Onmi* is instinctive. In a New Year's Day tradition, everyone visits a shrine and takes "Omikuji", where one selects a piece of paper to check one's luck for the coming year. Hibino overlapped *Onmi* with Omikuji. The action of picking one of 26 characters is like Omikuji, and a meaning has been created for each one, located on the FUSE 13 disk's movie file.

ABCDEFGHIJKLMNOPQRSTUVWXYZ
!$&{}´.?,¡'"¿

SANTO DOMINGO DE CHILE

ABCDEFGHIJKLMNOPQRSTUVWXYZ
ABCDEFGHIJKLMNOPQRSTUVWXYZ
!$&{}´.?,¡'"¿

SANTO DOMINGO DE DULCE

ABCDEFGHIJKLMNOPQRSTUVWXYZ
ABCDEFGHIJKLMNOPQRSTUVWXYZ
!$&{}´.?,¡"¿

SANTO DOMINGO DE MANTECA

SANTO DOMINGO PATZCUARO

FUSESUPERSTITION: Pablo Rovalo Santo Domingo

Santo Domingo is a loving appropriation, inspired by the strength of expressions and traditions in Mexico. It is a sad witness that sees our painful conversion, based on ignorance on both sides, to foreign standards, superstitions and values. *Santo Domingo* is open to all kinds of improvement but it is against any cultural impositions that might come attached. The poster commemorates the 15th anniversary of the murder of El Salvador's Archbishop Oscar Romero; the times of death and fear in which he lived and loved his people are not over; his strength and spirit still live on in Latin America.

OSCAR
ARNULFO
ROMERO
XV AÑOS
MARZO MCMXCV.

F Santo Domingo © Pablo Rovalo ℗ 1995 FontShop International Poster printed on recycled paper

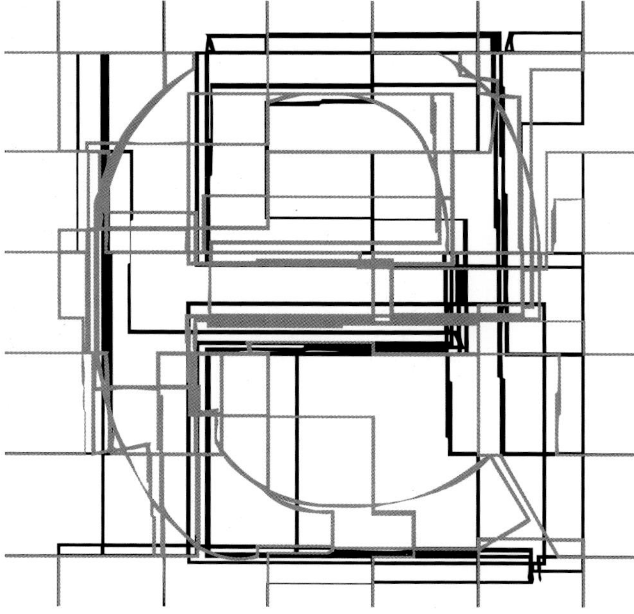

FUSESUPERSTITION: Tomato Newcracks 13

Newcracks 13, where angels fear to tread; cracks in pavements, avoiding them. Font designed to equate visually with plan view of a pavement. Each character constructed using thirteen lines; lines start and finish at six points on each axis of em square, making twelve. One floats free, equalling thirteen. Resultant grid creates a text impossible to access without crossing a line. Poster, crucifix in cracks. Thirteenth parallel.

"The dead... are concrete. They're part of the sidewalk."
Norman Mailer, Pavement & Religion

F Newcracks 13 © 'Tomato' © 1995 FontShop International Poster printed on recycled paper

FUSE

FUSE 14: 2@odds.com Jon Wozencroft

SUMMER 1995

CYBER

'Cyber' comes from the Greek for 'to steer'. The French *'cybernétique'* means 'the art of governing'. Mutation into the scientific term 'cybernetics' did not happen until 1948 and 'cyborg', the mechanical man, appeared only recently, in 1960. The new term 'cyberspace' is often defined as 'the place you go to when you're talking on the telephone', a nostalgic way of representing the destination of the future; the concept of 'directing' a call has been outmoded by the fibre-optic speed of a digital connection.

Plug-in: Live/Neutral/Earth.
www.Switch. Map Ref 0°N 52°W

For the past twelve months, it has been impossible to look at newspaper or magazines without seeing articles and news items about the Internet. Advocates of the online revolution cite McLuhan as their mentor. This is very strange. You'd expect a thorough reappraisal of his warnings... the "space between" the transmission of a message and its reception could be explored and examined as never before... one would hope... to take time for thought before plunging headlong into the latest media must-have... but no. Very few voices actively question the cyberspace promise. Who has the time to think? Who will admit that there could be many people who, given the choice, would reject the cyberspace experience if it has you stuck at home with the VR headset, trapped in mental curfew, afraid to walk the streets.

For a long time there seems to have been an unspoken rule in force that any active critique of the Internet should wait whilst the new medium was "sized up" according to the conflicting concerns of freedom of speech and corporate strategy. Next in the media dynamic comes the backlash and moral panic, made visible by the present furore over cyberporn. Nobody really knows what's going to happen, but even if the dubious claims for utopian democratic connectivity are cast aside, it is tempting to shrug one's shoulders and agree with Bruce Sterling when he says we should be thankful we have the Internet and not the anticipated outcome developed by ARPA in the early 1970s... a communications channel designed for military use in the event of nuclear war.

Global media continues to act local in the way that various items and personalities become (at least for a time) Protected Species. You know that certain records or films are going to be released and praised to the nines: whether they're any good or not has little to do with it. In a world saturated with products and posturings it is much easier to go with the flow – the flow of promotional activity – rather than risk upsetting the advertisers (unless of course they are sponsoring you to be outrageous), or seeming out of touch.

The journalist's technique of "build them up then knock them down" is familiar enough. Today, the frequent use of binary editorial orientations – backwards/forwards, left/right, up/down – blinds through repetition and also sanctions those arguments that are based on nothing more than *Schadenfreude* and envy. *Mathematician Reads the Newspaper*, a new book by John Allen Paulos, examines the way in which journalists and columnists have incorporated this conceit into critical analysis to create fatuous arguments by using the method of "contrarianism". He cites the example of the reporter who puts together a news story on the latest evidence for global warming, only to be followed a few days later by another article that argues that global warming is a complete myth invented by scientists to gain lucrative funding. It is not difficult to think up other examples: Modern Art is rubbish/no it isn't; O.J. Simpson is guilty/not guilty; the Bosnian crisis can only be solved by diplomacy/armed intervention. And so on. Paulos upholds the need for alternative viewpoints and animated debate, while suggesting that a basic awareness of arithmetic, of probability and games theory reveals the pattern. "The odds that someone is American, given that they speak English, are clearly not the same as the odds that someone speaks English, given they are American".

The arguments that Paulos puts forward are developments of a tactic previously used in television broadcasting known as "the empty chair". Any filmmaker or TV journalist who wished to make a programme promoting a singular point of view would have to be subject to "balancing material" that upheld "the consensus". And if no one could create or be commissioned to come up with the counterclaim, if no "expert" could be interviewed to contradict the initial item, then "the empty chair" effectively vetoed the possibility of the programme's transmission.

Appositioning opposites used to be primarily an avant-garde and structuralist device. Positive and negative were used to acknowledge the presence and power of the Double. Now assimilated into the mainstream, the current media practice of using ideas and arguments like checkers in a loop has the opposite effect. Left at the level of "No it isn't Yes it is", debate stays in a kindergarten. It fuses the mundane to the monumental, and paves the way for authoritarianism to look friendly and fair. Freedom of Speech is not the same thing as freedom of thought, yet the one cannot exist without the other. Who – what – creates the consensus? How can you claim a consensus if the process is promoting fragmentation and maintaining social divisions?

Cyberspace, "A consensual hallucination... unthinkable complexity. Lines of light ranged in the nonspace of the mind, clusters and constellations of data. Like city lights, receding...". For William Gibson, cyberspace was not a zone which encouraged radical new art forms, nor even a digital shopping arcade to browse through at leisure, but the acme of arcade games, with "animals wired into test systems, helmets feeding into fire control circuits of tanks and war planes". As far as its inventor was concerned, cyberspace came with a warning sign, representing a dystopian vision of the future, "a drastic simplification of the human sensorium".

In the eleven years since *Neuromancer* was published, the meaning of 'cyberspace' has been turned inside out to become a refuge, like a crowded nightclub full of expectation. A place to lose yourself... to who knows where... into a compact of computer game, reference library and brothel? Maybe hazard is all that people look for, but neatly boxed with an illusion of safety. At a time of rootlessness and fluent paranoia, cyberspace can be a mobile home for anyone who wants to get lost without having to go anywhere.

In the eleven years since *Neuromancer* was published, the meaning of 'cyberspace' has been turned inside out to become a refuge, like a crowded nightclub full of expectation. A place to lose yourself... to who knows where... into a compact of computer game, reference library and brothel?

Navigation is a keyword in the lexicon of new media. Comparisons are frequently made between the building of rail and road networks and the establishment of the online universe. Human interaction depends on a compatible relationship with time and space. Rail and then air travel quickly transformed and compressed the sense of space. Electronic distribution has the same effect on time... increasing confusion (cyberfusion) to support the production of inertia.

"There is no *Pattern of Things to Come*. Our universe is not merely bankrupt; there remains no dividend at all; it has not simply liquidated; it is going clean out of existence, leaving not a wrack behind. The attempt to trace a pattern of any sort is absolutely futile".
H.G. Wells, *Mind at the End of its Tether*, William Heinemann Ltd. 1945

Alas the man best remembered for *The Time Machine* and *War of the Worlds* (prophecies since softened by their film versions) had no faith in the future. Wells' dread is nowhere to be seen in a new set of stamps recently issued by the Royal Mail; they simply use his titles like adverts for futurity. *The Time Machine* is depicted as a one-way vortex to tomorrow. The Superhighway... are you on it? Safety codes stress the importance of adequate stopping distance. "Leave plenty of space between your car and the vehicle in front of you". The stamps, adopting the livery of the overtaking lane, wear the same Go Faster stripes as car adverts, tins of soft drink and professional footballers. Packaging is warpaint.

In a recent interview, ex-Prime Minister, the now Baroness Thatcher admitted, "I cannot leave the future alone... I don't want it to go wonky"... a remarkable statement from a politician whose speciality during the last decade has been crash-creation schemes. John Major, on "resigning", demanded his detractors "put up or shut up". He was challenged by an unknown, John Redwood, a man on the right wing of the Tory party who was nevertheless accorded the futuristic nickname "Vulcan". What was he all about? "It was hard to tell. Thanks to the information revolution, in which yet more news is balanced by still less enlightenment, Britain now has what the Americans call 'goat-fucks', those swaying edifices of cameramen, snappers, sound recorders and hacks which lurch perilously round press conferences like the towers used to besiege medieval cities"
Simon Hoggart, *The Guardian*, 27–6–95

"Exterminate all rational thought"
William Burroughs

Reference:

Mathematician Reads the Newspaper, John Allen Paulos, Basic Books 1995
Heroes, John Pilger, Jonathan Cape Ltd. 1986
Neuromancer, William Gibson, Victor Gollancz Ltd. 1984

FUSE 14: Bonus Fonts

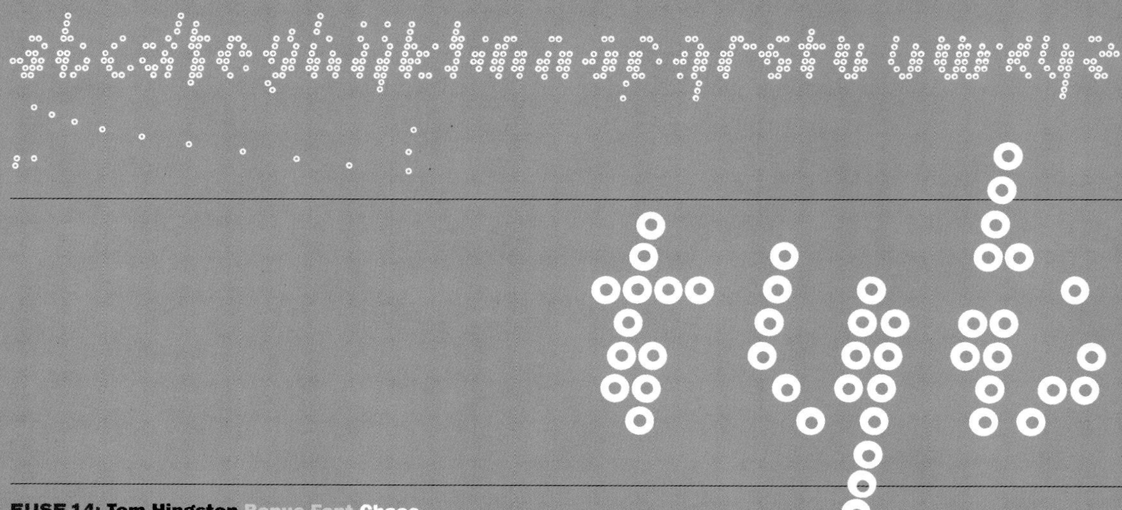

FUSE 14: Tom Hingston Bonus Font Chaos

Chaos is not designed to be used in isolation but provides the raw material for a background that would render any website inoperable!

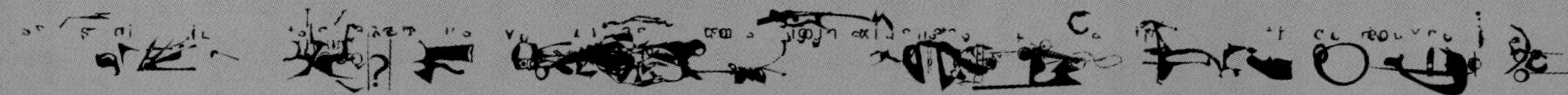

FUSE 14: Vera Daucher & Francis Stebbing Bonus Font Trinity

Trinity results from the opinion that every NEW phenomenon is the result of the combination or the meeting point of 3 different or opposing forces, we decided to produce a digital manifesto according to this natural principle or law of 3, created by the interaction of 3 people – the designers (male and female) and you.

The alphabet consists of 23 characters, located in the lower case and randomly arranged on the keyboard. The user must explore and experiment with them to find the correct order. It is only when this has been achieved, when the 11 "male" symbols alternate with 11 "female" symbols and the final character is located elsewhere on the keyboard, that the statement is legible. Good luck.

Tom Hingston for Research Studios (TOP). Vera Daucher & Francis Stebbing RCA student competition winners (ABOVE).

JOHN CRITCHLEY & JON WOZENCROFT EDITORIAL POSTER

CYBERFUSE

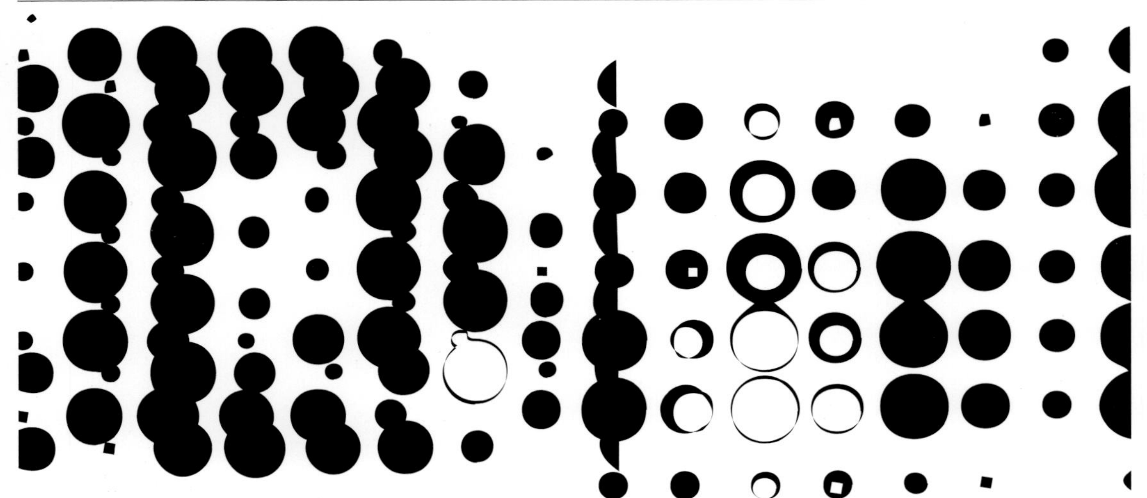

FUSE 14: Neville Brody Bonus Font Cyber

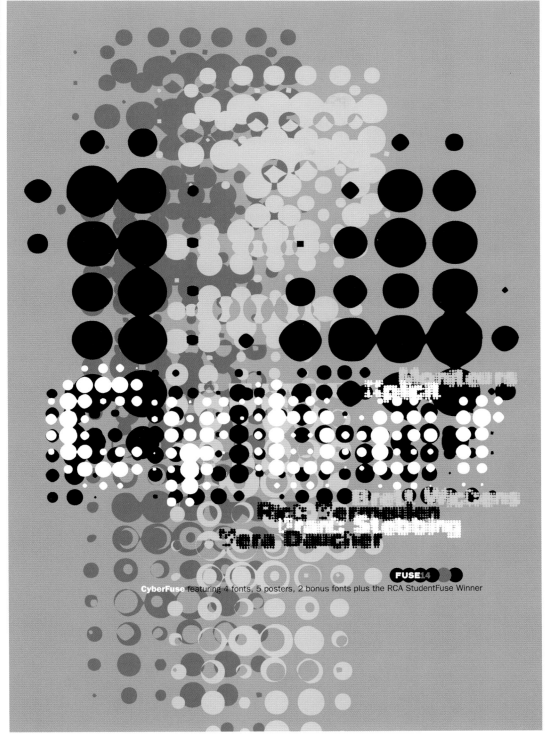
FUSE14
CyberFuse featuring 4 fonts, 5 posters, 2 bonus fonts plus the RCA StudentFuse Winner

```
=   =)  =  \ /  =¬  =)  =¬  =)   =  \ /  =)  =¬  =)
|   =   |    =  =¬  =   =¬  =\   |    =  =   =¬  =\
=   =)  =    =  =¬  =)  =¬       =    =  =)  =¬

=  \ /  =)  =¬  =)  =)   =  \ /  =)  =¬  =)  \ /  =
|    =  =   =¬  =\  =\   |    =  =   =¬  =\    =  |
=    =  =)  =¬           =    =  =)  =¬        =  =
```

FUSE 14: 'Moniteurs' MMMteurs-Cyber/MMMteurs-Real

MMMteurs-Cyber/MMMteurs-Real enables you to switch between the real world and cyberspace, but when you're in cyberspace you won't get very far with your text and will have to get used to another aesthetic... and you cannot watch the cyber world from the outside. The Internet is the first stage of cyberspace. "ASCII art" is an attempt to bring emotion to a medium which is ill prepared to transport feelings. And the output always looks different to the input.

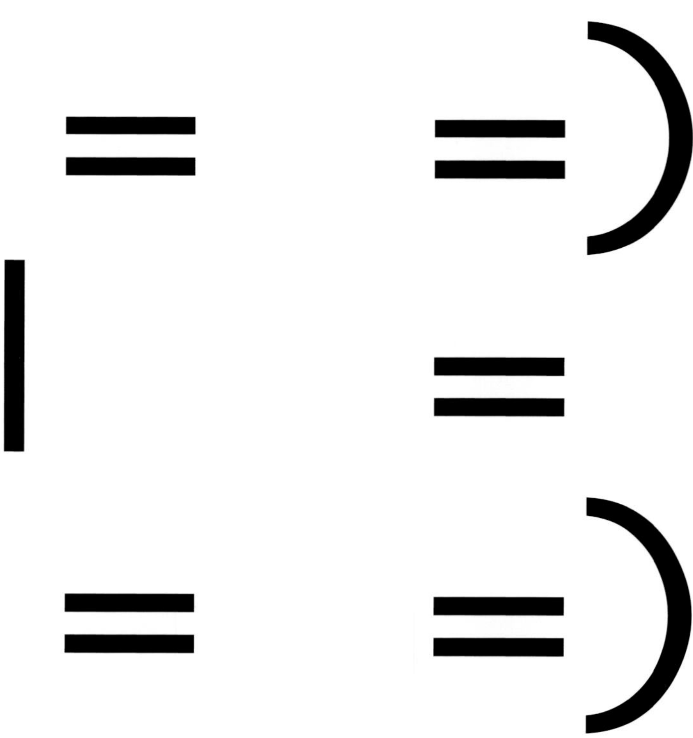

WITH MMMTEL'S YOU CAN
SWITCH FROM REAL WORLD TO
CYBERSPACE, BUT WHEN YOU ARE
IN CYBERSPACE YOU DON'T GET
[illegible]

YOU WILL ACHIEVE ANOTHER
AESTHETIC [illegible]
[illegible]
WATCH CYBERSPACE FROM THE
OUTSIDE [illegible] CYBERSPACE
[illegible]
[illegible] ON THE INTERNET
[illegible]

OUTPUT LOOKS DIFFERENT FROM
THE INPUT.

MMMTEL'S-REAL
MMMTEL'S-CYBER

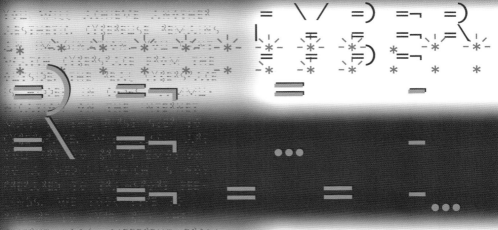

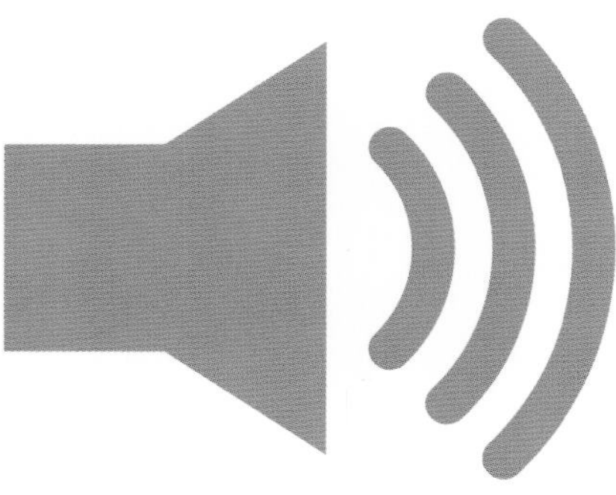

BIG EYED BEANS WAS PRODUCED AS AN AUDIO FILE WHICH IS NO LONGER COMPATIBLE WITH TODAY'S OPERATING SYSTEMS.

FUSE 14: Rick Vermeulen Big Eyed Beans

Big Eyed Beans is the result of experiments into the way we communicate. We use the same instruments but not the same sounds. The vocal chords, palate and uvula, the throat, our tongue, teeth, not forgetting the lips. Even the rhythm of our breathing plays a role in our speech.

Our spoken language consists of vowels and consonants, which we can divide into three distinct groups of sound: Lip-letters: b, f, m, p, v and w. Teeth/tongue-letters: c, d, l, n, r, s and t. Throat-letters: g, h, j, k, q and x. The consonant sounds connect with vowel sounds creating understandable words. In *Big Eyed Beans* the vowels have their own sounds (rustle) and the letters of each group of consonants share a sound.

This compresses the alphabet to 9 (letterforms/sounds). In cyberspace the difference between shape and sound doesn't exist. By touching a letter on the keyboard it is immediately sent to the receiver. When the keyboard isn't touched, nothing is sent. The length and transmission time of the message depends on the speed of the sender, who is also able to personalise the message by touching the keys in their own 'speaking' mode and making the sounds longer or shorter (loud, slurry, high-pitched, slow, fast).

The small visuals in the middle of the screen serve to remind us that we still look at something that represents type. The ever-moving 'hair' is there to make the now-and-then imperfect functioning of man-machine noticeable.

Thank you Albert and Angelique.

Hit

Fantasy.

that

is

long

reality,

lunar

I

note,

love

and

my

let

fantasy.

it

Reality is fantasy. Just don't call it reality. (Brian Wilson)

float.

'Big-eyed beans from Venus' (Don van Vlient)

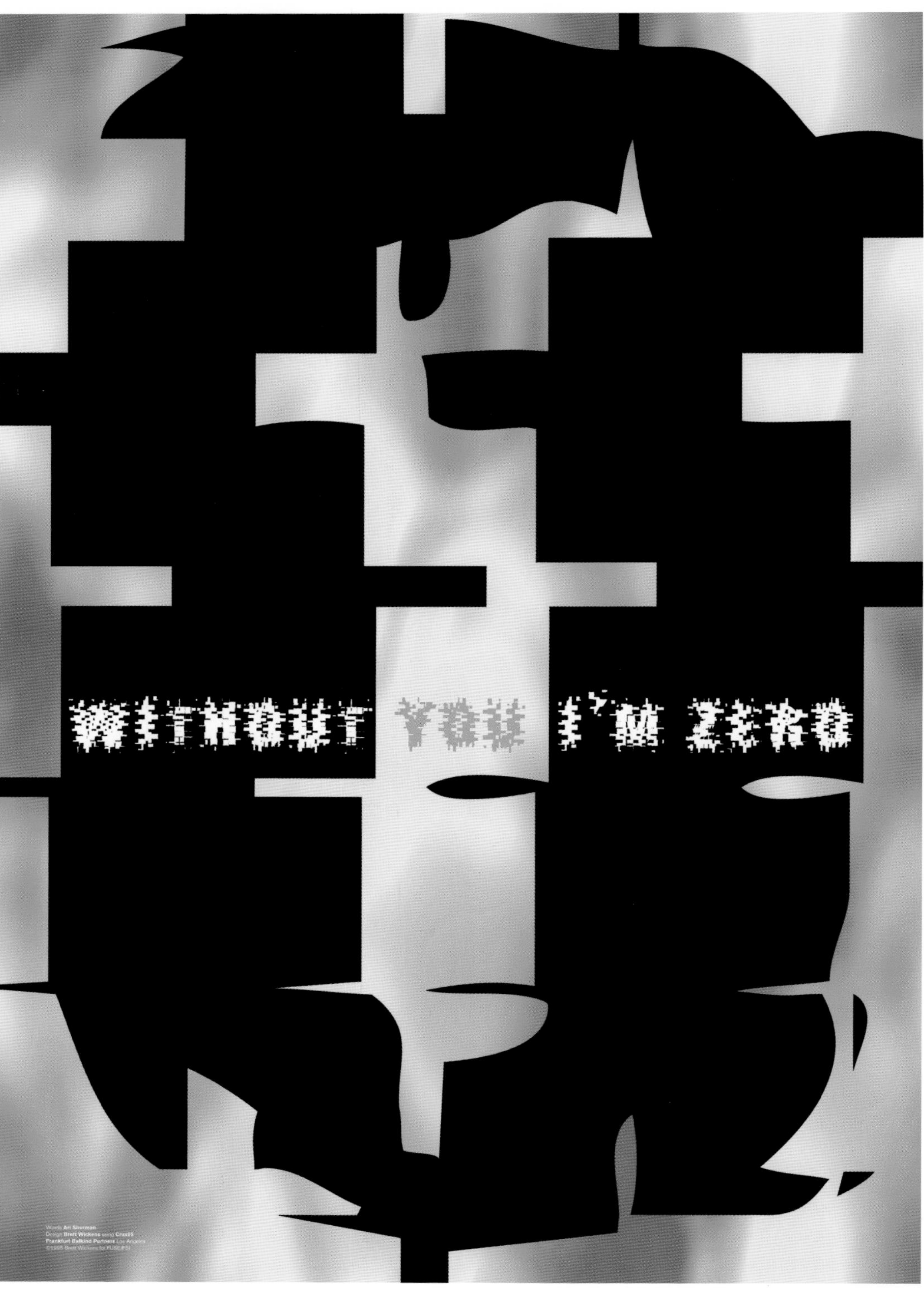
WITHOUT YOU I'M ZERO
Words Ari Sherman
Design Brett Wickens using Crux95
Frankfurt Balkind Partners Los Angeles
©1995 Brett Wickens for FUSE/FSI

FUSE 14: Brett Wickens Crux95

The seeds of *Crux95* were sown on the pages of *Typographica* in its June 1962 issue. One article, "Reading by Machine", discussed the process of designing fonts for optical character recognition, illustrated with examples of bizarre fonts such as *E13B*, *Solartron*, *Farrington Selfchek*, *CMB* and *EMI Fred*. This last typeface interested me the most – there were examples of how far you could degrade *Fred* before a machine could no longer read it. I built *Crux95* around the concept of a typeface in transit. A sequence of 1s and 0s, ons and offs, ups, downs and sideways.

The shapes started to remind me of images fractured through stained-glass, infusing the font with a quasi-religious aspect.

When communication is binary, it has no audience. The process of modulating/demodulating communication gives it meaning, but can also lead to fascinating, nonsensical errors. Binary pictures corrupted in transit. Words scrambled into machine-induced code. This is the spirit of *Crux95*. *"Without you, I am zero."*

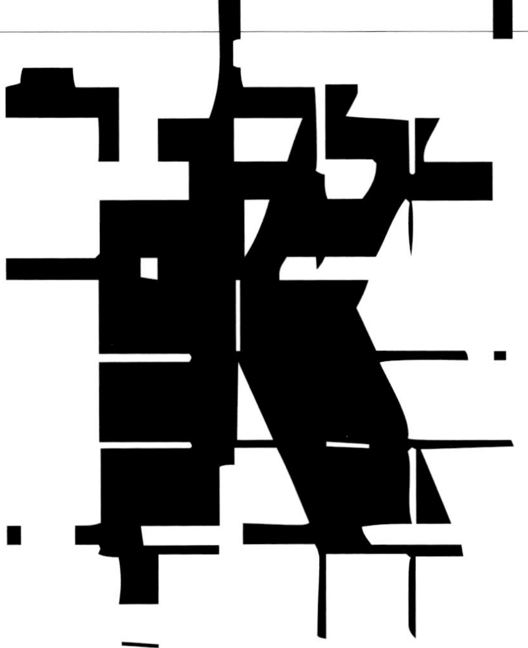

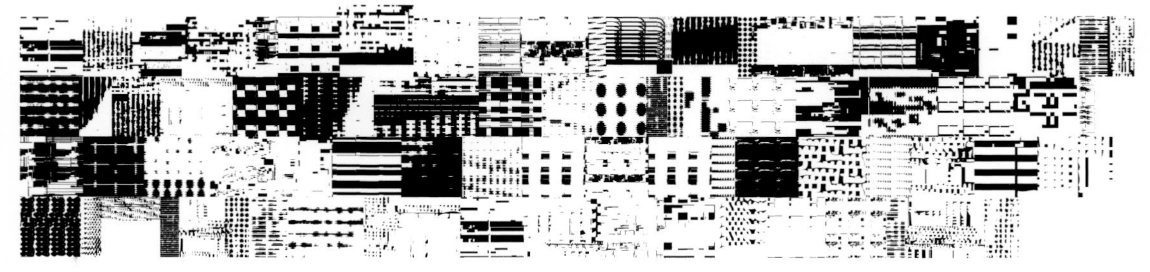

FUSE 14: Xplicit FFM Synaesthesis

Synaesthesis is inspired by the phenomenon of *synaesthesia*, the ability to "see sounds", "smell colours", "hear shapes". Amongst those who have used this perception are Messiaen, who linked his compositions to painting, and Kandinsky, who talked about his paintings in musical terms and even wrote an opera, *Yellow Sound*. Isaac Newton attempted a mathematical correlation between sound and colour; Oskar Fischinger created a "colour organ" to visualise music. Synaesthesia seems to be a function latent in the cortex and limbic system of us all, yet accessible only to a few. It may well be that cyber technologies and prosthetics will make this phenomenon available to us all.

Synaesthesis tries to translate the sensory modality of sound into form. It is more a collection of patterns than a font and has no aspirations towards the Roman alphabet. Make your own music!

FUSE
FUSE 15: Optical Illusions Jon Wozencroft

5 CITIES

1. ZHHRNROZGRLM Go upwards and backwards from where you are standing. Operating 917 kilometres above your head, in the time it takes to read this sentence, a Landsat spacecraft will have photographed and updated information on the well-being of 10,000km^2 of the earth's surface. Every 18 days, every city is scanned for signs of ecological disturbance, population growth, for any abnormalities... To the satellite eye, the (Western) city is seen as greenish grey, rescued by brief outbursts of red (park areas, woods and heathland) and meandering lines of blue/black (rivers and waterways). The image field looks like a body scan. The data is relayed to earth via communication relay satellites, in orbit 35,000km above the equator: earthbound receiving stations can then choose to zoom in on details as small as the slogan on a baseball cap. The electronic trawler is nothing if not ambitious. The global sight-test is, in essence, non-means tested, which is to say London, New York and Tokyo can expect the same standard of service and care as Lusaka, Rangoon and Shanghai. But the First World is hardly running a welfare state. The motive is not emancipation but through surveillance, omnivision and assimilation.

Imagine, for a moment, clusters of life dotted around the planet with no idea nor any desire to know what the other is doing. Does this sound human to you? Landsat could be seen as global technology's update of the village gossip, except the city is no longer an arena for the spoken word. Alphabet and printed word no longer frame the city limits.

2. HGIFTTOV In November 1895, Professor W.C. Röntgen of Würzburg invented the X–ray. His centenary is being written up in the usual way in this week's quality press. What would he have thought had he watched *Total Recall* in widescreen? For Paul Virilio, to visit the cinema is to undergo "cataract surgery".[1] At the Empire Leicester Square in London, after the intro-advert for the THX sound system, the audience applauds in anticipation of more sledgehammer-through-the-skull treatment. The body is a machine, as the Nazis insisted; it can take a lot of punishment. Throughout the century, imaging technology has steadily improved its accuracy in mapping the physical body, and in the process, science and technology have drained the wonder out of wonder and the rage out of outrage. Having created this void, science moves towards its reconciliation, and redetermination.

What about mental space? Historically, the only satellite in orbit is Heaven, and God the ultimate listening station. God, according to science, has not been able to cope with the build-up of messages on the astral answering machine and His self-appointed satellites now monitor the calls. This will seem to you, the reader, an awkward allusion. But if you still accept that there is something magical deep within us as human beings, then what to call it and how to objectify it ceases to matter. But it always does, and curiously, the more far-reaching the optical bias, at the expense of the other five senses, the more we limit our understanding of what it is we see. We lose so much energy through our eyes. Maybe the X-ray we apply to images of the external world would be better turned upon ourselves.

Around 4am in London, the schedule that controls city behaviour pauses, just briefly before dawn, before the first alarm clocks mobilise the suburbs. In the half-light the streets look like X-rays. The city, crowdless, sharpened by the noise of the sleepers.

3. HVIERXV Michael Sorkin assessed the damage caused by the corporate redesign of public space as follows: "The issue for cities is simple: if there's a Coke machine everywhere, how do you know where you are?". He switches the TV on in his hotel room to find out which language the American soap has been dubbed into.[2] "It is more or less widely recognised today that there are some essential ingredients missing from artificial cities. When compared with ancient cities that have acquired the patina of life, our modern attempts to create cities artificially are, from a human point of view, entirely unsuccessful..."[3] How do we visualise non-linear activity across a network? "For the human mind, the tree is the easiest vehicle for complex thoughts. But the city is not, cannot and must not be a tree. The city is a receptacle for life. If the receptacle severs the overlaps of the strands of life within it, because it is a tree, it will be like a bowl full of razor blades on edge, ready to cut up whatever is entrusted to it. In such a receptacle life will be cut to pieces. If we make cities which are trees, they will cut our lives within to pieces". Christopher Alexander, writing in *Zone 1|2* about urban structures, presents a critique that can also be applied perfectly to the current policy of using video surveillance cameras to fight crime.

In a U.K. survey, 74% of respondents called for more video cameras to be installed, and at the recent Tory party conference in Britain, the government pledged another 10,000 to the nation. Already, cities like Birmingham, Newcastle-Upon-Tyne and Kings Lynn 'Landsat themselves' from ground level, so that it is now possible to observe the curious phenomenon of satellites taking photographs of video cameras taking photographs of citizens taking photographs of cities. The process even proceeds to the processing – if you develop your film through a chain store like Boots, anything deemed dubious is passed on to the police. It might then get published in the papers and broadcast on the news. When the present is right out of hand, "the future is better protected than the past" (Chris Marker).[4]

4. NZMRUVHGZGRLM Today's big cities are the hometowns of the minority. Most urban dwellers arrive from outside, running on empty, in need of protection. The city plays host to refugees of misfortune. Cities also develop a volatile series of inter-relationships that would like to be left as chaotic. Disorder is again the natural condition of the world.

Driven to develop a more efficient and "hygienic" environment, Le Corbusier turned the world into a building site.[5] What to do now, lacking the resources? "Words are useless, especially sentences,

Imagine, for a moment, clusters of life dotted around the planet with no idea nor any desire to know what the other is doing. Does this sound human to you? Landsat could be seen as global technology's update of the village gossip, except the city is no longer an arena for the spoken word.

don't function any more..."[6] For those caught in the receptacle of service industry jobs, "let's get unconscious" is the least they can do. Elsewhere, "In restless despair, the hopeless masses of the periphery witness the spectacle of another hemisphere's wealth". In *Millennium*, Jacques Attali warns of marauding barbarians that will soon flood in from the abandoned South to wreak havoc on the paranoid North – an escalation of the France vs. Algerian fundamentalist terrorist.[7] More cameras are installed. Explosives set on timer. Façade fights façade. Glass everywhere.

Cameras can deal with individual deviation but not with collective attack. Slack behaviour, if not criminal activity, forms the basis of so many social rituals and ceremonies – such as 'sweeteners', sexual encounters, drug deals etc. Crime is magnesium. Oppression is tin foil. If the situation seems hopeless, it is, but in a binary world the opposite can also be true. For example, the more multicultural a city becomes, the more that subcultures – and not multinationals – will define urban experience. Time to check what's on TV...

Night time. A man, well-dressed, looks furtively around. He selects keys from his pocket and enters the apartment block. He pauses for a moment. A soft clunk, smothered by his handkerchief, as he fixes the silencer onto the revolver.

Fearful of a creak, he tiptoes up the stairs and moves towards the door...

"All this light is killing me, driving me crazy" (Le Corbusier's wife, speaking about living in his architecture).[5]

5. IVXVKGRERGB This realisation of a need for unity is increasingly visible through the emphasis of late-capitalism on what might loosely be termed 'service', or the lack of it. The Service Economy is at the cusp of a curve that must eventually deal with its excluded. At present, nothing seems more daring than the idea of a Caring Economy, because of the prevailing mindset accelerating to the year 2000 that thinks things can only get worse. This is a false economy. The refusal of any system to "Let the Power Fall" sows the seeds of its own inevitable collapse. In the city, it is easy to see how the demand for goodwill outstrips its supply. Once, the direction of social policy was towards the disadvantaged – today, it seeks to consolidate the comfort of the restless middle class (stuck as always between two extremes, wealth and poverty – a perfect breeding ground for such ideas as the National Lottery and private health insurance). In this space you find the prime mental voyagers.

This too is an oversight. If you make the privileged even more privileged in the eyes of the deprived, then the bubble bursts from within. The privileged use the image world of the oppressed as a buffer, they make it an aesthetic, and start an involution.

6. HFYNRHHRLM The homeless crunch their teeth, the sales assistant smiles. You walk on. With immediate notice, begin to keep a count of how often, each day, you pay somebody a compliment, even in your own domain, and how often you criticise somebody or make an offhand remark, even if it is not to their face. Or to put it another way, do you believe stress comes in piecemeal amounts or does it rise cumulatively as the day goes on? How might we modify our behaviour if instead of the CCTV cameras, the city was cordoned with a series of sensitive microphones, smart enough to separate speech from muzak? How gifted have you become at distorting the differences between what you say and what you actually do? The outcome is like a currency transaction where everyone loses out because of the lousy exchange rate.

7. KFIRGB In the city, as it has always been, human life swings between the two poles of movement and settlement. The nomadic urge might have reached its apogee when the speed of intercity travel became synonymous with an increasing immobility – standing on escalators, pushing the buttons of a high-speed lift, quartered up and thirsty in Economy Class. The next stage in the process will see physical movement finally give way to mental projection (of which the online activity of the Internet gives just a glimpse). For those with a good credit rating, the domestic living-room will be transformed into a cockpit (and

How might we modify our behaviour if instead of the CCTV cameras, the city was cordoned with a series of sensitive microphones, smart enough to separate speech from muzak? How gifted have you become at distorting the differences between what you say and what you actually do?

who said anything of air traffic control?). In this space, all artforms fuse with technology to create a "*trompe-la-vie*". For Jean Baudrillard, this could relegate the artist's work to being "an ephemeral luxury of the species", which is just the point. 'Double or quits', he insists: "One must rediscover through illusion, a fundamental form of seduction".[8]

Think back to the movement documented in Rodchenko's photographs of 1920s Berlin, taken from the rooftops, transposed 60 years forward to Wim Wenders' film *Himmel Über Berlin* ('Wings of Desire'), where the camera is a guardian angel that can read people's thoughts. Ten years from now, across the Great Lake of 2000, what will your thoughts be, how hard and fast our illusions, and who will be taping everything?

Reference:
1. Paul Virilio, 'Cataract Surgery: Cinema in the Year 2000', in *Alien Zone*, ed. Annette Kuhn, Verso 1990 **2.** Michael Sorkin, 'Cartoon Cities', in *I.D.* November – December 1992 **3.** *Zone 1|2*, eds. Michel Feher & Sanford Kwinter, Zone Books 1988 **4.** Chris Marker, *La Jetée*, Argos Films 1962 (available on Academy Video from the BFI) **5.** *Hidden Hands: A Different History of Modernism*, Channel 4 TV, 5 November 1995 **6.** Madonna, *Bedtime Stories*, Maverick/Sire Records 1995 **7.** Jacques Attali, *Millennium – Winners and Losers in the Coming World Order*, Times Books (US) 1992 **8.** Jean Baudrillard, 'The Aesthetic Illusion', in *Parkett* 37 1993

"Urban society has come to a parting of the ways. Here, with a heightened consciousness of our past and a clearer insight into decisions made long ago, which often still control us, we shall be able to face the immediate decision that now confronts man and will, one way or another, ultimately transform him: namely, whether he shall devote himself to the development of his own deepest humanity, or whether he shall surrender himself to the now almost automatic forces he himself has set in motion and yield place to his dehumanised alter ego, 'Post-historic Man'. That second choice will bring with it a progressive loss of feeling, emotion, creative audacity, and finally consciousness."
Lewis Mumford, *The City in History*, Martin Secker & Warburg Ltd. 1961

FUSE 15: Bonus Fonts

BONUS FONTS THE RESULTS OF A STUDENT FUSE PROJECT SET BY DAVID CROW AT UNIVERSITY COLLEGE SALFORD.

FUSE 15: Darren Scott Bonus Font Berliner

Berliner is based on the stencil art found on the now-demolished Berlin Wall, powerful messages full of emotion and conviction. The stencil art style is combined with traditional German letterforms.

FUSE 15: John Randle Bonus Font Mayaruler 1

Mayaruler 1 is sourced from ancient carvings made in 5 limestone steps of a great staircase of a royal plaza in the ancient Maya city of Guatemala. The future of typography depends upon our understanding of the way various forms of typography have functioned in the past.

FUSE 15: Sam Jones Bonus Font Smog

Smog is a typeface based on the physical and emotional aspects of London.

JOHN CRITCHLEY & JON WOZENCROFT EDITORIAL POSTER

FUSE CITIES

OPTICAL ILLUSIONS

"Urban society has come to a parting of the ways. Here, with a heightened consciousness of our past and a clearer insight into decisions made long ago, which often still control us, we shall be able to face the immediate decision that now confronts man and will, one way or another, ultimately transform him: namely, whether he shall devote himself to the development of his own deepest humanity, or whether he shall surrender himself to the now almost automatic forces he himself has set in motion and yield place to his dehumanised alter ego, 'Post-historic Man'. That second choice will bring with it a progressive loss of feeling, emotion, creative audacity, and finally consciousness."

Lewis Mumford, The City in History, Martin Secker & Warburg Ltd, 1961

1 ZHHRNROZGRLM Go upwards and backwards from where you are standing. Operating 917 kilometers above your head, in the time it takes to read this sentence, a Landsat spacecraft will have photographed and updated information on the well-being of 10.000km² of the earth's surface. Every 18 days, every city is scanned for signs of ecological disturbance, population growth, for any abnormalities...

FUSE CITIES
Editor & writer: Jon Wozencroft
Design: John Critchley

ABENDGLOCKE
FUSE fonts do not always carry a full set of upper and lower case characters; nor does every font cover a full range of accents and special characters. FUSE fonts are experimental typefaces that should be extended by users... and abuse is part of the process.

SUBMIT
Please send us any comments and proposals to the address below. Please remember to enclose an SAE/IRC where appropriate.

FUSE EDITORIAL
Unit 2, White Horse Yard,
78 Liverpool Road, London N1 0QD
Fax: +44 171 704 2447

The future city transcends the city limits. Urban activity takes place indoors, the streets once ablaze, fall quiet, but not till the voice becomes a touch.

fuse 15 cities features twelve experimental typefaces plus five posters by
distributed exclusively through the fontshop network

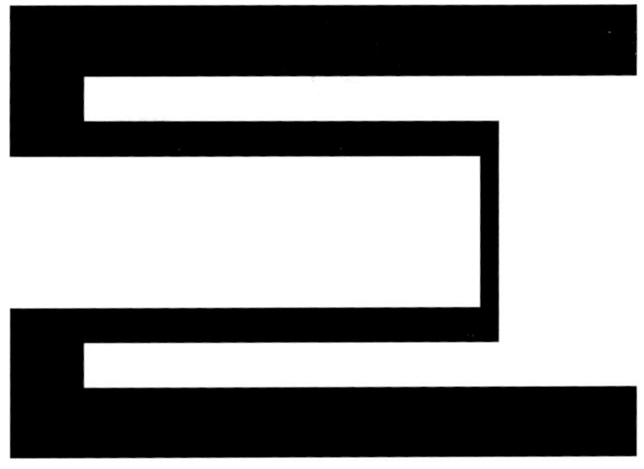

CITY ARCHITECTURE

CITY AVENUE

CITY HABITATION

CITY HOMELESS

CITY HOMELESS

abcdefgh

ijklm

nopqrst

uvwxyz.

0123456789

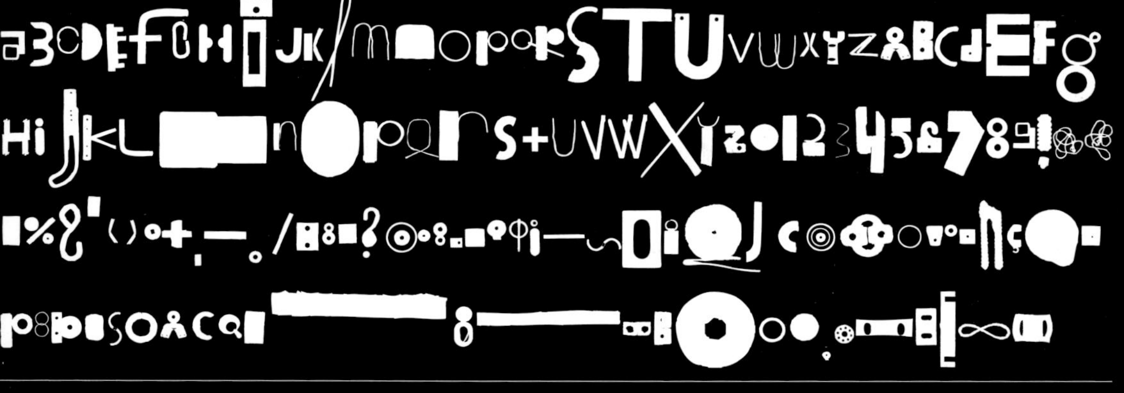

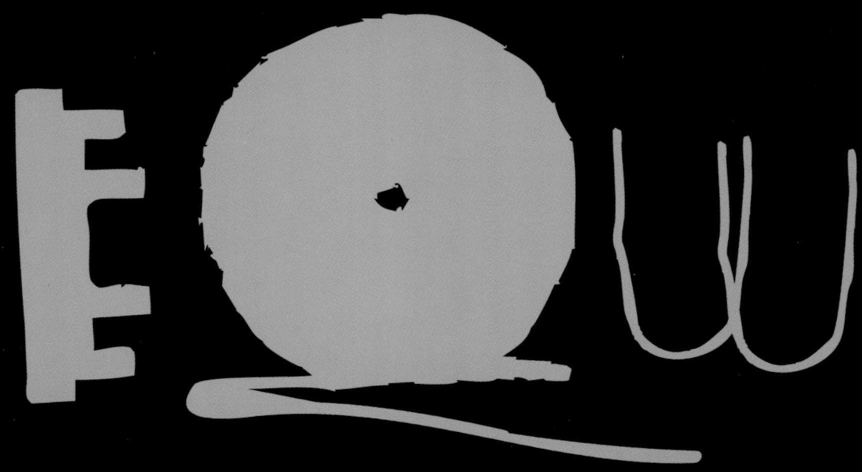

FUSE 15: Paul Elliman Bits

Bit. n. Anything that curbs or restrains. Bit. n. A small piece of something.

Bit. n. (Computers) A single, basic unit of information (binary digit).

The office next to mine in the department of Art History at the University of Texas was occupied by the brilliant communications historian Denise Schmandt-Besserat. Her discoveries have shown how writing evolved, with the development of agriculture, as systems of counters, small geometric clay forms used mainly in the accounting of goods. These encoded tokens are a key stage in the development of writing, which evolved further only with the emergence of cities. This kind of change doesn't happen overnight, but post-industrial typography is a notable indication of the cultural shift brought about by the advance of information technology. My tokens are not clay counters but shards of industrial waste; pieces of die-cast metals and heat-resistant plastics, sections of zintec, polypropylene, chromium, butyl, PVA and perspex, samples of 'memory' plastics, a coil of black-annealed wire, a disc of bright spangled galv. Our communication is changing again, but what could describe the city, life within it, and the writing system used to express that life, better than a nugget of well-milled titanium?

TWO FORTY-NINE ten-sixteen ON SCHEDULE but if the public realizes he'll get over it it's not enough

GIMME THAT you ASK ME it's always the same I just hope no, I can't go back CAN'T WAIT ANY LONGER

it's not getting any better and do you know what she said? GET OVER HERE just because STOP you're looking for a pistol, right?

I just can't deal with it that is just how they act I'll give you an example half of my money it's a big decision

nobody cares as fast as possible where is it? can you help me out? it's so beautiful you're not going to do that, are you? RIGHT IN THE MIDDLE OF THE STREET

I've been here waiting what's it like? THEY TRICKED YOU but I know you just take it NEXT IN LINE what are you looking at?

they know you'll do it if you have to I need you know, like RIGHT NOW oh God he's like that, though

I never like to touch HE'S RUNNING AWAY FROM SOMETHING I can't help it IT'S HOPELESS

YOUR ATTENTION, PLEASE you can hear it miles away pretty embarrassing, isn't it? I CAN'T DO ANYTHING

that's what it looks like NOW hello OK but

---

and do you know what she said? STOP NEXT IN LINE

FUSE 15: Tobias Frere-Jones Microphone

"There are six million stories in the naked city". *Microphone* approaches the city from a social angle, focusing on how its inhabitants talk to each other. Tobias Frere-Jones walked around Boston, eavesdropping on people's conversations as they passed by. In *Microphone*, a single character will trigger an entire phrase, with a style, size and spacing to reflect the voices heard on the street. Rather than treating text as content to be rendered, *Microphone* treats text as a sequence or plot enerator. Text set in *Microphone* becomes a readymade ecording of conversations in the street. More than anything else, here is a short story, which uses the digital font format for its ability for re-arrangement.

ten-sixteen

t go back

you're looking for a pisto, right

ON SCHEDULE

no, I can't go back

he'll get

it's not enough

just because

but I know you

STOP

u know what s

RIGHT NOW

it's not

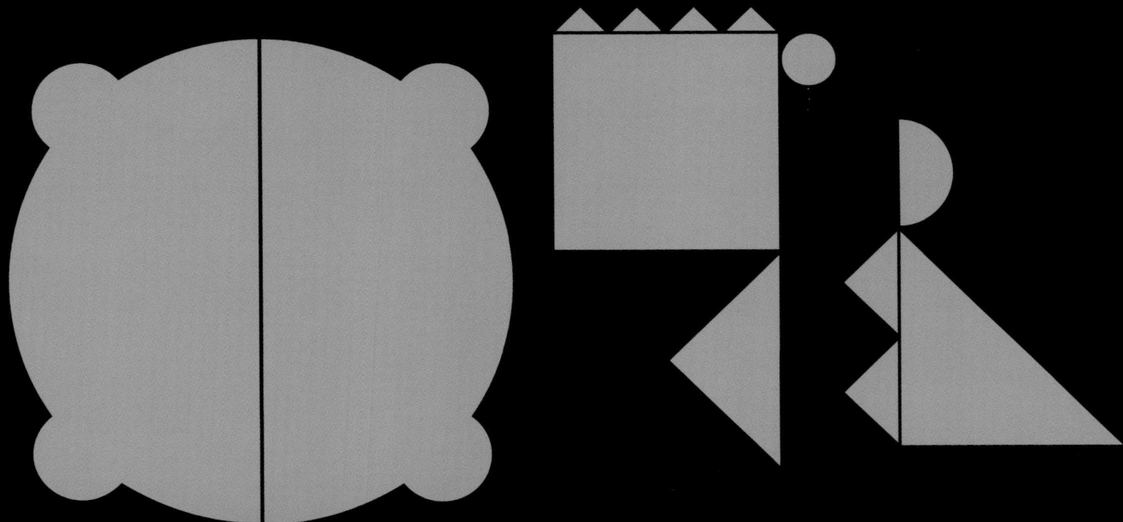

FUSE 15: Peter Grundy DIY

DIY is a development of an idea first produced as a large poster, *Architects Language*. *DIY* investigates type as landscape. Letterforms and buildings are both constructed from a library of systemised modules arranged strategically in space to provide function and expression.

DIY (Design it Yourself) continues that connection. You can choose two options: *DIY Foundations* creates mysterious silhouettes, over which *DIY Skeleton* can be overlaid to create a cityscape of complex detail and engineering. You can take the process further by using the letterforms as modular drawing tools to create pictures such as 'City Entity', seen on the poster enclosed.

SNAP OFF ▸

NR

CHECKED

121

CHESTER

42

FUSE 15: Frank Heine Determination

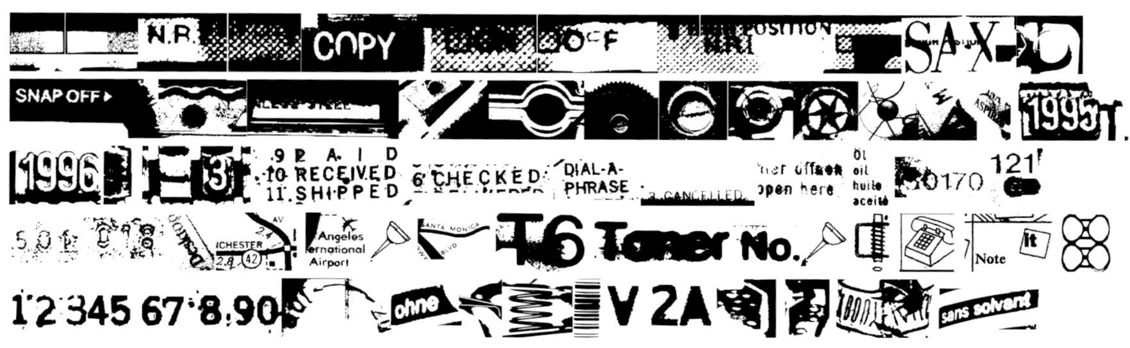

Determination is based on the book *Objects On a Desk* produced by my partner, Lutz Eberle. The book offers a kaleidoscope of randomly chosen sunglasses/cutter/waterglass/perforator/keys etc. These were scanned and then transformed into a "cubist" version of reality, showing details from simultaneously different points of view and enhancing the initial procedure of noticing distinctive details on quite trivial items.

The results serve as icons for the modern world... Words like POSITION, COPY, ON, OFF, NO., OIL, CHECKED and CANCELLED cover many contexts in the computer world. NUMBERS and DEADLINES cannot be avoided. Randomly set, *Determination* reflects the chaos, yet the "morbidity" and roughness of these characters show the hidden terror that can also emerge from the pretty, harmless visual appearance of the digital-industrial.

FUSE 16: Trace Elements Jon Wozencroft

WINTER 1996

GENETICS

A lifelong agnostic, as he lay on his deathbed, the comedian W.C. Fields was asked by a friend "Why are you reading The Bible?". "I'm looking for a loophole", he replied.
Quoted by Les Dawson on *The Michael Parkinson Show*, a 1970s series repeated in September 1996

With the information assumed from our postcodes, market research companies already build up consumer profiles linked to lifestyle behaviour and particular spending habits. The now-digital telecom companies can offer a Caller Display function that lets you know who is on the phone before you've picked it up. Should you not have this facility, dial 1471 in the U.K. and a computerised voice will tell you the number of the last caller who tried to get hold of you. Many people already own ansaphone machines — these days, more often used as a *won'tansathephone* machine, to invert their original purpose. British Telecom advertises its Caller Display service with a comforting photo of Granny, linked to this caption: "Hey look, everyone! Granny's back from her holiday. Let's pick up the phone and shout, 'Welcome Home'". BT liken this to "having a crystal ball". In fact they are looking through the wrong end of a telescope. All of this will make people communicate less freely rather than more so. In no time, we will have access to OCR transcripts of any phone conversation we ever have. Just press a button.

Surveillance of one kind or another is an intrinsic tool of social and political control. The technology has been the by-product of military espionage and police-regulated forensic science. Add to this the sophisticated imaging techniques of the medical profession and the soon-to-be completed breakthroughs in genetic profiling and the potential for intrusion and interference is greatly enhanced.

"The ultimate aim of the Human Genome Project is to read every letter of every word in the library that is the human genome – including the vast volumes of nonsense – to obtain the complete set of instructions on how to put together a human being. A different way of gauging the magnitude of the enterprise is to

consider the Human Genome Project as akin to conducting a census of every human being living on this earth today. Biologists are confident not only that they can conduct that census, but that they can do the equivalent of writing down every individual's full address, and their relationships with other members of their family."
Tom Wilkie, *Perilous Knowledge*, Faber and Faber 1993

Gene. Origin. Literally, "the place of formation".

Genetic engineering is more like telecommunications because like mobile phone companies its exponents are forcefully convinced that any expansion in their operational reach is by definition good. This is also the science of presenting a few steps on the path of the trace as a substitute for ever having control over the full picture.

Genetic information is digital, cellular and existential dynamite. The Human Genome Project hopes to complete the genetic mapping of the human body shortly after the year 2000. The technology that enables our numerous strands of DNA to be sequenced has been around since 1975, developed by Frederick Sanger at Cambridge University. Genomic laboratories are little more than number-crunching facilities, because this they have to be — there are between 50,000 and 100,000 genes hidden in the human genome (and, as Wilkie points out, many of them completely meaningless, but who is to be sure which ones?). The pieces of DNA contained within hold some 3 billion chemical letters that instruct each of our 100 trillion cells to produce the proteins or enzymes that maintain our essential bodily fluids. And just to sequence this information is the easy part of the operation. Here is an updated version of Alan Turing's decoding of the Enigma Machine during World War Two — a breakthrough that ushered in the digital age. Cracking the human genome is the next step, even more significant and accordingly hazardous.

The project has been funded and fêted because great hopes ride on its promised medical benefits. However, even if hundreds of 'single fault' genetic disorders such as Huntington's chorea (a rare but fatal neurological disease) and haemophilia were to be eradicated, they would amount to "less than 2% of the world's disease burden" (*The Economist*, 14 September 1996). Common diseases like cancer are caused by the mutation of several genes and result from more volatile environmental/behavioural patterns as much as they do from inherited genetic flaws. Treatment comes by introducing a gene that produces the correct protein to encourage the body's immune system to attack cancerous cells, but not only is the means of pinpointing this corrective gene hotly disputed, its delivery method has yet to be refined so that it allows the new gene to produce the requisite amount of protein over a sufficient period of time to be effective. Nevertheless, a cure is said to be within reach. A new technique is to package the gene in a virus which has had its pathogenic elements removed: a neat idea, like alcohol-free lager. Gene therapists like Dr. Michael Fossil at Michigan State University even break the optimism barrier, believing that the control of the one key gene that produces an enzyme called telomerase will not only enable doctors to destroy all types of cancer cell — telomerase treatment will prevent all ageing-related diseases and even halt the ageing process itself.

"Life would be intolerable if we knew everything"
Tony Hancock, 'The Blood Donor',
BBC Television 1958

In another day and age, not quite laid to rest by pager phones and unreliable hospital tests, the common feeling was "I'd rather not know". In the manner of an HIV test, this will soon become "I'd rather I didn't have to know", giving increased octane to Information Fatigue (a slump, already, from Anxiety) and inevitably, with selective breeding, to paraknowledge (a kind of omnipotence) on the side of the select, and subliteracy for the masses. Is this not the prime ingredient of fascism... a 'Welcome Home' to the very force for which the medical revolution and the Welfare State was the common prize for having conquered in 1945?

If political non-intervention were not enough, the access to genetic information will undermine any health care system. The insurance industry will become as selective as the National Lottery. Already,

Genetics brings with it the danger of a fundamental philosophical misconception – namely, that a person's actions are no longer determined by free will, but by their genes. The confirmation that "genetics is destiny" will certainly be an attractive one to the so-called Victim Culture that has steadily promoted the standpoint of "It's not my fault"

the U.S. model of private health insurance is adopting a policy of "Preferred lives", a rationing of coverage granted only to the screened and fit, at the same time as "Wrongful life" suits are being successfully brought on behalf of infants with birth defects whose parents had not been fully informed of their risk. Litigation is in process in the U.S.A., but can it be anything but a stop-gap? Imagine your local doctor, armed with a full run-down of your genetic profile, hired to advise you of the likely genetic outcome of your coming child. Does the world become China, with its tolerance of infanticide, or like the U.S.A., whose Pro-Life lobby clouds such issues in a smog of self-righteous fanaticism.

Medical advances are assumed to be, by definition, beneficial, but today they have to coexist with the legacy of BSE, the abuse of pesticides, and in the case of genes, the legacy of eugenics — the short distance earlier in this century between selective breeding, the U.S. Immigration Laws of the 1920s, and Nazism. The diagnosis, analysis and access to the comprehensive genetic map that the Genome Project intends to deliver raises questions that cut to the quick, when there are so many other agents of change "with massive implications for the future". How to see the wood for the trees? In newspaper features and on television documentaries, they appear so distinct and categorical: the violent pleasures of virtual reality, the processing paradise to come from nanotechnology, cybernetics, neural networks... but they all point to one central confusion — the promise that new technologies will bring us closer to the source and the font of wisdom that delivers us the information we need to know about anything, at the very time that we pull further and further away from what we have felt it to be to be human, and to have space.

Genetics brings with it the danger of a fundamental philosophical misconception — namely, that a person's actions are no longer determined by free will, but by their genes. The confirmation that "genetics is destiny" will certainly be an attractive one to the so-called Victim Culture that has steadily promoted the standpoint of "It's not my fault": murderers who plead a history of child abuse, through to cancer patients who sue tobacco companies. What about Education? What about Nutrition? The idea that people do not control their own actions can come as a comforting escape in the short term. Eventually, it can only lead to a new and effortlessly upheld form of slavery.

Of course, Walt Disney, the great believer in hygiene as moral value would disagree; the Human Genome Project's very name rings like a Disney production, where tradition — the Past — can be mitigated and indeed replaced by constant modification in the Present: in other words, the dream of the surgeon splicer, the reanimator who becomes the true policeman and politician of the 21st century.

"Since people are going to be living longer and getting older, they'll just have to learn how to be babies longer. I think that's what's happening now. Some kids I know personally are staying babies longer."
Andy Warhol, *From A to B and Back Again*, Michael Dempsey/Cassell & Co. 1975

The surgeon need not work in a hospital, nor run an exclusive clinic overlooking Lake Geneva. You might as easily find him or her in the role of television presenter, cutting and splicing and surfing a channel through a tidal wave of top entertainment to bring it in on time and in good ratings health for the network bosses. In Britain, we can barely run a Health Service, but we can count on TV surgeons and anaesthetists.

Every Friday, at 6 o'clock and then repeated after the pub shuts, comes Chris Evans' new show, ginger hair and glasses his natural props for a caricature of the rampant energy of a hyperactive child. Great innovations in the tabloid gene pool, there are two slots, "I'M AN UGLY BLOKE" and "FAT LOOKALIKES" that should make Darwinians smile in their clippers. The idea is to invite viewers to submit themselves to this address, "I'M AN UGLY BLOKE", PO Box so on and so forth, and then help to make public humiliation an artform by concocting some embarrassing circumstance that bonds itself effortlessly with Postmodern Irony. Nobody knows what that is until it is too late, and so the primal urges

"We're just having a laugh" says Chris Evans, beaming an infectious smile across his Operating Theatre, here decked out to look like a trendy pub with a dancefloor attached, backed up by its range of anaesthetics — beer, football, celebrity populism, as well as non-stop laughing gas — guaranteed to cure the blues by pumping that base but contagious emotion, schadenfreude, into the nation's homes. "And now, with his new single, it's Jamiroquai and 'Virtual Insanity'"...

of bread and circuses, soapbox and self-satisfaction urge everyone onwards, if hardly upwards.

This particular week, Del wrote in. He looked gormless, and just what the doctor ordered for this gregarious stunt. The producers of the show packed him off with a socialite blonde to the London première of *Emma*, the new Hollywood costume drama starring Gwyneth Paltrow, held at the Chelsea Cinema with rows of minor celebrities and beautiful people in attendance. The event was video'd, and then played back to Del and the TV studio audience. As Del, dressed in a dinner suit and tie for the occasion, is introduced to Greta or Tamara or Caprice or whoever, the look on their well-heeled faces all says the same thing... *"What the **** is he doing here??"*. Del's expression, to his credit, does not reveal whether he is as bemused as everyone else or absolutely mortified. He is on TV. And he is famous for at least half a minute. He slopes off as quickly as he has sloped on (like a mutant lifeform that can only be exposed to the atmosphere for a passing moment). Later on in the show, Chris Evans introduces two contestants for "FAT PERSON LOOKALIKE", a "Fat André Agassi" and "Fat Claudia Schiffer". They get to be famous for about 10 seconds.

"We're just having a laugh" says Chris Evans, beaming an infectious smile across his Operating Theatre, here decked out to look like a trendy pub with a dancefloor attached, backed up by its range of anaesthetics – beer, football, celebrity populism, as well as non-stop laughing gas — guaranteed to cure the blues by pumping that base but contagious emotion, schadenfreude, into the nation's homes. "And now, with his new single, it's Jamiroquai and 'Virtual Insanity'"... Whatever the contents of this delivery system, the links can be vital or overwhelmingly meaningless. They too are packaged in a virus, but one that has *not* had its pathogenic elements removed.

Chris Evans cries out "Coming up next, don't go away...". The National Lottery reassures its weekly clientele of millions that "It could be you". Before he died, Warhol modified his catchphrase that "Everybody will be famous for fifteen minutes"... "No, what I really meant to say was 'Everybody will be famous *in* fifteen minutes...'". The medical and the telematic converge to make every one of us a hologram of our former selves.

FUSE 16: Genetics **Dr. Rachel Armstrong**

"I was born... eight hundred and ten years ago... I was probably bottled but it may have been a natural birth. I don't know... I was looking for ways to design a whole society from scratch. There were plenty of examples – mostly miserable failures. Part of the problem was that it was impossible to start with brand-new human beings. The converts to the new society always brought along a cultural hangover from their areas of origin. Most of the very worst failures were those based on religions and airy moral convictions. I decided that mine would be based firmly on self-interest."
Bruce Sterling, *The Artificial Kid*, ROC publishers 1980

The Body Machine

The whole of Nature was considered in mechanical terms for the first time in the 17th century. This viewpoint took hold increasingly among investigators and was developed into a comprehensive theory to include the human body by René Descartes (1596–1650). Descartes was a mathematician and philosopher who approached the study of human physiology with a strong mechanistic bias. He believed that the processes of human life, except for mental processes, could be explained by the simple application of physical laws and through the understanding of the structure of matter. Descartes proposed that the mind was separate from the body and believed that intellect was the gift of God to mankind. He thought that mind existed outside of the body and was independent of it, although the two could interact through the pineal gland. This dualistic view of the human body is the philosophical basis of scientific thinking.

In this age of information technology, a new model of how the human body works is emerging. The body can now be thought of as a mind-body-machine.

This transformation of the body is not an artificial process, on the contrary it is a natural extension of our humanity. Our species has elevated itself on the Earth by its capacity to use machines, not by its innate genetic programming.

We increasingly depend on machines, particularly computers, to carry out our daily activities. Our individual bodies are already being extended through the use of technological devices. These new technologies provide a meeting place, like the pineal gland, for the genetic body and mind to interact. In some ways we already are the computers that we metaphorically refer to not just at a functional level, but at a higher, spiritual level.

"There is no such thing as either man or nature now, only a process that produces the one within the other and couples the machines together."
Deleuze and Guattari, *Anti-Oedipus: Capitalism and Schizophrenia*, Athlone Press, 3rd edition 1994

The mechanical and the biological body are being united through biotechnological techniques. On medical wards we have already created symbiosis between biological bodies and machines. Intensive Care Units have nurtured a generation of independent cyborgs whose mechanical arterial balloon pumps and artificial respiratory systems keep the organic body alive. Even our elderly are mechanised individuals using wheelchairs, pacemakers, steel hips, reading glasses, hearing aids and false teeth which re-establish these previously dependent individuals as autonomous mechanised bodies. However, all mechanised individuals, regardless of their degree of integration with technology, remain fundamentally human.

This transformation of the body is not an artificial process, on the contrary it is a natural extension of our humanity. Our species has elevated itself on the Earth by its capacity to use machines, not by its innate genetic programming. However, genes play an important role. They are the organic body's software and serve to program the component molecules to build and run the body's hardware. The fine control of how genes work is still not fully understood but they have popularly been accepted as the modern-day custodians of human identity and responsible for the transmission of heritable characteristics to our offspring. The "Gene Theory" of heredity has been the most successful 20th-century metaphor of the body and in both scientific and artistic practice – the expression of our self-understanding has become reliant on the metaphorical use of and imagery associated with genes.

The strange new images produced by the new technologies to give the genes an identity have already gained much authority. Genes are invisible to the naked eye, residing within the protection of the nuclear membrane, the 'brain' of the cell. In the attempt to understand how they work, genes have been given both a real and metaphorical value. The real genes that we encounter are simply bands of ultraviolet jelly seen on an electrophoretic gel or banded strands seen under a high-powered microscope. The metaphorical genes are given properties such as heritable characteristics and it is more difficult to characterise the gene structure with a predicted set of physical attributes. The difficulty arises because the properties genes are alleged to carry cannot be directly confirmed as the DNA molecules orchestrate vast numbers of different processes, none of which can be simply isolated. All our knowledge of genes has been accumulated through indirect methods of study in order to observe something scientifically tangible so that the study of genetic heritability is based on probabilities, rather than absolute knowledge.

Genetics as a science has been given increasing status in the scientific community and the principles defining the expression of 'genes' have become established theories. The notion of a 'pure' science of genetics, however, raises a number of important questions since the issues have a direct effect on society; and the 'theory' supporting their impartiality is drawn from the prevailing models of civilised society. Far from being 'objective' interpretations of human behaviour they are loaded with political and social references.

"Humanity will gradually destroy itself from within, will decay in its very core and essence, if this slow but relentless process is not checked... dealing with defectives in the present system can be at best palliative. We must pick out the genetically inferior stocks with more certainty, and we must set in motion

counter-forces making for faster reproduction of superior stocks, if we are to reverse or even arrest the trend..."
J. Huxley, *The Uniqueness of Man*, Readers Union/ Chatto & Windus 1943

One contemporary theory proposes that genes are autonomous organisms which have actually created our biological bodies as a means of self replication. This Selfish Gene Theory proposes that strands of DNA have created and continue to manipulate our bodies for the sole means of their evolutionary survival.

In his 1976 book *The Selfish Gene* the biologist Richard Dawkins inverted the accepted relationship of the body to the gene. His theory promoted a worldview that placed the gene as the driving force of human evolution. Rather than establishing the gene as an integral part of human anatomy, Dawkins positioned genes as distinct, primordial entities. He proposed that they actually built us, not to keep the human species going but for their own purpose, to enslave our bodies for their survival. Dawkins proposes that our organic bodies, according to the Selfish Gene Theory, are actually robot vehicles, blindly programmed to preserve and propagate the molecules driving them. Successful genes are the ones that survive at all costs: they are immoral and immortal following the same principles of the ideal anatomical bodies.

This model is reflective of a post-Christian society where it is clear that there is a dehumanising process in our culture, marked by a loss of care for one another. Closely linked is the decline in any real belief or truth. Governments and power structures have become in the most literal sense, incredible. As compassion has died, so we have ceased to expect the truth to be told and we are not surprised when it is not. We have become hardened, desensitised and uni-dimensional, in other words "Selfish".

It is difficult to challenge these genetic scientific theories, or propose alternatives, as the evidence needed to contest them requires specific tools to conduct the genetic investigations. These techniques are only available to those who have access to and knowledge of the technology. However, until other methods of conducting genetic experiments are devised, it will be a laborious task to challenge these cardinal scientific theories.

Digital Body

"In this age of information overload, what is significant is no longer freedom of ideas but rather freedom of form – freedom to modify, freedom to mutate your body. The question is not whether a society will allow [the] freedom to express yourself but whether the human species will allow you to break the bonds of your genetic parameters – the fundamental freedom to determine your own DNA destiny."
More, 'Self Transformation'; Stelarc, *Obsolete Body/suspensions/Stelarc*, Davis, Calif: J.P. Publications 1984

Without shedding blood and without resistance, medical technology has already achieved its invasion of the body with the assistance of new imaging appliances such as: Computer Assisted Tomography (CAT); Positron Emission Tomography (PET); Magnetic Resonance Imaging (MRI) and ultrasound. These intrusive cameras have converted the organic body from carbon molecules into three-dimensional digital blocks or 'voxels'. This digital body is a hollow structure, devoid of natural colour around which the once significant skin has been displaced as a crust. The body space contains a collage of increasingly smaller and seemingly unrelated parts and the amount of black space inside us suggests that our physical existence is mainly an interior one. It seems that, in Cyberspace, we inhabit new anatomical depths which were formerly invisible. These interior cavities have historically carried a negative association. The philosopher Antonin Artaud dreamed of a body without organs, considering these structures to be filthy parasites. He evaluated the relative time that we spend eating, defecating, urinating and washing in comparison to the creative act. His conclusion was that the organs of the body were a drain of creative energy out of all proportion to their significance.

Rather than establishing the gene as an integral part of human anatomy, Dawkins positioned genes as distinct, primordial entities. He proposed that they actually built us, not to keep the human species going but for their own purpose, to enslave our bodies for their survival.

"The body is the body/it is single/and has no need of organs/the body is never an organism/organisms are the enemies of the body"
Antonin Artaud 1948

However, the new spaces offered to us by medical scans provide a home for the very creative qualities that Artaud referred to which cannot be attributed to the outside. The public body can only exist at the level of the skin and more complex behaviour has to be derived. Second-hand interpretations of our actions have led to the observation that many human qualities are 'skin deep'.

"The skin is deceptive. In life one only has one's skin. There is an error in human relations because one is never what one has. I have an angel's skin and I am a jackal... a crocodile skin but I am a puppy. I have a black skin but I am white, a woman's skin but I am a man; I never have the skin of what I am. There is no exception to the rule because I am never what I have..."
Eugene Lemoine Luccioni, *The Dress*, from ORLAN, press conference, ICA, London, April 1996

Text originally continued on FUSE 16 disk, now continued on the FUSE 1-20 website.

TOM HINGSTON & JON WOZENCROFT EDITORIAL POSTER

F Cico Paco The basic premise behind the typeface is the main focus of genetics, which is the degree to which the observable trait (the phenotype) is attributable to the pattern of genes in the cells (the genotype) and to what extent it arises from environmental influence. When this premise is taken into the realm of political doctrines, the dominant ideology strives to become an "environmental influence".

Esperanto*, an attempt at "linguistic genetic engineering", and the Lamarckian theory of evolution** which found new life under Stalinist regime in the 40s and 50s both put emphasis on the strategically conducted environmental changes. Cico Paco contains both English and Russian characters, with added fragments of Esperanto (upper case is English, lower case is Russian and Esperanto). The user can write in English only, or in Russian. In addition, a set of crossections of a human body is available for easy manipulation (the option+numbers contain progressive slices of the body divided into 9 equal parts from head to toe). On a formal level, the letters (uc and lc) are impressions of flesh, liquid and plastic, referring to the "phenotype=reason" ("mating" as "influence"). The X-Ray corpus crossections and tools refer to the "genotype=result" ("meat" as "evidence").

Alexei Tylevich (b.1972, Minsk), US resident. Graphic designer, artist, director working in a variety of media, including high-end computer animation and web design. Studied painting before coming to the United States in 1980, received BFA degree in graphic design from Minneapolis College of Art and Design in 1994. List of freelance clients includes Sega, Nike, Airwalk and ISEA (International Symposium on Electronic Art, Rotterdam, NL). Work has been featured on Canal+ and Television Española, and has received awards at SIGGRAPH'94, Prix Ars Electronica'95 and the American Center for Design 100 Show, among others. Recent projects include Electra'96 electronic art exhibition at the Henie-Onstad Kunstsenter, Norway and a Nike campaign for 1996 Summer Olympics in Atlanta, Georgia. Currently senior art director at Channel 1 TV station in Los Angeles.

* *Esperanto: an artificial international language based upon words common to the chief European languages. Dr. Zamenhof's "Fundamento de Esperanto", containing over 3,500 roots, was published in 1905 and quickly became very popular with the Bolsheviks (Josef Stalin was an avid esperantist).*

** *Jean-Baptiste de Lamarck, a pioneering 19th century French evolutionist, formulated a theory of organic evolution according to which environmental changes cause structural changes in animals and plants (by inducing new or increased use of organs or parts resulting in adaptive modification or greater development, and similarly cause disuse and eventual atrophy of other parts whose changes are transmitted to offspring).*

The quarter of the century roughly between 1938 and 1963 marked the dark ages in Soviet genetic research (after it's flowering in the 30s due to such important figures as Dubinin and Vavilov). The agronomist Trofim Lysenko was able to make his own brand of Lamarckism (asserting the fundamental influence of environmental factors on heredity) the official creed of the Soviet Union, having suppressed most of the teaching and research in orthodox genetics. His theories complemented the dominant ideological concepts of "social engineering" and "turning rivers upstream" very well. One of the favourite epithets used to characterize Stalin at the time was "The Engineer of Human Souls".

F Mega Family2 The alphabet keys contain elements of the female portrait and the shift alphabet keys hold the male portrait. By typing a selection the user can produce genetic mixes between these parents. The numerals and shift numerals contain non-physical information in the form of words; some of these attributes are dominant and will override others, removing them. A thumbnail can be fixed at the end of a sequence by typing either shift X or shift Y; this will also determine the gender of the thumbnail.

A parental preview is on the x and y keys and the manufacturer's logo on =. A talisman can be created for each character using the option numeral keys. To fix your talisman, use opt 1 or the space bar.

The font functions as a game for one or two players and suggests a move towards leisure-based activity as a cellular growth within what we understand as typography. Its rules are self-generated and not imposed.

David Crow Studied Graphic Design at Manchester Polytechnic. Worked as a designer at Assorted Images (London) and Island Records (London) before running a freelance practice (also in London) for 3 years. Clients included Sony UK, Sony USA, Rolling Stones Records, Phonogram Records, Virgin Records, Island Records, IBM, Royal Shakespeare Company, Fosters Lager, MTV. Published eight issues of *Trouble* Magazine. Guest speaker at Fuse 94 in London, Fuse 95 in Berlin and Festivital 96 in Tel Aviv. Currently Subject Leader in Graphic Design at Liverpool John Moores University.

F Killis Heredity reveals itself through the medium of a cell of a specific appearance and character, inherited from generation to generation. However, the familiar pattern of the giraffe differs even between parent and child. It is really a graphic art created by a gene. This font comprises samples of a giraffe's pattern – while all of letters are recognizable as alphabetical, they have been selected without any intentional manipulation.

Naomi Enami Born in 1956 in Osaka. Founded PROPELLER ART WORKS Ltd. in 1981 whilst art directing magazines such as *Number* (1982-84), *Marie Claire* (1984-88) and *ELLE JAPON* (1989-90). In 1992 he opened the Macintosh gallery DIGITALOGUE in Tokyo, and cofounded DIGITALOGUE Inc. with the photographer Akiro Gomi and designer Neville Brody in 1993. Has published many multimedia works such as the CD-ROM collection, Yellows. His awards include the Disk Of The Year 95 USA and a Multimedia Grand Prize Excellence Award in 1992.

F Condition is built on 4 levels, the first exploring the etymology of over-familiar links in language, next, the use of those elemental parts in coining new words to form the *lingua franca* (or technobabble) of new information technologies. These 'clusters' of (signified) meaning are then visually mutated to suggest a genetics of shape. Finally, all the elements are reduced to their line width, the 'heartbeat' and rhythm of a language machine which, like the economy, seems forever on the point of collapse.

Tom Hingston & Jon Wozencroft met at Central Saint Martins in London in 1993. Shortly after graduating, Hingston came to work at Research Studios, where they have collaborated on a number of projects. Wozencroft currently teaches at the Royal College of Art.

Dr. Rachel Armstrong Qualified as a doctor in 1991 and practiced medicine for 2 years. After a series of collaborations with artists such as Helen Chadwick, Orlan and Stelarc she now uses her medical knowledge and alternative visions of the body to work as a producer in multimedia and desktop virtual reality.

"I was born... eight hundred and ten years ago... I was probably bottled but it may have been a natural birth. I don't know... I was looking for ways to design a whole society from scratch. There were plenty of examples – mostly miserable failures. Part of the problem was that it was impossible to start with brand-new human beings. The converts to the new society always brought along a cultural hangover from their areas of origin. Most of the very worst failures were those based on religions and airy moral convictions. I decided that mine would be based firmly on self-interest."
Bruce Sterling, *The Artificial Kid*, ROC publishers 1980.

THE BODY MACHINE

The whole of Nature was considered in mechanical terms for the first time in the 17th century. This viewpoint took hold increasing among investigators and was developed into a comprehensive theory to include the human body by René Descartes (1596–1650). Descartes was a mathematician and philosopher who approached the study of human physiology with a strong mechanistic bias. He believed that the processes of human life, except for mental processes, could be explained by the simple application of physical laws and through the understanding of the structure of matter. Descartes proposed that the mind was separate from the body and believed that intellect was the gift of God to mankind. He thought that mind existed outside of the body and was independent of it, although the two could interact through the pineal gland. This dualistic view of the human body is the philosophical basis of scientific thinking.

In this age of information technology, a new model of how the human body works is emerging. The body can now be thought of as a mind-body-machine. We increasingly depend on machines, particularly computers, to carry out our daily activities. Our individual bodies are already being extended through the use of technological devices. These new technologies provide a meeting place, like the pineal gland, for the genetic body and mind to interact. In some ways we already are the computers that we metaphorically refer to not just at a functional level, but at a higher, spiritual level.

"There is no such thing as either man or nature now, only a process that produces the one within the other and couples the machines together."
Deleuze and Guattari, *Anti-Oedipus: Capitalism and Schizophrenia*, Athlone Press 3rd Edition 1994.

The mechanical and the biological body are being united through biotechnological techniques. On medical wards we have already created symbiosis between biological bodies and machines. Intensive Care Units have nurtured a generation of independent cyborgs whose mechanical arterial balloon pumps and artificial respiratory systems keep the organic body alive. Even our elderly are mechanised individuals using wheelchairs, pacemakers, steel hips, reading glasses, hearing aids and false teeth which re-establish these previously dependent individuals as autonomous mechanised bodies. However, all mechanised individuals, regardless of their degree of integration with technology, remain fundamentally human.

This transformation of the body is not an artificial process, on the contrary it is a natural extension of our humanity. Our species has elevated itself on the Earth by its capacity to use machines, not by its innate genetic programming. However, genes play an important role. They are the organic body's software and serve to programme the component molecules to build and run the body's hardware. The fine control of how genes work is still not fully understood but they have popularly been accepted as the modern-day custodians of human identity and responsible for the transmission of heritable characteristics to our offspring. The 'Gene theory' of heridity has been the most successful 20th century metaphor of the body and in both scientific and artistic practice – the expression of our self-understanding has become reliant on the metaphorical use of and imagery associated with genes.

The strange new images produced by the new technologies to give the genes an identity have already gained much authority. Genes are invisible to the naked eye, residing within the protection of the nuclear membrane, the 'brain' of the cell. In the attempt to understand how they work, genes have been given both a real and metaphorical value. The real genes that we encounter are simply bands of ultraviolet jelly seen on an electrophoretic gel or banded strands seen under a high-powered microscope. The metaphorical genes are given properties such as heritable characteristics and it is more difficult to characterise the gene structure with a predicted set of physical attributes. The difficulty arises because the properties genes are alleged to carry cannot be directly confirmed as the DNA molecules orchestrate vast numbers of different processes, none of which can be simply isolated. All our knowledge of genes has been accumulated through indirect methods of study in order to observe something scientifically tangible so that the study of genetic heritability is based on probabilities, rather than absolute knowledge.

Genetics as a science has been given increasing status in the scientific community and the principles defining the expression of 'genes' have become established theories. The notion of a 'pure' science of genetics, however, raises a number of important questions since the issues have a direct effect on society; and the 'theory' supporting their impartiality is drawn from the prevailing models of civilised society. Far from being 'objective' interpretations of human behaviour they are loaded with political and social references.

"Humanity will gradually destroy itself from within, will decay in its very core and essence, if this slow but relentless process is not checked... dealing with defectives in the present system can be at best palliative. We must pick out the genetically inferior stocks with more certainty, and we must set in motion counter-forces making for faster reproduction of superior stocks, if we are to reverse or even arrest the trend..."
J. Huxley, *The Uniqueness of Man*, Readers Union/Chatto & Windus 1943

One contemporary theory proposes that genes are autonomous organisms which have actually created our biological bodies as a means of self replication. This Selfish Gene Theory proposes that strands of DNA have created and continue to manipulate our bodies for the sole means of their evolutionary survival.

In his 1976 book *The Selfish Gene* the biologist Richard Dawkins inverted the accepted relationship of the body to the gene. His theory promoted a worldview that placed the gene as the driving force of human evolution. Rather than establishing the gene as an integral part of human anatomy, Dawkins positioned genes as distinct, primordial entities. He proposed that they actually built us, not to keep the human species going but for their own purpose, to enslave our bodies for their survival. Dawkins proposes that our organic bodies, according the Selfish Gene Theory, are actually robot vehicles, blindly programmed to preserve and propagate the molecules driving them. Successful genes are the ones that survive at all costs: they are immoral and immortal following the same principles of the ideal anatomical bodies. (See > THE VISIBLE HUMAN PROJECT)

This model is reflective of a post-Christian society where it is clear that there is a dehumanising process in our culture, marked by a loss of care for one another. Closely linked is the decline in any real belief or truth. Governments and power structures have become in the most literal sense, incredible. As compassion has died, so we have ceased to expect the truth to be told and we are not surprised when it is not. We have become hardened, desensitised and uni-dimensional, in other words 'Selfish'.

It is difficult to challenge these genetic scientific theories, or propose alternatives, as the evidence needed to contest them requires specific tools to conduct the genetic investigations. These techniques are only available to those who have access to and knowledge of the technology. However, until other methods of conducting genetic experiments are devised, it will be a laborious task to challenge these cardinal scientific theories.

Genetic experiments > go to 'EXPERIMENTS'

DIGITAL BODY

"In this age of information overload, what is significant is no longer freedom of ideas but rather freedom of form – freedom to modify, freedom to mutate your body. The question is not whether a society will allow [the] freedom to express yourself but whether the human species will allow you to break the bonds of your genetic parameters – the fundamental freedom to determine your own DNA destiny."
More, "Self Transformation"; Stelarc, Obsolete Body/suspensions/Stelarc, Davis, Calif: J.P. Publications 1984

Without shedding blood and without resistance, medical technology has already achieved its invasion of the body with the assistance of new imaging appliances such as: Computer Assisted Tomography (CAT); Positron Emission Tomography (PET); Magnetic Resonance Imaging (MRI) and ultrasound. These intrusive cameras have converted the organic body from carbon molecules into three dimensional digital blocks or 'voxels'. This digital body is a hollow structure, devoid of natural colour around which the once significant skin has been displaced as a crust. The body space contains a collage of increasingly smaller and seemingly unrelated parts and the amount of black space inside us suggests that our physical existence is mainly an interior one. It seems that, in Cyberspace, we inhabit new anatomical depths which were formerly invisible.

These interior cavities have historically carried a negative association. The philosopher Antoin Artaud dreamed of a body without organs, considering these structures to be filthy parasites. He evaluated the relative time that we spend eating, defecating, urinating and washing in comparison to the creative act. His conclusion was that the organs of the body were a drain of creative energy out of all proportion to their significance.

"The body is the body/it is single/and has no need of organs/the body is never an organism/organisms are the enemies of the body"
Antoin Artaud 1948

However, the new spaces offered to us by medical scans provide a home for the very creative qualities that Artaud referred to which cannot be attributed to the outside. The public body can only exist at the level of the skin and more complex behaviour has to be derived. Second hand interpretations of our actions have led to the observation that many human qualities are 'skin deep'.

"The skin is deceptive. In life one only has one's skin. There is an error in human relations because one is never what one has. I have an angel's skin and I am a jackal... a crocodile skin but I am a puppy. I have a black skin but I am white, a woman's skin but I am a man; I never have the skin of what I am. There is no exception to the rule because I am never what I have..."
Eugeno Lemoine Luccioni, *The Dress*, from ORLAN, Press conference, ICA, London, April 1996.

© Dr. Rachel Armstrong

Continued on READ ME file on FUSE16 disk...

TRACE ELEMENTS

A lifelong agnostic, as he lay on his deathbed, the comedian W.C. Fields was asked by a friend "Why are you reading The Bible?".
"I'm looking for a loophole", he replied.
Quoted by Les Dawson on *The Michael Parkinson Show*, a 1970s series repeated in September 1996.

With the information assumed from our postcodes, market research companies already build up consumer profiles linked to lifestyle behaviour and particular spending habits. The now-digital telecom companies can offer a Caller Display function that lets you know who is on the phone before you've picked it up. Should you not have this facility, dial 1471 in the UK and a computerized voice will tell you the number of the last caller who tried to get hold of you. Many people already own ansaphone machines—these days, more often used as a *won'tansathephone* machine, to invert their original purpose. British Telecom advertises its Caller Display service with a comforting photo of Granny, linked to this caption: "Hey look, everyone! Granny's back from her holiday. Let's pick up the phone and shout, 'Welcome Home'". BT liken this to "having a crystal ball". In fact they are looking through the wrong end of a telescope. All of this will make people communicate less freely rather than more so. In no time, we will have access to OCR transcripts of any phone conversation we ever have. Just press a button.

Surveillance of one kind or another is an intrinsic tool of social and political control. The technology has been the by-product of military espionage and police-regulated forensic science. Add to this the sophisticated imaging techniques of the medical profession and the soon-to-be completed breakthroughs in genetic profiling and the potential for intrusion and interference is greatly enhanced.

"The ultimate aim of the Human Genome Project is to read every letter of every word in the library that is the human genome – including the vast volumes of nonsense – to obtain the complete set of instructions on how to put together a human being. A different way of gauging the magnitude of the enterprise is to consider the Human Genome Project as akin to conducting a census of every human being living on this earth today. Biologists are confident not only that they can conduct that census, but that they can do the equivalent of writing down every individual's full address, and their relationships with other members of their family."
Tom Wilkie, *Perilous Knowledge*, Faber and Faber 1993

Gene. Origin. Literally, "the place of formation".

Genetic engineering is more like telecommunications because like mobile phone companies its exponents are forcefully convinced that any expansion in their operational reach is by definition good. This is also the science of presenting a few steps on the path of the trace as a substitute for ever having control over the full picture.

Genetic information is digital, cellular and existential dynamite. The Human Genome Project hopes to complete the genetic mapping of the human body shortly after the year 2000. The technology that enables our numerous strands of DNA to be sequenced has been around since 1975, developed by Frederick Sanger at Cambridge University. Genomic laboratories are little more than number-crunching facilities, because this they have to be—there are between 50,000 and 100,000 genes hidden in the human genome, (and, as Wilkie points out, many of them completely meaningless, but who is to be sure which ones?). The pieces of DNA contained within hold some 3 billion chemical letters that instruct each of our 100 trillion cells to produce the proteins or enzymes that maintain our essential bodily fluids. And just to sequence this information is the easy part of the operation. Here is an updated version of Alan Turing's decoding of the Enigma Machine during World War Two—a breakthrough that ushered in the digital age. Cracking the human genome is the next step, even more significant and accordingly hazardous.

The project has been funded and fêted because great hopes ride on its promised medical benefits. However, even if hundreds of 'single fault' genetic disorders such as Huntington's chorea (a rare but fatal neurological disease) and haemophilia were to be eradicated, they would amount to "less than 2% of the world's disease burden" (*The Economist*, 14th September 1996). Common diseases like cancer are caused by the mutation of several genes and result from more volatile environmental/behavioural patterns as much as they do from inherited genetic flaws. Treatment comes by introducing a gene that produces the correct protein to encourage the body's immune system to attack cancerous cells, but not only is the means of pinpointing this corrective gene hotly disputed, its delivery method has yet to be refined so that it allows the new gene to produce the requisite amount of protein over a sufficient period of time to be effective. Nevertheless, a cure is said to be within reach. A new technique is to package the gene in a virus which has had its pathogenic elements removed: a neat idea, like alcohol-free lager. Gene therapists like Dr Michael Fossil at Michigan State University even break the optimism barrier, believing that the control of the one key gene that produces an enzyme called telomerase will not only enable doctors to destroy all types of cancer cell—telomerase treatment will prevent all ageing-related diseases and even halt the ageing process itself.

"Life would be intolerable if we knew everything"
Tony Hancock, 'The Blood Donor', BBC Television 1958

In another day and age, not quite laid to rest by pager phones and unreliable hospital tests, the common feeling was "I'd rather not know". In the manner of an HIV test, this will soon become "I'd rather I didn't have to know", giving increased octane to information fatigue (a slump, already, from Anxiety) and inevitably, with selective breeding, to paraknowledge (a kind of omnipotence) on the side of the select, and subliteracy for the masses. Is this not the prime ingredient of fascism... a 'Welcome Home' to the very force for which the medical revolution and The Welfare State was the common prize for having conquered in 1945?

If political non-intervention were not enough, the access to genetic information will undermine any health care system. The insurance industry will become as selective as the National Lottery. Already, the US model of private health insurance is adopting a policy of "Preferred lives", a rationing of coverage granted only to the screened and fit, at the same time as "Wrongful life" suits are being successfully brought on behalf of infants with birth defects whose parents had not been fully informed of their risk. Litigation is in process in the USA, but can it be anything but a stop-gap? Imagine your local doctor, armed with a full run down of your genetic profile, hired to advise you of the likely genetic outcome of your coming child. Does the world become China, with its tolerance of infanticide, or like the USA, whose Pro-Life lobby clouds such issues in a smog of self-righteous fanaticism.

Medical advances are assumed to be, by definition, beneficial, but today they have to coexist with the legacy of BSE, the abuse of pesticides, and in the case of genes, the legacy of eugenics—the short distance earlier in this century between selective breeding, the US Immigration Laws of the 1920s, and Nazism. The diagnosis, analysis and access to the comprehensive genetic map that the Genome Project intends to deliver raises questions that cut to the quick, when there are so many other agents of change "with massive implications for the future". How to see the wood for the trees? In newspaper features and on television documentaries, they appear so distinct and categorical: the violent pleasures of virtual reality, the processing paradise to come from nanotechnology, cybernetics, neural networks... but they all point to one central confusion—the promise that new technologies will bring us closer to the source and the font of wisdom that delivers us the information we need to know about anything, at the very time that we pull further and further away from what we have felt it to be to be human, and to have space.

Genetics brings with it the danger of a fundamental philosophical misconception—namely, that a person's actions are no longer determined by free will, but by their genes. The confirmation that "genetics is destiny" will certainly be an attractive one to the so-called Victim Culture that has steadily promoted the standpoint of "It's not my fault"; murderers who plead a history of child abuse, through to cancer patients who sue tobacco companies. What about Education? What about Nutrition? The idea that people do not control their own actions can come as a comforting escape in the short term. Eventually, it can only lead to a new and effortlessly upheld form of slavery.

Of course, Walt Disney, the great believer in hygiene as moral value would disagree; the Human Genome Project's very name rings like a Disney production, where tradition—the Past—can be mitigated and indeed replaced by constant modification in the Present: in other words, the dream of the surgeon splicer, the reanimator who becomes the true policeman and politician of the 21st century.

ONE IS NEVER WHAT ONE HAS...

CONTACT
FUSE is published quarterly by *FontShop International*, distributed via the FontShop network.

BINDEGLIED
FUSE fonts do not always include a full set of upper and lower case characters. They are experimental ideas and should be extended by users... abuse is part of the process!

FUSE EDITORIAL
Unit 2 Whitehorse Yard
78 Liverpool Road London N1 0QD
Fax: +44 (0) 1 71 704 2447
e-mail: ag62@cityscape.co.uk

ISSUE 16
Editor & writer: Jon Wozencroft
Design: Tom Hingston

"Since people are going to be living longer and getting older, they'll just have to learn how to be babies longer. I think that's what's happening now. Some kids I know personally are staying babies longer."
Andy Warhol, *From A to B and Back Again*, Michael Dempsey/Cassell & Co. 1975

The surgeon need not work in a hospital, nor run an exclusive clinic overlooking Lake Geneva. You might as easily find him or her in the role of television presenter, cutting and splicing and surfing a channel through a tidal wave of top entertainment to bring it in on time and in good ratings health for the network bosses. In Britain, we can barely run a Health Service, but we can count on TV surgeons and anaesthetists.

Every Friday, at 6 o'clock and then repeated after the pub shuts, comes Chris Evans' new show, ginger hair and glasses his natural props for a caricature of the rampant energy of a hyperactive child. Great innovations in the tabloid gene pool, there are two slots, "I'M AN UGLY BLOKE" and "FAT LOOKALIKES" that should make Darwinians smile in their clippers. The idea is to invite viewers to submit themselves to this address, "I'M AN UGLY BLOKE", PO Box so on and so forth, and then help to make public humiliation an artform by concocting some embarrassing circumstance that bonds itself effortlessly with Postmodern irony. Nobody knows what that is until it is too late, and so the primal urges of bread and circuses, soapbox and self-satisfaction urge everyone onwards, if hardly upwards.

This particular week, Del wrote in. He looked gormless, and just what the doctor ordered for this gregarious stunt. The producers of the show packed him off with a socialite blonde to the London première of *Emma*, the new Hollywood costume drama starring Gwyneth Paltrow, held at the Chelsea Cinema with rows of minor celebrities and beautiful people in attendance. The event was video'd, and then played back to Del and the TV studio audience. As Del, dressed in a dinner suit and tie for the occasion, is introduced to Greta or Tamara or Caprice or whoever, the look on their well-heeled faces all say the same thing... *"What the **** is he doing here??"*. Del's expression, to his credit, does not reveal whether he is as bemused as everyone else or absolutely mortified. He is on TV. And he is famous for at least half a minute. He slopes off as quickly as he has sloped on (like a mutant lifeform that can only be exposed to the atmosphere for a passing moment). Later on in the show, Chris Evans introduces two contestants for "FAT PERSON LOOKALIKE", a "Fat André Agassi" and "Fat Claudia Schiffer". They get to be famous for about 10 seconds.

"We're just having a laugh" says Chris Evans, beaming an infectious smile across his Operating Theatre, here decked out to look like a trendy pub with a dancefloor attached, backed up by its range of anaesthetics—beer, football, celebrity populism, as well as non-stop laughing gas—guaranteed to cure the blues by pumping that base but contagious emotion, schadenfreude, into the nation's homes. "And now, with his new single, it's Jamiroquai and 'Virtual Insanity'"... Whatever the contents of this delivery system, the links can be vital or overwhelmingly meaningless. They too are packaged in a virus, but one that has *not* had its pathogenic elements removed.

Chris Evans cries out "Coming up next, don't go away...". The National Lottery reassures its weekly clientele of millions that "It could be you". Before he died, Warhol modified his catchphrase that "Everybody will be famous for fifteen minutes"... "No, what I really meant to say was 'Everybody will be famous *in* fifteen minutes...'". The medical and the telematic converge to make every one of us a hologram of our former selves.

Jon Wozencroft

FUSE 16: Type Design Comes to Life **Zaid Hassan**

Over the last few decades type design has changed. The changes have been more in the tools of design than any intrinsic shift of purpose or methodology. The tools have changed from hot metal presses all the way to Apple Macs and laser printers. The prevailing attitude towards the tools of type design is summarised by Robert Bringhurst in *The Elements of Typographic Style*; "Meaning resides... in the firmness and grace of the gesture itself, not in the tool with which it was made".

Today's tools, software packages, faster and faster machines, are a long way from the "medieval" scribes' stone tablets and chisel. Has the quality of type been affected by such radical shifts? If this point is at all debatable then we have our answer. Yes? No? We don't know. Yet the grace and the tools have both changed...

The digitisation of type has paved the way for the manipulation of typefaces in a way never seen before. Bypassing every tradition of type design, we have now reached the stage where an hour or so spent doodling on a computer can produce a new typeface. The dividing line between the scribe and a Barry Deck is simply that of slow and fast rather than ancient and modern.

The further acceleration of type design comes from the Genetic Algorithm (GA). A product of the infant field of artificial life, the GA is evolution harnessed. From the study of how genes combine, duplicate, reproduce and die, researchers have created a simple algorithm that can be used to optimise systems, in much the same way evolution weeds out the weakest organisms. The irony is that where evolution takes millions of years, computers have given us the power to press a button and speed up this artificial evolutionary process to match our liking.

A digital typeface is a mathematical expression that is presented in a form acceptable to binary computers. This form, Postscript, is ideal for digital manipulation. Computers and modern printers survive on this process.

The typeface has become a number.

A GA can be used to produce new typefaces through a rendering process. Indicate the style of type you are interested in, anything from Mannerist to Baroque, then give the GA a typeface to use as a starting point and it will generate populations of new typefaces using the rules of evolution. As new typefaces are generated, a set of rules, known as the fitness test, are applied. This test determines which typefaces are to be used as "parent" generations, and which typefaces are to be rejected. "Parent" generations determine the aesthetics of future generations. The process is random, unpredictable and unique.

For an artist this reductionism seems obscene, impersonal and it exemplifies modern technology and science. Speed and numbers. The antithesis of art!

This process raises a number of issues. These issues are paralleled in everything we see around us, order and chaos, science and art. Divisions that, fortunately, are no longer applicable. Science and art embody a common creative process, and type design increasingly reflects this fact.

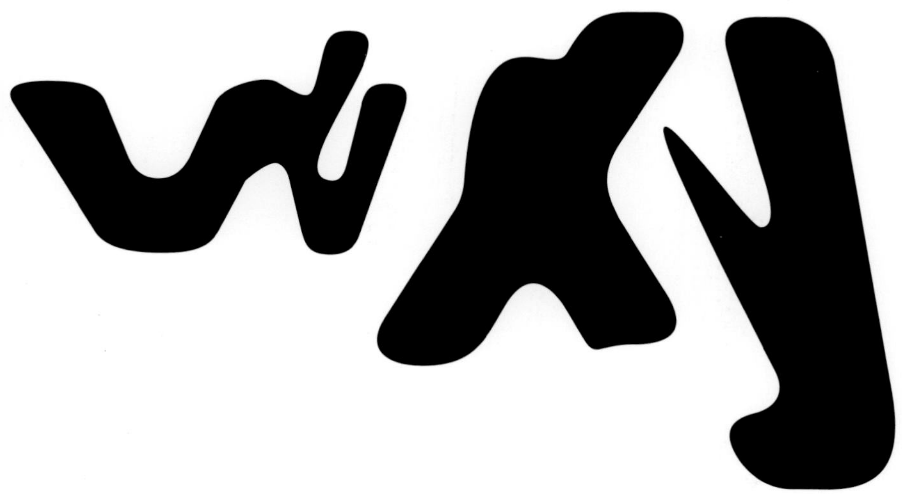

FUSE 16: Neville Brody Bonus Font Genetics Second Generation

TOM HINGSTON @ RESEARCH STUDIOS ISSUE POSTER

DESIGN: TOM HINGSTON @ RESEARCH STUDIOS

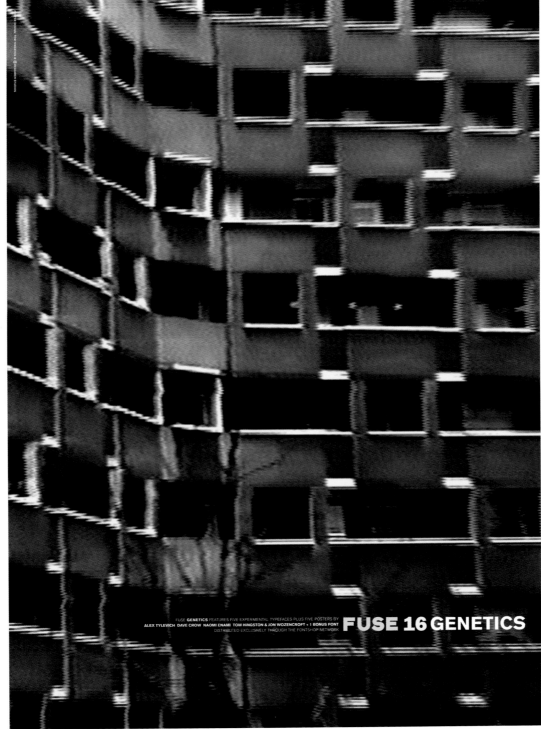

FUSE **GENETICS** FEATURES FIVE EXPERIMENTAL TYPEFACES PLUS FIVE POSTERS BY
ALEX TYLEVICH DAVE CROW NAOMI ENAMI TOM HINGSTON & JON WOZENCROFT + 1 BONUS FONT
DISTRIBUTED EXCLUSIVELY THROUGH THE FONTSHOP NETWORK

FUSE 16 GENETICS

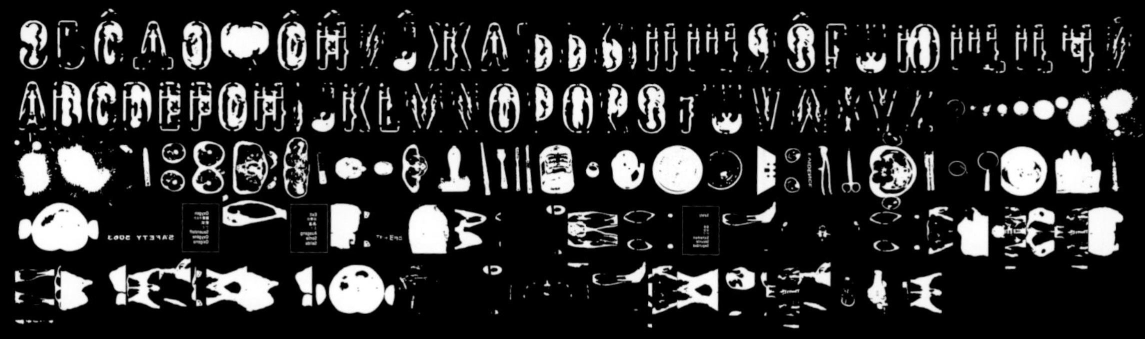

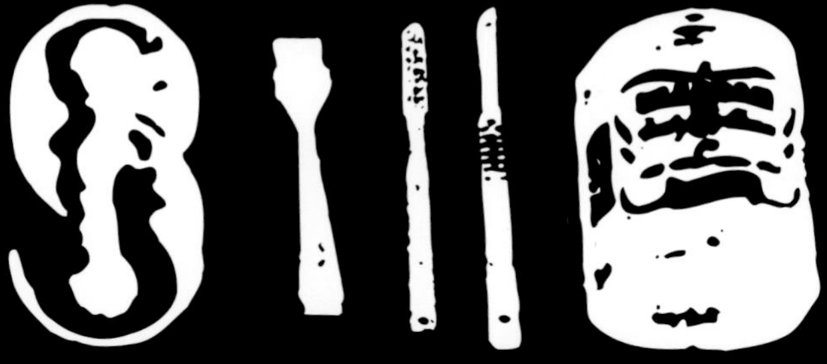

FUSE 16: Alex Tylevich Cico Paco

The basic premise behind the typeface is the main focus of genetics, which is the degree to which the observable trait (the phenotype) is attributable to the pattern of genes in the cells (the genotype) and to what extent it arises from environ-mental influence. When this premise is taken into the realm of political doctrines, the dominant ideology strives to become an "environmental influence".

Esperanto,* an attempt at "linguistic genetic engineering", and the Lamarckian theory of evolution** which found new life under the Stalinist regime in the '40s and '50s both put emphasis on the strategically conducted environmental changes.

Cico Paco contains both English and Russian characters, with added fragments of Esperanto (upper case is English, lower case is Russian and Esperanto). The user can write in English only, or in Russian. In addition, a set of cross-sections of a human body is available for easy manipulation (the option+numbers contain progressive slices of the body divided into 9 equal parts from head to toe). On a formal level, the letters (uc and lc) are impressions of flesh, liquid and plastic, referring to the "phenotype=reason" ("mating" as "influence"). The X–ray corpse cross-sections and tools refer to the "genotype=result" ("meat" as "evidence").

* Esperanto: an artificial international language based upon words common to the chief European languages. Dr. Zamenhof's *Fundamento de Esperanto*, containing over 3500 roots, was published in 1905 and quickly became very popular with the Bolsheviks (Josef Stalin was an avid esperantist).

**Jean-Baptiste de Lamarck, a pioneering 19th-century French evolutionist, formulated a theory of organic evolution according to which environmental changes cause structural changes in animals and plants (by inducing new or increased use of organs or parts resulting in adaptive modification or greater development, and similarly cause disuse and eventual atrophy of other parts whose changes are transmitted to offspring). The quarter of the century roughly between 1938 and 1963 marked the dark ages in Soviet genetic research (after its flowering in the '30s due to such important figures as Dubinin and Vavilov). The agronomist Trofim Lysenko was able to make his own brand of Lamarckism (asserting the fundamental influence of environmental factors on heredity) the official creed of the Soviet Union, having suppressed most of the teaching and research in orthodox genetics. His theories complemented the dominant ideological concepts of "social engineering" and "turning rivers upstream" very well. One of the favourite epithets used to characterise Stalin at the time was "The Engineer of Human Souls".

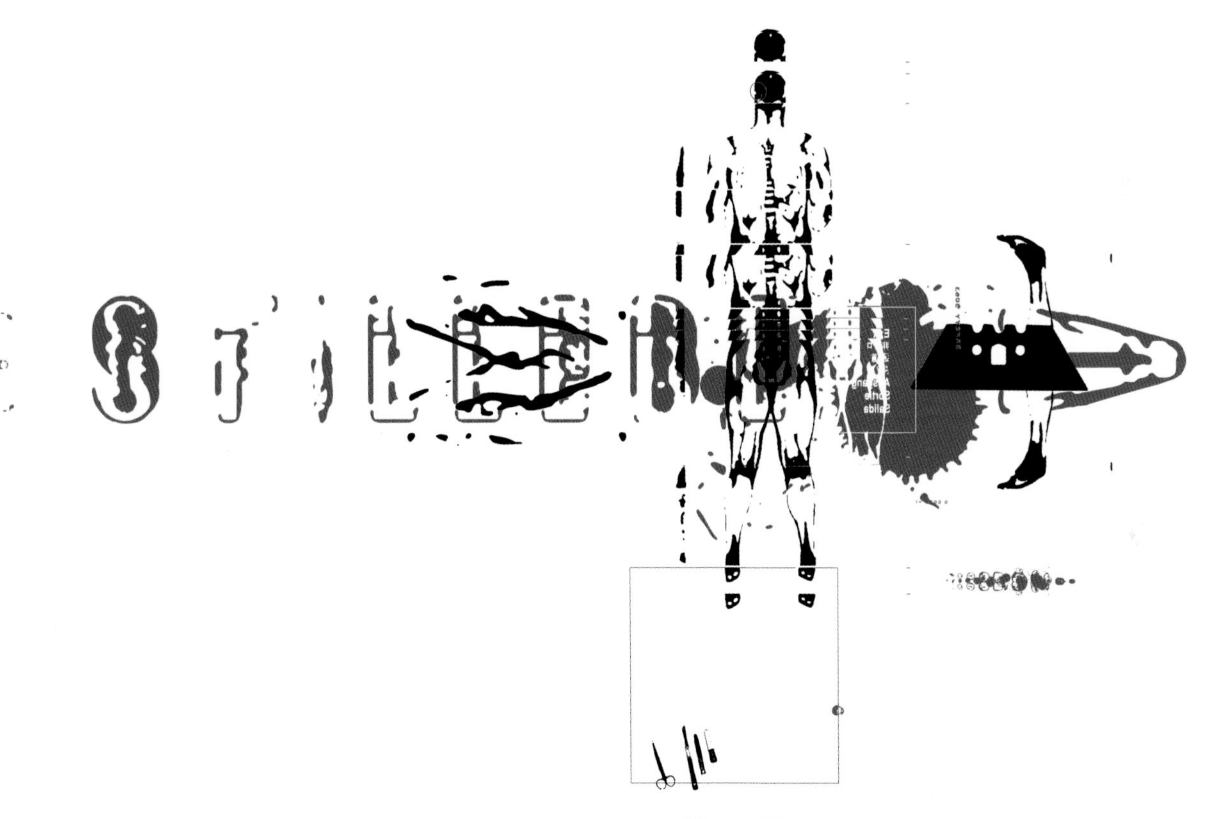

active••••
idealistic
uncertain•
organised•
creative••
logical

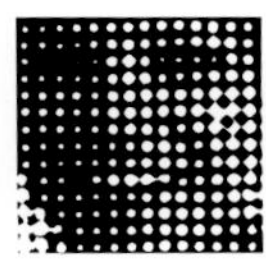

active••••
idealistic
uncertain•
organised•
creative••
logical

emotional
unpredictable•
passionate•••
inflexible
reclusive
reserved

gentle
loyal
loving
loving
shy•••
proud

blonde
brown
white
white
green
brown

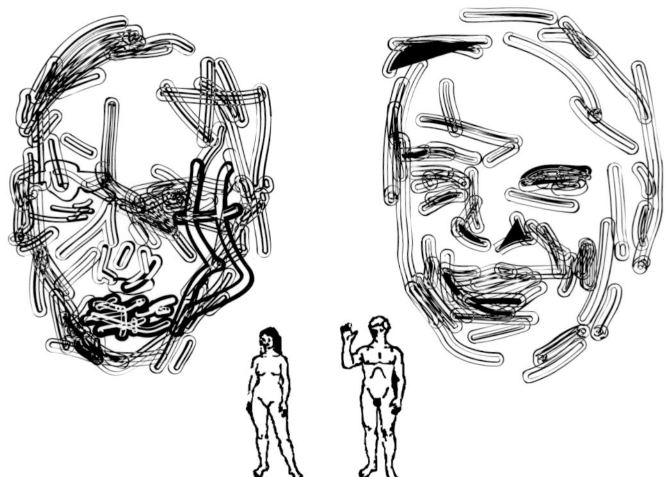

FUSE 16: David Crow Mega Family 2

The alphabet keys contain elements of the female portrait and the shift alphabet keys hold the male portrait. By typing a selection the user can produce genetic mixes between these parents. The numerals and shift numerals contain non-physical information in the form of words: some of these attributes are dominant and will override others, removing them. A thumbnail can be fixed at the end of a sequence by typing either shift X or shift Y; this will also determine the gender of the thumbnail. A parental preview is on the x and y keys and the manufacturer's logo on +.

A talisman can be created for each character using the option numeral keys. To fix your talisman, use opt 1 or the space bar.

The font functions as a game for one or two players and suggests a move towards leisure-based activity as a cellular growth within what we understand as typography. Its rules are self-generated and not imposed.

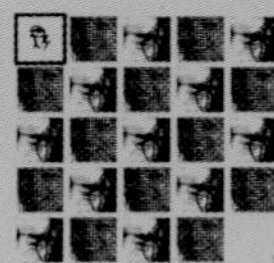

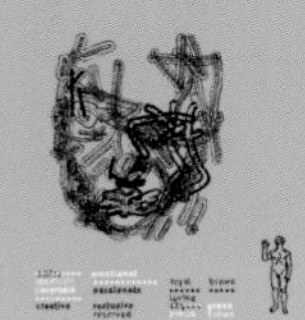

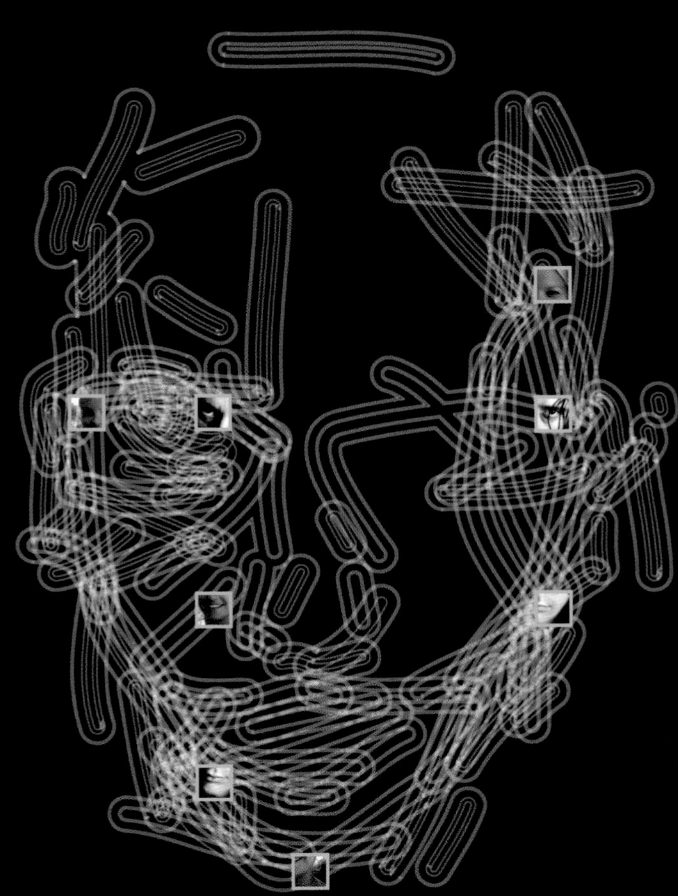

F Mega Family 2 © David Crow ® 1996 FontShop International Poster printed on recycled paper

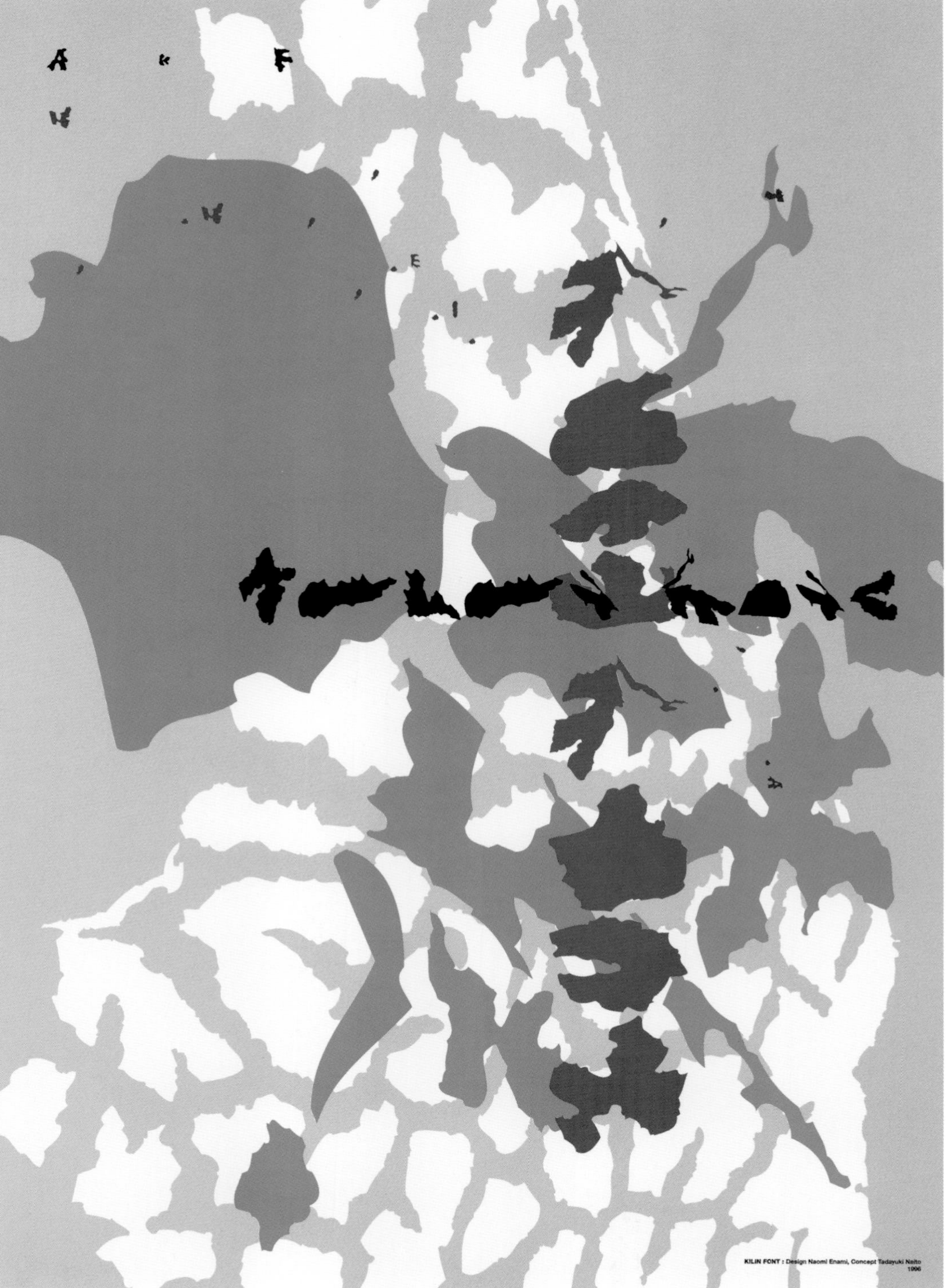
KILIN FONT : Design Naomi Enami, Concept Tadayuki Naito
1996

ABCDEFG HIJK LMN
OPQRSTU VWX YZ ,.

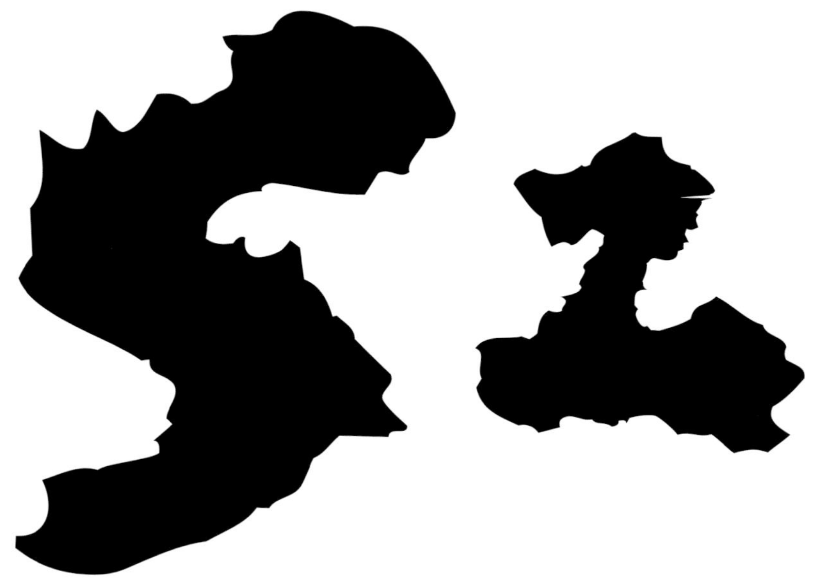

FUSE 16: Naomi Enami Kilin

Heredity reveals itself through the medium of a cell of a specific appearance and character, inherited from generation to generation. However, the familiar pattern of the giraffe differs even between parent and child. It is really a graphic art created by a gene. This font comprises samples of a giraffe's pattern – while all of the letters are recognisable as alphabetical, they have been selected without any intentional manipulation.

altautocondigidisextrafungenhyperinterlogmanminimodmultinetoptipropararefsigsynteletransunivirable

actallyationcesscomdentfaceformfulframilitlesslinementmeternalologysivesizedtexttivetrontypewarework

CONDITION CONCEPTION

altautocondigidisextrafungenhyperinterlogmanminimodmultinetoptipropararefsigsynteletransunivirable

actallyationcesscomdentfaceformfulframilitlesslinementmeternalologysivesizedtexttivetrontypewarework

CONDITION BIRTH

CONDITION MUTATED

CONDITION PULSE

FUSE 16: Tom Hingston & Jon Wozencroft Condition

Condition is built on 4 levels, the first exploring the etymology of over-familiar links in language, next, the use of these elemental parts in coining new words to form the *lingua franca* (or technobabble) of new information technologies. These 'clusters' of (signified) meaning are then visually mutated to suggest a genetics of shape. Finally, all the elements are reduced to their line width, the 'heartbeat' and rhythm of a language machine which, like the economy, seems forever on the point of collapse.

. = X
, = IT
: = ON
; = NO
? = A
“ = @
” = @ (inverted)
‘ = CO
’ = INC

numerals = newly designed set of directional symbols

VIS
RIX

ALT–high, in an exalted state
AUTO–self, independent(ly)
CON–together, with
DIGI–finger, numeral
DIS–apart, between
EXTRA–beyond, outside
FUN–basis, foundation
GEN–that which produces
HYPER–over, above and exceeding
INTER–among, between
LOG–reckoning, ratio
MAN–the human race, adult male
MINI–small, minor
MOD–of form not substance
MULTI–many, abundance
NET–complex system, mesh
OPTI–of sight, ultimate view
PARA–beyond, wrong, irregular
PRO–in front of, supportive
REF–make allusion, football referee
SIG–mark, indicate
SYN–alike, two into one
TELE–recording at a distance
TRANS–to the other side
UNI–singular, of only one
VIR–man, not yet used or tried
ABLE–holding, having the means to
ACT–to do, thing done
ALLY–allied with another
ATION–create, the appearance
CESS–ceasing, rate
COM–completely, connected
DENT–subordinate, free
FACE–outward show, front
FORM–having the shape of
FUL–to utmost capacity, complete
GRAM–thing written, letter
ILITY–of the tendency
LESS–without, missing
LINE–of ancestry, pedigree
MENT–expressing result
METER–of measuring instrument
NAL–of the body, before
OLOGY–of any science, theory
SIVE–having the nature of
SIZED–regulate, act like
TEXT–original words, of weaving
TIVE–tending to, towards
TRON–balance, pair of scales
TYPE–class, structure
WARE–of manufactured material
WORK–operations in building

to the other side
having the shape of

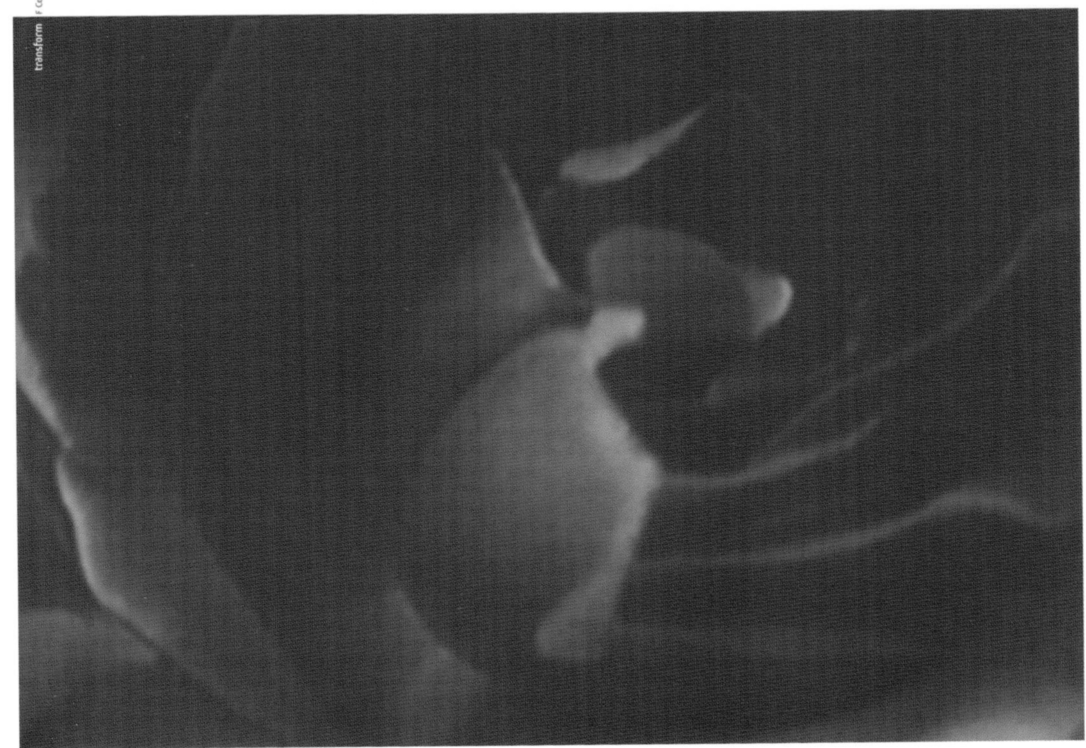

transform

17
FUSE
FUSE 17: Echoes Jon

SUMMER 1997

ECHO

"Don't quote me on that", the politicians say, and then take cover behind soundbites. "Quotations. I hate quotations" wrote the American poet Emerson over a century ago. But books are published entirely of them – and few you read, even works of fiction, seem to do without them in this day and age. This is understandable, of course. Writing is an elementary form of echo location, and books are the echo chambers. The problem – maybe – is that quotations are being used increasingly like shields rather than springboards, their range held back by the over-categorised domain of critical writing. The echo goes backwards. 'Connectivity' promises so much in the way of lateral outcomes, but it encourages the scatter-shot of issue-based agendas. The net tightens. Have today's writers and philosophers failed to provide the tools that enable people to understand what is at stake in the post-digital world? Such works *do* exist, if not in abundance (the less the merrier); they are simply awaiting more of 'the right readers' – echoes into the near and distant – because it is this part of the bargain, the willingness to take time over 'serious' texts that has disappeared into the screen. From Milton's *Pandaemonium* and Mary Shelley's *Frankenstein*, humanity has been shadowed by the fracture of new technologies, and is ill-equipped to negotiate the impact of the new before its passing and replacement by the next. When everything is transitional, who can find the time to piece the stories together? But it's not just that. Echoes involve the idea of tracing a signal back to its source. Quotations are suspect devices because they are easy fodder, slipping all too easily into 'pop biog' cut and pastes, where nothing very much is said about anything.

My eyes are doing somersaults, staring at my shoe.
Siouxsie and the Banshees, 'Jigsaw Feeling', Polydor Records 1978

These echoes imply expanded texts. "The future is not what it used to be" comments Arthur C. Clarke. The range of the echo is shortening... The here and now as expressed by the off-beat on a drum and bass record, and in the gap that separates a techno rhythm patten from a distorted guitar riff, to swallow a letter of the alphabet and then wait for its ricochet.

Joy Divison, 'Transmission', Factory/London Records 1979
Wire, '40 Versions', EMI Records 1979
Public Image Limited, 'Memories', Virgin Records 1980

Clear Reception (The Idea of Camouflage)

"Wishing to render the things that can be verified, I limited myself to my inner life."
Entry in Klee's diary, quoted in Paul Klee, *Notebooks Volume 1 – The Thinking Eye*, Lund Humphries 1961

Search Engines and Censorship

"The programme uses complex algorithms – relating to shape and the distributions and ratios of colour mass – to determine whether the image is indeed that of a naked person.

Of course, it's by no means perfect – just as word-censor packages screen out not just pornography but articles attacking it, so Image Censor can't necessarily distinguish between a bikini-clad Spice Girl, your grandma sunbathing, a hardcore centrefold or a pile of uncooked sausages."
Chris Jones, 'Flesh-eating Bug', in *Sight and Sound*, July 1997

Shrink-wrapped Experience

"You can't get sick from too much knowledge — but we can suffer from the virtualization of knowledge, its alienation from us and its replacement by a weird dull changeling or simulacrum — the same 'data', yes, but now dead — like supermarket vegetables; no 'aura'. Our malaise arises from this: we hear not the language but the echo, or rather the reproduction ad infinitum of the language, its reflection upon a reflection-series of itself, even more self-referential and corrupt. The vertiginous perspectives of this VR datascape nauseate us because they contain no hidden spaces, no privileged opacities."
Hakim Bey, 'Silence', in *Immediatism*, AK Press 1994

Down Memory Lane

"But — what? ... the buzzing? ... yes... all the time the buzzing... so-called... in the ears... though of course actually... not in the ears at all... in the skull... dull roar in the skull..."
Samuel Beckett, *Not I*, Faber & Faber 1973

The Ripple of Artificial Intelligence

"You cannot think about thinking without thinking about thinking about something."
Seymour Papert, in *The Society of Mind*, Marvin Minsky, Picador 1988

Art is not for Liking

"My idea was to choose an object that wouldn't attract me either by its beauty or its ugliness – to find a point of indifference in my looking at it... you see, after a while, when you look at something, it becomes very interesting and you can even like it.

And the minute that I liked it, I would discard it."
Marcel Duchamp, discussing his first readymade sculpture, *Fountain*, 1917, on BBC TV in 1966; *The Works*, BBC2 15 June 1997

Echoes involve the idea of tracing a signal back to its source. Quotations are suspect devices because they are easy fodder, slipping all too easily into 'pop-biog' cut and pastes, where nothing very much is said about anything.

Making Them Redundant

"Police called to a break-in at a B&Q store in Darlington, Co. Durham, resorted to an aircraft equipped with infra-red, heat-detecting equipment to track down the perpetrator. He was caught hiding in shrubbery, along with his loot – a £1.75 paintbrush."
The Guardian, 28 June 1997

Triple Echo

"Art as I see it has to do with changing the mind, turning it away from the confines of ego (art in my opinion is not self-expression) ... My notion of how to proceed in a society to bring change is not to protest the thing that is evil, but rather to let it die its own death.

And I think we can state that the power structure is dying because it cannot make any inspiring statements about what it is doing. I think that protests about these things, contrary to what has been said, will give it the kind of life that a fire is given when you fan it, and that it would be best to ignore it, put your attentions elsewhere, take actions of another kind of positive nature, rather than to continue to give life to the negative by negating it."
John Cage, in *Conversing with Cage*, ed. Richard Kostelanetz, Limelight Editions NY 1988

Temporarily Blinded

"I feel we are in a situation where we can't foresee the future, we can't make any predictions since we are already in a kind of 'real time'. There's no longer any history, any continuity, any future. Before, you could have a perspective. Nowadays, we are in an area of the instantaneous, of immediacy, of information, so we can't respond to the future because everything is here and now.

We can see everything, and when we can see everything we can't foresee anything. I particularly have the feeling that this millennium, this 'judgement day' is not a time of communion, but more one of withdrawal... We would like to have a period of purification, purification of the century gone by."
Interview with Jean Baudrillard by Michael Fordham, *Dazed & Confused*, June 1997

Downloaded

"The archaic 'tyranny of distances' between people who have been geographically scattered increasingly gives way to this 'tyranny of real time' that is not merely a matter for travel agencies, because the more the speed of commerce grows, the more unemployment becomes globally massive. In the nineteenth century, the muscular force of the human being is literally 'laid off' when automation of the 'machine tool' is employed.

Then, with the recent growth of computers, 'transmission machines', comes the laying off or ultimate shutdown of human memory and conscience. Automation of post-industrial production is coupled with the automation of perception."
Paul Virilio, 'The Third Interval: A Critical Transition', in V.A. Conley (ed.), *Rethinking Technologies*, University of Minnesota Press 1993

Boys will be Beuys

"I used to look forward to the era when everybody would be an artist. Sorry. It's a nightmare."
Laurie Anderson, interviewed by Michael Pye, *The Daily Telegraph*, 19 June 1997

***Curriculum Vitae* Give it the Once Over**

"You have got to reach on up, never lose your soul,
You have got to reach on up, never lose control."
The Spice Girls, *Who Do You Think You Are?*, Virgin Records 1996

"The new technologies feed on a diet of mass passification. Compliance and dependance give the Superhighway its strength. In an age of obedience, the information age will thrive. In a different time, it will become a target for losers. The race is on to develop an information infrastructure that becomes invisible and inviolable, before the trouble begins."

Bell Ringer

"The new technologies feed on a diet of mass passification. Compliance and dependance give the Superhighway its strength. In an age of obedience, the information age will thrive. In a different time, it will become a target for losers. The race is on to develop an information infrastructure that becomes invisible and inviolable, before the trouble begins."
Simon Davies, *Big Brother*, Pan Books, 1996

Local Swelling

"Insects can see discrete events that follow each other at a very high frequency. Whereas, for us, events separated by less than one thirty-fifth of a second become fused, in an 'insect cinema' the projector would have to race along at 350 frames per second to give the 'insect audience' the illusion of smooth continuity in time. This enables insects to appreciate movement to an extent quite unimaginable to us."
Otto Lowenstein, *The Senses*, Penguin Books 1966

Optical Sound ("Blind as a Bat")

"The experience (of sustained depth-charging) has often been described from the German side: the sound of the propellers above, the metallic chirp of not only the hydrophones but the increasing volume throughout the hull, the regular intervals of the sonar shortening as the still and silent, feet clad only in socks, wait. The propeller noise reaches intensity overhead, anticipation building until the boat becomes like the skin of the men inside."
Peter Padfield, *War Beneath the Sea*, John Murray Ltd. 1995

The Echo Reversed

"The eyes are the most exposed part of the brain. We do have these eyelids that protect the eye, and we have the pupil that protects it, but basically the eye is a pea-processor of visual information. It is very difficult to 'see' our seeing, as we do not see the blind spots, we arc them in... A lot of my work is about exploring this quality of seeing yourself see. So literally, when you are presented or confronted with a work of mine, it is something for your seeing and about your seeing, not about mine."
Interview with James Turrell, in *Sensing Space*, Seattle, University of Washington/Henry Gallery 1992

A Law of Diminishing Returns

"Content is a glimpse of something, an encounter like a flash. It's very tiny — very tiny, content."
Willem De Kooning, quoted by Susan Sontag, *Against Interpretation*, André Deutsch Ltd. 1987

Lottery Success

"Eclecticism is the degree zero of contemporary general culture: you listen to reggae, you watch a western, you eat McDonald's at midday and local cuisine at night, you wear Paris perfume in Tokyo and dress retro in Hong Kong, knowledge is the stuff of TV game shows. It is easy to find a public for eclectic works. When art makes itself kitsch, it panders to the disorder which reigns in the 'taste' of the patron. Together, artist, gallery owner, critic and public indulge one another in the Anything Goes – it's time to relax, But this realism of anything goes is the realism of money... This realism accommodates every tendency just as capitalism accommodates every 'need' – so long as these tendencies and needs have buying power. As for taste, these is no need to be choosy when you are speculating or amusing yourself. Artistic and literary investigation is doubly threatened: by 'cultural politics' on one side, by the art and book market on the other."

Jean-François Lyotard, *The Postmodern Explained to Children*, Turnaround 1992

"A 17 fuse was a clockwork delay fuse that was set for anything up to four days by the armourer who put the bomb in the plane. The Germans realised that delayed action really disturbed the area that they were bombing because people had to move out and stay out until the bomb was gone. A delayed-action fuse could put a factory out of action for days or weeks. We started endeavouring to remove these fuses and at first we would simply take it out by hand."

Lieutenant Stuart Archer, 105 Bomb Disposal Section, Royal Engineers
Quoted in *Joshua Levine, Forgotten Voices of the Blitz...*, Ebury Press 2007

SIMON GRIFFIN & ROBERT WILKINSON @ RESEARCH STUDIOS & JON WOZENCROFT EDITORIAL POSTER

CLEAN RECEPTION (THE IDEA OF CAMOUFLAGE)

"Wishing to render the things that can be verified, I limited myself to my inner life."

17 ECHO

F Surveillance
F Where The Dog Is Buried
F Spell Me
F White No Sugar
F Page Three

SEARCH ENGINES AND CENSORSHIP

"The programme uses complex algorithms – relating to shape and the distributions and ratios of colour mass – to determine whether the image is indeed that of a naked person.
Of course, it's by no means perfect – just as word-censor packages screen out not just pornography but articles attacking it, so Image Censor can't necessarily distinguish between a bikini-clad Spice Girl, your grandma sunbathing, a hardcore centrefold or a pile of uncooked sausages."

FUSE 17 ECHO

SHRINK-WRAPPED EXPERIENCE

"You can't get sick from too much knowledge—but we can suffer from the virtualization of knowledge, its alienation from us and its replacement by a weird dull changeling or simulacrum—the same 'data', yes, but now dead—like supermarket vegetables; no 'aura'. Our malaise arises from this: we hear not the language but the echo, or

rather the reproduction ad infinitum of the language, its reflection upon a reflection-series of itself, even more self-referential and corrupt. The vertiginous perspectives of this VR datascape nauseate us because they contain no hidden spaces, no privileged opacities."

Hakim Bey, 'Silence', in Immediatism, AK Press 1994

"Don't quote me on that", the politicians say, and then take cover behind soundbites. "Quotations. I hate quotations", wrote the American poet Emerson over a century ago. But books are published entirely of them—and few you read, even works of fiction, seem to do without them in this day and age. This is Understandable, of course. Writing is an elementary form of echo location, and books are the echo chambers. The problem – maybe – is that quotations are being used increasingly like shields rather than springboards, their range held back by the overcategorised domain of critical writing. The echo goes backwards. 'Connectivity' promises so much in the way of lateral outcomes, but it encourages the scatter-shot of issue-based agendas. The net tightens. Have today's writers and philosophers failed to provide the tools that enable people to understand what is at stake in the post-digital world? Such works *do* exist, if not in abundance (the less the merrier); they are simply awaiting

more of 'the right readers' — echoes into the near and distant — because it is this part of the bargain, the willingness to take time over 'serious' texts, that has disappeared into the screen. From Milton's *Pandaemonium* and Mary Shelley's *Frankenstein*, humanity has been shadowed by the fracture of new technologies and is ill-equipped to negotiate the impact of the new before its passing and replacement by the next. When everything is transitional, who can find the time to piece the stories together? But it's not just that. Echoes involve the idea of tracing a signal back to its source. Quotations are suspect devices because they are easy fodder, slipping all too easily into 'pop blog' cut and pastes, where nothing very much is said about anything.

My eyes are doing somersaults, staring at my shoe.
Siouxsie and the Banshees, 'Jigsaw Feeling', Polydor Records 1978.

These echoes imply expanded texts. "The future is not what it used to be", comments Arthur C. Clarke. The range of the echo is shortening... The here and now as expressed by the off-beat on a drum and bass record, and in the gap that separates a techno rhythm pattern from a distorted guitar riff, to swallow a letter of the alphabet and then wait for its ricochet.

Joy Division, 'Transmission', Factory/ London Records 1979.
Wire, '40 Versions', EMI Records 1979.
Public Image Limited, 'Memories', Virgin Records 1980.

DOWN MEMORY LANE

"But – what? ... the buzzing?... yes... all the time the buzzing... so-called... in the ears... though of course actually... not in the ears at all... in the skull... dull roar in the skull..."

Samuel Beckett, Not I, Faber & Faber 1973.

THE RIPPLE OF ARTIFICIAL INTELLIGENCE

"You cannot think about thinking without thinking about thinking about something."

Seymour Papert, in The Society of Mind, Marvin Minsky, Picador 1988.

BOYS WILL BE BEUYS

"I used to look forward to the era when everybody would be an artist. Sorry. It's a nightmare."

ART IS NOT FOR LIKING

"My idea was to choose an object that wouldn't attract me either by its beauty or its ugliness—to find a point of indifference in my looking at it... You see, after a while, when you look at something, it becomes very interesting and you can even like it. And the minute that I liked it, I would discard it."

CURRICULUM VITAE GIVE IT THE ONCE OVER

"You have got to reach on up, never lose your soul. You have got to reach on up, never lose control."

BELL RINGER

"The new technologies feed on a diet of mass passification. Compliance and dependence give the Superhighway its strength. In an age of obedience, the information age will thrive. In a different time, it will become a target for losers. The race is on to develop an information infrastructure that becomes invisible and inviolable, before the trouble begins."

MAKING THEM REDUNDANT

"Police called to a break-in at a B&Q store in Darlington, Co. Durham, resorted to an aircraft equipped with infra-red, heat-detecting equipment to track down the perpetrator. He was caught hiding in shrubbery, along with his loot – a £1.75 paintbrush."

TRIPLE ECHO

"Art as I see it has to do with changing the mind, turning it away from the confines of ego (art in my opinion is not self-expression) ... My notion of how to proceed in a society to bring change is not to protest the thing that is evil, but rather to let it die its own death.
And I think we can state that the power structure is dying because it cannot make any inspiring statements about what it is doing. I think that protests about these things, contrary to what has been said, will give it the kind of life that a fire is given when you fan it, and that it would be best to ignore it, put your attentions elsewhere, take actions of another kind of positive nature, rather than to continue to give life to the negative by negating it."

LOCAL SWELLING

"Insects can see discreet events that follow each other at a very high frequency. Whereas, for us, events separated by less than one thirty-fifth of a second become fused. In an 'insect cinema' the projector would have to race along at 350 frames per second to give the 'insect audience' the illusion of smooth continuity in time. This enables insects to appreciate movement to an extent quite unimaginable to us."

OPTICAL SOUND ("BLIND AS A BAT")

"The experience (of sustained depth-charging) has often been described from the German side: the sound of propellers above increasing in volume, the metallic chirp of the not only through the hydrophones but throughout the hull; its regular interval shortening as the still and silent, feet clad only in socks, the weep-weeping propeller noise reaches maximum intensity overhead, and the silent wait, anticipation building until boat becomes like the skin of the men inside, the smallest noise

TEMPORARILY BLINDED

"I feel we are in a situation where we can't foresee the future, we can't make any predictions since we are already in a kind of 'real time'. There's no longer any history, any continuity, any future. Before, you could have a perspective. Nowadays, we are in an area of the instantaneous, of immediacy, of information, so we can't respond to the future because everything is here and now.

We can see everything, and when we can see everything we can't foresee anything. I particularly have the feeling that this millenium, this 'judgment day' is not a time of communion, but more one of withdrawal... We would like to have a period of purification, purification of the century gone by."

THE ECHO REVERSED

"The eyes are the most exposed part of the brain. We do have these eyelids that protect the eye, and we have the pupil that protects it, but basically the eye is a pre-processor of visual information. It is very difficult to 'see' our seeing, as we do not see the blind spots, we are them in... A lot of my work is about exploring this quality of seeing yourself see. So literally, when you are presented or confronted with a work of mine, it is some thing for your seeing and about your seeing, not about mine."

SEARCH ENGINES AND CENSORSHIP

"The programme uses complex algorithms – relating to shape and the distributions and ratios of colour mass – to determine whether the image is indeed that of a naked person. Of course, it's by no means perfect – just as word-censor packages screen out not just pornography but articles attacking it, so Image Censor can't necessarily distinguish between a bikini-clad Spice Girl, your grandma sunbathing, a hardcore centrefold or a pile of uncooked sausages."

A LAW OF DIMINISHING RETURNS

"Content is a glimpse of something, an encounter like a flash. It's very tiny—very tiny, content."

DOWNLOADED

"The archaic 'tyranny of distances' between people who have been geographically scattered increasingly gives way to this 'tyranny of real time' that is not merely a matter for travel agencies, but especially for employment agencies, because the more the speed of commerce grows, the more unemployment becomes globally massive. the nineteenth century, the muscular force of the human being is literally 'laid off' when automation of the 'machine tool' is employed.

Then, with the recent growth of computers, 'transmission machines', comes the laying off or ultimate shutdown of human memory and conscience. Automation of post-industrial production is coupled with the of perception."

LOTTERY SUCCESS

"Eclecticism is the degree zero of contemporary general culture: you listen to reggae, you watch a western, you eat McDonald's at midday and local cuisine at night, you wear Paris perfume in Tokyo and dress retro in Hong Kong, knowledge is the stuff of TV game shows. It is easy to find a public for eclectic works. When art makes itself kitsch, it panders to the disorder which reigns in the 'taste' of the patron. Together, artist, gallery owner, critic and public indulge one another in the Anything Goes – it's time to relax. But this realism of anything

goes is the realism of money... This realism accommodates every tendency just as capitalism accommodates every 'need' – so long as these tendencies and needs have buying power. As for taste, there is no need to be choosy when you are speculating or amusing yourself. Artistic and literary investigation is doubly threatened: by 'cultural politics' on one side, by the art and book market on the other from one or other of these channels, is to provide works of art which, first, relate to subjects eyes of the public."

CONTACT
FUSE is published by *FontShop International* and distributed via the FontShop network.

FUSE fonts do not upper and lower case characters. They are experimental ideas and should be extended by users... abuse is part of the process!

Unit 2, Whitehorse Yard, 78 Liverpool Road, Islington, London, N1 0QD.
Fax: +44 (0) 171 704 2445
e-mail: ag62@cityscape.co.uk

ISSUE 17
Editor & Writer: Jon Wozencroft
Design: Simon Griffin & Robert Wilkinson @ Research Studios

capitalism accomm- need to be choosy when you are speculating or amusing yourself. Artistic and literary investigation is doubly eyes of the public."
As for taste, there is no threatened: by 'cultural politics' on one side , by the art and book market on the other. **Jean-François Lyotard, The Postmodern Explained to Children, Turnaround 19**
from one or other of these channels, is to provide works of art which, first, relate to subjects

LOTTERY SUCCESS "The archaic 'tyranny of distances' between people who have been geographically scattered of commerce grows, the more unemployme
92. increasingly gives way to this 'tyranny of real time' that is not merely a matter for travel the nineteenth century, the muscular force of t
agencies, but especially for employment agencies, because the more the speed 'laid off' when automation of the 'macl

"Eclecticism is the degree zero ofcontemporary general culture: and dress retro in Hong Kong, knowledge is the stuff of TV game shows.
you listen to reggae, you watch awestern, you eat McDonald's at It is easy to find a public for eclectic works. When art makes itself kitsch, it
midday and loca cuisine at night you wear Parisperfume in Tokyo panders to the disorder which reigns in the 'taste' of the patron. Together, artist,
gallery owner, critic and public indulge one another in the Anything Goes – it's time to
relax. But this realism of anything goes is the realism of money... This realism accommodates every tendency just as
odates every 'need' – so long as these tendencies and needs have buying power.

nt becomes globally massive. human memory and conscien
he human being is literally Then, with the recent growth of computers, 'transmission industrial production
nine tool' is employed. machines', comes the laying off or ultimate shutdown of
thinking Technologies, **DOWNLOADED**ce. Automation of post- is coupled with the of perception." **Paul Virilio, 'The Third Interval: A Critical Transition', in V.A. Conley (ed.), Re University of Minnesota Press 1993.**

ECHO DOWNLOADED

eal lerol scthal lUI eliefat pattinpleasure
e before pairJoirat aparchangemy lifeIt allow me tocontrol

r, Dr Edwardbut also thres to the lettents have tolda. But it was through his allows me**Asthma:** The hemotherapy.problem with High School.ters, Croydd were wholly
from Rochdal tar and five te expect the his can help research one of 16, durinpain. It allowsfound to wideled Nabilone ave been presys' comprehnine staff at Ingram has b
e dangerousarbon mono their membe e not just go e of its illegal of the diseasen other sleepthe lung. But tol can be used you take enf 18 schools "that they facerming and it is

widen the airv eye socket in nd to reduce rs Society. ent **three tiblaster for v finds that llows him to lowe, from Flent three ti'Cannabis is n open 1**
But the tar amuse of blindnand tremors. Iief executive e **is still foland still as him to dealy with theshire, was e is still fos little dru**
es cause problowing down thd in other conid: "People w ut there is also **alleviatewith the illh now keep ths last yearut there is aut there is s example**

ex. Thertracks c pain. Itallowsme to sleep' **Flexible friend** 'If emplyers feel able to t the **ad donen open**
decadd once t ....able to tar up agreem **street. exampl**

ECHO PAGE THREE

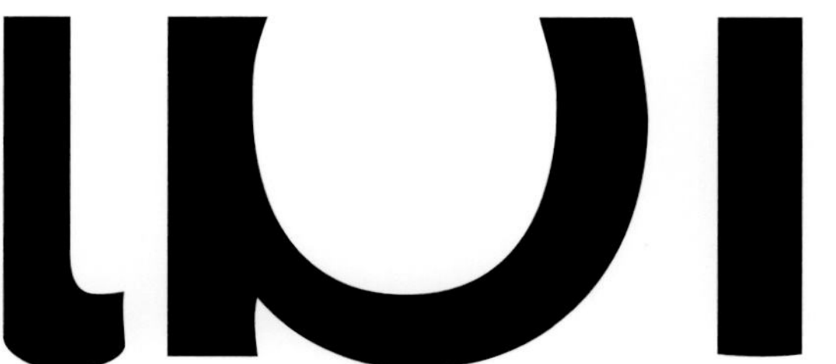

FUSE 17: Neville Brody Bonus Font Echo

Echo Download produces complete little scraps of text that make up 3 lines of blind copy when assembled, and *Echo Three* offers various copy sizes. Both fonts together form amazing collages that show without a doubt the message of this FUSE edition: Information gets shredded by echoes.

l thepain. Itallowsme to sleep' **Flexibl friend** 'If emplyers feel able to t

able to tar up agreem

eliefat putting

pleasure before pairJoirat apartchangemy

life It allow me tocontrol

r, Dr Edwardbut also thres to the lettnts have tolda. But it was through his
from Rochdal tar and five te expect the Nis can help research one of 16, during
e dangerousarbon mono their membe not just go-e of its illegal of the diseas
allows meAsthma: The hemotherapy.problem with High Schoolters, Croydd were whollywiden the airv eye socket in nd to reduce n
pain. It allowsfound to wideled Nabilone ave been presys' comprehnine staff at Ingram has bBut the tar anuse of blindnand tremors. I
en other sleethe lung. But tol can be used you take enf 18 schools "that they facming and it ises cause problowing down tld in other con
Society. plaster for v finds that llows him to owe, from Flent three ti 'Cannabis is **n open tex. Thertracks c**
ief executive and still avs him to dealy with theshire, was e is still fos little dru
id: "People wilso alleviatewith the illh now keep nths last yearut there is aut there is s **exampls decadd once t**

FUSE 17 : **echo** : featuring exploratory fonts and posters from Dave Crow, Etcetaera Plus, Etcetaera Plus, Etcetaera Plus

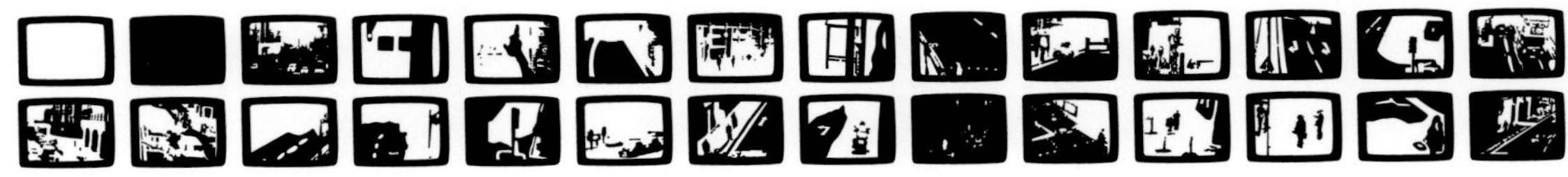

SURVEILLANCE SCENES

SURVEILLANCE SUSPICIOUS PEOPLE

SURVEILLANCE VICTIMS

SURVEILLANCE WITNESS

0123456789 0123456789

SURVEILLANCE DATE AND TIME

FUSE 17: Florian Heiß Surveillance

For graphic designer Florian Heiß, monitoring is the perfect example of echoing information. His typeface family *Surveillance* consists of five fonts depicting everyday situations monitored by video cameras and shows victims, suspects, witnesses, crime scenes and time displays. The rigid black and white drawings appear ominous and vulgar.

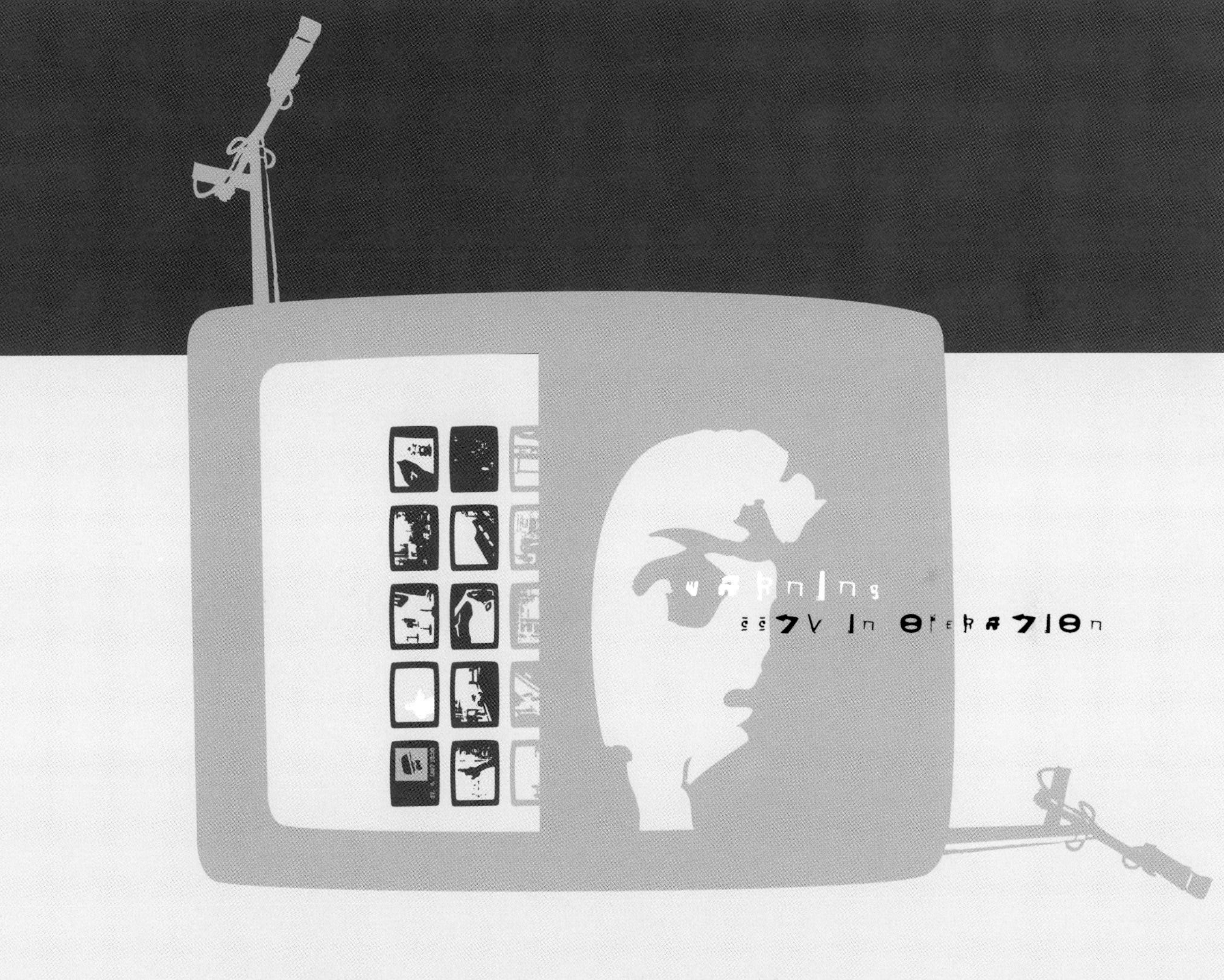
warning
ccTV in operation

WHERE THE DOG IS BURIED MOUNTAIN TOP

ABCDEFGHIJKLMNOPQRSTUVWXYZ
RGI 0123456789

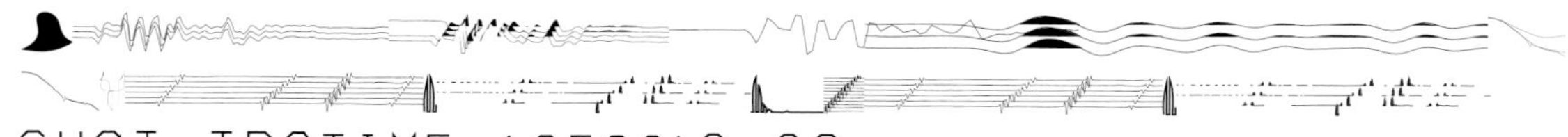

SHOT.TRCTIME (SECS)2.39

WHERE THE DOG IS BURIED SEA BOTTOM

FUSE 17: Function Where the Dog is Buried

Where the Dog is Buried by Norwegian design-group Function interprets Echo in two ways: Mountain Top as a bird's eye view and Sea Bottom from the opposite direction. Function describes their bonus font *Shinjuku* as a Tokyo-graffiti-hip-hop-culture-travel-the-world-echo-font.

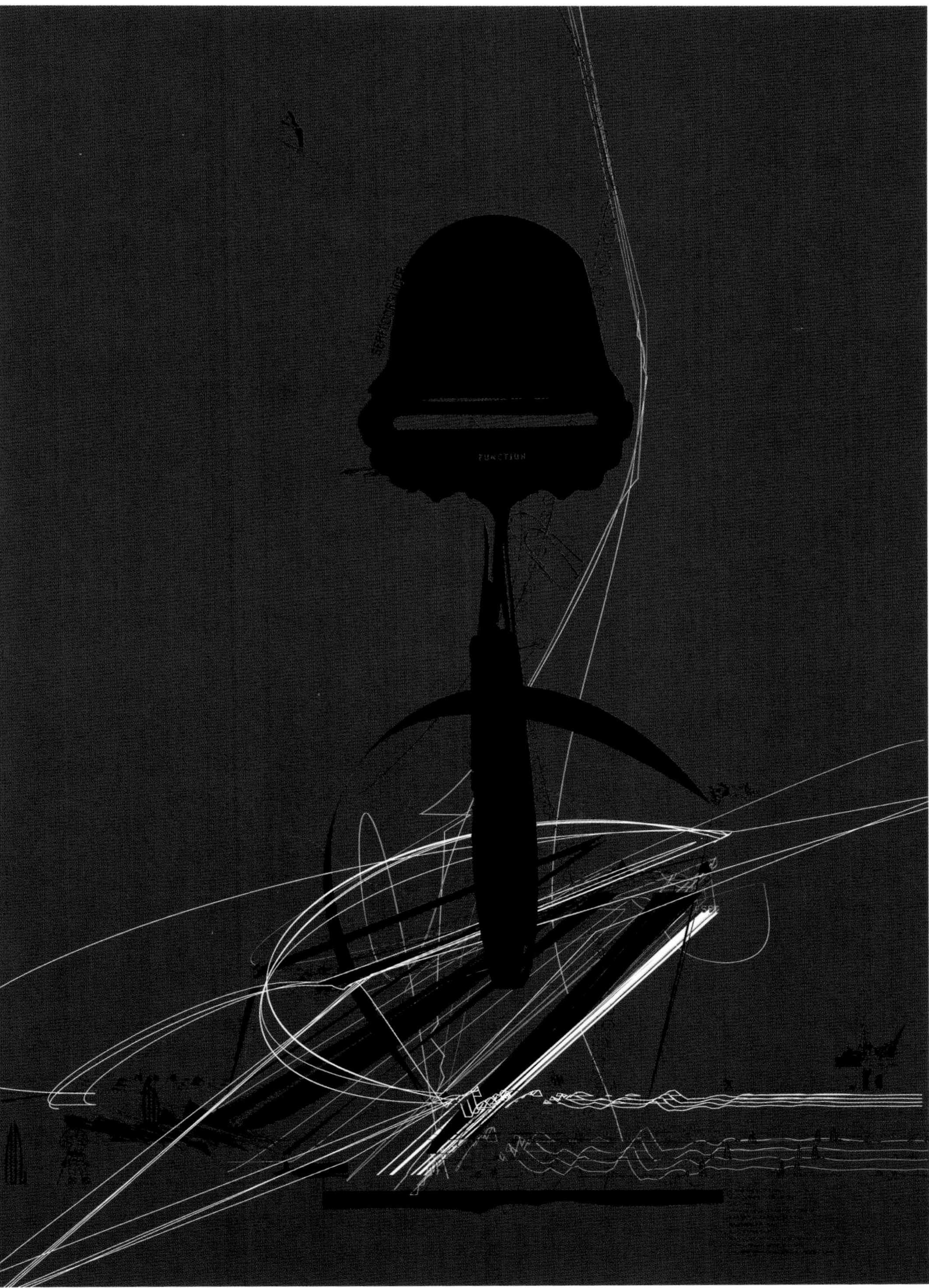

FUSE 17: Pierre di Sciullo Spell Me

Spell Me took a phonetic approach to the subject and visualised the English alphabet with spelling echoes.

yamiu?

yrume?

wy aem I you?
y.a.m.i.u.?

wy are you emee¿
y.r.u.m.e.?

Pourquoi je suis toi moi ? Pourquoi t'es moi toi ?

Tu t'en tiens une de ces couches, je peux pas le croire

I jayyouesstee ceeaen'tee beeeeellieeveeee

I jayyouesstee ceeaen'tee beeeeellieeveeee wyohyou aareee essyouceeaitch a efohohel !!

wyohyou aareee essyouceeaitch a efohellell!

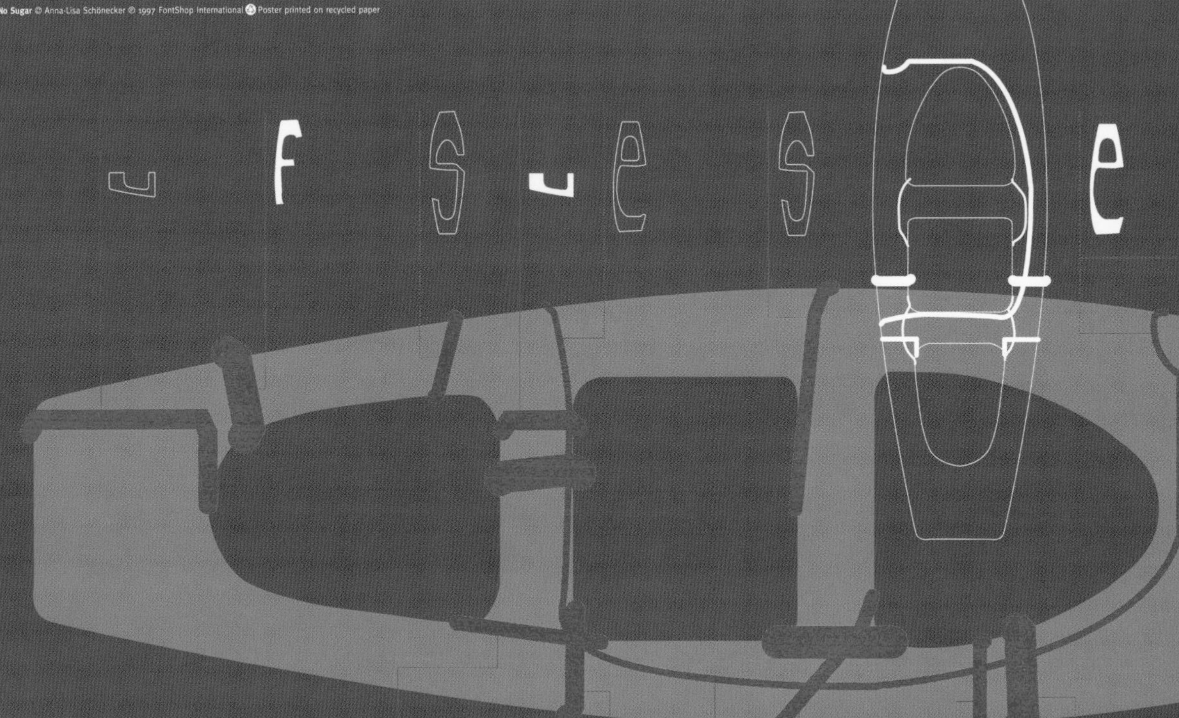
F White No Sugar © Anna-Lisa Schönecker ℗ 1997 FontShop International Poster printed on recycled paper

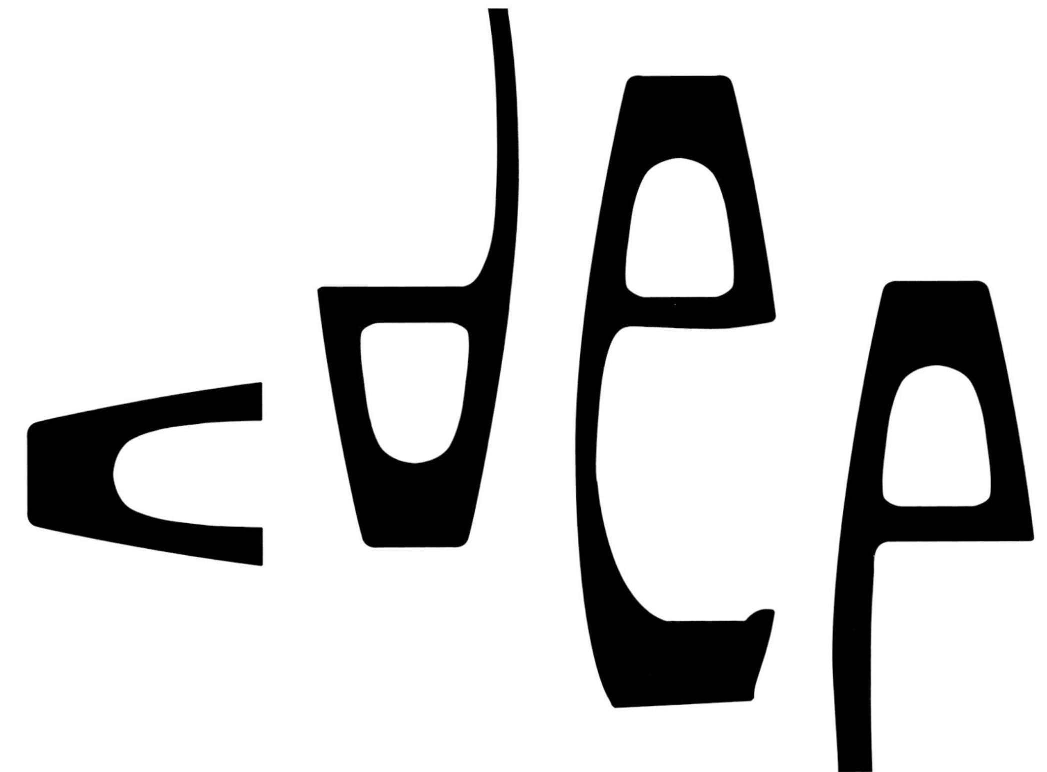

FUSE 17: **Anna-Lisa Schönecker** White No Sugar

White No Sugar will seem familiar to all who have drunk coffee from styrofoam cups. Anna-Lisa Schönecker took the famous plastic coffee cup stirrer and broke little bits off until she got a complete alphabet with milk, but without sugar.

FUSE

FUSE 18: Fit in Window Jon Wozencroft

AUTUMN 2000

SECRETS

3 short takes on interactivity

1 "This is the past that somebody in the future is longing to get back to". The phrase is not a readily identifiable quotation by a French philosopher of time and space, but one of a series of 'Thought provoking ads' to promote Radio Taxis, 'strategically' placed on the doors of licensed black cabs in London throughout June last year. Asking a driver who had this particular message on his cab what he thought of it, he spoke out immediately against the perils of "cowboy operators and their dodgy vehicles", plus the reminder that most of them had "got previous" (i.e. criminal records) and that he "wouldn't touch 'em with a barge pole". All very revealing, because at no point did he give his opinion about the actual message, only about whom it advertised. When pressed about the intriguing thought that his cab broadcast to the outside world, "in actual fact", he "couldn't give a monkey's", "haven't given it a second thought" because, as he went on to explain, he rarely had any say about which advertisements he had to carry, "they're all the same anyway" (he has a point there), "so I just get on with it".

SECRET: orig. Latin from *secretus*, derived from *secernere*, 'to separate, divide off'.

also SECRETARY: a notary, scribe; one who is entrusted with confidential matters.

SECRETE: *transitive*, to place in concealment; *reflexive*, to remove secretly.

We had escaped the 'Ring of steel', the police surveillance operation that has covered an area of the City of London with 47 CCTV cameras, number-plate reading systems and photo-matching technologies since February 1997, checking over 100,000 vehicles and their occupants per day... now we were stuck in Goodsway, the backside of King's Cross. This is where, notoriously, the Director of Public Prosecutions under a previous Tory government was caught kerb-crawling. Graffiti knowingly attests to this; and because the road is still a favourite cruising spot in a grim shadowland beneath a skeleton of gas towers, Goodsway is a nirvana of grafitti. In block white capitals, another rush of paint spells out RAVE IS BEST. Next, barely legible today, JESUS LOVES YOU. The cab turns left into York Way, past the nightclubs and the Camden car pound, then right into Copenhagen Street, back to the world of authorised text. On the corner, a model blonde beams a luscious smile from a billboard, whose slogan says 'FCUK ME'.

Wherever you are, you are exposed to an interplay of warnings, signals and messages that are carnal yet discreet in their motives – just as information involves its shadow of disinformation, they encourage the cult of the individual to turn into sour disindividualism (could 'road rage' be linked to the intense advertising campaigns that the captive audience of a traffic jam has to endure?). Everyone is challenged to be both the codified and code-breaker at one and the same time. The subconscious becomes discord.

2 "Arrangement, configuration, organisation, structure, ordering – these are now key words. What underlies this verbal fashion? Greater attention to complexity." Lancelot Law Whyte, 'Atomism, Structure and Form', in *Structure in Art and Science*, ed. Gyorgy Kepes, Braziller, New York, 1965

Complexity needs the time for reflection, the luxury of being able to think, totally against the momentum of the messages that swarm through the jungle of signs. Today, if and when people do get the time to think, all they want to do is "chill out", which might seem like resignation in the face of brutalism, and another symptom of a mass disenfranchisement currently under way – almost the mirror opposite of the socialist struggle that marked the first part of the 20th century. It is also a question of survival in the face of what can seem overwhelming odds.

"Since 1994 the number of people working in the media – including TV, radio, film and newspapers – has exploded from 118,000 to 154,000. In the same period, the number of jobs in advertising has gone from 69,000 to 80,000, and in market research from 152,000 to 188,000. For every U.K. fisherman, there are 37 market researchers." Office of National Statistics quoted by Anthony Browne, 'From the farmyard to the finance house', *The Observer*, 15 November 1988

More media has not been matched by more access – if anything, the broadcaster and journalist elites have become more entrenched in the last 10 years. Philosophies of media, Marxist theory and cultural studies programmes have failed to create media literacy in the manner that late Victorian culture was able to foster reading and writing. What has been achieved is a sophisticated and distancing cynicism amongst the producers of media, whose primary audience is its immediate competition, whilst knowing what it all means to your average mug punter – nothing. So much for "The people", whose lives were to be transformed in Blair's New Vision for Britain. The dissenting voice is first mocked then stifled, and in the absence of any collective spirit, the social outcome is that everybody becomes their own secret police force, looking out for number one.

Orwell's concept of 'doublespeak' has turned out to be conservative in its prophecy: in the *1984* scenario, leadership and its media are one and the same, whereas in every democratic/mediatised society in the late 1990s, the powerplay between media and government is subject to many of the same off/on perceptions as the attitude of individual opinion to marketing campaign – classic master slave relationship.

The current obsession with the delivery of its message (always singular, please note) by Britain's Labour government is a powerful indicator of the perceived media literacy of its people. Its strategists and spin doctors can never commit themselves to the idea that A) the country is either one of the most media-savvy in the world, producing as it does a plethora of pop stars, designers, fashion icons etc., or, B) the nation is populated by a bunch of morons, a few of whom get famous, but mostly they lie prostrate in front of the telly waiting for the football to come on. The principal emotion that comes from the communications of the Western world's leadership is one of trepidation. New Labour have fashioned the art of being both arrogant and fearful in the same breath, which strangely fits the zeitgeist (a key New Labour concept).

The principal emotion that comes from the communications of the Western world's leadership is one of trepidation. New Labour have fashioned the art of being both arrogant and fearful in the same breath, which strangely fits the zeitgeist (a key New Labour concept).

Recently, the chaotic relationship between the Government and the media was brought sharply into relief by a remark that Tony Blair made at the Labour Party Conference (in October 1998) when questioned about his plans for the much-forecasted coming recession (another key feature of the on/off shadowplay: worst-case scenarios, meltdowns and global catastrophes that exonerate the locally affected). In flagrant contradiction of everything that had gone before, he said... "It is better to be unpopular than to be wrong".

In its way, Blair's reply competes with the Margaret Thatcher claim that "There is no such thing as society", but it has passed universally without comment. This could be pure luck, or the triumph of spiel over analysis where anyone with the means of response throws their hands up in the air and retreats to a familiar byline. What we might observe is a period not of pre-millennial tension, but pre-millennial fatigue. So Tony Blair does connect with the taxi driver, but neither hears the other... the heart of the matter exists in the spinning silence of the anti-matter. A decade ago, the pop group Depeche Mode sang tellingly, "Everything Counts in Large Amounts". Very soon, the opposite will be true. Perhaps it always has been, and we are coming to the apogee of one classic hallucination.

3 "The infosphere – the sphere of information – is going to impose itself on the geosphere. We are going to be living in a reduced world. The capacity of interactivity is going to reduce the world, real space to nearly nothing. In the near future, people will have the feeling of being enclosed in a small, confined environment. In fact, there is already a speed pollution which reduces the world to nothing. Just as Foucault spoke of this feeling among the imprisoned, I believe that there will be for future generations a feeling of confinement in the world, of incarceration which will certainly be the limit of tolerability, by virtue of the speed of information. If I were to give a last image, interactivity is to real space what radioactivity is to the atmosphere."

'Is the author dead?' An interview with Paul Virilio by James Der Derian in *The Virilio Reader*, Blackwell 1998

The age of broadcasting is dead. The socialist dream that you might reach the masses and convince them of the validity of your argument has reached its last post with New Labour. Volatile like never before, and yet placid in the face of amazing changes on civil liberties, everyday life has become the secret affair that science fiction always said it would be.

In its present guise interactive media is no solution. It could have been, but deep in the hearts of the producers is a hybrid of *Look and Learn* and the first computer ping-pong game. Interactivity could, still might offer a window for publishing material that dissolves the authority of its construction and delivery, but this is likely to be low-key, "off message". Already, the majority of so-called interactive product is little more than a wonderfully elaborate multiple-choice question, where the once restricted diet becomes a supermarket display of chargeable options.

Last year, the BBC promoted its case as a public service by repeatedly broadcasting 'Perfect Day', a collage of celebrity voices each singing a line from the Lou Reed song, which won the corporation industry awards and a number one hit single. Taking advantage of this success, the BBC has since been advertising its new digital operation, BBC Choice. In one key scene, the actor Stephen Fry is seen sitting at a restaurant table with a TV monitor in front of him: "I'll even be able to interact with my television", he gleefully informs us, before the punchline "Can you pass the salt please darling?".

This is a classic example of the New being dressed up in the Emperor's Old Clothes — in this case, the labour-saving devices of the 1950s (Kenwood mixers, hoovers, washing machines). The couch potato connotation of BBC Choice presents us with a ridiculously slack image of how Interactive TV might develop, but well exposes the brake that media producers would like to apply to the idea of more and more varied voices entering their exclusive orbit. But nothing is obvious and never has been, and it is just as well that the communications media has become such a travesty, because it has made itself open to imminent collapse, just like the banking system. When broadcasting fragments into thousands of tiny lights, will we see the breakdown of the equation Coverage beats Quality?

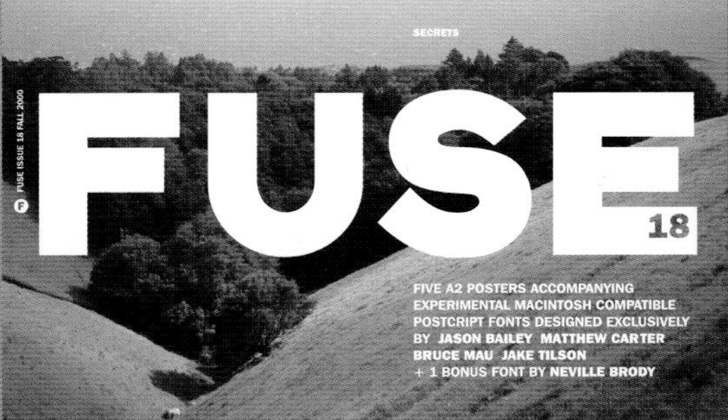

DANIEL BORCK & JON WOZENCROFT STICKER

DANIEL BORCK & JON WOZENCROFT EDITORIAL POSTER

FUSE 18: Neville Brody Bonus Font Lies

zabcdefghijklmnopqrstuvwxyz
ZABCDEFGHIJKLMNOPQRSTUVWXYZ
9012345678 9

LIES LIGHT

z abcdefghijklmnopqrstuvwxyz
Z ABCDEFGHIJ KLMNOPQRSTUV
VWXYZ0123456789

LIES BOLD

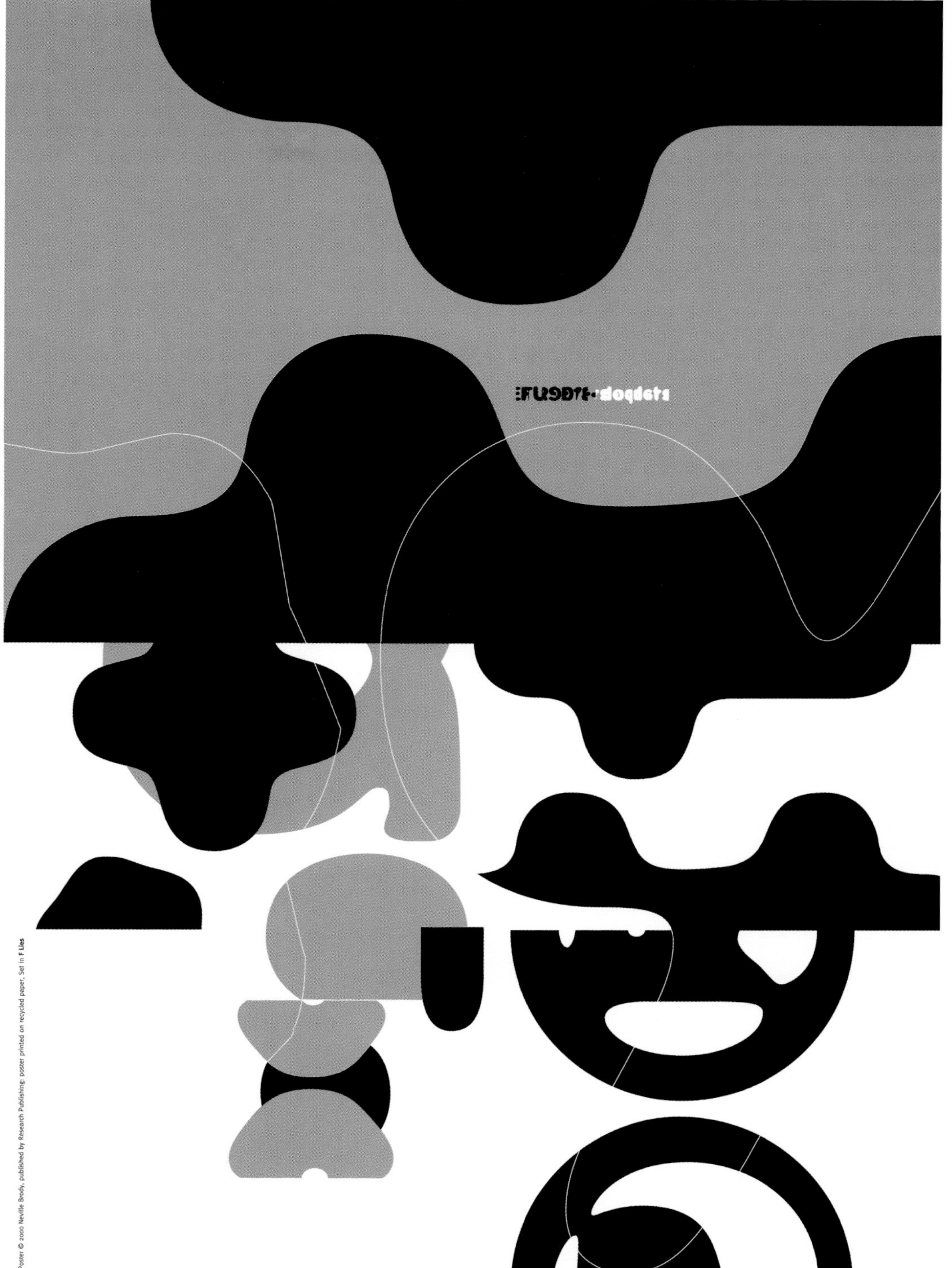
Poster © 2000 Neville Brody, published by Research Publishing; poster printed on recycled paper, Set in **F Lies**

FUSE 18: Jason Bailey Sclerosis Script

Multiple Sclerosis is a cruel disease that randomly attacks the central nervous system, eroding the control a sufferer has over their body. The symptoms of MS can range from slurred speech and numbness through to paralysis and even blindness. The severity and rate at which these symptoms manifest themselves is totally unpredictable. As yet there is no known cure for the illness.

My mother, Faith Bailey, had MS for nearly thirty years. She was diagnosed as having the condition before I was born, so the effects of MS have always been a part of my life. As a child I was aware that there was something wrong with her health, but the specifics and implications of the illness were rarely discussed. This was not because the subject was taboo or shrouded in secrecy, simply that my mother wanted to lead as 'normal' a life as possible. That was always her aim, right up to the time of her death in the summer of 1999.

One of the most frustrating aspects of MS is the way in which one's ability to communicate is impaired. I have tried to translate this frustration into the font *Sclerosis Script*. The letterforms that make up the font are digitised examples of my mother's handwriting, with certain characters having had their 'natural' kerning relationships with other characters greatly exaggerated. Thus, like the condition itself, the experience of using *Sclerosis Script* cannot be completely controlled.

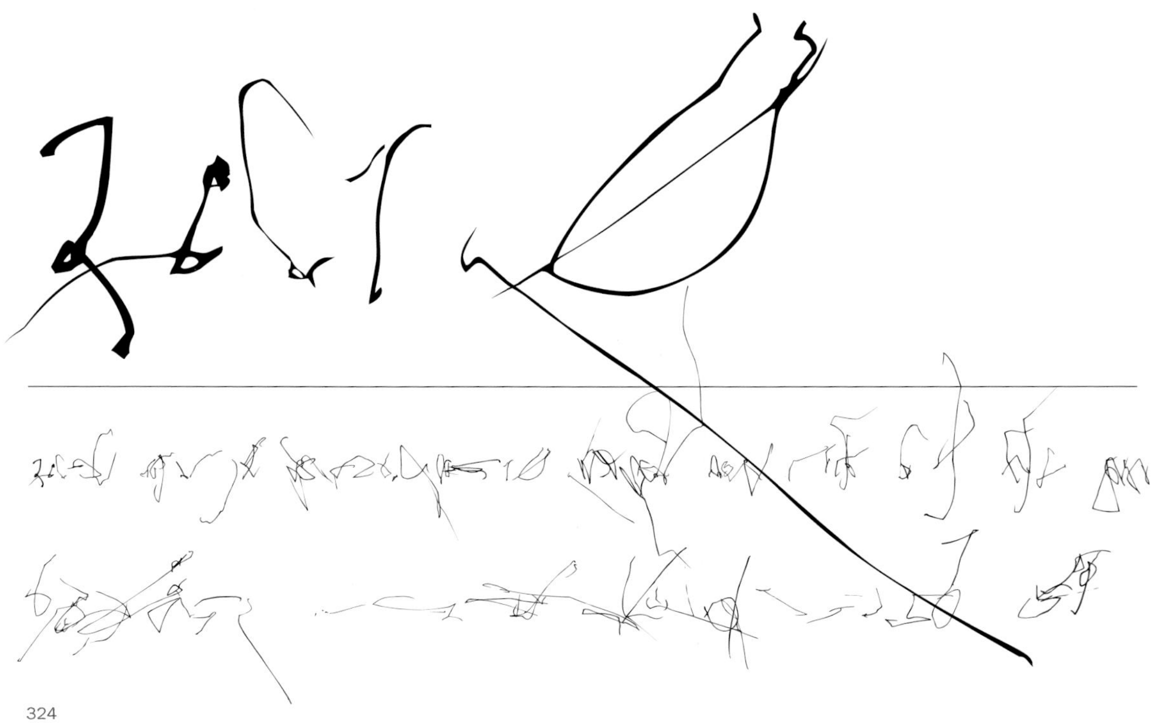

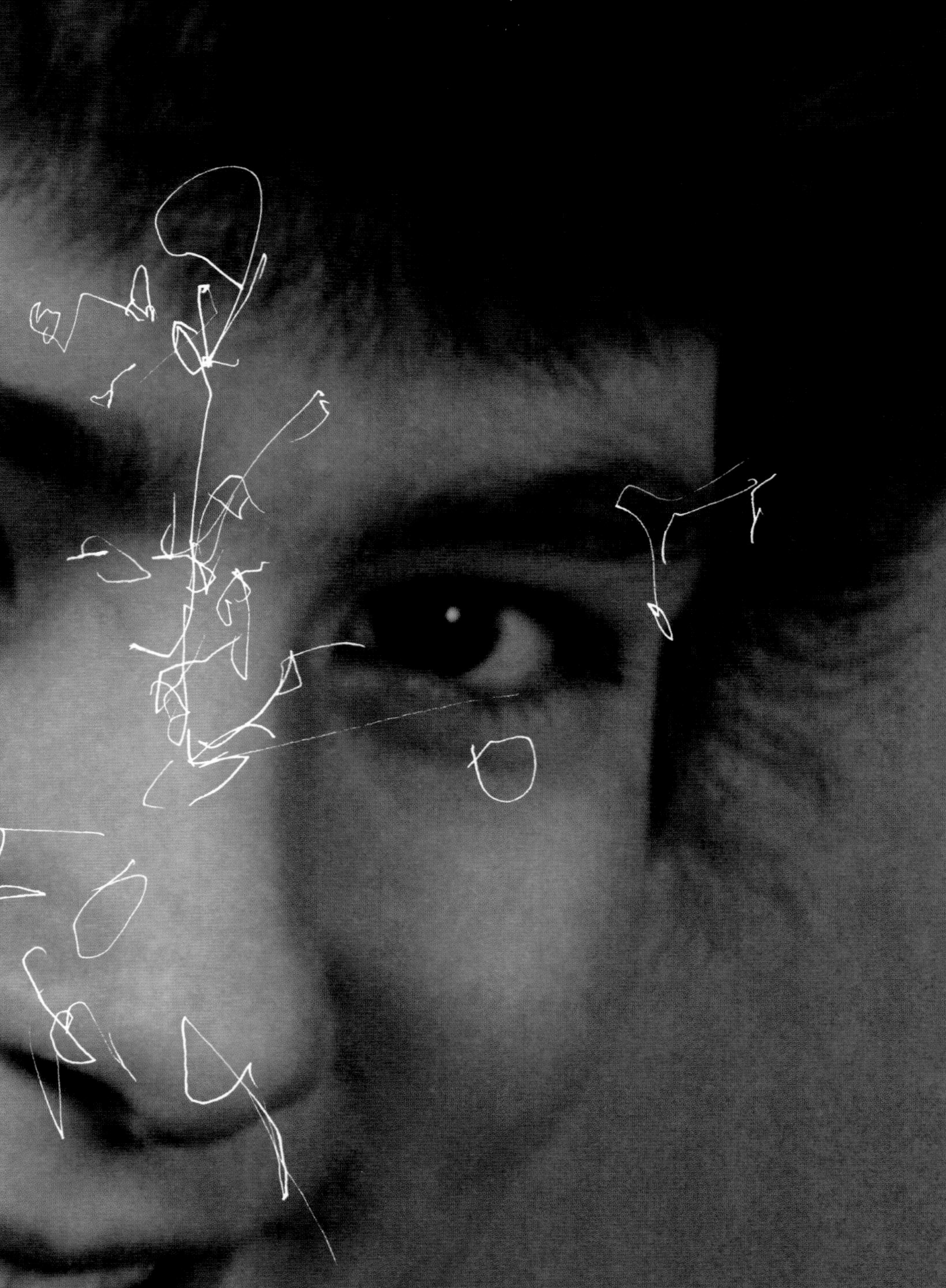

GARAMOND ROGERS

DEKLM

ARRIGHI
AVSTIN

FUSE 18: Matthew Carter DeFace

It is interesting to me that certain forms of lettering that are intended to perpetuate memory, such as inscriptions on public memorials, tombstones and cornerstones, become defaced in time to the point of illegibility. What was once accessible reverts to a state of concealment and secrecy. The defacement can be caused naturally (by weathering, erosion, subsidence) or deliberately (by demolition or vandalism). This typeface, named *DeFace*, contains a set of inscriptional capitals that are self-vandalising: each letter has graffiti associated with it that deface neighbouring letters. Depending on the text, the graffiti can vandalise both the underlying capitals and other graffiti to make a palimpsest of marks that are individually legible but obscure in combination. The urge to write on monuments, to add something personal to something public, or to subvert meaning, seems to be at least as old as Pompeii. The vandals responsible for the graffiti in *DeFace* have the names of eminent typographers, leaving evidence here of their love-hate of the classical capitals from which all Latin types ultimately derive. Is nothing sacred? Is anything secret?

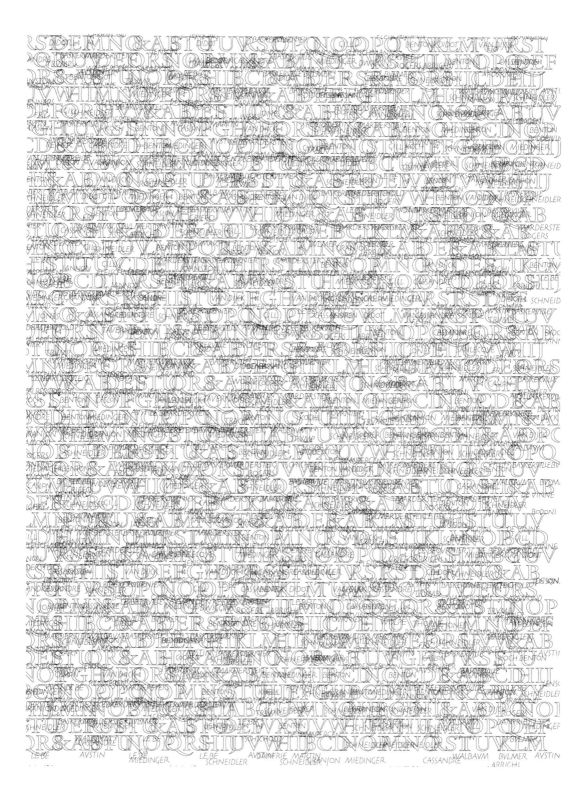

A font unaffected by the force of gravity and the weight of human history

CAN YOU IMAGINE

A font that sounds as good as it looks

CAN YOU IMAGINE

A font that responds to your touch

CAN YOU IMAGINE

FUSE 18: Bruce Mau Can We Imagine

When we look at the current state of design practice, we find most of the activity confined within a small zone, crackling at maximum volume on the surface of the page. It is the goal of our practice to get beneath the surface and furrow new courses of inquiry. In the field of typography we believe it's time for a new question. Or 100 of them. By asking instead of answering, we imagine new behaviours and tendencies for type. We discover new spaces for our practice to travel.

Can we envision 1. a font that asks more questions than it answers 2. a font that has projective memory, that reminds you to remember 3. a font with a limited life span 4. a font with an expiry date 5. a font that has gone bad 6. a font without temporal inflection, without the imprint of its time 7. an apolitical font, a font that doesn't care 8. a font unaffected by the force of gravity and the weight of human history 9. a font without family, without ancestry 10. a Marshall McLuhan font that stubbornly persists in bidding farewell to itself 11. a font that is something other than a recording 12. a font that is different every time you "play" it 13. a font that takes advantage of all that promised "processing power" 14. a font that does something other than sit on its ass in a digital museum 15. a font with the capacity to breed with other fonts 16. a recombinant font, every letterform the unruly child of a predictable but random process 17. a font that sounds as good as it looks 18. a font that writes its own script 19. a font that thickens the plot 20. a font that responds and reacts to the meaning it carries and conveys 21. a font that assumes intelligence on the part of its reader 22. a font that senses your level of agitation, fear or aggression 23. a font prone to sudden outbursts and tantrums 24. a font that exceeds the typographic genome 25. ___________ 26. a font whose parents are father time and the mother of invention 27. an ambient font, a font without qualities 28. a font that slows the pace of reading for the difficult passages (and skips along through the easy bits) 29. a font that writes between the lines 30. a font that refuses to utter imperatives or commands 31. a karaoke font, a lip-synching font, a font without a voice of its own 32. a font that listens while it speaks 33. a font that toggles effortlessly between languages 34. a font that simultaneously translates 35. a font for speaking in tongues 36. a metropolitan font for uptown, the ghetto and suburbia alike 37. a font that sings the plaintive songs of lonely whales 38. a font that grows 39. a font that learns 40. an evolutionary font 41. an entropic font 42. a "live" font 43. a promiscuous font, a font-fucking-font 44. a monogamous font, forever faithful and unerring 45. a font that emerges, unfolds, performs, evolves, and passes away 46. the font of youth 47. twin fonts, identical but distinct 48. a generative font that renders itself according to behavioural tendencies 49. a font with the metabolism of a fly 50. a font with a demographic algorithm that projects itself onto you, the average reader 51. a font that recognizes you 52. an unfinished font 53. a font that is not an etymological fallacy, that says what it means and means what it says 54. an ergonomic font that reduces discomfort and fatigue 55. a slang font 56. a pidgin font 57. a pheromonic font 58. a phatic font 59. a game font that takes you to the next level 60. an amnesiac font, a font that forgets to write itself 61. a font of doubt, uncertainty and indeterminacy, endlessly postponing clarity 62. a local font, a font to which you have to travel 63. a font for airports, a ruthless average of distinctive character 64. a font with ambitions, dreams, and expectations of its own 65. a font with cuts, [illegible] zooms, and close-ups 66. a font trapped in the present tense, erasing as it writes itself 67. a font changing states — melting, crystallizing, [illegible] sublimating 68. a colloid font, a font between states 69. a font immaculately conceived 70. a font with a Brooklyn accent 71. a font that only [illegible] 72. a seasonal font, a font for this spring 73. a model-year font 74. a font that becomes you, a font with boundless empathy for your desires 75. a font that constantly reinvents and renews itself, shedding its crusty old skin with every new thought-76. a font that witnesses, testifies, mourns, and [illegible] memory across itself 77. a font that perforates the surface of things 78. a font that responds to your touch 79. a porous, absorbent font 80. a font that is atmospherically sensitive, registering environmental shifts 81. a font that is yours and yours alone, that grows and ages with you, and with your passing, also dies 82. a font that sees itself reflected in the searching eyes of the reader 83. a font that looks up to you 84. a font that "stuffs" meaning onto the printed page 85. a dream font 86. a deadpan font 87. a slow-motion font 88. a dirt[illegible] 89. a big-budget, full-colour, star-studded, wide-screen, Oscar-winning, surround-sound, larger-than-life-sized font 90. a scathingly funny, tenderly moving, blissfully surreal, blazingly original, hugely entertaining font 91. an action-packed, eye-popping, over-the-top font 92. a glossy font 93. a "lite" font 94. a facelift-gone-wrong font 95. a fluid font that oozes, bleeds and leaks and weeps 96. a viral font 97. an unstable font, in need of constant intervention to maintain appearances [illegible] torture font, that interminably drip drip drips its meaning onto your forehead 99. a tragic American font of youthful promise [illegible] to an abrupt and violent end 100. a font whose uniqueness lies in its program, not merely in its image?

[illegible]

35/ 37/ 38/ 40/ 41/ 43/ 52/ 53/ 58/ 61/ 63/ 67/ 70/
72/ 77/ 80/ 81/ 82/ 90/ 93/ 98/ 10/ 14/ 16/ 20/ 25/
34/ 36/ 39/ 42/ 44/ 48/ 51/ 53/ 55/ 62/ 69/ 66/ 71/
74/ 75/ 83/ 84/ 89/ 92/ 95/ 99/ 14/ 17/ 18/ 21/ 26/

FUSE 18: Jake Tilson httpwc MEN ONLY

Three elements combine to produce *httpwc*: poster, font and website. The font acts as a translator between the poster and website. Each typed character reveals a two-digit code that when added to the website address "www.thecooker.com/fuse18/" reveals a new screen image. There are fifty-two images to find. The hidden nature of cities appears in the smallest evidence.

93/ 98/

httpwc

jake tilson
www.thecooker.com/fuse18/

FUSE

FUSE+

About this section

The second half of the book features a small selection of the different activities that the FUSE project promoted over its 20+ year history.

The conferences reflect the international and critical debate that FUSE was part of; the competitions demonstrate the importance of FUSE to contemporary and emerging graphic designers throughout this period.

Also listed in the last section of the book are reproductions of contributors' biographies submitted at the time of each edition's publication. Its purpose is two-fold. It provides an index and a timeline for the graphic designers whose fonts have defined FUSE as a seminal typographic record of its time.

FUSE 1 INVENTION
Neville Brody Issue Poster
Phil Baines Can You...?
Neville Brody State
Malcolm Garrett Stealth
Ian Swift Maze 91

FUSE 2 RUNES
Neville Brody Issue Poster
Max Kisman Linear Konstrukt
Gerard Unger D'coder
Erik Van Blokland Niwida
Just van Rossum Flixel

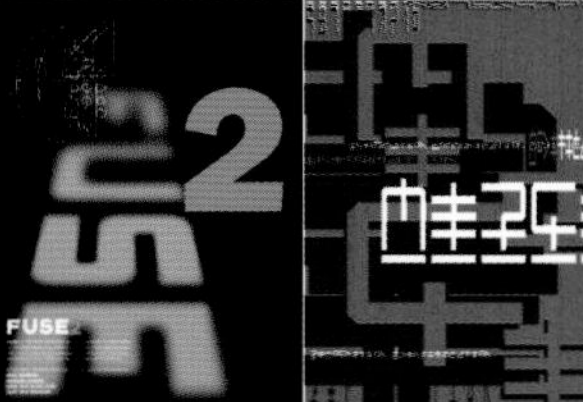

FUSE 3 (DIS)INFORMATION
Neville Brody Issue Poster
Barbara Butterweck DearJohn
Erik Spiekermann Grid
Martin Wenzel InTegel
Cornel Windlin Moonbase Alpha

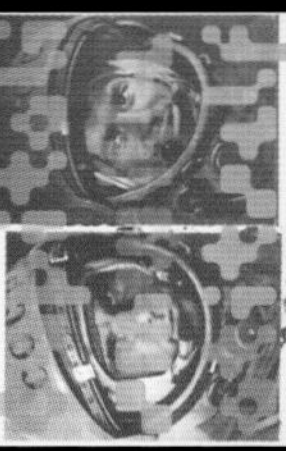

FUSE 4 EXUBERANCE
Neville Brody Issue Poster
David Berlow Yurnacular
Barry Deck Caustic Biomorph
Jeffrey Keedy LushUS
Rick Valicenti Uck N Pretty

FUSE 5 VIRTUAL
Neville Brody Bonus Font Virtual
Peter Saville FloMotion
Lo Breier & Florian Fossel Spherize
Paul Elliman Alphabet
Pierre di Sciullo Scratched Out

RIEN DE
DURABLE DANS
CE MONDE

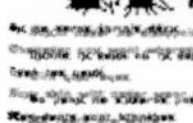

FUSE 6 CODES
Neville Brody Bonus Font Code Bold
Ian Anderson Dr No-B
Paul Sych Box
Martin Wenzel Schirft
Rick Vermeulen Morsig

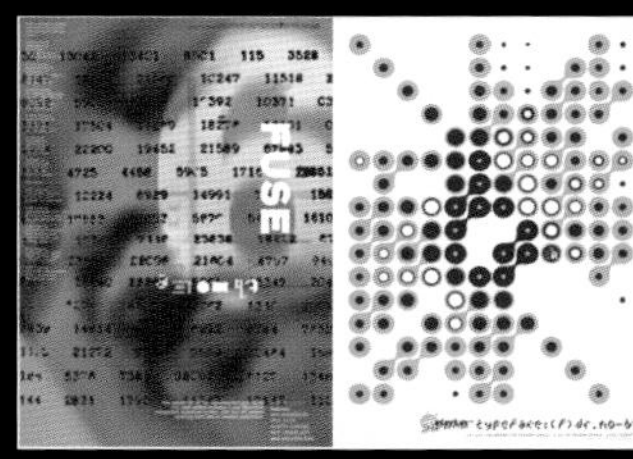

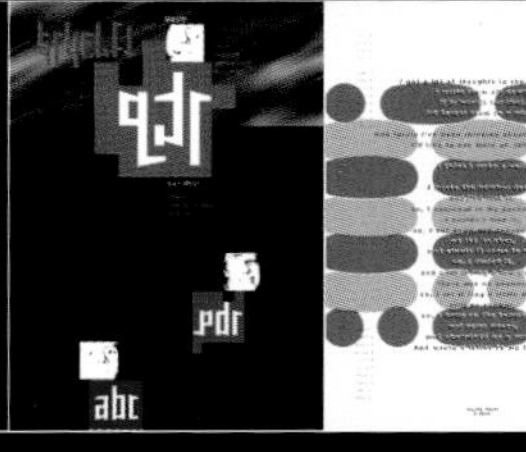

FUSE 7 CRASH
Neville Brody Bonus Font Crash
Phil Bicker Illiterate
David Carson Fingers
Tobias Frere-Jones Reactor
Cornel Windlin Mogidischu

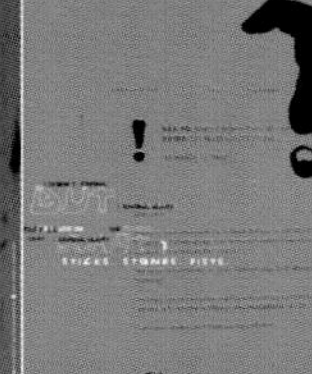

FUSE 8 RELIGION
Neville Brody Bonus Font Religion
Phil Baines Ushaw
Dave Crow Creation 6
M&Co What The Hell
Chu Uroz X-Pain

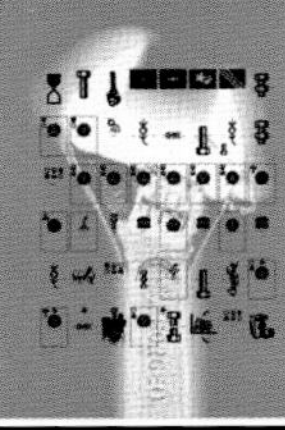
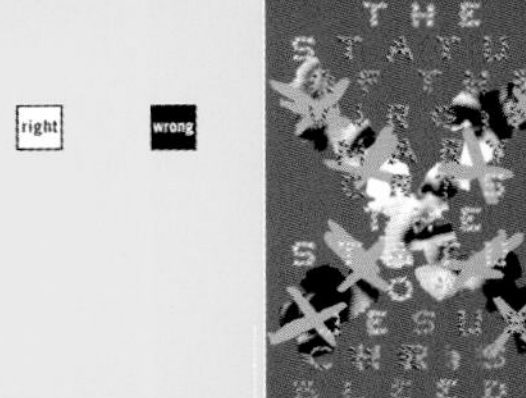

FUSE 9 AUTO
Neville Brody Bonus Font Autosuggestion
Vaughan Oliver Currency
Margaret Calvert A26
Russell Mills Metal
Mario Beernaert TV27HN

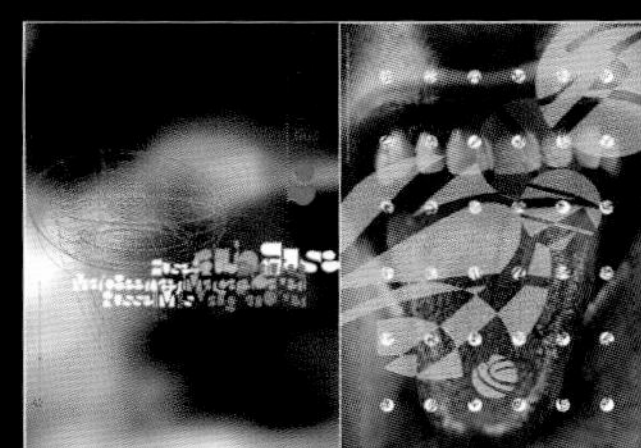

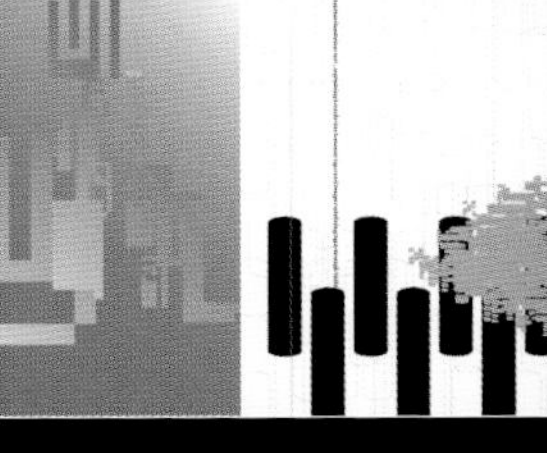

FUSE 10 FREEFORM
Neville Brody Freeform
Jon Wozencroft Restart
John Critchley Mutoid
Tobias Frere-Jones Fibonacci
Sylke Janetzky Atomic Circle
Cornel Windlin Robotnik

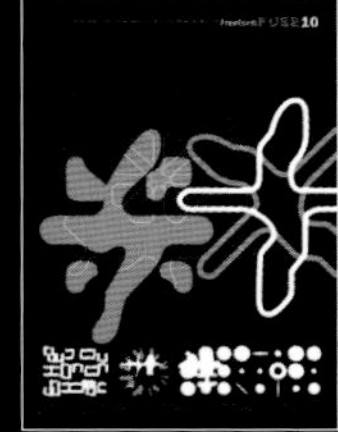

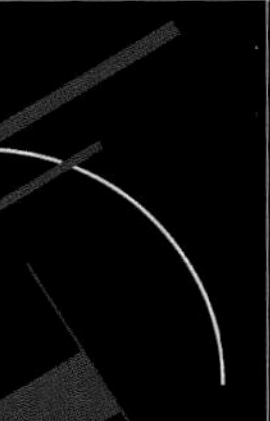
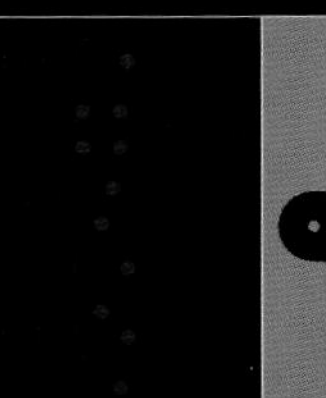
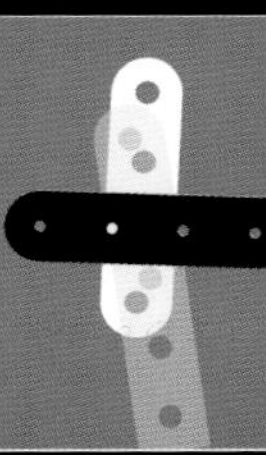

FUSE 11 PORNOGRAPHY
Neville Brody Bonus Font Peep
Lucas de Groot Move Me MM
Fuel Tape Type
LettError WhatYouSee/WhatYouGet
Ian Wright Hand Job

FUSE 12 PROPAGANDA
Neville Brody Bonus Font Populist
Matthew Butterick Agitprop
Malcolm Garrett Instrument
Simon Staines Trojan
'WD + RU' Pussy Galore

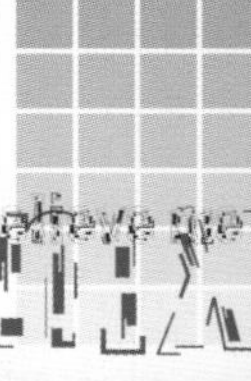

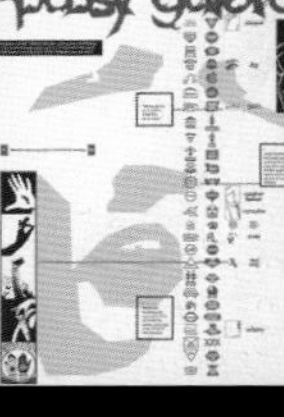

FUSE SUPERSTITION
Neville Brody Bonus Font Ritual
Scott Clum Burnfont
Katsuhiko Hibino Onmi
Pablo Rovalo Flores Santo Domingo
Tomato Newcracks 13

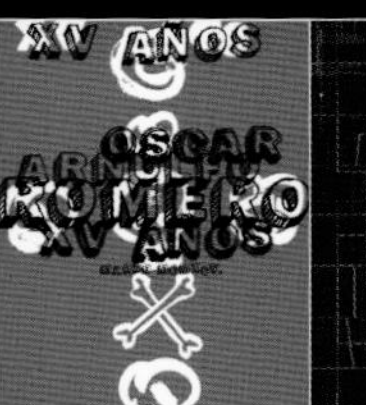

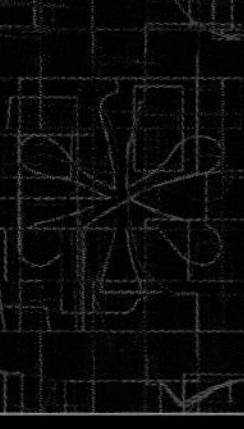

FUSE 14 CYBER
Neville Brody Bonus Font Cyber
'Moniteurs' MMMteurs-Cyber/MMMteurs-Real
Rick Vermeulen Big Eyed Beans
Brett Wickens Crux95
Xplicit FFM Synaesthesis

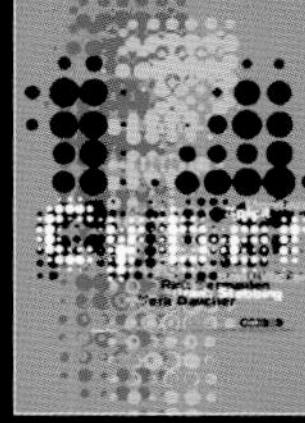

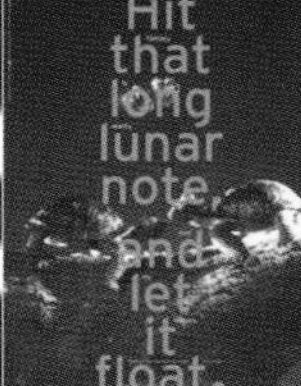

Hit
that
long
lunar
note,
and
let
it
float.

FUSE 15 CITIES
Neville Brody Bonus Font City
Paul Elliman Bits
Tobias Frere-Jones Microphone
Peter Grundy DIY
Frank Heine Determination

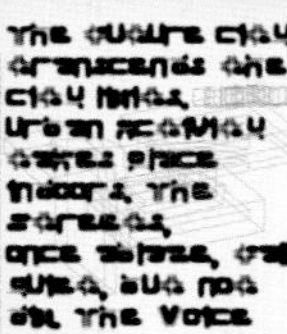

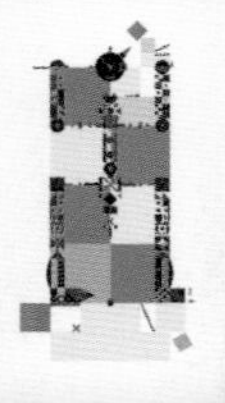

FUSE 16 GENETICS
Neville Brody Bonus Font Genetics Second Generation
Alex Tylevich Cico Paco
David Crow Mega Family 2
Naomi Enami Kilin
Tom Hingston & Jon Wozencroft Condition

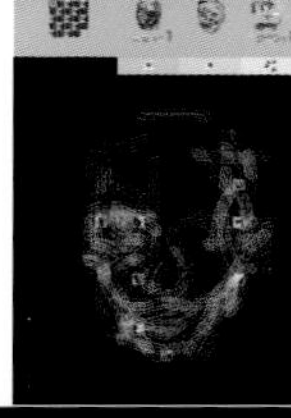
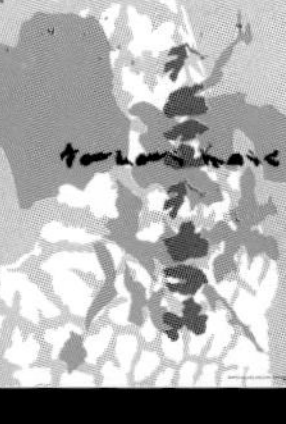

FUSE 17 ECHO

Neville Brody Bonus Font Echo
Florian Heiß Surveillance
Function Where the Dog is Buried
Pierre di Sciullo Spell Me
Anna-Lisa Schönecker White No Sugar

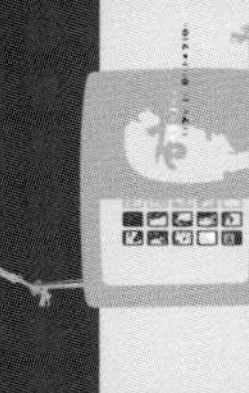

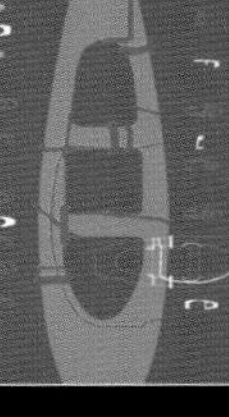

FUSE 18 SECRETS
Neville Brody Bonus Font Lies
Jason Bailey Sclerosis Script
Matthew Carter DeFace
Bruce Mau Can We Imagine
Jake Tilson httpwc Men Only

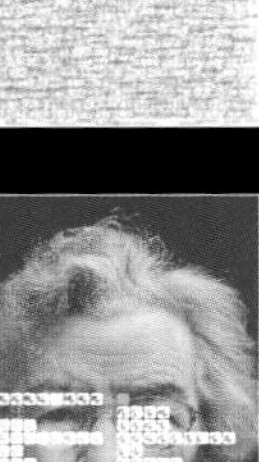
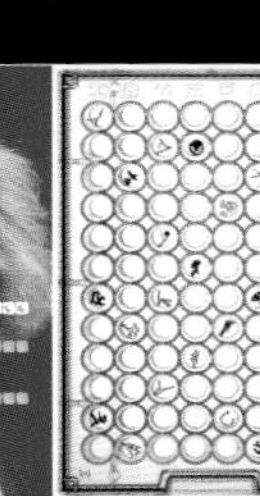

FUSE 19 REVOLUTION
Neville Brody Bonus Font Neural
eBoy Camou
Bob Wilkinson & Lucienne Roberts Equality/Individuality/Community
Stefan Sagmeister Bazillus
Erik van Blokland Data Mine

FUSE 20 ANTIMATTER
Neville Brody Bonus Fonts Antisans
Tom Balchin Cogdis
Barnbrook Rattera
Neville Brody Antimatter
RAD HOC Landwriting

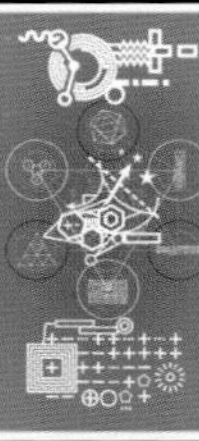

FUSE Competition: Security Research Studios 2005

Brief for FUSE Competition by Jon Wozencroft

In 2005, Research Studios ran a competition via its website with the idea of extending FUSE through open submission. The overwhelming response attested to the latent creativity and need for experimental outlet in our current communications space.

The work is shown here in print for the first time.

Freedoms fought for during the liberation struggles of the 20th century are being replaced by new struggles, the fight for Independence giving way to a state of perpetual instability and First World indifference to the question of survival.

New technologies celebrate the nomadic lifestyles that laptop computers, mobile phones and net access offer. For the majority, however, the reality is for progressive restrictions to be placed upon freedom of movement, in the regions of the world that easyJet does not reach.

Home: the fear of crime, congestion charges, loyalty cards, mirror this growing pattern of restriction. The U.K. is the proud owner of more CCTV cameras per metre than any country in the world. The paranoia enables further research into biometric systems and 3D mapping /// don't move, we've got you covered. A thin line separates an asylum seeker from the suspected terrorist.

Liberation these days is viewed through the lens of protection, no life worth living without the presence of insurance. If you could measure insecurity in the same way you fix an interest rate, we'd probably be paying 300% – how much of it is manufactured by the media and how much of it is down to the new nature of our modified perceptions we can argue about. How often is it that you see your thoughts published?

Sensing the need to nurture initiatives that speak about the current state of communications in a context which is expansive... the FUSE project started in 1990 to investigate the switch from analogue working methods to digital systems, and chose typography as a means of expressing this transitional time. Chaos and new order made one question reading habits... visual recognition, and time-based notions in a medium previously "set in stone".

The themes explored thus far include runic alphabets, transport systems for the new typography, genetic visual form. This latest FUSE project presents an opportunity for a new generation of designers to consider the implications of new technologies on language, and their relation to social and psychological conditions.

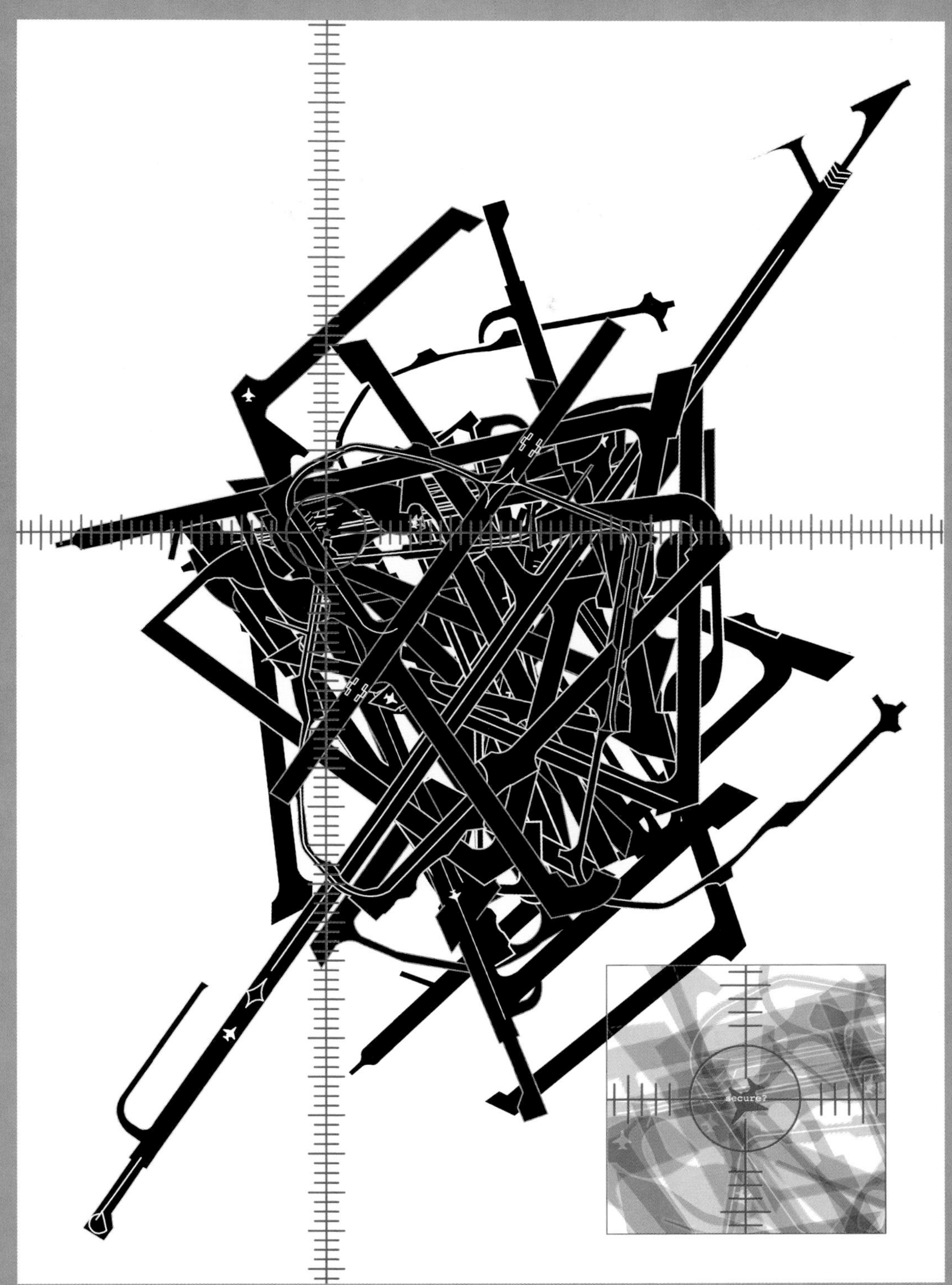
secure?

FUSE Competition: Winner Adam Graveley Landing Strip (PREVIOUS PAGE)

The government/state keeps us secure and protects us from 'the enemy'... or do they? I took my inspiration for the typeface from a satellite image of an airfield taken by a commercial satellite. The most 'secure' of all commercial travel areas is able to be photographed and infiltrated, open to a number of unknown sources. The concept was to create an uneasy, slightly awkward display type out of something that we perceive to be secure. Ironic.

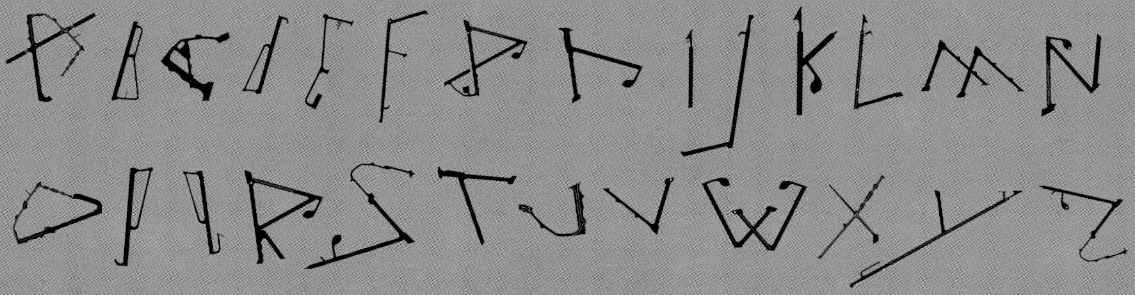

FUSE Competition: Winner Lee Hasler Env (FACING PAGE)

Envelope patterns and the information they try to conceal have an interesting place in our lives. Although still in use today within most envelopes, this basic form of security has become increasingly ineffectual. Ironically all that's ever been necessary to gain access to our secrets, is a finger or steam. Where once we were concerned with hiding our pin numbers and medical history, we now find ourselves in a society where someone can hide themselves in our identity. Is it possible that we still hold onto these patterns as a reminder of simpler more trusting times?

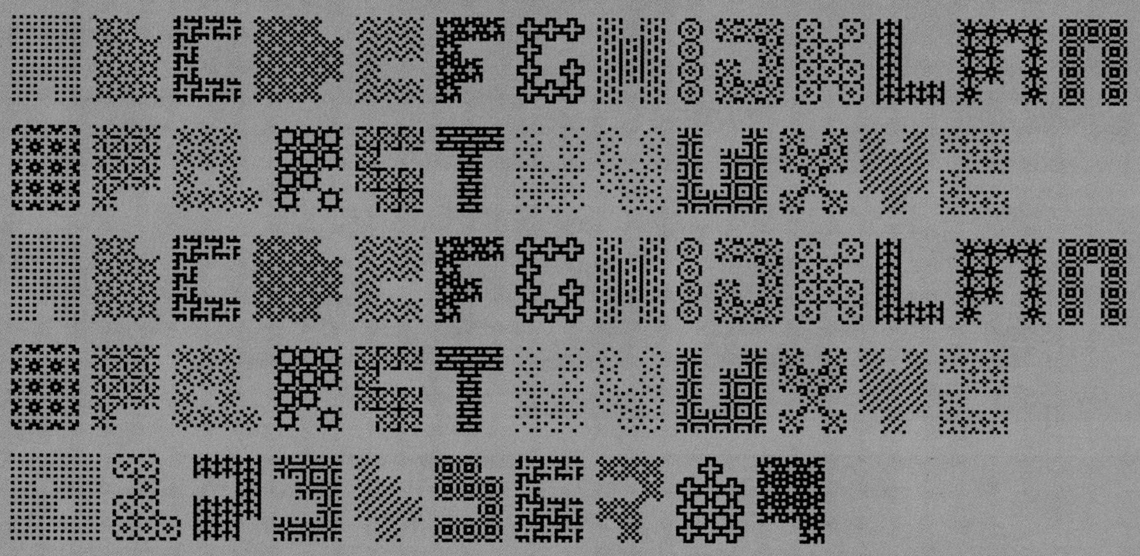

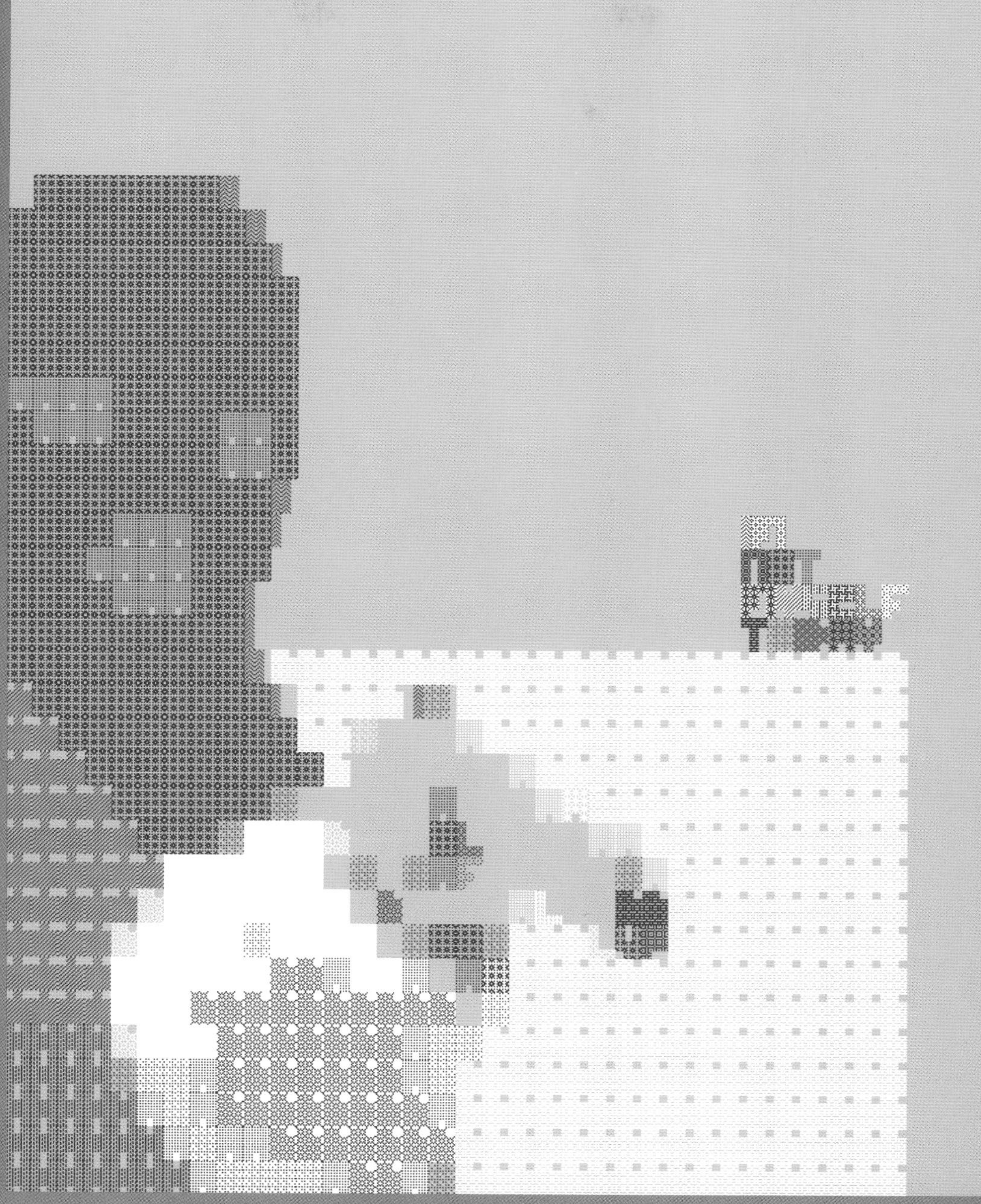

security ©2005 coilgraphics / www.coilgraphics.com

FUSE Competition: Winner
Coil Graphics SystemG (FACING PAGE)

The font family (*SystemG*) is made by imaging a network. It also considers the old-age characteristics of a neon bulb. It works best three-dimensionally, displaying a type of modern retro.

SYSTEMG 1

SYSTEMG 2

SYSTEMG 3

FUSE Competition: Winner
François Moissette The Birth of a Nation (NEXT PAGE)

To ensure the place of your incipient nation, use the deterrent power of a flag, federator emblem of the people. *The Birth of a Nation** enables you to create your own flag starting from completely flexible elements resulting in contemporary flags. A great number of combinations are possible. The *Background* will enable you to mark the to mark the founding and guiding lines of your fatherland, whereas *Star Wars* allows you to show with character your force and your ambitions. You can thus produce a sufficiently effective standard to galvanise your country, and state your power in the face of all your enemies. *Merci à Xavier Dupré pour son aide technique...*

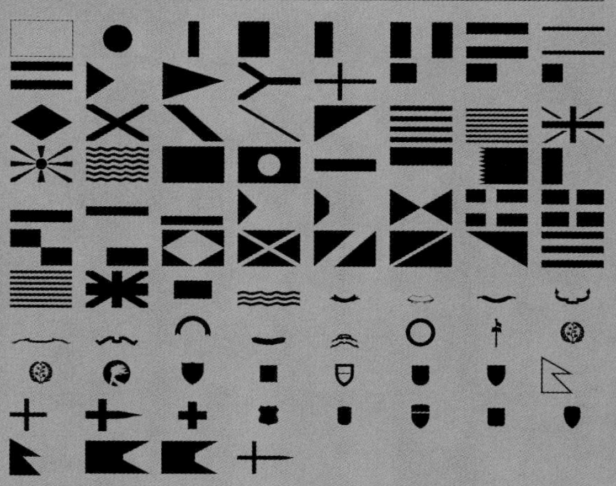

THE BIRTH OF A NATION BACKGROUND

THE BIRTH OF A NATION STAR WARS

FUSE

wanted reg: abcdefghijklmnopqrstuvwxyz[äöüßaæœç]ABCDEFGHIJKLMNOPQRSTUVWXYZ1234567890(.,;:?!$&-*)(ÄÖÜÅÆŒÇ)

Eye

Nose

Mouth

Head

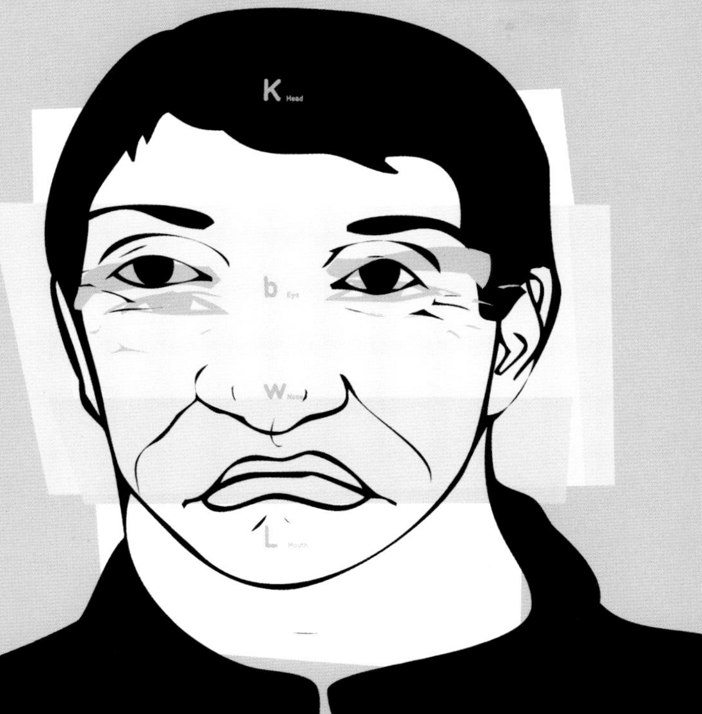

Nr. 073/341

FUSE Competition: Bonus Volcano Type Mr. J. Smith (PREVIOUS PAGE)

When there's no picture of a "most wanted" or "Missing Persons", photofit pictures are used. Once drawn by hand, they are now more and more substituted by photomontage.

The personality is created with different modules like head, eyes, nose and mouth. The vague memory of a witness leads to the image of a "concrete" person. Sometimes different combinations of possible looks are attributed to the same person. This new virtual image finds itself soon in thousands of archives and databases. Anyone can easily have access to those images by the Internet. To increase security and help track criminals the government asks its citizens to help search for unknown deaths (Mr. J. Smith), or lost and kidnapped people.

Mr. J. Smith is a font-family consisting of 4 portrait-fonts and one letter-font. The portrait-font *Mr. J. Smith* is a portrait-construction-kit. By layering the fonts *"Head"*, *"Eye"*, *"Nose"*, *"Mouth"* one over the other, you can design over 7 million different faces. The font *"Wanted"* gives you the possibility to join names and registration numbers to the unknown or most wanted persons.

What is nice about this font is the "surprise moment". Just write a word, e.g. "security", and you'll get a nice shot of 8 different characters!

FUSE Competition: Commended
A-Bombe Nøgleord

The initial concept for *Nøgleord* came from the way that governments 'flag' certain library books to obtain 'intelligence' on potential murderers, terrorists, anti-government factions, etc. in order to protect their citizens. From the way in which the information is collected, barcodes, the structure of the letterforms took their basic shape. By creating a font using a grid of blocks and then overlaying a barcode horizontally the characters developed into forms that resembled the negative spaces of cut keys. This observation led to developing the font into an illustrative form with the emphasis placed on a stylised key structure. The idea that we place so much faith/security in a simple 'fashioned' piece of metal is frightening, yet all of us do it on a daily basis. We give no thought to the fact that this simple 'device' is the 'thing' that is responsible for protecting our homes and our belongings. *Nøgleord* is a Danish word that when directly translated into English means *keyword*. This felt appropriate when applied to the finished font because of the playfulness of the meaning due to the font's structure being based on cutting elements away from another shape and then its ability to create words.

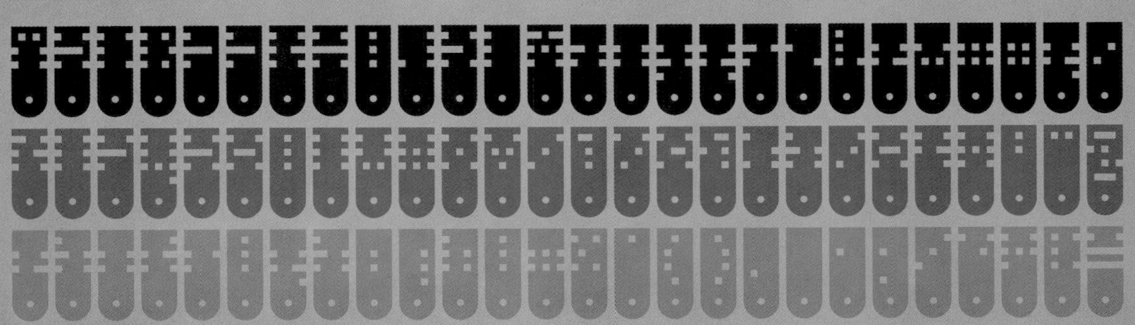

FUSE Competition: Commended
Keith Bates Insecurity

This font is *demi-dingbat*, part readable, part pictorial. Its appearance derives partly from children's spelling books or alphabet cards, and partly from its ancestors, the *Mailart Typeface* and *Mailart Graphics* font of 2004.

It has been compiled in a Pop Art fashion using images trawled from Internet searches, entering various expressions relating to 'Security'. The aim was to reflect the theme intuitively and eclectically, without concern for restrictions of copyright or weighty documentation.

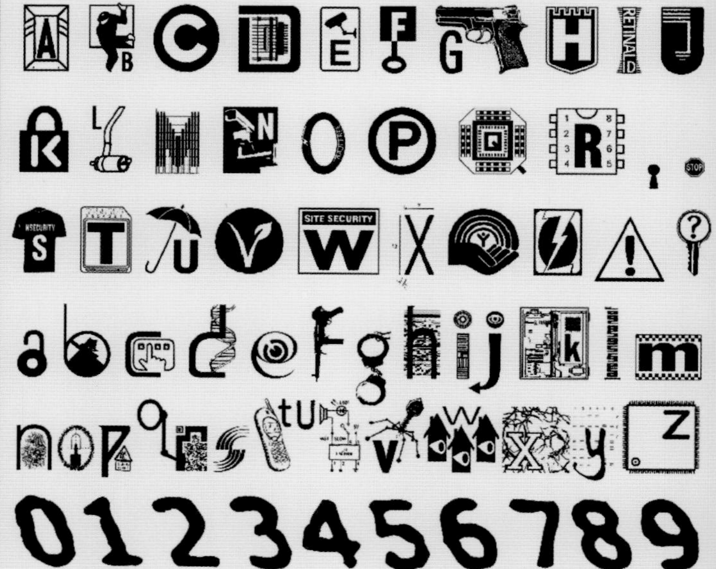

Surveillance cameras may be in use. Plain clothes and uniformed police patrol this font.

FUSE Competition: Commended
Jose Chamorro Code Secure

Code Secure is a vision of men involved in their own social cells, and the insurrection/liberation intentions that he could dream.

The font works as a background -caps- and a first layer where something is contained. The numbers are a box, a safe zone. The text works by adding a bottom layer of caps and lower-case text, forming zones of cells into individual groups.

Code Secure 2 is geometrical, *Code Secure* is more irregular.

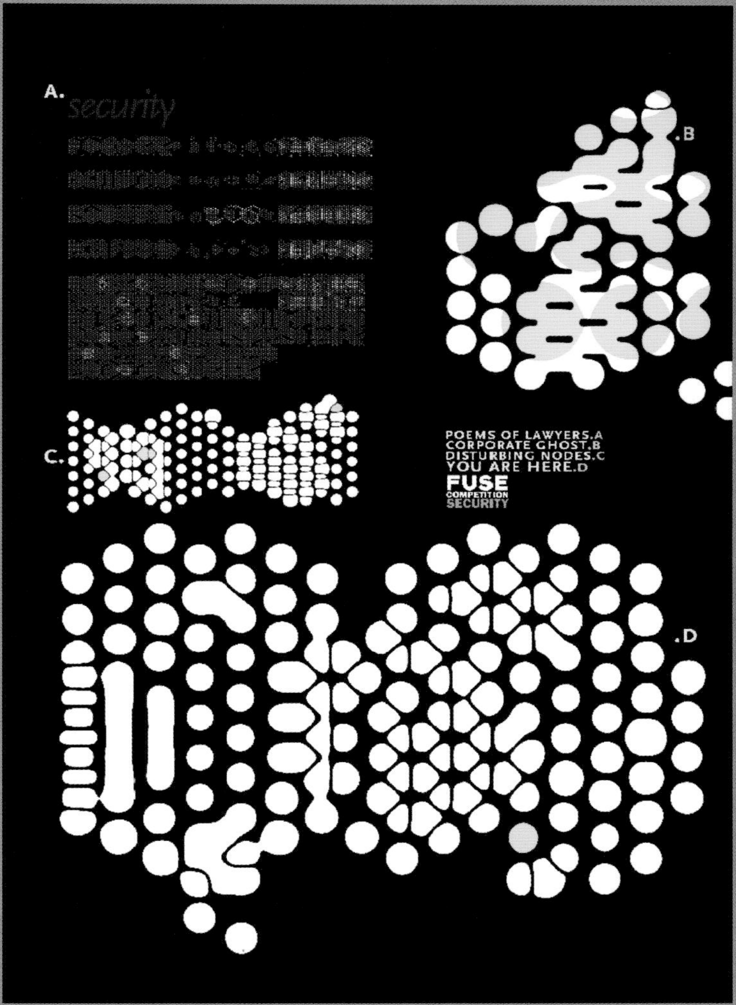

A. security

.B

C.

POEMS OF LAWYERS.A
CORPORATE GHOST.B
DISTURBING NODES.C
YOU ARE HERE.D
FUSE
COMPETITION
SECURITY

.D

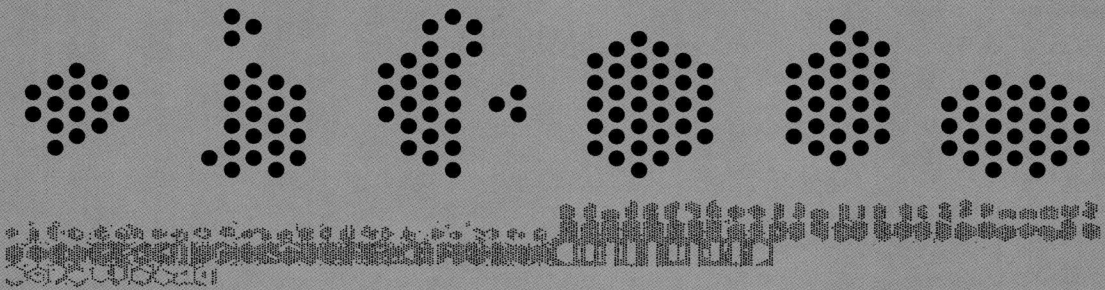

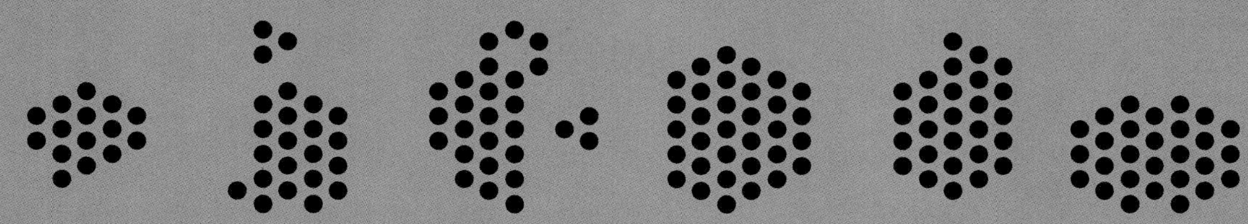

FUSE Competition: Commended
Rory McCartney Don't Listen

The idea for this font came out of thinking about communication and how it is affected by fears about security. Words and type are used to communicate messages to an audience or readership, but when fear of the 'other' mounts, it is necessary to communicate secretly, limiting the audience, or readership, by shutting out the 'other'. The 'other' stands for the real or supposed cause of fear. The medium therefore is changed into codes. Scrambled or altered messages, encryption and secret languages become the mode of graphic communication in times of security alerts and silent wars. The font has been created by recording the audible (analogue) alphabet from Morse Code signals, and saving them as .RAW sound files. These files were then imported directly into Photoshop. This translated the information from the audio files into images. As a result, this has changed the once analogue Morse Code into a visual, scrambled digital format, and made an encrypted code.

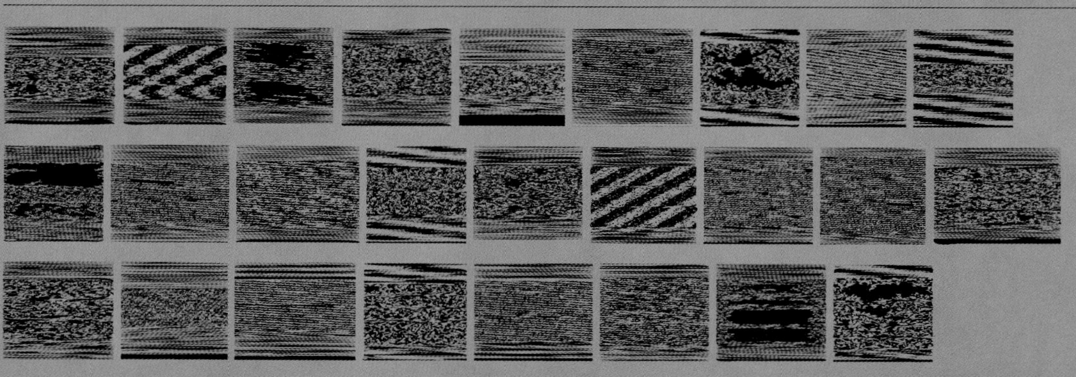

FUSE Competition: Commended
Nikpalj Polondak Monitoring

The primary goal was to design a font, but for now, the result is a sign system. Motivation has derived from three sources. One was the subject of restraining access to information, such as passwords and security levels. Other motivations were safety sign systems, in accordance with my usual designer research interests – mass systems for open spaces – for example, IALA and IMO signalling and orientation signs at sea. In the end I used a third source: monitoring. Issues that are also appealing are pictogram systems, geographical and nautical chart signs. Inside my own sign system there are satellite monitoring and air surveillance signs, in the form of a doubled rounded element that is drawn into the sign structure, made up of symbols that suggest direction note or movement curve as linear entry, arrows, dots, arrays of lines, warning signs.

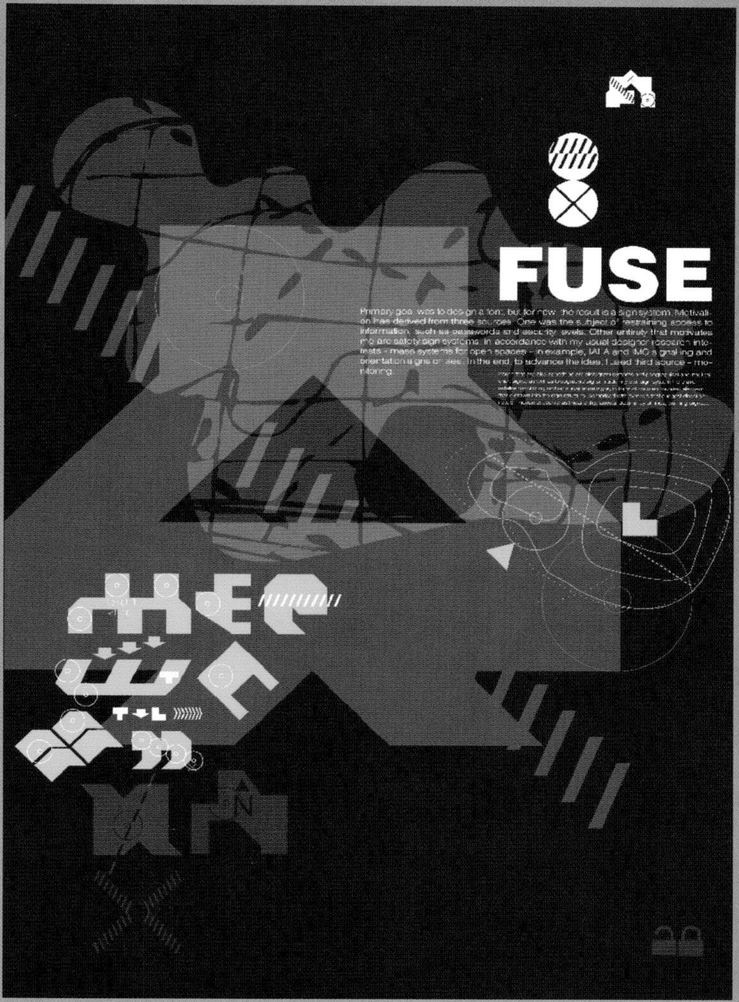

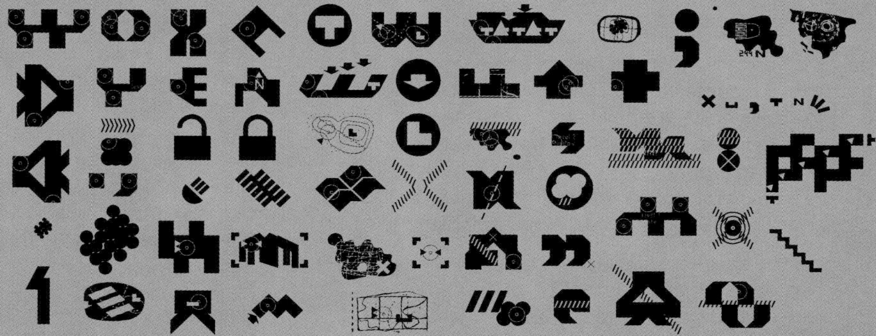

FUSE Conferences/Events **You talking to me? (Memory of Stagefright)** Jon Wozencroft

FUSE had its own international distribution network through the various FontShops; one way to promote the project was to take it on the road. The 1990s saw a growth industry in design conferences, therefore the challenge for us was to present something different, something brave and true to the context of the revolution that was taking place in terms of design's profile and designers' working practices.

We were idealistic and we believed that the design industry was undergoing a sea change after the hype of the 1980s. Coming from an independent mode of operation, the gradual emergence of more discreet studio set-ups with a Mac, a scanner and a laserwriter, instead of the more corporate context of Wolff Olins/ Michael Peters/Fitch, gave us the idea that a non-industry based conference would be a strong addition to the existing discourse.

The first FUSE conference was set up largely through the connection with the Royal College of Art. Their main lecture theatre was not big enough, so an exhibition of FUSE 1-10, a student competition, and a 'FUSELAB' was set up in the college's Gulbenkian Galleries, while the lectures for **FUSE94** were held in the auditorium at Imperial College, across the road.

The introduction to this book admits to a certain naïvety; here are the most Technicolor examples of that. When it comes to the FUSE conferences we were in at the deep end – a small team, doing the work of 20, underestimating the scale of the operations we were about to embark upon. To work out what to charge financially, how to deal with the logistics of 750 delegates for FUSE94, we proceeded with high hopes.

Many of the speakers at the first conference had never spoken in public before. Criticisms came that certain presentations were "unprofessional". Of course they were. That was one of the operating conditions, and we had to quickly learn from the situation. Failure was part of the process.

Just before the conference in November 1994, Michael Rock had published his overview of FUSE in *Eye* magazine, who were one of our "media supporters". It is solid with base-level questions about typography and its usage but we felt that it was missing the point, or in any case a spirit of generosity. Rock's analysis was a reminder that *Eye*'s emphasis was on design history and criticism before anyone was in the clear, free to go forward. The article used "old wives'/craft-based" proverbs to illustrate the fonts, which was a fine idea in terms of postmodern irony – we felt it was belittling something we had been quite dedicated to. This issue of *Eye* was unexpectedly given away free on a subscription drive at the top of the stairs to the lecture theatre at Imperial College, as the conference was being set up, and we wondered, "these are our friends?". This version was the entry point for many, who wanted to know more.

The over-abiding mood of any conference is nervous energy, ego and frustration, and shards of wisdom if you are attentive long enough to hear them. There were moments at FUSE94 where the auditorium looked up in horror as inexperienced presenters struggled to find their stride. In spite of everything, great things were achieved and the feedback seemed alive to it. FUSE94 formed the seed-bed of the TYPO conferences run by Jürgen Siebert that continue to this day. A few weeks later a review in *Eye* magazine by William Owen was a body-blow, overly aggressive about the conference's shortcomings and a personal attack in its detail. It was a shock. We wondered if it was worth continuing. Don't believe the hype when they say reviews mean nothing. Curiously this review is not to be found online. Be thankful for small mercies!

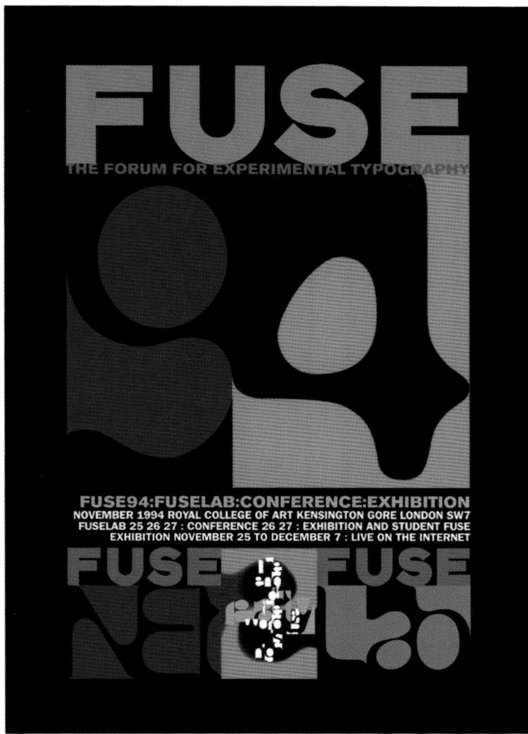

FUSE94 SPEAKERS DAVID BERLOW, PHIL BICKER, ERIK VAN BLOKLAND, NEVILLE BRODY, DAVID CROW, TOBIAS FRERE-JONES, MALCOLM GARRETT, LUCAS DE GROOT, TIBOR KALMAN, JEFF KEEDY, VAUGHAN OLIVER, JUST VAN ROSSUM, PETER SAVILLE, ERIK SPIEKERMANN, IAN SWIFT, RICK VERMEULEN, CORNEL WINDLIN, JON WOZENCROFT.

If FUSE is an attempt to weave tradition and expertise with the new, it is no surprise that it should meet resistance. We had persuaded Erik Spiekermann to go on early, hoping his talk would modify this direction. It was the second day, the Saturday afternoon, when Vaughan Oliver, having never spoken in public before and missing his slides, came out of the Queen's Arms with Graham Wood, straight onto the stage, that things got hairy. Next up, Neville Brody ended his talk by saying he'd rather be outside having a cigarette, before Rick Vermeulen outlined such a conceptual idea of a typeface that the audience by this time were visibly restless. Where was David Carson? Would he turn up? He didn't.

As the conference broke up on the Saturday evening, I tried to suppress the mounting tension of knowing I was going on last, the next day. I had this crazy plan to get mobile phone technology involved somehow.

Touch had recently started a new label, *Ash International*, whose first releases were based around phone interceptions recorded by Robin Rimbaud, aka Scanner. I asked Robin to play his scanning device live during my talk, for which I had prepared a 10-minute film and soundtrack that he interacted with, picking up the sounds of liaisons in Mayfair and drug deals in Piccadilly intermittently. After 3 days, maybe it was too much information.

Someone came up afterwards complaining "This has nothing to do with typography". Five seconds later another attendee rushed up saying, "Fucking brilliant, fucking brilliant". It was all very confusing.

FUSE94 was framed by a great energy and student project. We produced an edition of 100 with the RCA Dept. of Communication Design, as it was then. For the students, such an event on their doorstep doesn't happen easily; across the country we saw an immediate response in student portfolios and attitudes to type design as a result of the conference.

FUSE95 in Berlin had to be of a different dimension. Firstly, the organisation was blessed by the more experienced hands of the Berlin FontShop who, with MetaDesign, made the set-up that much smoother. Secondly, we were wiser. [17–19 November 1995] Haus am Köllnischen Park, Berlin Mitte... East not West...

The conference was opened by Günter Gerhard Lange whose soft and commanding voice was lost to those arriving first thing before coffee. FUSE95 had a different spell, there were 900 attendees and the majority were students.

There is a reflective process that goes on at any critical transition. Many attend conferences because of the perceived allure of the 'Designer as Hero', and critics and audience alike then pick that up easily as 'ego'. It can be. It can also be stagefright, for which there is little preparation.

It isn't 'Rock and Roll' – but here is Max Kisman, one of the presenters at FUSE95 on the subject. "When I was invited to be a speaker at the FUSE conference in Berlin, the first thought I had was: Gee, this is Woodstock!... When you look at the list of speakers, you realise that typography and graphic design is a cult of its own. Type design isn't much different from songwriting and composing... An audience of about a thousand heads seemed as much as a pop festival to me".

Max made a revealing set of drawings for each speaker that you can see on http://www.typ.nl/TYP01/fuse/fuse00.html

The memory of FUSE95 was one of exuberance and freezing cold – minus 25 by the Sunday night. On this occasion Brody and I had the joy of not speaking at the front and back of the conference; in Berlin we had more time to observe the experience. There were more professional presentations from the stage. What emerged at this juncture was the desire of the audience to be more involved. They wanted an all-nighter.

How do you do that? Curating a conference, to sell tickets, has to be based on a set menu and the event has to run on time, as much as is possible. This became the legacy of FUSE95, a distinct improvement on FUSE94, but difficult to reconcile

NEVILLE BRODY FUSE95 PROMOTIONAL POSTER

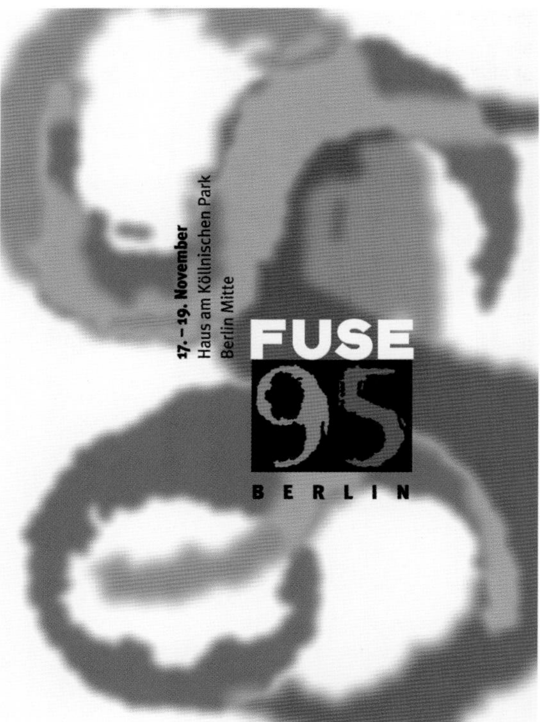

FUSE95 SPEAKERS IAN ANDERSON, DAVID BERLOW, ERIK VAN BLOKLAND, ALEXANDER BRANCZYK, THOMAS NAGEL, LO BREIER, NEVILLE BRODY, MATTHEW BUTTERICK, DAVID CARSON, DAVID CROW, TOBIAS FRERE-JONES, MALCOLM GARRETT, LUCAS DE GROOT, JEFF KEEDY, MAX KISMAN, GÜNTER GERHARD LANGE, HEIKE NEHL, JUST VAN ROSSUM, HEIDI SPECKER, SIBYLLE SCHLAICH, PIERRE DI SCIULLO, ERIK SPIEKERMANN, IAN SWIFT, TEAL TRIGGS, GERARD UNGER, RICK VALICENTI, CORNEL WINDLIN, GRAHAM WOOD, JON WOZENCROFT.

FUSE98 SPEAKERS DAVID BERLOW, ERIK VAN BLOKLAND, NEVILLE BRODY, ANDY CAMERON, DAVID CARSON, MATTHEW CARTER, DAVID CROW, TINA FRANK, SASHA FRERE-JONES, TOBIAS FRERE-JONES, MALCOLM GARRETT, MATHIAS GMACHL, ZAHA HADID, RUSSELL HASWELL, BILL HILL, KARRIE JACOBS, JEFF KEEDY, SANFORD KWINTER, BRUCE MAU, REBECA MÉNDEZ, [PANASONIC], JUST VAN ROSSUM, SKOT, MICHAEL SORKIN, ERIK SPIEKERMANN, LUCILLE TENAZAS, CHRIS WATSON, MIKE WILLIAMS, JON WOZENCROFT.

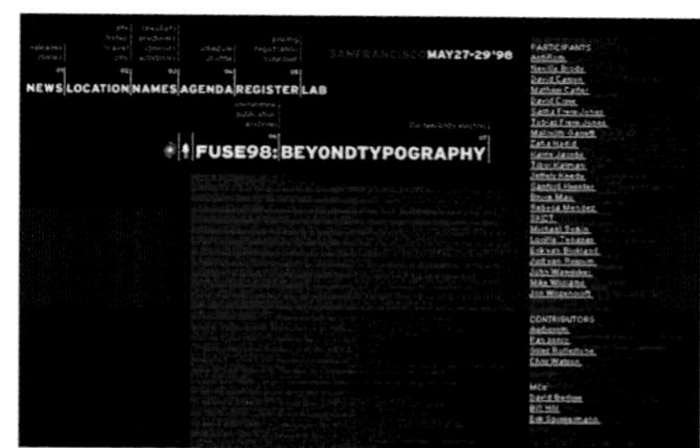

OLVIER CHÉTELAT, SHAWN HAZEN, DAVID PETERS, JOSEPH TERNES, EVA WALTER FOR METADESIGN SF FUSE98 WEBSITE

the performative aspects with the desire for discussion and debate. In this respect it's not like a pop festival at all, nor a rave. It was social networking years ahead of its time.

Chicago was going to be the next conference venue, but it became San Francisco... MetaDesign SF took up the challenge. **FUSE98** was extremely ambitious; and almost every last detail was taken care of in the preparation, until the difficulties of securing an overall sponsor reached the point of no return. We expanded our range of speakers to include architects, sound artists and film intermissions. There was an exhibition and installations of interactive media, "The New Body Electric", evening events, a lavish catalogue and website. The theme, "Beyond Typography", was echoed in the composition and the location – The Masonic Hall, opposite Grace Cathedral. As well as the shadow of the '60s, the cinema of *Vertigo*, *Bullitt* and *Basic Instinct* seemed to cast its spell on the proceedings.

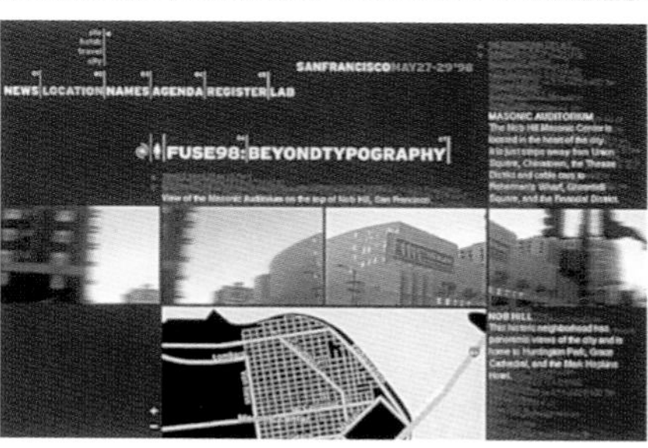

Late May, and strange weather. The first day of FUSE98 went like a dream, 1200 delegates high on expectation, California and caffeine. Actually it started badly. Brody's film didn't show up on screen as he was talking – this would have been a shining start. Nevertheless, the talks throughout the day were generally great and after screening a Dumb Type/Ryoji Ikeda excerpt from *OR*, we felt exhilarated.

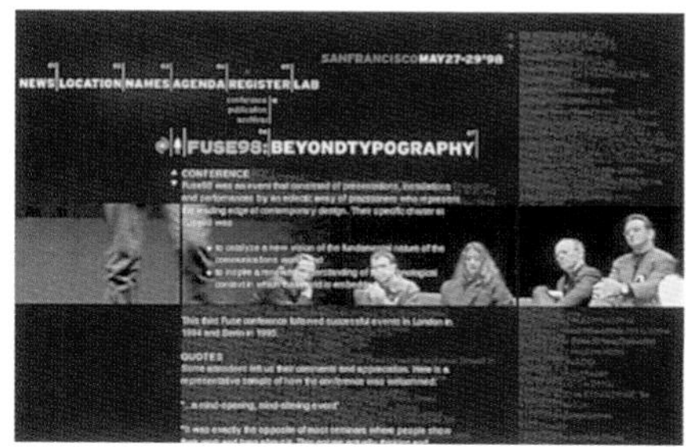

Simultaneously the problems started to flare up. David Carson only had his film on Digi-SP when he wanted it to be shown on DigiBeta; his talk had to be rescheduled, a new machine hired at great expense and an overnight courier arranged from his NY studio, otherwise he wouldn't speak. This, you've guessed, was becoming a pattern. Panasonic had shipped over their equipment, much of it custom-made from electronics sourced in the ex-U.S.S.R. and China, only to have it impounded by U.S. customs in Memphis. We were more worried about that.

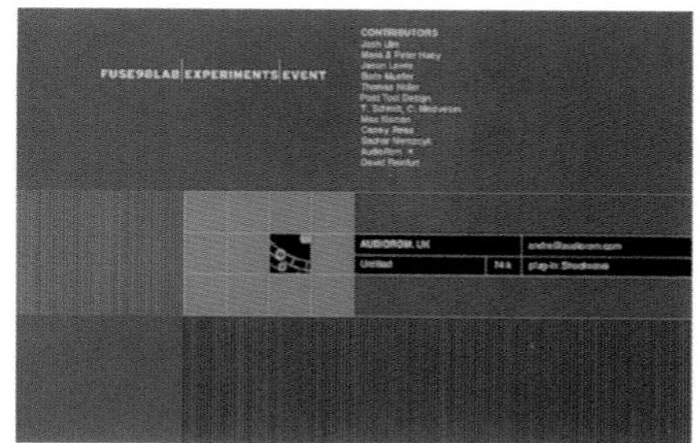

A prime ambition was to bring some spirit of the European avant-garde to the West Coast. There were so many levels to the event. At the end of the first day many of us were feeling the full effects of jetlag and retired early from the post-presentation drinking/discussions.

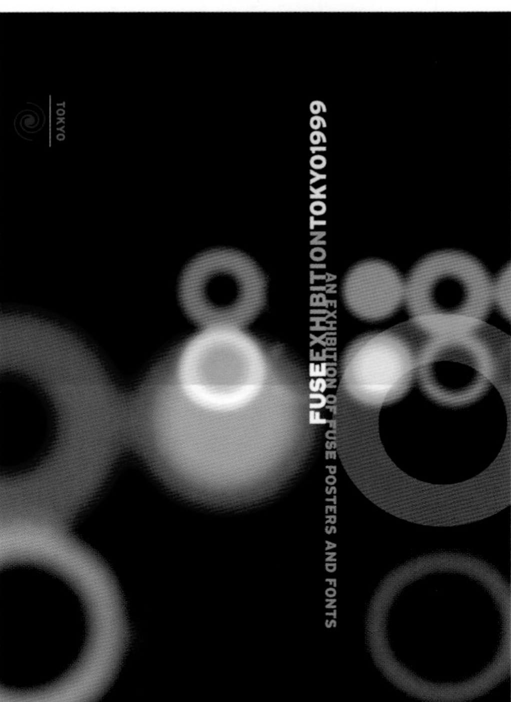

FUSEDAY MANCHESTER SPEAKERS NEVILLE BRODY, ERIK VAN BLOKLAND, JUST VAN ROSSUM, IAN SWIFT

FUSEDAY TOKYO SPEAKERS NEVILLE BRODY, NAOMI ENAMI, SUZUNG KIM, JOHN MAEDA

NEVILLE BRODY FUSEDAY PROMOTIONAL POSTERS

The following morning, the atmosphere changed and requests for more discussion slots steadily increased in proportion to the difficulties in accommodating them. When David Carson took to the stage in the afternoon, it was as the self-elected "voice of the people", his mixture of holiday snaps, Nazi propaganda posters and acerbic asides taking us on a journey to a crash.

One of the intersection films was a classic structural work by the Austrian film-maker, Peter Kubelka. He had made *Arnulf Rainer* in 1960 as the last of his "Metric films". It consists of black and white frames, flickering at great intensity alongside a soundtrack that alternates silence with white noise. It was impossible to soundcheck any of these pieces. The print was a new one Kubelka had supplied to the New York Film-makers Co-op, and it came out of the speakers like a tornado.

It is 6 minutes long. A minute in, a section of the audience started booing, and this became the breaking point of the conference on the part of those who took it as a personal attack. My response to this was far from my finest moment, but faced with what seemed to be 'beyond displeasure', I could only think about stupidity and then became a mirror to it.

The final day saw the most extreme interventions by the Viennese video/noise group SKOT and the architect/writer Michael Sorkin whose talk was delivered like a mutant TV show. Somehow by the end of the third day we came to a calm resolution – the audience wasn't ripping up seats and screaming at the organisers – and at the closing night-time event we were welcomed with the opposite. Many said it was the best conference they had ever attended.

Looking back on this learning curve, we mismanaged audience expectations... we hadn't understood the basic instinct. Because of this, we achieved more – for everyone it was something of the first time.

We get reminded now that these conferences were 'seminal events'. Hopefully they will continue. FUSE conferences did feel like festivals after all – and being indoors, we had to recreate our own version of mud, bad acid and epiphany. You had to be there. Both sides of the story are true.

GGGTOKYO
JOHN MAEDA SUZUNG KIM
ENAMI NAOMI NEVILLE BRODY
FUSEDAY TOKYO1999

TOKYO

NEVILLE BRODY FUSEDAY PROMOTIONAL POSTER

FUSE98 San Francisco Beyond Typography Neville Brody

The opening unabridged speech as presented on 27 May 1998 (CONTINUED FROM PAGE 3)

Traditionally, we had all been taught that typography is more or less a fixed form, with specific rules and behaviours.

These fixed patterns were developed at a different point in history to our own by different peoples to solve very different needs. This formulaic approach led to a way of thinking that design only exists to be problem solving, leading inevitably to a situation where all that was being communicated in society was the problem itself. The concept that problems were to be solved led to an elimination of all other ways of thought. Abstract and more intuitive approaches to communications were left on the sidelines and dismissed to a fringe position as Art. Type design and usage was taught as a tradition, almost an occult activity.

At the same time, in western society, typographic creation and design had been largely placed in the hands of a few highly-trained practitioners, in a monastic fashion. This closed-shop practice fuelled a self-referential elitism at the heart of the control mechanism governing our typographic systems and core elements. This elitism was challenged by the advent of the PC, when tools for designing fonts became readily available, and led to a democratisation of the typographic process. Suddenly, anyone could design their own font, and just as the invention and distribution of the camera took away the sole responsibilty for visual representation from the artists and painters, so the advent and availability of the computer achieved the same for design.

FUSE was born out of this process of liberalisation. But the freedom this gives us is also quite frightening in its possibilities.

The other key factor was that through this process of democratisation, as with Dadaism and Duchamp, designers were left with one burning question: *'why design?'*

The computer takes away from the designer the sole responsibility for the formulation of our visual communications. Grids are now predefined, and templates are prepared in advance. Mass availability of fonts means that uniqueness is short-lived, and that a reliance solely on the choice of font to differentiate oneself is no longer possible. The voice, not the words, is becoming indistinguishable and interchangeable.

Most people can now produce and publish professional-looking documentation, and many companies have become self-sufficient in their visual communications.

This means that, as with the post-impressionists, a great freedom from the shackles of needing to maintain accurate representation was now possible. As Jeff Keedy has stated, we now have the cultural possibilty of using abstract form in Art, in Literature, even in Architecture, but this had never before been possible in Typography.

Language | Firstly, though, we must ask the question *'what is language?'*

Essentially, language is a contract, a form of legislation. For any form of communication to be effective, there must be an agreed set of components or elements that both parties, broadcaster and receiver, can visualise and understand. This given set of elements is combined to form meaning. These elements can number 2 or 2000. The elements can be anything with a variable value, from colours to materials, sizes, shapes, objects, sounds, distances, textures or functions. The variables can be sensory or logistic, abstract or pragmatic. Either way, the core result is one of a set of perceptually differentiable elements. The relationship between the forms, or structure, is key. It could be a relationship based on time or temperature, space or sequence. The resultant combination of these elements in relation to each other we use to signal meaning, and this

NEVILLE BRODY FUSE98 PROMOTIONAL POSTER

FUSE98:
CONFERENCE
BEYOND
TYPOGRAPHY
SANFRANCISCOMAY27-291998
INSTALLATION
TOWARDS
THENEW
BODY
ELECTRIC

can be to do with conveying fact or emotion, data or feeling – information in any case.

FUSE takes the structure of the font, a number of boxes to be filled with elements that will later be combined to form new elements, as a way of creating new language forms. In liberating typography from the need to represent words, new dynamic possibilities appear and a way of developing our languages to embrace the joining of digital and organic matter occur.

Language is a process of editing. By the very nature of the social need to share a common understanding, language must be limited in order to be widespread. Localisation brings specialisation, and the smaller the group, the more detailed the frame of reference. The more global the group, or the more total the intent, the more the language becomes homogenised.

All cultures are defined by their languages. A philosophy of a people is encapsulated in the words they speak and the way they express them. Language evolves from culture. When we attempt to dictate language, we destroy culure.

Responsibility | We are here today the unquestioned translators of invisible ideas into tangible form. In today's society, we increasingly define ourselves through input. TV, Radio, Fax, Email, Cellular phones, Digital TV, Internet, Film, Advertising hoardings, Newspapers, Magazines, Books, Theme parks, Shopping.

As visual communicators, we have been handed the responsibility to formulate those messages. Our output becomes someone else's input. We take abstract invisible concepts such as emotions, directions, drives, desires, needs and hopes, and give them solidity. In the translation process, in the transferral of matter from invisible to visible form, we inevitably invoke a subjective process. Our interpretation becomes part of the form. We are imbued with such a high degree of trust because the power of the tools we have access to in order to manipulate desire is terrifying.

Advertising reverses the process of listening. It takes an original language from a target culture and incorporates key points into its own language which it then feeds back, thus freezing and then replacing the culture through the conversion of it into cliché or stereotype.

The choice of typeface is one of the tricks we use from our visual toolbox to enable this apparent 'speaking the same language' as the target audience. Hip-hop and punk culture are clear examples of counter-cultures in the west being annulled through the process of absorption. Non-European cultures are weakened through integration and regurgitation as westernised languages. British Airways is no longer a world airline but is now a world culture. Today we colonise through language.

Communication must allow cultures to breathe freely, to grow naturally. Visual language must be more organic, allowing evolution through respect – a celebration of the diversity of life and experience.

Information | Information is not information. Information is how a fact is presented, how we are informed about a fact. This means that sets of variables exist, that choices are being made by someone as to how a fact is given form and therefore as to how a fact should actually be perceived.

In this sense, information is a form of censorship.

We therefore control people's perceptions. Choice of font or typeface is one of the key variables in this mix. It signals to us before we have read a single word exactly how we should interpret a message. Largely, the presentation of a signal obscures the signal itself, and increasingly the presentation becomes the signal. There is more noise than signal in the process today, the box becomes the content.

Web | We are currently creating an increasingly richer web of promise. The Internet is a series of roads to nowhere, inhabited by roadside motels with flashing neon lights. This notion of electric promise means that it is no surprise that the single largest online activity is pornography. The same was true at the advent of home VCR machines. No, we are today obsessed with building new roads and towns. Most of life is relatively uneventful and most of us lead relatively repetitive life patterns. Design and advertising are part of an

MIKE ABBINK FOR METADESIGN SF FUSE98 CONFERENCE CATALOGUE

industry that creates a temporary escape route where we don't have to think too deeply. The obsession with the Internet is another great hope that the web of communications we are building will somehow save us from the belief that the world is flat.

When the Internet first became a visual possibility, design was in a state of collapse. The net has been seized upon as an employment opportunity, a self-propelled, self-generating job shop. The tragedy is that we have become so singularly obsessed with the glitter that we have glossed over the message.

We are currently in a state of what I call Desktop Web, DTW. As in DTP, the main object of communication is the object of communication itself. We look no further than the latest technological tricks as content, and we use quickly-established clichés as our visual language. As the first televisions looked like radios and behaved like theatre, we generally relate to electronic media as if we were reading newspapers or books using VCR controls.

Also, as in DTP, part of the current creative limitation to the expressive content of the web is due to the fact that we imagine as designers that we can do everything. On the web we flatter ourselves to be not only designers and engineers, but also writers, photographers, film directors, illustrators and publishers. The only way we can break into a greater content base is by incorporating specialists.

We must move beyond the obsession with the how and deal with the what and why. We are more concerned with the choice of typeface than the choice of text.

We continually make the mistake of assuming that information is content. It is not. It is simply the excuse to produce more and more electronic noise to keep us all in business.

Maps | As we increasingly define ourselves through input, through the machines we use and the messages we receive on them, the obsession with surface maps is reaching a crescendo. The Internet represents a new geography, one with no national boundaries. New geopolitics are creating new towns, new cities. Our bodies stretch out into extended forms, imagining real space where it is only light on screen.

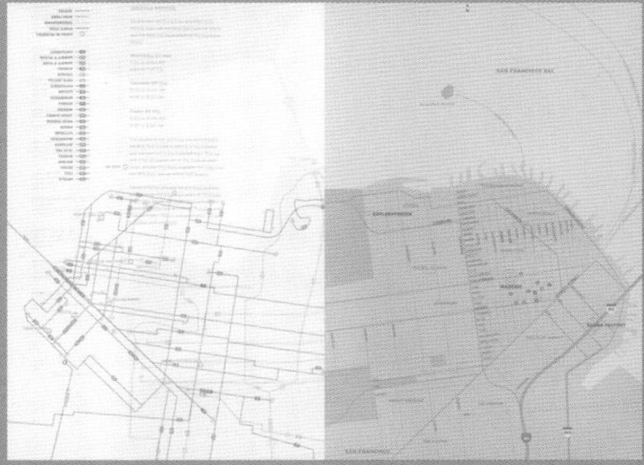

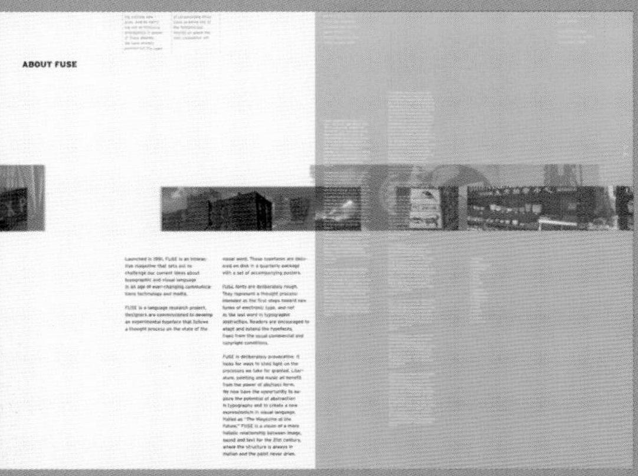

Information is not information. Information is how a fact is presented, how we are informed about a fact. This means that sets of variables exist, that choices are being made by someone as to how a fact is given form and therefore as to how a fact should actually be perceived.

In this sense, information is a form of censorship.

Interaction | Type is culture. Type is fact. Type is trust. Type is faith. Type is entertainment. Appropriateness is everything, and our responses define ourselves.

The message needs to be more of a dialogue. Keep the packaging away from the message. If we really believed in the idea that our readers and market were intelligent, and that we could speak to them intelligently, we would create real interaction, not just a choice between pre-edited, pre-defined solutions.

We can use the tools we are developing for the promotion of other ideas. We can use them for the good of people, not for the exploitation of them. We can embrace compassion, we can use our tools to help enable the billion powerless poverty-stricken peoples of our own planet. We can bring love to the table, we can respect our audience and listen to them, allowing them access and the power to change the message.

We can educate instead of dictate. If type is money, then it belongs to everyone. Democracy is apparently a one-way process of communication. Type is not money, red is not a soft drink. William Burroughs in *The Soft Machine* lambasts Coca-Cola for stealing the colour red as its own. Blue is not IBM. Life exists in the gap between words, the silence between sounds and the space between objects. Life exists in the space beyond definitions, intuition is all.

FUSE98 | Love is all there is.

This conference is intended to be experiential. There is enough in life that is observational, and there is more than enough that is referential. This conference seeks to be something greater than that. It seeks to take you into your own experience, to experience what is true for you rather than observe, or be referred to, what is true for others. The biggest choice you will make is the choice between your truth and the truth of another.

Context is all. There is no such thing as Objective or Factual truth in this reality. All truth in our world is created by the context in which it is experienced or observed. Information is just a point of view.

In some ways, media forbids you to seek your own personal experience. It is the job of media not to invite you to experience what is true for you, but to tell you outright what should be true for you. In order for this conference to be experiential, you will have to allow it to be. You will need to be willing to be a part of the conference's unfolding.

We keep repeating behaviours, and failed behaviours at that, instead of inventing new ones. It is clear now that the reason we as a race continue to exhibit

NEVILLE BRODY DESIGNS FOR FUSE98 BEYOND TYPOGRAPHY

old behaviours is that we have not given ourselves permission to stop listening to old instructions. We need to encourage, stimulate or produce real behavioural change. The human revolution begins with you. Feeling is the language of the soul, and the purpose of the soul is evolution. In order to change our behaviour, and therefore our experience, we need to embark on a forward journey of reversals. Reversing the process is necessary.

FUSE98 : BEYOND TYPOGRAPHY : TOWARDS THE NEW BODY ELECTRIC : THE VITAL DESIGN EVENT OF THE YEAR

We need to move from broadcaster to receiver, in order to hear what we transmit. We are both publisher and reader, and we always have been. We need to approach language from the ground up, allowing growth and evolution, rather than decreeing from the top down with the viewpoint of short-term gain.

We need to educate, not dictate.

We need to learn and listen, not shout all the time.

We need to move from monologue to dialogue, where we risk that the message itself can be altered.

We need to stop, to move from speed to motion, from continual movement to a state of stillness, from spiralling out to spiralling inwardly.

We need to move away from anti-matter to matter, from re-invention to growth, from doing to being.

FUSE 1-20: Designers Biographies/Index

The index includes original biographies provided by contributors for each issue of FUSE. To remain faithful to the FUSE compendium contributors featured in more than one issue have been listed with multiple biographies.

Text has been left as it was originally provided and published. Any errors, mistakes, or omissions are authentic to the original publication of that issue.

Biographies were not listed in issues 17, 18, 19 & 20.

Page numbers in italic.

A-BOMBE

***Nøgleord*, commended**
FUSE Competition (2005) *347*

Was born Simon Graham in Glasgow, Scotland in 1973. He studied in Glasgow and Edinburgh focusing on type design and experimental typography. After graduating with a degree in Visual Communication he briefly taught font design and development at Edinburgh College of Art. Now working as a freelancer out of Denmark his clients include Deaconn Clothing, Edinburgh International Film Festival, Icon and Sony.

IAN ANDERSON

Dr No-B
FUSE 6 Codes (1992) *112*

My name is Ian Anderson. I was born in Croydon before England won the World Cup and now I'm lucky enough to be here with you. Somewhere in between came Thunderbirds, Captain Scarlet, Scooby Doo, The Trigan Empire, Bubblegum and Andy Warhol; Dave & Ansel Collins, Slade, Roxy Music, Parlifunkadelicament, The Clash, The Pop Group, Eno, On-U and Miles Davies; the Young Socialists, the Anti-Nazi League, the Marx Brothers and Russian Constructivism; Infra Red Helicopters, *Voodoo Voodoo* magazine, a Philosophy degree, playing records for money and managing bands; Nobby, friends & family, Fulham, Sheffield Wednesday and DR Sokka; *Helvetica*, Burroughs, technology, "Crash", Tokyo and sci-fi consumerism.

I never studied design formally, I am not a typographer, I hate religion, I love my wife and I love my Designers Republic.

DR. RACHEL ARMSTRONG

***The Body Machine*, editorial text**
FUSE 16 Genetics (1996) *282*

Qualified as a doctor in 1991 and practised medicine for 2 years. After a series of collaborations with artists such as Helen Chadwick, Orlan and Stelarc she now uses her medical knowledge and alternative visions of the body to work as a producer in multimedia and desktop virtual reality.

JASON BAILEY

Sclerosis Script
FUSE 18 Secrets (2000) *324*

PHIL BAINES

Can You (and Do You Want to) Read Me?
FUSE 1 Invention (1991) *26*

Phil Baines was born in Kendal in the English Lake District in 1958. Since studying Graphic Design at St. Martin's School of Art and at the Royal College of Art between 1982 and '87, he has worked as a freelance designer for various clients, including Monotype Typography and The Craft's Council. He teaches letter-press techniques one day a week at Central St. Martin's College of Art & Design in London and is currently editing and designing *Rookledge's International Handbook of Type Designers*, due to be published in late 1991.

***Between the Book & the Vernacular*, editorial text**
FUSE 4 Exuberance (1992) *70*

Ushaw
FUSE 8 Religion (1993) *148*

Phil Baines (born 1958) studied graphic design at St. Martin's School of Art (1982–85) and the Royal College of Art (1985–87) in London. Much college work hand-set and printed letterpress, and some personal projects are still produced this way (the recently self-published STоneUTTERS for example). Currently combines freelance work for arts organisations and small publishers with teaching typography part-time at Central St. Martin's College of Art and Design. His first typeface *Can You...?* appeared in FUSE 1 and he is currently working on a sans serif type family with four weights.

TOM BALCHIN

Cogdis
FUSE 20 Antimatter (2011)

BARNBROOK

Rattera
FUSE 20 Antimatter (2011)

KEITH BATES

Insecurity, commended
FUSE Competition (2005) 348

Was born in Liverpool, England in 1951 and currently works as an Art & Design teacher at a Salford High School. He is well-known for his Mail Art activities since 1983, his postal art projects include The Abstract Realist Show (2002), The English Suppressionists (1993), and the recent Mailart Typeface (2004). His Ersatz Ephemera pieces turn humble tickets into mailartworks and can be seen at www.keithbates.co.uk together with three downloadable mailart inspired songs, the documentation for recent projects, and some of his fonts.

Keith fell in love with Fontographer in 2001. The K-Type foundry was established in 2003, and fonts available from the website at www.k-type.com include *English* (2003–04), initially an attempt to combine the power of *Helvetica* with the home-grown elegance of *Gill Sans*, *Context* (2002), an exercise in omission, and the freebie *Lexia Readable* (2004), based on *Comic Sans* for legibility, but casting off the American comic-book styling.

Having created *Gill New Antique* in 2003, an imaginary, undiscovered second sans of Eric Gill, Keith continued to study Gill's work and made the first digital version of *Solus*, originally cut in 1929, the following year (available as *Non Solus* for copyright reasons).

The Mailart Typeface is an experiment in eclecticism, created in 2004 from 150 contributions from mailartists worldwide. Mail Art continues to feed his type design – *Mailart Rubberstamp* (2004) is based on the rubberstamped envelopes sent by several mailartists, and *Susanna* (2004) was drawn as a typo-diary in response to Susanna Lakner's mail art project, 22 Days. *Susanna* and another recent work, *Plasterboard*, are currently under consideration by the FontFont Typeboard.

Some recent Keith Bates free fonts are available from: www.1001fonts.com

MARIO BEERNAERT

TV27HorizontalNormal
FUSE 9 Auto (1994) 170

Born in 1971. Currently studying Graphic Design at St. Lucas, Ghent (in Belgium, the creative desert), after four years of Informatics. I haven't done much of interest yet in graphic design, I'm just starting. I'm working with Cloaca Maxima; our logo is a chicken. I saw Jungle Book yesterday and my next typeface will be called 'Tarzan'. Too bad there's no chicken in it.

DAVID BERLOW

Yurnacular
FUSE 4 Exuberance (1992) 78

David Berlow began his career in the type industry in 1977 with Mergenthaler Linotype where he developed such legible typeface revivals as *New Century Schoolbook* and *New Caledonia*. He moved to the newly formed Bitstream Inc. in 1982 before forming The Font Bureau Inc. with Roger Black in 1989. The Font Bureau have developed over 200 typefaces, new designs and revivals for custom clients, the retail market and for equipment manufacturers like Apple Computer Inc.

Berlow has won no major awards and is not a member of any prestigious organisation. His hobbies include taking time off, collecting rubber bands and counting grains of sand.

PHIL BICKER

Illiterate
FUSE 7 Crash (1993) 130

As art director of his London-based company, Village, Bicker has sought to encourage and work towards a creative community. Working to the ideals of a collaborative spirit, he has and continues to actively support and collaborate with a new generation of young maverick photographers.

Originally working as an illustrator, he has a strong editorial background having previously been art director at *New Socialist* and *The Face* magazines. Since setting up Village two years ago, he has worked on more diverse projects. Presently he is consciously trying to accentuate the more human elements in his work, whilst developing further ideas through a series of non-design projects.

ERIK VAN BLOKLAND

Niwida
FUSE 2 Runes (1991) 48

Born 1967, studied at the Royal Academy for Fine and Applied Arts in The Hague from 1985 to 1989. Worked for a few months at MetaDesign in Berlin, travelled across The States, grew up and is now a graphic designer in The Hague.

[With van Rossum] Their work involves typography, graphic design and illustration. In 1989, they started the LettError group as a small magazine about typography, which has since grown into a label for experimental typography and type design. "The *RandomFonts* (published by FSI) are perhaps the most shocking thing we've done so far, at least judging from the reaction we've had". The magazine itself will probably resume publication towards the end of this year.

WhatYouSee/WhatYouGet
FUSE 11 Pornography (1994) *204*

Independent designers from The Netherlands, Erik van Blokland and Just van Rossum graduated from the Royal Academy for Fine and Applied Arts in The Hague. After working separately together at various design companies in Europe and the U.S. they are now working separately together under the name of LettError (Pronounced Let-Error), still in The Hague. Projects: corporate design, animation and interactive thingies, illustration, animation, TV design, interface design for applications and online services, CD covers, music stuff, typography, magazine stuff. They are the creators of the recently-released *Kosmik*, "one of the world's leading *Flipper*™ fonts".

Data Mine
FUSE 19 Revolution (2003)

LO BREIER

Spherize
FUSE 5 Virtual (1992) *98*

Hello, my name is Lo Breier and I fly from Vienna to Hamburg and from Hamburg to Vienna. You can get in touch with me through the number registered in the phonebook under Büro X. After I had discovered the "Vienna-Layout-Bacillus" I brought Germany face to face with the "Tempo-Layout-Bacillus". This has led to various and most severe infections among art-directors in Germany. Some of them are still suffering badly. At the moment I devote my time to organising the so-called "Art-Directors-Mafia". I think this might be a rather thrilling job.

NEVILLE BRODY

State
FUSE 1 Invention (1991) *28*

Neville Brody did his best to avoid typography until he was forced to look for new ways of treating type whilst Art Director of *The Face* from 1982–86. During this time he designed a series of typefaces, of which the recently published *Industria* and *Typeface Six* are the best known. Having since been Art Director of *Arena*, *Per Lui* and *Lei* magazines, he is presently Art Director of *Actuel*.

Recent commissions have included the station identity for Premiere, a national German TV Channel, and the 1991 calendar for Parco, one of the largest department stores in Tokyo. A Thames and Hudson book was published to coincide with a touring exhibition of his work, which has so far been seen in England, Scotland, Germany and Japan. Brody runs his own studio in London.

***Virtual*, bonus font**
FUSE 5 Virtual (1992) *94*

***Code Bold*, bonus font**
FUSE 6 Codes (1992) *111*

***Crash*, bonus font**
FUSE 7 Crash (1993) *128*

***Religion*, bonus font**
FUSE 8 Religion (1993) *146*

***Autosuggestion*, bonus font**
FUSE 9 Auto (1994) *162*

***Freeform*, bonus font**
FUSE 10 Freeform (1994) *182*

Neville Brody is currently working on a new FontShop International series, Dirty Faces, a midpoint between FontFont and FUSE. Recent font releases have included *Harlem*, *Tokyo* and *World*. His next project is to create a CD-ROM version of *The Graphic Language of Neville Brody 2*.

***Peep*, bonus font**
FUSE 11 Pornography (1994) *198*

***Populist*, bonus font**
FUSE 12 Propaganda (1994) *216*

***Ritual*, bonus font**
FUSE Superstition (1995) *232*

***Cyber*, bonus font**
FUSE 14 Cyber (1995) *248*

***City*, bonus font**
FUSE 15 Cities (1995) *266*

***Genetics Second Generation*, bonus font**
FUSE 16 Genetics (1996) *288*

***Echo*, bonus font**
FUSE 17 Echo (1997) *306*

***Lies*, bonus font**
FUSE 18 Secrets (2000) *322*

***Neural*, bonus font**
FUSE 19 Revolution (2003)

Antimatter
FUSE 20 Antimatter (2011)

Antisans, bonus font
FUSE 20 Antimatter (2011)

MATTHEW BUTTERICK

Agitprop
FUSE 12 Progaganda (1994) 218

Matthew Butterick abandoned an early mathematics career at Harvard for one which has encompassed graphic design, type design, multimedia and programming. He began work as a letterpress printer, then became a type designer, working with Font Bureau and Carter & Cone, producing work for clients such as Apple, *Esquire*, Microsoft, *Rolling Stone* and Ziff-Davis. He is the founder of Atomic Vision, a new studio which incorporates design and technology for digital media projects, such as Websites, CD-ROMs and interactive presentations.

BARBARA BUTTERWECK

DearJohn
FUSE 3 (Dis)information (1993) 62

Was born in Soest, Germany, in 1961. After school, she studied at the design department of the Fachhochschule Bielefeld and gained a diploma in Graphic Design under Professor Gerd Fleischmann. Since 1990, she has worked as a freelance designer in Bielefeld: her main income is from work for a local Apple dealer.

MARGARET CALVERT

A26
FUSE 9 Auto (1994) 166

Born in South Africa in 1936. Studied Illustration at Chelsea School of Art from 1953 to '57. Joined Jock Kinnear as an assistant designer in 1958 working principally on lettering and signage systems for Gatwick Airport; Britain's new motorways, 1961; the U.K.'s all-purpose roads, 1963; British Rail; British Airports; and the Tyne and Wear Metro in 1981.

Margaret Calvert now works independently and since 1966 she has taught at the Royal College of Art in London, where from 1987 to '89 she was Head of Graphic Design and Acting Course Director from 1989 to '91. She is a member of the Alliance Graphique Internationale.

DAVID CARSON

Fingers
FUSE 7 Crash (1993) 132

Based in Del Mar California, Carson's work with *Beach Culture* magazine received numerous awards. Here, he has his own design studio, where he currently produces *Ray Gun* magazine. He has been art director for *Billboard's Musician* magazine, a senior designer for Condé Nast's *Self*, and is currently art director at Surfer Publications in Dana Point California. Carson's clients include MTV, Suzuki, Converse shoes, Scripto pens, Sony and Kentucky Fried Chicken.

MATTHEW CARTER

DeFace
FUSE 18 Secrets (2000) 326

JOSE CHAMORRO

Code Secure, commended
FUSE Competition (2005) 349

Jose Chamorro Salas, graphic designer, graduated in 2002, University Nacional de Colombia.

SCOTT CLUM

Burnfont
FUSE Superstition (1995) 234

Was born in 1964. Studied advertising and design and received a degree in Fine Art from Munson Williams Proctor Institute of Fine Art in NY.

"I have always been captivated by art, its complexities and the ability it has to move people. All of my time is spent in the studio [ride dsgn.] Silverton, Oregon, where I handle the design direction for *Blur* magazine, *Bikini* magazine and Morrow Snowboards, as well as other freelance work".

COIL GRAPHICS

SystemG, winner
FUSE Competition (2005) 342

1987 opened design office in Tokyo – Coilgraphics

1991 established company – Coil Corporation

1993 elected by *International Typography 2*, Robundo

1998 Mac font brand *Grid System* start
www.coilgraphics.com

JOHN CRITCHLEY

Mutoid
FUSE 10 Freeform (1994) 184

Graduated from Manchester Polytechnic in 1990 and after a brief spell at The Designers Republic in Sheffield, joined Neville Brody Studios where he works on a variety of projects including FUSE. Other fonts include *Childs Play*, a series based on children's handwriting.

Ollie, bonus font
FUSE 12 Propaganda (1994) 214

DAVID CROW

Creation 6
FUSE 8 Religion (1993) *150*

Born Galashiels, Scotland in 1962. Published 8 issues of *Trouble* magazine, an exploration of consumer imagery. Currently a lecturer in graphic design at University College Salford. About to begin an MA programme in Environmental Graphics at Manchester.

Mega Family 2
FUSE 16 Genetics (1996) *292*

Studied Graphic Design at Manchester Polytechnic. Worked as a designer at Assorted Images (London) and Island Records (London) before running a freelance practice (also in London) for 3 years. Clients included Sony UK, Sony USA, Rolling Stones Records, Phonogram Records, Virgin Records, Island Records, IBM, Royal Shakespeare Company, Foster's Lager, MTV. Published eight issues of *Trouble* magazine. Guest speaker at FUSE '94 in London, FUSE '95 in Berlin and Festivital '96 in Tel Aviv. Currently Subject Leader in Graphic Design at Liverpool John Moores University.

VERA DAUCHER

***Trinity*, student bonus font**
FUSE 14 Cyber (1995) *246*

Cup size B, astronaut.

BARRY DECK

Caustic Biomorph
FUSE 4 Exuberance (1992) *80*

Grew up in an American suburb, where he contemplated world domination while mowing the lawn. After studying briefly at six different colleges and pursuing almost as many majors, he settled on graphic design as 'a creative way to make money'. In 1986 he took his first job at a firm where work was routinely typeset in *Goudy*, then centred. He worked there for only six months before realising the fatal flaw in his career choice. The next autumn, he found himself enrolled at California Institute of the Arts where he caught on to a particularly loud-mouthed rationale for his hyper-individualism in design.

Today he can't hold a job and does everything he can to make ends meet. In addition to designing type, Barry does photo-illustration, graphic design and even design production.

LUCAS DE GROOT

Move Me MM
FUSE 11 Pornography (1994) *200*

Studied at the Royal Academy of Fine Arts in The Hague under Gerrit Noordzij and then spent four years with the Dutch design group BRS Premsela, mainly on corporate identity work. He taught at the Art Academy in Den Bosch and freelanced before moving to Berlin in 1993 to join MetaDesign. A self-confessed font fanatic who spent 5 years on his typeface *Thesis*, he compensates such hard work and sweat with quickly programmed novelty faces.

PIERRE DI SCIULLO

Scratched Out
FUSE 5 Virtual (1992) *102*

Is neither artist nor typographer, yet his work has always been based on the relationship between text and image. In 1983, he started to publish *Qui? Résiste*, of which there have been nine issues so far – 'manuals' on seduction, truth, death, zoology, the square, clouds, reading and elementary logic. Today, his explorations have led him to the limits of type with the creation of a range of signs, typefaces, or rather a system which creates endless variations from a basic repertoire, which he refers to as a "sign machine". Pierre di Sciullo tries to balance type with text and text with type, striving to avoid any superficial illustration of the one by the other.

Spell Me
FUSE 17 Echo (1997) *312*

EBOY

Camou
FUSE 19 Revolution (2003)

PAUL ELLIMAN

Alphabet
FUSE 5 Virtual (1992) *100*

Born 1961, self-taught designer of *Wire* magazine (1986) and now a member of the East London University Visual Communication think-tank. Mistrustful of the written word and suspicious of Graphic Design in general, he is occasional publisher/editor of *BoxS pace*, international magazine for electronic mail systems, which took Gold and Silver medals in the 1991 D&AD awards. More interested in Design as socio-linguistic assemblage and initiator of change, he is presently working with choreographer Rosemary Butcher on a performance that will tour Europe in 1993.

***Reading Typography Writing Language*, editorial text**
FUSE 10 Freeform (1994) *174*

Bits
FUSE 15 Cities (1995) *268*

Paul Elliman's favourite city is Liverpool, city of his childhood. He has recently returned to London after taking on a proper job for a year at the University of Texas, and is actively developing a programme for his own online school of communication design, the University of Nowhere. "I ask my students to research typography as a working relationship between the alphabet and our language. My FUSEwork is a contribution to this research."

NAOMI ENAMI

Kilin
FUSE 16 Genetics (1996) *294*

Born in 1956 in Osaka. Founded PROPELLER ART WORKS Ltd. in 1981 whilst art-directing magazines such as *Number* (1982–84), *Marie Claire* (1984–85) and *ELLE Japon* (1989–90). In 1992 he opened the Macintosh gallery DIGITALOGUE in Tokyo, and cofounded DIGITALOGUE Inc. with the photographer Akira Gomi and designer Neville Brody in 1993. Has published many multimedia works such as the CD-ROM collection, *Yellows*. His awards include the Disk of the Year 85 U.S.A. and a Multimedia Grand Prize Excellence Award in 1992.

FLORIAN FOSSEL

Spherize
FUSE 5 Virtual (1992) *98*

My name is Florian Fossel. Together with Lo, I tortured *Franklin*. There will be further violations, cruel and merciless, right to reincarnation. Death to design, what follows is the expression of sensory perception, communication that gets you. So take your mind and run. Hide if you can. You'll have no chance, we'll find you anywhere.

TOBIAS FRERE-JONES

Reactor
FUSE 7 Crash (1993) *134*

Born 1970 in New York, graduated from the Rhode Island School of Design in 1992. He is currently working as a type designer for the Font Bureau Inc. in Boston. Previous designs include *Dolores* (FontFont), *Garage Gothic* and *Nobel* (The Font Bureau). He enjoys walking around on train tracks late at night.

Fibonacci
FUSE 10 Freeform (1994) *186*

Born in New York in 1970, graduated from the Rhode Island School of Design in 1992. He is currently working as a senior type designer for The Font Bureau, Inc. in Boston. Previous designs include *Dolores* (FontFont), *Garage Gothic*, *Nobel*, *Cafeteria*, *Reiner Script*, *Stereo*, *Interstate*, *Epitaph*, *Armada* (at the Font Bureau) and *Reactor* (FUSE 7).

He relaxes by banging on sheet metal with a sledgehammer, and enjoys chewing on styrofoam.

Microphone
FUSE 15 Cities (1995) *270*

Tobias Frere-Jones is Senior Managing Designer at the Font Bureau Inc. in Boston. In addition to his numerous contributions to the Font Bureau retail library, he has worked for dozens of custom clients in the U.S. and Europe. After *Reactor* (FUSE 7) and *Fibonacci* (FUSE 10), this is his third.

He enjoys smashing bottles against his head, and has discovered the secret of levitation.

FUEL

Tape Type
FUSE 11 Pornography (1994) *202*

Fuel are Peter Miles, Damon Murray and Stephen Sorrell. A design group based in London's East End.

FUNCTION

Where the Dog is Buried
FUSE 17 Echo (1997) *310*

Function is Marius Watz, Kim Hiorthoy & Havin Bodin.

OLÖF BIRNA GARDARSDOTTIR

XFuse, student bonus font
FUSE 12 Propaganda (1994) *213*

MALCOLM GARRETT

Stealth
FUSE 1 Invention (1991) *30*

Is design director of the U.K. consultancy Assorted Images. He studied typography at Reading University 1974–75 and Graphic Design at Manchester Polytechnic between 1975 and '78. In 1977 he began a long period of working with the music industry, with clients such as Buzzcocks, Simple Minds, Culture Club and Duran Duran. In 1983, Garrett formed a partnership with Kasper de Graaf, former editor of *New Sounds New Styles*, to develop the wider potential of the creative team at Assorted Images along with an increasing commitment to the use of electronic design tools. Garrett has judged for the D&AD annual awards each year from 1988 to 1990; a book of his work is planned for later this year, to coincide with an exhibition in Tokyo and at the Design Museum in London.

Instrument
FUSE 12 Propaganda (1994) *220*

Malcolm Garrett was director of the design consultancy Assorted Images [London] and consultant designer at Protocol Creative Consultants [Manchester] until 1994, his work involving graphic identity, exhibition design, television graphics, and design for literature of all kinds, as well as for artists such as Duran Duran, Boy George, Simple Minds and more recently Peter Gabriel. His work in TV includes designs for the first three series of *The Last Resort*, and the identity and weekly on-screen graphics for the influential Network 7. He is an acknowledged enthusiast of the use of computers in design having worked with Apple, Scitex and Macintosh since the early '80s; he has authored a number of controversial articles in the trade press welcoming new developments in digital publishing. Garrett is now partner with Alasdair Scott in the newly formed interactive media production company AMX digital [London], so far commissioned to develop CD-based multimedia titles for EMI Records, News International and Kodak Image Bank. He designed the recently published Phaidon book, *The Cyberspace Lexicon*.

ADAM GRAVELEY

***Landing Strip*, winner**
FUSE Competition (2005) *340*

Studied Graphic Design at London Guildhall University – 2000–2003. Graduated with a BA Hons 2.1. Worked for 6 months in a design/marketing agency working on commercial projects for clients such as Wella and Vodafone. Won the Design Indaba competition from CR and spent 6 days in Cape Town networking and meeting international designers. 6 months' freelance working on marketing material for restaurants and marketing companies in and around the Newbury area. At present am the Designer for a design/print company based in Newbury, Berks.

PETER GRUNDY

DIY
FUSE 15 Cities (1995) *272*

Born England 1954. Bath Academy of Art 1973–76. Royal College of Art 1976–79. Grundy & Northedge to the present day. Grundy works as a typographer and illustrator. With his partner Tilly Northedge, they are known internationally for the flair they bring to graphic information. As Peter Grundy Ownworks, he has produced a series of typographic works that "bridge the gap between lettering and illustration", an area he calls "iconography".

LEE HASLER

***Env*, winner**
FUSE Competition (2005) *340*

Lee Hasler studied at Kent Institute of Art & Design, graduating in 1993 with an honours degree in illustration/graphics. Pursued his illustration via old technology (Commodore Amiga) later combining old and new with an Apple Mac. Has designed many fonts since leaving college, of which *Env* is his most recent.

ZAID HASSAN

***Type Design Comes to Life*, editorial text**
FUSE 16 Genetics (1996) *287*

FRANK HEINE

Determination
FUSE 15 Cities (1995) *274*

1964 born on February 15. 1969 I could read *Akzidenz Grotesk*, so when I was sent to school I was quite irritated with the script type that was used in our primers. 1983 Practical courses with a silk-screen printer, a graphics studio and an offset litho printer. 1986 Studies at the Staatliche Akademie der Bildenden Künste Stuttgart. Work in a graphic design studio for 4 years. 1991 My first Macintosh, a IICi. 1992 Release of the *Remedy* font (thru Emigre). 1993 *Motion* font (thru Emigre). *Contrivance*, *Cutamond*, *Schablone*, *Signaler* fonts (thru FontHaus). 1994 Founding of my own company (together with Lutz Eberle): U.O.R.G. in Stuttgart. *Chelsea* and *Instanter* fonts (thru FontShop), *Kracklite*, *Whole Little Universe* (thru T–26). 1995 *Amplifier* and *Indecision* (thru T–26).

FLORIAN HEIß

Surveillance
FUSE 17 Echo (1997) *308*

KATSUHIKO HIBINO

Onmi
FUSE Superstition (1995) *236*

Born in Gifu City, Japan, 1958. 1982 graduated from the Design Course, Faculty of Fine Arts, Tokyo National University of Fine Arts and Music. 1984 gained Master's Degree in Design from the Faculty of Fine Arts. 1990 International Broadcasting Award, then Governor's Prize, Tokyo Metropolitan Outdoor Advertisement Awards for Excellence. Hibino does not see alphabets as linguistic devices but shapes. He does not have the ability to understand each character because he was brought up in Japan and our linguistic culture is not accustomed to incorporating Roman alphabets into our daily lives. With special thanks to Propeller Art Works in Tokyo for their assistance.

TOM HINGSTON

Chaos, **bonus font**
FUSE 14 Cyber (1995) 246

Condition
FUSE 16 Genetics (1996) 296

Tom Hingston & Jon Wozencroft met at Central Saint Martin's in London in 1993. Shortly after graduating, Hingston came to work at Research Studios, where they have collaborated on a number of projects.

RAD HOC

Landwriting
FUSE 20 Antimatter (2011)

SYLKE JANETZKY

Atomic Circle
FUSE 10 Freeform (1994) 188

24 years old, born in Neuss and still living there. After leaving school I worked in several theatres in Neuss and Cologne. At present I am studying graphic design – *Atomic Circle* was the result of a student FUSE project.

SAM JONES

Smog, **student bonus font**
FUSE 15 Cities (1995) 264

ASGEIR JÓNSSON

Dofus, **student bonus font**
FUSE 12 Propaganda (1994) 213

TIBOR KALMAN

What the Hell
FUSE 8 Religion (1993) 152

Tibor Kalman is a Hungarian-American Jew raised as a Roman Catholic.

JEFFREY KEEDY

A Type of Death, **editorial text**
FUSE 4 Exuberance (1992) 74

LushUS
FUSE 4 Exuberance (1992) 82

Mr. Keedy is a graphic designer living in Los Angeles. His clients include the Museum of Contemporary Art, Los Angeles Contemporary Exhibitions, Santa Monica Museum of Art and other such artsy-fartsy organisations. He also designs typefaces soon to be released through his company 'Cipher'. Currently he is Acting Program Director in Graphic Design at California Institute of the Arts.

MAX KISMAN

Linear Konstrukt
FUSE 2 Runes (1991) 44

Max Kisman has worked as a freelance graphic designer in Amsterdam since 1977. In the early 1980s, the Dutch music magazine *Vinyl* gave Kisman the chance to develop his experimental design and typography, and from 1982 to 1989 he designed the posters for the Paradiso, a music venue in Amsterdam. As a DTP pioneer, in 1986 he began using a computer for his designs for the Dutch PTT's Red Cross stamps, and in his work as art director for *Language Technology* magazine. At this time, he also founded the typography magazine *Typ* and taught graphic design at the Rietveld Academy in Amsterdam. He now lives and works in Barcelona.

M&CO

What the Hell
FUSE 8 Religion (1993) 152

M&Co used to be a multi-disciplinary, non-denominational design studio in New York City. From 1979 to 1993, M&Co produced graphic, industrial, film/video and environmental design for clients such as Talking Heads, Knoll, Chiat/Day, the 42nd Street Development Project and Benetton.

BRUCE MAU

Can We Imagine
FUSE 18 Secrets (2000) 328

RORY MCCARTNEY

Don't Listen, **commended**
FUSE Competition (2005) 350

RUSSELL MILLS

Metal
FUSE 9 Auto (1994) 168

Since graduating from the Royal College of Art in 1977 with an MA degree, Russell Mills has worked extensively in many areas, especially those related to the music industry. He has produced numerous record covers for amongst others Brian Eno, David Sylvian, Youssou N'Dour, etc. He has made many book covers, images for editorial, magazine and corporate bodies, stage sets and lighting designs for contemporary dance and rock musicians, video and environmental installations.

He has lectured in art colleges and architectural schools in Europe, America and Japan. His paintings have been exhibited in numerous solo and group shows in the U.K., U.S.A., Japan, Germany, France and Denmark. He currently lives and works near Ambleside in Cumbria, the English Lake District.

FRANÇOIS MOISSETTE

The Birth of a Nation, **winner**
FUSE Competition (2005) 343

François Moissette was born in 1972 in France. After training in communication and in graphic design, he worked at Michel Lepetitdidier (AGI), then for the Triways agency. Today he's responsible for graphic design at the Infinirouge agency in Metz. In parallel, he collaborates at Images d'écritures and creates greetings postal ufos with Lezorangesgivrées. Recently he designed a character for Building Letters (*Fleurons of Hope*) and a page in the 2005 Fontfont calendar for Xavier Dupré with whom he collaborates regularly.

MONITEURS

MMMteurs-Cyber/ MMMteurs-Real
FUSE 14 Cyber (1995) *250*

'Moniteurs' is based in Berlin. Since May 1994, Heike Nehl (31), Sibylle Schlaich (31) and Heidi Specker (32) have worked on corporate design projects, magazines and interface design for TV and online services, with a distinctive bias towards music. Moniteurs has designed typefaces for magazines such as *1000 Clubzine*, *Frontpage* and *SENSE*. Many of their corporate designs (E-Werk, the techno art exhibitions Chromapark '94 and '95, EarthBeats) are based on self-made typefaces.

VAUGHAN OLIVER

Currency
FUSE 9 Auto (1994) *164*

Born 1957. Studied Graphic Design, specialising in Illustration at Newcastle-Upon-Tyne under Terry Dowling, who exposed me to his photographs of East European shop-front typography. Touched but not fully comprehending, I was further inspired by the lettering on a Quay Brothers film poster, seen during their college visit. Otherwise missed the History of Typography lectures and was later left to furthering my interest through practical experience, designing drink labels at a packaging design company in London, and through an intuitive and eclectic taste. Today I'm a freelance art director/designer working in the music business, television, publishing and theatre, looking forward to my first interior design commission from France and a personal retrospective exhibition in Los Angeles in September.

This project has been my debut with digital technology (partially used) and I might even consider using it again in 1994.

NATALIJA NIKPALJ POLONDAK

***Monitoring*, commended**
FUSE Competition (2005) *351*

Name: Natalija Surname: Nikpalj Polondak. I was born in 1971, in Zagreb, Croatia. I graduated from the Academy of Fine Arts in Zagreb, in Applied Arts. Now I work in the same department as Assistant for Applied Arts. At the same time, I'm currently in the second year of a master's degree in ALU, Ljubljana, Slovenia, in the department of Visual Communications Design. My tutor is Prof. Ranko Novak. Subject: Space orientation systems with analysis of current situation. More precise: information system for orientation in the Adriatic, including safety signs, harbour access signs and nautical signalling for small tourist vessels. Last standalone exhibition I had was "Sign and logo", and currently I'm preparing for typography exhibition in October. I featured in group and standalone exhibitions, and also lead autonomous design projects. References: Hewlett Packard Croatia, Fujitsu Siemens Croatia, Ministry of Science of Croatia. From collaborations in particular I note Croatian Scientist project created with Boris Ljubièiæ.

JOHN RANDLE

***Mayaruler*, student bonus font**
FUSE 15 Cities (1995) *264*

LUCIENNE ROBERTS

equality/individuality/community
FUSE 19 Revolution (2003)

JUST VAN ROSSUM

Flixel
FUSE 2 Runes (1991) *50*

Just van Rossum (born 1966) studied at the Royal Academy for Fine and Applied Arts in The Hague from 1984 to 1988. Worked for a year at MetaDesign in Berlin, and is now a graphic designer in The Hague as well.

[With van Blokland] Their work involves typography, graphic design and illustration. In 1989, they started the LettError group as a small magazine about typography, which has since grown into a label for experimental typography and type design. "The *RandomFonts* (published by FSI) are perhaps the most shocking thing we've done so far, at least judging from the reaction we've had". The magazine itself will probably resume publication towards the end of this year.

WhatYouSee/WhatYouGet
FUSE 11 Pornography (1994) *204*

Independent designers from The Netherlands, Erik van Blokland and Just van Rossum graduated from the Royal Academy for Fine and Applied Arts in The Hague. After working separately together at various design companies in Europe and the U.S. they are now working separately together under the name of LettError (Pronounced Let-Error), still in The Hague. Projects: corporate design, animation and interactive thingies, illustration, animation, TV design, interface design for applications and online services, CD covers, music stuff, typography, magazine stuff. They are the creators of the recently-released *Kosmik*, "one of the world's leading *Flipper*™ fonts".

PABLO ROVALO

Santo Domingo
FUSE Superstition (1995) 238

Born 1969, Mexico City. Work experience: design of the Mexican Yellow Pages for Telmex, 1995. Head of design direction of the corporate image vicepresidency of Televisa from 1993–95. Corporate image and internal promotion for Cablevisión cable network in 1992, 1993 and 1994; corporate image and internal promotion for channels 2, 5 and 9 in Mexico in 1993 and 1994; digital and printed promotion for the 1994 World Cup transmissions in Mexico. Images for the Jesuit community in Puebla. Images for human rights at the University Iberoamericana. Dropped out of the graphic design department at the University Iberoamericana with only one subject to finish. Disenchanted, Pablo Rovalo abandoned his career in graphic design after eight years' freelance work in Mexico for a trip around Europe, Africa and Asia.

STEFAN SAGMEISTER

Bazillus
FUSE 19 Revolution (2003)

Designer: Eva Hueckmann

PETER SAVILLE

FloMotion
FUSE 5 Virtual (1992) 96

Peter Saville is a partner of Pentagram in London. After graduating from the faculty of Art and Design at Manchester Polytechnic in 1978, he was co-founder of Factory Communications. He has remained Factory's art director for 14 years, working particularly with New Order. Over this time he has worked with many major record companies; other clients include Yohji Yamamoto, Jil Sander, Whitechapel Art Gallery, Centre Georges Pompidou and The French Ministry of Culture.

ANNA-LISA SCHÖNECKER

White No Sugar
FUSE 17 Echo (1997) 314

DARREN SCOTT

***Berliner*, student bonus font**
FUSE 15 Cities (1995) 264

ERIK SPIEKERMANN

***Information Design: Who needs it, what is it, and the Catch 22?*, editorial text**
FUSE 3 (Dis)information (1992) 58

Grid
FUSE 3 (Dis)information (1992) 64

Insatiable curiosity, wanting to find out why things look the way they do, is what Erik Spiekermann gives as his motivation for experimenting with his first printing press at the age of twelve, studying Art History at university, designing typefaces and writing books about typography, as well as travelling the world as typographic evangelist. Though known as a writer and international authority on type, he frequently serves as a judge in design competitions and names designing complex information systems as his hobby. After seven years in London, Erik returned to Berlin in 1979 to set up MetaDesign, now a studio employing more than 25 designers. In 1989, he founded FontShop together with his wife, Joan.

SIMON STAINES

Trojan
FUSE 12 Propaganda (1994) 222

Is an art director at the recently-formed Research Studios and has worked with clients such as *Arena*, *The Face* and *Actuel* magazines, ORF and Premiere television channels, *The Guardian*, Closed and Fiorucci clothing companies, Agfa, Haus der Kulturen der Welt, and IKEA over the last seven years. He has just finished a project to create several interactive sequences for the forthcoming movies *Hackers* and *Judge Dredd*. He is also a director of the CD-ROM publishing company Digitalogue.

FRANCIS STEBBING

***Trinity*, student bonus font**
FUSE 14 Cyber (1995) 246

Shoe size 10, custard.

IAN SWIFT

Maze 91
FUSE 1 Invention (1991) 32

Studied Graphic Design at Manchester Polytechnic between 1983–86 before joining *The Face* and then *Arena*, for whom he became Art Director in 1990. Swifty currently runs his own studio in London, specialising in work for dance labels Talking Loud and SBK

Records. He has been design director of the quarterly jazz magazine *Straight No Chaser* since 1989.

PAUL SYCH

Box
FUSE 6 Codes (1992) *114*

I spent three years at the Ontario College of Art in Toronto, and because of my interest in jazz, I studied concurrently at York University, doing a Jazz Studies Program. Having left college, I worked for a number of design companies, most recently with Reactor. As senior Art Director, I began to explore and concentrate on type design – however, my work there was restricted by the need to maintain the 'look' that Reactor had already established for itself.

I felt there to be an ample opportunity in Toronto to develop my own look, or 'voice', hence the creation of Faith – a leap, as it were, into the unknown. The main emphasis is still on typography – a discipline that seems to be in decline in Canada. At the moment, Faith can count almost every major advertising agency in Canada amongst its clients: the campaigns we have worked on include Coca-Cola, General Motors, McDonald's, Letraset and IBM. My work has been featured in issues of *Print* magazine, *International Design*, *Step by Step*... It is possible to challenge even the most conservative of clients, and doing this has opened up many opportunities for me to provide a voice in Canada and elsewhere.

JAKE TILSON

httpwc Men Only
FUSE 18 Secrets (2000) *330*

TOMATO

Newcracks 13
FUSE Superstition (1995) *240*

Ten lines travelling in a similar direction, sometimes (but not always) crossing, and in their crossing, specifying if not creating events, and in the process laughing.

ALEX TYLEVICH

Cico Paco
FUSE 16 Genetics (1996) *290*

(b.1972, Minsk), U.S. resident. Graphic designer, artist, director working in a variety of media, including high-end computer animation and web design. Studied painting before coming to the United States in 1989; received BFA degree in graphic design from Minneapolis College of Art and Design in 1994. List of freelance clients includes Sega, Nike, Airwalk and ISEA (International Symposium on Electronic Art, Rotterdam, NL). Work has been featured on Canal+ and Television Española, and has received awards at SIGGRAPH'94, Prix Ars Electronica'95 and the American Center for Design 100 Show, among others. Recent projects include Electra'96 electronic art exhibition at the Henie-Onstad Kunstsenter, Norway and a Nike campaign for 1996 Summer Olympics in Atlanta, Georgia. Currently senior art director at Channel 1 TV station in Los Angeles.

GERARD UNGER

***Chocolate Runes*, editorial text**
FUSE 2 Runes (1991) *42*

D'coder
FUSE 2 Runes (1991) *46*

Gerard Unger was born in Arnhem, Holland, in 1942 and studied graphic design at the Rietveld Academy in Amsterdam, where he has been a part-time teacher since 1970. He worked in advertising with Wim Crouwel and Messrs. Joh. Enschedé en Zonen before going freelance in 1973. He has designed typefaces for the Amsterdam Metropolitan Railway, Joh. Enschedé en Zonen, Dr.-Ing, Rudolf Hell GmbH, Philips Data Systems, Océ, Bitstream and a set of special numerals for Dutch phonebooks. Amongst his recent type designs are *Swift*, *Bitstream Amerigo* and *Bitstream Oranda* for desktop publishing. Otherwise he works on the standard fare of any graphic designer, doing calendars, annual reports, postage stamps, routing systems, magazines etc. He also works as a typographic consultant, lectures extensively and writes for the trade press.

CHU UROZ

X–Pain
FUSE 8 Religion (1993) *154*

Born 30-01-61. In 1974, won 4 design awards for the magazine *SOLO MOTO*. Studied at the Barcelona School of Architecture before going on to study at the Elisava School of Industrial Design. In 1986 he joined Basi S.A. Lacoste. In 1986 he designed Armand Basi Barcelona. In 1987–88 he won 3 "LAUS" awards for the catalogues for the "Dinamo" and "Blue Moon" collections, plus a line of women's underwear. In 1989 he worked with architects. In 1992 he designed work for The Mediterranean Suite, performed by La Fura Dels Baus theatre company at the opening ceremony of the Barcelona Olympic Games, also designing the image for the human components of that work, as well as the design of the electronic imagery for the Olympic archer who lit the flame, commissioned by the ASICS company, and for the fibre-optic costumes for the Stadium Muses. He also designed the concept of raising the mascot 'Petra' for the Paralympics with an indoor trials motorbike, plus the design of the wheelchairs and the outfits for the carriers of the Paralympic Flag. He designed the clothes for the soprano, Virginia Perramon, and the centre stage for the opening ceremony in association with Naomi Campano. He art directed the Bigas Luna film *Jamon, Jamon* (Ham, Ham), once again with Naomi Campano; the film was awarded the Silver Lion at the Venice Film Festival. In 1993, Campano and Uroz worked with Bigas Luna on his new film, *Huevos De Oro* (Golden Eggs).

At the present time, Uroz is working on a convertible motorbike suggested by the Suzuki Company (Japan).

RICK VALICENTI

Uck N Pretty
FUSE 4 Exuberance (1992) *84*

Rick Valicenti lives and works in Chicago. He is principal and principle of Thirst, a group devoted to the creation of Art with Function. Thirst clientele vary in their respective businesses, but all share a deep commitment to design's ability to make a difference.

RICK VERMEULEN

Morsig
FUSE 6 Codes (1992) *118*

Briefly... Born 1950. Studied design at the College of Fine Arts in Rotterdam from 1967–72. In-house designer at publishers Bert Bakker in Amsterdam from 1975 until 1977. In 1979, co-founded *Hard Werken* magazine, and since 1981, one of the partners along with Gerard Hadders, Willem Kars, Tom van den Haspel and Bart Jan Jansen.

The design company evolved out of the magazine to become a multi-disciplinary organisation working within the areas of corporate, literature, packaging and interior design, with a full-time staff of fifteen. My main work is for print-catalogues for museums, book jackets, magazine and book design, architectural monographs, posters, postage stamps, etc. Hard Werken works on an international level and has become known for its outspoken attitude to the design industry. Hard Werken designers have lectured at educational institutions in Europe and the United States – the Rietveld Academy in Amsterdam. Les Ateliers Paris, Cranbrook Academy of Art, Cal Arts in LA, amongst others.

Big Eyed Beans
FUSE 14 Cyber (1995) *252*

Born 1950. Studied design at the College of Fine Arts in Rotterdam from 1967–72. In-house designer at publishers Bert Bakker in Amsterdam from 1975 until 1977, co-founded *Hard Werken* magazine in 1979, and since 1981 has been one of the partners. Between 1993–95 was in charge of the Hard Werken L.A. desk, Los Angeles. Currently working with Inizio/Hard Werken in Amsterdam. The design company evolved out of the magazine to become a multi-disciplinary organisation. My work is concerned mainly with print. From 1980 onwards I have lectured and taught at various educational institutions and design conferences in Europe and the United States.

VOLCANO TYPE

Mr. J. Smith, **bonus font**
FUSE Competition (2005) *346*

No. 1:
Mr. J. Smith alias Nikolai Renger

1.89 m, blond hair, blue eyes

He was born in 1982 in Karlsruhe and refused to go into military service. Right now he would like to study design. N.R. is the youngest of the crew and designed the faces of this font. Dangerous.

No. 2:
Mr. J. Smith alias Ulrich Weiß

1.72 m, black hair, brown eyes

He is co-leader of MAGMA [Büro für Gestaltung]. After his studies in Pforzheim he worked as art-director in Baden-Baden for JG & Partners. He is married and has two kids. He designed the poster of this font. Dangerous sniper.

No. 3:
Mr. J. Smith alias Lars Harmsen

1.93 m, blond hair, green-brown eyes, big scar on his left leg

He is wanted for being one of the leaders of MAGMA [Büro für Gestaltung]. Since he was 12 years old he has lived in Karlsruhe. As a child his parents took him to Chicago and Geneva. After his studies of graphic-design in Pforzheim and Basel he founded MAGMA. He conceived this font. Aggressive, very fast. Extremely dangerous.

No. 4:
Mr. J. Smith alias Boris Kahl

1.75 m, brown hair, green eyes

This 30-year-old designer has worked with MAGMA since 2001 and designed over 30 fonts for MAGMA's font-label VOLCANO-TYPE, most of them published in the book *VERSUS*. He digitised this font. Very athletic, close-combat adept.

PETRA WALDEYER

***Kwarthel*, student bonus font**
FUSE Superstition (1995) *230*

WD+RU

Pussy Galore
FUSE 12 Propaganda (1994) *224*

'WD+RU' – Women's Design + Research Unit – is a new design initiative set up by Siân Cook, Liz McQuiston and Teal Triggs, based at Ravensbourne College of Design and Communication.

Cook is a consultant designer for Me Company, amongst others; McQuiston is the author of the recently published *Graphic Agitation*; Triggs is the editor of the upcoming Batsford publication, *Communicating Design*.

MARTIN WENZEL

InTegel
FUSE 3 (Dis)information (1992) *66*

Was born in Berlin on 1969. After school, he trained to be a pastry cook but quit six months later. His education in type came at City-Satz in Berlin, where he started working in 1986. With five years' experience on Apple Macintosh, in 1989 he designed the typeface *Marten*, published by FontShop in 1991.

Schirft
FUSE 6 Codes (1992) *116*

Born on the 6th of June (1969) in Berlin. Still living there. 2 years experience in digital typographic design. Has designed several faces, including *Marten* for FontShop International.

BRETT WICKENS

Crux95
FUSE 14 Cyber (1995) *254*

Is an art director with Frankfurt Balkind Partners in Los Angeles. He designs publicity campaigns for Hollywood studios, ad campaigns for clients including Nike, and interactive products such as the forthcoming United Nations CD-ROM.

Prior to joining Pentagram Design in London as an associate partner in 1990, Brett was a partner in Peter Saville Associates for nine years. His expertise in design technology eventually led him to LA in 1993 to pursue his interest in the convergence of entertainment, information and technology. He is contributing design technology editor for *Eye* magazine and is currently visiting teacher of interactive graphics at the California Institute of the Arts in Valencia, California.

BOB WILKINSON

equality/individuality/community
FUSE 19 Revolution (2003)

MARINA WILLER

***Babel*, student bonus font**
FUSE Superstition (1995) *230*

CORNEL WINDLIN

Moonbase Alpha
FUSE 3 (Dis)information (1992) *68*

Was born in Switzerland in the early mid-Sixties. First personal heroes – Bernhard Russi and Johan Cruyff; first record bought – SOS by Abba. Too many schools, or not enough of them: one was the Schule für Gestaltung in Lucerne. Later went to England to work for Neville Brody. Got bored and left to become art editor at *The Face* magazine. Got bored again and left to work on his own in London. Gets bored easily. Tends to work late at night. Reads papers. Travels by Tube. Misses his girlfriend. Currently working on *Baader Meinhof*, an anti-imperialistic typeface with an inbuilt anti-alienation-device™ (Patent Pending). Plans a solo exhibition in an out-of-town supermarket to coincide with the publication of *The Corporate Cornel Windlin*.

Mogidischu
FUSE 7 Crash (1993) *136*

Born in Switzerland in 1964, where he grew up on an unhealthy diet of "understanding and caring Catholicism" and, like most middle-Europeans, very dodgy pop music and outdated afternoon TV shows: Daktari, Skippy, Flipper and the Brady Bunch. Does anyone remember Arpad, the Gipsy?

He studied graphic design and visual communication at the Schüle für Gestaltung in Lucerne, where he met Hans-Rudolf Lutz, whom he describes as "the only good teacher I have ever known in my life".

In 1987 he started to work with Neville Brody, and moved to England a year later to join his studio on a permanent basis. Eager to learn about magazine design, he left the Brody Bunch to work for *The Face* magazine in 1990. A year later he set up his own studio and has since been living and working as a freelance art director/designer in London and Zürich.

Robotnik
FUSE 10 Freeform (1994) *190*

After 5 years in London working for, amongst others, Neville Brody

Studios and *The Face*, I am currently running my own studio in Zürich. Recently I have done work for Peter Gabriel, NTT Data Corporation, Museum für Gestaltung Zürich and Kunsthaus Zürich.

JON WOZENCROFT

Why FUSE?, **editorial text**
FUSE 1 Invention (1991) *20*

Wind Blasted Trees: A Short History of Runes, **editorial text**
FUSE 2 Runes (1991) *34*

Point to Line and Plane..., **editorial text**
FUSE 3 (Dis)information (1992) *52*

The Great Escape, **editorial text**
FUSE 5 Virtual (1992) *86*

It may be wrapped, but will it warp...?, **editorial text**
FUSE 6 Codes (1992) *104*

The Fast Lane, **editorial text**
FUSE 6 Codes (1992) *108*

Pandemonium, **editorial text**
FUSE 7 Crash (1993) *120*

Astronomy Dominé/Scramble!, **editorial text**
FUSE 8 Religion (1993) *138*

Auto Focus, **editorial text**
FUSE 9 Auto (1994) *156*

Freeform: A Trojan Horse, **editorial text**
FUSE 10 Freeform (1994) *172*

Restart
FUSE 10 Freeform (1994) *180*

Extratransubstantiationism, **editorial text**
FUSE 11 Pornography (1994) *192*

An Extra Zero (Careless Type Costs Lives), **editorial text**
FUSE 12 Propaganda (1994) *208*

We Live In Hope, **editorial text**
FUSE Superstition (1995) *226*

2@odds.com, **editorial text**
FUSE 14 Cyber (1995) *242*

Optical Illusions, **editorial text**
FUSE 15 Cities (1995) *258*

Trace Elements, **editorial text**
FUSE 16 Genetics (1996) *276*

Condition
FUSE 16 Genetics (1996) *296*

Echoes, **editorial text**
FUSE 17 Echo (1997) *298*

Fit in Window: 3 short takes on interactivity, **editorial text**
FUSE 18 Secrets (2000) *316*

IAN WRIGHT

Hand Job
FUSE 11 Pornography (1994) *206*

Has worked as an illustrator for over 15 years. He has produced record sleeves for artists as diverse as Madness (in the early '80s) and the Talking Loud label (in the early '90s). His work is regularly seen in *Esquire* and *Straight No Chaser* magazine. He is best known for his use of hi-tech equipment: "I'm fascinated by fax machines, photocopiers, digital scanners, the Paintbox... They are designed to produce slick, high-quality results, but it excites me to use them in the most inappropriate way. I might start with a life drawing, and then process it any number of ways – what I end up with is very low-tech, if not no-tech." He reads "tons of American crime novels", is a reggae fanatic and a compulsive record buyer. A collection of his portrait works, *Headcase*, has recently been published in Japan.

XPLICIT FFM

Synaesthesis
FUSE 14 Cyber (1995) *256*

Alexander Branczyk (*1958) and Thomas Nagel (*1962) are the founders of xplicit ffm, based in Frankfurt. Both studied Visual Communication at the Hochschule für Gestaltung in Offenbach. Their careers have run in parallel – after graduating, they moved to Berlin joined MetaDesign, worked for FontShop, Berthold, Zanders and the public transport authorities of Potsdam and Berlin.

Branczyk lives in planes and trains between Frankfurt, Berlin and Munich. In '92 he became art director of the techno-house magazine *Frontpage*, which became a forum for experimental layout and type design. He also art directs *SENSE* and *Camel Silver Pages*, both of them related to the German techno scene.

Nagel lives in Frankfurt, where he works for Linotype-Hell, the clubwear label Bad & Mad, the mail-order house Topdeq and other clients mainly in the print sector. In '94 Branczyk and Nagel started to publish their experimental font collection *Face2Face* featuring more than 100 fonts that challenge possibilities of legibility and PostScript!

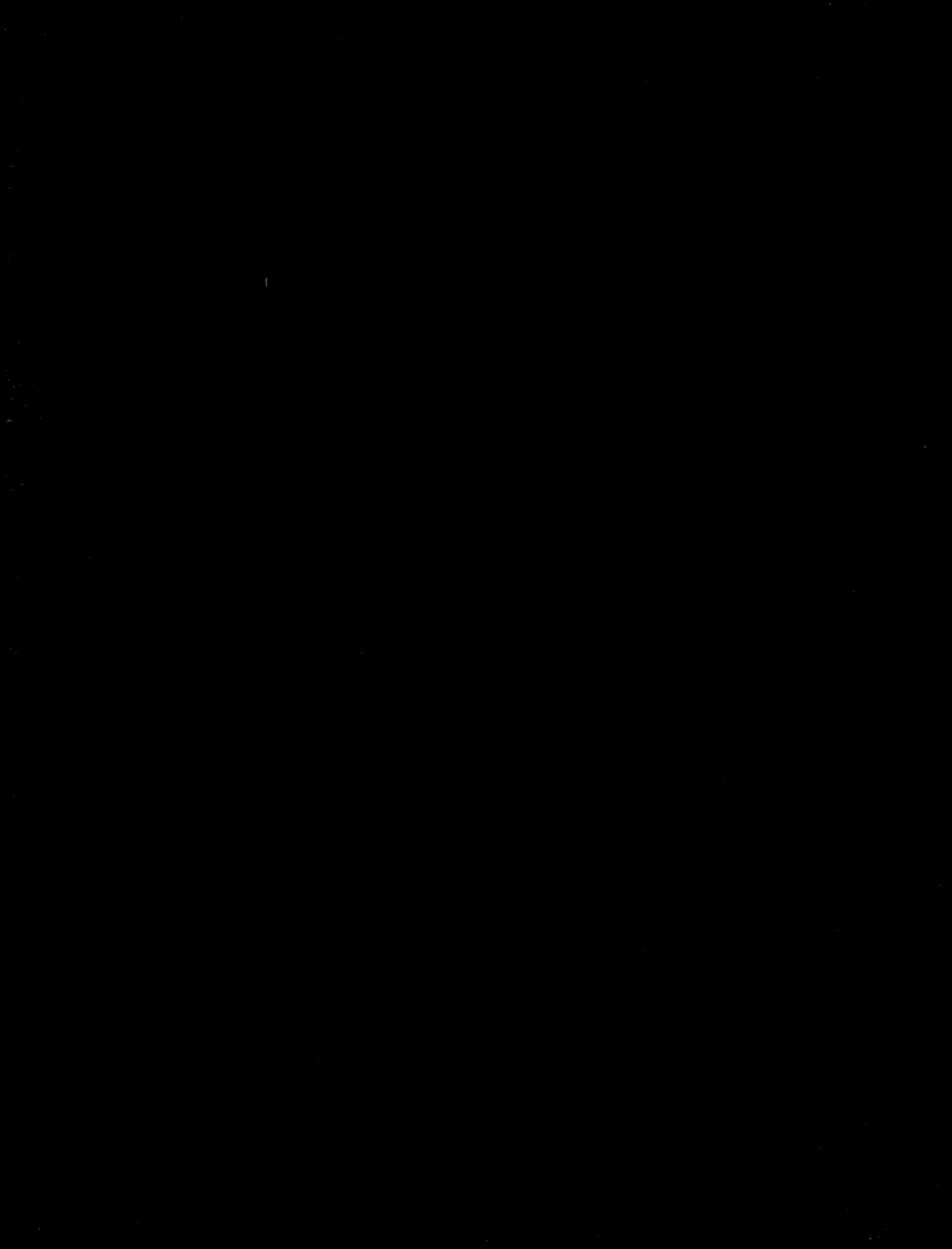

Translations

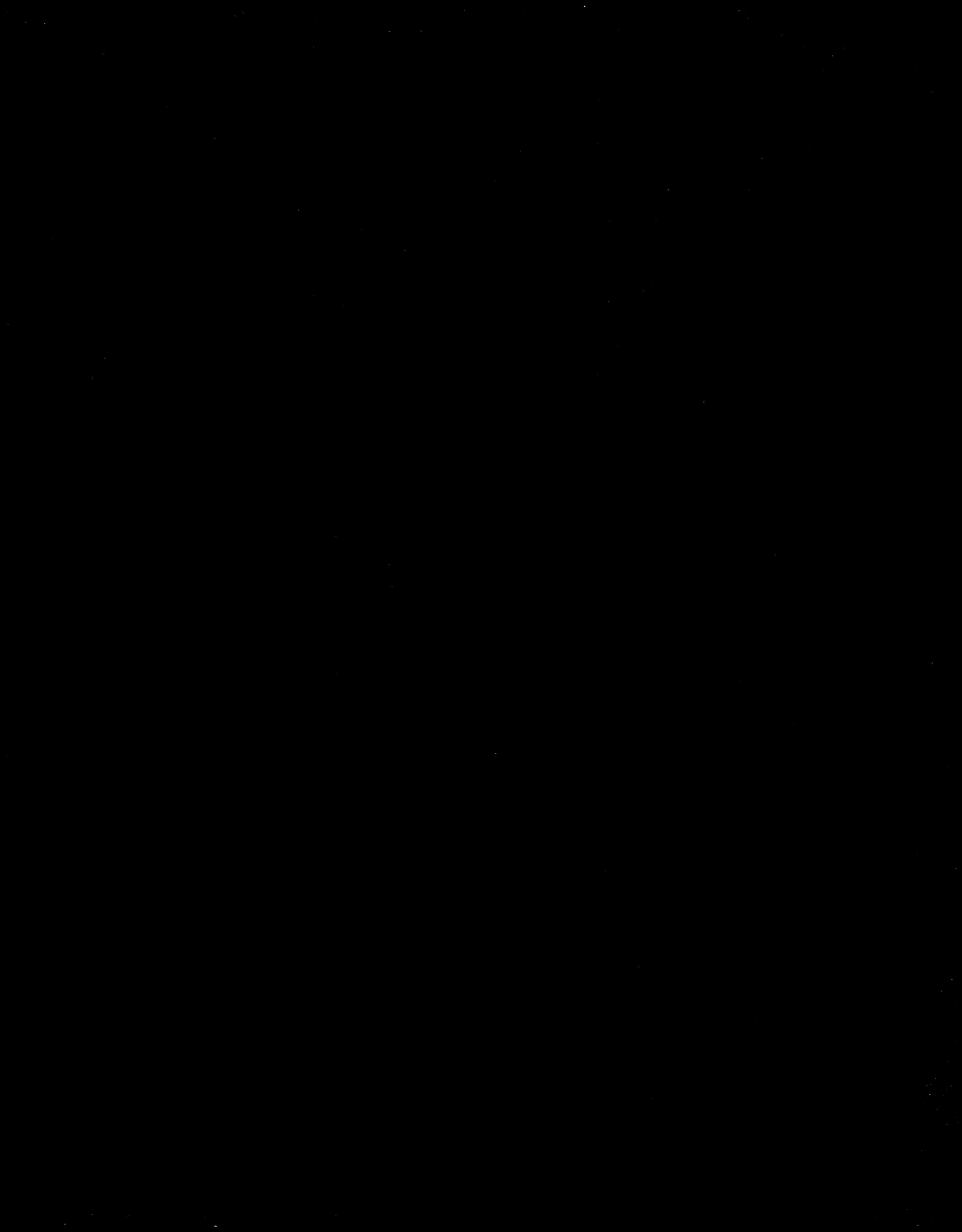

DEUTSCH

Was ist FUSE?

Über dieses Buch

FUSE 1-20 ist eine Anthologie des FUSE-Projekts seit Erscheinen der ersten Ausgabe 1991.

Zum ersten Mal werden hier alle Ausgaben von FUSE versammelt und gemeinsam als eine Art visuelles und historisches Nachschlagewerk veröffentlicht. Beschränkte Auflagen, überaltete Techniken und eine 20-jährige Software-Entwicklung führten dazu, dass FUSE bis jetzt noch nie in ganzer Vollständigkeit vorlag.

Wir beschlossen, die einzelnen Ausgaben so zu reproduzieren, wie sie bei Ersterscheinung aussahen, und aus diesem Grund ist das Buch in zwei Abschnitte geteilt. Teil 1 umfasst die FUSE-Ausgaben 1 bis 18. Die redaktionellen Essays und Beschreibungen der Schriften folgen detailgenau den Texten, wie sie auf den ursprünglichen Postern erschienen sind. Gewisse Abweichungen mussten vorgenommen werden und führen die sich verändernden Versionen bei DTP-Standards beispielhaft vor Augen.

Die FUSE-Ausgaben 19 und 20 sind dem Buch als Poster beigelegt, die Fonts und der redaktionelle Inhalt lassen sich online mit der in der Box enthaltenen Key Card downloaden.

Zu diesem Abschnitt

In der zweiten Hälfte des Buchs wird eine kleine Auswahl der Aktivitäten vorgestellt, die das FUSE-Projekt im Lauf seiner gut 20-jährigen Geschichte unterstützt hat. Die Konferenzen zeigen, an welchen internationalen kritischen Diskussionen sich FUSE beteiligte, während die Wettbewerbe die Bedeutung von FUSE für zeitgenössische und aufstrebende Grafiker in dieser Zeit verdeutlichen.

Zudem finden sich in diesem letzten Abschnitt die Biografien, die die beitragenden Autoren und Grafiker für die jeweiligen Ausgaben eingereicht hatten. Diese Angaben erfüllen zwei Zwecke: Zum einen dienen sie als Verzeichnis, zum anderen als Timeline der Grafiker, deren Schriften FUSE zum wegweisenden typografischen Medium seiner Zeit gemacht haben.

FUSE wurde 1990 gegründet und ist dem Augenschein nach ein vierteljährlich erscheinendes Magazin, in London hergestellt und zunächst von FontShop International verlegt. Jede Ausgabe besteht aus einem einfachen Kartonumschlag, der neben fünf gedruckten Plakaten auch eine Diskette bzw. CD mit vier oder mehr Schriften enthält. Jede Ausgabe befasst sich mit einem bestimmten Thema, das mit der einen oder anderen Tendenz in der Kommunikationswissenschaft und deren Konsequenzen zu tun hat. Vier Grafiker, sowohl aus dem Druckgewerbe als auch aus anderen Bereichen, gestalten dazu eine Schrift. Jeder Grafiker veranschaulicht deren kreative Anwendung an Hand eines Plakats oder einer Animation. Die vier Entwürfe begleiten ein Editorial sowie eine unbestimmte Zahl zusätzlicher Schriften.

Das ist die nüchterne Beschreibung des haptischen Produkts namens FUSE. Doch im Grunde sagt sie nichts über FUSE aus.

Letztlich versteht sich FUSE als Forschungsprogramm. Es ist ein Labor, ein Spielplatz, auf dem Fachleute und Laien mit den visuellen Sprachformen unseres täglichen Gebrauchs experimentieren können. In gewisser Hinsicht funktioniert FUSE vor allem als Katalysator. Jede Ausgabe ist ein Weißbuch, ein Forschungsbericht von neuen Expeditionen.

Ausgangspunkt ist das Konzept, dass jede Sprache unentwegt im Wandel begriffen, dass sie nicht fixiert ist, und dass digitale Vertriebssysteme uns ermöglichen, Ideen zu verbreiten, die insbesondere in ihrer visuellen Form veränderlich sind.

Aus der Eröffnungsrede Neville Brodys bei FUSE98, San Francisco (FORTSETZUNG AUF SEITE 358)

20 Jahre, 20 Ausgaben, 100 gedruckte Plakate, 114 Schriften!

Seit seiner Gründung vor 21 Jahren ist FUSE ein Schauplatz für Experimente, ein Gedanken- und Sprachlabor, in dem Diskussionen über sehr vielschichtige Themen eine Form innerhalb der Form finden sollen, innerhalb genau der Strukturen, in die wir unsere Systeme zur Verbreitung von Ausdruck und Information einbinden. Dieser Raum, der stets im Fluss ist und ständig zwischen Vertrautheit und Abstraktion mäandert, macht es möglich, dass durch intensives Hinterfragen und Aufgliedern unserer herkömmlichen Kommunikationswerkzeuge und -strukturen neue visuelle Sprachmuster entstehen. Eine Gesellschaft ist Form im Fluss und verlangt laufend nach neuen, evolutionären Sprachsystemen, die alle Versuche unterminieren, den Status quo hypnotisch erstarren zu lassen. Anti = Materie.

In einer Welt, in der durchgängig Mittelmaß und Konzernhörigkeit herrschen, können sich neue Blüten der Exzentrik nur in dunklen Nischen entfalten. FUSE ist ein solcher Riss in der Mauer, eine genetische Mutation, aus der neue Lebensformen entspringen können. Unsere Sprache bestimmt, was wir sind, und unser Denken wird durch unsere Sprachen beschränkt. Nur wenn diese erweitert werden, können wir auch die Grenzen des uns Möglichen erweitern. Was als trotzige, explosive Auseinandersetzung mit der typografischen Sprache begann – möglich allein dank der digitalen Technik –, bildete später einen differenzierteren, umfassenderen Anspruch heraus.

Die 21 Jahre mit FUSE kommen mir vor wie ein unvermittelter Ausbruch kreativer Fragmente. Manche Schriften waren vandalistisch, manche dekorativ, manche verspielt. Manche waren investigativ, manche architektonisch und manche der reinste Überschwang. Alle waren sie für sich sowohl Frage als auch Möglichkeit, emotiv oder auch formalistisch, und sie alle gewährten neue Blicke in neue Räume, die durch neue Sprachen eröffnet worden sind. Neue Formen wurden in neuen Strukturen ausgerichtet, die neue Gedanken ermöglichten. Viele waren ein Erfolg, einige scheiterten, und das Experiment geht weiter. Nie zuvor war FUSE derart relevant und derart notwendig.

Einleitung 1

Dieser Aspekt des „Heiligen“ mag deshalb als heilig empfunden werden, weil es der modernen Welt offenbar an einem Äquivalent mangelt. Das ist ein Rückschritt. Stimmt es, dass wir Entkörperlichung erleben, Entfremdung, einen psychischen Machtverlust … das langsame Verschwinden der Poesie? Das würden nur wenige zugeben, denn in der Raumfähre der zeitgenössischen Kommunikation käme das der Häresie gleich.

FUSE 1-20: Der Kreis und das Quadrat Jon Wozencroft

Der Unterschied zwischen Analog und Digital wird gemeinhin mit einem Verweis auf Formatwechsel erklärt – von Vinyl zu CD, von Film und VHS zu DVD, in neuester Zeit von Taschenbuch zu Kindle. Dahinter verbirgt sich allerdings eine ganz grundsätzliche Veränderung in der Reproduktion und Mustergenerierung. Das erklärt, weshalb die Typografie ein wesentliches Umfeld geworden ist, um diese Fragen zu erläutern.

Betrachten wir für den Anfang, was mit dem Buchstaben O passiert ist. In *Garamond* folgen die Rundung und das harmonische Gefüge einer jahrhundertelangen Entwicklung. Digital gedruckt gaukelt eine Ansammlung von Quadraten/Pixeln dem Auge vor, es sehe keine Pixel ... es hat den Anschein eines Os, ist aber keines. Das digitale *Garamond*-O hat einen völlig anderen Aufbau und gibt bloß vor, wie der Buchstabe O auszusehen. Schuld ist die serifenlose Vorgängerschrift, aus der binnen vierzig Jahren *Helvetica* und *Univers* geworden sind. Deren Os bilden perfekte Kreise, die nur darauf warten, eine Delle abzubekommen.

Digitale Systeme beruhen zu einem großen Maß auf optischer Illusion. Einer Art Magie, wiewohl zum falschen Zweck eingesetzt. Im Bereich des Fantastischen gehört es heute zum Alltag, dass wir eine Sache erkennen, obwohl wir eigentlich etwas anderes sehen. Diese Täuschung erstreckt sich auf immer mehr Bereiche und ist der Ursprung unserer Wahrnehmungsmalaise. Instinktiv glauben wir gar nichts mehr. Wie könnten wir auch – außer den Frommen? Für die anderen unter uns sollte die Welt am 21. Mai 2011 untergegangen sein, aber das ist sie nicht. Wir leben in der Welt endloser Veränderung.

„Die Reproduktionstechnik, so ließe sich allgemein formulieren, löst das Reproduzierte aus dem Bereich der Tradition ab.“[1]

Nachdem das erste *Graphic Language*-Buch erschienen war, verbrachte ich 1989/90 über ein Jahr damit, für den von uns angedachten Folgeband *The Death of Typography* zu recherchieren und Konzepte zu schreiben. Ausgangspunkt dafür war eine Seite, die Brody 1986 für das Projekt Touch *Ritual* entworfen hatte. Wir verstanden das neue Buch auch als flammende Replik auf die Minuten des Ruhms, die unser Studio 1988, nach dem Jahr mit *Graphic Language* und der Ausstellung im Victoria & Albert Museum, kurzzeitig genossen hatte. In den dazwischenliegenden Monaten hatten wir mit dem PC und dem Nadeldrucker experimentiert und deren Möglichkeiten ausgelotet, die uns aber nicht überzeugten. Ich halte es immer noch für einen höchst merkwürdigen Zufall, dass die Segnungen des Computers zuerst auf uns Gebrauchsgrafiker herabkamen und dann erst auf Filmemacher, Musiker und bildende Künstler.

Wir interessierten uns für Druckverarbeitung. Wir bewegten uns zwischen typografischen Büchern und dem Fotokopierer, zwischen Millimeterpapier und Rotring, wir pressten typografische Formen in mehr oder minder gequälte Konturen. Das Projekt wurde für uns zur Leidenschaft. Brody sprach in Interviews über *The Death of Typography*, während ich in der Hampstead Heath unter einem Baum saß und mich in der Geschichte und Philosophie nach Ideen umtat, insbesondere in den Kommunikationsstrategien des Zweiten Weltkriegs: Da klang nämlich, von Goebbels bis zu Churchills *Black Propaganda*, schon vieles an, was heute in unserer Kultur passiert.

Ich habe gerade „Death of Typography“ gegoogelt. Der Begriff kommt häufig vor, und natürlich findet sich kein einziger Hinweis auf die Version von 1986, was nur poetische Gerechtigkeit ist. Die wirkliche Herausforderung bestand darin, ein Update von Walter Benjamins wegweisendem *Kunstwerk im*

Zeitalter seiner technischen Reproduzierbarkeit zu formen. Wenn man allerdings „technische Reproduzierbarkeit“ durch „digitale Erfahrung“ ersetzt, kommt man zu dem Schluss, dass das eine schier unlösbar Aufgabe ist angesichts des Tempos, mit dem sich Kommunikationssysteme verändern.

Die digitale Typografie kam uns nach dem, was wir von Hand gemacht hatten, wie ein Rückschritt vor, und es dauerte Monate, bis uns aufging, wie wir sie in eine andere Dimension heben konnten. Und dann bekam die Arbeit plötzlich neuen Impetus durch die Frage, wie visuelle Sprache überhaupt zu verstehen sei.

Manche nahmen den Titel *Death of Typography* für bare Münze und fragten wie Idioten in Texten von T.S. Eliot: „Was meint ihr damit?“ Wir hatten nie eine schlagfertige Antwort parat. Gleichzeitig war immer häufiger vom papierlosen Büro die Rede, vom Ende des Buchs und von virtueller Realität. Gerade war die erste Abhandlung über Nanotechnologie erschienen[2], ganz zu schweigen von *The End of History* und *A Thousand Plateaus.*[3]

Zu der Zeit artete die Theorienflut in eine Überschwemmung aus, aber die hatte ebensoviel mit den Folgen des Zweiten Weltkriegs zu tun wie mit dem Weg in die digitale Zukunft. Adorno und Warhol hätten den Begriff „Rhizom“ verstanden, sie verwendeten ihn nur nicht.

Das gedruckte Wort, das bislang in die Zukunft geschickt worden war, konnte auf einmal in Echtzeit gesendet werden. Das Faxgerät, 1987 auf die Welt gekommen, war ein Kind der Drucktechnik und der Digitalität/Telefonie. Es war mehr als ein Telegramm und so unmittelbar wie das Fernsehen.

Es gab keine E-Mail und, abgesehen vom lokalen JANET-System, das die akademische Zunft verwendete, kein Internet. Dem Fax schien die Zukunft zu gehören – und was ist aus ihm geworden?

Trotzdem, das Fax war ein Katalysator: hitzeempfindliches Papier, eckige Formen wie beim früheren Tiefdruckverfahren, die beim Kontakt mit dem Papier unscharf wurden und in der Vergrößerung eine neue Ästhetik verführerischer Fragmentierung annahmen, so weichgezeichnet, wie die heutige Bilderwelt hart und leblos ist.

FUSE ist eine untergegangene Erzählung aus dieser wilden Zeit, wenn „you know something is happening but you don't know what it is“, um Bob Dylan zu zitieren.

Eines versuchten wir bei diesem Projekt immer wieder durchzusetzen, nämlich, dass es ein Forum für Diskussionen wäre, und wir hofften auf lebhafte Debatten. Die wurden unweigerlich abgebrochen, Perspektiven waren nicht möglich – bis heute. Von den Traditionalisten, die nie verstanden, dass wir uns der Tradition sehr wohl bewusst waren, kam Kritik. Was herrschte, war das reinste Chaos. In der Zeit, in der wir FUSE tatsächlich herausbrachten, war alles irgendwie immer außer Kontrolle, gab es immer Panik in letzter Minute.

Der Hase wurde zu einer Schildkröte. Es stimmte nicht mehr, dass „alle Wege nach Rom führen.“ Die Linien zum Cyberspace drehen sich im Kreis.

„Die Grenze gibt dem Grenzenlosen Form.“[4]

In älteren Zivilisationen schätzten die Menschen den Kreis mehr als das Quadrat. Es gab sogar einen quadratischen Kreis: Er bestand aus der harmonischen Anordnung von Maß und Zahl – das zumindest könnte man einer Analyse der Mathematik und der heiligen Geometrie entnehmen, die zum Goldenen Schnitt führte und zur pythagoreischen Vorstellung einer kosmischen Harmonie. Das alles steht den Grafikern nach wie vor zu Gebote, der modernen Welt mit metrischen Maßen und DIN-Vorgaben zum Trotz. „Deswegen versuchten die Menschen jener Zeit auch, derartige Harmonien im Muster ihres Alltags umzusetzen, wodurch sie das Leben zur Kunst erhoben.“[5] Tatsächlich haben nur wenige heutige Grafiker eine Ahnung vom Goldenen Schnitt, und wie sollten sie auch, wenn er nicht mehr zum Handwerkszeug eines jeden Grundkurses gehört?

Überall auf den Britischen Inseln kann man Steinkreise besichtigen, die uns vor Augen führen, was Menschen früher in ihrer Beziehung zu Formen als

Unser Denken ist heute um keinen Deut digitaler als vor zwanzig Jahren. Das heißt, es geht weniger um Intuition als vielmehr um Rechenleistung und um Reichweite, die man über Netzwerke, Facebook und Twitter erreicht, wo aber trotz der angeblich so mühelosen Vernetzung alles eher beiläufig und oberflächlich geworden ist.

strahlend und fortschrittlich empfunden haben. Astronomie, astrale Projektionen, Rituale – derartige Konzepte deuten darauf hin, dass Intuition und Divination überlebensnotwendige Fähigkeiten waren. „Jeder Steinkreis hatte eine Affinität zu einem bestimmten Teil des menschlichen Körpers ... und [dieses Konzept] stellt ein gemeinsames Merkmal des poetischen Ausdrucks dar.“ [6]

Dieser Aspekt des „Heiligen“ mag deshalb als heilig empfunden werden, weil es der modernen Welt offenbar an einem Äquivalent mangelt. Das ist ein Rückschritt. Stimmt es, dass wir Entkörperlichung erleben, Entfremdung, einen psychischen Machtverlust ... das langsame Verschwinden der Poesie? Das würden nur wenige zugeben, denn in der Raumfähre der zeitgenössischen Kommunikation käme das der Häresie gleich. Ein Pixel kann nie mehr sein als ein bloßer Tropfen im Ozean, doch er lässt Kräusel auf dem Wasser entstehen, die Kreise nach sich ziehen. Die beste Möglichkeit, um im Zustand des steten Flusses zu leben, haben wir noch nicht gefunden.

Dieser recht neue Übergang vom Kreis zum Quadrat ist als Wendepunkt bezüglich der „Zukunft“ nicht minder folgenschwer als die Römer es für das frühe Britannien waren. Er stellt alles in Frage, was folgt, und besitzt die verblüffende, bislang unbekannte Fähigkeit, von sich selbst ertränkt zu werden, ohne je tatsächlich unterzugehen. Wir erleben weniger das Ende der Geschichte als vielmehr den Anfang eines ewigen Wandels. Fakten und Zahlen werden im nie versiegenden Dialog zwischen der Realität und ihren Fiktionen verändert.

Die alten Briten müssen recht kurzsichtig gewesen sein, wenn man bedenkt, wie mühelos die römischen Eindringlinge anno 43 n. Chr. in Britannien quadratische Formen verwenden konnten, um die Stammeshäuptlinge und Clans in der Schlacht mit ihrer Schildkrötenformation und in Friedenszeiten mit ihren quadratischen Plätzen und schnurgeraden Straßen zu erobern ... oder auch weitsichtig angesichts dessen, was sich Jahrtausende später entwickeln sollte. Die Römer bauten ihre Straßen auf den bestehenden „Geraden“, die auf prähistorische Art als Verbindung zwischen den heiligen Stätten gezogen worden waren.

Deutsch

Dabei gaben sie das Muster für Pferd und Wagen vor, für die Eisenbahn, für den Asphalt, wo das Alte das Neue in seiner neuesten Form ersticken konnte – Kraft wird verwässert –, doch die Kraft ist nach wie vor da, versucht mit aller Macht durch die Risse in den Pflastersteinen nach oben zu dringen.

In Vor-PC-Zeiten nahm bis auf die wenigen Auserwählten niemand leichtfertig Gestaltungswerkzeuge in die Hand. Der PC veränderte alles, und zwar in einem Maße, wie es Schreibmaschine und Elektrogitarre einst zwar verheißen, aber nie erfüllt hatten. Unser Denken ist heute um keinen Deut digitaler als vor zwanzig Jahren. Das heißt, es geht weniger um Intuition als vielmehr um Rechenleistung und um Reichweite, die man über Netzwerke, Facebook und Twitter erreicht, wo aber trotz der angeblich so mühelosen Vernetzung alles eher beiläufig und oberflächlich geworden ist.

Eine Kultur der Pixel und der abgeschnittenen Ecken ist ein sehr anderes Konzept als das römische Ideal von quadratischen Marktplätzen, dem Forum, und selbst als das der Gartenstädte der Nachkriegsmoderne. Auch sie wurden noch im großen Maßstab angelegt, sie waren für jeden Bürger sichtbar, sie hatten einen praktischen Nutzen und waren die Verheißung einer hoffnungsvollen Zukunft. Unser heutiges gepixeltes Universum erinnert eher an einen Fluchtpunkt, nach dem jeder auf seine Art sucht, wie auch immer er sich durch die Antimaterie vortastet.

1990, als wir mit FUSE begannen, hatten wir in Tokio ein Gespräch: Tokio ist für das Londoner Empfinden eine Megastadt des Wahnsinns, damals nicht inder dem Geschwindigkeitsrausch erlegen als heute:) – der Grad an Informationssurrealismus: ein atemberaubendes Wunderland dessen, was passierte und was später auf dem Bildschirm erscheinen konnte. Man konnte sehen, wie Geschwindigkeit und Zeit sich zuneigten. Später fand ich heraus, dass dieses Phänomen viel mit den Benzolabgasen zu tun hat. Die Lösung für unsere Zusammenarbeit bestand darin, parallel zu arbeiten, und FUSE war ein Musterbeispiel dafür.

FUSE 1 war im Grunde ein Schlag vor den Latz des Universums. Die Ausgabe ist naiv, wie Manifeste es gemeinhin sind. Aber ab FUSE 2 *RUNES* taten wir unser Bestes, unsere Arbeit zu etwas Dauerhafterem als nur einer Zeitschrift zu gestalten. Aber wir schossen ein Eigentor. Wir wollten die Exemplare in regelmäßigen Abständen herausbringen, aber das wurde sehr bald undurchführbar, und letztlich bedeutet das Vermächtnis von FUSE, dass es immer noch ein „Work in Progress" ist.

Immer hatten wir irgendein Problem ... wen wir fragen sollten ... wir wollten gerne auch Grafikerinnen engagieren ... Wo das alles hinführte, sehen Sie an FUSE 3/9/12. Das mag zwar nach Party aussehen, aber so war es, FUSE herauszubringen. Es war schwierig, über ein paar treue Verbündete hinaus Leute zu überreden, etwas für uns zu machen, und (das werden Sie jetzt nicht glauben) ziemlich viele der hier vertretenen Grafiker lehnten zuerst dankend ab. Wenn Sie sich überlegen: „Warum hat denn Soundso keine Schrift für FUSE gemacht?", dann lautet die Antwort höchstwahrscheinlich, dass wir Soundso gefragt, aber eine Absage bekommen hatten!

Zurückblickend wird auch die zunehmende Besessenheit für Grafikdesign deutlich, vom „Designer als Autor" Ende der 1990er Jahre bis hin zur neueren Leidenschaft für die Geschichte des Designs, für das „Who's who" und dafür, was in Vergessenheit geraten ist.

Am Anfang bekamen wir endlos Presse und verkauften die dreitausend Exemplare der Auflage locker. Als sich das Projekt entwickelte, waren es mit Mühe fünfhundert, weil jeder die Ausgabe umsonst haben wollte.

Unsere größte Leistung bei FUSE ist der Finger am Puls der Zeit. Das ist immer noch so, auch wenn das nicht richtig dokumentiert ist. Immerhin, *Moonbase Alpha* war in den 1990er Jahren für Techno-Flyer sehr beliebt, *Reactor* wurde oft in der bildenden Kunst eingesetzt, und *White No Sugar* war eine der vielen prämierten Schrifttypen. Letztlich endeten die Fonts völlig abseits ihres Kontextes, von Firmenlogos bis hin zu Arztpraxen.

Wer die Texte heute noch einmal liest, dem sei der Gedanke verziehen, FUSE habe eine pessimistische Zukunftsvision vertreten. Das Surreale unserer

Immerhin, *Moonbase Alpha* war in den 1990er Jahren für Techno-Flyer sehr beliebt, *Reactor* wurde oft in der bildenden Kunst eingesetzt, und *White No Sugar* war eine der vielen prämierten Schrifttypen. Letztlich endeten die Fonts völlig abseits ihres Kontextes, von Firmenlogos bis hin zu Arztpraxen.

Situation – was Repräsentation und Reproduktion betraf, lebten wir in der Überzeugung, dieser Moment wäre vergleichbar mit den Grabenkämpfen zwischen Fotografie und Malerei zu Anfang des vorletzten Jahrhunderts – sollte nicht darüber hinwegtäuschen, dass wir uns als Abenteurer fühlten. Und was die Zukunft betrifft: An unseren Kindern beobachten wir Anzeichen für ein digitales Verständnis, das wir nie hatten und auch nie haben konnten. Also halten wir die Luft an.

Irgendwann 1991 abstrahierte ich unter der Reprokamera die Schrift *Akzidenz Grotesk* für ein Logo, das ich für Kudos Productions entwarf, ein in London ansässiges Fernsehstudio. Und Brody sagte zu mir: „Was machst du denn da? Das kann ich doch auf dem Computer machen …"

Blur, eine Schrift, die Brody über Nacht konfigurierte, wurde eine Leitform des FUSE-Projekts. Neulich sah ich sie irgendwo im Ausland am Schaufenster eines Optikers.

Quellenangabe:

1. Walter Benjamin, *Das Kunstwerk im Zeitalter seiner technischen Reproduzierbarkeit*, Frankfurt/Main (Suhrkamp) 1963 **2.** Eric Drexler, *Engines of Creation: The Coming Era of Nanotechnology*, New York u.a. (Doubleday) 1986 **3.** Francis Fukuyama, *The End of History and the Last Man*, London (Penguin) 1993; Gilles Deleuze und Felix Guattari, *A Thousand Plateaus: Capitalism and Schizophrenia*, Minneapolis (University of Minnesota Press) 1988 **4. und 5.** György Doczi, *The Power of Limits*, Boston u.a. (Shambhala Publications) 1981 **6.** John Michell, *The New View Over Atlantis*, London (Thames and Hudson) 1983; John Michell, *The Dimensions of Paradise*, London (Thames and Hudson) 1988

Einleitung 2

Überzeugender als je zuvor zeigten sie, dass die visuelle und semantische Kommunikation durch computergestütztes Design zu einer neuen Zukunft finden konnte, die über lateinische Buchstabenformen hinausging und den Quantensprung von gedruckter Seite zu elektronischem Bildschirm bewältigte.

FUSE 1-20: Die Vandalen der typografischen Zivilisation
Adrian Shaughnessy

Grafiker, die den ersten Ausgaben von FUSE begegneten, hatten den Eindruck, ein neues Land würde auf die Weltkarte gesetzt: Zwei Forscher – Brody und Wozencroft – wagten sich in die eisige Steppe des neuen digitalen Königreichs hinaus. Die Berichte, die sie – verpackt zwischen schlichten Kartons – von dort nach Hause schickten, waren prophetisch und vielfach schockierend.

Wozencrofts provokant-spritzige Texte lasen sich damals bisweilen wie Science-Fiction. Heute allerdings, mehr als zwanzig Jahre später, führen sie uns seine fast unheimliche Fähigkeit vor Augen, die großen Fragen unserer Gegenwart zu umreißen: die kulturelle Bedeutung von Informationstechnologie, Überwachung, Propaganda, Genetik, das Internet und andere Themen mehr. Gleichzeitig war FUSE unter Art Director Brody in der Anfangszeit ein Dorn im Auge der typografischen Traditionalisten und beschwor unbekümmert die Missbilligung der selbst ernannten herrschenden Grafikerelite auf sich herab, indem es demonstrierte, dass die Typografie dank Computer allen Nutzern offenstand. Und es bewies überdies die Befreiung der Schrift von ihrem herkömmlichen Zweck, linguistische Bedeutung zu vermitteln.

Die Grafiken in frühen FUSE-Ausgaben bezogen ihr Schockpotenzial aus dem Versuch Brodys, Wozencrofts und ihrer Mitstreiter, die neuen Tools – Software, Tastatur, Ausgabegeräte – so zu bearbeiten, dass diese die Aussagen vermittelten, die man unter die Menschen bringen wollte. Die Ergebnisse waren oft ungeschliffen und auch unfertig, einige wirkten unreif, aber etwa mit dem Erscheinen von FUSE 10 kam es zum qualitativen Sprung: Die Grafik überwand die digitale Feuerschneise und mutierte vom zufälligen Experiment zum kontrollierten Ausdruck. Das wird auf den Seiten dieses Buchs augenfällig: ein Moment der digitalen Transsubstantiation, als die Nutzer schließlich die Tools meisterten und visuelle Statements schufen, die solide und integer waren und den Vergleich mit anderen Sternstunden der Grafikgeschichte nicht zu scheuen brauchten.

In seinem Artikel für FUSE 10 benannte Wozencroft die Gründe für diesen qualitativen Sprung: „Seit einiger Zeit reden wir von unserer Absicht, die Tastatur eher als Musikinstrument oder Farbpalette zu nutzen und ihr Potenzial nicht auf die immerwährende Verbesserung, Verfeinerung und Abstraktion lateinischer Buchstabenformen zu beschränken." Von da an war bei Brody und Wozencroft – und bei den vielen anderen Gebrauchsgrafikern und Schriftsetzern, die sie zur Mitarbeit einluden – eine neue Macht über digitale Werkzeuge und Vernetzungen nicht zu übersehen. Überzeugender als je zuvor zeigten sie, dass die visuelle und semantische Kommunikation durch computergestütztes Design zu einer neuen Zukunft finden konnte, die über lateinische Buchstabenformen hinausging und den Quantensprung von gedruckter Seite zu elektronischem Bildschirm bewältigte.

Auch Brody sprach über diesen Moment. Im Interview für *Eye* (Nr. 6, 1992) fragte ihn Rick Poynor, ob er im Umgang mit seinem Computer einen Moment erfahren konnte, die Oberhand erlangt zu haben. Daraufhin erwiderte Brody: „Aber ja. Ich weiß sogar genau, wann das passiert ist. Es war halb zwölf Uhr nachts, und ich hatte dagesessen und auf den Computer eingehackt. Und plötzlich wurde mir klar, dass ich das Sagen hatte, dass die Kontrolle irgendwann tatsächlich auf mich übergegangen war."

Unter heutigen Gebrauchsgrafikern findet die digitale Technologie nahezu uneingeschränkte Akzeptanz. Sich im Kommunikationsdesign gegen den Computer auszusprechen, gilt als häretisch. Allerdings gab es eine Zeit, als das Digitale – die DTP-Revolution – als Beweis dafür galt, dass die Barbaren die Festung gestürmt hatten. In seinem Essay „Computer, Pencils and Brushes“ von 1992 schrieb Paul Rand: „... die Sprache des Computers ist die Sprache der Technik, nicht die des Designs. Es ist auch die Sprache der Herstellung. Der Computer findet Eingang in die kreative Welt nur als Hilfsmittel, als Werkzeug – ein Gerät, das Zeit spart, das Experimente ermöglicht, das Bilder abrufbar macht und anspruchslose Arbeiten übernimmt –, aber nicht als Hauptakteur.“ Auf den Seiten von FUSE und auch anderswo wollte Brody beweisen, dass der Computer in der Grafik eine weit zentralere Rolle spielen konnte, als Rand ihm zugestehen wollte.

Selbst ein scharfsinniger Beobachter wie der amerikanische Grafiker Michael Rock – den man kaum als eingefleischten Traditionalisten bezeichnen kann – erlaubte sich ein Quäntchen Bedauern angesichts der Vorstellung, dass die Schriftgestaltung in die Hände der neuen digitalen Ungläubigen fiele. So schrieb er in *Eye* (Nr. 15, 1994) über FUSE: „Schrift wird nie wieder von einer zunftähnlichen Bruderschaft entworfen werden. Die konservative Handwerkermentalität und der Gewerkschaftsgeist, die die Buchstabenproduktion prägten, sind unwiederbringlich Vergangenheit. Doch so spannend die Ergebnisse der typografischen Revolution sind, empfindet man doch ein gewisses Bedauern ob der Entwertung eines weiteren Berufsstands und einer weiteren Handwerkerzunft durch eine Handvoll junger Punks mit PCs.“

Hehre Vorstellungen von Buchstaben als geheimer Handwerkskunst, als „unsichtbarem“ Gefäß, denen ausschließlich die Aufgabe zukam, linguistische Inhalte zu vermitteln, wurden von Brody und anderen „jungen Punks mit PCs“ und deren geometrisch spitzen Ellbogen rüde hinweggefegt. Brody trug mehr dazu bei als jeder andere, der in den 1980er und 1990er Jahren im grafischen Bereich arbeitete, die Typografie ins Rampenlicht zu rücken. Er machte sie zu einem visuellen Ausdruck. Damit soll nicht gesagt sein, dass es vor Brody keine ausdrucksstarken Schriften gab. Die Konstruktivisten der 1920er und die psychedelischen Plakatkünstler der 1960er

Die Digitalisierung bedeutete aber noch mehr, nämlich Interaktion. Durch den PC konnten Nutzer jetzt das Mittel – und die Art – der Kommunikation selbst bestimmen. FUSE ist voll von nutzergenerierten „Schriften“.

Jahre verwendeten ausgesprochen exzentrische Schriftarten, und zwar auf eine Weise, die jeder Norm orthodoxer Typografie spottete. Diese antiformalistischen Spielereien sollten allerdings vorwiegend eine Botschaft übermitteln. Brody und die anderen jedoch schufen – um mit Michael Rock zu sprechen – „eine neue typografische Rhetorik ... die die Buchstabenform als Objekt für visuelle Experimente begreift und das Alphabet als Leinwand, auf die Grafiker ihre Kreativität projizieren können."

Aber sie taten etwas anderes. Sie zeigten, dass es möglich war, Schriften zu entwerfen und gleichzeitig als Grafiker zu arbeiten. Bis zu dem Zeitpunkt hatte man gemeinhin entweder das eine oder das andere getan. Neue Softwares wie Fontographer gaben den Grafikern mit ihren zahlreichen Optionen – optische Skalierung etwa oder einheitliche Strukturen für Schriftfamilien – Mittel an die Hand, den mühseligen Prozess zu überspringen, ganze Zeichensätze händisch auszuarbeiten. Das war die neue Grafikergeneration, die nach Belieben eigene Schriften und Buchstabenformen gestalten und sich damit von den bestehenden typografischen Systemen lösen konnte. Das bedeutete, dass die Arbeit dieser Grafiker eine ihnen eigene Optik erhielt – am augenfälligsten bei Brody selbst. Der Grafiker, der seine eigenen Fonts verwendete, war eher ein Urheber-Grafiker als ein Kollege, der auf existierende Schriften zurückgriff.

Sicher hatten Grafiker bereits vor dem digitalen Aufbruch der 1980er und 1990er Jahre eigene Buchstabenformen entworfen, der berühmteste ist zweifellos Wim Crouwel. *New Alphabet*, das er 1967 als Reaktion auf das Aufkommen der ersten bildschirmorientierten Kommunikationssysteme entwarf, ist wohl die bekannteste seiner Schriften. Allerdings war *New Alphabet* eine Ausnahme und ungewöhnlich für Crouwel insofern, als er selten ein ganzes Alphabet ausarbeitete – meist beschränkte er sich auf die Buchstaben, die er für bestimmte Worte benötigte. Erst in den 1990er Jahren konnte der Schriftenhersteller The Foundry dank der Digitalisierung Crouwel anbieten, seine Buchstabenformen zu einem vollständigen Zeichensatz auszuarbeiten.

Die Digitalisierung bedeutete aber noch mehr, nämlich Interaktion. Durch den PC konnten Nutzer jetzt das Mittel – und die Art – der Kommunikation selbst bestimmen. FUSE ist voll von nutzergenerierten „Schriften". David Crows Font *Mega Family 2* funktioniert wie ein Zeichenwerkzeug, aus dem die Nutzer Porträts herstellen können: „Die Schrift ist eine Art Spiel für ein bis zwei Personen", schrieb Crow in FUSE 16, „und weist auf eine Entwicklung wie beim Zellwachstum hin zu Freizeitaktivitäten innerhalb dessen, was wir als Typografie verstehen. Die Spielregeln sind nicht vorgegeben, sondern werden selbst erstellt." Bei John Critchleys *Mutoid* (FUSE 10) wird auf der Tastatur „eine Reihe untereinander austauschbarer Körperteile – Köpfe, Beine, Rümpfe – [eingefügt], die zu einer ganzen Serie ‚mutierter' Gestalten zusammengesetzt werden können. Bau dir dein eigenes Monster!"

Brody, Wozencroft und ihre Mitstreiter – Grafiker wie Cornel Windlin, David Crow, Pierre di Sciullo und andere – nutzten FUSE als Plattform, um typografische Dogmen zu hinterfragen. Sie zeigten, dass man Schrift auf dieselbe Art einsetzen kann, wie Illustratoren Striche, Kritzel, Schattierungen und Formen für abstrakte und semi-abstrakte visuelle Aussagen verwenden. Illustratoren waren bisweilen sehr klar in ihrem Ausdruck, dann wieder eher mehrdeutig, aber sie standen nicht unter demselben Zwang wie Grafiker, semantischen Sinn zu vermitteln. Brody und seine Leute, und tausende Grafiker nach ihnen, reklamierten ein Stück dieser Freiheit für sich. Sie verwendeten amorphe Kleckse, Wellenlinien, gezackte und verzerrte Bitmaps mit einer Freiheit, wie sie bislang nur Illustratoren zugestanden hatte. Sie entwarfen eine neue, frei verfügbare Typografie für das Zeitalter des Bildes – und, wichtiger noch, für das Zeitalter der bildschirmorientierten Kommunikation.

Die Mischung von Texten und visuellen Experimenten in FUSE war potenziell subversiv. Wozencroft beschäftigte sich in seinen Essays auf Art eines James Graham Ballard mit dem Stoff, der uns umgibt. Seine Texte waren selten beifällig, oft weitblickend sowie ein flammendes Manifest für eine bestimmte Gruppe:

denkende Grafiker, die ihre symbiotische Beziehung zu Industrie und Kommerz hinterfragten. Für die überwiegende Zahl der Grafiker, dem Konsumboom der Thatcher-Reagan-Jahre erlegen, müssen Wozencrofts Gedanken fast wie Verrat geklungen haben, doch andere begriffen sie als Vorlage für eine alternative Denkweise.

Seine Texte legten ganz ungezwungen großes Wissen an den Tag. In einem Essay („Runes", FUSE 2) erwähnt er unter anderem die etruskische Schrift, die nordischen Legenden, die Runen der Druiden in Wales und Irland, Abzeichen und Uniformen der SS, Heavy-Metal-LPs, „New Age"-Kultur, grüne Themen, die Gaia-Philosophie und LED-Zuganzeiger. Dann wieder verstand er es, aufschlussreich über Fragen der sozialen Gerechtigkeit zu schreiben: „Früher hatte die Sozialpolitik eher die Benachteiligten im Blick, heute geht es ihr vermehrt darum, den Komfort der unruhigen Mittelschicht zu gewährleisten (die, wie immer, zwischen zwei Extremen gefangen ist: Wohlstand und Armut – der ideale Nährboden für Ideen wie die National Lottery und private Krankenversicherungen)." Hier wie auch in anderen FUSE-Essays spricht Wozencroft in einer Grafikzeitschrift gesellschaftsrelevante Themen auf eine Art an, die damals sehr selten war – erst heute, nach der Bankenkrise, begegnet man ihr häufiger.

Die größte Leistung von FUSE besteht aber vielleicht in seinem vehementen Widersprechen der weitverbreitete Meinung, dem Grafikdesign gehe die Fähigkeit zur Selbstkritik ab, es sei ein Feld der stilvollen Pose und der Eigenwerbung. In regelmäßigen Abständen beklagen Kritiker und Historiker die mangelnde Tiefe und Substanz in den Beiträgen der Gebrauchsgrafiker zur Diskussion über ihr Gewerbe. Meiner Ansicht nach wird diese Behauptung kaum überzeugender widerlegt als von FUSE, und doch wird das Projekt selten erwähnt, wenn es um Grafikdesign und dessen Kultur geht. Es können auch nur sehr wenige von Grafikern herausgebrachte Publikationen mit dem Anspruch in Wort und Bild mithalten, der Brodys und Wozencrofts selbst verlegtes Projekt auszeichnet – vergleichbar war vielleicht überhaupt nur *Emigre*.

Nicht nur ideologisch und von der Polemik wurde FUSE vernachlässigt. In der modernen Typografie gibt es auch nur wenige Nachfolger mit Brodys waghalsigem Erfindungsgeist. Heutige Schriftgrafiker haben offenbar nur noch Sinn für den Formalismus der Vergangenheit, konservative typografische Werte sind die Norm. Diese Entwicklung sagte Jeffrey Keedy bereits früh – nämlich 1992 in FUSE 4 – voraus: „Um die Sterblichkeit des Stils zu vermeiden, lassen viele heutige Grafikdesigner die Toten auferstehen. Die typografischen Kadaver werden aus der fernen Vergangenheit zurückgeholt (klassische Mumien), aus der neueren Vergangenheit (Zombie-Moderne) oder à la Frankenstein aus kürzlich ausgegrabenen Fundstücken zusammengesetzt (Post-mortem-Moderne). Welche Methode auch immer, es läuft immer auf dasselbe hinaus, nämlich eine Art typografischer Nekrophilie. Dabei sollten Schriftenentwerfer mit ihrer Zeit Besseres anstellen, als eine schöne Leiche weiter auszuschmücken, und sich lieber von den neuen digitalen Möglichkeiten begeistern lassen, wie die Grafiker des Industriezeitalters es angesichts des technischen Fortschritts taten."

In Interviews und in seiner neuen Rolle als Pädagoge hat Brody seine Nachfolger wiederholt aufgefordert, sich „von den neuen digitalen Möglichkeiten begeistern zu lassen" und „gefährlich zu denken". Er wünscht sich explizit, jemand möge die Fackel weitertragen und dasselbe tun wie er vor zwanzig Jahren. Er möchte wieder hören, wie die Abrissbirne die Mauern der typografischen Zivilisation niederreißt, aber er glaubt nicht, dass es dazu kommen wird. Vielmehr bescheidet sich das Gros der Typografen offenbar damit, sich den sterilen Klängen der Kaufhausmusik anzupassen, zu der wir unserer täglichen Arbeit nachgehen, und dabei, um Wozencroft zu zitieren, „durch einen saumlosen Quilt von Shoppingmalls, Bankterminals, Telekomzentren, Restaurants und Bars zu treiben, die die modernen Nomaden im Niemandsland auf Trab und bei Laune halten."

Die größte Leistung von FUSE besteht aber vielleicht in seinem vehementen Widersprechen der weitverbreiteten Meinung, dem Grafikdesign gehe die Fähigkeit zur Selbstkritik ab, es sei ein Feld der stilvollen Pose und der Eigenwerbung. In regelmäßigen Abständen beklagen Kritiker und Historiker die mangelnde Tiefe und Substanz in den Beiträgen der Gebrauchsgrafiker zur Diskussion über ihr Gewerbe. Meiner Ansicht nach wird diese Behauptung kaum überzeugender widerlegt als von FUSE, und doch wird das Projekt selten erwähnt, wenn es um Grafikdesign und dessen Kultur geht.

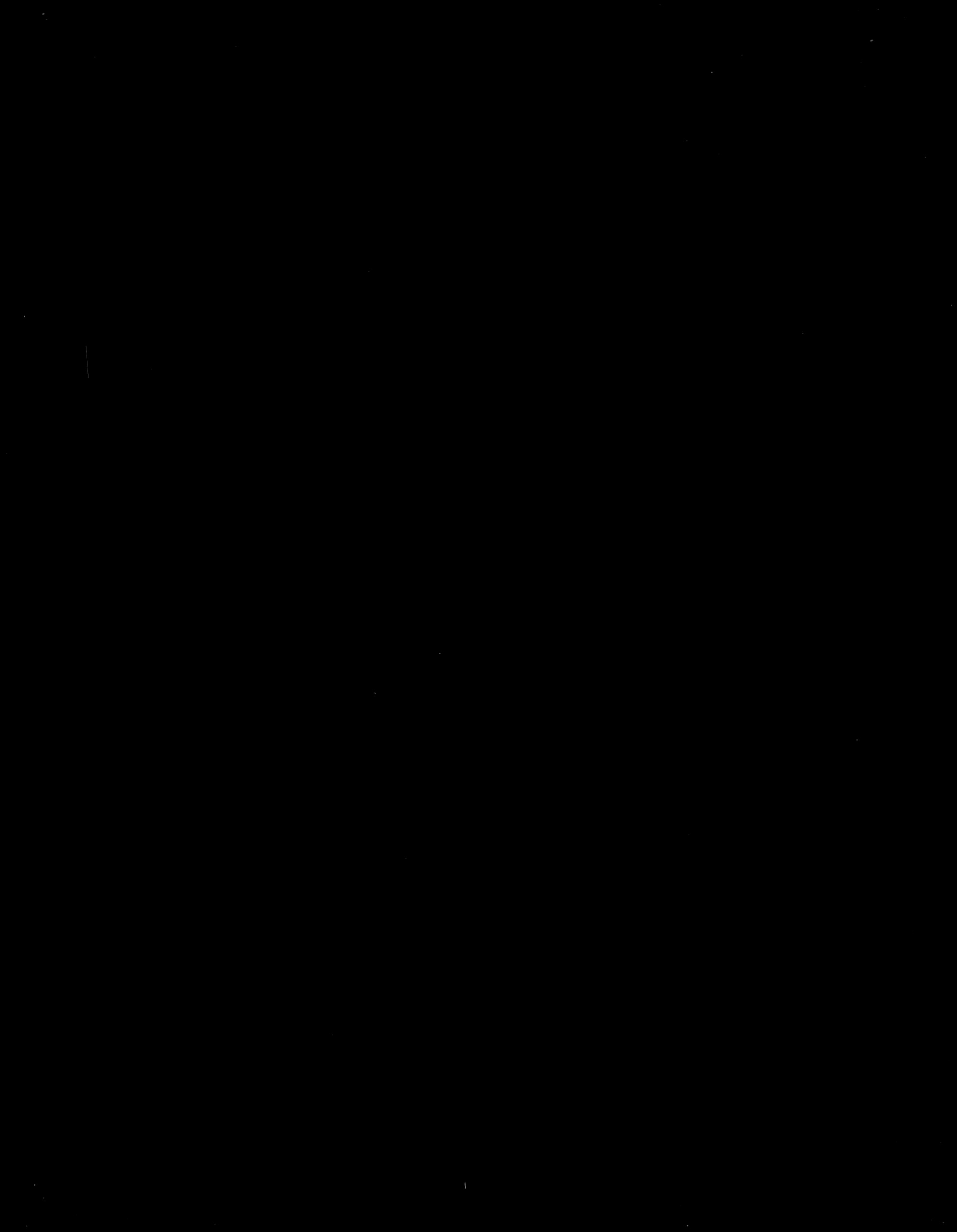

FRANÇAIS

Qu’est-ce que FUSE

À propos de ce livre

FUSE 1-20 est une anthologie du projet FUSE depuis sa première édition en 1991.

C’est la première fois que tous les numéros de FUSE ont été rassemblés et publiés en un même volume, œuvre de référence visuelle et historique. Les tirages limités, les technologies obsolètes et vingt ans d’évolution des logiciels avaient jusqu’à présent empêché FUSE de se montrer sous sa forme complète et entière.

Nous avons décidé de rester fidèles aux différents numéros tels qu’ils sont parus à l’époque, c’est pourquoi le livre a été divisé en deux sections principales. La première partie présente les numéros 1 à 18 de FUSE. Les éditoriaux et les descriptions des polices de caractères respectent le texte paru sur les affiches d’origine. Toute modification apportée reflète l’évolution des normes de la PAO.

Les numéros 19 et 20 de FUSE accompagnent ce livre sous forme d’affiches. Les polices et les articles sont disponibles en ligne, la carte incluse dans le coffret fournit les codes nécessaires pour leur téléchargement.

À propos de cette section

La deuxième moitié de ce livre présente une petite sélection des différentes activités que le projet FUSE a promues au cours de son histoire sur plus de deux décennies.

Les conférences reflètent le débat international et critique auquel FUSE a participé ; les concours démontrent l’importance de FUSE pour les graphistes contemporains et émergents tout au long de cette période.

La dernière section du livre reproduit également les biographies des collaborateurs envoyées au moment de la publication de chaque numéro. Son objectif est double. Elle fournit un index et une chronologie des graphistes dont les polices de caractères ont fait de FUSE un document d’archives essentiel.

FUSE est un magazine trimestriel lancé en 1990, édité à Londres et publié à l’origine par FontShop International. Chaque numéro se compose d’une boîte en carton brut contenant un disque avec au moins quatre polices de caractères et cinq affiches imprimées. Chaque numéro est consacré à un thème lié à différentes tendances sous-jacentes du domaine de la communication, et à leurs conséquences. Quatre graphistes issus de la typographie et d’autres secteurs sont chargés d’explorer ce thème en créant une police de caractères. Chaque graphiste passe ensuite à l’application créative de cette police en créant une affiche ou une animation. Les quatre créations sont accompagnées d’un éditorial, et d’un nombre imprévisible de polices supplémentaires.

C’est ainsi que l’on peut décrire FUSE en tant que produit matériel. Mais cela ne dit rien sur FUSE.

Depuis l’origine, l’intention qui sous-tend le projet de FUSE a toujours été l’exploration. C’est un laboratoire, un espace où les praticiens et les non-praticiens sont invités à entrer pour faire des expériences sur les formes de langage visuel que nous utilisons. D’une certaine manière, ce n’est rien de plus qu’un catalyseur, et chaque numéro est comme une feuille blanche, un document de recherche qui révèle de nouvelles explorations.

FUSE se base sur le concept selon lequel tout langage est fluide et non pas figé, et les systèmes de distribution numérique nous permettent de diffuser des idées qui sont modifiables, particulièrement sous leur forme visuelle.

Tiré du discours d’inauguration de Neville Brody pour FUSE98, San Francisco (SUITE EN PAGE 358).

20 ans, 20 numéros, 100 affiches imprimées, 114 polices !

Depuis son invention il y a 21 ans, FUSE a toujours été un champ de bataille et d'expérimentation, un laboratoire de la pensée et du langage, où la discussion de questions bien plus larges ont pris forme dans la forme, dans les structures où nous plaçons nos systèmes pour la distribution de l'expression et du fait. Fluctuant constamment entre la familiarité et l'abstraction, cet espace liquide a permis l'émergence de nouveaux modes de langage visuel à travers le questionnement intense et le démantèlement de nos outils et structures de communication conventionnels. La société est une forme fluide, et exige des systèmes de langage évolutifs capables de saper toute tentative de perpétuer le statu quo dans une stase exploitative à travers l'hypnose. L'anti est essentiel.

Dans un monde de médiocrité généralisée et d'obéissance à des entreprises décrépites, de nouvelles fleurs d'exubérance poussent dans l'ombre des crevasses. FUSE est une brèche dans le mur, une mutation génétique qui fera jaillir de nouvelles formes de vie. Notre langage est notre être, et nos pensées sont limitées par nos langages ; ce n'est que par l'extension que nous pouvons repousser les limites de nos possibilités. Ce qui a commencé comme une exploration explosive et sauvage du langage typographique dans le cadre de la technologie numérique s'est ensuite raffiné et approfondi.

Les vingt-et-un ans de FUSE font l'effet d'une rafale inattendue de tessons créatifs. Certaines polices étaient iconoclastes, d'autres décoratives, d'autres encore étaient ludiques. Certaines relevaient de l'investigation, d'autres de l'architecture, ou encore de l'exubérance pure. Toutes étaient intrinsèquement question et possibilité tout à la fois, tour à tour émotives et formalistes, mais toutes offraient de nouvelles perspectives sur de nouveaux espaces créés par de nouveaux langages. Des formes nouvelles ont été arrangées dans de nouvelles structures qui ont donné naissance à de nouvelles pensées. Beaucoup ont réussi, certaines ont échoué, et l'expérience se poursuit. Jamais FUSE n'a été aussi pertinent et nécessaire.

Introduction 1

Cet aspect du «sacré» peut sembler s'imposer comme sacré parce que le monde moderne n'offre aucun équivalent. C'est un problème. Est-il vrai que nous sommes en train de vivre une désincarnation, une aliénation, une perte psychique de pouvoir… la lente disparition de la poésie ? Rares sont ceux qui seraient prêts à le reconnaître, car ce serait une hérésie dans la navette spatiale de la communication moderne.

FUSE 1-20: Le cercle et le carré Jon Wozencroft

La différence entre l'analogique et le numérique est souvent envisagée sous l'angle d'un changement de format: du vinyle au CD, du celluloïd et du VHS au DVD, et plus récemment du livre relié au Kindle. Mais cela néglige un changement plus fondamental en termes de reproduction et de génération de schémas, et indique pourquoi la typographie est devenue un contexte essentiel pour approfondir cette question.

On pourrait commencer par une démonstration de ce qui est arrivé à la lettre «O». En *Garamond*, sa structure courbe et harmonique est alimentée par des siècles d'évolution, en numérique un ensemble de carrés/pixels donne à l'œil l'illusion que ce ne sont pas des pixels qu'il voit… Cela ressemble à un «O», mais ce n'est pas un «O». C'est un ordre de construction différent, qui ressemble à la lettre «O». Il faut blâmer le précédent des polices sans empattement, qui ont mis moins de 40 ans à devenir *Helvetica* et *Univers*, et dont le «O» est un cercle parfait qui ne demande qu'à être écrasé!

Les systèmes numériques sont basés sur un ordre supérieur d'illusion optique. C'est une sorte de magie, mais utilisée à mauvais escient… Dans le domaine du fantastique, le cours de la vie moderne vous fait voir certaines choses alors qu'en réalité vous avez vu autre chose, et cela s'applique à tout et constitue la racine de notre malaise perceptuel. Notre instinct nous pousse à ne plus croire en rien. Et qui donc pourrait croire en quoi que ce soit (à part les religieux)? Pour nous autres, le monde devait arriver à sa fin le 21 mai 2011, mais il en a été autrement. Nous vivons dans un monde de Changement Perpétuel.

«La technique de reproduction sépare l'objet reproduit du domaine de la tradition.»[1]

Après la publication du premier livre de la série *Graphic Language*, j'ai passé une bonne année en 1989-90 à faire des recherches et rédiger un plan pour la suite que nous voulions lui donner – *The Death of Typography*. La genèse de cette idée était une page que Brody avait réalisée pour le projet Touch *Ritual* en 1986. C'était aussi pour nous une réaction à la bouffée de notoriété qui avait enveloppé notre studio après une année de publications intenses et l'exposition V&A en 1988… Dans ce court intervalle, nous avions expérimenté sur ce que le PC et l'imprimante matricielle avaient à offrir. Pas grand-chose, en ce qui nous concernait, et il me semble toujours extrêmement étrange et accidentel que les ordinateurs aient été utilisés par les graphistes avant les cinéastes, les musiciens et les artistes.

Nous étions intéressés par le traitement de l'impression – passant des catalogues de polices de caractères et de la photocopieuse au papier quadrillé et au Rotring, forçant les formes typographiques à adopter des états extrêmes.
Ce projet étant une passion, Brody mentionnait *The Death of Typography* dans les entretiens qu'il accordait tandis que je m'asseyais sous un arbre dans le parc de Hampstead Heath et que je cherchais des indices dans l'histoire ou la philosophie, et en particulier dans les stratégies de communication de la Deuxième Guerre mondiale: entre Goebbels et l'unité de «propagande noire» de Churchill, cette époque avait beaucoup de points communs avec ce que nous voyons dans la culture actuelle.

Je viens juste de rechercher «Death of Typography» dans Google. Les résultats se répètent sur la page, et il n'y a bien sûr pas trace de la version de 1986, ce qui relève d'une sorte de justice poétique. Le véritable défi était de donner forme à une sorte de mise à jour du texte fondateur de Walter Benjamin, «L'Œuvre d'art à l'époque de sa reproductibilité mécanique». Remplacez «reproductibilité mécanique» par

« expérience numérique », et la conclusion est/était que c'est une tâche pratiquement impossible lorsque les systèmes de communication mutent à une telle vitesse.

La typographie numérique semblait représenter un pas en arrière par rapport à ce que nous faisions à la main, et il a fallu de nombreux mois pour que nous réalisions comment tout cela pouvait se transférer à une autre dimension. Tout à coup, notre travail s'est trouvé revitalisé par ce défi direct : comment devions-nous comprendre le langage visuel ?

Certains ont pris *The Death of Typography* au sens littéral et, à l'instar du « questionneur idiot » de T. S. Eliot, demandaient « Que voulez-vous dire ? » Nous n'avons jamais réussi à trouver une bonne répartie. Au même moment, des dialogues s'engageaient sur la dématérialisation des documents dans les bureaux, la fin des livres et la réalité virtuelle; Drexler venait de publier le premier traité de nanotechnologie[2] ; sans compter *La Fin de l'histoire* et *Mille plateaux*.[3]

À partir de là, la théorie s'est emballée, mais elle avait autant à voir avec les conséquences de la Deuxième Guerre mondiale qu'avec les progrès du numérique. Adorno et Warhol comprenaient les « rhizomes », mais ils n'utilisaient simplement pas ce mot-là.

Dans le domaine des supports imprimés, les mots qu'il fallait auparavant envoyer dans le futur pouvaient tout à coup être envoyés en temps réel. Le fax, né en 1987, était un mariage entre l'impression et le numérique/la téléphonie. C'était plus qu'un télégramme, et aussi instantané que la télévision.

Il n'y avait pas d'e-mail ni d'Internet, à part le système local JANET utilisé par les universités. Le fax semblait représenter le futur, et voyez ce qui en est advenu.

C'était néanmoins un catalyseur ... Le fax, et non les faits – papier thermique, formations carrées comme dans le processus d'impression plus ancien de la gravure, qui bavait au contact du support en papier, et qui avec l'agrandissement formait une esthétique nouvelle de fragmentation séduisante, aux contours aussi flous que les images d'aujourd'hui sont nettes et virtuellement dénuées de vie.

FUSE est un récit souterrain de cette époque haute en couleurs, quand « on sait que quelque chose est en train de se passer, mais on ne sait pas quoi » (B. Dylan).

Nous avons essayé d'insister sur le fait que le projet devait être un « forum » de discussion. Nous espérions un débat vigoureux. Mais le dialogue a toujours tourné court, et jusqu'à maintenant il a été impossible de dégager une perspective. Les traditionalistes se sont montrés critiques, et ont toujours prétendu que nous ne comprenions pas vraiment la tradition. Le projet est devenu viral, et pendant l'époque où nous avons réussi à le maintenir, FUSE était relativement impossible à contrôler, et le bouclage se faisait toujours à la dernière minute et dans la panique.

Le lièvre est devenu tortue. Il n'est plus vrai que « toutes les routes mènent à Rome ». Les lignes du cyberespace tournent en rond.

« La limite donne forme à l'illimité. »[4]

Dans les civilisations antiques, on préférait les formes rondes aux formes carrées. Le cercle carré était une réalité, faite de l'alignement harmonique de la mesure et du nombre – c'est ce que l'on peut déduire de l'analyse des mathématiques et de la géométrie sacrée qui ont donné le nombre d'or et la notion pythagoricienne d'harmonie cosmique, auxquels les graphistes peuvent toujours avoir recours, en dépit du monde moderne des valeurs métriques et des formats normalisés. « C'est également l'origine de leurs efforts pour comprendre les harmonies de ces proportions dans les structures de la vie quotidienne, ce qui a élevé la vie au rang d'art. »[5] En fait, peu de graphistes modernes savent quoi que ce soit sur le nombre d'or, et pourquoi devraient-ils connaître cette notion, puisqu'elle ne fait plus l'objet d'un module obligatoire dans les cours d'introduction ?

On peut visiter dans les îles Britanniques des cercles de pierres qui témoignent d'une perception ancienne de la relation humaine rayonnante et progressive avec les formes. Astronomie, projection astrale, rituel ... ces pratiques font de l'intuition et de la divination des compétences essentielles pour la

Nous ne sommes toujours pas plus proches de « l'alphabétisation numérique » qu'il y a vingt ans. Ce n'est pas tant une question d'intuition que de puissance de traitement et de l'exposition que vous pouvez obtenir sur les réseaux, Facebook et Twitter, où malgré la facilité d'accès supposée, tout est devenu plus aléatoire et éphémère.

survie. « Chaque cercle de pierres avait une affinité avec une certaine partie du corps humain ... et forme un élément commun d'expression poétique. »[6]

Cet aspect du « sacré » peut sembler s'imposer comme sacré parce que le monde moderne n'offre aucun équivalent. C'est un problème. Est-il vrai que nous sommes en train de vivre une désincarnation, une aliénation, une perte psychique de pouvoir ... la lente disparition de la poésie ? Rares sont ceux qui seraient prêts à le reconnaître, car ce serait une hérésie dans la navette spatiale de la communication moderne. Un pixel ne peut jamais prétendre être autre chose qu'une goutte dans l'océan, mais il cause des remous, forme des cercles, et il nous faut encore trouver le meilleur moyen de vivre dans un état liquide.

Cette transition récente du cercle au carré est un tournant aussi crucial en termes de « futur » que les Romains l'ont été pour la Grande-Bretagne de l'Antiquité. Elle remet tout en question sur son sillage et a cette nouvelle capacité étonnante de se noyer en elle-même, sans jamais vraiment disparaître. Ce n'est pas tant la Fin de l'Histoire que le Commencement du Changement Perpétuel. Les faits et les chiffres mutent dans le dialogue continu entre la réalité et ses fictions.

Les Anciens doivent avoir manqué de vision, si l'on en juge par la facilité avec laquelle les envahisseurs romains de la Grande-Bretagne en 43 av. J.-C. ont eu recours à des formes carrées pour conquérir les clans et tribus autochtones, avec leurs formations « en tortue » pour la bataille, ou les places carrées et les routes rectilignes en temps de paix. Ou au contraire, ils avaient une vision extraordinaire, confirmée par ce qui allait arriver des milliers d'années plus tard. Les Romains ont construit leurs routes sur les « pistes droites » préhistoriques qui reliaient les sites sacrés entre eux. Ce faisant, ils ont défini le gabarit qui allait servir pour les charrettes à chevaux, les chemins de fer, les routes goudronnées, où l'ancien pouvait étouffer la nouveauté sous sa dernière forme. Le pouvoir se dilue, mais le pouvoir est quand même là, luttant pour se frayer un passage à travers les fissures dans les pavés.

Avant le PC, personne ne pouvait accéder facilement aux outils, à part quelques privilégiés. L'ordinateur personnel a tout changé. La machine à écrire et la guitare électrique avaient elles aussi promis de tout changer, mais ne l'ont jamais fait à une telle échelle. Nous ne sommes toujours pas plus proches de « l'alphabétisation numérique » qu'il y a vingt ans. Ce n'est pas tant une question d'intuition que de puissance de traitement et de l'exposition que vous pouvez obtenir sur les réseaux, Facebook et Twitter, où malgré la facilité d'accès supposée, tout est devenu plus aléatoire et éphémère.

Cette culture de pixels et de raccourcis est très différente de l'idée romaine des places, du forum, et même des cités-jardins du modernisme d'après-guerre. Ces idées avaient également été conçues à grande échelle, visibles et concrètes pour tous les citoyens, signes de confiance en l'avenir. De nos jours, notre univers pixélisé ressemble davantage à un point de fuite que tout le monde a sa propre façon de chercher, en se frayant un passage à travers l'antimatière.

Nous avons eu une conversation à Tokyo en 1990 lorsque nous commencions FUSE : pour le regard londonien, Tokyo est une ville complètement folle, tout aussi dominée par la vitesse aujourd'hui qu'à l'époque :) – le niveau de surréalisme de l'information ... un extraordinaire pays des merveilles qui reflétait ce qui se passait alors, et ce qui pouvait apparaître sur l'écran. On pouvait voir la vitesse et le temps se replier sur eux-mêmes. Plus tard, j'ai appris que ce n'était pas étranger aux vapeurs de pétrole-benzène qui flottaient dans l'air. Nous avons conclu que pour travailler ensemble, la solution était de travailler en parallèle, et FUSE en a été le fruit.

FUSE 1 était en fait un brûlot contre l'univers. Il était naïf, comme les manifestes le sont en général. Mais à partir de FUSE 2 *RUNES* nous nous sommes efforcés de transformer ce travail en quelque chose de plus durable qu'un magazine. En fin de compte, nous nous sommes tiré une balle dans le pied. Nous avons commencé à publier des numéros régulièrement, mais il est vite devenu impossible de continuer et finalement FUSE est toujours un projet inachevé.

Il y avait toujours un problème ... Réfléchir à qui l'on allait pouvoir demander ... essayer d'inviter des graphistes femmes ... Vous pouvez voir ce qu'il en était en consultant FUSE 3/9/12 ... Cela ressemble peut-être à un club, mais c'était tout simplement dû à la nécessité de publier les numéros. Nous avons eu du mal à convaincre des tas de gens à faire quelque chose pour nous, au-delà des quelques alliés que nous avions, et (vous n'allez pas le croire), un bon nombre des graphistes qui apparaissent dans cette collection ne voulaient pas participer au début. Si vous vous demandez « pourquoi Untel n'a pas fait une police pour FUSE ? », eh bien il y a de bonnes chances que nous le lui ayons proposé, et qu'il ou elle ait refusé !

Rétrospectivement, il y a également dans ces travaux un fort courant sous-jacent de ce qui est ensuite devenu une obsession dans le graphisme, depuis l'argument du « graphiste auteur » de la fin des années 1990 jusqu'à toutes ces récentes préoccupations sur l'Histoire du graphisme, qui est qui, et ce qui a été oublié.

Lorsque nous avons commencé, la presse a énormément parlé de nous et nous vendions les 3 000 exemplaires sans problème. Lorsque le projet a gagné en profondeur, nous avons eu du mal à écouler 500 exemplaires parce que tout le monde voulait les avoir gratuitement.

La dimension temporelle de FUSE est notre plus grande réussite. Le projet poursuit sa floraison, et n'a pas été documenté à proprement parler. Mais *Moonbase Alpha* a été fréquemment utilisée dans les flyers techno des années 1990. *Reactor* était très appréciée dans les applications liées aux beaux-arts, et *White No Sugar* est l'une des nombreuses polices qui ont remporté une récompense de design typographique, et qui se sont retrouvées dans des contextes surréalistes, logos d'entreprise ou cabinets de médecins.

En relisant les textes, je me rends compte que l'on ne pourrait pas en vouloir au lecteur de penser que FUSE représente une vision pessimiste de l'avenir. Le surréalisme de la situation (en termes de

Mais *Moonbase Alpha* a été fréquemment utilisée dans les flyers techno des années 1990. *Reactor* était très appréciée dans les applications liées aux beaux-arts, et *White No Sugar* est l'une des nombreuses polices qui ont remporté une récompense de design typographique, et qui se sont retrouvées dans des contextes surréalistes, logos d'entreprise ou cabinets de médecins.

représentation et de reproduction, nous avions la sensation de vivre un événement du même calibre que le schisme photographie/peinture du début du siècle dernier) ne doit pas éclipser le sentiment d'aventure que nous éprouvions. En ce qui concerne l'avenir, lorsque nous regardons nos enfants nous pouvons discerner les signes d'une conscience numérique que nous n'avons jamais eue, et que nous n'aurions jamais pu avoir. Alors nous sommes impatients de voir ce que cela va donner.

Un jour, en 1991, j'étais en train de travailler à une extraction photomécanique de la police *Akzidenz Grotezk* pour un logo que je faisais pour Kudos Productions, une société de télévision basée à Londres. Brody m'a dit : « Qu'est-ce que tu fais ? Je peux faire ça sur l'ordinateur »...

Blur, une police que Brody a configurée en une nuit, est devenue une référence pour le projet FUSE. Je l'ai vue il y a peu à l'étranger, sur l'enseigne d'un opticien.

Référence :

1. *Illuminations*, Walter Benjamin, Harcourt, Brace and World Inc. 1968 **2.** *Engins de création : l'avènement des nanotechnologies*, Eric Drexler, Vuibert 2005 **3.** *La Fin de l'histoire et le dernier homme*, Francis Fukuyama, Flammarion 2009; *Capitalisme et schizophrénie : Mille Plateaux*, Gilles Deleuze et Félix Guattari, Éditions de Minuit, 1980 **4 et 5.** *The Power of Limits*, György Doczi, Shambhala Publications 1981 **6.** *The New View Over Atlantis*, John Michell, Thames et Hudson 1983; *The Dimensions of Paradise*, John Michell, Thames et Hudson 1988

Introduction 2

Ils ont montré avec plus de force que jamais que le graphisme informatique pouvait servir à façonner un nouvel avenir pour la communication visuelle et sémantique, au-delà des caractères romains, en opérant un saut évolutif de la page imprimée à l'écran électronique.

FUSE 1-20: Les fossoyeurs de la civilisation typographique
Adrian Shaughnessy

Les graphistes qui sont tombés sur les premiers numéros de FUSE ont eu le sentiment qu'un nouveau terrain s'ouvrait devant eux: deux explorateurs, Brody et Wozencroft, s'enfonçaient à grandes enjambées dans les steppes glacées du nouveau royaume numérique. Les rapports qu'ils envoyaient dans de modestes boîtes en carton étaient prophétiques et souvent choquants.

Les textes de Wozencroft bouillonnaient de provocations qui ressemblaient parfois à de la science-fiction mais qui aujourd'hui, plus de vingt ans plus tard, démontrent une capacité troublante à définir les grandes questions qui nous préoccupent actuellement – l'impact culturel des technologies de l'information, la surveillance, la propagande, la génétique et Internet, entre autres. Dans le même temps, sous la direction artistique de Brody, FUSE a dès ses débuts planté des épingles dans les yeux des typographes traditionalistes, et s'est fait une joie de s'attirer les foudres de l'élite régnante autoproclamée du graphisme en montrant que, grâce à l'ordinateur, la typographie était désormais ouverte à tous *et* s'était libérée de son objectif traditionnel, la transmission de la signification linguistique.

Le facteur choc visuel des premiers numéros de FUSE venait des tentatives de Brody, Wozencroft et leurs collaborateurs à forcer les nouveaux outils – logiciels, claviers, systèmes d'impression – à composer les déclarations qu'ils voulaient diffuser de toute urgence. Le résultat était souvent brut et imparfait, et trahissait parfois une certaine immaturité, mais à l'époque de la publication de FUSE 10, il s'est passé quelque chose: l'expression graphique a franchi le pare-feu numérique et, d'expérimentation désordonnée, est devenue expression maîtrisée. Les pages de ce livre s'en font témoin : dans ce moment de transsubstantiation numérique, les utilisateurs ont acquis la maîtrise des outils et ont fait surgir des œuvres visuelles porteuses de substance et d'intégrité, que l'on peut comparer à d'autres grands moments de l'histoire du graphisme.

Dans FUSE 10, Wozencroft a identifié les raisons de cette révolution: « Nous parlons depuis un certain temps de notre intention de créer un moyen d'expression qui utilise le clavier comme un instrument de musique ou une palette de couleurs, et ne restreint pas son potentiel au perfectionnement, au raffinement ou à l'abstraction sans fin des caractères romains. » Depuis, Brody et Wozencroft, ainsi que les nombreux designers et typographes qu'ils ont invités à travailler avec eux, ont fait preuve d'une nouvelle maîtrise des outils et réseaux numériques. Ils ont montré avec plus de force que jamais que le graphisme informatique pouvait servir à façonner un nouvel avenir pour la communication visuelle et sémantique, au-delà des caractères romains, en opérant un saut évolutif de la page imprimée à l'écran électronique.

Brody a lui aussi parlé de ce moment: dans *Eye* (n° 6, 1992), Rick Poynor lui demandait s'il avait atteint un stade d'aisance suffisant pour être le maître de l'ordinateur... » Brody a répondu: « Absolument. Je me souviens même du moment où c'est arrivé. Il était 23h30 et j'avais passé des heures à m'acharner sur cette machine. Tout à coup, j'ai réalisé que c'était moi qui avais le contrôle, et qu'il y avait eu un renversement. »

Chez les designers d'aujourd'hui, le rôle de la technologie numérique est presque universellement accepté. Dans le design, être contre l'ordinateur relèverait maintenant de l'hérésie, mais il y a eu une époque où le numérique (la révolution de la PAO) était considéré comme un signe que les Barbares avaient pénétré la citadelle. Dans un essai intitulé *Computer, Pencils and Brushes* (« Ordinateur, crayons et pinceaux», 1992), Paul Rand remarquait que «l'ordinateur est le langage de la technologie, et non le langage du design. C'est aussi le langage de la production. Il entre dans le monde de la créativité en tant que simple outil ou accessoire, un moyen de gagner du temps, d'expérimenter, de rétablir, et d'exécuter des tâches laborieuses. Ce n'est pas l'acteur principal.» Brody, dans les pages de FUSE et ailleurs, a entrepris de prouver que l'ordinateur pouvait jouer dans le design un rôle bien plus significatif que Rand ne le pensait.

Même un commentateur aussi fin que le graphiste américain Michael Rock – que l'on ne saurait accuser de biais traditionaliste – a pu s'autoriser un petit soupir de regret devant la perspective de voir la typographie tomber aux mains des nouveaux infidèles numériques. Dans un article à propos de FUSE publié dans *Eye* (nº 15, 1994), il écrivait: «Les polices de caractères ne seront plus jamais produites par une confrérie assemblée en corporation ; le républicanisme de l'artisanat et le syndicalisme du travail qui caractérisaient cette activité ont disparu pour toujours. Aussi électrisants que les résultats de la révolution typographique puissent avoir été, il est bien difficile de ne pas éprouver une pointe de remords devant la décimation d'un métier, d'un groupe organisé d'artisans, par une poignée de jeunes morveux armés d'ordinateurs de bureau.»

Les représentations de la typographie en tant qu'art secret et sacré, vaisseau «invisible» chargé d'une seule mission, transmettre du sens linguistique (la «coupe de cristal» de la tradition typographique) ont été balayées par la géométrie de Brody et des autres «morveux armés d'ordinateurs de bureau». Plus que tout autre graphiste des années 1980 et 1990, Brody a contribué à mettre la typographie sur le devant de la scène en faisant des polices de caractères un mode d'expression visuelle. Cela ne veut pas dire que la typographie n'ait jamais été expressive avant Brody. Les constructivistes des années 1920 et les créateurs des affiches psychédéliques des années 1960 ont utilisé des lettres aux formes extravagantes qui se jouaient des limites de l'orthodoxie typographique. Mais ces concepts antiformalistes servaient avant

La numérisation signifiait également autre chose: l'interaction. Grâce à l'ordinateur personnel, les utilisateurs pouvaient contrôler les moyens (et les modes) de communication. FUSE regorge de «polices de caractères» créées par les utilisateurs.

tout à véhiculer des messages, des instructions et des annonces. Selon les termes de Michael Rock, Brody et ses compagnons ont créé « une nouvelle rhétorique typographique... qui conçoit la lettre comme un site d'expérimentation visuelle et l'alphabet comme un écran sur lequel les designers projettent leur créativité. »

Mais ils ont aussi fait autre chose. Ils ont montré qu'il était possible de créer des polices de caractères et, en même temps, d'être graphiste. Jusqu'à ce moment crucial, on pouvait exercer un métier ou l'autre, mais pas les deux. Mais de nouveaux logiciels tels que Fontographer ont donné aux designers les outils nécessaires pour s'épargner le processus laborieux de créer à la main des polices de caractères entières, avec leurs nombreuses propriétés telles que la correction d'échelle visuelle et les structures de familles unifiées. Une nouvelle génération était née, qui pouvait créer à volonté ses propres fontes, polices de caractères et lettres individuelles, et n'avait plus besoin des systèmes typographiques existants. Cela signifiait aussi que ce travail (et particulièrement dans le cas de Brody) pouvait acquérir la « patte » unique de son créateur. Le designer qui utilisait ses propres fontes était un meilleur designer/auteur que ceux qui dépendaient des fontes créées par d'autres.

Avant l'explosion numérique des années 1980 et 1990, d'autres graphistes avaient créé leurs propres caractères, dont le plus célèbre est Wim Crouwel. *New Alphabet* (1967), créée en réponse à l'arrivée des premiers systèmes de communication par écran, est peut-être l'exemple le plus célèbre des polices de caractère de Crouwel. Mais *New Alphabet* était une exception, et il était rare que Crouwel fasse un alphabet entier – en général il ne dessinait que les lettres dont il avait besoin pour composer certains mots. Ce n'est que dans les années 1990, avec l'arrivée de la numérisation, que la fonderie typographique The Foundry a pu approcher Crouwel et lui proposer de transformer ses lettres en polices de caractères fonctionnelles.

La numérisation signifiait également autre chose: l'interaction. Grâce à l'ordinateur personnel, les utilisateurs pouvaient contrôler les moyens (et les modes) de communication. FUSE regorge de « polices de caractères » créées par les utilisateurs. La police *Mega Family 2* de David Crow fonctionnait comme une trousse à outils de dessin, et permettait aux utilisateurs de faire des portraits: « Cette fonte fonctionne comme un jeu pour un ou deux joueurs » a-t-il écrit dans FUSE 16, « et suggère une tendance vers une activité de loisir en tant que croissance cellulaire au sein de ce que nous concevons comme étant la typographie. Ses règles sont autogénérées, et non imposées. » La police *Mutoid* de John Critchley (FUSE 10) utilisait le clavier pour stocker « une série de parties du corps – têtes, jambes et torses – qui peuvent être combinées pour former une collection de figures "mutantes". Créez votre propre créature ! »

Brody, Wozencroft et leurs collaborateurs – des designers tels que Cornel Windlin, David Crow et Pierre di Sciullo, entre autres – ont utilisé FUSE comme une plateforme pour se confronter au dogme typographique. Ils ont montré que la typographie pouvait être utilisée de la même manière qu'un illustrateur utilise des lignes, des gribouillis, des ombres et des formes pour composer une déclaration visuelle abstraite ou semi-abstraite: avec des intentions tour à tour claires ou ambigües, les illustrateurs étaient dégagés de la nécessité du sens sémantique, contrairement aux graphistes. Brody et ses collaborateurs, ainsi que les milliers de graphistes qui leur ont succédé, se sont approprié une partie de cette liberté. Ils ont utilisé des masses amorphes, des lignes sinueuses, des bitmaps tordus et en dents de scie avec la même liberté que les illustrateurs. Ils ont créé une nouvelle typographie débarrassée de contraintes pour l'ère de l'image et, ce qui est encore plus important, pour l'ère de la communication sur écrans.

Le cocktail de textes et d'expérimentation visuelle de FUSE était un breuvage puissant. Les essais de Wozencroft étaient des investigations ballardiennes sur les choses qui nous entourent. Ils relevaient rarement de la jubilation, mais souvent de la prescience, et fonctionnaient comme des manifestes incandescents pour un groupe – les graphistes pensants – qui remettait en question sa relation symbiotique avec le commerce et le consumérisme.

Pour la vaste majorité des graphistes, subjugués par le boom de la consommation sous Thatcher et Reagan, le ton de Wozencroft a pu résonner comme une trahison. Mais pour d'autres, ses mots ont posé les bases d'une pensée anticonformiste.

Ses textes affichaient une érudition aisée et naturelle: dans un essai («Runes», FUSE 2), il fait référence à l'écriture étrusque, aux légendes scandinaves, aux trois langues des druides gallois et irlandais, aux insignes et uniformes des SS, aux disques de heavy metal, à la culture New Age, aux questions écologiques, à la philosophie de Gaia et aux indicateurs ferroviaires en LED. Ailleurs, il écrit avec un sens de la justice sociale bien informé: «Il fut un temps où la politique sociale devait servir les défavorisés. Aujourd'hui, elle cherche à consolider le confort de la classe moyenne inquiète (toujours coincée entre deux extrêmes, la richesse et la pauvreté – un terrain propice pour des idées telles que la loterie nationale et l'assurance maladie privée).» Ici, comme il le fait dans d'autres essais publiés dans FUSE, Wozencroft aborde des questions sociales dans une publication consacrée au graphisme, ce qui était rare à l'époque mais aujourd'hui, après la crise du système financier, est plus courant.

Cependant, le plus grand accomplissement de FUSE est peut-être le démenti cinglant qu'il oppose à l'opinion largement répandue selon laquelle le graphisme serait un domaine qui manque sévèrement d'autocritique, un espace d'affectation stylistique et d'autopromotion. Les critiques et les historiens se sont systématiquement plaints de la superficialité et de la pauvreté des contributions que les designers apportaient au discours de leur discipline. Il me semble que FUSE est l'une des rares réfutations efficaces de cette allégation. Pourtant ce magazine est rarement mentionné lorsque la culture du graphisme est évoquée, et seule une poignée de publications réalisées par des graphistes peuvent se mesurer à l'ambition textuelle et visuelle de l'aventure auto-éditée de Brody et Wozencroft. *Emigre* est peut-être la seule qui puisse soutenir la comparaison.

Mais ce n'est pas seulement dans les domaines de l'idéologie et de la polémique que FUSE a souffert de négligence. La typographie moderne n'a produit que peu de successeurs à Brody et son jaillissement d'invention pure. Les typographes actuels semblent n'avoir d'yeux que pour le formalisme du passé: le conservatisme typographique est la norme. Jeffrey Keedy, l'un des premiers à avoir participé au magazine, avait prédit cette évolution. Dans FUSE 4 (1992), il remarquait: «Pour éviter la mortalité du style, de nombreux designers actuels ont ressuscité les morts. Les cadavres typographiques sont ramenés du lointain passé (momies classiques), du passé récent (zombies modernes) ou raccommodés à la Frankenstein, avec des parties fraîchement déterrées (modernes post-mortem). Quelle que soit la démarche adoptée, cela revient au même: une sorte de nécrophilie typographique. Au lieu de perdre du temps à fignoler un cadavre exquis, les typographes devraient se passionner pour les nouvelles possibilités du numérique, tout comme ceux de l'ère industrielle se sont passionnés pour les progrès de leur époque.»

Dans les entretiens qu'il a accordés et dans son nouveau rôle d'éducateur, Brody a souvent appelé ses successeurs à «se passionner pour les nouvelles possibilités numériques» et à «penser dangereusement». Il souhaite ardemment que quelqu'un entreprenne d'imiter le travail qu'il a commencé il y a vingt ans. Il veut entendre encore une fois le bruit des boulets démolissant les murs de la civilisation typographique, mais il n'est pas sûr que cela arrive. La plupart des typographes semblent plutôt aspirer à égaler les notes stériles de la musique de supermarché qui nous accompagne dans notre tâche quotidienne consistant, selon Wozencroft, à errer dans «une suite sans fin de centres commerciaux, services bancaires, centres de télécommunications, restaurants et bars qui veillent à ce que les nomades modernes soient constamment occupés et animés dans un véritable no man's land.»

Cependant, le plus grand accomplissement de FUSE est peut-être le démenti cinglant qu'il oppose à l'opinion largement répandue selon laquelle le graphisme serait un domaine qui manque sévèrement d'autocritique, un espace d'affectation stylistique et d'autopromotion. Les critiques et les historiens se sont systématiquement plaints de la superficialité et de la pauvreté des contributions que les designers apportaient au discours de leur discipline. Il me semble que FUSE est l'une des rares réfutations efficaces de cette allégation.

FUSE 1-20: Acknowledgements

Thanks to **Joan Spiekermann, Erik Spiekermann,** and **Jürgen Siebert** at FontShop Berlin/FontShop International for supporting the project from the outset. In London, this could never have happened without the dedication of all at Research Studios who worked with us – in particular, **Fwa Richards** and **John Critchley. Rudy Geeraerts** at FontShop Benelux, **Stuart Jensen** at FontWorks UK and all members of the FontShop network... **Ed Cleary** (FontShop Canada), **David Michaelides** (FontShop Canada), **Michael Gorman** (FontShop Italy), **Yves Peters** (FontFeed), **Roland Henß** (Student FUSE), **Beth Russell** (FUSE production), **Frank Hentschker** (FUSE95), **Jons Michael Voss** (Photographer), **Karola Menzel** et al. (Schoepe Display, cardboard boxes), **Carmen Dormann** et al. (Buhl Data Service, disk production), **Peter Stumpe** et al. (MetaDesign, poster production). **Hedley Finn** for his help with FUSE94. **Shel Perkins, Bill Hill, Terry Irwin** and **Billy Hill** at MetaDesign SF (FUSE98). **Bill Thompson** at Pipex and **John Welsh,** who created the FUSE website and to all three members of **The Barr Family. Orange Communications Ltd.** in London for repro services. **Erik van Blokland, Peter van Blokland** and **Just van Rossum** for technical support. **Jeff Knowles** archived the files at Research Studios in the late 2000s and organised the FUSE security project. **Sarah Temple** set up the 2004 LCC exhibition in London which subsequently travelled the world, thanks to FontShop Berlin.

Our gratitude to all FUSE contributors.

This book is dedicated to **Frank Heine, Tibor Kalman** and **Ed Cleary** who are sorely missed.

Credits

Produced by Neville Brody and Jon Wozencroft

Design and production: www.researchstudios.com

Adaptation and completion: Sam Renwick
Project manager: Phil Rodgers
Editorial assistant: Dani Admiss
Editorial consultant: Adrian Shaughnessy

Design support: Jeff Knowles

For TASCHEN:

Editor: Julius Wiedemann
Editorial coordination: Daniel Siciliano Bretas
Production: Stefan Klatte

English revision: Chris Allen
German translation: Ursula Wulfekamp
French translation: Aurélie Daniel

Research support from the Royal College of Art

Printed in China

www.researchstudios.com

Royal College of Art
Postgraduate Art and Design

Lost in History

Compiling this book, we returned to the original floppy disks only to discover that previously unopened/archival copies had content that has vaporised into thin air. Specialist archival services have been unable to retrieve this. We have rebuilt everything we can, faithfully, from ancient Quark files and SyQuest disks from Outer Space.

This book is also about memory, and the short-termism of digital formats. Only FUSE 18 was issued on a CD rather than a floppy. Now it looks as though that format is going the way of the Gods as well.

In 1995/96 we worked on a CD-ROM of FUSE1-10 which was one of the best demonstrations of the early fonts in digital animation. Mike Williams did the Director/software architecture, and Mia Sabel the animations, directed by our feeling for the format, which soon disappeared just like the fax machine. The FUSE CD-ROM has great sound and 4 interactive fonts designed especially for this medium.

Neville Brody's *Untitled 1 & 2* was an animation of every FUSE poster, like a flicker-book. John Critchley and Just van Rossum programmed a font, *Censor*, that self-erased. Simon Griffin and Mike Williams did an interactive font, *Transmission*, based on cybernetics. Tom Hingston and Jon Wozencroft made *Terminal 5* out of aircraft assembly parts; as you moved the cursor across each section it revealed a sound clip of an in-cabin safety announcement or an air traffic control signal.

Due to financial pressures, it never came out.

The CD-ROM was made on Mac Operating System 7. It works, just, on Mac OS9. It is incompatible with OS10.

The first few issues of FUSE were made available in PC format, but this became an uneconomical option, so we stopped it after FUSE4.

If FUSE1-20 is a hidden history it is also a challenge to the question of what we want to retrieve from the short digital past.

Do we have to conclude that anything you distribute now, in digital, has the lifespan of a fruit fly?

US FUSE

US FUSE 2

US FUSE 3

US FUSE 7

US FUSE 8

US FUSE 9

US FUSE

US FUSE 14

US FUSE 15

US FUSE 4

US FUSE 5

US FUSE 6

US FUSE 10

US FUSE 11

US FUSE 12

US FUSE 16

US FUSE 17

US FUSE 18